WITHDRAWN

The Student's Introduction to *Mathematica*® and the Wolfram Language™

Third edition

The unique feature of this compact student's introduction to *Mathematica* and the Wolfram Language is that it presents concepts in an order that closely follows a standard mathematics curriculum, rather than structure the book along features of the software. As a result, the book provides a brief introduction to those aspects of the *Mathematica* software program most useful to students. Used as a supplementary text, it will aid in bridging the gap between *Mathematica* and the mathematics in the course. In addition to its course use, this book will serve as an excellent tutorial for former students.

There have been significant changes to *Mathematica* since the publication of the second edition, and all chapters in this third edition have been updated to account for new features in the software, including natural language queries and the vast stores of real-world data that are now integrated through the cloud. This third edition includes many new exercises and a new chapter on 3D printing that utilizes concepts introduced in earlier chapters to showcase new computational geometry capabilities that will equip readers to design and print in 3D.

Bruce F. Torrence and Eve A. Torrence are both Professors in the Department of Mathematics at Randolph-Macon College, Virginia.

The Student's Introduction to *Mathematica*® and the Wolfram Language™

Third edition

Bruce F. Torrence
Eve A. Torrence

CAMBRIDGE
UNIVERSITY PRESS

CAMBRIDGE
UNIVERSITY PRESS

University Printing House, Cambridge CB2 8BS, United Kingdom

One Liberty Plaza, 20th Floor, New York, NY 10006, USA

477 Williamstown Road, Port Melbourne, VIC 3207, Australia

314–321, 3rd Floor, Plot 3, Splendor Forum, Jasola District Centre, New Delhi – 110025, India

79 Anson Road, #06–04/06, Singapore 079906

Cambridge University Press is part of the University of Cambridge.

It furthers the University's mission by disseminating knowledge in the pursuit of
education, learning, and research at the highest international levels of excellence.

www.cambridge.org
Information on this title: www.cambridge.org/9781108406369
DOI: 10.1017/9781108290937

First edition © Cambridge University Press 1999
Second and Third editions © Bruce F. Torrence and Eve A. Torrence 2009, 2019
Page design and composition: Paul Wellin

First published 1999
Second edition 2009
Third edition 2019

Printed in the United Kingdom by TJ International Ltd. Padstow Cornwall

Mathematica® and Wolfram Alpha® are registered trademarks of Wolfram Research, Inc.
Wolfram Language and Wolfram One are trademarks of the same company.

A catalogue record for this publication is available from the British Library.

ISBN 978-1-108-40636-9 Paperback

Additional resources for this publication at www.cambridge.org/torrence3.

For

Alexandra and Robert

Contents

Preface

The mathematician and juggler Ronald L. Graham has likened the mastery of computer programming to the mastery of juggling. The problem with juggling is that the balls go exactly where you throw them. And the problem with computers is that they do exactly what you tell them.

This is a book about *Mathematica* and the Wolfram[1] Language™. *Mathematica* is a comprehensive technical computing environment that has long been the flagship product of Wolfram Research. With a functional programming language at its core, *Mathematica* is an ambitious project that has always taken the long view regarding structure and design. And with 30 years of continuous development, it has grown into something far beyond its original concept. Interactive mathematical typesetting arrived in 1996, and dynamically interactive computation was incorporated in 2007. The introduction of Wolfram Alpha® in 2009 brought natural language queries into the fold, and a decade of data curation has brought in the entire world. The underlying symbolic language, now called the Wolfram Language, has maintained its syntactical structure while permitting access to both natural language inputs and a huge wealth of curated data and algorithms. It is a truly unique and powerful platform.

As software programs go, *Mathematica* is big—really big. We said that back in 1999 in the preface to the first edition of this book. And it has gotten a good deal bigger since then. The printed user manual was abandoned after version 5 as it was approaching 1000 pages in length. Now in version 12, the program is many times larger. Yes, *Mathematica* will do exactly what you ask it to do, and it has the potential to amaze and delight—but you have to know how to ask.

That's where this book comes in. Originally intended as a supplementary text for high school and college students using *Mathematica* in their mathematics classes, it introduces the reader to the Wolfram Language in an order that roughly coincides with the usual mathematics curriculum. The idea is to provide a coherent introduction to *Mathematica* that does not get ahead of itself mathematically. Most of the available reference materials make the assumption that the reader is thoroughly familiar with the mathematical concepts underlying each Wolfram Language command and procedure, many of which are rather advanced. This book does not. It presents *Mathematica* as a means not only of solving mathematical problems, but of exploring and clarifying the underlying mathematical ideas. It also provides examples of procedures that students will need to master, showing not just individual commands, but sequences of commands that together accomplish a larger goal.

But a funny thing happened. While written primarily for students, the first editions were well-received by many non-students who just wanted to learn *Mathematica*. Because the book follows the standard mathematics curriculum, we were told, the presentation exudes a certain familiarity and coherence. What better way to learn a computer language than to rediscover the beautiful ideas from your foundational mathematics courses? In seeing how *Mathematica* deals with familiar concepts, its underlying principles become clearer and more transparent.

1. www.wolfram.com

What's New in this Edition?

The impetus for a third edition was driven by the software itself. Since the second edition we have seen the launch of Wolfram Alpha[2], the development of the Wolfram Knowledgebase and the corresponding incorporation of Entities into the language, and the introduction of *Mathematica* Online and cloud computing. Just as the second edition was rewritten from the ground up, so too has the third edition been extensively revised to reflect these and other enhancements to the software.

In addition, a new chapter has been added (Chapter 9) on the topic of 3D printing. While *Mathematica* has never been a CAD program, its inherent capabilities have been enhanced with the active development of new tools for computational geometry, and the net result is impressive. The chapter provides a fitting showcase for the techniques introduced earlier.

How to Use this Book

Of course, this is a printed book and as such is perfectly suitable for bedtime or beach reading. But in most cases you will want to be interacting with *Mathematica* as you read the book. You can mimic the inputs and then try variations.

The first chapter provides a brief tutorial for those just getting started with the software, be it a desktop or cloud platform. The second delves a bit deeper into the fundamental design principles and can be used as a reference for the rest of the book. Chapters 3 and 4 provide information on those *Mathematica* commands and procedures relevant to the material in a precalculus course, including some basic data science. Chapter 5 adds material relevant to single-variable calculus, and Chapter 6 deals with multivariable calculus. Chapter 7 introduces commands and procedures pertinent to the material in a linear algebra course, and Chapter 8 provides an introduction to programming in the Wolfram Language. Chapter 9 wraps things up with an introduction to 3D printing.

> ⚠ Some sections of the text carry this warning sign. These sections provide slightly more comprehensive information for the curious reader. They can be skipped by less hardy souls.

Beginning in Chapter 3, each section has exercises. Solutions to *every* exercise can be freely downloaded from the Cambridge University Press website at www.cambridge.org/torrence3.

Mathematica runs on every major operating system, from Macs and PCs to machines running Linux®, and with cloud-based versions it is now accessible from mobile touchscreen devices. For the most part it works with admirable consistency across platforms. There are, however, a few procedures (such as certain keyboard shortcuts) that are platform-specific. In such cases we have provided specific information for both the Mac OS® and Microsoft® Windows® platforms, as well as for cloud-based environments. If you find yourself running *Mathematica* on some other platform, you can be assured that the procedure you need is virtually identical to one of these.

---

2. www.wolframalpha.com

Acknowledgments

Time flies. When we wrote the first edition of this book our children were toddlers who wanted to sit on our laps while we worked. When we wrote the second edition they were teenagers who just wanted our laptops. Now they are young adults with laptops and lives of their own. We are so proud of the wonderful people they have become and love the creativity, energy, joy, and spark they bring to our lives.

We extend our thanks to Randolph-Macon College and the Chenery and Rashkind Family Endowments for the support we received throughout this project. We are especially grateful to Paul Wellin, who handled the page design and composition and who dealt tirelessly with countless other issues, both editorial and technical.

1

Getting Started

1.1 Launching *Mathematica*

The first task you will face is opening your copy of *Mathematica* or Wolfram|One™. If you are using a desktop version of *Mathematica*, you are looking for an icon that looks something like this:

Just click it to launch. A window titled "Welcome to Wolfram Mathematica" will appear. In the top left corner there is a "New Document" button. Click it and an empty document window will appear. This is your *Mathematica notebook*, where you will carry out your work.

Cloud-based products such as *Mathematica* Online require only a web browser and an active account at WolframCloud.com. Once launched, the interface is nearly identical to that of the desktop version.

The remainder of this chapter is a quick tutorial that will enable you to get accustomed to the syntax and conventions of *Mathematica*, and demonstrate some of its many features.

1.2 The Basic Technique for Using *Mathematica*

A *Mathematica* notebook is an interactive environment. You type a command (such as 2 + 2) and instruct *Mathematica* to execute it. *Mathematica* responds with the answer on the next line. You then type another command, and so on. Each command you type will appear on the screen in a **boldface** font. *Mathematica*'s output will appear in a plain font.

> 💡 **Entering Input**
>
> After typing a command, you must enter it. To do this hold down the `SHIFT` key and then hit the `ENTER` key. Your keypad may say "Return" on this key, or "Enter," or just have the ↵ symbol. Regardless, when we say the `ENTER` key we mean the key that takes you to a new line when you are typing.
>
> Beware that you can't just hit the `ENTER` key. Hitting this key alone will insert a line break in your input. It will not process your input.

There is one exception to this rule: If you happen to have an extended keyboard with a numeric keypad on the right, you can use the ⌊ENTER⌋ key in the bottom right corner to enter your commands. But using ⌊SHIFT⌋⌊ENTER⌋ on the main part of the keypad will still work. It is probably easiest to get used to using ⌊SHIFT⌋⌊ENTER⌋ from the beginning since this will work on any keyboard.

1.3   The First Computation

For your first computation, type

> **2 + 2**

then hit the ⌊SHIFT⌋⌊ENTER⌋ combination.

> In[1]:=   **2 + 2**
>
> Out[1]=   4

Notice the gray bar that appeared just below the output. This is the "Suggestions Bar." *Mathematica* is trying to be helpful by providing a few suggestions related to your input that you may want to explore. Feel free to follow its suggestions to create and evaluate new inputs, or feel free to ignore them. A new Suggestions Bar will appear every time you enter a command. To prevent this from happening simply click on the small "×" button on the far right of the bar and *Mathematica* will turn off this feature for the current session.

When you enter your input, it is processed by an auxiliary program called the kernel. *Mathematica* really consists of two programs: the notebook front end where you type your commands and where output, graphics, and text are displayed, and the kernel, where your inputs are evaluated. Even though you will probably never interact directly with the kernel, it is useful to be aware of this structural dichotomy in *Mathematica*'s architecture. We will discuss some implications in the next chapter in Section 2.6.

1.4   Commands for Basic Arithmetic

Mathematica works much like a calculator for basic arithmetic. Just use the +, −, *, and / keys on the keyboard for addition, subtraction, multiplication, and division. As an alternative to typing *, you can multiply two numbers by leaving a space between them (the × symbol will automatically be inserted when you leave a space between two numbers). You can raise a number to a power using the ^ key. Use the dot (i.e., the period) to type a decimal point. Here are a few examples:

> In[1]:=   **17 − 1**
>
> Out[1]=   16

In[2]:= **123 456 789 ✶ 123 456 789**

Out[2]= 15 241 578 750 190 521

In[3]:= **123 456 789 × 123 456 789**

Out[3]= 15 241 578 750 190 521

In[4]:= **123 456 789 ^ 2**

Out[4]= 15 241 578 750 190 521

In[5]:= **9.1 / 256.127**

Out[5]= 0.0355292

In[6]:= **34 / 4**

Out[6]= $\dfrac{17}{2}$

This last line may seem strange at first. What you are witnessing is *Mathematica*'s propensity for providing exact answers. *Mathematica* treats decimal numbers as approximations, and will generally avoid them in the output if they are not present in the input. When *Mathematica* returns an expression with no decimals, you are assured that the answer is exact. Fractions are displayed in lowest terms.

1.5 Input and Output

You've surely noticed that *Mathematica* is keeping close tabs on your work. Each time you enter an expression, *Mathematica* gives it a name such as In[1]:=, In[2]:=, In[3]:=. The corresponding output comes with the labels Out[1]=, Out[2]=, Out[3]=. At this point, it is enough to observe that these labels will appear all by themselves each time you enter a command, and it's okay:

In[1]:= $\left(\dfrac{1}{2}\right)^6$

Out[1]= $\dfrac{1}{64}$

You've surely noticed something else too (you'll need to be running a live session for this): those brackets along the right margin of your notebook window. Each input and output is written into a *cell*, whose scope is shown by the nearest bracket directly across from the respective input or output text. Cells containing input are called *input cells*. Cells containing output are called *output cells*. The brackets delimiting cells are called *cell brackets*. Each input–output pair is in turn grouped with a larger bracket immediately to the right of the cell brackets. These brackets may in turn be grouped together by a still larger bracket, and so on. These extra brackets are called *grouping brackets*.

At this point, it's really enough just to know these brackets are there and to make the distinction between the innermost (or smallest, or leftmost) brackets which delimit individual cells and the others which are used for grouping. If you are curious about what good can possibly come of them, try positioning the tip of your cursor arrow anywhere on a grouping bracket and double-click. You will *close the group* determined by that bracket. In the case of the bracket delimiting an input–output pair, this will have the effect of hiding the output completely (handy if the output runs over several pages). Double-click again to open the group. This feature is useful when you have created a long, complex document and need a means of managing it. Alternately, you can double-click on any output cell bracket to *reverse-close* the group. This has the effect of hiding the input code and displaying only the output.

Since brackets are really only useful in a live *Mathematica* session, they will not, by default, show when you print a notebook. Additional details about brackets and cells will be provided in Section 2.2.

One last bit of terminology is in order. When you hit the SHIFT-ENTER combination after typing an input cell, you are *entering the cell*. You'll be seeing this phrase quite a bit in the future.

1.6   The Basic Math Assistant Palette

There may already be a narrow, light-gray window full of mathematical symbols along the side of your screen. If so, you are looking at one of *Mathematica*'s palettes, and chances are that it is the Basic Math Assistant palette. If you see no such window, go to the Palettes dropdown menu at the top of your screen and select Basic Math Assistant to open it.

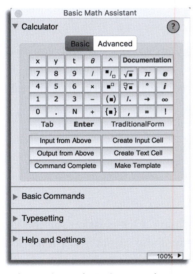

The Basic Math Assistant palette

This palette is currently available only on desktop versions of *Mathematica*. If you are using *Mathematica* Online, look in the menu for Insert ▷ Special Characters. This will open a palette with a simpler interface that allows you to insert special symbols one character at a time. To simulate many of the buttons on the Basic Math Assistant palette, online users can take advantage of *command completion* and *command templates*; these are discussed in Section 1.11.

The Basic Math Assistant palette is a handy tool. You will use it to help typeset your *Mathematica* input so that it looks like traditional mathematical notation. The palette will also help you construct your inputs easily by providing a template with correct syntax for you to fill in. And if you need to submit a technical paper it will help you to typeset your notebook into a beautifully formatted document that contains all your *Mathematica* computations.

The top section of the Basic Math Assistant palette is called Calculator. If this section is not open, click on the ▸ to open it. You can toggle between the Basic and Advanced calculators by hitting the tabs with those labels. We will start with the Basic Calculator and discuss other sections of this palette in Section 1.10.

To type an exponential expression such as 17^{19}, use the $\blacksquare^{\square}$ button in the middle of the Calculator. To do this, first type 17 into your *Mathematica* notebook, then highlight it with your mouse. Next, push the $\blacksquare^{\square}$ palette button with your mouse. The exponent structure shown on that button will be pasted into your notebook, with the 17 in the position of the black square on the palette button (the black square is called the *selection placeholder*). The text insertion point will move to the placeholder in the exponent position. Your input cell will look like this:

$$17^{\blacksquare}$$

Now type the value of the exponent, in this case 19, into the placeholder, then enter the cell:

In[1]:= 17^{19}

Out[1]= 239 072 435 685 151 324 847 153

> ⚠ Another way to accomplish the same thing is this: First hit the palette button, then type 17 into the first placeholder. Next hit the [TAB] key to move to the second placeholder (in the exponent position). Now type 19 and enter the cell. This procedure is perhaps a bit more intuitive, but it can occasionally get you into trouble if you are not careful with grouping. For instance, if you want to enter $(1 + x)^{8}$, and the first thing you do is push the $\blacksquare^{\square}$ button on the palette, then you must type $(1 + x)$ with parentheses, then [TAB], then 8. By contrast, you could type $1 + x$ with or without parentheses and highlight the expression with your mouse, then hit the $\blacksquare^{\square}$ palette button, and then type 8. If needed, the parentheses are added automatically when this procedure is followed.

If you don't understand what some of the palette buttons do, don't fret. Just stick with the ones that you know for now. For instance, you can take a cube root like this: Type a number and highlight it with the mouse, then push the $\sqrt[\square]{\blacksquare}$ button on the Basic Math Assistant palette, then hit the [TAB] key, and finally type 3. Now enter the cell:

In[2]:= $\sqrt[3]{50\,653}$

Out[2]= 37

This is equivalent to raising 50 653 to the power 1/3:

In[3]:= $50\,653^{1/3}$

Out[3]= 37

And of course we can easily check the answer to either calculation:

In[4]:= 37^3

Out[4]= 50 653

You may have noticed the Classroom Assistant palette and the Writing Assistant palette options at the top of the Palettes menu. The Classroom Assistant palette is quite similar to the Basic Math Assistant palette, but it also contains a Navigation section and a Keyboard section, as well as all the sections of the Writing Assistant palette.

> 💡 **Using Palette Buttons**
>
> Speaking in general terms, all palette buttons that contain a solid black placeholder ■ are used in this way:
>
> - Type an expression into a *Mathematica* notebook.
> - Highlight all or part of the expression with your mouse (by dragging across the expression).
> - Push a palette button. The structure on the face of the button is pasted into your notebook, with the highlighted text appearing in the position of the solid black square.
> - If there are more placeholders in the structure, use the TAB key or forward arrow (or move the cursor with your mouse) to move from one to the next.

1.7   Decimal In, Decimal Out

Sometimes you don't want exact answers. Sometimes you want decimals. For instance, how big is this number? It's hard to get a grasp of its magnitude when it's expressed as a fraction:

In[1]:= $\dfrac{17^{19}}{19^{17}}$

Out[1]= $\dfrac{239\,072\,435\,685\,151\,324\,847\,153}{5\,480\,386\,857\,784\,802\,185\,939}$

And what about this?

In[2]:= $\sqrt[3]{59\,875}$

Out[2]= $5 \times 479^{1/3}$

Mathematica tells us that the answer is 5 times the cube root of 479 (remember that raising a number to the power 1/3 is the same as taking its cube root). The output is exact, but again it is difficult to grasp the magnitude of this number. How can we get a nice decimal approximation, like a calculator would produce?

If any of the numbers in your input is in decimal form, *Mathematica* regards it as approximate. It responds by providing an approximate answer, that is, a decimal answer. It is handy to remember this:

In[3]:= $\dfrac{17.0^{19}}{19^{17}}$

Out[3]= 43.6233

In[4]:= $\sqrt[3]{59\,875.0}$

Out[4]= 39.1215

A slightly quicker way to accomplish this is to type a decimal point after a number with nothing after it. That is, *Mathematica* regards "17.0" and "17." as the same quantity. This is important for understanding *Mathematica*'s output:

In[5]:= $\sqrt[3]{59\,875.}$

Out[5]= 39.1215

In[6]:= $\dfrac{30.}{2}$

Out[6]= 15.

Note the decimal point in the output. Since the input was only "approximate," so too is the output. Get in the habit of using exact or decimal numbers in your input according to the type of answer, exact or approximate, you wish to obtain. Adding a decimal point to any single number in your input will cause *Mathematica* to provide an approximate (i.e., decimal) output. A detailed discussion on approximate numbers can be found in Section 8.3.

1.8   Use Parentheses to Group Terms

Use ordinary parentheses ( ) to group terms in algebraic expressions. This is *very* important, especially with division, multiplication, and exponentiation. Being a computer program, *Mathematica* takes what you say quite literally; operations are performed in a definite order, and you need to make sure that it is the order you intend. Get in the habit of making a mental check for appropriate parentheses before entering each command. Here are some examples. Can you see what *Mathematica* does in the absence of parentheses?

In[1]:= **3 * (4 + 1)**

Out[1]= 15

In[2]:= **3 * 4 + 1**

Out[2]= 13

In[3]:= **$(-3)^2$**

Out[3]= 9

In[4]:= **-3^2**

Out[4]= -9

In[5]:= **(3 + 1) / 2**

Out[5]= 2

In[6]:= **3 + 1 / 2**

Out[6]= $\dfrac{7}{2}$

The last pair of examples shows one benefit of using the Basic Math Assistant palette instead of typing from the keyboard. With the typesetting capability afforded by the palette there is no need for grouping parentheses, and no chance for ambiguity:

In[7]:= $\dfrac{3 + 1}{2}$

Out[7]= 2

In[8]:= $3 + \dfrac{1}{2}$

Out[8]= $\dfrac{7}{2}$

The lesson here is that the order in which *Mathematica* performs operations in the absence of parentheses may not be what you intend. When in doubt, add parentheses.

Note also that only round brackets can be used for the purpose of grouping terms. *Mathematica* reserves different meanings for square brackets and curly brackets, so never use them to group terms.

1.9 Three Well-Known Constants

Mathematica has several built-in constants. The three most commonly used are π, the ratio of the circumference to the diameter of a circle (approximately 3.14); e, the base of the natural logarithm (approximately 2.72); and i, the imaginary number whose square is −1. You can find each of these constants near the top of the Basic Calculator section of the Basic Math Assistant palette.

In[1]:= π

Out[1]= π

In[2]:= π + 0.

Out[2]=   3.14159

Again, note *Mathematica*'s propensity for exact answers. You will often use π to indicate the radian measure of an angle to be input into a trigonometric function. There are examples in the next section.

It is possible to enter each of these three constants directly from the keyboard, as well. You can type [ESC]p[ESC] for π, [ESC]ee[ESC] for e, and [ESC]ii[ESC] for i.

⚠ You can also type Pi for π, E for e, and I for i. The capitalization is important. These do not look as nice, but it illustrates an important point: It is possible to type any *Mathematica* input using only the characters from an ordinary keyboard. That is, every formatted mathematical expression that can be input into *Mathematica* has an equivalent expression constructed using only characters from the keyboard. Indeed, versions 1 and 2 of *Mathematica* used only such expressions. These days, the keyboard, or InputForm, of an expression is used when you include a *Mathematica* input or output in an email message (say, to a friend or to your professor). If you copy a formatted expression such as $\pi^{1/3}$ from *Mathematica* and paste it into an email or text editor, you'll find that it becomes Pi^(1/3) (or just π^(1/3) if the editor has the π symbol available). The point is that it is exceedingly simple to include formatted *Mathematica* expressions in plain text environments. Note that you can display any input cell in InputForm from within *Mathematica* by clicking on its cell bracket to select it, and going to the Cell menu and choosing ConvertTo ▷ InputForm.

1.10 *Mathematica* Commands from Palettes

Mathematica contains thousands of *commands*. Commands provide a means for instructing *Mathematica* to perform all sorts of tasks, from computing the logarithm of a number, to simplifying an algebraic expression, to solving an equation, to plotting a function. *Mathematica*'s commands are more numerous, more flexible, and more powerful than those available in any hand-held calculator, and in many ways they are easier to use.

Commands can be typed from the keyboard, but if you are using a desktop version of the software it is easiest to start by using the palette buttons. The Basic Commands section of the Basic Math Assistant palette contains many of the commands you are likely to use. If this section of the palette is not open, click on the ▸ to open it. At the top of this section there is a bar with seven tabs. If you hover over one of these tabs with your mouse, the name of its sub-palette will appear. The seven sub-palettes are shown in Table 1.1.

Icon	Sub-palette Name	Topics
$\sqrt{x}$	Mathematical Constants and Functions	Trigonometric, exponential, and logarithmic functions
$y = x$	Algebra Commands	Factoring, expanding, and simplifying algebraic expressions
$d \int \Sigma$	Calculus Commands	Computing derivatives, integrals, sums, and limits
$\begin{pmatrix} \Box & \Box \\ \Box & \Box \end{pmatrix}$	Matrix Commands	Entering matrices and linear algebra computations
List	Table, List, Vector Commands	Creating tables and working with data
2D	2D Plot Commands	Creating two-dimensional graphs
3D	3D Plot Commands	Creating three-dimensional graphs

Table 1.1   **Basic Commands.** The seven tabs in the Basic Commands section of the Basic Math Assistant palette.

We will start with the Mathematical Constants and Functions sub-palette. This appears when you click on the $\boxed{\sqrt{x}}$ tab.

Numerical Approximation and Scientific Notation

The first command we will introduce is N. It is the first button under Numeric Functions, just below the Mathematical Constants buttons. Click on the button labeled $\boxed{\text{N}}$ and the following will appear in your notebook at the position of the cursor:

> N[*expr*]

Now type an expression, such as 5/3, and it will be inserted where *expr* appears in the input. Then enter the cell by hitting $\boxed{\text{SHIFT}}$ $\boxed{\text{ENTER}}$. By default, the approximation will have six significant digits:

> In[1]:= **N[5 / 3]**
>
> Out[1]= 1.66667

The palette is not strictly necessary here; if you type the input above directly from the keyboard, the result is the same. The point here is that the palette provides easy access to many commonly used commands. As you use the palette and gradually become familiar with these commands, you may eventually find it is simpler to type them directly from the keyboard.

N is a command you are likely to use frequently. Very large or very small numbers will be put in scientific notation:

In[2]:= 17^{30}

Out[2]= 8 193 465 725 814 765 556 554 001 028 792 218 849

In[3]:= $N[17^{30}]$

Out[3]= 8.19347×10^{36}

In[4]:= $N\left[\dfrac{1}{2^{50}}\right]$

Out[4]= 8.88178×10^{-16}

If you were wondering, yes, typing 17.^{30} has the same effect as typing $N[17^{30}]$. But the command N is more flexible. If you add a comma after your quantity followed by a positive integer m the output will have m significant digits. In other words, enter $N[x, m]$ to get a numerical approximation to x with m significant digits:

In[5]:= $N[\pi, 50]$

Out[5]= 3.1415926535897932384626433832795028841971693993751

In[6]:= $N[17^{30}, 20]$

Out[6]= $8.1934657258147655566 \times 10^{36}$

If you let your cursor hover over the $\boxed{N}$ button on the palette you will see the proper syntax specification for the N command, N[*expr, digits*]. Every N command must contain a number, typed where *expr* is shown. You can then, at your discretion, add an optional second argument to specify the number of significant digits. Because this second argument is optional, this part of the syntax specification is shown in gray.

Mathematica commands always conform to a strict syntactical structure, whether they are rendered using a palette button or by typing from the keyboard. It is useful to understand this basic syntax as you begin working with *Mathematica*. Commands take one or more *arguments*. The typical syntax for a command is:

Command [*argument*] or **Command** [*argument1*, *argument2*]

💡 **Rules for *Mathematica* Syntax**

   Mathematica commands always follow strict syntax rules. The three most important are:

   - Every built-in command begins with a capital letter. Furthermore, if a command name is composed from more than one word (such as ArcSin or FactorInteger) then each word begins with a capital letter, and there will be no space between the words.
   - The arguments of commands are enclosed in square brackets.
   - If there is more than one argument, they are separated by commas.

Logarithms

Logarithmic functions are found in the next section of the Mathematical Constants and Functions sub-palette under Elementary Functions. When we write log(x) we generally mean $\log_{10}(x)$, also called the common logarithm. But in *Mathematica*, Log is the *natural* logarithm. We can confirm this while using the ⬚Log⬚ button to do a few calculations:

In[7]:= **Log[e]**

Out[7]= 1

In[8]:= **Log[e^{45}]**

Out[8]= 45

It is possible to build up input by nesting one command inside another. This is done by starting with the innermost command, in this case the Log[π]. The N command can be added to the Log command by highlighting Log[π] and then hitting the ⬚N⬚ button. The Log[π] will become the *expr* for the N command. You can add the optional second argument specifying the number of significant digits using the keyboard.

In[9]:= **N[Log[π]]**

Out[9]= 1.14473

In[10]:= **N[Log[π], 30]**

Out[10]= 1.14472988584940017414342735135

For log base 10, or common log, use the ⬚Log10⬚ button:

In[11]:= **Log10$\left[\dfrac{1}{1000}\right]$**

Out[11]= −3

Clicking ⬚More ▾⬚ below the ⬚Log10⬚ button will reveal more functions such as log base 2:

In[12]:= **Log2[8]**

Out[12]= 3

You can compute logarithms with any base using Log[*base*, *expr*]:

In[13]:= **Log[17, 83 521]**

Out[13]= 4

Of course you can always check an answer:

In[14]:= 17^4

Out[14]= $83\,521$

Trigonometric Functions

Trigonometric functions are also shown on the Mathematical Constants and Functions sub-palette. All trigonometric functions assume angles are given in *radian* measure. You enter radian values such as $\frac{\pi}{4}$ using the Calculator section of the Basic Math Assistant palette.

In[15]:= $\cos\left[\dfrac{\pi}{4}\right]$

Out[15]= $\dfrac{1}{\sqrt{2}}$

If you wish to use degrees you must add the degree symbol, $^\circ$, by clicking the $\boxed{^\circ}$ button under Mathematical Constants. It may seem strange that this symbol is listed with the constants, but the symbol $^\circ$ in *Mathematica* is equivalent to $\frac{\pi}{180}$. Placing $^\circ$ after a number simply multiples the number by $\frac{\pi}{180}$ and thus converts the angle measurement to radians.

In[16]:= $\sin[120\,^\circ]$

Out[16]= $\dfrac{\sqrt{3}}{2}$

In[17]:= $\sin\left[120*\dfrac{\pi}{180}\right]$

Out[17]= $\dfrac{\sqrt{3}}{2}$

In[18]:= $N\left[\dfrac{\pi}{180}\right]$

Out[18]= 0.0174533

In[19]:= $N[^\circ]$

Out[19]= 0.0174533

Inverse trigonometric functions can be found on this portion of the palette. The output is given in radians.

In[20]:= $\arcsin\left[\dfrac{-1+\sqrt{3}}{2\sqrt{2}}\right]$

Out[20]= $\dfrac{\pi}{12}$

In[21]:= $\mathsf{Sin}\left[\dfrac{\pi}{12}\right]$

Out[21]= $\dfrac{-1+\sqrt{3}}{2\sqrt{2}}$

Integer Functions

Under the Integer Functions section you can find commands for finding divisors and prime factorization of integers, checking whether a number is a prime, and finding the greatest common divisor (GCD) or least common multiple (LCM) of two integers. The Divisors command lists all the integers that divide your input integer

In[22]:= **Divisors[4 832 875]**

Out[22]= {1, 5, 23, 25, 41, 115, 125, 205, 575, 943, 1025, 1681, 2875, 4715, 5125, 8405, 23 575, 38 663, 42 025, 117 875, 193 315, 210 125, 966 575, 4 832 875}

You can factor any integer as a product of prime numbers using the command FactorInteger, which is found under the | More ▼ | button in this section.

In[23]:= **FactorInteger[4 832 875]**

Out[23]= {{5, 3}, {23, 1}, {41, 2}}

The output here needs interpretation. It means that $4\,832\,875$ can be factored as $5^3 \times 23 \times 41^2$. Note the form of the output: a list whose members are each lists of length two. Each list of length two encloses a prime number followed by its exponent value. Again, it is easy to check the answer:

In[24]:= $\mathbf{5^3 * 23 * 41^2}$

Out[24]= 4 832 875

> ⚠ You may wonder why the output to FactorInteger appears in a form that at first glance is somewhat cryptic. Why isn't the output just $5^3 * 23 * 41^2$? The rationale is subtle, but important. The designers of *Mathematica* put the output in the form they did to make it easier for the user to work programmatically with it. That is, it is easy to extract just the primes 5, 23, and 41, or just the exponents 3, 1, and 2, from this output, and to input those values into another command for further analysis. Remember that *Mathematica* is a sophisticated programming language that is used by experts in many disciplines. In this and in many other cases, commands are designed to allow their output to be easily operated on by other commands. It makes the task of assembling many commands into a single program much simpler for the user. For the beginner, however, these advantages may not be immediately obvious.

Factoring and Expanding Polynomials

Clicking on the $\boxed{y = x}$ tab will bring up the Algebra Commands sub-palette. *Mathematica* is very much at home performing all sorts of algebraic manipulations. For example, you can factor just about any imaginable polynomial using the command `Factor[`*polynomial*`]` (recall that a polynomial is an expression consisting of a sum of terms, each of which is the product of a constant and one or more variables each raised to a nonnegative whole number power). Typically, lowercase letters such as x or t are used to represent the variables in a polynomial. Here's an example that you could probably do by hand:

In[25]:= `Factor`$\left[t^2 - 9\right]$

Out[25]= $(-3 + t) \ (3 + t)$

But here's one that you probably couldn't do by hand:

In[26]:= `Factor`$\left[64 - 128\,x + 48\,x^2 + 144\,x^3 - 292\,x^4 + 288\,x^5 - 171\,x^6 + 61\,x^7 - 12\,x^8 + x^9\right]$

Out[26]= $(-2 + x)^6 \ \left(1 + x + x^3\right)$

Note that you do not need to type a space between a number and a variable to indicate multiplication as long as the number is written first; *Mathematica* will insert the space automatically in this case.

You can also have *Mathematica* expand a factored polynomial by typing `Expand[`*polynomial*`]`. Below we confirm the output above:

In[27]:= `Expand`$\left[(-2 + x)^6 \ \left(1 + x + x^3\right)\right]$

Out[27]= $64 - 128\,x + 48\,x^2 + 144\,x^3 - 292\,x^4 + 288\,x^5 - 171\,x^6 + 61\,x^7 - 12\,x^8 + x^9$

These commands can be used on any mathematical expression, not just polynomials. The commands `Factor`, `Expand`, and a host of others that perform various algebraic feats are explored in Chapter 4.

Plotting Functions

Clicking on the $\boxed{2\,\text{D}}$ tab will bring up the 2D Plot Commands sub-palette. *Mathematica* has a variety of commands that generate graphics. One of the most useful is the `Plot` command, which is used for plotting functions. Click on the $\boxed{\text{Plot}}$ button and you will see the template for this command, which takes two arguments.

`Plot[`*function*`, {`*var*`, `*min*`, `*max*`}]`

The first is the *function* to be plotted (it will be highlighted, indicating it will be replaced by whatever you type next), the second is something called an *iterator*, which specifies the span of values that the independent variable is to assume. It is of the form {*var*, *min*, *max*}. Remember to use the $\boxed{\text{TAB}}$ key to advance to the next placeholder as you type your input into the template.

Here's an example. We see the function $x^2 - 1$ on the domain where the variable x ranges from -3 to 3. *Mathematica* determines appropriate values for the y axis automatically:

In[28]:= $\text{Plot}\left[x^2 - 1, \{x, -3, 3\}\right]$

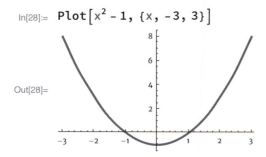

Out[28]=

Here's a more interesting example:

In[29]:= $\text{Plot}\left[x \, \text{Cos}\left[\dfrac{10}{x}\right], \{x, -2, 2\}\right]$

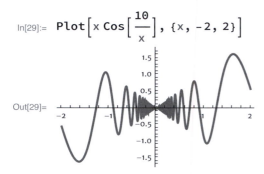

Out[29]=

If you want to specify the viewing window for your graph you can use one of the options found under the Range ▾ button. Place your cursor just before the closing square bracket of your command and then click on one of the PlotRange options to get a template such as PlotRange $\to$ {{$x\,min$, $x\,max$}, {$y\,min$, $y\,max$}}.

In[30]:= $\text{Plot}\left[x^2 - 1, \{x, -3, 3\}, \text{PlotRange} \to \{\{-3, 3\}, \{-5, 15\}\}\right]$

Out[30]=

The Plot command is explored in greater depth in Section 3.2.

Manipulate

The Manipulate command allows the user to create a dynamic interface (with sliders or buttons that can be manipulated in real time). The Manipulate button can be found on the 2D Plot Commands sub-palette in the section titled Interactive Tools, just below the rainbow of Color Names. Like Plot, Manipulate takes two arguments.

$$\texttt{Manipulate}[expr, control]$$

The first is the expression to be manipulated, the second is an iterator which specifies the span of values that the controller variable is to assume. Here's a simple example:

In[31]:= $\texttt{Manipulate}\left[x^2 - 1, \{x, -3, 3\}\right]$

Out[31]=

You can move the slider with your mouse to control the value assumed by x, and watch as the value of $x^2 - 1$ is displayed in real time. This is far more interesting to play with than it is to read about, so be sure to try it! Click on the ⊞ button to the right of the slider to reveal a more sophisticated user control panel:

As you hover over each button on the panel, a tooltip message will display on screen with a brief explanation of that button's function. Go ahead and try each button in turn to get a feel for what you can do. You can even type a value for the variable x into the input field and hit [ENTER] (not [SHIFT]-[ENTER]) to see the value of $x^2 - 1$ in the display area.

Here's a more interesting example:

In[32]:= $\texttt{Manipulate}\left[\texttt{Plot}\left[a \; x \; \texttt{Cos}\left[\dfrac{10}{x}\right], \{x, -2, 2\}, \texttt{PlotRange} \rightarrow 2\right], \{a, -2, 2\}\right]$

Out[32]=

As you type this input, be sure to leave a space between the a and x, and between x and Cos. The option PlotRange → 2 has been added after the second argument in the Plot command to fix the viewing rectangle between −2 and 2 in both the x and y directions. A fixed PlotRange is needed so that the scaling on the *y* axis does not change as the slider moves. `Manipulate` is explored in greater depth in Section 3.4.

Naming Things

It is easy to assign names to quantities in *Mathematica*, and then use those names to refer to the quantities later. This is useful in many situations. For instance, you may want to assign a name to a complicated expression to avoid having to type it again and again. To make an assignment, type the name (perhaps a lowercase letter, or a Greek character, or even an entire word), followed by =, followed by the quantity to which the name should be attached. Greek letters, like θ, can be found in

the Typesetting section toward the bottom of the Basic Math Assistant palette by clicking on the $\boxed{\infty\,\beta}$ tab. For example:

In[33]:= $\theta = \dfrac{\pi}{6}$

Out[33]= $\dfrac{\pi}{6}$

Now whenever you place θ in an input cell, *Mathematica* will replace it with $\dfrac{\pi}{6}$:

In[34]:= θ

Out[34]= $\dfrac{\pi}{6}$

In[35]:= `Sin[`θ`]`

Out[35]= $\dfrac{1}{2}$

In[36]:= `Sin[2 `θ`]`

Out[36]= $\dfrac{\sqrt{3}}{2}$

In[37]:= `Tan[4 `θ`]`

Out[37]= $-\sqrt{3}$

You can (and should) clear an assignment when you are done. This is accomplished with the `Clear` command, which can be found in the Advanced Calculator section of the Basic Math Assistant palette.

In[38]:= `Clear[`θ`]`

No output will be produced when you enter the `Clear` command. You can check that no value is attached to the symbol θ by typing it into an input cell:

In[39]:= θ

Out[39]= θ

For a second example, we can assign to p the value of π rounded to 39 decimal places (the 3 followed by 39 decimal places makes a total of 40 significant digits):

In[40]:= `p = N[π, 40]`

Out[40]= `3.141592653589793238462643383279502884197`

Using this approximation of π, we can approximate the area of a circle of radius 2:

In[41]:= `p * 2²`

Out[41]= `12.56637061435917295385057353311801153679`

Note how *Mathematica*, in performing a calculation involving an *approximate* number p and an *exact* number 2^2, returns an approximate number with the same number of significant digits as p.

Finally, we demonstrate that it is possible to assign values to entire words (such as `data`), and to special characters (such as the script letter $\mathcal{R}$, found on the Special Characters palette, or typed from the keyboard as ⎡ESC⎤ scR ⎡ESC⎤).

In[42]:= `data = {23, 27, 21, 34, 25, 21, 28, 22}`

Out[42]= `{23, 27, 21, 34, 25, 21, 28, 22}`

In[43]:= `ℛ = MengerMesh[3]`

Out[43]=

We can clear all of these assignments in one shot with the `Clear` command—just put a comma between each successive pair of names if there is more than one:

In[44]:= `Clear[θ, p, data, ℛ]`

Since every built-in *Mathematica* command begins with a capital letter from the standard alphabet, it is good practice to use lowercase letters for your names, or words that begin with lowercase letters, or special symbols such as θ or $\mathcal{R}$. This ensures that you will never accidentally assign a name that *Mathematica* has reserved for something else. The only Greek character that has a built-in value is π. All others make perfectly good names. If you really want to use an uppercase letter, use the script version.

It is also permissible to use numbers in your names, provided a number is not the first character. For instance, you might use the names x1 and x2. It is not alright to use the name 2x, for that means 2 times *x*.

1.11   Let *Mathematica* Do Your Typing

Command Completion

You may have noticed that *Mathematica* will offer to finish typing a command for you as soon as you type the first few letters. In both the online and desktop versions a popup appears near the cursor with a list of all built-in and user-defined symbols that begin with the letters you have typed so far. Just move the cursor to the appropriate choice and click, or ignore the popup and keep typing until your command percolates to the top of the list, then hit ENTER to paste the full command into your notebook. Try it—type Expa in an input cell. You will find that there are five *Mathematica* commands that start with these letters: Expand, ExpandAll, ExpandNumerator, ExpandDenominator, and ExpandFileName.

Command Templates

After typing a command name, the next character expected by the Wolfram Language is typically the left square bracket [. But rather than typing this, you can have *Mathematica* paste a template of the complete syntax structure for your command, including both square brackets and everything in between. You can then just TAB from item to item within the square brackets to complete your input.

For example, type Plo into an input cell and use the command completion popup to complete it to Plot. At this point another popup will appear. Hit the double down arrow to see the syntax options:

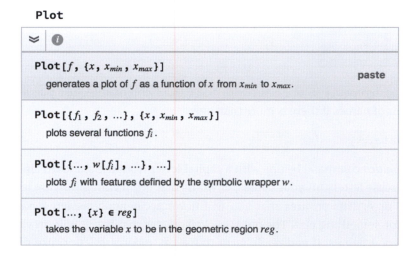

The first option is the most basic and typically the most common, and it is highlighted. Just hit ENTER to paste this template into your input cell. It will look like this:

$$\text{Plot}[f, \{x, x_{min}, x_{max}\}]$$

You can now complete the input (replacing f with the function *you* want to plot, x with your variable, x_{min} with the lower bound for *your* domain, etc.) using the TAB key to jump from item to item.

Command completion and templates used together are a powerful tool. Type a few letters, complete the command, then choose an appropriate template for your application. It is an easy way to speed up your workflow and avoid syntax errors.

1.12 Free-Form Input

The Wolfram Language has a mechanism for translating informal natural language into correctly formatted *Mathematica* input. This can be extremely useful if you know what you want to do but are not sure which *Mathematica* command will accomplish the task. As a simple example, position the cursor below or between existing cells in your notebook so that a thin horizontal line appears across your screen, and click on the small + sign on the left side of the line. In the popup menu that appears, select Free-form Input. The cursor will change to a colored equal sign. Now type a query in ordinary language, like this:

⊟ x^2-1

Hit ENTER (or SHIFT┫ENTER), and you will see *Mathematica*'s best guess at the input required to complete your request, properly formatted, along with the resulting output:

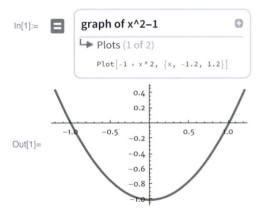

Click on the properly formatted input and it will replace your original query.

1.13 Computing with Real Data

The Wolfram Language is enhanced by the availability of a huge repository of curated data in the Wolfram Knowledgebase that can be input directly into *Mathematica*. An internet connection is needed to access this repository. And in a manner similar to the free-form input discussed earlier, curated data can often be accessed with a simple text query; the method for doing this is discussed in Section 2.8. The net result is a computing environment of unparalleled sophistication, utility, and elegance. Below we show a few examples to give you a sense of what is possible.

Get a 3D plot of any anatomical structure. You can rotate the plot with your mouse.

In[1]:= **AnatomyPlot3D**[left hand ANATOMICAL STRUCTURE]

Out[1]=

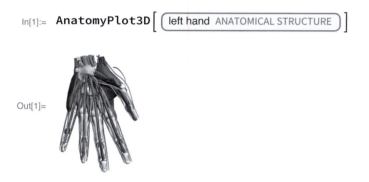

How large an area did the Roman Empire encompass at its peak?

In[2]:= **GeoListPlot**[Roman Empire HISTORICAL COUNTRY]

Out[2]=

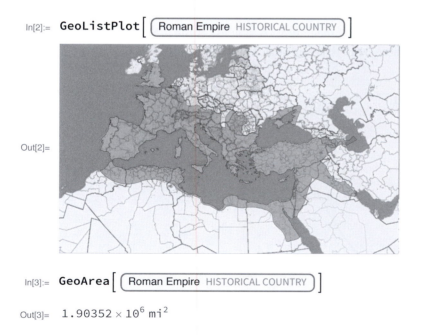

In[3]:= **GeoArea**[Roman Empire HISTORICAL COUNTRY]

Out[3]= $1.90352 \times 10^6 \text{ mi}^2$

How many words were spoken in each State of the Union address, from George Washington's first address in 1790 to the present? (The plot below shows word counts for each address up to and including Donald Trump's second in 2018.)

In[4]:= `DateListPlot[ResourceData["State of the Union Addresses"][`
`All, {"Date", "Words"}], PlotRange → All, AspectRatio → 1 / 3]`

Out[4]=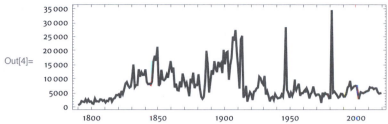

1.14 Saving Your Work and Quitting *Mathematica*

Say you want to save a notebook that you created. If you are using *Mathematica* Online or any cloud–based product, this is automatic. Just exit your session and the most recent version of your work will be saved. But with a standalone desktop version of *Mathematica*, you will need to actively save your notebook. Let's suppose that it is a freshly created notebook that has not been saved previously. Go to the File menu and select Save. You will be prompted by the computer and asked two things: What name do you want to give the notebook, and where would you like the computer to put it? Give it any name you like (it is good form to append the suffix ".nb" which stands for "notebook"), and save it to an appropriate location. The details of this procedure vary somewhat from one platform to the next (Mac OS, Windows, etc.), so ask a friendly soul for assistance if you are unfamiliar with the computer in front of you. Keep in mind that the saving and naming routine isn't a *Mathematica* thing; it's a process that will be similar for every program on the computer you are using. Anyone who is familiar with the platform will be able to help.

⚠ The file size of a *Mathematica* notebook tends to be quite small unless the notebook contains lots of graphics. Notebook files are also portable across computer platforms, as the files themselves are plain text (ASCII) files. The *Mathematica* front end interprets and displays notebook files in much the same way that a web browser interprets and displays HTML files. For information on the actual structure of the underlying notebook file, select **Wolfram Documentation** from the **Help** menu, type "notebooks as Wolfram Language expressions" in the text field, then read the tutorial Notebooks as Wolfram Language Expressions.

If you have created a large notebook file, and want to shrink its file size (for instance to make it small enough to attach to an email), do this: Open the notebook and delete the graphics cells. To do this, click once on a graphic's cell bracket to select it, then choose **Cut** in the **Edit** menu. Do not cut out the input cells that generated the graphics. Now save the notebook. When you open the notebook next time, you can regenerate any graphic by entering the input cell that created it. An even simpler approach is to select **Cell ▷ Delete all Output**, and then save your notebook. When you open the file later, select **Evaluation ▷ Evaluate Notebook** to re-evaluate every input cell in the notebook.

After a notebook has been saved once, the title bar will bear its filename. Note that desktop versions of *Mathematica* do not "auto-save" your work, so you should get in the habit of saving your notebooks often, as you are writing them. This is easy to do: choose Save from the File menu. This will write the latest version of the notebook to the location where the file was last saved. Should the power fail during a session, or should your computer crash for some reason, it is the last saved version of your notebook that will survive. Experienced users understand that it's best to save your work every few minutes, just in case.

To end a *Mathematica* session, select Quit from the application's main menu. If you have modified your notebook since it was last saved, you will be prompted to save the changes you have made: Answer Yes.

1.15 Frequently Asked Questions About *Mathematica*'s Syntax

Why Do All *Mathematica* Command Names Begin with Capital Letters?

Mathematica is case-sensitive, and every one of the thousands of built-in *Mathematica* commands begins with a capital letter. So do all built-in constants, built-in option settings, and so on. In fact, every built-in *Mathematica* symbol of any kind that has a name begins with a capital letter (or the $ or \ characters). Taken together, there are over 6000 such objects.

```
In[1]:=  Length[Names["*"]]
Out[1]=  6407
```

Why capital letters? The main reason is that you will find yourself assigning names to quantities, such as x = 3 or pi = 3.14. Since you don't know the name of every built-in object, there is a danger that you may choose a name that coincides with the name of a built-in command or constant. Without getting into the technicalities, that wouldn't work. But the issue can be avoided if you simply stick to the convention of beginning all your assignment names with lowercase letters or by using special symbols like $\mathcal{R}$ or σ. By doing this you guarantee that you will never choose a name that conflicts with an existing *Mathematica* symbol.

Why Does My Input Appear in Color as I Type?

Mathematica will not be able to process your input unless it is grammatically correct. Syntax coloring is an aid to help you navigate these perilous waters in real time as you type. Any symbol that is not in the system's memory will appear in blue in your notebook. So as you type a command such as Factor, it will be blue until the final r is added, at which point it turns black. If it doesn't turn black—oops, you mistyped it. When you use = to define your own symbols, they too will turn black upon being entered. Brackets need to come in pairs, so that each opening bracket is paired with a matching closing bracket somewhere down the line. An opening bracket appears brightly colored, and turns black only when its matching closing bracket has been appropriately placed. If your input has any brightly colored brackets, then it is not ready for entry.

Why Are the Arguments of Commands Enclosed in Square Brackets?

The numerical approximation command N is an example of what a mathematician calls a function; that is, it converts an argument *x* to an output N[*x*]. In *Mathematica*, all functions enclose their arguments in square brackets [ ], always.

You may recall that in our usual mathematical notation, we often write $f(x)$ to denote the value of the function f with argument x. This won't do in *Mathematica*, for parentheses ( ) are reserved for grouping terms. In a world where round brackets are used for both delimiting function arguments and for algebraic grouping, expressions such as $f(12)$ are ambiguous: It is not clear whether you intend for a function named f to be evaluated at 12, or whether you want the *product* of a variable named f with the number 12. You and I can usually flesh out the meaning of the notation $f(12)$ from its context, but a computer needs unambiguous grammatical rules to make such distinctions. Hence in *Mathematica*, square brackets are used to enclose function arguments, while parentheses are used to group terms.

When working with *Mathematica*, never use round parentheses for anything other than grouping terms, and never use square brackets for anything other than enclosing the arguments to functions.

What Happens If I Use Incorrect Syntax?

If you want to find the natural log of 7.3, you must type Log[7.3], not log(7.3), not Log(7.3), not log[7.3], not ln[7.3], and not anything else.

What happens if you slip and muff the syntax? First of all, don't worry. This *will* happen to you. The computer won't explode. For example, behold:

In[2]:= **Log[7.3**

Here our input is close enough to the correct syntax that *Mathematica* suspects that we goofed, and tells us so. Upon entering an incomplete or erroneous input, *Mathematica* will show a warning flag in the expression's cell bracket, and will often highlight or brightly color the offending part of the input. Click once on the warning flag and any relevant warning messages will be displayed.

In[3]:= **Log[7.3**

••• Syntax: Expression "Log[7.3" has no closing "]".

You will certainly generate messages like this at some point, so it's good to acquaint yourself with some. Error messages may be somewhat cryptic to interpret, and are rarely a welcome sight. But do read the text of these messages, for you will often be able to make enough sense of them to find the source of the problem. In this case we left off the closing square bracket. Note that as you type your input, each opening bracket will appear brightly colored until the corresponding closing bracket is added, at which time both brackets will turn black. This makes mistakes of this type easy to spot. If an expression has one or more brightly colored brackets, it is incomplete and should not be entered.

But worse than getting an error message or input flag is getting neither. It is not difficult to enter syntactically correct but meaningless input. For example, consider this:

In[4]:= **ln (7.3)**

Out[4]= **7.3 ln**

No warning is given (other than the command name ln appearing in blue before the cell is entered), but the output is *not* the natural logarithm of 7.3. *Mathematica* has instead multiplied the meaningless symbol ln by the number 7.3 (remember round brackets are for grouping only). *Always* look carefully and critically at your output. There will certainly be times when you need to go back and edit and reenter your input before you get the answer you desire.

2
Working with *Mathematica*

2.1   Opening Saved Notebooks

You can open any *Mathematica* notebook stored on your computer or in the cloud by double-clicking its icon. It will appear on your screen exactly as it was when it was saved. You can open several notebooks at the same time if you wish.

2.2   Adding Text to Notebooks

Text Cells

Mathematica has a full-featured, integrated word processor that is simple to use once you are familiar with the cell structure of a *Mathematica* notebook. In Section 1.5, "Input and Output," we discussed input and output cells. To add text to a notebook, you need to create a *text cell*. To do this, click once beneath an existing cell (or anywhere in the notebook window if you are working in a new notebook), and look for a small "+" sign on the far left of the horizontal insertion bar. Click on it and select Plain Text, and you are ready to begin typing. It is common practice to use a new text cell for each paragraph of text. Note that with the desktop version of *Mathematica*, using the key combination $\boxed{\text{OPTION}}\!\!-\!\!\boxed{\text{ENTER}}$ from within a cell (Mac OS) or $\boxed{\text{ALT}}\!\!-\!\!\boxed{\text{ENTER}}$ (PC) will create a new cell of the same type, so use this key combination when you finish typing one paragraph and are ready to create the next one.

In both online and desktop versions of *Mathematica*, another way to create a text cell is to look within the Format menu. In addition to text cells, here you will find many possible cell styles, including Title and Section.

Mathematica's text environment is simple to use. It wraps lines for you within each text cell, and you can use a palette to paste a mathematical symbol or expression into your text, just as you paste into an input cell. The desktop version includes a full-featured spell checker—it will underline words that do not appear in its dictionary; hover the cursor over such a word and suggestions will appear in a popup, allowing you to choose the word you intended to type. You can change the size, face, font, and color of a text selection by choosing the appropriate item in the Format menu. In the desktop version you may bring up a formatting toolbar by choosing Window ▷ Toolbar ▷ Formatting. There are buttons on the toolbar to control the centering and justification of your text. Use these features to make your notebook a masterpiece.

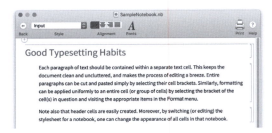

A Notebook with the Formatting Toolbar Displayed

You can cut, copy, paste, and format entire cells or groups of cells. You *select* a cell or group of cells by positioning the tip of the cursor arrow on a cell bracket or grouping bracket along the right side of the notebook window. SHIFT -click to select several adjacent cells at once. The cell bracket of the selected cell or cells will be highlighted. Now choose Cut or Copy from the Edit menu, position the mouse where you wish to paste the selection (in the current notebook or in any other notebook that is open), click once, and select Paste from the Edit menu. Similarly, the commands in the Format menu will be applied to the text in any cell or group of cells whose bracket is selected.

Mathematica's cell structure makes it easy to organize your notebook into collapsible sections. You simply add Title or Section headings. To do this, click between existing cells (or below the last cell in the notebook, or above the first cell), and then go to the drop-down menu in the toolbar (or in the Format menu) and select Title, or Section, or Subsection, and start typing. Upon adding a title cell to a notebook, you will notice a gigantic grouping bracket on the far right of your notebook window that spans the entire notebook. Place the cursor anywhere along this bracket and double-click to *close the group.* You will see the title, but the rest of the notebook will disappear. Don't worry, it's still there; double-click again on the bracket to *open the group.* When you create sections or subsections, grouping brackets will appear to show their scope, and these too can be toggled open or closed with a double-click on the appropriate grouping bracket. These features allow you to keep your work organized, and minimize the amount of scrolling needed to navigate a large document.

If you click between cells in a notebook and then start typing, you will by default create a new input cell. This makes it easy to enter input during a *Mathematica* session; as soon as you get output from one computation, you can just start typing to generate a new input cell. You only have to specify cell type (Text, Title, Section, etc.) when you want to create some type of cell other than input.

If you accidentally start typing text in an input cell, don't despair. The fix is simple: Click once on the cell's bracket to select it, then use the toolbar (or go to the Format menu) to change the cell to a text cell. In the desktop version its even simpler: After typing a few words of text into an input cell, a popup will ask if you want to convert the cell to a text cell.

Adding Mathematical Expressions to Text

If you wish to place a mathematical formula or symbolic expression (such as $f(x) = x^2$) within a sentence of text, there is a simple means for doing so. While typesetting mathematics is an inherently subtle business, *Mathematica* is an excellent platform for producing beautifully typeset equations. Its prowess in this regard far exceeds that of standard word processing programs such as Word, and rivals that of specialty programs such as LATEX. We advise you to read carefully the procedure outlined below, as the method for adding mathematical expressions to text, while not difficult, is not immediately obvious. At the time of this writing, this procedure works only for desktop versions of *Mathematica*.

To typeset a mathematical expression within a sentence of text, begin by creating a text cell (as outlined in the previous section) and typing the text that will precede the mathematical expression. When you are ready to insert the math, from the menus select Insert ▷ Typesetting ▷ Start Inline Cell, or hit CTRL 9 on the keyboard. The state of the cursor will change to a placeholder within a lightly colored box. This colored box delimits what is called an *inline cell.* Now type your mathematics, using palettes if you like, being careful not to exit the inline cell as you add the mathematics (if you exit the colored box, use the back-arrow key to get back into it). When you are finished typing the mathematical expression, hit the forward-arrow to exit the inline cell. You can also exit the inline cell by hitting CTRL 0. It's easy to remember these keyboard shortcuts as CTRL (to start a mathematical expression and CTRL) to end it.

When you are typing in an inline cell, you'll notice that what you type is displayed differently than ordinary text. For instance: any single letter will be italicized, a hyphen will change subtly to a minus sign, and spacing will be different. For example, here is an equation typeset *without* using an inline cell: f(x)-x=0. And here is what is produced by the same keystrokes when typeset within an inline cell: $f(x) - x = 0$. The difference is striking. The inline cell environment will automatically handle these and countless other subtleties to make your mathematics clear and readable.

Modifying the Stylesheet

You can change the look of an entire notebook by changing the *stylesheet.* A stylesheet contains different formatting parameters for each cell type. One stylesheet might render all input cells with light purple backgrounds; another might render all titles, sections, and subsections in 18-point Helvetica font, with 12-point Times New Roman as the default font in Text cells. By choosing a new stylesheet, your notebook will take on a completely new look. Go to Format ▷ StyleSheet to select a stylesheet for your notebook; there are several from which to choose, or you may make a new one.

Note that whenever you switch stylesheets, the items in the Format ▷ Style menu will change to reflect the cell styles available in that stylesheet. Note also that stylesheets can be used to control both the on-screen and print versions of notebooks, and even to make each look different from the other if you wish. Stylesheets may also be used to change what the default cell style is in a particular notebook (the type of cell that will be created if you just start typing). In order to see just how powerful these concepts are, try this: Open a new blank notebook, and switch to the Format ▷ Stylesheet ▷ Utility ▷ Correspondence stylesheet. Now pay attention: you are going to write a formal letter. First type your name and address, using carriage returns to create new lines. It appears in a special "Sender" cell, complete with a gray label to remind you of that fact. Now hit the *down-arrow* on the keyboard to jump to the insertion point for the next cell. Immediately start typing. This time a "Date" cell will be created, so type today's date. Again, when you're done hit the down-arrow. Now type the recipient's name and address. Down-arrow. Type a salutation, such as "Dear Stephen," then down-arrow. Now type the body of your letter, using the carriage return to create new paragraphs. Down-arrow. Type your closing, such as "Sincerely" or "Cheers." Down-arrow. And finally, add your signature. Now have a look at a print preview of the document. All the gray cell labels are scrubbed from the printed version; the formatting is just right. If you have to write a lot of letters, this stylesheet streamlines your workflow. That's exactly what a stylesheet should do. *Creating* a sophisticated stylesheet like this one takes a bit of work, but *using* it takes almost none. And if you just wish to modify an existing stylesheet to better suit your purposes, well that's a breeze. Read on.

Suppose you wish to modify an existing cell style, for instance, to change the look of the Section headings in your current notebook. Or suppose you wish to create an entirely new cell style, say a custom text cell that puts a light gray background shading behind your text. To do this you add a local modification to the notebook's stylesheet as follows: Create a notebook, and either apply one of the included stylesheets or just stick with the default. Now choose Format ▷ Edit Stylesheet…, and the stylesheet for your notebook will appear. At the top of this notebook you may either choose an existing style to modify (if, for instance, you just want to change the default text font), or type the name of a new style you would like to create (if, for instance, you want to keep the default text style, and add a second text style for some other purpose). In either case, a cell will appear in this new notebook, and its cell bracket will be selected. Go directly to the Format menu and apply the formatting changes you desire to this selected cell. You can change the font, the font size, the font slant, the font color, the background color, the alignment, etc. When you are finished, close the stylesheet window and return to your notebook. If you created a new style, its name will appear at the bottom of the Format ▷ Style menu, so you may easily apply it to any cell in your notebook at any time. If you modified an existing style, all cells of that style in your notebook will now reflect that change.

2.3   Printing

As long as your computer is connected to a printer (and the printer has ink and paper and is turned on!) you can print your current notebook by going to the File menu and choosing Print…. If your notebook contains graphics or two-dimensional input using special math fonts, it may take a moment to start printing, so be patient.

You can also select one or more cells to print, rather than printing an entire notebook. This can save vast quantities of paper, so we repeat: You don't have to print the entire notebook. To print a single cell or any group of cells delimited by a grouping bracket, position the tip of the cursor arrow on the cell or grouping bracket and click once. This *selects* the cell or group. Now go to the File menu and choose Print Selection….

To select several adjacent cells when there is no grouping bracket, hold down the SHIFT key and click on their cell brackets one by one. They will all become selected. To select several nonadjacent cells, hold down the ⌘ key (Mac OS), or the CTRL key (Windows) while clicking on cell brackets. You can then print your selection as above: Go to the File menu and choose Print Selection….

Printing a notebook that has graphics can sometimes lead to less-than-optimal page breaks. It is easy to add more page breaks, but it can be tricky to force pages not to break. To add a page break, simply click between the cells where you would like the break to occur and select Insert ▷ PageBreak. To remove a break above or below a graphic, try resizing the graphic. It is often the case that smaller graphics look better in print, so this may be a good idea in any event. If this does not help, or if the unwanted page break is not adjacent to a graphic, select the bracket of the first cell to appear after the unwanted break, then summon the Option Inspector by visiting Format ▷ Option Inspector.... Make sure that the first drop-down menu reads **Selection** (which it should by default). Now type "pagebreak" into the text field. Change the **PageBreakAbove** setting for the selected cell to **False**. Repeat as necessary for nearby cells. If you are working on a Mac, be sure to make use of the PDF button in the Print dialog to view a preview before committing your notebook to paper.

It is possible to control what is printed in the header and footer areas on each page of a printed notebook. By default, the header is composed of the filename of the notebook and the page number. To change this, go to the File menu and select Printing Settings ▷ Headers and Footers.... The resulting dialog box gives you the option of not displaying a header on the first page, which is handy if you have a nicely typeset title page. There are also text fields for the content of the left, right, and center portion of each header and footer. The dialog allows you to display the filename, page number, date, or running text of your choice in the headers or footers.

2.4 Creating Presentations

Desktop versions of *Mathematica* have a presentation environment, analogous to PowerPoint or Keynote, but with the unique advantage of providing access to live computation and dynamic elements. You can wow your audience with a `Manipulate`, grab and rotate a 3D graphic in real time, and of course you can evaluate input on the fly. This is possible because a Presenter Notebook is really just a *Mathematica* notebook with some special display features.

To get started, select File ▷ New ▷ Presenter Notebook... in the menus. A window will appear where you can choose a theme and a color scheme for your presentation. Check the box "Prefill slides with sample content" and then click the Create button to open your Presenter Notebook, which will have several sample pages for you to peruse. Use these as templates, editing the content rather than creating new cells from scratch.

There is a toolbar at the top of your Presenter Notebook, and the controls that reside there are generally self-explanatory. You will see a label above each slide, reading "Slide 1 of 6," "Slide 2 of 6," and so on, and you will be able to scroll through the slides. You can select, cut, and copy the elements in your slides to change the content. Or you may add new elements: Use the Cell Style control near the upper left of the toolbar to set the cell style. To add a new slide, position the cursor between existing slides (or at the bottom of the last slide) and push the Insert New Slide button on the left side of the toolbar. To play your presentation, push the Start Presentation button on the right side of the toolbar. To end the presentation, click the contextual menu in the upper right corner and select End Presentation.

You can create a Side Notes window to display presentation notes that you will see but your audience will not. The button to access this window is under the Start Presentation button. You can also create a slideshow outline window with thumbnails of all your slides. Play with these, and explore the other features.

Presenter Notebooks were introduced in version 11.3 of *Mathematica*. It may be useful to understand that earlier versions of *Mathematica* included a "SlideShow" environment for presentations. While that technology still works, its primary purpose these days is to display legacy documents created on older versions of the software. If you are creating a new presentation, we recommend utilizing the more full-featured Presentation Notebook environment.

2.5   Sharing a Notebook

If you are working in a cloud platform such as *Mathematica* Online, sharing is simple: Go to the Share menu and provide the emails of the people with whom you will share the document, or you can instead elect to make it a public webpage.

If you are working on a desktop platform, you can simply save your notebook and send it as an email attachment. The recipient will need to have a working copy of *Mathematica*, or a cloud subscription (the recipient can simply upload it to her cloud account in that case). Be mindful that graphics in your document can greatly increase the file size. It is common practice to delete output cells, especially those containing graphics, before saving to keep your file lean. Remember that you can delete all output cells in your notebook by choosing the menu item Cell ▷ Delete All Output. The recipient can re-evaluate the entire notebook with the menu item Evaluation ▷ Evaluate Notebook.

If your correspondent does not have a *Mathematica* license, you can save your notebook in Computable Document format (go to File ▷ Save As... and select *.cdf). Once saved as a CDF file, you can load it on any device that has the Wolfram CDF Player (a free download available at wolfram.com) or the Wolfram Player app for iOS. CDF documents allow you to keep interactive dynamic elements in your document, such as those produced with *Mathematica*'s `Manipulate` command. It is not possible to evaluate inputs with the player apps, so be sure to leave your outputs intact before saving to the CDF format.

Other common conversion formats available in the Save As... menu include PDF and HTML. We once had a student who was getting nowhere trying to explain a mathematics problem over the phone to a fellow student. He then typed the equations he was thinking of into *Mathematica*, saved the notebook as HTML, posted it to his website, and had the fellow student go to the freshly minted page. This seems a bit extreme, but if you maintain a website and are handy with posting web pages, it's nice to know that it's a simple matter to compose web content in *Mathematica*.

2.6   *Mathematica*'s Kernel

When you enter a command in *Mathematica*, it is processed by an essentially separate computational engine, called the *kernel*. In the early days, the kernel was a completely separate program and this client–server relationship was explicit: You typed and entered a command in a notebook window, and once entered your input was whisked away to the kernel, where it was processed, and the output was then returned to your notebook for display. These days things are not quite so clear-cut (for instance, multi-core hardware may run a separate subkernel on each processor, and dynamic interactive interfaces can blur the line between user interface and computation), but the conceptual dichotomy between the front end, where you type your input, and the kernel, where computation occurs, still persists. This makes it possible, for instance, to run your kernel on a completely separate machine (a massively parallel super computer, for instance). It also makes it possible to abort a calculation that seems to be taking too long to finish without disturbing your notebook contents.

Numbering Input and Output

The inputs that you send to the kernel, and the outputs delivered by the kernel, are numbered in your notebook. They are numbered in the order that they are received by the kernel. When you first launch *Mathematica*, the first input that you enter will be labeled In[1]:=, and its output will be labeled Out[1]=. The next input will be labeled In[2]:=, and so on.

Be mindful that the numbering is determined by the sequential order in which the commands are received by the kernel, and not necessarily by their location within the notebook. For instance, if you were to start a *Mathematica* session by opening an existing notebook, then scroll down to some input cell in the middle of that notebook, click in that cell and enter it, it would be labeled In[1]:=.

Re-evaluating Previously Saved Notebooks

When you first launch *Mathematica* and open a notebook that you saved earlier, you will notice that none of the inputs or outputs will be numbered in that notebook, even if they had been when you saved it. That's because the numbering refers to the order in which input cells were sent to the kernel and in which output cells were delivered from the kernel *in your current session*. When you quit *Mathematica*, the kernel shuts down and this information is discarded. So when you launch *Mathematica* and open a previously saved notebook, you are free to click in any input cell and enter it. That cell will acquire the label In[1]:=, and its output will be called Out[1]=.

For instance, suppose you start a new *Mathematica* session by opening a notebook that contains the following input and output cells (they are not numbered, since they have not been entered in this session):

```
a = 90
90

a^2
8100
```

What would happen if you were to click on the second input cell (containing the text a^2) and enter it? The kernel would be unaware of the cell containing the assignment a = 90 since that cell has not been entered in the current session. The resulting notebook would look like this:

In[1]:= **a = 90**

Out[1]= 90

In[2]:= **a^2**

Out[2]= 8100

In practice this means that when reopening an old notebook to continue work that you started in a previous session, you should reenter, one by one and in order, all the inputs to which you will refer later in the session.

You can automate this procedure if you like. Upon opening a previously saved notebook to continue working on it, go to the Evaluation menu and select Evaluate Notebook. This will instruct the kernel to evaluate every cell in the notebook, in order, from top to bottom. It's a handy way to pick up your work where you left off. Alternately, you may OPTION-click on the cell bracket of any cell (Mac OS), or ALT-click (Windows), to select *all* cells of that type in the notebook. Do this to an input cell, and all input cells will be selected. Now go to the Evaluation menu and choose Evaluate Cells.

⚠ Many notebooks contain certain input cells that will be evaluated each time the notebook is used; this is often the case with notebooks created for students by teachers. Such notebooks utilize special types of input cells called initialization cells. When a cell is an initialization cell, it will be automatically evaluated before any other input cells in the notebook. Typical initialization cells will define a special command to be used throughout the notebook, or load a *Mathematica* package, which will typically define a suite of commands that are designed to extend *Mathematica*'s core capabilities. When you send your first input to the kernel from a notebook containing one or more initialization cells, you will be prompted and asked if you want to automatically evaluate all initialization cells in the notebook. If you ever see such a prompt, answer "Yes." Moreover, if you want to make an input cell in one of your own notebooks an initialization cell, select the cell by clicking once on its cell bracket (or SHIFT-click on several cell brackets), then go to the Cell menu and choose Cell Properties ▷ Initialization Cell.

You will notice that the cell gets a light-gray background, and its cell bracket gets little vertical tick mark at the top. Now when you reopen this notebook in a new session you will be prompted to evaluate the initialization cells.

2.7 Tips for Working Effectively

Referring to Previous Output

In a typical *Mathematica* session you will enter a cell, examine the output, enter a cell, examine the output, enter a cell, examine the output, and so on. There are numerous little tricks that make it easier to deal efficiently with *Mathematica*'s input–output structure. Perhaps the most important is the percentage sign. When you need to use the output of the previous cell as part of your input to the current cell, just type %. *Mathematica* interprets % as the output of the last cell processed by the kernel (i.e., % represents the contents of the output cell with the highest label number):

In[1]:= $\dfrac{21^{20}}{20^{21}}$

Out[1]= 278 218 429 446 951 548 637 196 401 / 2 097 152 000 000 000 000 000 000 000

In[2]:= N[%]

Out[2]= 0.132665

If you prefer to copy and paste an input or output from above, of course that will work as well. The percentage sign is just quick way to refer to the most recent output, a tool to streamline your work-flow. Note also that %% can be used to represent the second-most-recent output.

Finally, note that since referring to previous output is so commonplace, there is yet another way to copy and paste output to an input cell: click below an old output cell and select Insert ▷ Output from Above from the menu. This will paste the contents of the output cell that resides *directly above* the p osition of the cursor into a new input cell (regardless of when that cell was processed by the kernel). Y ou can then edit the new input cell and enter it.

Referring to Previous Input

You will often enter a cell and later want to enter something very similar. The simplest way to deal with this is to click on the former input cell and edit it, then reenter it. The cursor can be anywhere in the input cell when you enter it; it need not be at the far right. Once the edited cell is entered, its label number will be updated (for example from In[5]:= to In[6]:=). The old output will be replaced with the output from the edited input cell. While simple and effective, this technique will destroy your previous input cell.

If you want to keep (rather than overwrite) a previous input and output, click below the old output c ell, go to the menu, and select Insert ▷ Input from Above. The content of the old input cell will be c opied into a new input cell, which you can then edit and enter.

Of course you may also simply copy and paste your old input into a new cell.

Postfix Command Structure

The typical structure for *Mathematica* commands is:

Command [*argument*] or Command [*argument1*, *argument2*]

We've seen examples such as Sin$\left[\frac{\pi}{4}\right]$ and Log[10, 243]. When a command has only one argument, another way to apply it is in *postfix* form. The postfix form for a command is:

argument // Command

This form is useful when the command is applied to an existing expression as an afterthought. For instance, if you copy the contents of an earlier input or output cell into a new input cell, you can easily apply a command in postfix form to the entire copied expression. Here are some examples:

In[3]:= $\mathsf{Sin}\left[\dfrac{\pi}{12}\right]$ // N

Out[3]= 0.258819

This is equivalent to entering $\mathsf{N}\left[\mathsf{Sin}\left[\frac{\pi}{12}\right]\right]$.

In[4]:= (x - 1) (2 + 3 x) (6 - x) // Expand

Out[4]= $-12 - 4\,x + 19\,x^2 - 3\,x^3$

This is equivalent to entering Expand[(x - 1) (3 x + 2) (6 - x)].

Prefix Command Structure

When a command accepts a single argument, it can also be given in *prefix* form. The prefix form for a command is:

> Command@*argument*

Like the postfix form, this form can useful when the command is applied to an existing expression as an afterthought. It allows you to type the new command to the left of the previous input, without worrying about adding a closing square bracket. Here are some examples:

In[5]:= First@{2, 4, 6, 8}

Out[5]= 2

This is equivalent to entering First[{2, 4, 6, 8}].

In[6]:= TraditionalForm@Sin[x]^2

Out[6]//TraditionalForm=

$\sin^2(x)$

This is equivalent to entering $\mathsf{TraditionalForm}\left[\mathsf{Sin[x]}^2\right]$.

Undoing Mistakes

If you make a *bad* mistake in typing or editing, the kind that makes you say, "I wish I could undo that and return my notebook to its former state," the chances are that you can. Look for Undo in the Edit menu. It will reverse the previous action. You can undo multiple mistakes by applying the procedure more than once.

For desktop versions at the time of this writing, *Mathematica* does not auto-save your notebooks. So another option is to visit the File menu select Revert... and answer Yes to the popup. You will find your notebook in the state that it was in when it was last saved. Of course, you should only do this if you have saved the notebook recently, and before the mistake was introduced.

A more frightening scenario is entering an input cell and finding that *Mathematica* appears to be stuck. For a long time you see the text "Running…" in the notebook's title bar, but no output is being generated. You may have inadvertently asked *Mathematica* to perform a very difficult calculation, and after a few minutes you may get tired of waiting. How can you make it stop? Go to the Evaluation menu and select Abort Evaluation. Depending on the situation, it may halt immediately or you may have to wait a moment before it stops. Be patient. If more than a few minutes pass with no response, refer to Section 2.10, "Troubleshooting."

Keyboard Shortcuts

As you become a regular user, you will likely find it easier to use keyboard shortcuts than to make repeated trips to menus and palettes. Next to many menu items you will find annotations for keyboard shortcuts that will perform the same task. We summarize some of the most common tasks in Table 2.1.

Task	Mac OS	Windows
Save your notebook	CMD s	CTRL s
Cut	CMD x	CTRL x
Copy	CMD c	CTRL c
Paste	CMD v	CTRL v
Undo an editing or typing mistake	CMD z	CTRL z
Create free-form input	CTRL =	CTRL =
Create a new cell of the same type	OPTION ENTER	ALT ENTER
Copy input from above	CMD l	CTRL l
Copy output from above	SHIFT CMD l	SHIFT CTRL l
Complete a command	CMD k	CTRL k
Make a command template	SHIFT CMD k	SHIFT CTRL k
Look up selected command	SHIFT CMD f	SHIFT CTRL f
Abort an evaluation	CMD .	ALT .
Quit	CMD q	ALT F4

Table 2.1 **Keyboard Shortcuts.** When reading this table, CMD q means hitting the command key and the q key at the same time. On a Mac, the command key is marked ⌘.

Typesetting Input: More Shortcuts

A typical input cell contains symbols and structures created both from the keyboard and from palettes (such as the Basic Math Assistant palette). As you get more familiar with *Mathematica*, you will want to find the easiest way to typeset your input. It is helpful to know that there are ways to get many symbols and structures directly from the keyboard without invoking the use of a palette at all. Table 2.2 shows some of the most often used. You can find others by opening the SpecialCharacters palette. Hover the cursor over a symbol on the palette to reveal its keyboard entry sequence.

For instance, you can produce the input

$$\pi^2 + \frac{x}{y}$$

by typing the following key sequence:

`ESC` p `ESC` `CTRL`-`6` 2 `CTRL`-`SPACE` + `CTRL`-`/` x `TAB` y

And you can produce the input

$$\frac{\pi^2 + x}{y}$$

by typing the following key sequence:

`CTRL`-`/` `ESC` p `ESC` `CTRL`-`6` 2 `CTRL`-`SPACE` + x `TAB` y

Type	To get
`ESC` p `ESC`	the symbol π
`ESC` ee `ESC`	the symbol e
`ESC` ii `ESC`	the symbol i
`ESC` inf `ESC`	the symbol ∞
`ESC` deg `ESC`	the symbol $^\circ$ (for entering angles in degrees)
`ESC` elem `ESC`	the symbol $\in$ (is an element of)
`ESC` th `ESC`	the symbol θ (no built-in meaning, but often used)
`ESC` * `ESC`	the symbol $\times$
`CTRL`-`^` or `CTRL`-`6`	to the exponent position
`CTRL`-`/`	into a fraction
`CTRL`-`2`	into a square root
`CTRL`-`SPACE`	out of an exponent, denominator, or square root
`TAB`	from one placeholder to the next

Table 2.2   Keyboard Shortcuts for Typesetting. When reading this table, `CTRL`-`2` means hitting the control key and the 2 key *at the same time*, while `CTRL` 2 means hitting the control key *followed by* the 2 key.

Of course, if you consider yourself a poor typist, you may want to use palettes more rather than less. Check out the Basic Math Assistant palette (in the Palettes menu). It contains buttons that will paste templates of commonly used commands into your notebook. This keeps your typing to a minimum, and helps you remember the correct syntax for commands. Whichever approach you take, you'll eventually find the way to typeset *Mathematica* input that works best for you.

Suppressing Output and Entering Sequences of Commands

There will be times when you don't want *Mathematica* to produce output. For instance, suppose you need to carry out several calculations involving the quantity $\frac{\pi}{12}$. Rather than type this expression each time it is needed, you can assign its value to a letter and type this letter instead. When you make this assignment and enter it, *Mathematica* will display the value as its output:

In[7]:= $x = \dfrac{\pi}{12}$

Out[7]= $\dfrac{\pi}{12}$

Here the output is not necessary. If you would like to suppress the output of any input cell, simply type a semicolon ; after typing the contents of the cell. The kernel will still process the input, but the output will not be displayed in your notebook. So here is the best way to make an assignment, for instance:

In[8]:= $x = \dfrac{\pi}{12}$;

You can type a sequence of several commands in a single input cell by putting semicolons between them. Only the output of the final command will be displayed. When you are typing, you can use the character return key ([RET] on a Mac or [ENTER] on a PC) to move to a new line in the same input cell, or you can keep it all on one line if it will fit:

In[9]:= $x = 3$;
$\text{Expand}\left[(x - y)^8\right]$

Out[10]= $6561 - 17\,496\,y + 20\,412\,y^2 - 13\,608\,y^3 + 5670\,y^4 - 1512\,y^5 + 252\,y^6 - 24\,y^7 + y^8$

In[11]:= $\text{Clear}[x]; \text{Expand}\left[(x - y)^8\right]$

Out[11]= $x^8 - 8\,x^7\,y + 28\,x^6\,y^2 - 56\,x^5\,y^3 + 70\,x^4\,y^4 - 56\,x^3\,y^5 + 28\,x^2\,y^6 - 8\,x\,y^7 + y^8$

Mathematica will sometimes suppress, or perhaps diminish, output even when you do not ask it to. For instance, this might happen if the output would require the equivalent of a few hundred printed pages. Don't laugh! It's very easy to produce such output, and you could easily do so accidentally. Here's an example that makes use of *factorials*. The factorial of a positive integer n is the product of n with every other positive integer less than n. So the factorial of 5 is $5 \times 4 \times 3 \times 2 \times 1 = 120$. The common mathematical notation for the factorial of n and the *Mathematica* notation agree: Simply type n !, as we do below. Note that factorials grow quickly, so quickly in fact that a million factorial is a number with over five million digits.

In[12]:= **1 000 000 !**

Out[12]=   826 393 168 833 124 006 237 664 610 317 266 629 113 534 797 896 387 304 516 ⋮
           777 588 556 337 961 103 564 508 444 653 051 ⟨··· 5 565 528 ···⟩
           0 000 000 000 000 000 000 000 000 000 000 000 000 000 000 000 000 000 000 ⋮
           000 000 000 000 000 000 000 000 000 000 000 000

           large output | show less | show more | show all | set size limit...

Here *Mathematica* does not display the full output. Rather, it displays the first several digits, and the final few digits, and in the gray area in the center it tells us how many digits are missing. The buttons on the bottom of the output permit you to show more or less. If you really want to see all those digits, choose "show all."

If you want to find out whose device has the faster processor for a particular calculation, or if you want to know how long it takes *Mathematica* to arrive at an answer, use the Timing command. Wrap any input with this command, and the output will be a list containing two items (separated by a comma). The first item in the list is the number of seconds that it took the kernel to process your answer (it doesn't include the time it takes to format and display the answer in your notebook, or to download information if that is required), and the second item is the answer itself. If the input to the Timing command is followed by a semicolon, the second item in the list will be the word Null rather than the answer. This is useful when the output is large:

In[13]:= **50 ! // Timing**

Out[13]= $\{8. \times 10^{-6},$
          30 414 093 201 713 378 043 612 608 166 064 768 844 377 641 568 960 512 000 000 ⋮
          000 000$\}$

In[14]:= **1 000 000 !; // Timing**

Out[14]= $\{0.182402, \text{Null}\}$

Master the Triple-Click

The Wolfram Language is highly structured, and this allows for a really efficient way to select all or part of your input or output with your mouse or trackpad: Place the cursor on a single digit or letter in an input or output cell and double-click to select the full number or word containing that character. That's true in pretty much any word processor. But triple-clicking in *Mathematica* will take you out one level in the structural hierarchy, expanding your selection. Quadruple-clicking expands your selection still further, and so on. If you ever want to copy and paste a portion of your input or output, this method of selection is typically far superior to clicking and dragging.

Perhaps the essential takeaway is this: Triple-click on a command name to select the entire scope of that command.

2.8 Working with Entities and Units

Entities

The Wolfram Language includes huge stores of curated real-world data that can be incorporated seamlessly into the standard command syntax. This is a distinguishing feature of the Wolfram Language, and the possibilities it creates are enormous. Yet at the same time, it presents challenges to the new user: How do I access this store of information, and how do I incorporate it in computations?

The basic unit for stored knowledge is the `Entity`, which is typically displayed as an icon. The simplest way to call up an entity is to ask for it in ordinary language: Hit CTRL = on desktop and browser-based versions, or use the designated key on touchscreen devices, and type the name of the thing you seek, then hit ENTER (not SHIFT ENTER). We typed the text "Alan Turing" and the system recognized this as a person.

In[1]:= ⎡ Alan Turing PERSON ✓ ⎤ ;

Click on the checkbox to accept this interpretation. This compact yellow box is an easy-to-use icon that represents the Alan Turing entity. While you will rarely need to see the underlying `InputForm` of an entity, it is useful to understand its structure, and it is nice to know that it is not hard to type it directly:

In[2]:= `Entity["Person", "AlanTuring"]`

Out[2]= ⎡ Alan Turing ⎤

Every `Entity` has a host of associated *properties*:

In[3]:= `EntityProperties[` ⎡ Alan Turing PERSON ⎤ `]`

Out[3]= { other names , astrological sign , date of birth , place of birth , brothers , children , Chinese zodiac sign , daughters , date of death , place of death , father , full name , gender , height , husbands , image , space missions , mathematical contributions , mother , notable film appearances , notable film direction credits , notable film production credits , notable film writing credits , name , nationality , net worth , notable artworks , astronomical discoveries , notable books , famous chemistry problems , notable facts , notable inventions , physics contributions , occupation , parents , siblings , sisters , sons , spouses , weight , wives }

Note that if you hover your mouse over the icon for an `Entity` or `EntityProperty`, a tooltip will show its underlying `InputForm`.

There are two common ways to evaluate a particular property for an entity. One is to treat the `Entity` as a command, and the `EntityProperty` as its argument:

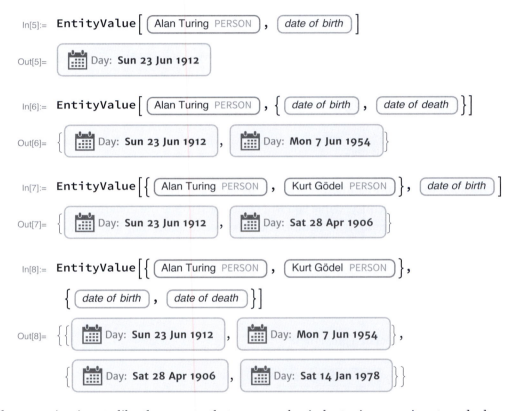

The other is to use the command `EntityValue`. This is handy for evaluating several properties for an entity, or for evaluating a single property for several entities.

When creating inputs like these, note that you may begin by typing your input, and when you reach the point where an `Entity` should appear, type [CTRL]=[=] and use ordinary language to call up the appropriate object, hitting [ENTER] (not [SHIFT]-[ENTER]) to resolve the `Entity` into its icon without evaluating the entire cell. Or if the icon has appeared previously, just copy it and paste it where you like.

It is also handy to understand that `EntityProperty` objects may be called up with a simple text string (in double quotations). When entering the text string, as soon as you type the opening double quotation, a popup will display all legal strings for that position, and after you type each additional character the list will be refined, so in practice only a few characters are required to complete the string. For example, here is another way to ask for Turing's birth date:

In[9]:= `EntityValue[` Alan Turing PERSON `, "BirthDate"]`

Out[9]= ▦ Day: **Sun 23 Jun 1912**

Note that in addition to date objects, entity values can be numerical quantities, text, images, graphics, and even other entities.

In[10]:= `EntityValue[` Alan Turing PERSON `,` image `]`

Out[10]=

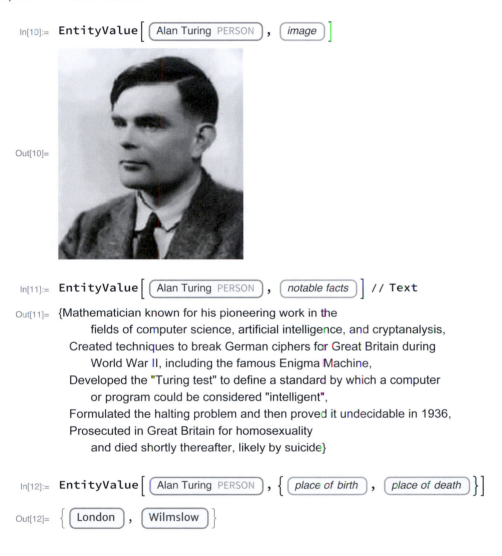

In[11]:= `EntityValue[` Alan Turing PERSON `,` notable facts `] // Text`

Out[11]= {Mathematician known for his pioneering work in the
fields of computer science, artificial intelligence, and cryptanalysis,
Created techniques to break German ciphers for Great Britain during
World War II, including the famous Enigma Machine,
Developed the "Turing test" to define a standard by which a computer
or program could be considered "intelligent",
Formulated the halting problem and then proved it undecidable in 1936,
Prosecuted in Great Britain for homosexuality
and died shortly thereafter, likely by suicide}

In[12]:= `EntityValue[` Alan Turing PERSON `, {` place of birth `,` place of death `}]`

Out[12]= { London `,` Wilmslow }

Units

It is very common for `EntityValue` to return a numeric quantity.

In[13]:= `EntityValue[` [Eiffel Tower BUILDING] `, "Height"]`

Out[13]= `1062.99 ft`

Numeric `EntityValue` output always comes with a unit—it is a `Quantity` object. The `InputForm` for the quantity above is:

In[14]:= `Quantity[1062.99, "Feet"]`

Out[14]= `1062.99 ft`

Mathematica understands thousands of standard units. Units are most easily specified using the same CTRL = technique used for producing entities. For instance, typing "1062.99 ft" into a free-form input produces the same result.

Below we use `GeoGraphics` to produce a map showing the locations of the birthplaces of Archimedes, Euler, Gauss, and Turing. `GeoRange` allows you to control the extent of the region displayed. When it comes time to enter this distance in the input, hit CTRL = and type "800 miles" and hit ENTER . As before, click the checkbox to accept the interpretation. Finally, type the closing bracket and enter the cell.

In[15]:= `EntityValue[{` [Archimedes PERSON] `,` [Leonhard Euler PERSON] `,`
[Carl Friedrich Gauss PERSON] `,` [Alan Turing PERSON] `}, "BirthPlace"]`

Out[15]= `{` [Syracuse] `,` [Basel] `,` [Brunswick] `,` [London] `}`

In[16]:= `GeoGraphics[GeoMarker[%], GeoRange → 800 mi]`

Out[16]=

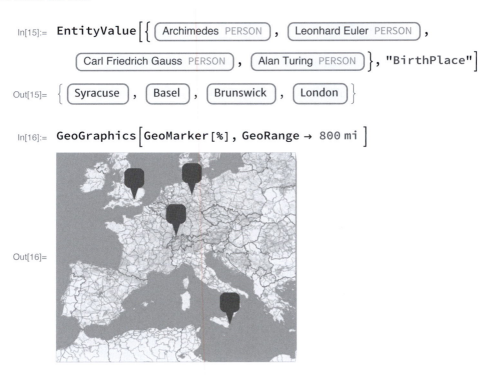

Typing `Quantity[800, "Miles"]` will work in the input, but the spelling must be perfect. As with an `Entity`, as soon as you type the opening double quotation, a popup will appear showing all legal strings. Even so, it is typically easier, when specifying the string to represent the unit, to use the CTRL = paradigm to enter this string, since you can specify your units in natural language (you may use "mi" or "mile" or "miles" or "Miles") and let *Mathematica* interpret your intentions. This is especially useful when you are using a unit for the first time. For example, it is typically easier to type "degrees F" than it is to guess, or to look up, the precise string required to express a `Quantity` in degrees Fahrenheit.

If you hover your mouse over a `Quantity` object, a tooltip will display the full unit name. Note that some disparate units share the same common symbol, such as the US dollar and the Mexican peso, both of which are expressed with $. The tooltip can be very helpful to distinguish such units.

It is a simple matter to convert quantities. Use `UnitConvert` to express the answer as a `Quantity` in the new units, or use `QuantityMagnitude` to strip the units and express the answer as a pure number.

In[17]:= `UnitConvert[ 26.2 mi , km ]`

Out[17]= `42.1648 km`

In[18]:= `QuantityMagnitude[ 26.2 mi , km ]`

Out[18]= `42.1648`

In[19]:= `QuantityMagnitude[ 26.2 mi ]`

Out[19]= `26.2`

The command `CurrencyConvert` works like `UnitConvert`, and will use the current conversion rate to do its thing. Its output is dependent on when you enter it.

In[20]:= `CurrencyConvert[ $10.00 , € ]`

Out[20]= `€8.55`

2.9 Getting Help from *Mathematica*

Command Completion

You have probably noticed that *Mathematica* will offer to finish typing a command for you as soon as you type the first few letters. A popup appears near the cursor with a list of all built-in and user-defined symbols that begin with the letters you have typed so far. Just move the cursor to the appropriate choice and click, or ignore the popup and keep typing until the command you want is at the top of the list, then hit ENTER to paste the full command into your notebook. Try it—type `Expa` in an input cell and attempt the completion. You will find that there are five *Mathematica* commands that start with these letters: `Expand`, `ExpandAll`, `ExpandNumerator`, `ExpandDenominator`, and `ExpandFileName`.

Command Templates

After typing a command name, the next character expected by the Wolfram Language is typically the left square bracket [. But rather than typing this, you can have *Mathematica* paste a template for the complete syntax structure of your command, including both square brackets and everything in between. You can then just TAB from item to item within the square brackets to complete your input.

For example, type `Plo` into an input cell and use the command completion popup to complete it to `Plot`. At this point another popup will appear. Hit the double down-arrow to see the syntax options:

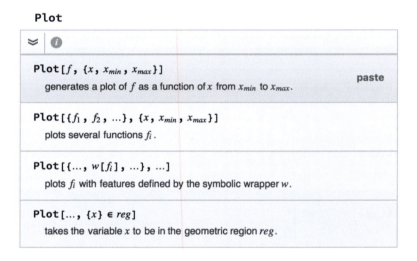

The first option is the most basic and typically the most common, and it is highlighted. Just hit or ENTER to paste a template into your input cell. It will look like this:

$$\texttt{Plot}\Big[\,f\,,\;\Big\{\,x\,,\;x_{min}\,,\;x_{max}\,\Big\}\Big]$$

You can now complete the input (replacing f with the function *you* want to plot, x_{min} with the lower bound for *your* domain, etc.) using the TAB key to jump from item to item.

Command templates and command completions work well together. Type a few letters, complete the command, then make the template. It's an easy way speed up your workflow and avoid syntax errors. See Table 2.1 for keyboard shortcuts.

Getting Information on a Command whose Name You Know

Begin typing the name of the command, and a popup will suggest completions. Hit the little *i* in the popup and you will be directed to the reference page for that command in the Documentation Center, where you will find the correct syntax structure for the command and several usage examples. You may also type ? followed by a *Mathematica* command name, and then enter the cell to get information on that command. For example:

In[1]:= **? N**

> N[*expr*] gives the numerical value of *expr*.
>
> N[*expr, n*] attempts to give a result with *n*-digit precision. ≫

You can click on the ≫ symbol at the end of this output to get more detailed information in the Documentation Center.

Note that the ∗ character may be used as a "wild card" in such a query. The following input, for instance, will return a list of all built-in symbols that include the string "Plot" in their names. We do not show the output here, as there are over 50 such commands and symbols. Click on any name in the output to see its documentation.

In[2]:= **? ∗Plot∗**

Syntax Coloring
Mathematica uses colors to help you type your input. Any symbol that is not in the system's memory will appear in blue in your notebook. So as you type a command such as Factor, it will be blue until the final r is added, at which point it turns black. If it doesn't turn black—oops, you mistyped it. When you use = to define your own symbols, they too will turn black upon being entered.

Brackets need to come in pairs, so that each opening bracket is paired with a matching closing bracket somewhere down the line. An opening bracket appears brightly colored, and turns black only when its matching closing bracket has been appropriately placed. If your input has any brightly colored brackets, then it's not ready for entry.

The Documentation Center
The Wolfram Language Documentation Center is the most useful feature imaginable; learn to use it and use it often. Go to the Help menu and choose Wolfram Documentation. A window will appear displaying the documentation home page. You may either type a keyword in the text field at the top, or follow links from the main page. Every one of the thousands of built-in symbols has its own individual reference page. For example, if you type "Plot" into the text field (with a capital P), the reference page for the Plot function will appear. At the top of the page you will find drop-down menus titled "See Also," "Related Guides," and "Tutorials." These provide paths to supplemental information that can be incredibly useful. And note that there are forward and back buttons to the left of the search field at the top of the page, so it's easy to follow a few links then return to the reference page where you started. Just below these navigation features at the top of the page there is information on syntax for your command, and a "Details and Options" section that will provide comprehensive information on every conceivable option and setting for the command. Finally, there

will be several usage examples. These are live cells that you are free to edit and enter, or you may just want to copy and paste an example input directly into your notebook, where you can edit it to your heart's content.

One could spend the rest of his or her natural life wading through the Documentation Center; it's a big place.

2.10 Troubleshooting

The most common challenge when learning *Mathematica* is adapting to a system in which spelling and syntax must be perfect. What happens if your syntax is wrong (say you typed a period instead of a comma, or forgot to capitalize a command name)? Usually you will get an error message. Don't panic. Most error messages can be traced to a simple typing mistake. Just go back to your last input cell, edit it, and reenter it. If you can't find your mistake, ask a friend or your instructor. You may also want to try the online help features discussed earlier.

In any event, if your input is either generating error messages or not generating the output you want, look first for spelling or syntax problems. If you are reasonably certain that the command has been entered correctly, there are a few other things you might try. If *Mathematica* beeped when you attempted to enter your input cell, you can go to the Help menu and select Why the Beep?…. This will provide you with an explanation that may be quite helpful. Another tactic that cures a common source of problems is to clear the names of any variables appearing in your input, then try reentering the cell. For instance, if your current input involves a variable called *x*, and somewhere long ago you typed x = 3, then *Mathematica* will substitute 3 for *x* every chance it gets for as long as the current kernel is running. You may have forgotten that you made such an assignment, and no longer want it. Type and enter Clear[x] to remove any previous assignment to *x*, then reenter your input cell (you will need to clear the values of all symbols that have been assigned values in *your* current session; such expressions may or may not be called *x* in *your* notebook). Get in the habit of clearing variable names as soon as you are done with them.

Another reality that you may encounter at some point is that your computer can *crash*. This occurs only rarely under ordinary usage on a computer of recent vintage, but it's good to be able to recognize one should it occur.

Recognizing a Crash

When you enter a command to *Mathematica*'s kernel, the title bar to the notebook window will display the text "Running…." This label will vanish when the output appears. It is *Mathematica*'s way of telling you that it is working on a calculation. Some calculations are fast, but some are slow, and some are *very* slow (hours, days, even weeks). How much time a calculation will require depends on the complexity of the calculation and the type of computer being used. If you have entered a command and nothing seems to be happening, don't despair. It is likely that you have simply asked a difficult question (intentionally or not) and it will take *Mathematica* a bit of time to answer.

If you don't have time to wait and just want *Mathematica* to stop, read on.

Or if (heaven forbid) the cursor does not respond when you move the mouse, and the keyboard does not seem to work, it is likely that a crash has occurred. Don't panic, and don't pull the plug just yet. Read on…

Aborting Calculations and/or Recovering from a Crash

Under ordinary circumstances (the computer hasn't crashed), simply select Abort Evaluation from the Evaluation menu. This will usually work, but not always. Wait a minute or two and take a deep breath. Relax. If all goes well you should eventually see the message $Aborted in your notebook window where the output would ordinarily appear. Mission accomplished.

If nothing happens when you attempt to abort, you will have to take slightly more decisive action: You will have to quit the kernel. To do this, go again to the Evaluation menu, but this time select Quit Kernel (you then have to select the kernel that is running, usually the local kernel), then hit the Quit button when it asks if you *really* want to quit the kernel. The only consequence here is that if you wish to continue working, you will have to start a new kernel. This will happen automatically when you enter your next input. Remember that the new kernel will not be aware of any of your previous calculations, so you may have to reenter some old cells to bring the new kernel up to date (if your new commands make reference to any of your previous work).

Now for those of you who have lost control of the mouse and keyboard due to a crash, none of the above is possible. Ideally, you would like to be able to quit *Mathematica* without losing any of your unsaved work. It's not always possible; this is why it's a good idea to save your work often.

The action that you should take depends to some extent on what type of computer you are using. Let's proceed by platform.

Mac OS Procedure

First, try simultaneously hitting ⌘ and . (that's the period key). This is just the keyboard equivalent of selecting Abort Evaluation from the Evaluation menu as described above. It probably won't work, but give it a try. We've seen instances in which the mouse failed in the middle of a long calculation. No crash, just a worn mouse that died at an inopportune time.

If that doesn't work, try simultaneously hitting ⌘ and q. If this works you will be presented with a dialog box asking if you wish to save your work. Answer "Yes." In this case, the result will be quitting the entire *Mathematica* program (front end and kernel).

If that doesn't work, simultaneously hit the ⌘ OPTION ESC keys. A dialog will appear asking which application you wish to Force Quit. Choose *Mathematica.* This is almost always effective. The front end and kernel will quit, but you will not have an opportunity to save your work.

As a last resort, you will have to turn off your computer manually. Any unsaved changes will be lost. If the computer has a reset button, use it. Otherwise find the "off" button (often on the back of your computer) and use it. Wait a few seconds and restart the computer in the usual way.

Windows Procedure

First, try simultaneously hitting [ALT] and . (that's the period key). This is just the keyboard equivalent of selecting Abort Evaluation from the Evaluation menu as described above. It probably won't work, but give it a try. We've seen instances in which the mouse failed in the middle of a lengthy computation. No crash, just a worn mouse that died at an inopportune time.

If that doesn't work, simultaneously hit the [CTRL]-[SHIFT]-[ESC] keys. This will call up the Task Manager. Look under the Applications Tab for *Mathematica*. Select it, and hit the End Task button to quit *Mathematica* altogether. It may be possible to save your notebook before quitting. You should restart your computer before launching *Mathematica* again. This will decrease the likelihood of another crash.

As a last resort, you may have to restart your computer. Again, any unsaved changes will be lost.

Running Efficiently: Preventing Crashes

Mathematica can make heavy demands on your computer's resources. In particular, it benefits from large amounts of random access memory, or RAM. You should be aware of this so that you can help it along. Here are some tips to consider if you find yourself pushing your system's resources.

First, quit other programs (such as your web browser) when using *Mathematica*. Other programs also require RAM, so running them at the same time steals valuable memory from *Mathematica*. Also, even though it is possible to have multiple notebooks open at one time, avoid having more notebooks open than necessary. Each open notebook will consume memory. You should also save your notebooks often. Doing so will allow *Mathematica* to store part of it on your computer's hard drive, rather than storing all of it in RAM. Finally, if you work on your own computer and are in the habit of leaving *Mathematica* running for days or weeks at a time, quit the kernel from time to time to flush out any symbols that are not being used.

3

Functions and Their Graphs

3.1 Defining a Function

A *function* is a rule that assigns to each input exactly one output. Many functions, such as the natural logarithm function Log, are built into *Mathematica*. You provide an input, or argument, and *Mathematica* produces the output:

In[1]:= **Log[1]**

Out[1]= 0

You can define your own function in *Mathematica* like this (use the Basic Math Assistant palette to type x^2; see Section 1.6):

In[2]:= **f[x_] := x^2 + 2 x - 4**

This function will take an input x, and output $x^2 + 2x - 4$. For instance:

In[3]:= **f[1]**

Out[3]= -1

In[4]:= **f[π]**

Out[4]= -4 + 2 π + π^2

As a second example, here is a function that will return the multiplicative inverse of its argument (again, use the Basic Math Assistant palette to type the fraction):

In[5]:= **inv[x_] := $\dfrac{1}{x}$**

Let's try it:

In[6]:= **inv[45]**

Out[6]= $\dfrac{1}{45}$

You can also create functions by combining existing functions:

In[7]:= `g[x_] := N[inv[x]]`

In[8]:= `g[45]`

Out[8]= `0.0222222`

> ## 💡 Defining a Function
>
> Follow these rules when defining a function:
>
> - The name of the function (such as f or inv) should be a lowercase letter, or a word that begins with a lowercase letter. This is because all built-in functions (such as Log and N) begin with capital letters. If your function begins with a lowercase letter, you will never accidentally give it a name that already belongs to some built-in function.
> - The function argument (in these examples x) must be followed by an underscore _ on the left side of the definition.
> - Use square brackets [ ] to enclose the function argument.
> - Use the colon-equal combination := to separate the left side of the definition from the right.

After typing the definition, enter the cell containing it. Your function is now ready for action.

> ⚠ The := operator (called the SetDelayed operator) used in defining functions differs in a subtle way from the = operator (called the Set operator) used for making assignments (the = operator was discussed in Section 1.10). Essentially, when you use := the expression appearing to its right is evaluated anew by the kernel each time that the expression appearing to its left is called. The = operator, by contrast, evaluates the expression on its right only once, at the time the assignment is made. In many settings = and := can be used interchangeably; however, there are cases when one is appropriate and the other is not. Using SetDelayed for function definitions will work in virtually every setting, and we will use it consistently for that purpose throughout this book.
>
> An illustrative example is the following: Type and enter
> `x = RandomInteger[100]; {x, x, x}`. Then change = to := and do it again. In the first case, x is set to be a single (randomly chosen) integer, so the output is a list in which that same number appears three times. In the second case, each x causes a new random integer to be chosen, so the output is a list of three (probably) distinct numbers.
>
> For more information, go to Wolfram Documentation (in the **Help** menu) and type "immediate" in the search field, then scroll down to find the link to the tutorial titled "Immediate and Delayed Definitions."

Clearing a Function

A word to the wise: Once you are finished working with a function, Clear it. Why? One reason is that you may forget about the function and later in the session try to use the name for something else. But

Mathematica won't forget, and all sorts of confusion can result. Another is that in getting rid of a function you will clear out a little bit of memory, leaving more room for you to work. To see if a letter or word has been defined as a function, use the ? command just as you would for a built-in *Mathematica* command:

In[9]:= ? f

Global`f

$$f[x\_] := x^2 + 2 x - 4$$

This indicates that *f* is still retained in memory. You can use the Clear command to erase it, just as you would to erase the value of a constant:

In[10]:= Clear[f]

Now if you use the ? command you will find no such definition:

In[11]:= ? f

Global`f

⚠ To clear out *every* user-defined symbol from the current session, enter this input: Clear["Global`*"]. The asterisk is a wild-card symbol; this essentially says, "Clear all symbols defined in the Global context" (the Global context is the default location where user-defined symbols are stored).

3.2 Plotting a Function

In[1]:= $f[x\_] := x^2 - 2 x + 4$

In[2]:= Plot[f[x], {x, -1, 3}]

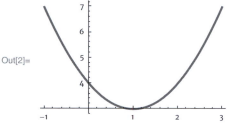

Out[2]=

The Plot command takes two arguments, separated (as always) by a comma. The first (in this case f[x]) is the function to be graphed, and the second (in this case {x, -1, 3}) is called an *iterator*. It describes the span of values that the variable *x* is to assume; that is, it specifies the domain over which the plot will be constructed. The curly brackets are essential in describing this domain. In fact, *Mathematica* uses this iterator structure in numerous commands, so it warrants a bit of discussion. The first item (x) names the variable, and the next two items give the span of values that this variable will assume (−1 through 3). Values in this domain are displayed along the horizontal axis, while the values that the function assumes are displayed along the vertical axis.

Note that the axes in this plot do not intersect at the origin, but rather at the point (0, 3). Every time you use the Plot command *Mathematica* decides where to place the axes, and they do not always cross at the origin. There is a good reason for this. As often as not you will find yourself plotting functions over domains in which the graph is relatively far from the origin. Rather than omit one or both axes from the plot, or include the axes together with acres of white space, *Mathematica* will simply move the axes into view, giving your plot a frame of reference. If you really want to produce a plot with the axes intersecting at the origin, you can. The details are provided in the next section of this chapter, "Using *Mathematica*'s Plot Options."

You can zoom in on a particular portion of a plot simply by editing the domain specified in the iterator, then reentering the cell. Let's take a close look, so to speak, at the function in the last example, this time with *x* values near 2. Notice how "flat" the graph becomes:

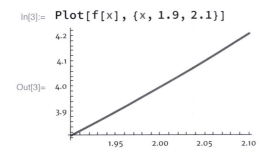

In[3]:= `Plot[f[x], {x, 1.9, 2.1}]`

You could zoom in even more (say, with a domain from 1.99 to 2.01) and get a more detailed view of the function's behavior near the point *x* = 2. In the plot below we show an extreme zoom (and make use of the lowercase Greek letter δ, which mathematicians often use to denote small quantities). Here we also employ the With command, a device that allows you to make *local* assignments; the assignment $\delta = 10^{-10}$ will only be utilized within the Plot expression, and will not be remembered by *Mathematica* later.

In[4]:= `With[{δ = 10⁻¹⁰}, Plot[f[x], {x, 2 - δ, 2 + δ}]]`

Note that the numerical values on each axis display identically; this is simply because so many decimal places (ten in this case) are needed to distinguish them that there isn't room for their display. In principle you could keep zooming in forever, but in practice this is not possible. See Exercise 2 for a discussion on the limits of zooming.

Another little trick that's good to know about is how to resize a graphic. This technique is best learned by trying it, so get yourself in front of the computer and produce a plot. Position the cursor anywhere on the graph and click once. A rectangular border with eight "handles" appears around the graph. Position the cursor on a handle and drag (hold down the mouse button and move the mouse) to shrink or enlarge the graphic. It's easy; try it.

Let's look at another example:

In[5]:= **Clear[f];**

In[6]:= **f[x_] :=** $\dfrac{x^5 - 4\,x^2 + 1}{x - \frac{1}{2}}$

In[7]:= **Plot[f[x], {x, -2, 2}]**

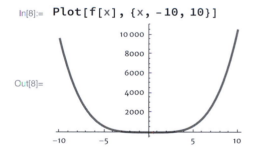

Out[7]=

You'll notice this graph has an asymptote at $x = \frac{1}{2}$ since the denominator of f is zero when $x = \frac{1}{2}$ while the numerator is not zero. But we cannot assume that *Mathematica* will clearly display every feature of a graph. Vertical asymptotes (and other "narrow" features) in a plot will change in appearance as the specified domain changes. Asymptotes may disappear or become barely noticeable. For instance, here is another view of the function f, this time zoomed out to accommodate the domain from -10 to 10. The asymptote appears to have vanished:

In[8]:= **Plot[f[x], {x, -10, 10}]**

Out[8]=

In order to understand *Mathematica*'s graphical output, it is important to understand how the Plot command works. Plot samples several values of x in the specified domain and numerically evaluates $f(x)$ for each of them. After refining its selection of sample points via an adaptive algorithm, it then plots these points and "connects the dots" with little line segments. There are so many that the graph appears in most places like a smooth curve. In this case *Mathematica* did not notice the asymptote because the set of sample points allowed the algorithm to miss this feature of the graph. Never trust the output of the computer as gospel; it always demands scrutiny.

The "true" graph of f still approaches positive infinity to the right of the asymptote at $x = \frac{1}{2}$ and negative infinity to the left of it. The point of all this is to make clear that the graphs *Mathematica* produces are approximations. They may hide important features of a function if those features are sufficiently narrow relative to the domain over which the function is graphed. When it comes to finding a function's asymptotes, for instance, looking for them on a plot is not necessarily the best approach. We'll discuss better methods for finding vertical asymptotes (by finding explicit values of x for which the denominator is equal to zero) in the next chapter. If you know the precise numerical position of a function's vertical asymptote(s) you can omit such points from a graph and draw the asymptotes by using the `Exclusions` option, which will be introduced in the next section.

Be Careful with Odd Roots

A more subtle issue may arise from the manner in which *Mathematica* utilizes the complex number system. There are cases in which there are two potential definitions for a function: one which disallows complex numbers, and another which embraces them. *Mathematica* will always embrace them, and this can lead to some unexpected results. In particular, students in precalculus or calculus often work in a setting that disallows non-real numbers. A classic example is the cube root function, $f(x) = x^{1/3} = \sqrt[3]{x}$. Here is a plot of this function on the domain $-8 \le x \le 8$:

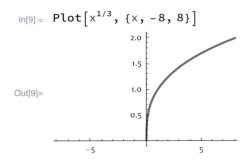

In[9]:= `Plot[x^1/3, {x, -8, 8}]`

Out[9]=

The left side of the plot is empty. That seems odd; don't negative numbers have cube roots? We know that $(-2)^3 = -8$, so the cube root of -8 should be -2, shouldn't it? The issue is a subtle one. In the complex number system there are *three* numbers whose cube is -8 (they happen to be -2 and the two complex numbers $1 \pm \sqrt{3}\, i$). *Mathematica*, savvy as it is regarding the complex numbers, takes one of the *complex* numbers to be the cube root of -8. In a similar manner, it regards the cube root of every negative real number to be complex. It can't plot a complex number, and so the left half of the plot is empty. A thorough discussion of why *Mathematica* chooses complex values as the cube roots of negative numbers can be found in Section 4.4. Suffice it to say that there are very good reasons for doing so, but that it can be an annoyance to those who would like to study the real-valued cube root function (and remain blissfully ignorant of the complex number system).

If you would like to see the plot of the real-valued cube root function found in many precalculus and calculus texts (where the cube root of -8 is taken to be -2), you can use `CubeRoot[x]` instead of $x^{1/3}$ or $\sqrt[3]{x}$.

In[10]:= `Plot[CubeRoot[x], {x, -8, 8}]`

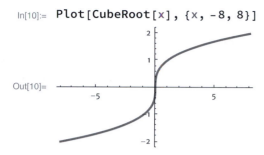

Out[10]=

Or you can use `Surd[x, 3]` for the real cube root. The command `Surd[x, n]` is the real-valued *n*th root of *x*:

In[11]:= `Surd[-32, 5]`

Out[11]= `- 2`

There is a symbol for this strangely named command (derived from an old-fashioned word for roots) that looks like an *n*th root but has a slight difference:

In[12]:= $\sqrt[5]{-32.}\,^\rceil$

Out[12]= `- 2.`

Do you see the extra little overhang at the end of the radical above? To get this symbol type ⎹ESC⎸ surd ⎹ESC⎸ in an input cell.

Again, notice that when you use the ordinary *n*th root symbol $\sqrt[\square]{\blacksquare}$ from the palette to find a root of a negative number you will get a complex number:

In[13]:= $\sqrt[5]{-32.}$

Out[13]= `1.61803 + 1.17557 i`

Any negative number raised to a fractional power with an odd denominator will have this issue:

In[14]:= $(-8.)^{\frac{2}{3}}$

Out[14]= `- 2. + 3.4641 i`

When working in real numbers, fractional exponents can be computed by taking the power first and then the root, or the root first and then the power. That is, $x^{\frac{m}{n}} = \sqrt[n]{x^m} = \left(\sqrt[n]{x}\right)^m$. But this is not always true when complex numbers are allowed.

In[15]:= $\sqrt[3]{(-8.)^2}$

Out[15]= `4.`

In[16]:= $\left(\sqrt[3]{-8.}\right)^2$

Out[16]= $-2. + 3.4641\ \mathrm{i}$

To avoid these complex issues (pun intended) use Surd for all computations involving odd roots of negative numbers, either as a command or with the fancy radical symbol, $\sqrt[\Box]{\blacksquare}$:

In[17]:= $\mathtt{Surd[-8,\ 3]}^2$

Out[17]= 4

In[18]:= $\left(\sqrt[3]{-8}\right)^2$

Out[18]= 4

In[19]:= $\left(\sqrt[3]{-8}\right)^2$

Out[19]= 4

Exercises 3.2

1. Plot the following functions on the domain $-10 \le x \le 10$.

   a. $\sin(1 + \cos(x))$

   b. $\sin(1.4 + \cos(x))$

   c. $\sin\left(\frac{\pi}{2} + \cos(x)\right)$

   d. $\sin(2 + \cos(x))$

2. One can zoom in toward a particular point in the domain of a function and see how the graph appears at different zoom levels. For instance, consider the square root function $f(x) = \sqrt{x}$ when x is near 2.

   a.   Enter the input below to see the graph of f as x goes from 1 to 3.

   $$\mathtt{With\Big[\{\delta = 10^0\},\ Plot\Big[\sqrt{x}\,,\ \{x,\ 2 - \delta,\ 2 + \delta\}\Big]\Big]}$$

   b.   Now zoom; change the value of δ to be 10^{-1} and reenter the input above to see the graph of f as x goes from 1.9 to 2.1. Do this again for $\delta = 10^{-2}, 10^{-3}, 10^{-4}$, and 10^{-5}.

   c.   Use the last plot to approximate $\sqrt{2}$ to six significant digits. Check your answer using N.

   d.   When making a Plot, the lower and upper bounds on the iterator must be distinct when rounded to machine precision. Enter the previous Plot command with $\delta = 10^{-20}$. An error message results. Read the error message and speculate as to what is happening. The bottom line is that zooming has its limits.

3. Use the Surd command to plot the real-valued function $f(x) = x^{4/5}$ on the domain $-32 \le x \le 32$. What is the value of $f(32)$?

3.3   Using *Mathematica*'s Plot Options

Many of *Mathematica*'s commands accept *option settings*; you can add additional arguments into a command to modify the behavior of that command. In this section, we'll see how to tweak the `Plot` command so that you get the most out of your graphs. For example, here is the plot of the function $100 \cos(x) + e^{(x^2)}$:

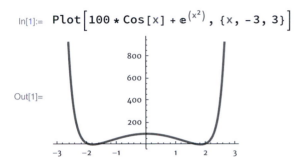

In[1]:= `Plot[100 * Cos[x] + e^(x²), {x, -3, 3}]`

Out[1]=

One can change the appearance of such a plot by choosing a `PlotTheme` setting, such as `PlotTheme → "Business"`. To add this option setting, position your cursor just inside the closing square bracket of your `Plot` command, add a comma, then type a few letters of the word `PlotTheme` until a popup appears and allows you to complete it. At this point the arrow → will be added and another popup menu will appear with a list of available themes. Choose one, or just type `"Business"`.

In[2]:= `Plot[100 * Cos[x] + e^(x²), {x, -3, 3}, PlotTheme → "Business"]`

Out[2]=

Each `PlotTheme` applies a bundle of individual plot option settings. The `"Business"` setting thickens the plot, adds dotted horizontal grid lines, removes the vertical axis, and places the vertical scale along the left side of the plot. If this or any of the other themes appeals to you, use it. If you instead wish to tweak one or more individual settings, read on.

There is a `PlotRange` option, for instance, that gives you control of the span of *y* values for your plot. Notice in the plots above how *Mathematica* only showed us a portion of what we asked for—the graph only spans the domain from roughly −2.5 through 2.5. This is because beyond the portion shown *Mathematica* observed no interesting behavior; the graph just kept going up on the left and on the right. The (boring) information near the edges was clipped off to give a better view of the middle portion of the plot. *Mathematica* will do such clipping by default.

But suppose you really want to see the function over the *full* domain from −3 to 3. You can indicate this by adding `PlotRange → Full` as an additional argument to the `Plot` command. Typically, an option like this is added after producing and viewing a plot with no options. Just go back to your input, add the option setting after the requisite arguments, and re-enter it.

In[3]:= $\texttt{Plot}\left[\texttt{100 * Cos[x] + e}^{\left(x^2\right)}, \texttt{\{x, -3, 3\}, PlotRange} \rightarrow \texttt{Full}\right]$

Out[3]=

Look at the output. The left and right sides of the plot now climb almost ten times higher, and as a result the detail in the middle is harder to surmise. It is a very different picture.

After exploring this function in the previous graphs, it is clear that the interesting behavior occurs above the x axis and below roughly $y = 250$. You can specify the exact range of values you wish to display using $\texttt{PlotRange} \rightarrow \texttt{\{ymin, ymax\}}$. If your desired range is $-n$ to n, $\texttt{PlotRange} \rightarrow n$ will suffice.

In[4]:= $\texttt{Plot}\left[\texttt{100 * Cos[x] + e}^{\left(x^2\right)}, \texttt{\{x, -3, 3\}, PlotRange} \rightarrow \texttt{\{0, 250\}}\right]$

Out[4]=

If you want to have complete control over the viewing window for your plot use $\texttt{PlotRange} \rightarrow \texttt{\{\{xmin, xmax\}, \{ymin, ymax\}\}}$ to specify the values for both the domain and range.

In[5]:= $\texttt{Plot}\left[\texttt{100 * Cos[x] + e}^{\left(x^2\right)}, \texttt{\{x, -3, 3\}, PlotRange} \rightarrow \texttt{\{\{-10, 10\}, \{0, 500\}\}}\right]$

Out[5]=

This brings up an important distinction between the values entered into the required $\texttt{\{var, min, max\}}$ iterator of the $\texttt{Plot}$ command and the values entered in $\texttt{\{\{xmin, xmax\}, \{ymin, ymax\}\}}$ for the $\texttt{PlotRange}$ option. The values entered for the iterator delimit the interval of values *Mathematica* will plug into the function to create the graph. The values in {{*xmin*, *xmax*}, {*ymin*, *ymax*}} do not need to match, but the graph will only be displayed for values in the iterator, even when the viewing window is larger.

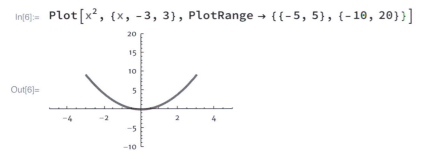

In[6]:= `Plot[x`^{2}`, {x, -3, 3}, PlotRange → {{-5, 5}, {-10, 20}}]`

Many of the options for the `Plot` command can be found in the Basic Math Assistant palette. In the Basic Commands section, look in the 2D Plot tab for Options: Automatic Positioning. Templates for the `PlotRange` option can be found in the Range ▾ menu. Note that if you ever wish to type the arrow → from the keyboard, you can find it on the palette, or you can just type a dash followed by "greater than" > and on the next keystroke it will morph into an arrow.

The philosophy of allowing commands such as `Plot` to accept options is simple: very little typing is required for the command to be used in its default form. If the default output is not entirely to your liking, you may use options to tweak the various default settings to your heart's content. There are over 60 options for the `Plot` command, several of which are discussed below. You may add multiple option settings to a command, and in any order you wish (provided each optional argument is listed *after* the required arguments); just use commas to separate them.

How to Get the Axes to Intersect at the Origin

To get the axes to intersect at the origin, use the option `AxesOrigin → {0, 0}`, which can be found in the Axes & Frame ▾ menu. You can use `AxesOrigin → {`*x coordinate*, *y coordinate*`}`, in fact, to make the axes intersect at any point.

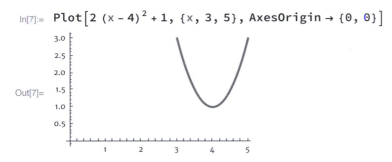

In[7]:= `Plot[2 (x - 4)`^{2}` + 1, {x, 3, 5}, AxesOrigin → {0, 0}]`

Note that the domain specified is $3 \leq x \leq 5$, yet the option setting extends the viewing window beyond these values.

How to Get the Same Scaling on Both Axes

In order to get both sets of axes to use the same scale, use the option `AspectRatio → Automatic` from the `Other ▾` menu.

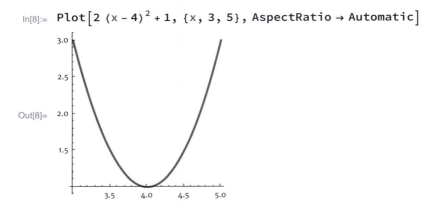

In[8]:= `Plot[2 (x - 4)² + 1, {x, 3, 5}, AspectRatio → Automatic]`

Be mindful that in some cases you definitely do not want your axes to have the same scale. You could, for instance, very easily ask for a plot that was a few inches wide and a few miles high. Imagine the plot at the beginning of this section if you are skeptical. That is why the default aspect ratio (the ratio of height to width) is set to a fixed value. In other words, by default `Plot` will scale the axes in such a way that the graph will fit into a rectangle of standard proportions. It's best to add the `AspectRatio → Automatic` option only after you have viewed the plot and determined that its use won't result in a plot that is too long and skinny.

Note that you can also set `AspectRatio` to any positive numerical value you like. The plot will have the *height* to *width* ratio that you specify. For instance, the setting `AspectRatio → 3` will produce a plot that is three times as high as it is wide. Widescreen televisions are advertised to have a 16 : 9 aspect ratio. We can get these dimensions using the option `AspectRatio → 9 / 16`.

How to Display Mesh Points

To show the points that are sampled when you enter a `Plot`, use the option `Mesh → All`.

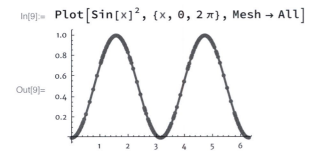

In[9]:= `Plot[Sin[x]², {x, 0, 2π}, Mesh → All]`

Note that more points are sampled in regions where the function bends sharply. The graph itself is composed of line segments joining adjacent pairs of the sampled points.

To show points whose *x* coordinates are regularly spaced, use the option Mesh → Full or Mesh → *n* where *n* is the desired number of points (not counting endpoints).

In[10]:= `Plot[Sin[x]², {x, 0, 2 π}, Mesh → Full]`

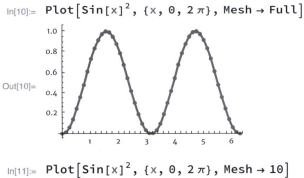

Out[10]=

In[11]:= `Plot[Sin[x]², {x, 0, 2 π}, Mesh → 10]`

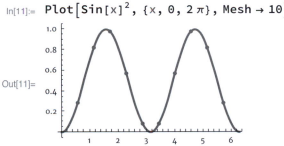

Out[11]=

⚠ One can display *any* finite collection of mesh points by setting Mesh to a double-bracketed *list* of *x* coordinates, such as Mesh → {{1, 2, 3}}. One can program-matically generate such a list of *x* coordinates using Range (for equally spaced *x* coordinates), or Table (see Section 3.5 for a discussion of the Table command). Even more control can be garnered by setting the MeshFunctions option, which specifies which function or functions are to be set to the list of Mesh values. Typically such functions are given as *pure functions* (see Section 8.4 for a discussion of the Function command). By default, MeshFunctions is set to {#1 &}, meaning that the list of Mesh values is a list of *x* coordinates. With the setting MeshFunctions → {#2 &}, the list of Mesh values becomes a list of *y* coordinates. See Exercise 5 for examples.

How to Add Color and Other Style Changes: Graphics Directives

It's not hard to make a plot any color you like using the PlotStyle option (there is a template in the Style ▾ menu). The output below will appear red on your monitor:

In[12]:= `Plot[2 (x - 4)² + 1, {x, 3, 5}, PlotStyle → Red]`

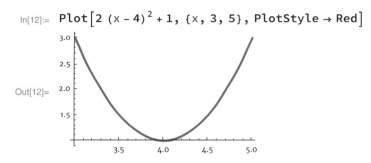

Out[12]=

You can choose a color by typing a color name, or by clicking on the colored buttons below Color Names on the palette. For a broader collection of colors, bring up the Color Schemes palette and look in the Named section. For a list of all colors go to Wolfram Documentation, type "colors" in the search field, and navigate to the guide page of that name.

You can easily create a lighter or darker version of any color; just replace `Red`, for instance, with `Lighter[Red]`, or `Lighter[Red, .7]` or `Darker[Red, .2]`. The second numerical argument may be omitted. If present, it determines the extent of the lightening or darkening, and should be set to a value between 0 (no effect) and 1 (maximal effect). You can also blend two or more colors. Setting `PlotStyle` to `Blend[{Blue, Red}, .3]` will produce a blend of 70% blue and 30% red. And one could nest these settings, for example: `Lighter[Blend[{Blue, Red}, .3], .4]`. Other color settings are discussed in Exercise 3.

These color settings are examples of *graphics directives*. The `PlotStyle` option may be set to any single graphics directive (such as the color directives outlined above), or simultaneously to several such directives. A few of the many possible directives can be found in the Directives ▾ menu in the Combining Graphic Objects section of the palette. Multiple directives should be wrapped in the `Direc` `tive` command. For instance, one can apply the directives `Thick`, `Gray`, and `Dashed` as follows:

In[13]:= `Plot[2 (x - 4)² + 1, {x, 3, 5}, PlotStyle → Directive[Thick, Gray, Dashed]]`

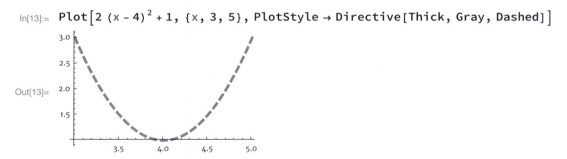

Out[13]=

Dashes may be fine-tuned by replacing `Dashed` with the directive `Dashing[Small]`, `Dashing[Large]`, or `Dashing[{.02, .01}]`. This last setting has the effect of breaking the plot into dashed segments each of which is 2 percent of the width of the entire graphic, and where the space between consecutive dashes is 1 percent of the width of the graphic. To fine-tune the thickness, try `Thickness[.01]`. This will adjust the plot's thickness to 1 percent of the width of the entire graphic.

Other common `Plot` options that accept graphics directive settings are `AxesStyle`, `Background`, `FillingStyle`, `FrameStyle`, and `MeshStyle`.

How to Remove the Axes or Add a Frame

To remove axes simply add the option `Axes → False` from the Axes & Frame ▼ menu.:

In[14]:= `Plot[2 (x - 4)² + 1, {x, 3, 5}, Axes → False]`

Out[14]=

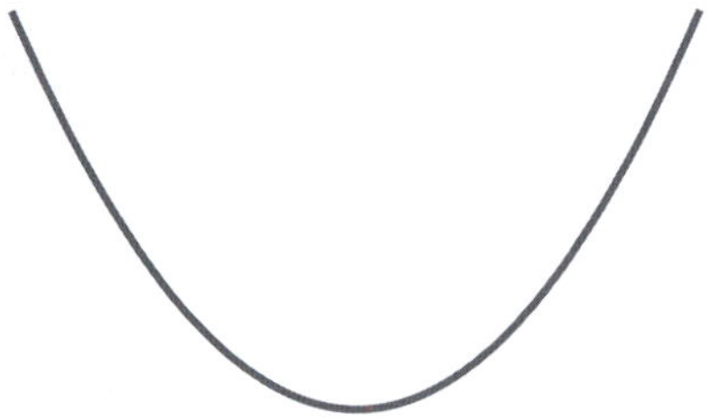

To replace the axes with a frame around the entire graph, add the option `Frame → True`:

In[15]:= `Plot[2 (x - 4)² + 1, {x, 3, 5}, Frame → True]`

Out[15]=

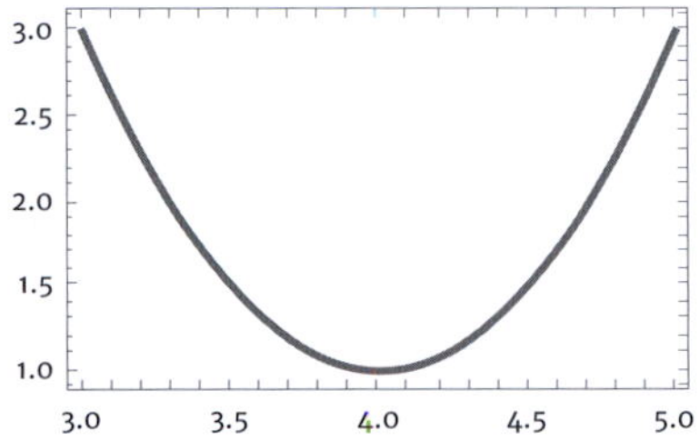

How to Place Arrowheads on the Axes

Add the option `AxesStyle → Arrowheads[.05]` to put arrowheads on the top and right only, or `AxesStyle → Arrowheads[{-.05, .05}]` to put arrowheads on both ends of each axis. The value .05 means that the arrowheads will be scaled to be 5 percent of the width of the entire plot.

In[16]:= `Plot[2 (x - 4)² + 1, {x, 3, 5},`
`        AxesStyle → Arrowheads[.05], AxesOrigin → {2, 0}]`

Out[16]=

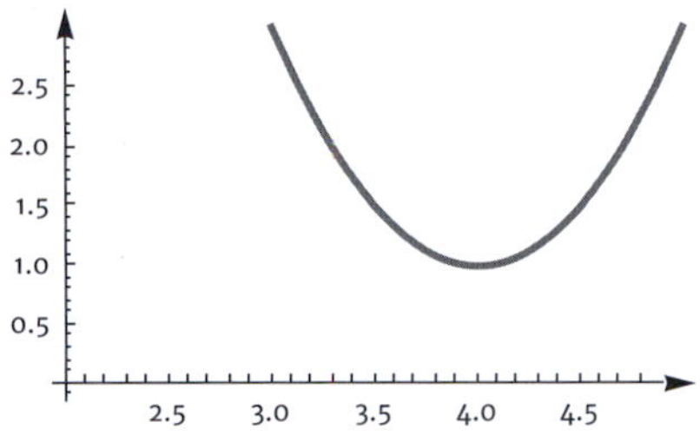

In[17]:= `Plot[x² - 1, {x, -2, 2}, AxesStyle → Arrowheads[{-.05, .05}]]`

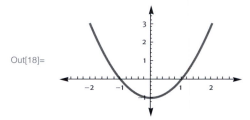

Out[17]=

When adding arrowheads, it may be desirable to manually increase the `PlotRange` for both axes to place the arrowheads farther from the center of your plot. This will allow room to display more tick marks on the axes.

In[18]:= `Plot[x² - 1, {x, -2, 2}, AxesStyle → Arrowheads[{-.05, .05}],`
         `PlotRange → {{-3, 3}, {-2, 4}}]`

Out[18]=

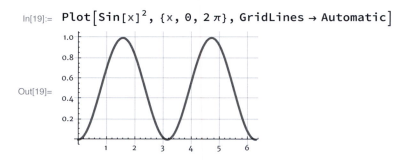

How to Add Grid Lines and Adjust Ticks on the Axes

To add a grid to your plot, as if it were plotted on graph paper, add the option `GridLines → Automatic` from the ⬚ Grids ▾ menu.

In[19]:= `Plot[Sin[x]², {x, 0, 2 π}, GridLines → Automatic]`

Out[19]=

The appearance of the grid lines is controlled by the `GridLinesStyle` option, which can be set to any graphics directive.

In[20]:= Plot$\left[\text{Sin}[x]^2, \{x, 0, 2\pi\}, \text{GridLines} \to \text{Automatic},\right.$
  $\text{GridLinesStyle} \to \text{Directive[Thin, Gray, Dotted]}\big]$

Out[20]=

To adjust the placement and number of grid lines, set GridLines to a list of two lists: the first consists of *x* values indicating the positions of the vertical lines, and the second consists of *y* values indicating the positions of the horizontal lines:

In[21]:= Plot$\left[\text{Sin}[x]^2, \{x, 0, 2\pi\},\right.$
  $\text{GridLines} \to \left\{\left\{\dfrac{\pi}{2}, \pi, \dfrac{3\pi}{2}, 2\pi\right\}, \{.2, .4, .6, .8, 1\}\right\}\big]$

Out[21]=

For finer grids, use Range to generate each of the *x* and *y* lists. Range is used to generate a list of evenly spaced numerical values. For example, Range[0, 1, .1] generates a list of numbers from 0 to 1 in increments of one-tenth:

In[22]:= Range[0, 1, .1]

Out[22]= {0., 0.1, 0.2, 0.3, 0.4, 0.5, 0.6, 0.7, 0.8, 0.9, 1.}

In[23]:= Plot$\left[\text{Sin}[x]^2, \{x, 0, 2\pi\},\right.$
  $\text{GridLinesStyle} \to \text{Directive[Thin, Lighter[Gray]]},$
  $\text{GridLines} \to \left\{\text{Range}\left[0, 2\pi, \dfrac{\pi}{8}\right], \text{Range}[0, 1, .1]\right\}\big]$

Out[23]=

Numerical tick marks on the axes are controlled via the `Ticks` option from the `Ticks ▾` menu. It works in a manner similar to `GridLines`. If you are happy with the default list of tick marks on one of the axes, just use `Automatic` instead of a specific list of values.

In[22]:= `Plot[Sin[x]², {x, 0, 2 π},`

  `GridLinesStyle → Directive[Thin, Lighter[Gray]],`

  `GridLines → {Range[0, 2 π, π/4], Range[0, 1, .1]},`

  `Ticks → {Range[0, 2 π, π/2], Automatic}]`

Out[22]=

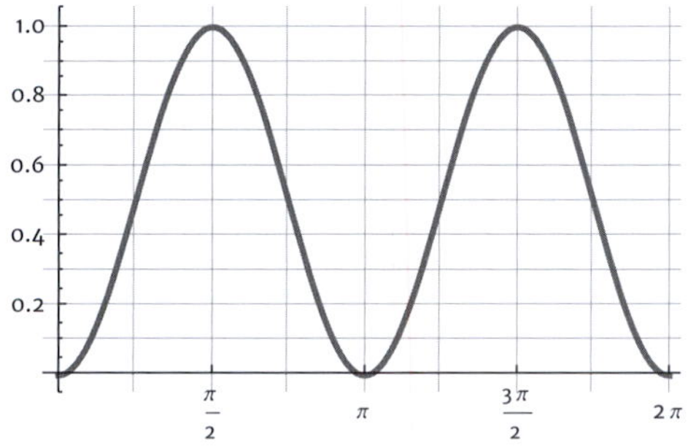

How to Add Labels

Labels can be added to the axes via the option `AxesLabel` from the `Axes & Frame ▾` menu. By default, it will apply `TraditionalForm` to your label expressions. So, for instance, `Sin[x]²` will be displayed using the traditional notation, $\sin^2(x)$.

In[23]:= `Plot[Sin[x]², {x, 0, 2 π},`

  `Ticks → {{0, π, 2 π}, {0, .5, 1}}, AxesLabel → {x, Sin[x]²}]`

Out[23]=

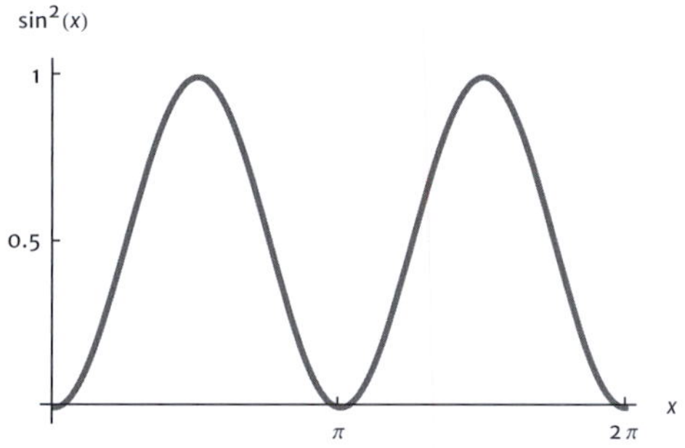

You can put a label on the entire plot with the option `PlotLabel` from the Other ▾ menu.

In[24]:= `Plot[Sin[x]`^{2}`, {x, 0, 2` π`}, Ticks → {{0,` π`, 2` π`}, {0, .5, 1}},`
`AxesLabel → {x, y}, PlotLabel → Sin[x]`^{2}`]`

Out[24]=

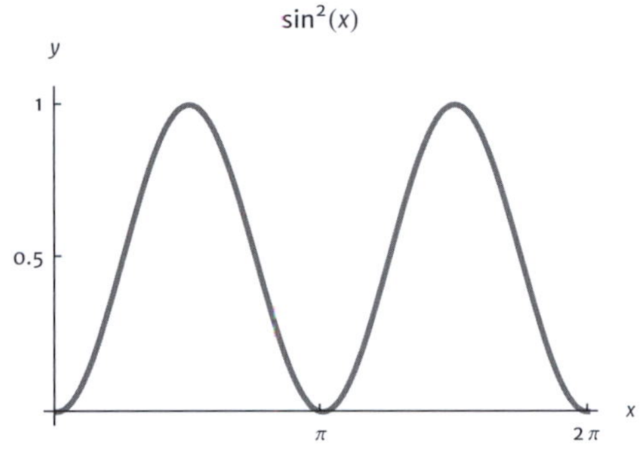

Labels that include operators (such as =), or that are composed of more than one word, should be entered as a `String`, i.e., put in double quotation marks. In this case, the text between the quotation marks will be reproduced *exactly* as you write it. Below, for instance, we italicized the *x* and the *y* as we typed the label text.

In[25]:= `Plot[Sin[x]`^{2}`, {x, 0, 2` π`}, Ticks → {{0,` π`, 2` π`}, {0, .5, 1}},`
`AxesLabel → {x, y}, PlotLabel → "`y `=` `sin`^{2}`(`x`)"]`

Out[25]=

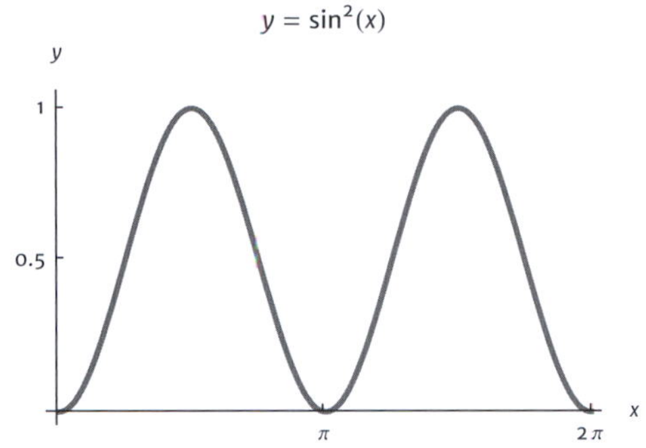

If one had not used double quotation marks for the label above, *Mathematica* would have actually made the nonsensical assignment $y = \sin^2 x$, possibly causing confusion later in the session. When in doubt, wrap your plot labels in double quotes.

An alternate means of labeling will work not only for plots, but for labeling any *Mathematica* expression. Simply wrap the expression to be labeled in the `Labeled` command, and add a second argument that specifies the text for the label. The label appears at the bottom by default, but a third argument may be given to specify the position of the label. Look up `Labeled` in Wolfram Documentation for information about micro-positioning the label text.

In[26]:= `p = Plot[Sin[x]², {x, 0, 2π},`
`    Ticks → {{0, π, 2π}, {0, .5, 1}}, AxesLabel → {x, y}];`
`Labeled[p, Text["y = sin²(x)"], Right]`

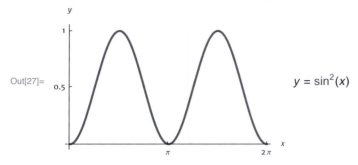

Out[27]=

Exclusions and Vertical Asymptotes

You can add vertical asymptotes to a plot using the options `Exclusions` and `ExclusionsStyle` from the bottom of the ⎢ Other ▾ ⎢ menu. `Exclusions` can be set to a list containing an equation or equations whose solution(s) you wish to exclude. Use two equal signs back to back `==` when typing an equation. `ExclusionsStyle` specifies the directive(s) applied to the vertical line(s) through the points to be excluded. Multiple directives should be wrapped in the `Directive` command, as was done earlier with `PlotStyle`.

In[28]:= $\mathtt{Plot}\left[\dfrac{(x-3)\ (x-4)}{(x-2)\ (x-5)},\ \{x,\ 0,\ 7\},\right.$
$\left.\mathtt{Exclusions} \to \{x == 2,\ x == 5\},\ \mathtt{ExclusionsStyle} \to \mathtt{Dashed}\right]$

Out[28]=

The benefit of expressing exclusions as *equations* is illustrated in the following example, where a single equation has many solutions in the specified domain:

In[29]:= `Plot[Tan[x], {x, 0, 4 π}, Exclusions → {Cos[x] == 0},`

`ExclusionsStyle → Directive[Gray, Dashed],`

`Ticks → {Range[0, 4 π, `$\frac{π}{2}$`], Automatic}]`

Out[29]=

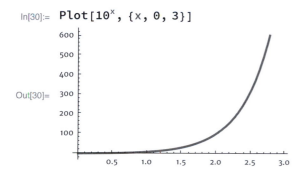

Note that `Exclusions` has little visible effect at a point unless there is an essential discontinuity there. See Exercise 4.

Putting a Logarithmic Scale on One or Both Axes

While `Plot` may use different scales on the horizontal and vertical axes, it will always put a uniform scale on each (in which there are equal distances between successive numbers). The commands `LogPlot`, `LogLinearPlot`, and `LogLogPlot`, found under More ▼ to the right of the Plot button, may be used to put a logarithmic scale (in which there are equal distances between successive powers of 10) on one or both axes. Each of these commands has the same syntactical structure as `Plot`, and will accept the `Plot` options discussed above.

Compare the two graphs below:

In[30]:= `Plot[10`^{x}`, {x, 0, 3}]`

Out[30]=

In[31]:= **LogPlot[10^x, {x, 0, 3}]**

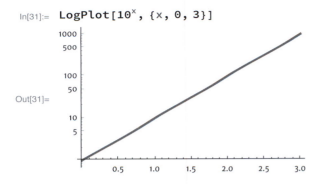

Out[31]=

The `LogPlot` command puts a logarithmic scale on the vertical axis. The graph of exponential function, 10^x, appears linear since $\log(b^x) = x \log(b)$.

`LogLinearPlot` will put a logarithmic scale on the horizontal axis so that logarithmic functions appear linear:

In[32]:= **Plot[Log10[x], {x, 1, 1000}]**

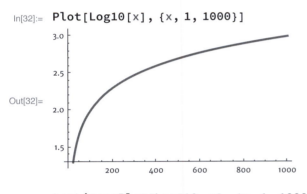

Out[32]=

In[33]:= **LogLinearPlot[Log[10, x], {x, 1, 1000}]**

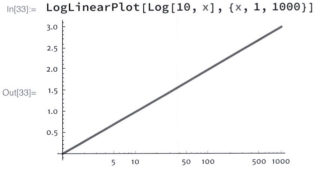

Out[33]=

To put a logarithmic scale on both axes, use the command LogLogPlot:

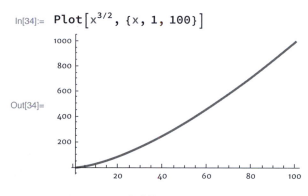

In[34]:= **Plot**[x$^{3/2}$, {x, 1, 100}]

Out[34]=

In[35]:= **LogLogPlot**[x$^{3/2}$, {x, 1, 100}]

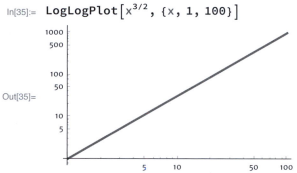

Out[35]=

Exercises 3.3

1. Use the GridLines and Ticks options, as well as the setting GridLinesStyle → Lighter[Gray], to produce the following Plot of the sine function:

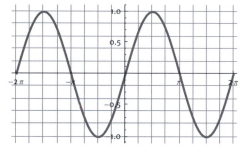

2. Use the Axes, Frame, Filling, FrameStyle, PlotRange, and AspectRatio options to produce the following plot of the function $y = \frac{\cos(15\,x)}{1+x^2}$:

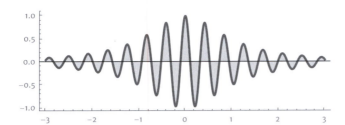

3. Color values such as Red, Blue, and Orange are easy to type and to remember, but they present you with a very limited color palette. Standard color spaces used in graphic design, such as RGB (for red–green–blue) and HSB (for hue–saturation–brightness), are supported. The command RGBColor takes three arguments, each a number between 0 and 1. They represent the relative amounts of red, green, and blue, respectively, in the final color. Hue takes either one argument (the color setting), or three, where the second and third are saturation and brightness levels. Each is a number between 0 and 1. You may type in values yourself (such as RGBColor[.2, .8, .8] or Hue[.6, .5, .5]), or you may do this: Type an option setting such as PlotStyle →, and with the cursor still at the tip of the arrow go to the Insert menu and select Color…. A dialog box appears, and you can use it any way you like to choose the color you're after. When you have it, hit the OK button. You'll find the appropriate RGBColor setting pasted in your notebook at the position of the cursor. Experiment with both methods, direct typing and using the menu, to custom-color the Plot of a function of your choosing.

4. Plot the function $f(x) = x^2$ on the domain $-2 \le x \le 2$, and set Exclusions to {x == 1} using the input below. Note that f has no vertical asymptote at $x = 1$. Why not? Now try $f(x) = x^2 - 1/(x - 1)$ with the same domain and Exclusions setting.

In[1]:= **Plot[x², {x, -2, 2}, Exclusions → {x == 1}]**

Out[1]=

5. In order to place mesh points on the graph so that their y coordinates are equally spaced, one may set the MeshFunctions option to {#2&}. This notation is explained in depth in Section 8.4, but for our purposes it will suffice to understand that #1 refers to x and #2 refers to y, and that the ampersand character & is needed to make it a *function*. The mesh points will be displayed at the specified values for this function. For example, a numerical Mesh setting of 9 indicates that there should be 9 equally spaced values. A *list* of Mesh values indicates that the specific values in the list should be used as values for the function. For instance, consider the input and output:

In[2]:= `Plot[x`^{2}`, {x, 0, 10}, Mesh → 9, MeshFunctions → {#2 &},`
      `GridLines → {None, Range[0, 100, 10]}]`

Out[2]=

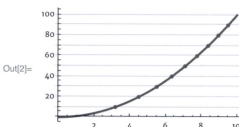

a. Replace the `None` in the input above with the appropriate list of *x* values to add vertical `GridLines` that pass through these same mesh points.

b. Add a `GridLines` setting to the input below so that the output includes (equally spaced) vertical grid lines that pass precisely through the mesh points, and (unequally spaced) horizontal grid lines that pass through the same mesh points.

In[3]:= `Plot[x`^{2}`, {x, 0, 10}, Mesh → 9]`

Out[3]=

6. Add `Mesh` and `MeshFunctions` options to the input below so that the mesh points are precisely the points where the graphs of the two functions intersect.

In[4]:= $\text{Plot}\left[\left\{\text{Sin}[2\,x], \frac{1}{2}\,\text{Cos}[5\,x]\right\}, \{x, 0, 2\,\pi\}\right]$

Out[4]=

3.4   Investigating Functions with Manipulate

The Manipulate command is used to manipulate an expression in real time using the mouse or trackpad (or even a gamepad controller; see Exercise 8). On the Basic Math Assistant palette, the Manipulate button can be found in the 2D Plot Commands tab in the section titled Interactive Tools just below the rainbow of Color Names. But as always, one may type it directly from the keyboard instead. One of the most basic uses of Manipulate is to evaluate a function defined over an interval, say $1 \leq x \leq 10$. In such a case, the syntax is identical to that of the Plot command:

In[1]:= **Manipulate$\left[x^2,\ \{x,\ 1,\ 10\}\right]$**

Out[1]=

The controller, aptly called a *manipulator*, initially displays as a slider. Clicking on the ⊞ button to the right of the slider, however, will reveal additional controls beneath:

Now operate the slider. It ranges over the values from 1 to 10 in this example, and the current value is displayed in the input field directly under the slider. The function value $f(x) = x^2$ is displayed below. Try it. As you position the cursor over any control button, a tooltip will appear that describes that button's function. For instance, the Play/Pause button ▶ is used to start and stop an animation, while the buttons on either side of it will advance it forward or backward one frame at a time. The double up- and down-arrow buttons are used to adjust the speed of the animation, and the direction button on the far right is used to determine whether the animation will play forward, backward, or oscillate (forward to the end, then backward to the beginning, and so on). You may also type a specific numerical value directly into the input field, followed by the Return/Enter key. Note that if you hit SHIFT⎻ENTER after typing in the input field, you will generate a second output cell. So just use ENTER when interacting with a Manipulate object.

The Manipulate command in its most basic form takes two arguments, separated by a comma. The first (in this case x^2) describes the expression to be manipulated. The second (in this case $\{x,\ 1,\ 10\}$) is the Manipulator Control. Templates for a few of the many possibilities are in the Manipulator Control ▼ menu. If you wish to have your variable increase in unit steps only, you can add a fourth element to the iterator that will specify the amount by which the variable will skip from one value to the next. For example, here we increment the variable x in steps of size 5. When the slider is moved, x jumps from 0 to 5 to 10, etc.

In[2]:= `Manipulate[x², {x, 0, 50, 5}]`

Out[2]=

In the next example, we make a plot of the function $f(x) = x \sin(1/x)$, the right endpoint of which is controlled with a slider, while the left endpoint is fixed at 0. When the controller is moved to the left, the plot's domain narrows, and the user is afforded a zoomed-in view of the function's behavior near $x = 0$.

In[3]:= `Manipulate[Plot[x * Sin[1 / x], {x, 0, r}],`
       `{r, .1, 2}]`

Out[3]=

In cases such as this it would be nice to put a more descriptive label on the slider. This can be accomplished either by giving the controller variable a more descriptive name (e.g., one might use `xmax` or `rightEndpoint`), or by replacing the controller variable r in the iterator above by a *list* of the form {*var*, *init*, *label*}. Here *var* is the variable name, *init* is the initial value to be assumed by the variable upon evaluation, and *label* is the label you want to be displayed on the interface. For instance, below we generate the same output as above, except that we create a slider with the label right endpoint, and whose initial value will be 0.2.

In[4]:= `Manipulate[Plot[x * Sin[1 / x], {x, 0, r}],`
       `{{r, 0.2, "right endpoint"}, .1, 2}]`

Out[4]=

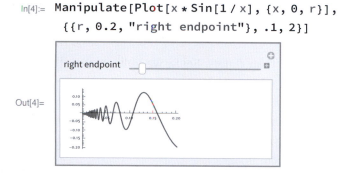

It is possible to place several controller variables in a single `Manipulate`. It is also possible to simultaneously animate all of them using their individual controls. Below we explore three directive settings for `PlotStyle`.

In[5]:= `Manipulate[Plot[x Sin[x], {x, -10, 10}, PlotStyle →`
`Directive[Thickness[t], Dashing[{d}], Blend[{Red, Blue}, b]]],`
`{{t, .01, "Thickness"}, .001, .02}, {{d, .02, "Dash Size"}, 0, .04},`
`{{b, .5, "Percent Blue"}, 0, 1}]`

Out[5]=

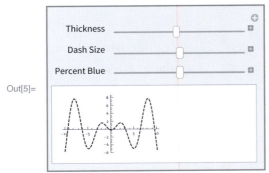

When manipulating a function inside a `Plot`, it is often desirable to include a `PlotRange` setting to maintain a fixed viewing rectangle as the controllers are moved. Here we use three controls to adjust some coefficients on a parabola:

In[6]:= $\texttt{Manipulate}\Big[\texttt{Plot}\Big[\texttt{a (x - b)}^2 \texttt{+ c, \{x, -5, 5\}},$
$\texttt{PlotRange} \rightarrow \texttt{5, PlotLabel} \rightarrow \texttt{"y = a (x-b)}^2\texttt{+c"}\Big],$
$\texttt{\{a, -1, 1\}, \{\{b, -1\}, -3, 3\}, \{\{c, 2\}, -3, 3\}}\Big]$

Out[6]=

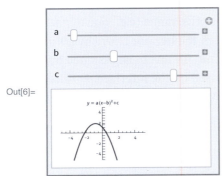

There are numerous control types available other than sliders. Below we force `Manipulate` to use a `SetterBar` (a row of buttons, only one of which can be selected at a time) simply by changing the syntax of the iterator. The values to be assumed by the controller variable are given explicitly as a list. This example is useful for exploring the roles of the `PlotPoints`, `MaxRecursion`, and `Mesh` options in producing a `Plot`. Note that the default setting for `PlotPoints` is 50, so most of the settings for this option below force *Mathematica* to produce a poor image.

```
In[7]:= Manipulate[
          Plot[ Sin[4 / x], {x, -2 π, 2 π}, PlotPoints → pp, MaxRecursion → mr,
            Mesh → m], {{pp, 64, "PlotPoints"}, {4, 8, 16, 32, 64}},
          {{mr, 4, "MaxRecursion"}, {0, 1, 2, 3, 4}},
          {{m, Full, "Mesh"}, {Full, All, None}}]
```

Out[7]=

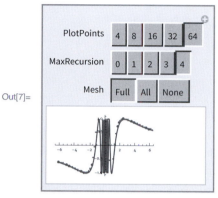

The control type adapts to the syntax used in the iterator for that control. For instance, if a list of values associated with a controller variable contains six or more items, the controller will change from a SetterBar (as in the previous example) to a PopupMenu. While a PopupMenu is desirable if there is a *very* long list of choices, we prefer a simple SetterBar as long as there is room for it. In the next example we override the default behavior with an explicit ControlType option setting.

```
In[8]:= Manipulate[
          Plot[f[x], {x, 0, 4 π},
            Ticks → {Range[0, 4 π, π / 2], Automatic}, PlotLabel → f[x]],
          {{f, Tan, "function"}, {Sin, Cos, Sec, Csc, Tan, Cot},
            ControlType → SetterBar}]
```

Out[8]=

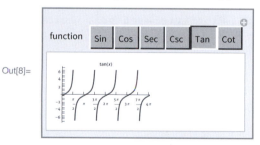

There are many other useful controller types. For instance, you can produce the controller known as Slider2D by creating a Manipulate variable whose value is set to an *ordered pair* of the form {*x*, *y*} (i.e., a point in the plane), and specifying its bounds as {*xmin*, *ymin*} and {*xmax*, *ymax*}. Below we illustrate this by letting the user manipulate the AxesOrigin setting with a two-dimensional slider:

In[9]:= `Manipulate[`
`Plot[x Sin[x], {x, -20, 20}, AxesOrigin → pt, PlotRange → 20],`
`{{pt, {0, 0}, "Move the axes: "}, {-20, -20}, {20, 20}},`
`ControlPlacement → Left]`

Out[9]=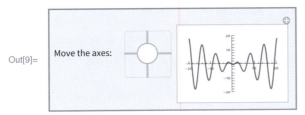

Another means of manipulating a point in a graphic is to use an iterator of the form {*var*, `Locator`}, as shown below. Drag the `Locator` icon with your mouse to move it directly across the graph, or simply click on the graphic to move the `Locator` to that location. The {0,0} in the input below specifies the initial position of the locator when the cell is first evaluated.

In[10]:= `Manipulate[Plot[x Sin[x], {x, -20, 20},`
`AxesOrigin → pt, PlotRange → 20], {{pt, {0, 0}}, Locator}]`

Out[10]=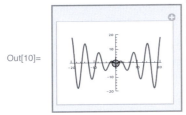

The simple iterator structure {*var*, *color*} will produce a color slider. You can drag over the color field with the mouse to adjust the color continuously in real time.

In[11]:= $\text{Manipulate}\left[\text{Plot}\left[\frac{\text{Sin}[x]}{x}, \{x, 0, 20\}, \text{PlotStyle} \rightarrow \text{color}\right], \{\text{color}, \text{Blue}\}\right]$

Out[11]=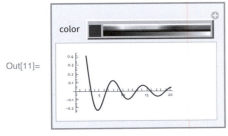

A complete listing of permissible iterator syntax structures and their corresponding default controller types can be found in the Details and Options section of the documentation page for `Manipulate`. We summarize this information in Table 3.1.

Iterator Form	Default Control Type
$\{u, u_{min}, \infty\}$	Animator
$\{u, u_{min}, u_{max}\}$	Manipulator
$\{u, u_{min}, u_{max}, du\}$	Discrete Manipulator with step du
$\{u, \{x_{min}, x_{max}\}, \{y_{min}, y_{max}\}\}$	Slider2D
$\{u, \{x_{min}, x_{max}\}, \{y_{min}, y_{max}\}, \{dx, dy\}\}$	Discrete Slider2D with horizontal step dx, vertical step dy
$\{u, \text{Locator}\}$	Locator
$\{u, \{\text{True}, \text{False}\}\}$	Checkbox
$\{u, \{value_1, value_2, \ldots\}\}$	PopupMenu (or SetterBar if fewer than 6 items)
$\{u, color\}$	ColorSlider
$\{u\}$	InputField

Table 3.1   Iterator structures for Manipulate variables and default control types they produce.

When making a `Manipulate` object it is important to put the right controllers in place for the task at hand. Options may be added to any of the iterator forms so that one may specify a controller other than the default. For example, one could replace the `Manipulate` iterator list `{u, 0, 10}` by `{u, 0, 10, ControlType → VerticalSlider, ControlPlacement → Left}`. We summarize some valid `ControlType` settings for each iterator form in Table 3.2 (default setting underlined).

Other Dynamic Display Commands

While `Manipulate` is the single most flexible and powerful command for creating dynamic user environments, there are a number of other commands which produce dynamic output of some kind. For instance, one may use the command `Animate` to produce an animation. The syntax is identical to that of `Manipulate`.

Each of the commands `ListAnimate`, `FlipView`, `PopupView`, `OpenerView`, and `SlideView` accepts a list of expressions, and creates an environment in which the user can dynamically interact with the individual expressions. `OpenerView` accepts a list containing only two expressions: a header and an expression to display when it is in the "open" state. You simply click the triangle to open it.

```
In[12]:=  OpenerView[{Style["click the triangle", "Text"],
            Style["Hah, you did it!", "Section"]}]
```

Out[12]=   ▶ click the triangle

The commands `MenuView` and `TabView` accept lists of the form $\{label_1 \to expression_1, label_2 \to expression_2, \ldots\}$, and return a menu of labels or a collection of tabs, respectively, associated with their corresponding expressions.

In[13]:= `TabView[{"sine" → Plot[Sin[x], {x, 0, 2 π}],`
         `   "cosine" → Plot[Cos[x], {x, 0, 2 π}]}, ImageSize → Automatic]`

Out[13]=

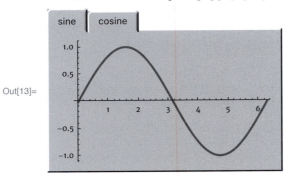

Iterator Form	Valid Control Type Settings
$\{u, u_{min}, u_{max}\}$	Animator, InputField, <u>Manipulator</u>, Slider, Slider2D, VerticalSlider, None
$\{u, u_{min}, u_{max}, du\}$	Animator, InputField, <u>Manipulator</u>, PopupMenu, RadioButtonBar, SetterBar, Slider, Slider2D, VerticalSlider, None
$\{u, \{x_{min}, x_{max}\}, \{y_{min}, y_{max}\}\}$	InputField, Locator, <u>Slider2D</u>, None
$\{u, \{x_{min}, x_{max}\}, \{y_{min}, y_{max}\}, \{dx, dy\}\}$	InputField, Locator, <u>Slider2D</u>, None
$\{u, \text{Locator}\}$	<u>Locator</u>, None
$\{u, \{\text{True}, \text{False}\}\}$	Animator, <u>Checkbox</u>, CheckboxBar, InputField, Manipulator, Opener, PopupMenu, RadioButtonBar, SetterBar, Slider, VerticalSlider, None
$\{u, \{value_1, value_2, \ldots\}\}$	Animator, Checkbox, CheckboxBar, InputField, Manipulator, <u>PopupMenu</u>, RadioButtonBar, SetterBar, Slider, TogglerBar, VerticalSlider, None
$\{u, color\}$	ColorSetter, <u>ColorSlider</u>, InputField, None
$\{u\}$	<u>InputField</u>, None

Table 3.2 Valid control type settings for the various iterator structures used in Manipulate.

Exercises 3.4

1. The following simple `Manipulate` has two sliders: one for *x* and one for *y*, and it displays the pair $\{x, y\}$. Make a `Manipulate` that also has output $\{x, y\}$, but that has a single `Slider2D` controller.

In[1]:= `Manipulate[{x, y}, {x, 0, 1}, {y, 0, 1}]`

Out[1]=

2. Make a `Manipulate` of a `Plot` where the user can adjust the `AspectRatio` in real time, from a starting value of 1/5 (five times as wide as it is tall) to an ending value of 5 (five times as tall as it is wide). Set `ImageSize` to `{Automatic, 128}` so the height remains constant as the slider is moved.

3. Make a `Manipulate` of a `Plot` where the user can adjust the `Background` in real time.

   a. Use the setting `Background → RGBColor[r, g, b]`, where *r*, *g*, and b are `Manipulate` variables that range from 0 to 1. They will control the relative amounts of red, green, and blue in the background, respectively. This allows you to interactively explore the RGB color space.

   b. Use the setting `Background → Hue[h, s, b, a]`, where *h*, *s*, *b*, and *a* are `Manipulate` variables that range from 0 to 1. They will control the values of hue, saturation, brightness, and opacity in the background, respectively. This allows you to interactively explore the HSBcolor space.

4. It is often the case that one wants to create a `Manipulate` that includes some sort of explanatory text that can be manipulated. A robust means of accomplishing this is to (1) transform any variable quantity in the text to a `String` using `ToString`, and (2) join together the static and variable text strings with `StringEx` `pression`.

   a. You can type `~~` between two text strings to sew them together into a single string. Technically, you are invoking the `StringExpression` command when you do this. Try it; type and enter the following. We use `FullForm` so that the double quotes will display.

   In[2]:= `"This is a string" ~~ " and so is this." // FullForm`

   Out[2]//FullForm=
   `"This is a string and so is this."`

   b. Now explain what's going on here:

   In[3]:= `Manipulate[Style["The square root of " ~~ ToString[x] ~~`
   `" is " ~~ ToString[N[√x]] ~~ ".", "Subsubsection"],`
   `{{x, 2}, 1, 10}]`

   Out[3]=

   c. Create a `Manipulate` showing a `Plot` of the sine function, with a `PlotLabel` that indicates the value of the function for any value of *x* between $-\pi$ and π. The user can control *x* with a slider.

5. When a `Manipulate` has a `Locator` controller, it's possible (and often desirable) to modify the `Locator`'s default appearance in the image pane. A simple way to do this is to display a `Graphics` object of your choosing at the position of the `Locator`, and add the option setting `Appearance → None` to the iterator for the `Locator` control. Enter the following input, explore the output, and then change things so that the `Locator` appears as a `Thick`, `Blue`, `Circle`.

```
Manipulate[Graphics[
    {Directive[PointSize[.03], Red], Point[pt]}, Axes → True, PlotRange → 1],
    {{pt, {0, 0}}, Locator, Appearance → None}]
```

6. The following input will create a useful interactive interface in which every available option for the `Plot` command appears in a popup menu. Select an option in this menu, and the usage message for that option is displayed. Try it (courtesy of Lou D'Andria, Wolfram Research).

```
Manipulate[ToExpression[SymbolName[option] ~~ "::usage"],
    {option, Map[First, Options[Plot]]}]
```

   a. Modify the input above to create an option explorer for the `Grid` command, and use it to get information on the `ItemSize` option.

   b. See if you can figure out how this `Manipulate` works. This will entail finding information in the Documentation Center on the commands `Map`, `First`, `Options`, `SymbolName`, `ToExpression`, and `StringExpression` (~~). Note that by replacing `Plot` (near the end of the input) by any other command that accepts options, an option explorer for that command can be generated.

7. Use `TabView` with two tabs to produce the output below. You'll have to find the answer to the riddle on your own, or look at the solution. (Riddle by Alexandra Torrence, age 10.)

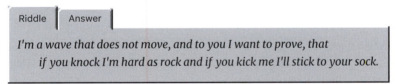

8. This exercise discusses the use of gamepad controllers to operate a `Manipulate` output. If you have a gamepad for your computer, the first thing to do is to plug it in, select the cell bracket for a `Manipulate` and try it. In most cases it's plug and play. To bind a particular `Manipulate` local variable to a given controller axis, replace the iterator {*var*, *spec*} for that variable with *axisName* → {*var*, *spec*}, where *axisName* is the string name of the given controller axis. Typical axis names are given below. Create a `Manipulate` where you bind a specific local variable to a specific controller axis.

> one-dimensional: X1, Y1, Z1, X2, Y2
> two-dimensional: XY1, XY2
> buttons: Button 1, Button 2

3.5 Producing a Table of Values

It is often handy to produce a table of function values for various inputs. The Table command can be found on the Basic Math Assistant palette in the Basic Commands section by clicking on the List button. Alternately, it's a simple matter to enter the input below directly from the keyboard. Here is a table of the squares of the first ten positive whole numbers:

In[1]:= **Table**$\left[x^2, \{x, 1, 10\}\right]$

Out[1]= $\{1, 4, 9, 16, 25, 36, 49, 64, 81, 100\}$

Like Plot and Manipulate, the Table command takes two arguments, separated by a comma. The first is an expression that will evaluate to the entries in your table, while the second (in this case $\{x, 1, 10\}$) is an iterator. Unlike Plot and Manipulate, however, the values of the variable will increment by 1 (by default) in a Table. As with Manipulate, a fourth number can be added to the iterator to specify the step size.

In[2]:= **Table**$\left[x^2, \{x, 0, 50, 5\}\right]$

Out[2]= $\{0, 25, 100, 225, 400, 625, 900, 1225, 1600, 2025, 2500\}$

You can also shorten the iterator to contain only two items—the name of the variable and a stopping number. When you do this, *Mathematica* starts at 1 and increments the variable in steps of 1 until the stopping number is reached. So for instance, using the iterator $\{x, 10\}$ is the same as using the iterator $\{x, 1, 10\}$:

In[3]:= **Table**$\left[x^2, \{x, 10\}\right]$

Out[3]= $\{1, 4, 9, 16, 25, 36, 49, 64, 81, 100\}$

Templates for several forms of input for the Table command can be found in the Tables ▼ menu in the palette.

The output of the Table command is a basic data structure in *Mathematica* called a *list*. A list is composed of an opening curly bracket, individual items (such as numbers) separated by commas, and a closing curly bracket.

Table will also accept a special iterator structure of the form $\{var, \{value_1, value_2, ...\}\}$. In this case the variable will assume the explicit values in the given list.

In[4]:= **Table**$\left[x^2, \{x, \{1, 7, 12, 20\}\}\right]$

Out[4]= $\{1, 49, 144, 400\}$

One of the most useful applications of the Table command is producing something that actually looks like a table. We accomplish this by constructing a Table where the first argument is itself a list. The result is a list of lists. We then apply Grid to the result in order to create a two-dimensional display in which each inner list becomes a row. Here's an example where both the input value x and the output value $f(x) = x^2$ are given in each row:

In[5]:= `data = Table`$\left[\{x, x^2\}, \{x, 5\}\right]$

Out[5]= $\{\{1, 1\}, \{2, 4\}, \{3, 9\}, \{4, 16\}, \{5, 25\}\}$

In[6]:= `Grid[data]`

Out[6]=
```
1  1
2  4
3  9
4  16
5  25
```

`Grid` will display any list of lists in a two-dimensional format like this; each sublist appears as a separate row. Numerous options are available that allow all manner of presentation possibilities. But perhaps the most simple formatting tip is to apply `Text` to an entire grid. This will apply textual formatting to the individual items (numbers in this case) that occupy each grid cell. Here we use the prefix form (@, see Section 2.7) instead of square brackets when applying the `Text` command, and add the `Grid` option setting `Alignment → Right` to align each column to the right.

In[7]:= `Text@Grid[data, Alignment → Right]`

Out[7]=
```
1  1
2  4
3  9
4  16
5  25
```

Another simple but valuable technique is to add headings to the columns of a table. There are a few different ways to accomplish this. One way is to simply *prepend* an additional row containing the column headings to your table data. Typically each item in the header row is a *string*; this is accomplished by enclosing each column header in double quotes.

In[8]:= `Prepend`$\left[\text{data}, \{"x", "x^2"\}\right]$

Out[8]= $\left\{\{x, x^2\}, \{1, 1\}, \{2, 4\}, \{3, 9\}, \{4, 16\}, \{5, 25\}\right\}$

In[9]:= `Text@Grid`$\left[\text{Prepend}\left[\text{data}, \{"x", "x^2"\}\right], \text{Alignment → Right},\right.$
$\left.\quad \text{Dividers → \{Center, \{False, True\}\}, Spacings → 2}\right]$

Out[9]=

x	x^2
1	1
2	4
3	9
4	16
5	25

The Spacings option can be used to add a bit of space between successive columns. The Dividers option is used above to add dividing lines in a Grid. The setting is of the form {*vertical dividers*, *horizontal dividers*}. The Center setting specifies that there are no vertical lines on the far left or far right, only between the columns. The {False, True} specifies the horizontal dividing lines: there is no line above the first row, while there is one above the second row, and none for any subsequent rows. The following syntax may also be used for Dividers. It can be handy in cases like this where few dividers are required. It simply specifies that only the *second* vertical divider and the *second* horizontal divider will be rendered, and no others.

In[10]:= `Text@Grid[Prepend[data, {"x", "x²"}], Alignment → Right,`
`        Dividers → {2 → True, 2 → True}, Spacings → 2]`

Out[10]=

x	x^2
1	1
2	4
3	9
4	16
5	25

Another means of introducing row or column headings to a table is to use the TableForm wrapper instead of Grid. They work the same way, but TableForm will automatically add a dividing line between the headings and the table contents, and easily permits row labels as well as column labels.

In[11]:= `TableForm[data, TableHeadings → {None, {"x", "x²"}},`
`        TableAlignments → Right]`

Out[11]//TableForm=

x	x^2
1	1
2	4
3	9
4	16
5	25

In the input above, the TableHeadings option is set to a list whose first member is the list of row headings, and whose second member is the list of column headings. Use None to leave out one set of headings or the other. TableForm also makes it easy to "transpose" the table, turning its columns into rows:

In[12]:= `TableForm[data, TableHeadings → {None, {"x", "x²"}},`
`        TableAlignments → Right, TableDirections → Row]`

Out[12]//TableForm=

x	1	2	3	4	5
x^2	1	4	9	16	25

With these tools in hand, you can create tables to your heart's content. Here we display a table with three columns, using `Grid` with the simple `Dividers → All` setting to put in all possible row and column dividers:

In[13]:= **Clear[data];**
        data = Table$\left[\left\{x, x^2, 2^x\right\}, \{x, 10\}\right]$

Out[14]= {{1, 1, 2}, {2, 4, 4}, {3, 9, 8}, {4, 16, 16}, {5, 25, 32}, {6, 36, 64},
        {7, 49, 128}, {8, 64, 256}, {9, 81, 512}, {10, 100, 1024}}

In[15]:= **Text@Grid$\left[\text{Prepend}\left[\text{data}, \left\{"x", "x^2", "2^x"\right\}\right]\right]$,**
        Alignment → Right, Dividers → All, Spacings → 2]

Out[15]=

x	x^2	2^x
1	1	2
2	4	4
3	9	8
4	16	16
5	25	32
6	36	64
7	49	128
8	64	256
9	81	512
10	100	1024

💡 **The three most common types of brackets**

Now is a good time to review the three most commonly used brackets in *Mathematica*. Parentheses ( ) are used to group terms in algebraic expressions. Square brackets [ ] are used to enclose the arguments of functions. And curly brackets { } are used to enclose lists.

Manipulating a Grid

Here is a grid with a header row, and a second row of content. The values in this second row can be manipulated. This gives a compact table that allows one to display the row of his or her choosing:

In[16]:= **Manipulate$\left[\text{Text@Grid}\left[\left\{\left\{"x", "x^2"\right\}, \left\{x, x^2\right\}\right\}, \text{Dividers → All},\right.\right.$**
        $\left.\left.\text{ItemSize → 4}\right], \{\{x, 5.3\}, 1, 10, .1\}\right]$

Out[16]=

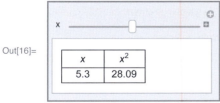

The following shows a simple Celsius to Fahrenheit conversion tool:

In[17]:= `Manipulate[Text@Grid[{{"C", "F"}, {c, 1.8 c + 32}},`
`        Dividers → Lighter[Gray], ItemSize → 4], {{c, 0}, -40, 100, 1}]`

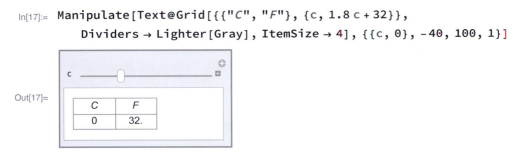

Out[17]=

Here is another version, using the built-in UnitConvert with appropriate Quantity objects, all inside a Grid with a single row:

In[18]:= `Manipulate[`
`        Grid[{{Quantity[c, "DegreesCelsius"], " = ", UnitConvert[`
`            Quantity[c, "DegreesCelsius"], Quantity["DegreesFahrenheit"]]}},`
`        ItemSize → {5, 3}, Alignment → {Center, Center}],`
`        {{c, 0}, -40, 100, 1}]`

Out[18]=

The two examples above make use of the ItemSize option to the Grid command. When set to a single numerical value (as in the first example) it specifies the width of each cell in the grid in *ems* (the width of the letter m). Other common settings for this option include All (which specifies that all cells have identical width and height values, determined by the content of the largest cells), or a list of two numerical values such as {4, 3} (which specifies the width of each cell in *ems* and the height of each cell in *line heights*, respectively). When manipulating a grid, it is a good idea to set ItemSize to a specific numerical value (or to a list of two such values) in order to keep the table dimensions steady as the controller is adjusted.

Exercises 3.5

1. The Partition command is used to break a single list into sublists of equal length. It is useful for breaking up a list into rows for display within a Grid.

   a. Enter the following inputs and discuss the outputs.

   `Range[100]`

   `Partition[Range[100], 10]`

b.   Format a table of the first 100 integers, with 20 digits per row. The first two rows, for example, should look like this:

1	2	3	4	5	6	7	8	9	10	11	12	13	14	15	16	17	18	19	20
21	22	23	24	25	26	27	28	29	30	31	32	33	34	35	36	37	38	39	40

c.   Make the same table as above, but use only the `Table` and `Range` commands. Do not use `Partition`.

d.   Make the same table as above, but use only the `Table` command (twice). Do not use `Partition` or `Range`.

2. The `Style` command is used to apply a particular style to an expression.

a.   Enter the following inputs and discuss the outputs.

```
Style[4, Red]
```

```
Style[4, 72]
```

```
Style[4, "Section"]
```

```
Style[4, FontFamily → "Helvetica", FontWeight → "Bold"]
```

b.   One can apply a particular style to *every* item in a `Grid` by using the entire `Grid` as the first argument to `Style`. Create an output that matches that below. The font is Comic Sans MS, and the text should be blue.

1	1	1	1
2	4	8	16
3	9	27	81
4	16	64	256
5	25	125	625

c.   Alternately, one can apply style elements to an entire grid by selecting the cell bracket of the cell containing the grid, and visiting the Format menu. For instance, Format ▷ Text Color ▷ Blue will make all the text blue. Reproduce the `Grid` above, this time using the menu items to change the style.

3. A statement that is either true or false is called a *predicate*; in *Mathematica* a predicate is any expression that evaluates to `True` or `False`. In this exercise you will learn how to use predicates to apply `Styles` selectively.

a.   There are many built-in predicate commands. Most end in the letter Q (for "Query"). Enter the following inputs and discuss the outputs.

```
? PrimeQ
```

```
? P*Q
```

b.   The `If` command is used to generate one output if a specified condition (i.e., a predicate) is true, and another if that condition is false. The predicate is the first argument to `If`. The next argument is what is returned if the predicate is true (`If` is discussed in Section 8.5). A third argument specifies the expression to be returned if the predicate is false. Enter the following input and discuss the output.

```
Table[If[PrimeQ[n], Style[n, Red], n], {n, 100}]
```

c.   Format a table of the first 100 integers, with ten digits per row. In this table, make all prime numbers red.

d. Format a table of the first 100 integers, with ten digits per row. In this table, make all *squarefree* numbers blue and underlined. Note: An integer is squarefree if none of its divisors (other than 1) are perfect squares.

e. Format a table of the first 100 integers, with ten digits per row. In this table, make all *prime powers* orange and italicized. Note: An integer is a prime power if it is equal to p^n, where p is prime and n is a positive integer.

4. The `Sum` command has a syntax similar to that of `Table`.

a. Use the `Sum` command to evaluate the following expression:
$$1^3 + 2^3 + 3^3 + 4^3 + 5^3 + 6^3 + 7^3 + 8^3 + 9^3 +$$
$$10^3 + 11^3 + 12^3 + 13^3 + 14^3 + 15^3 + 16^3 + 17^3 + 18^3 + 19^3 + 20^3$$

b. Make a table of values for $x = 1, 2, \ldots, 10$ for the function
$$f(x) = 1 + 2^x + 3^x + 4^x + 5^x + 6^x + 7^x + 8^x +$$
$$9^x + 10^x + 11^x + 12^x + 13^x + 14^x + 15^x + 16^x + 17^x + 18^x + 19^x + 20^x$$

c. Plot $f(x)$ on the domain $1 \le x \le 10$.

5. Comments can be inserted directly into your input code. Any text placed between the `(*` and `*)` tokens will be ignored by the kernel when an input is entered. Comments do not affect the manner in which your code is executed, but they can be helpful to you or someone else who has to read and understand the code later. Look at the *solution* to the *next* exercise to see an example in which comments are used to help a reader find each of four items in a somewhat complex two-by-two `Grid`.

6. In this exercise you will explore the syntax for applying options to a `Grid`. Mastery of this syntax will allow you to construct stunningly beautiful tables. There are two common syntax forms that work for several options. To illustrate the possibilities we use the `Dividers` option, which specifies the placement and style of vertical and horizontal dividing lines in a `Grid`. First enter the input below to generate a 10×10 table of invisible data (each entry is simply a string composed of a single space character). Note: The `Partition` command is discussed in Exercise 1.

```
emptyTable = Partition[Table[" ", {100}], 10]
```

a. The simple setting `Dividers → All` will insert every possible line. But other single-word settings such as `Gray` are permissible. Enter the inputs below, and discuss the outputs.

```
Grid[emptyTable, Dividers → Gray]
```

```
Grid[emptyTable, Dividers → Dotted]
```

```
Grid[emptyTable, Dividers → Thick]
```

```
Grid[emptyTable, Dividers → Directive[Thin, Orange]]
```

b. More control may be obtained with the syntax `Dividers → {x setting, y setting}`. Typically the x setting is a list of values relating to positions within a row, and is used to specify the style and placement of vertical items. Enter the input below. Here the x setting is `{Black, {Gray}, Black}`, and the y setting is `None`. What effect does this have?

```
Grid[emptyTable, Dividers → {{Black, {Gray}, Black}, None}]
```

c.   How would you produce the output below?

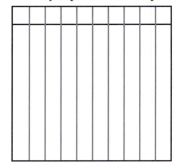

d.   Take your last input and add the following option setting, then explain the output.

Background →

{None, {Lighter[Gray, .7], {Lighter[Blue, .9], Lighter[Yellow, .9]}}}

e.   Other options that utilize these syntactical conventions are Alignment, Spacings, ItemSize, and ItemStyle. Some simple but useful Alignment settings to try are Alignment → Right or Align﹔ ment→"." (to align numbers at the decimal point). Produce the following Grid using the options mentioned. Once you can do this, you will be equipped to produce a rich assortment of useful tables.

10^{-5}	0.00001
10^{-4}	0.0001
10^{-3}	0.001
10^{-2}	0.01
10^{-1}	0.1
10^{0}	1.
10^{1}	10.
10^{2}	100.
10^{3}	1000.
10^{4}	10000.
10^{5}	100000.

7. Use a two-by-two Grid within Manipulate to create the interface below for zooming in on a graph of the sine function. The "Center" controller corresponds to a variable named x0, and the "Zoom Level" controller corresponds to a variable named δ. The iterator for the lower Plot is of the form {x0 – δ, x0 + δ}.

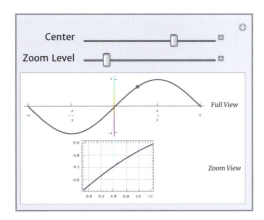

8. Use `Manipulate` to make a currency converter. The user enters a price in euros, and the converter shows the price in dollars. Hint: Model it after the Celsius to Fahrenheit converter at the end of this section, using either `CurrencyConvert` or `UnitConvert`. As long as you are connected to the internet, this will cause *Mathematica* to use the current conversion rates to compute the answer.

3.6 Working with Piecewise Defined Functions

Certain functions are defined differently over various disjoint pieces of their domain, so-called *piecewise defined functions*. For instance, a function may be defined by the rule $f(x) = x$ when x is between 0 and 1, inclusive; by the rule $f(x) = -x$ when x is strictly between -1 and 0; and by $f(x) = 1$ for all other values of x. In standard mathematical notation we write:

$$f(x) = \begin{cases} x & 0 \le x \le 1 \\ -x & -1 < x < 0 \\ 1 & \text{otherwise} \end{cases}$$

Here, "otherwise" means that either $x > 1$ or $x \le -1$. How can this be conveyed to *Mathematica*? It is a simple matter to enter a piecewise function directly from the keyboard in standard notation. To do so, first type `f[x_] :=`, then create the single bracket by typing [ESC]pw[ESC], and finally produce a grid to the right of the bracket by typing [CTRL] ,]. If more than two rows are needed, type [CTRL] ↵]. Each time you hit [CTRL] ↵] you will add one additional row. At this point your input looks like this:

$$f[x\_] := \begin{bmatrix} \square & \square \\ \square & \square \\ \square & \square \end{bmatrix}$$

Now move the cursor to the first placeholder and type in a function expression, then use the [TAB] key to move to the adjacent placeholder and type a logical expression. This is typically an inequality such as $0 \le x \le 1$, but in all cases is an expression that evaluates to either `True` or `False` when x is a specific real number. Fill in the remaining pairs of placeholders; the first in each pair holds a function expression, the second a logical expression. The following example shows how one would enter the function above. Note that the logical expression in the final row can simply contain the expression `True`, which conveys that this rule is applied to all values of *x* for which the logical expressions in earlier rows are False; that is, it behaves like the word "otherwise" in the example above. When you're finished typing, enter the cell.

$$\text{In[1]:= } \texttt{f[x\_] :=} \begin{cases} x & 0 \le x \le 1 \\ -x & -1 < x < 0 \\ 1 & \texttt{True} \end{cases}$$

Once entered, this function behaves like any other. You may Plot it, Manipulate it, apply to it any transformations that you might apply to any other function. In short, it behaves exactly as it should. For instance:

In[2]:= `Plot[f[x], {x, -2, 2}]`

Out[2]=

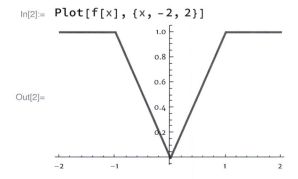

The underlying *Mathematica* command that is being utilized to create the function above is called Piecewise. In most cases it is easiest to use the syntax above, which has the effect of calling the Piecewise command. Equivalently, one can use Piecewise directly; the following example shows how to enter the function above using this syntax:

In[3]:= `f[x_] := Piecewise[{{x, 0 ≤ x ≤ 1}, {-x, -1 < x < 0}}, 1]`

This syntax can be useful when you are working with a function that has a large number of "pieces," for you can then use the Table command to generate the first argument programmatically. See Exercise 3.

Regardless of how a piecewise function is entered, it is important to understand some syntactical conventions regarding the logical expressions (such as $0 \le x \le 1$) that specify when the function rule is applied. In particular, the logical connective && can be used to mean "and," and || can be used to mean "or." The connectives allow complex conditions to be specified. Here's an example:

$$\text{In[4]:= } \texttt{g[x\_] :=} \begin{cases} x^2 & (-2 \le x \le -1) \;||\; (1 \le x \le 2) \\ 1 & -1 < x < 1 \\ 4 & \texttt{True} \end{cases}$$

Here is an equivalent formulation, using the absolute value function:

In[5]:= $g[x\_] := \begin{cases} x^2 & 1 \le \text{Abs}[x] \le 2 \\ 1 & \text{Abs}[x] < 1 \\ 4 & \text{True} \end{cases}$

In[6]:= **Plot[g[x], {x, -3, 3}, PlotRange → {0, 5}]**

Out[6]=

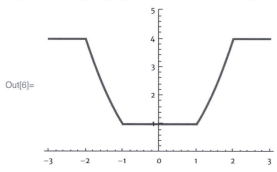

Piecewise functions provide a rich setting in which to explore *discontinuous* functions. Plot is aware of discontinuities appearing at the boundary between regions, and excludes such points. This leads to accurate plotting of such discontinuous functions.

In[7]:= $\text{Plot}\left[\left\{\begin{array}{ll} 1 & x \ge 1 \\ -1 & x < 1 \end{array}\right., \{x, -3, 3\}\right]$

Out[7]=

The ExclusionsStyle option works as it should in such cases:

In[8]:= $\text{Plot}\left[\left\{\begin{array}{ll} 1 & x \ge 1 \\ -1 & x < 1 \end{array}\right., \{x, -3, 3\}, \text{ExclusionsStyle} → \text{Dashed}\right]$

Out[8]=

Exercises 3.6

1. Show the second condition in the last example above could just as well be `True`.

2. Make a plot of the piecewise function below, and comment on its shape.

$$f(x) = \begin{cases} 0 & x < 0 \\ \dfrac{x^2}{2} & 0 \le x < 1 \\ -x^2 + 3x - \dfrac{3}{2} & 1 \le x < 2 \\ \dfrac{1}{2}(3-x)^2 & 2 \le x < 3 \\ 0 & 3 \le x \end{cases}$$

3. A *step function* assumes a constant value between consecutive integers n and $n + 1$. Make a plot of the step function $f(x)$ whose value is n^2 when $n \le x < n + 1$. Use the domain $0 \le x < 20$.

3.7 Plotting Implicitly Defined Functions

An *implicitly defined function* is given as an equation relating two variables, such as $x^2 + y^2 = 1$ (which describes a circle of radius 1). Here the y variable is not given *explicitly* as a function of the x variable, but rather the x and y terms appear in an equation; hence the term "implicitly" defined function. In order to plot an implicitly defined function, use the `ContourPlot` command; you can find a template at the bottom of the More ▾ menu to the right of the Plot button. Use the implicit equation for the first argument (with a double equal sign `==`), and include two iterators: one for x, and a second for y.

In[1]:= `ContourPlot[x² + y² == 1, {x, -1, 1}, {y, -1, 1}]`

Out[1]=

By default, a `ContourPlot` will display with a frame and no coordinate axes, but it is a simple matter to change this behavior.

In[2]:= **ContourPlot**$\left[x^2 + y^2 \; \text{==} \; 1, \; \{x, \; -1, \; 1\},\right.$

$\left.\{y, \; -1, \; 1\}, \; \text{Frame} \; \rightarrow \; \text{False}, \; \text{Axes} \; \rightarrow \; \text{True}\right]$

Out[2]=

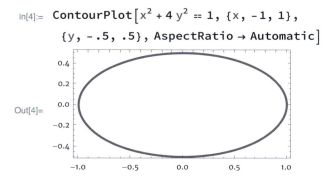

Note that by default the AspectRatio of a ContourPlot will be set to 1, meaning that the coordinate axes will be scaled as necessary to produce a perfectly square plot. Such a plot can be misleading; for instance, the ellipse below looks like a circle!

In[3]:= **ContourPlot**$\left[x^2 + 4\,y^2 \; \text{==} \; 1, \; \{x, \; -1, \; 1\}, \; \{y, \; -.5, \; .5\}\right]$

Out[3]=

Set the AspectRatio to Automatic to give your axes a uniform scale. We do not recommend this as a default setting, however, as it is all too easy to ask for a plot that is thousands of times higher than it is wide. But in cases such as the ellipse above, where a common scaling of axes is called for, this setting is important.

In[4]:= **ContourPlot**$\left[x^2 + 4\,y^2 \; \text{==} \; 1, \; \{x, \; -1, \; 1\},\right.$

$\left.\{y, \; -.5, \; .5\}, \; \text{AspectRatio} \; \rightarrow \; \text{Automatic}\right]$

Out[4]=

ContourPlot works in a fundamentally different way than Plot does, as there is no explicit expression to evaluate for each numerical value of *x*. Rather, it samples points in the rectangular region specified by the two iterators, and recursively applies an adaptive algorithm in an attempt to find a smooth curve (or curves) satisfying the given equation. It is possible that in some cases the default parameters governing the algorithm are insufficient to produce an accurate plot. For example, note the jagged appearance in some parts of the output below:

In[5]:= `ContourPlot[Sin[x²] + y² == Cos[x * y], {x, -10, 10}, {y, -1, 1}]`

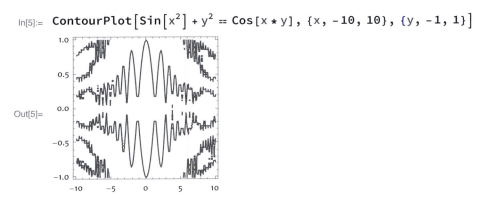

Out[5]=

To cure a case of "the jaggies," try setting the PlotPoints option to a large value such as 25, 50, or 100. PlotPoints controls how many points are initially sampled in the domain. Larger values tend to produce more accurate plots but may lead to significantly slower evaluation time, so use the lowest setting that produces a satisfactory plot.

In[6]:= `ContourPlot[Sin[x²] + y² == Cos[x * y],`
`        {x, -10, 10}, {y, -1, 1}, PlotPoints → 100]`

Out[6]=

Several implicitly defined functions can be simultaneously displayed by providing a *list* of equations as the first argument to ContourPlot. Mousing over a curve on the plot yields a tooltip displaying the equation corresponding to that curve, so it is easy to interpret the output when multiple equations are plotted.

In[7]:= $\texttt{ContourPlot}\left[\{2\,x^2 + y^2 == 1,\ 2\,x^2 - y^2 == 1\},\ \{x,\ -1,\ 1\},\ \{y,\ -1,\ 1\}\right]$

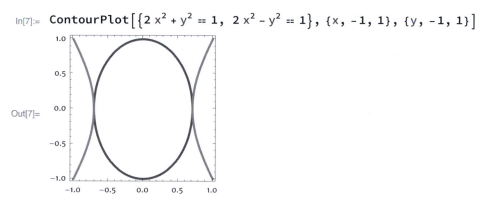

Out[7]=

As with the $\texttt{Plot}$ command, the option setting $\texttt{Mesh} \to \texttt{Full}$ will reveal which points are sampled initially, while the setting $\texttt{Mesh} \to \texttt{All}$ will reveal the final points used to construct the curves after the algorithm has run. The following $\texttt{Manipulate}$ is a useful aid for understanding how the options $\texttt{PlotPoints}$ and $\texttt{MaxRecursion}$ work in a $\texttt{ContourPlot}$. When $\texttt{MaxRecursion}$ is set to 0, no iterations take place and the initial and final meshes are the same. We saw a similar example for $\texttt{Plot}$ in Section 3.3.

In[8]:= $\texttt{Manipulate}\big[$
    $\texttt{ContourPlot}\big[2\,x^2 - y^2 == 1,\ \{x,\ -2,\ 2\},\ \{y,\ -2,\ 2\},$
      $\texttt{PlotPoints} \to \texttt{plotPoints},\ \texttt{MaxRecursion} \to \texttt{maxRecursion},\ \texttt{Mesh} \to \texttt{mesh}\big],$
      $\{\{\texttt{plotPoints},\ 4\},\ \{2,\ 3,\ 4,\ 8\}\},\ \{\{\texttt{maxRecursion},\ 2\},\ \{0,\ 1,\ 2,\ 3\}\},$
      $\{\texttt{mesh},\ \{\texttt{Full},\ \texttt{All}\}\}\big]$

Out[8]=

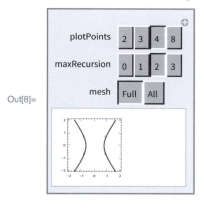

> ⚲ **The three types of equal signs**
>
> Now is a good time to review the three types of equal signs that are used in *Mathematica*. Each is used for a separate purpose, so it is imperative that they be used appropriately. A single equal sign = is used to assign a name to an expression, such as a = 3 or myPlot = Plot[2 x, {x, -2, 2}]. A colon-equal sign := is used to make a delayed assignment to an expression and is useful for defining functions, such as f[x_] := x². A double equal sign == is used to express an equation, such as $2x^2 - y^2 = 1$.

Exercises 3.7

1. The option ContourStyle (not PlotStyle) is used to change the style of a ContourPlot. Plot the implicit function $x^2 - \sin(x\,y) == 3$ as a thick, blue, dotted line.

2. If you ever wish to simultaneously view contour plots of implicitly defined functions of the form $f(x, y) == z_1$, $f(x, y) == z_2$, $f(x, y) == z_3$, and so on, where z_1, z_2, etc. are constants, the following syntax will work. Suppose, for instance, $f(x, y) = x^2 - y^2$, and the z-values are -2, -1, 0, 1, and 2. Enter the following input to see overlaid plots of $x^2 - y^2 = -2$, $x^2 - y^2 = -1$, $x^2 - y^2 = 0$, $x^2 - y^2 = 1$, and $x^2 - y^2 = 2$.

   ```
   ContourPlot[x² - y², {x, -2, 2}, {y, -2, 2},
     Contours → {-2, -1, 0, 1, 2}, ContourShading → False]
   ```

3. Piecewise functions may be implicitly defined. Let $f(x, y) = \begin{cases} x^2 - y^2 & x > y \\ 1 - \dfrac{x^2}{y^2} & x \le y \end{cases}$. Make a ContourPlot of the implicitly defined function $f(x, y) = \dfrac{1}{2}$ for $0 < x < 3$ and $0 < y < 3$.

3.8   Combining Graphics

So you want to combine two or more graphics together as one? There are many possibilities here, so we'll address each in turn.

Superimposing Plots

It is often desirable to view two or more plots together. If you simply want to plot several functions on the same set of axes, enter a *list* containing these functions as the first argument to the Plot command and you'll have it:

```
In[1]:=  Clear[f, g];
         f[x_] := 1 - x;
         g[x_] := x²;
```

In[4]:= `Plot[{f[x], g[x], f[x] * g[x]}, {x, -1, 1}]`

Out[4]=

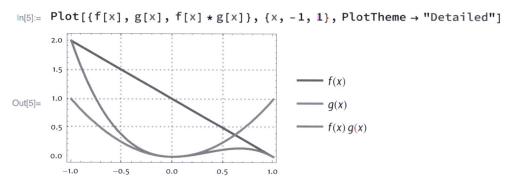

On your monitor the three functions are given three distinct colors. To tell which is which, one can add the option `PlotTheme → "Detailed"`.

In[5]:= `Plot[{f[x], g[x], f[x] * g[x]}, {x, -1, 1}, PlotTheme → "Detailed"]`

Out[5]=

One may also use the `PlotStyle` option to change the appearance of the three functions. This is sometimes useful for printed output when using a black and white printer. Just set `PlotStyle` to a list of three directives. These will be applied to the functions (in the order listed).

In[6]:= `Plot[{f[x], g[x], f[x] * g[x]}, {x, -1, 1},`
        `PlotStyle → {Black, Directive[Dashed, Black],`
            `Directive[Dotted, Black]}, PlotTheme -> "Detailed"]`

Out[6]=

If you need to superimpose a large number of plots, you can use *Mathematica*'s Table command to generate the list of functions:

In[7]:= $\texttt{Plot}\big[\texttt{Table}\big[\texttt{n x}^2, \{\texttt{n}, -40, 40\}\big], \{\texttt{x}, -2, 2\}, \texttt{PlotRange} \rightarrow 50\big]$

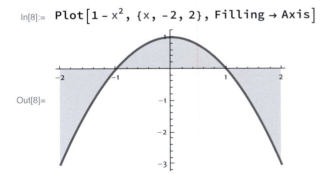

Out[7]=

⚠ In cases like this, where the expression appearing as the first argument to Plot is generated programmatically, it may be beneficial to wrap the expression with Evaluate. The necessity of the Evaluate command is a subtle business. Generally, Plot will hold the expression appearing as the first argument unevaluated, then evaluate it multiple times, once for each numerical value of *x* sampled in the domain. Evaluate forces Plot to first evaluate its initial argument before plugging in any values of *x*. In some settings this can lead to a plot that works versus one that does not. In other cases, Evaluate can reduce the time it takes to produce the plot. In the example above, the processing time is reduced (and curves become individually colored), if one replaces $\texttt{Table}\big[\texttt{n x}^2, \{\texttt{n}, -40, 40\}\big]$ by $\texttt{Evaluate}\big[\texttt{Table}\big[\texttt{n x}^2, \{\texttt{n}, -40, 40\}\big]\big]$.

Producing Filled Plots

One can shade the region between a plot and the *x* axis as follows:

In[8]:= $\texttt{Plot}\big[\texttt{1} - \texttt{x}^2, \{\texttt{x}, -2, 2\}, \texttt{Filling} \rightarrow \texttt{Axis}\big]$

Out[8]=

And one can shade the region between two curves like so:

In[9]:= `Plot[{Sin[x], 1 - x²}, {x, -2, 2}, Filling → {1}]`

Out[9]=

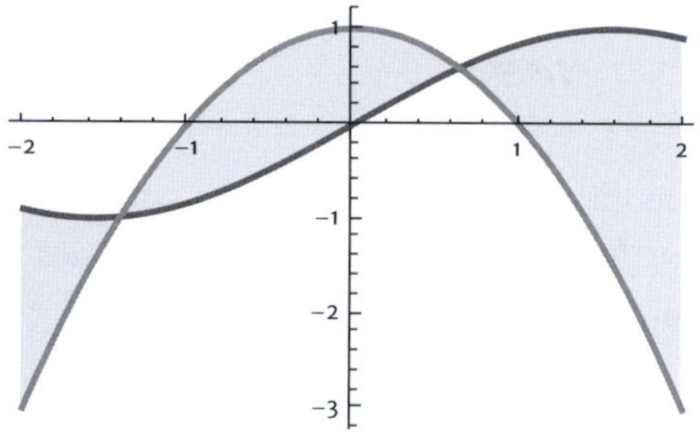

When there are more than two functions there are many ways to shade the various regions between them. Below, filling is added from the first function to the third, *and* from the second function to the top of the plot. Note that the filling is transparent, so the two filling styles can be layered one over the other. Look up `Filling` in the Documentation Center for more information.

In[10]:= `Plot[{x², x⁴, Sin[20 x]}, {x, 0, 1.2},`
      `PlotRange → {0, 1.2}, Filling → {1 → {3}, 2 → Top}]`

Out[10]=

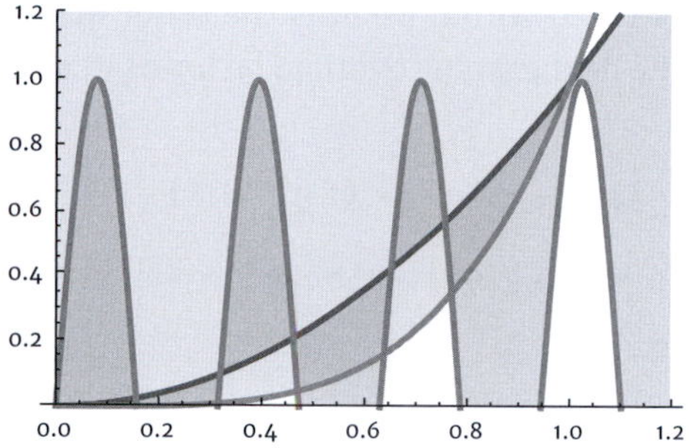

Superimposing Graphics

To overlay one graphic on top of another, simply feed the component images to the `Show` command. The individual images will be superimposed upon a common coordinate system. Below we demonstrate this by assigning names to the component images and suppressing their individual output with semicolons.

In[11]:= `p1 = Plot[Sin[x], {x, 0, 2 π}, AspectRatio → Automatic];`
      `p2 = ContourPlot[(x - π/2)² + y² == 1, {x, 0, 3}, {y, -1, 1}];`

In[13]:= `Show[p1, p2]`

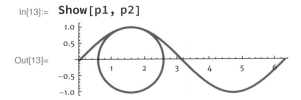

Out[13]=

The plot domain, and option settings, such as `AspectRatio`, `Axes`, and so on will be inherited from their settings in the *first* image listed within `Show`. Changing the order of the graphics listed within `Show` may therefore change the appearance of the output:

In[14]:= `Show[p2, p1]`

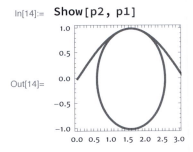

Out[14]=

Note also that the order of the component images listed within `Show` is the order in which they are rendered. The first graphic is rendered first, with the next graphic overlaid *on top* of it, and so on.

In[15]:= `ellipse = ContourPlot`$\left[\frac{x^2}{3} + 2\, y^2 == 1, \{x, -2, 2\}, \{y, -1, 1\}, \right.$

`ContourStyle → Directive[Thickness[.06], Black]`$\Big]$`;`

`squiggle = Plot[Sin[10 x], {x, -2, 2},`
`    PlotStyle → Directive[Gray, Thickness[.04]]];`

`Show[ellipse, squiggle]`

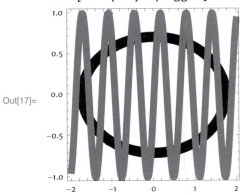

Out[17]=

In[18]:= **Show[squiggle, ellipse]**

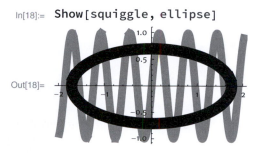

Out[18]=

One may also include within Show any options accepted by Graphics. Such options can be used to override settings inherited from the component images.

In[19]:= **Show[squiggle, ellipse, Axes → False]**

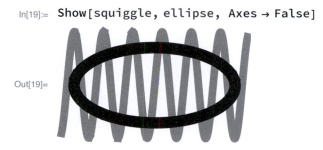

Out[19]=

Keep in mind also that while Show is an extremely useful and versatile command, it is often not needed. To plot two functions together, for instance, recall that one can simply provide a *list* of the two functions as the first argument to Plot. One may also use the Epilog option in commands such as Plot and ContourPlot to overlay primitive graphic elements on a plot (the Epilog option is discussed in Section 3.9).

Graphics Side by Side

A simple but rather primitive means of arranging graphics side by side is to simply create a *list* of graphics. Of course, the curly brackets enclosing the list will be displayed in the output, and there will be commas separating the images:

In[20]:= **{Plot[Sin[x] + Cos[x], {x, -π, π}], Plot[Sin[x] - Cos[x], {x, -π, π}]}**

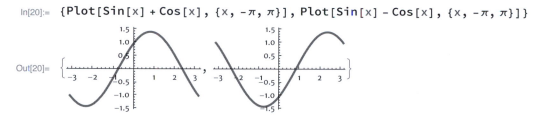

Out[20]=

A more polished way to accomplish a side-by-side display is to use GraphicsRow. Its argument is a list of graphics. It will integrate this list of individual Graphics objects into a single conglomerate graphic that can, for instance, be moved or resized as a whole.

In[21]:= `GraphicsRow[%]`

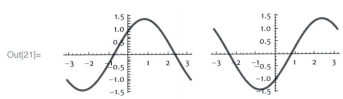

Out[21]=

The `Frame`, `FrameStyle`, and `Dividers` options may be used to add frames around each item, or to place divider lines between some of them. The syntax for these options works as it does in a `Grid`. The list of graphics can be generated programmatically, using `Table` for instance:

In[22]:= `GraphicsRow[Table[Plot[Sin[m * x], {x, 0, 2 π}], {m, 3}],`
        `Frame → All, FrameStyle → Dotted]`

Out[22]=

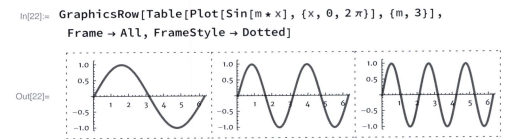

Graphics in a Grid

There is also a `GraphicsGrid` command to lay out graphics in a grid pattern. The syntax and many of the options are the same as for `Grid`.

In[23]:= `GraphicsGrid[{`
        `Table[Plot[Csc[m * x], {x, 0, 2 π}, Axes → False], {m, 5}],`
        `Table[Plot[Sec[m * x], {x, 0, 2 π}, Axes → False], {m, 5}]},`
        `Frame → All, FrameStyle → Gray]`

Out[23]=

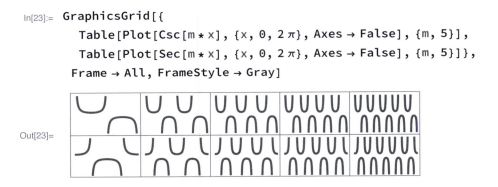

One could also use `Grid` instead of `GraphicsRow` or `GraphicsGrid`. The main difference is that the output of these latter commands is a *single* graphic that may be edited as such, for instance using the drawing tools. The entire output can be resized by selecting it and dragging a handle. In a plain `Grid`, only the *individual* component graphics can be edited.

Exercises 3.8

1. Name at least three strategies for determining which function is which in the graph below. You may alter the input and reenter it.

In[1]:= `Plot[{x² , x Sin[x]}, {x, -1, 1}]`

Out[1]=

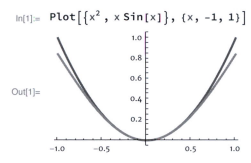

2. In this exercise you will examine the function $\frac{\sin(.4\,t)+\sin(1.6\,t)}{2\sin(t)}$ and the function $\cos(.6\,t)$.

   a. Simultaneously plot both functions on the domain $0 \le t \le 8\pi$ and describe what you find.

   b. Repeat for the functions $\frac{\sin(.3\,t)+\sin(1.7\,t)}{2\sin(t)}$ and $\cos(.7\,t)$. What do you find?

   c. How about for the functions $\frac{\sin(.2\,t)+\sin(1.8\,t)}{2\sin(t)}$ and $\cos(.8\,t)$?

   d. Make a conjecture as to the value of $\frac{\sin(k\,t)+\sin((2-k)\,t)}{2\sin(t)}$ for any real numbers k and t, where t is not an integer multiple of π.

   e. Enter the following, which illustrates the equivalence and allows the viewer to control k. Comment on the graphical implications of the fact that the third function is the sum of the other two. Note that in Exercise 2 in Section 4.6 we will return to this example and show why the equivalence holds.

In[2]:= `Manipulate[`
   `Plot[{`$\frac{\text{Sin}[k\ t]}{2\ \text{Sin}[t]}$`,` $\frac{\text{Sin}[(2 - k)\ t]}{2\ \text{Sin}[t]}$`, Cos[(1 - k) t]}, {t, 0, 8 π}, PlotRange → 2,`
      `PlotStyle → {Darker[Gray], Darker[Pink], Directive[Thick, Black]},`
      `GridLines → {Range[0, 8 π, π], {}}, Ticks → None,`
      `Filling → {1 → Axis, 2 → Axis}], {{k, .4}, 0, 2}]`

Out[2]=

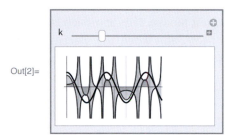

3. Make the following `Grid` showing the plots of power functions, i.e., functions of the form $f(x) = \pm p * x^n$, for real parameters p and n, with p positive and with domain $0 \le x \le 4$. Include text next to each plot indicating the values for the parameter n that will produce plots of the same general shape.

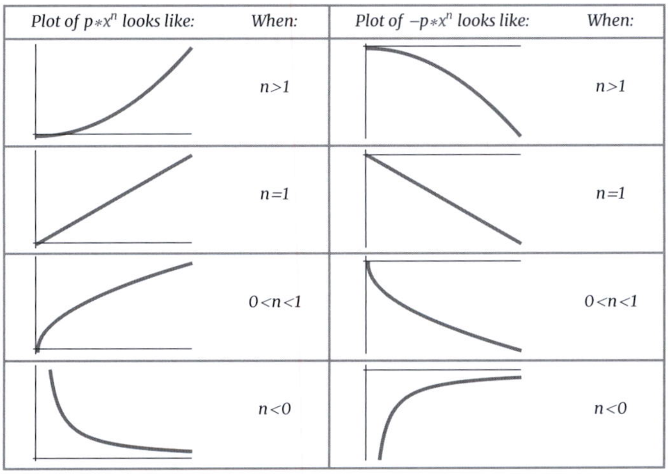

Plot of $p*x^n$ looks like:	When:	Plot of $-p*x^n$ looks like:	When:
	$n>1$		$n>1$
	$n=1$		$n=1$
	$0<n<1$		$0<n<1$
	$n<0$		$n<0$

3.9   Enhancing Your Graphics

The time will soon come when you feel the irresistible urge to add some sort of graphic enhancement to a plot. Maybe it will be something as minor as an arrow and some text. Maybe it will be a stick figure. Maybe it will be hundreds of circles, polygons, and lines. Whatever the need, the time will come. And if you read this section, you will be ready.

There are two basic ways to add information to an existing graphic: Use drawing tools and your mouse to interactively add the elements you desire, or use the `Graphics` command and primitive graphics elements to proceed programmatically. Each method has its advantages, and we'll address each in turn.

Drawing Tools
The Drawing Tools palette can be found in the Graphics menu. The idea is simple and intuitive: Elements are added to a graphic using the Drawing Tools and your mouse. This approach is appropriate when you are making a single image, or perhaps just a few, and when the placement of the elements on the graphic allows some leeway. It's great for adding labels with arrows pointing to items in a plot, for example.

Let's begin with a graphic produced by the `Plot` command.

In[1]:= `Plot`$\Big[$`{Sin[x], ArcSin[x]}`, $\Big\{$`x`, $-\frac{\pi}{2}$, $\frac{\pi}{2}\Big\}$, `PlotStyle` → `{Automatic, Dashed}`,

`AspectRatio` → `Automatic`, `AxesLabel` → `{x, y}`$\Big]$

Out[1]=

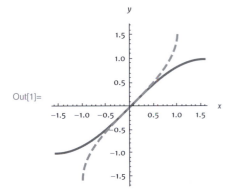

Now go to the Graphics menu and select Drawing Tools. Begin by clicking once on the graphic you wish to modify; an orange border appears around it. Now the tools on the palette are bound to this target image. Explore the Tools section of the palette by mousing over its buttons. As you do, a tooltip will give a brief description of that tool's function. Generally speaking, click a tool button once to use that tool once, or double-click it to keep it active. If you click a tool only once, the Select/Move/Resize tool will become active immediately after you use that tool. This is a good way to work in many cases; you push a palette button to activate a tool, use the tool to add an element to your graphic, then (without another trip to the palette) you can select and move or resize the new element.

For example, in the graphic above let's add labels for the two curves and an arrow pointing from each label to the appropriate curve. Click on the graphic. Then click the arrow button on the palette to activate the arrow tool (or just type the letter "a" after clicking on the graphic). Now position the cursor over the graphic where you want the tail of the arrow to appear, and click once. Holding the mouse button down, drag the cursor to where the arrowhead should be, and release. The arrow appears, with an orange bounding box around it. The palette has now reverted back to the default Select/Move/Resize tool (the cursor button in the upper left is now highlighted, not the arrow button). Click the middle of the orange box to move the arrow or grab one of the box handles to change the length or direction of the arrow. You really have to try this to get a feel for it. After you have finished, click outside the graphic. Note that you can continue to make adjustments on your arrow at any time in the future. Click once on the graphic to select it, then double-click on any element to select that element. The orange bounding box appears, allowing you to move or resize it. Alternately, if you just double-click on an element, you can edit it. You can use the Stroke section of the palette to change the thickness, color, opacity (how transparent it is when overlaid on another element), dashing, and other properties of your arrow. The Arrowheads section allows you to make double-headed arrows or place the arrowhead anywhere along the tail.

The best way to learn about the drawing tools is simply to use them. You can create a new (empty) graphic by pushing the button in the upper left corner of the Operations section of the palette or by choosing New Graphic in the Graphics menu. Then play with the tools to your heart's content.

To add text to a graphic, click the Text or Mathematical Text icon in the Tools section and click where you want to type your text. You can use the Typesetting section of the Basic Math Assistant palette to format mathematics. The Text section of the Drawing Tools palette allows you to change the text color, size and other formatting. Below we show a few simple labels added to our previously generated plot:

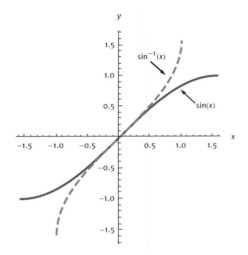

The Drawing Tools are a simple and powerful set of tools for creating all manner of creative and revealing information graphics. With no training whatever, and in a matter of minutes, our 13-year-old son added the archer to the plot below:

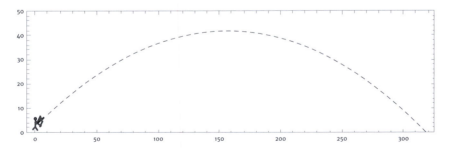

Detailed information on each drawing tool can be found in the Documentation Center in the Help menu. Type "Editing Wolfram Language Graphics Overview" in the text field and follow the link to the entry of that name. Some of the most commonly used keyboard equivalents for the drawing tools are given in Table 3.3.

Type	or click	to	Hold SHIFT to
CTRL t		open the Drawing Tools palette	
CTRL 1	⬚	create a new graphic at the current selection point	
o	▲	activate the Select/Move/Resize tool	move horizontally/vertically, or resize preserving aspect ratio
l	╱	activate the Line tool	make line horizontal or vertical
s	∿	activate the Line Segment tool	make any segment(s) horizontal or vertical
f	✍	activate the Freehand Draw tool	
a	↗	activate the Arrow tool	make arrow horizontal or vertical
t	T≡	activate the Text tool	capitalize text
m	Σ≡	activate the Mathematical Text tool	capitalize text
r	☐	activate the Rectangle tool	make a perfect square (aspect ratio 1)
g	⬠	activate the Polygon tool	make any side(s) horizontal or vertical
d	○	activate the Disk tool	make a circular disk (aspect ratio 1)
c	⬭	activate the Circle tool	make a perfect circle (aspect ratio 1)
p	•	activate the Point tool	

Table 3.3 Tools in the DrawingTools palette.

Graphics Objects

It is, of course, possible to forgo the freehand palette approach and work programmatically instead. This method is painstaking if you just want to add a simple label with an arrow, as above, but it is absolutely essential if you want to add many elements at precise locations. We ask the reader to be patient here; this section will introduce ideas that take some practice and perseverance to master. But it takes only a few moments to understand the basic structure and ingredients of a `Graphic`, and this is all that is needed to explore further.

Let's first meet the *graphics objects*, sometimes called *graphics primitives*. These are the building blocks from which all two-dimensional *Mathematica* graphics are constructed. They include, among many others: `Point`, `Line`, `Rectangle`, `Polygon`, `Circle`, `Disk`, and `Text`. Let's look at a few of these on their own. Later, we'll show how to combine them into a single graphic. We note that three-dimensional versions of some of these objects (and some new ones) exist as well; these will be discussed in Section 6.2.

The most common elements are points and lines. We will illustrate the ideas involved by drawing lines; the other objects work in a similar manner. Let's first construct the line segments joining the points (0, 0), (1, 1), and (2, 0). To join any finite collection of points in the plane, feed a list of the Cartesian coordinates of the points as the sole argument to the `Line` command. Individual points, such as (2, 0), are input as lists of length two, like this: {2, 0}.

In[3]:= `Line[{{0, 0}, {1, 1}, {2, 0}}]`

Out[3]= `Line[{{0, 0}, {1, 1}, {2, 0}}]`

Not too interesting yet. To *view* any primitive graphics element, wrap it in the `Graphics` command:

In[4]:= `Graphics[Line[{{0, 0}, {1, 1}, {2, 0}}]]`

Out[4]=

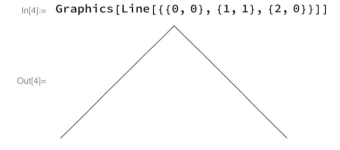

The visual appearance of objects can be tweaked using *graphics directives* (these were introduced in Section 3.3, in the subsection *How to Add Color, and Other Style Changes: Graphics Directives*). Some commonly used directives are `Red`, `Thick`, `Opacity[.5]`, and `Dashed`. The syntax works like this: Put the graphics object(s) in a *list* whose first item is the directive. If there is more than one directive, wrap them in the `Directive` command:

In[5]:= `Graphics[{Directive[Thick, Dashed], Line[{{0, 0}, {1, 1}, {2, 0}}]}]`

Out[5]=

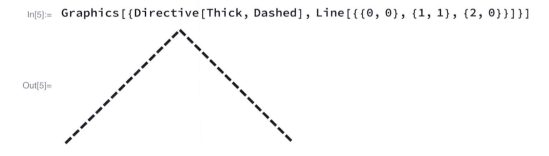

Note that Graphics will accept many of the same options discussed for the Plot command:

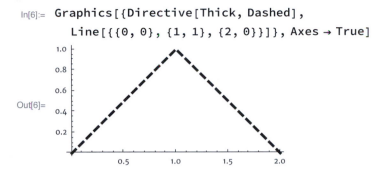

```
In[6]:= Graphics[{Directive[Thick, Dashed],
          Line[{{0, 0}, {1, 1}, {2, 0}}]}, Axes → True]
```

And combining objects is as simple as putting them all into one big list within the Graphics command:

```
In[7]:= Graphics[{
          {Directive[Thick, Gray], Line[Table[{x, Sin[x]}, {x, 0, 6.28, .1}]]},
          {Directive[Thin, Blue], Line[{{2, 0}, {2, Sin[2]}, {0, Sin[2]}}]},
          {Directive[PointSize[.02], Black], Point[{2, Sin[2]}]}
          }, Axes → True]
```

Note that the order in which the individual elements are specified matters. The first item is rendered first, and each additional item is placed "on top" of earlier items. The point above, for instance, would be obscured by the thick, gray sine curve had it been listed first.

Finally, it may be the case that you wish to include some primitive elements with the output of, say, the Plot command. There are a few ways to do this. One is to take advantage of the Epilog option in the Plot command. Set this option to any list of primitives that you could feed to the Graphics command. The effect is to overlay the primitives on top of the plot.

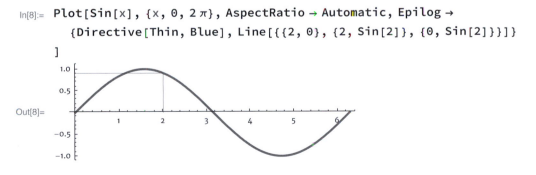

```
In[8]:= Plot[Sin[x], {x, 0, 2 π}, AspectRatio → Automatic, Epilog →
          {Directive[Thin, Blue], Line[{{2, 0}, {2, Sin[2]}, {0, Sin[2]}}]}]
          ]
```

And now, at last, we demonstrate the true benefit of understanding `Graphics` primitives. Below we combine a (static) plot of the sine function with a dynamically controlled point that the user can adjust with `Manipulate`:

In[9]:= `Manipulate[Plot[Sin[t], {t, 0, 2 π},`

        `Ticks → {Range[0, 2 π, ` $\frac{\pi}{6}$ `], Sin[Range[-` $\frac{\pi}{2}$, $\frac{\pi}{2}$, $\frac{\pi}{6}$ `]]},`

        `Epilog → {{Dashed, Line[{{x, 0}, {x, Sin[x]}, {0, Sin[x]}}]},`

        `{Red, PointSize[.015], Point[{x, Sin[x]}]}}], {{x, ` $\frac{2\pi}{3}$ `}, 0, 2 π}]`

Out[9]=

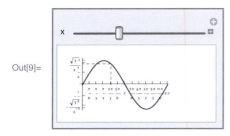

One final word is in order that pertains to printing. If you would like to produce a quality print of that beautiful graphic you spent hours getting just right, wouldn't it be nice to lose the cell label Out[117]= that appears to its left? There are two simple means of achieving this. First, you can highlight the cell label and hit the delete key. Mission accomplished. Alternately, wrap your input with the `Print` command, and the same output will appear but *without the label.* Note that `Print` will not send your output to a printer; rather, it "prints" an unlabeled cell in your notebook.

In[10]:= `Print@Plot[Sin[x]`^{5} `- Cos[x`^{5}`], {x, -3, 3}]`

The same comment applies to that wonderful table you produced with `Grid`. One may use `Print[Style[Grid[⋯], "Text"]]` to generate a table with textual styling in an unlabeled cell, suitable for inclusion in the finest of publications.

Exercises 3.9

1. Make the following figure using the commands `Graphics`, `Rectangle`, and `Circle`, and including the `Graphics` option setting `Frame → True`. You will want to look up `Circle` in the Documentation Center to find out how to draw an ellipse. Do not use the Drawing Tools palette.

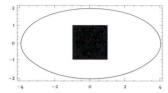

2. In this exercise you will explore various graphics directives using `Manipulate`.

   a. The following command will produce a red disk of radius 1 centered at the origin. Type and enter:

      `Graphics[{Red, Disk[]}]`

   b. Replace `Red` by `Lighter[Blend[{Blue, Red}, .3], .4]`.

   c. Finally, make this into a `Manipulate`, replacing .3 and .4 above by the control variables r and s, respectively. Investigate the effects.

   d. Make two disks of radius 1 centered at (0, 0) and (1, 0) with the commands `Disk[]` and `Disk[{1, 0}, 1]`, respectively. Make the first disk blue. Place them in a `Manipulate` with a single control variable that determines the `Opacity` of the second disk (with values that range from 0 to 1).

   e. Repeat the previous part, but make the second disk (the one with varying opacity) orange. If you are not a University of Virginia fan, feel free to use other colors.

3. Make a smiley face as follows:

   a. Create a `Manipulate` using `Circle[{0, 0}, {1, r}, {π, 2 π}]` for $.01 \le r \le 1$ and note the behavior.

   b. Using `Graphics` primitives such as `Disk`, create a yellow smiley face that can be manipulated.

   c. Add eyebrows that can be manipulated.

4. In this exercise we explore a family of ellipses.

   a. Using `Circle`, construct `Graphics` showing the ellipse $\frac{x^2}{4} + \frac{y^2}{9} = 1$ together with the coordinate axes.

   b. Construct `Graphics` showing together the family of ellipses $\frac{x^2}{\frac{k(n-k+1)}{n+2}} + \frac{y^2}{\frac{(n-k+1)(n-k+2)}{(n+1)(n+2)}} = 1$ with $n = 20$, and

      with k assuming integer values from 1 to 20. Note: The article cited below shows that for any real number r, the roots of the kth derivative of $f(z) = (z - r)^n (z^2 + 1)$ will either be real or will lie on the kth ellipse in this family (where $z = x + i y$ in the complex plane). See L. Lawson and B. Torrence, "Real polynomials, complex roots, and enchanting ellipses," *Pi Mu Epsilon Journal*, 12 No. 9 (2008), 541–546.

   c. For one of the values of k above, the ellipse appears to be an honest circle. Is it? Find the value of k, and investigate.

   d. For which value of k is the semimajor axis longest?

3.10 Working with Data

In situations where you have generated numerical data, you will want to enter the data into the computer to study it. How is this most easily accomplished with *Mathematica*? Here is an example. These data specify the temperature of a cup of coffee as it cools over time. The first column shows the number of minutes that have elapsed, while the second column indicates the temperature of the coffee, measured in degrees Fahrenheit:

$$
\text{In[1]:= } \textbf{data} = \begin{array}{c|c}
0 & 149.5 \\
\hline
2 & 141.7 \\
\hline
4 & 134.7 \\
\hline
6 & 128.3 \\
\hline
8 & 122.6 \\
\hline
10 & 117.4 \\
\hline
12 & 112.7 \\
\hline
14 & 108.5 \\
\hline
16 & 104.7 \\
\hline
18 & 101.3 \\
\hline
20 & 98.2 \\
\hline
22 & 95.4 \\
\hline
24 & 92.9 \\
\hline
26 & 90.5 \\
\hline
28 & 88.5 \\
\hline
30 & 86.6
\end{array};
$$

When recording data, a spreadsheet-type interface is desirable. To enter these data into *Mathematica*, first type data = (any name will do, but "data" seems convenient), then select Table/Matrix ▷ New... from the Insert menu. A dialog box will appear. In the top left portion select Table. To the right specify the number of rows (in this case 16) and columns (in this case 2). It is possible to add and delete more rows and columns later, so these numbers need not be exact. Ignore the remaining settings and hit the OK button. A rectangular array, a sort of mini-spreadsheet of the dimensions you specified, will appear in your notebook, and a very long, vertical, blinking cursor will appear to its right. Type ; so that when you eventually enter this cell the output will be suppressed. Now click on the placeholder in the upper left corner of your table (or hit the ⌷TAB⌷ key to jump there) and enter the first data value. When you are finished, use the ⌷TAB⌷ key to move to the next placeholder. Continue to enter your data in this fashion. Additional rows or columns can be added at any time; look in the Insert ▷ Table/Matrix menu for Add Row or Add Column. When all the data have been typed in, enter the cell.

When you enter data in this way, *Mathematica* stores it as a list of ordered pairs (one pair for each row in the table). Technically, it's a list of lists. If you don't put a semicolon after your data table, you will see it displayed in this form upon entering it. Or you will see it in this form if you ask for it by name:

In[2]:= **data**

Out[2]= {{0, 149.5}, {2, 141.7}, {4, 134.7}, {6, 128.3}, {8, 122.6}, {10, 117.4},
{12, 112.7}, {14, 108.5}, {16, 104.7}, {18, 101.3}, {20, 98.2},
{22, 95.4}, {24, 92.9}, {26, 90.5}, {28, 88.5}, {30, 86.6}}

You won't need to work with the data in this form, but it's good to see it once so you know how *Mathematica* interprets it.

Typical commands for plotting such a list of ordered pairs are ListPlot and ListLinePlot. Each of these commands takes a single argument: a list of two-tuples. Each two-tuple is interpreted as a point in the coordinate plane, and these points are then plotted. ListLinePlot will place line segments between successive points, but will not place the actual points on the plot unless the PlotMarkers option is utilized.

In[3]:= **GraphicsRow[**
{ListPlot[data], ListLinePlot[data, PlotMarkers → Automatic]}]

Out[3]=

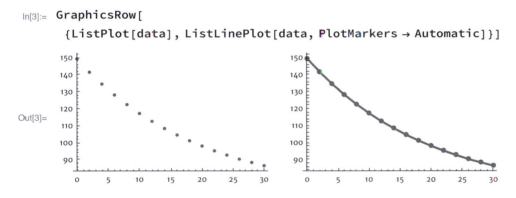

Both ListPlot and ListLinePlot also accept most of the options that the Plot command does, so it is a simple matter to produce as elaborate a graph as you desire. Here we assign the name *scatterplot* to our plot so that we can refer to it later. The *x* and *y* values in AxesOrigin were chosen just a bit smaller than the smallest *x* and *y* values appearing in the data; this pulls the axes off any data points. Finally, wrapping Tooltip around the data itself has the convenient effect of producing a tooltip showing a data point's exact coordinates when you mouseover that point (you'll have to try this to experience it).

```
In[4]:= scatterplot =
          ListPlot[Tooltip[data], AxesLabel → {"minutes", "temperature (°F)"},
            PlotStyle → Directive[PointSize[Small], Blue],
            Filling → Axis, AxesOrigin → {-1, 80}]
```

Out[4]=

You can have *Mathematica* find the best-fitting polynomial for your data (according to the criteria of least squares) using the Fit command. Here is the best-fitting linear function for the coffee cooling data. We assign it the name fitLine:

```
In[5]:= fitLine = Fit[data, {1, x}, x]
```

Out[5]= $141.332 - 2.03257 x$

Here is the best quadratic:

```
In[6]:= fitQuadratic = Fit[data, {1, x, x²}, x]
```

Out[6]= $148.465 - 3.56107 x + 0.0509498 x^2$

The Fit command takes three arguments. The first is the data (a list of two-tuples). The second is a list of the terms requiring coefficient values in the polynomial. The last is the name of the variable, in this case *x*. If you only wish to find a linear function, but plan to carry out a more complete statistical analysis, the best tool is called LinearModelFit.

```
In[7]:= linearModel = LinearModelFit[data, x, x]
```

Out[7]= $FittedModel\left[\;\boxed{141.332 - 2.03257\,x}\;\right]$

This gives the same line found by the Fit command, but the model includes a more complete set of information about the line and its relation to the data. For instance, we can get the *residuals* (the vertical distances from data points to the line—see Exercise 4) like this:

```
In[8]:= linearModel["FitResiduals"]
```

Out[8]= $\{8.16765, 4.43279, 1.49794, -0.836912, -2.47176,$
$\quad -3.60662, -4.24147, -4.37632, -4.11118, -3.44603,$
$\quad -2.48088, -1.21574, 0.349412, 2.01456, 4.07971, 6.24485\}$

And we can get the squared Pearson product-moment correlation coefficient r^2 like this:

In[9]:= `linearModel["RSquared"]`

Out[9]= `0.958741`

Whichever means we use to find our best-fit functions, we can view them against our data. A quick and dirty way to display the `Plot` of a function together with data points is as follows (the `Epilog` option is discussed in Section 3.9):

In[10]:= `Plot[fitQuadratic, {x, 0, 30}, Epilog → Point[data]]`

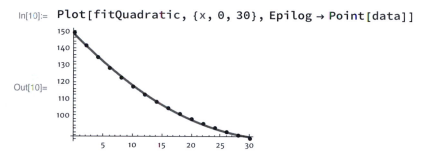

Out[10]=

A more nuanced image can be had by using `Plot` and `ListPlot` to generate separate graphics, and then using `Show` to display them together:

In[11]:= `Show[scatterplot,`
`    Plot[{fitLine, fitQuadratic}, {x, 0, 30}, Filling → True]]`

Out[11]=

Here we display them individually:

In[12]:= `GraphicsRow[{`
`    Show[scatterplot, Plot[fitLine, {x, 0, 30}],`
`      PlotLabel → Style[fitLine, 8]],`
`    Show[scatterplot, Plot[fitQuadratic, {x, 0, 30}],`
`      PlotLabel → Style[fitQuadratic, 8]]`
`  }]`

Out[12]=

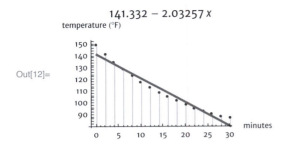 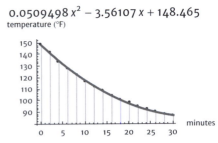

A slightly more efficient means of entering the input above, or in any situation where we wish to display a list of nearly identical items, is to use Table to generate the list:

```
In[13]:=  GraphicsRow[
            Table[Show[scatterplot, Plot[f, {x, 0, 30}], PlotLabel → Style[f, 8]],
              {f, {fitLine, fitQuadratic}}]
          ]
```

Out[13]=

The FindFit command may be used in place of Fit when a more complex form of approximating function is sought than a polynomial (or sum of basis functions). For instance, while the quadratic above seems to fit the coffee cooling data rather well, a moment's thought tells us that this function will fare poorly if we use it to predict the coffee's temperature, say, when the time x is equal to 60 minutes. This is because quadratics with a positive coefficient on the x^2 term are upward-opening parabolas, and so will eventually (for sufficiently large values of x) turn from decreasing to increasing functions. The coffee, on the other hand, is not going to get warmer as time progresses. It is a well-known principle of physics that bodies cool *exponentially* toward the ambient temperature of the surrounding medium. Hence the form of the cooling function *ought* to be $f(x) = a + b*c^x$, where a, b, and c are positive constants with $0 < c < 1$, and where a is the ambient temperature of the room.

FindFit requires four arguments. The first is the data. The second specifies the *form* of the fitting function (in this case $a + b*c^x$), the third is a list of the parameters whose values we seek in this expression (in this case $\{a, b, c\}$), and the last is the independent variable (in this case x). Any or all of the parameters in the third argument may be given as an ordered pair of the form {*parameter*, *guess*}, where *guess* is a rough estimate of the correct value of that parameter. Below we use 0.5 as an initial guess for the decay parameter c, since we know that c is between 0 and 1. This helps *Mathematica* refine its search for optimal values of the parameters in question.

In[14]:= `FindFit[data, a + b * c^x, {a, b, {c, .5}}, x]`

Out[14]= `{a → 69.348, b → 80.1489, c → 0.95015}`

The output of `FindFit` is a list of *replacement rules* giving the values of the parameters. Replacement rules are discussed in Section 4.2; for now we simply read off the values of the parameters, and note that the fit is excellent:

In[15]:= `Show[scatterplot, Plot[69.348 + 80.148 * 0.95015^x, {x, 0, 30}]]`

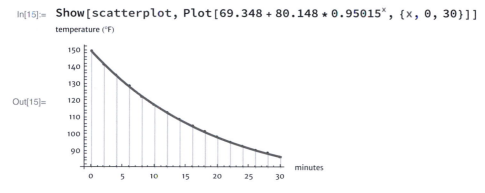

Out[15]=

Moreover, this approach allows us to use the coffee data to determine that the ambient temperature of the room is approximately $a = 69.35°$ Fahrenheit.

Exercises 3.10

1. For the data given below, find the best-fitting line (according to the criteria of least-squares), and plot this line together with the data.

x	1	2	3	4	5
y	1.2	2.3	3.6	4.9	5.9

2. For the same data used in the previous exercise, find the best-fitting *power function*. That is, find the best-fitting function of the form $f(x) = p * x^n$ for real parameters p and n.

3. For the functions in each of the previous two exercises, find the *residuals*. That is, for each x coordinate in the data, find the *difference* between the actual y value in the data and the value predicted by the fit function. Geometrically, these residuals indicate the vertical distance between a data point and the graph of the fit function. A residual is positive if and only if the data point lies above the graph of the fit function.

4. Enter the following input to create a command that will plot a collection of data, a fit function, and the residuals for the data and the given function. Test the command on the data from the first exercise and the fit function $f(x) = 3 - .25 x + .125 x^2$.

   ```
   residualPlot[data_, function_, {x_, xmin_, xmax_}, opts___Rule] :=
     Show[ListPlot[{data, Table[{x, function}, {x, data[[All, 1]]}]}, Filling →
       {1 → {2}}, FillingStyle → {Red, Green}, PlotMarkers → {"*", ""}, opts],
       Plot[function, {x, xmin, xmax}]]
   ```

3.11 Managing Data: An Introduction to Lists

You will often need to modify or transform the data with which you started. For instance, you might begin with a large table of data and wish only to work with a few rows or columns of it. Or you might wish to transform a particular row or column in a large table of data by applying the natural logarithm to each item in that row or column. In this section we introduce a few techniques to help with such tasks.

We mentioned in Section 3.5 that a *list* in *Mathematica* is a collection of items separated by commas and enclosed in curly brackets, such as $\{2, 5, 9, 7, 4\}$. Our first task will be to master the art of extracting one or more items from a list.

> In[1]:= `myList = Table[2`^{k}`, {k, 10}]`
>
> Out[1]= `{2, 4, 8, 16, 32, 64, 128, 256, 512, 1024}`

> In[2]:= `myList[[5]]`
>
> Out[2]= `32`

If you type the name of a list followed by `[[5]]`, you will extract the fifth item in the list. There are palette buttons for tidier versions of the double left and right square brackets in the Typesetting section of the Basic Math Assistant palette; these tidier versions work the same but they look a bit nicer. Click on the ⊠ tab to reveal the section containing the buttons ⟦ and ⟧ . You may also type ESC `[[` ESC to get a left double bracket and ESC `]]` ESC to produce the right double bracket.

> In[3]:= `myList⟦5⟧`
>
> Out[3]= `32`

We'll use this last notation throughout this section as it is easy to read, but remember that you may simply use double square brackets (which are easier to type). A negative number inside the double square brackets indicates an item's position relative to the end of the list. For instance, here is the second to last item:

> In[4]:= `myList⟦-2⟧`
>
> Out[4]= `512`

To extract a sequential portion of a longer list, one may indicate a Span of positions as follows:

> In[5]:= `myList⟦1 ;; 4⟧`
>
> Out[5]= `{2, 4, 8, 16}`

The most commonly specified items in a list are the first and last. There are, for convenience, special commands to extract these items (although `myList⟦1⟧` and `myList⟦-1⟧` work just as well):

In[6]:= `First[myList]`

Out[6]= 2

In[7]:= `Last[myList]`

Out[7]= 1024

Most of *Mathematica*'s arithmetic operations have the `Listable` attribute. This means they will be "mapped over lists." In other words, each item in the list will be operated upon individually by these commands, and the list of results will be displayed. This is extremely handy. For example:

In[8]:= `{1, 2, 3, 4} + 1`

Out[8]= `{2, 3, 4, 5}`

In[9]:= `2 * myList`

Out[9]= `{4, 8, 16, 32, 64, 128, 256, 512, 1024, 2048}`

In[10]:= `Log[2, myList]`

Out[10]= `{1, 2, 3, 4, 5, 6, 7, 8, 9, 10}`

⚠ To find out if a command has the `Listable` attribute, type `??` followed by the command name, and evaluate the cell. All the attributes of the command will appear (along with a brief description of the command and a list of its default option settings).

Recall that *Mathematica* stores a two-dimensional data table as a list of lists. That is, the data table is stored as one long list, the members of which are the rows of the table. Each row of the table is in turn stored as a list:

In[11]:= `data =`
$$\begin{array}{rr} 1 & 214 \\ 11 & 378 \\ 21 & 680 \\ 31 & 1215 \\ 41 & 2178 \\ 51 & 3907 \end{array}$$

Out[11]= `{{1, 214}, {11, 378}, {21, 680}, {31, 1215}, {41, 2178}, {51, 3907}}`

In[12]:= `data[[3]]`

Out[12]= `{21, 680}`

To extract the item in row 3, column 2, do this:

In[13]:= `data[[3, 2]]`

Out[13]= 680

To extract an entire column of a two-dimensional table, use `All` in the first position within the double bracket:

```
In[14]:=  data〚All, 2〛
Out[14]=  {214, 378, 680, 1215, 2178, 3907}
```

If your data happens to contain many columns, and you want to extract, say, only the second and fourth columns, type `data〚All, {2, 4}〛`.

The importance of these extraction commands manifests itself in situations that call for a transformation of the data. In most cases this will amount to performing some arithmetic operation on every item in a *column* of your data table. For instance, one column of a table may comprise the x coordinates of your data points, while another contains the corresponding y coordinates. You may want to subtract 70 from all the x coordinates, or take the logarithm of all the y coordinates. How can this be accomplished?

The simplest situation is one in which the same operation is to be applied to every member of a data table. The listable attribute of most operations makes this a one-step process. For instance:

```
In[15]:=  Log[data] // Grid

              0        Log[214]
          Log[11]   Log[378]
          Log[21]   Log[680]
Out[15]=  Log[31]   Log[1215]
          Log[41]   Log[2178]
          Log[51]   Log[3907]
```

If you wish to operate on just one of the columns, things are almost as simple. Suppose, for instance, that you want to take the logarithm of only the second column. One might proceed as follows (where we make a duplicate copy of the original data, then overwrite the second column in this copy):

```
In[16]:=  newData = data;
          newData〚All, 2〛 = Log[data〚All, 2〛];
          newData // Grid

           1   Log[214]
          11   Log[378]
          21   Log[680]
Out[18]=  31   Log[1215]
          41   Log[2178]
          51   Log[3907]
```

Another method of accomplishing the same task invokes the useful `Transpose` command, which switches rows and columns in a two-dimensional table.

In[19]:= `Transpose[{data[[All, 1]], Log[data[[All, 2]]]}] // Grid`

Out[19]=

1	Log[214]
11	Log[378]
21	Log[680]
31	Log[1215]
41	Log[2178]
51	Log[3907]

This latter approach suggests a useful means of extracting a few columns from a larger table of data and applying transformations to them selectively. Here, for example, is a somewhat random collection of data:

In[20]:= `data = Table[`
`    {x, RandomInteger[10], RandomReal[10], RandomComplex[]}, {x, 6}];`
`Grid[data, Dividers → Gray]`

Out[21]=

1	1	4.9005	0.893121 + 0.505061 i
2	7	4.46215	0.269457 + 0.382338 i
3	2	3.87718	0.208166 + 0.599303 i
4	1	5.9205	0.986883 + 0.524956 i
5	9	8.23348	0.514188 + 0.433528 i
6	1	5.14425	0.742723 + 0.0136656 i

And here is a new data table composed only of the first column and the natural logarithm of the third column:

In[22]:= `newData = Transpose[{data[[All, 1]], Log[data[[All, 3]]]}];`
`Grid[newData, Dividers → Gray]`

Out[23]=

1	1.58934
2	1.49563
3	1.35511
4	1.77842
5	2.10821
6	1.63788

So, for instance, one may now apply `ListPlot` or `Fit` to the `newData`, as discussed in the previous section.

Exercises 3.11

1. Suppose that data is input as a Table with 120 rows and 6 columns.

   a. What command could you use to extract only columns 2 and 6?

   b. What command could you issue to extract only the last 119 rows of columns 2 and 6 (for instance, imagine that the first row contains headings for the columns and not actual data)?

   c. What command could you issue to extract only the last 119 rows of columns 2 and 6, and then replace column 6 with the natural logarithm of its values?

3.12 Importing Data

The simplest means for computing with real-world data is to access the curated data collections in the Wolfram Knowledgebase. As long as you have internet access, many built-in commands will simply call up Wolfram servers and deliver hot, fresh data "paclets" to your current *Mathematica* session, chunks of up-to-date data that have been formatted to work with the Wolfram Language. The structure of data in the Wolfram Knowledgebase was first discussed in Section 2.8.

For example, the command CountryData is used to access data about countries. Like the other data commands, CountryData may be called with an empty argument to produce a list of its basic entities, in this case countries. You may notice a slight delay before the output appears, but this will only happen the first time a data command is evaluated in a session; this is when the data is transferred from the central server to your computer.

In[1]:= **RandomSample[CountryData[], 10]**

Out[1]= { Bulgaria , Burundi , Niue , Jamaica , Germany ,

Thailand , Egypt , Algeria , Vatican City , French Polynesia }

In[2]:= **Length[CountryData[]]**

Out[2]= 240

To call up a particular entity, the simplest approach is to type CTRL = to create a free-form input, and then type the name of the country and hit ENTER. Alternately, one may type the InputForm expression for a country Entity, like this:

In[3]:= **Entity["Country", "UnitedStates"]**

Out[3]= United States

At the time of this writing there are 750 properties available for the United States; we show 15 of them below.

In[4]:= **EntityProperties**[United States COUNTRY] // **Length**

Out[4]= 750

In[5]:= **EntityProperties**[United States COUNTRY][[201 ;; 215]]

Out[5]= { electricity from wind , falling water resources for electric power ,

   emigration rate of tertiary educated , employees compensation ,

   self-employed with employees , employers fraction ,

   employment , employment cost index , employment fraction ,

   employment to population ratio , school ending age , environmental agreements ,

   environmental issues , ethnic groups , ethnic mix }

The **InputForm** of an **EntityProperty** looks like this:

In[6]:= **EntityProperty["Country", "Employment"]**

Out[6]= employment

In the Wolfram Language, one typically treats an entity like a command, and a property like an argument:

In[7]:= United States COUNTRY [employment]

Out[7]= 1.55×10^{8} people

And again, the simplest way to create an input like the previous one is to type ⌐CTRL⌐=⌐ to create a free-form input, and then type a query in natural language, something like "employment in the USA." Or for the US population in 1970, you might type "population of US in 1970." This results in the following expression, where the **EntityProperty** for population has its "Date" option set for 1970. (When you hover your mouse over an **Entity** or **EntityProperty** icon, the **InputForm** for the underlying expression is displayed as a tooltip.)

In[8]:=  United States COUNTRY [population ➕   🗓 Year: **1970**]

Out[8]= 209 588 150 people

If you ask for a range of dates, you can then place the resulting expression in `DateListPlot`.

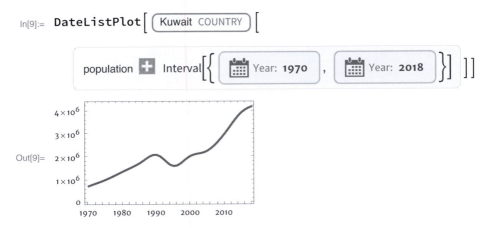

In[9]:= `DateListPlot[` Kuwait COUNTRY `[` population + Interval`[{` Year: 1970 `,` Year: 2018 `}]`]`]`

Out[9]=

Here is the gross domestic product of Germany per employed person, in US dollars, at the official exchange rate at the time of this writing:

In[10]:= Germany COUNTRY `[` GDP per employed person `]`

Out[10]= `$89 309 per person per year`

Here is the life expectancy for residents of Greenland:

In[11]:= Greenland COUNTRY `[` life expectancy `]`

Out[11]= `70.07 yr`

Note that numerical data are stored as `Quantity` objects, so the units are displayed. Next we generate a list giving the name, gross domestic product per person, and life expectancy for every country. To accomplish this we use `EntityValue`, which permits the retrieval of several properties. To save space, we use $[\![1 ; ; 6]\!]$ to take only the first six rows of data:

In[12]:= `EntityValue[CountryData[]` $[\![1 ; ; 6]\!]$ `,`

`{` name `,` GDP per employed person `,` life expectancy `}]`

Out[12]= `{{Afghanistan, $6382 per person per year , 60.947 yr },`

`{Albania, $32 266 per person per year , 77.392 yr },`

`{Algeria, $50 909 per person per year , 71. yr },`

`{American Samoa, Missing[NotAvailable], 73.72 yr },`

`{Andorra, Missing[NotAvailable], 82.51 yr },`

`{Angola, $17 281 per person per year , 51.899 yr }}`

Note the format for missing data. With a bit of effort one can tweak the input above to produce a nicely formatted table. To save space, we again take only the first six rows of data:

```
In[13]:=  Text@Grid[
            Prepend[%,
              Table[Style[x, FontWeight → "Bold"],
                {x, {"Country", "Gross Domestic Product", "Life Expectancy"}}]
            ],
            Dividers → {Center, {False, True}},
            Spacings → 2, Alignment → {{Left, Center}}]
```

Out[13]=

Country	**Gross Domestic Product**	**Life Expectancy**
Afghanistan	$6382 per person per year	60.947 yr
Albania	$32 266 per person per year	77.392 yr
Algeria	$50 909 per person per year	71. yr
American Samoa	Missing[NotAvailable]	73.72 yr
Andorra	Missing[NotAvailable]	82.51 yr
Angola	$17 281 per person per year	51.899 yr

In the exercises we illustrate how to Sort the rows of such a table, for instance by life expectancy, how to throw out rows containing missing data, and how to Select certain rows, for example those in which gross domestic product exceeds a certain value.

Here we display the complete, unabridged table as a scatterplot, with GDP per person per year on the horizontal axis, and life expectancy on the vertical axis. Since we wrapped the data coordinates in Tooltip, mousing over a data point will reveal the name of the associated country.

```
In[14]:=  ListPlot[Table[
            Tooltip[EntityValue[c, { GDP per employed person , life expectancy }],
              c[ name ]], {c, CountryData[]}], PlotRange → All]
```

Out[14]=

For a second example, consider the extensive information available in `FinancialData`. Every publicly traded company has its own `Entity` with over 60 properties, such as its last trading price, market capitalization, and price to earnings ratio. To access Microsoft, for instance, you can type the input `Entity["Financial", "NASDAQ:MSFT"]`, or you may type CTRL = to create a free-form input, and type "Microsoft."

In[15]:= `Entity["Financial", "NASDAQ:MSFT"]`

Out[15]= Microsoft

Here are the properties available for this entity:

In[16]:= `EntityProperties[` Microsoft FINANCIAL ENTITY `]`

Out[16]= { ask price , ask size , 200-day average , 50-day average ,

3-month average volume , bid price , bid size , change ,

200-day change , 50-day change , change from 52-week high ,

change from 52-week low , CIK , closing price , company ,

cumulative fractional change , cumulative return , market quote currency ,

dividend , dividend per share , dividend yield , earnings per share ,

earnings yield , EBITDA , exchange , shares outstanding , foreign listing ,

fractional change , 200-day fractional change , 50-day fractional change ,

fractional change from 52-week high , fractional change from 52-week low ,

financial statement currency , mutual fund family , mutual fund investment style ,

high price , 52-week high , company logo , initial public offering date ,

issue , last price , last trade size , latest trade , low price ,

52-week low , market capitalization , name , official name , opening price ,

original (split adjusted) closing price , price , P/E ratio , 52-week range ,

return , sector , share class description , short symbol , symbol , type ,

20-day volatility , 250-day volatility , 50-day volatility , volume , website }

And here is a plot showing the daily closing prices of Apple® and Microsoft from 1998 to 2018:

In[17]:= `With[{companies = { ( Apple  FINANCIAL ENTITY ), ( Microsoft  FINANCIAL ENTITY )}},`

    `DateListPlot[`

      `Table[c["Close", "Date" → Interval[{DateObject[{1998, 1, 1}],`

        `DateObject[{2018, 1, 1}]}]], {c, companies}], PlotLegends →`

      `Table[Show[c[ ( company logo ) ], ImageSize → {Automatic, 12}],`

        `{c, companies}], PlotTheme → "Detailed"]`

    `]`

Out[17]=

Many of the data commands can produce graphical content. It it easy to produce a map of each country, for example:

In[18]:= `CountryData["Greece", "Shape"]`

Out[18]=

```
In[19]:= GraphicsGrid[
          Transpose@Table[{CountryData[c, "Shape"], CountryData[c, "Name"]},
            {c, CountryData["G7"]}],
          Dividers → Lighter@Gray, ImageSize → Medium]
```

Out[19]=

Canada	France	Germany	Italy	Japan	United Kingdom	United States

Many of the data commands load gigantic collections of data. AstronomicalData, for instance, which has information on over 100,000 celestial bodies, is truly astronomical in size. ChemicalData has information on over 18,000 chemicals. Each such data command has its own set of properties, so the Documentation Center page for each such command is a must-read. But there are many similarities between commands; if you become familiar with one command, others will be easy to learn. For instance, after reading this section the input and output below should be self-explanatory.

```
In[20]:= ⎡ Earth  PLANET ⎤ [ ⎡ orbital period ⎤ ]
```

```
Out[20]= 365.25636 days
```

Here we illustrate a pattern first deduced by Kepler, that there is a mathematical relation between a planet's orbital period and its distance to the sun. We first list the planets:

```
In[21]:= AstronomicalData["Planet"]
```

```
Out[21]= {Mercury, Venus, Earth, Mars, Jupiter, Saturn, Uranus, Neptune}
```

Then turn them into entities:

```
In[22]:= Table[Entity["Planet", p], {p, AstronomicalData["Planet"]}]
```

```
Out[22]= { ⎡ Mercury ⎤ , ⎡ Venus ⎤ , ⎡ Earth ⎤ , ⎡ Mars ⎤ ,
           ⎡ Jupiter ⎤ , ⎡ Saturn ⎤ , ⎡ Uranus ⎤ , ⎡ Neptune ⎤ }
```

We next find the orbital period and distance to the Sun (approximated by semimajor axis length). Note that orbital periods for the outer planets use a different default unit, so in the second input we make a Table in which we convert all orbital periods to earth days.

In[23]:= `EntityValue[{` `Mercury PLANET` `,` `Venus PLANET` `,` `Earth PLANET` `,`
`Mars PLANET` `,` `Jupiter PLANET` `,` `Saturn PLANET` `,` `Uranus PLANET` `,`
`Neptune PLANET` `}, {` `orbital period` `,` `semimajor axis` `}]`

Out[23]= $\{\{$ 87.96926 days , 0.38709893 au $\}, \{$ 224.70080 days , 0.72333199 au $\}$,
$\{$ 365.25636 days , 1.00000011 au $\}, \{$ 1.8808476 a , 1.52366231 au $\}$,
$\{$ 11.862615 a , 5.20336301 au $\}, \{$ 29.447498 a , 9.53707032 au $\}$,
$\{$ 84.016846 a , 19.19126393 au $\}, \{$ 164.79132 a , 30.06896348 au $\}\}$

In[24]:= `data = Table[{UnitConvert[p[` `orbital period` `], "Days"], p[` `semimajor axis` `]},`
`{p, {` `Mercury PLANET` `,` `Venus PLANET` `,` `Earth PLANET` `,` `Mars PLANET` `,`
`Jupiter PLANET` `,` `Saturn PLANET` `,` `Uranus PLANET` `,` `Neptune PLANET` `}}]`

Out[24]= $\{\{$ 87.96926 days , 0.38709893 au $\}, \{$ 224.70080 days , 0.72333199 au $\}$,
$\{$ 365.25636 days , 1.00000011 au $\}, \{$ 686.97959 days , 1.52366231 au $\}$,
$\{$ 4332.8201 days , 5.20336301 au $\}, \{$ 10 755.699 days , 9.53707032 au $\}$,
$\{$ 30 687.153 days , 19.19126393 au $\}, \{$ 60 190.030 days , 30.06896348 au $\}\}$

A log-log plot of these data reveals a straight-line relationship, suggesting a power-law relationship between the underlying quantities.

In[25]:= `ListLogLogPlot[data, AspectRatio → 0.4]`

Out[25]=

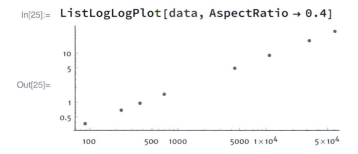

We can strip away the `Quantity` units from the data and work directly with the underlying numbers by applying `QuantityMagnitude`, and then find the power function that best fits the data. The true exponent appears to be 2/3.

In[26]:= `FindFit[QuantityMagnitude[data], a * x^b, {a, b}, x]`

Out[26]= $\{a \to 0.01956615, b \to 0.6667237\}$

In[27]:= `Show[Plot[.01956615 x^(2/3), {x, 0, 60 200}],`
`ListPlot[data, PlotMarkers → "◇"]]`

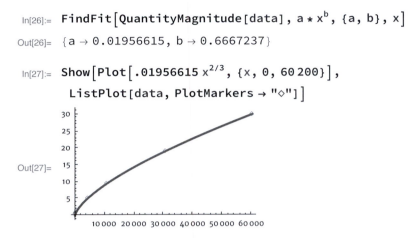

Out[27]=

Hence orbital "radius" is proportional to (orbital period)$^{2/3}$, or as Kepler put it, *radius^3 ∝ period^2*. The point here is simply that facility with one data command makes the other data commands a quick study, and that facility with lists and data fitting makes quick work of finding meaningful relations in data.

In addition to commands that access the Wolfram Knowledgebase, it is common practice to import data from other sources, such as a spreadsheet or text file, or directly from a web resource. For example, the URL shown below points to the raw data behind fivethirtyeight.com's "The Complete History of the NBA." It has information on every National Basketball League game from 1946 to the present. In order to bring it into *Mathematica*, we use `Import`. We then `Iconize` the imported file so we don't have to look at miles of raw data, and give it the label "FiveThirtyEight NBA data." We then type "nba=" in front of the icon and enter it.

In[28]:= `Iconize[Import[`
`"https://projects.fivethirtyeight.com/nba-model/nba_elo.csv"],`
`"FiveThirtyEight NBA data"]`

The raw data is now stored as an icon the current notebook, and in a future session we can simply enter the nba = line to load it into the kernel. Note that by clicking on the plus sign on the icon, the dimensions and structure of the data are revealed. Of course, we could ask for that information directly:

In[30]:= `Dimensions[nba]`

Out[30]= {67 095, 20}

There are over 67 000 rows of data here. The first row of the data gives descriptive column headings, briefly summarizing what will be found in each of the 20 columns. For instance, we could make a `DateListPlot` of the first team's score in the first 15 000 games listed. The game date is in the first column, while the first score is in the second-to-last column (column −2):

In[31]:= `DateListPlot[`
           `Transpose@{nba[2 ;; 15 000, 1], nba[2 ;; 15 000, -2]}, Joined → False]`

Out[31]=

This same import technique works for many types of raw files that are found online, even graphic files:

In[32]:= `pic = Import[`
           `"http://faculty.rmc.edu/btorrenc/bt-bikeclub/images/PoorFarm-`
           `ConesBW10-99.JPG", ImageSize → 180]`

Out[32]=

The `InputForm` of this image reveals it to be an `Image` constructed from a matrix of pixel values. Once imported, one may apply `ImageData` to extract the matrix of pixel values. We display them in a histogram below.

In[33]:= **InputForm[pic] // Short**

Out[33]//Short= Image[RawArray["UnsignedInteger8", {{<<180>>}, <<137>>}], <<4>>]

In[34]:= **Histogram[Flatten[ImageData[pic]]]**

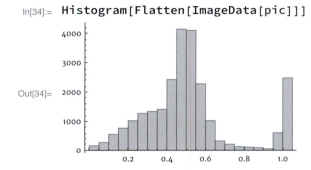

Out[34]=

When the data you're after is found in a *formatted* table pulled from a web page, add "Data" as a second argument to Import, like this: Import[" *URLstring* ", " Data "]. You may then have to manually select the table of data from the full web page that has been imported.

You may also Import data from a file on your local hard drive. Suppose, for instance, you have a spreadsheet or text file containing data that you want to analyze using *Mathematica*. The first step when importing a file is to tell *Mathematica* where to look for it. This is accomplished with the SetDi rectory command. We advocate the following simple approach: Save your notebook if you have not already done so, and then place the file you wish to import into the same directory as your *Mathematica* notebook. Then type and enter the following into your notebook:

In[35]:= **SetDirectory[NotebookDirectory[]];**

This will set the current directory, where *Mathematica* will look for your file, to be that of the notebook in which you are working. Even if you later move this directory to another location, even to a different computer running a different operating system, the command above will still set the directory correctly.

Now you are ready to Import your file. Here we use a csv text file that we downloaded from The Scripps Institution of Oceanography in San Diego (available at http://scrippsco2.ucsd.edu). It contains monthly readings for carbon dioxide concentration in the atmosphere, recorded at Mauna Loa Observatory in Hawaii since 1958. We placed this file into our notebook directory. Note that Import recognizes the file type by the suffix .csv, so no additional input is needed.

In[36]:= **co2data = Import["CO2data_MaunaLoaHI.csv"];**

Below we show the last ten rows of data (at the time of this writing). The first four columns give the date in three (redundant) formats. The fifth and sixth columns give the CO_2 concentration in parts per million, where column five is the raw measurement and column six introduces seasonal adjustments (since CO_2 levels fluctuate with the seasons). The final four columns provide outputs of various models for the data.

In[37]:= `Text@Grid[co2data[[-10 ;; -1]], Alignment → Left]`

Out[37]=

2017	7	42931	2017.54	407.2	406.36	407.45	406.64	407.2	406.36
2017	8	42962	2017.62	405.24	406.76	405.25	406.81	405.24	406.76
2017	9	42993	2017.71	403.27	406.76	403.45	406.97	403.27	406.76
2017	10	43023	2017.79	403.64	407.27	403.5	407.12	403.64	407.27
2017	11	43054	2017.87	405.17	407.45	405.01	407.26	405.17	407.45
2017	12	43084	2017.96	406.75	407.69	406.48	407.39	406.75	407.69
2018	1	43115	2018.04	408.05	408.02	407.56	407.52	408.05	408.02
2018	2	43146	2018.13	408.34	407.6	408.39	407.63	408.34	407.6
2018	3	43174	2018.2	409.26	407.71	409.3	407.73	409.26	407.71
2018	4	43205	2018.29	410.31	407.5	410.66	407.83	410.31	407.5

Here is a `ListPlot` showing the date (column 4) versus the seasonally adjusted CO_2 level (column 6). As the oldest continually recorded dataset on Earth for atmospheric CO_2 levels, these data show how dramatically this greenhouse gas is increasing.

In[38]:= `ListPlot[Transpose@{co2data[[All, 4]], co2data[[All, 6]]},`
          `   PlotRange → {300, 420}, AxesLabel → {"year", "ppm"},`
          `   PlotLabel → "Seasonally Adjusted CO2 Level"]`

Out[38]=

`Import` can accommodate roughly 200 file formats. File types are recognized by the suffix on the filename, so simply try `Import["filename"]` (where your filename includes the appropriate suffix) and chances are good that you will have success.

Exercises 3.12

1. This exercise makes use of the `ElementData` command.

   a. Construct a table with 118 rows and 3 columns. Each row should contain the name of an element, its atomic weight (in atomic mass units), and its molar volume (in moles, obviously). Use the first 118 elements listed in `ElementData`.

   b. Make a `ListPlot` of molar volume versus atomic weight for your data.

   c. Add a `Tooltip` to your `ListPlot` so that the name of each element is displayed as you mouseover it.

2. Visit the website www.census.gov/topics/population/genealogy/data/2010_surnames.html.

   a.   Find the file giving the top 1000 surnames reported in the 2010 census, and `Import` it into *Mathematica*.

   b.   What proportion of census respondents have one of the top 200 surnames? What proportion have one of the top 1000 surnames?

3. Visit the website http://research.stlouisfed.org/fred2/data/FEDFUNDS.txt. It shows the effective federal funds rate each month from 1954 to the present. Like the census site in the previous exercise, this page contains raw data suitable for display in a `Grid`. Unlike the census site, however, the first 13 lines of text on this page describe the data that follows. That is, the file contains more than just the straight data.

   a.   Use `Import` with the URL above as the first argument, and `"Table"` as the second argument.

   b.   Extract the data (starting on line 12, so that the column headers are included), and name it `data`.

   c.   Use `DateListPlot` and `Rest` to view the data.

4. The `Select` command will apply a function to each member of a list. The syntax is: `Select[list, function]`. It will return all items in the list for which the function returns the value `True`. Typically the function is given as a *pure function* (these are discussed in Section 8.4). For our purposes, just remember that the `Slot` character `#` represents the variable for the function, that is, the items in the list. Enter the input below to find all of the properties available to `CountryData` which contain the substring `"Product"`:

   In[1]:= `Select[CountryData["Properties"], StringMatchQ[#, ___ ~~ "Product" ~~ ___] &]`

   Out[1]= `{AgriculturalProducts, ElectricityProduction,`
   `          IndustrialProductionGrowth, NaturalGasProduction, OilProduction}`

5. Use `Select` to find all chemicals listed in `ChemicalData` that contain the substring `"ButylEther"`.

6. How many cities in the United States have a population exceeding 100 000? Hint: Use the `CityData` command together with `Select` to produce a list of such cities, then use `Length` to get the answer.

7. There are two standard ways of removing `Missing` data values from a list. One is to use `Select`, and another is to use `Cases` together with `Except`.

   a.   Enter the two inputs below to see an example of each.

   `Select[{1, 2, Missing["NotAvailable"], 4}, NumberQ[#] &]`

   `Cases[{1, 2, Missing["NotAvailable"], 4}, Except[Missing[_]]]`

   b.   List all countries in `CountryData` for which the `"OilConsumption"` property is given as numerical value (i.e., for which it is not `Missing`).

   c.   List all countries in `CountryData` for which both the `"OilConsumption"` and the `"Population"` properties are given as numerical values.

8. The `Sort` command is used to rearrange the items in a list. With a list given as its argument, `Sort` will arrange the list in standard order (ascending order for a list of numbers, alphabetical order for a list of strings, etc.)

   a.   Use `Sort` to put the list {10, 7, 9, 8} in ascending order.

b. A second argument may be added to Sort. It specifies the *sorting function* to use. This is typically given as a Function with two arguments, #1 and #2. Pairs of list members are given as the two arguments, and the function should return True precisely if item #1 should precede item #2 in the sorting order. Enter the inputs below to sort the rows of a table according to the values in the third column (by oil consumption). Note that we first remove missing values from the data as discussed in the previous exercise.

```
Select[CountryData[], NumberQ[CountryData[#, "OilConsumption"]] &&
    NumberQ[CountryData[#, "Population"]] &];

Table[{c, CountryData[c, "Population"],
    CountryData[c, "OilConsumption"]}, {c, %}];

Sort[%, #1[[3]] > #2[[3]] &] // Grid
```

c. Make a Grid with two columns. The first gives the name of a country. The second gives the oil consumption per capita, in units of *barrels per year per person*. Sort the rows of the table so that the countries with the greatest per capita oil consumption are listed first.

d. Where does the United States rank in per capita oil consumption?

3.13 Working with Difference Equations

A *sequence* is a function whose domain consists of the positive integers. In other words, it is a function *s* whose values can be listed: $s[1]$, $s[2]$, $s[3]$, …. A more traditional notation for these values is s_1, s_2, s_3, ….

It is often possible to define a sequence by specifying the value of the first term (say $s[1] = 3$), and giving a *difference equation* (also called a *recurrence relation*) that expresses every subsequent term as a function of the previous term. For instance, suppose the first term in a sequence takes the value 3, and each term that follows has a value twice that of its predecessor. We could express this via the difference equation $s[n] = 2\,s[n - 1]$ for each $n > 1$. A sequence defined this way is said to be defined *recursively*. Computers make it easy to calculate many terms of recursively defined sequences. Here's a means for harnessing *Mathematica* for such a purpose:

```
In[1]:= Clear[s, n];

        s[n_Integer] := {  s[1] = 3          n == 1
                           { s[n] = 2 * s[n - 1]   n > 1
```

Let's walk through this carefully, as it makes nontrivial use of all three types of equal signs. First, the left-hand side is of the form s[n_Integer]. This indicates that the variable *n* must be an integer in order for the definition that follows to be applied. This is a safety feature, as it will prevent the inadvertent use of the function *s* being applied, for instance, to $n = .5$ or to any other non-integer input. Next we see the SetDelayed operator :=. This indicates that the expression to its right will only be evaluated when the function *s* is called. We also see that the expression to its right is a Piece-wise defined function, as described in Section 3.6. There are two distinct definitions of *s* according to whether the input *n* is equal to 1 or greater than 1. These two conditions (on the far right) will, for any value of *n*, evaluate to either True or False. Note the double equal sign here; it is a condition to be tested, not an assignment being made to the symbol *n*, so the double equal sign is needed. Finally, what happens when *s*[*n*] is called with a specific value of *n*? Let's see:

In[3]:= **s[4]**

Out[3]= 24

Here is what is now stored in memory for the symbol *s*:

In[4]:= **? s**

Global`s

s[1] = 3

s[2] = 6

s[3] = 12

s[4] = 24

s[n_Integer] := Piecewise[{{s[1] = 3, n == 1}, {s[n] = 2 s[n - 1], n > 1}}]

Here's what happened: *s*[4] was evaluated as $2 \times s[3]$, which was in turn evaluated as $2 \times (2 \times s[2])$, which in turn was evaluated as $2 \times (2 \times (2 \times s[1]))$, which was finally evaluated as $2 \times (2 \times (2 \times 3)) = 24$, with the assignment s[1]=3 being made. At this point, the intermediate assignments s[2]=6, s[3]=12, s[4]=24 were made in turn. If you were to ask for *s*[4] again, it would be a one-step process and the value 24 would be returned immediately, for at this point the assignment s[4]=24 has already been made. This is very important, for if you were to then ask for, say, *s*[5], it would be a quick calculation: $2 \times s[4] = 2 \times 24 = 48$. This is the reason for the Set operator = in each of the two lines of the Piecewise definition of *s*; it prevents long chains of calculations being repeated.

The only downside to this approach is that after, for instance, *s*[20] is evaluated, the assignments s[1]=3, s[2]=6, ... , s[20]=1572864 are all stored in memory. If *s*[200] is called, you literally have hundreds of assignments stored in memory. Fortunately, they are all associated with the symbol s, and so can be Cleared in one line:

In[5]:= **Clear[s]**

In[6]:= **? s**

Global`s

Here are three things you can do with a sequence: compute an individual value (such as *s*[4] above); make a table of values; or make a plot. These are easy, and will be discussed below. More subtle is the task of trying to find a *solution* to a difference equation—an explicit representation of *s*[*n*] as a function of *n*. For instance, the function in our example above has the solution $s[n] = 3\left(2^{n-1}\right)$. The task of solving difference equations is addressed in Section 4.8.

Let us use a different example to illustrate the remaining topics. It is vitally important that we Clear the symbol s when moving from one function to the next, as the myriad of intermediate assignments from our earlier definition could easily pollute calculations made with a future definition. For this reason it is a good idea to always include a Clear statement when defining a function recursively.

In[7]:= `Clear[s];`

$$s[n\_Integer] := \begin{cases} s[1] = 2 & n == 1 \\ s[n] = 3\,s[n-1] - .05\,s[n-1]^2 & n > 1 \end{cases}$$

Finding individual values is simple. For instance:

In[9]:= `s[20]`

Out[9]= `37.0838`

However, there is one subtlety. *Mathematica* has a safety mechanism in place to prevent calculations from falling into an infinite loop. It will not allow, by default, any recursively defined command from calling itself more than 256 times. In practice, this means that you cannot ask for $s[n]$ when n is more than 256 units greater than the largest n with which s was previously called. For example, if you want to know $s[1000]$, you can't just ask for it and receive an answer. But you can work up to it by evaluating $s[250]$, then $s[500]$, then $s[750]$, and *then* $s[1000]$:

In[10]:= `{s[250], s[500], s[750], s[1000]}`

Out[10]= `{39.1038, 39.3646, 39.481, 39.5505}`

> ⚠ The system parameter $RecursionLimit is by default set to 256. Another means of making more than this number of recursive calculations is to assign a new value to this parameter. For instance, you may simply type $RecursionLimit = 1024, or whatever value you need, prior to evaluating your sequence term.

Making a table of sequence values is accomplished exactly as it is for any other type of function:

In[11]:= `Text@Grid[Table[{n, s[n]}, {n, 10}],`
`        Alignment → {{Right, Left}}, Spacings → 2]`

Out[11]=

1	2
2	5.8
3	15.718
4	34.8012
5	43.8474
6	35.4125
7	43.5353
8	35.8398
9	43.2948
10	36.1624

`ListPlot` may be used as discussed in Section 3.10 for plotting the values of a sequence.

In[12]:= `ListPlot[Table[{n, s[n]}, {n, 50}],`
      `AxesLabel → {"n", "sₙ"}, AxesOrigin → {0, 0}, PlotRange → All]`

Out[12]=

The option setting `Joined → True` will connect the dots. In this case, it helps to clarify the oscillatory nature of this sequence. We note that `ListLinePlot` may also be used to produce a plot with the points joined by line segments. Keep the arguments exactly as they are below, but remove the setting `Joined → True`.

In[13]:= `ListPlot[Table[{n, s[n]}, {n, 50}], AxesLabel → {"n", "sₙ"},`
      `AxesOrigin → {0, 0}, PlotRange → All, Joined → True]`

Out[13]=

⚠ To generate several terms of a sequence defined by a first-order difference equation it is quite efficient to use `NestList` with a pure function as its first argument, rather than using `Piecewise` to define the sequence and `Table` to generate values. `NestList` is discussed in Section 8.7 and pure functions are discussed in Section 8.4. Below is an example showing how to generate the first ten terms of the sequence in the last example with only a few keystrokes. The first argument is a pure function that will generate the next term of the sequence from the previous term. The second argument is the initial value in the sequence. The final argument is how many iterations you desire.

In[14]:= `NestList[3 # - .05 #² &, 2, 9]`

Out[14]= `{2, 5.8, 15.718, 34.8012, 43.8474,`
        `35.4125, 43.5353, 35.8398, 43.2948, 36.1624}`

Exercises 3.13

1. Consider the sequence $s[n]$ with $s[1] = 100$, and with the remaining terms defined by the difference equation $s[n] = 1.05\, s[n-1]$.

   a.   Enter this into *Mathematica*.

   b.   Find $s[20]$.

   c.   Make a ListPlot of the first 30 terms of the sequence.

   d.   Assuming that the solution to this difference equation is of the form $s[n] = p * b^n$ for real parameters p and b, use FindFit and the data used in the ListPlot above to find a solution.

2. Suppose that the value of a new automobile is $30\,000$, and that it loses 10 percent of its value each year. That is, at the end of each year it is worth only 90 percent of what it was worth at the beginning of that year.

   a.   How much is the car worth after ten years?

   b.   How many years will it take before the car is worth $8000?

4

Algebra

4.1 Factoring and Expanding Polynomials

A *polynomial* in the variable x is a function of the form:

$$f(x) = a_0 + a_1 x + a_2 x^2 + \cdots + a_n x^n,$$

where the coefficients a_0, a_1, ..., a_n are real numbers. Polynomials may be expressed in expanded or in factored form. Without a computer algebra system, moving from one form to the other is a tedious and often difficult process. With *Mathematica*, it is quite easy; the commands needed to transform a polynomial are called Expand and Factor. There are buttons for these commands in the Algebra Commands section of the Basic Math Assistant palette.

```
In[1]:= Clear[f, x];
        f[x_] := 12 - 3 x - 12 x^3 + 3 x^4
```

```
In[3]:= Plot[f[x], {x, -2, 5}]
```

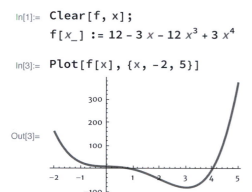

Out[3]=

Here we see the graph of a polynomial that appears to have *roots* at $x = 1$ and $x = 4$ (that is, the function appears to assume the value 0 when $x = 1$ and $x = 4$). We can confirm this by factoring the polynomial:

```
In[4]:= Factor[f[x]]
```

Out[4]= $3 (-4 + x) (-1 + x) (1 + x + x^2)$

Observe that when x assumes the value 4, the *linear factor* $(-4 + x)$ is zero, making the entire product equal to zero. Similarly, if $x = 1$ the linear factor $(-1 + x)$ is zero, and again the product is zero. Roots of a polynomial are often easily identified by determining the linear factors in the factored form of the polynomial.

The task of finding the roots of a given function f is a vitally important one. Suppose, for instance, that you need to solve an equation in one variable, say $-12 x^3 + 3 x^4 = 3 x - 12$. Equations such as this arise in a wide variety of applied contexts, and their solution is often of great importance. But solving such an equation is equivalent to finding the roots of a function—just subtract from each side of the given equation everything on the right-hand side. In this case we get $12 - 3 x - 12 x^3 + 3 x^4 = 0$, so the solutions of this equation are the roots of the function $f(x) = 12 - 3 x - 12 x^3 + 3 x^4$, which we have just found (via factoring) to be 4 and 1. Solving equations and finding roots are essentially the same task.

You can expand a factored polynomial with the Expand command. This will essentially "undo" the factoring. Use your mouse to highlight the factored output above, then push the ⬚Expand⬚ button. Another way is to type:

In[5]:= **Expand[%]**

Out[5]= $12 - 3 x - 12 x^3 + 3 x^4$

The expanded form gives us different information about the function. The constant term (in this case 12) represents the y intercept of the polynomial's graph. It's simply the value of the function when $x = 0$. The leading coefficient (in this case 3, the coefficient of x^4) is positive. Since the $3 x^4$ summand will dominate the others for large values of x, a positive leading coefficient tells us that the function values will get large as x gets large.

Note that some polynomials have real roots that will not be revealed by the Factor command:

In[6]:= **Plot$\left[-1 + 3 x + x^2, \{x, -5, 3\}\right]$**

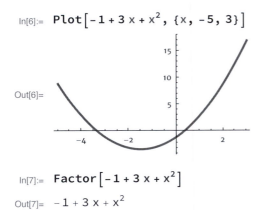

Out[6]=

In[7]:= **Factor$\left[-1 + 3 x + x^2\right]$**

Out[7]= $-1 + 3 x + x^2$

The graph clearly indicates two real roots, the x intercepts, yet there are no linear factors present in the factored form of the polynomial. Why? The Factor command will not extract factors that involve irrational or complex numbers unless such numbers appear as coefficients in the polynomial being factored. Since the coefficients in the above polynomial are all integers, only factors with integer coefficients will be extracted. To get *approximations* to the real roots, simply replace one of the integer coefficients in the original polynomial by its decimal equivalent by placing a decimal point after it. In doing this you are telling *Mathematica* that decimals are acceptable in the output:

In[8]:= $\mathbf{Factor}\left[-\mathbf{1.}+\mathbf{3}\,\mathbf{x}+\mathbf{x}^2\right]$

Out[8]= $\mathbf{1.}\ (-\mathbf{0.302776}+\mathbf{1.}\,\mathbf{x})\ (\mathbf{3.30278}+\mathbf{1.}\,\mathbf{x})$

The real roots are approximately .302776 and −3.30278. You can easily check that this is consistent with the graph (and, of course, you should).

Lastly, note that, as always, *Mathematica* makes a distinction between decimals and fractions when factoring:

In[9]:= $\mathbf{Factor}\left[\mathbf{x}^2-\mathbf{0.25}\right]$

Out[9]= $\mathbf{1.}\ (-\mathbf{0.5}+\mathbf{1.}\,\mathbf{x})\ (\mathbf{0.5}+\mathbf{1.}\,\mathbf{x})$

In[10]:= $\mathbf{Factor}\left[\mathbf{x}^2-\dfrac{\mathbf{1}}{\mathbf{4}}\right]$

Out[10]= $\dfrac{\mathbf{1}}{\mathbf{4}}\ (-\mathbf{1}+\mathbf{2}\,\mathbf{x})\ (\mathbf{1}+\mathbf{2}\,\mathbf{x})$

Exercises 4.1

1. Let $f(x) = 1 + 5x + 2x^3 + 10x^4$.

    a. Use a Plot to estimate the real roots of $f(x)$.

    b. Use Factor to find the real roots of $f(x)$.

2. Factor the following expressions and explain the differences in the resulting factorizations.

    a. $1 + x^n + x^m + x^{n+m}$ and $1 + x + x^3 + x^4$

    b. $1 + x^3$ and $1 + x^n$

    c. $1 - x^4$ and $1 - x^{2n}$

4.2 Finding Roots of Polynomials with Solve and NSolve

The Factor command together with the Plot command forms a powerful set of tools for discovering the real roots of polynomials. But there are a few shortcomings. Notice, for instance, that we can only *approximate* real roots that happen to be irrational (inexpressible as a quotient of integers). In addition, complex roots (involving the imaginary number i, the square root of −1) are completely inaccessible. For these reasons we introduce the NSolve and Solve commands.

Let's take another look at the polynomial $-1 + 3x + x^2$ from the previous section:

In[1]:= $\mathbf{NSolve}\left[-\mathbf{1}+\mathbf{3}\,\mathbf{x}+\mathbf{x}^2==\mathbf{0},\ \mathbf{x}\right]$

Out[1]= $\{\{\mathbf{x}\rightarrow-\mathbf{3.30278}\},\ \{\mathbf{x}\rightarrow\mathbf{0.302776}\}\}$

NSolve provides approximate numerical solutions to equations. It takes two arguments, separated as always by a comma. The first argument is an *equation*. Note that the double equal sign == is used for equations; this is because the single equal sign = is used to assign values to expressions, an essentially different operation. The second argument in the NSolve command (x in the example above) specifies the variable for which we want to solve. It may be obvious to you that you wish to solve for *x*, but it's not to the computer. For instance, there may be occasions when the equation you are solving involves more than one variable (we'll see an example later in this section). Lastly, the NSolve command can take an optional third argument which specifies the number of digits of precision that you desire:

In[2]:= $\mathtt{NSolve}\left[-1 + 3\,x + x^2 == 0,\ x,\ 15\right]$

Out[2]= $\{\{x \to -3.30277563773199\},\ \{x \to 0.302775637731995\}\}$

Now what about the output? First notice that it is in the form of a *list* (a sequence of items separated by commas with a set of curly brackets around the whole thing). This is because there are typically numerous solutions to a given equation, so it is sensible to present them in a list. Now let's focus on the items in this list. Each is of the form {*x → solution*}. This looks strange at first, but it is easy enough to interpret. It is an example of a structure called a *replacement rule*, which will be explored later in this section.

You can smarten the appearance of the list of solutions by making a Grid of the results. As discussed in the last chapter, in Section 3.5, when Grid is applied to such a list it will produce a neatly formatted column:

In[3]:= $\mathtt{NSolve}\left[-1 + 3\,x + x^2 == 0,\ x,\ 35\right]\ //\ \mathtt{Grid}$

Out[3]=
$x \to -3.3027756377319946465596106337352480$
$x \to 0.30277563773199464655961063373524797$

Can *Mathematica* produce *exact* solutions to polynomial equations? The answer is sometimes. It is a mathematical fact that some polynomial equations involving powers of *x* that exceed 4 cannot be solved algebraically, period. However, if an equation can be solved algebraically, the Solve command is the ticket. Here are the precise roots of the polynomial above:

In[4]:= $\mathtt{Solve}\left[-1 + 3\,x + x^2 == 0,\ x\right]\ //\ \mathtt{Grid}$

Out[4]=
$x \to \frac{1}{2}\left(-3 - \sqrt{13}\right)$
$x \to \frac{1}{2}\left(-3 + \sqrt{13}\right)$

Remember the quadratic formula? That's all that's happening here. In fact, if you ever forget the quadratic formula, you can have *Mathematica* derive it for you:

In[5]:= `Clear[a, b, c, x];`
`Solve[a x`^{2}` + b x + c == 0, x] // Grid`

Out[6]=
$$x \to \frac{-b - \sqrt{b^2 - 4\,a\,c}}{2\,a}$$

$$x \to \frac{-b + \sqrt{b^2 - 4\,a\,c}}{2\,a}$$

Note the space between a and x^2, and between b and x in the last input line; they are needed to indicate multiplication. This example also makes it clear why the second argument to the `Solve` command is so important; this is an equation that could be solved for *a*, for *b*, for *c*, or for *x*. You have to specify the variable for which you wish to solve.

Let's look at a few more examples of these commands in action. We'll start with the `NSolve` command and later address some special considerations for using the `Solve` command:

In[7]:= `Plot[x + 3 x`^{2}` + x`^{3}`, {x, -3, 1}]`

Out[7]=
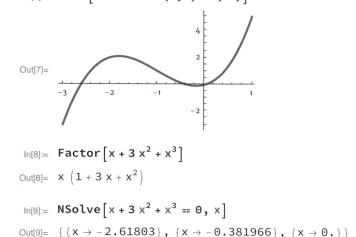

In[8]:= `Factor[x + 3 x`^{2}` + x`^{3}`]`
Out[8]= $x \left(1 + 3\,x + x^2\right)$

In[9]:= `NSolve[x + 3 x`^{2}` + x`^{3}` == 0, x]`
Out[9]= $\{\{x \to -2.61803\}, \{x \to -0.381966\}, \{x \to 0.\}\}$

Note that the factor *x* corresponds to the root *x* = 0, but that the other roots are not revealed by the `Factor` command (although they would have been found had we replaced the x by `1.*x` in the polynomial). The `NSolve` command reveals all roots, always.

Now let's tweak things a little. We can shift the graph of this function up by one unit by adding 1 to its expression, and the resulting function should have only one real root (the dip on the right of the graph will be entirely above the *x* axis):

In[10]:= $\text{Plot}\left[1 + x + 3\, x^2 + x^3,\ \{x,\ -3,\ 1\}\right]$

Out[10]=

In[11]:= $\text{Factor}\left[1 + x + 3\, x^2 + x^3\right]$

Out[11]= $1 + x + 3\, x^2 + x^3$

This didn't do a thing; the new function has no rational roots. What happens if we replace one of the integer coefficients with its decimal equivalent?

In[12]:= $\text{Factor}\left[1. + x + 3\, x^2 + x^3\right]$

Out[12]= $1.\ (2.76929 + 1.\ x)\ \left(0.361103 + 0.230708\, x + 1.\ x^2\right)$

This reveals a real root near $x = -2.76929$. But what about the quadratic factor?

In[13]:= $\text{NSolve}\left[1 + x + 3\, x^2 + x^3 == 0,\ x\right]$

Out[13]= $\{\{x \to -2.76929\},\ \{x \to -0.115354 - 0.589743\ i\},$
$\{x \to -0.115354 + 0.589743\ i\}\}$

Mathematica is reporting three roots. The first root reported is the x intercept that we see in the plot. The second two are complex numbers; they are each expressions of the form $a + bi$, where i is the imaginary number whose square is -1. They are purely algebraic solutions to the polynomial equation, bearing no obvious geometric relationship to its graph. It is a fact that every polynomial whose highest power of x is n will have exactly n roots, some of which may be complex numbers (see the *fundamental theorem of algebra* in Section 4.4). It is also true that any complex roots of a polynomial (whose coefficients are all real) come in *conjugate pairs*; one will be of the form $a + bi$, the other $a - bi$, as in the output above.

Often we are only interested in real-valued solutions to an equation. We can add the optional argument `Reals` to `Solve` or `NSolve` to suppress complex output.

In[14]:= $\text{NSolve}\left[1 + x + 3\, x^2 + x^3 == 0,\ x,\ \text{Reals}\right]$

Out[14]= $\{\{x \to -2.76929\}\}$

Here is another example:

In[15]:= $\text{Solve}\left[12 + 4\, x + 3\, x^2 + x^3 == 0,\ x\right]$

Out[15]= $\{\{x \to -3\},\ \{x \to -2\ i\},\ \{x \to 2\ i\}\}$

In[16]:= `Solve[12 + 4 x + 3 x^2 + x^3 == 0, x, Reals]`

Out[16]= `{{x → -3}}`

If there are no real solutions, `Solve` will return `{ }`.

In[17]:= `Solve[x^2 == -4, x, Reals]`

Out[17]= `{}`

You can specify other domains for `Solve`, such as `Integers`. The equation below has three solutions, two of which are integers.

In[18]:= `Solve[` $\frac{x^2}{3}$ `+` $\frac{92\,x}{3}$ `- x^3 == -20, x]`

Out[18]= $\left\{ \{x \to -5\}, \left\{ x \to -\frac{2}{3} \right\}, \{x \to 6\} \right\}$

In[19]:= `Solve[` $\frac{x^2}{3}$ `+` $\frac{92\,x}{3}$ `- x^3 == -20, x, Integers]`

Out[19]= `{{x → -5}, {x → 6}}`

If we only want positive solutions we can use `&&` to specify another condition on the first argument (`&&` stands for the word "and").

In[20]:= `Solve[` $\frac{x^2}{3}$ `+` $\frac{92\,x}{3}$ `- x^3 == -20 && x > 0, x]`

Out[20]= `{{x → 6}}`

You can extract a single solution from the list of solutions using double square brackets. This was discussed in Section 3.11. Here is an example to illustrate:

In[21]:= `sols = Solve[x^2 - 225 == 0, x]`

Out[21]= `{{x → -15}, {x → 15}}`

We have given the list of solutions the name `sols` (note the assignment operator `=` assigns the name `sols` to the output, while the equation operator `==` is used to produce equations). Here is how to extract the second element from a list (type ESC `[[` ESC to get ⟦, or you may also just use two square brackets back to back):

In[22]:= `sols⟦2⟧`

Out[22]= `{x → 15}`

To use one of the solutions provided by the `NSolve` or `Solve` command in a subsequent calculation, you need to understand the syntax of *replacement rules*. The symbol `/.` tells *Mathematica* to make a replacement. It is shorthand for a command called `ReplaceAll`. You first write an expression

involving x, then write /. and then write a replacement rule of the form $x \rightarrow solution$. The arrow
button   →   is found on the Basic Math Assistant palette in the Basic Calculator section. You may type
-> (the "minus" sign followed by the "greater than" sign) in place of the arrow if you wish:

> In[23]:= x^2 /. x → 3
>
> Out[23]= 9

This last input line can be read as "Evaluate the expression x^2, replacing x by 3."

Here is how you can use replacement rules to extract solutions generated by the Solve command:

> In[24]:= x /. sols⟦1⟧
>
> Out[24]= −15

> In[25]:= x /. sols⟦2⟧
>
> Out[25]= 15

> In[26]:= x^2 /. sols⟦2⟧
>
> Out[26]= 225

If you don't specify which solution you want, you will get a list where x is replaced by each solution in
turn:

> In[27]:= x /. sols
>
> Out[27]= {−15, 15}

You can do all of this in one step, generating output that is a list of solutions rather than a list of
replacement rules:

> In[28]:= x /. Solve$\left[x^2 - 225 == 0, x\right]$
>
> Out[28]= {−15, 15}

You may also use replacement rules to test whether an equation holds for a particular value of x:

> In[29]:= $x^2 - 225 == 0$ /. sols⟦1⟧
>
> Out[29]= True

> In[30]:= $x^2 - 225 == 0$ /. x → 10
>
> Out[30]= False

Replacement rules take some getting used to, but they are enormously convenient. Here, for instance,
we plot a polynomial, and include an Epilog to place a Point at each of the roots (this will work
when all roots are real):

> In[31]:= f[x_] := $12 + 4x - 15x^2 - 5x^3 + 3x^4 + x^5$

In[32]:= `Plot[f[x], {x, -4, 3},`
`Epilog → {PointSize[.02], Point[{x, 0}] /. NSolve[f[x] == 0, x]}]`

Out[32]=

Now let's look at the `Solve` command in greater detail. Note that you can find the exact roots (without any decimal approximations) for any polynomial whose degree is four or less:

In[33]:= `Grid[Solve[x⁴ - x - 2 == 0, x], Alignment → Left]`

Out[33]=

$$x \to -1$$

$$x \to \frac{1}{3}\left(1 - 2\left(\frac{2}{47 + 3\sqrt{249}}\right)^{1/3} + \left(\frac{1}{2}\left(47 + 3\sqrt{249}\right)\right)^{1/3}\right)$$

$$x \to \frac{1}{3} + \frac{1}{3}\left(1 + i\sqrt{3}\right)\left(\frac{2}{47 + 3\sqrt{249}}\right)^{1/3} - \frac{1}{6}\left(1 - i\sqrt{3}\right)\left(\frac{1}{2}\left(47 + 3\sqrt{249}\right)\right)^{1/3}$$

$$x \to \frac{1}{3} + \frac{1}{3}\left(1 - i\sqrt{3}\right)\left(\frac{2}{47 + 3\sqrt{249}}\right)^{1/3} - \frac{1}{6}\left(1 + i\sqrt{3}\right)\left(\frac{1}{2}\left(47 + 3\sqrt{249}\right)\right)^{1/3}$$

Wow, this is powerful stuff! But be careful when using the `Solve` command. If you just need an approximate decimal solution to an equation you will be better served using `NSolve`. In particular, if you want a numerical approximation to a solution generated by the `Solve` command, as you might with the output generated above, it is *not* a good idea to apply the `N` command to the result. In some cases, for instance, you may end up with complex numbers approximating real roots (try solving $x^3 - 15x + 2 = 0$; it has three real roots, yet applying `N` to the output of the `Solve` command produces complex numbers—see Exercise 2). The moral of the story: Use `Solve` to generate exact answers; use `NSolve` to generate numerical solutions to any required degree of accuracy.

Another consideration to be aware of when using the `Solve` command is that equations involving polynomials of degree 5 or more (i.e., where the highest power of x is 5 or more) may not have explicit algebraic solutions. This is a mathematical fact; there are equations of degree 5 with roots that cannot be represented in radicals. Here is what the output will look like in these situations:

In[34]:= `Solve[x⁵ - x + 1 == 0, x]`

Out[34]= `{{x → Root[1 - #1 + #1⁵ &, 1]},`
`{x → Root[1 - #1 + #1⁵ &, 2]}, {x → Root[1 - #1 + #1⁵ &, 3]},`
`{x → Root[1 - #1 + #1⁵ &, 4]}, {x → Root[1 - #1 + #1⁵ &, 5]}}`

The output here is composed of `Root` objects, which are a means of cataloging the (in this case five) roots that cannot be expressed in algebraic form using radicals. When `Root` objects arise, it is always possible to apply N to the output to get numerical approximations. Alternately, NSolve can be used to get the same result:

In[35]:= `Grid[NSolve[x`^{5}` - x + 1 == 0, x], Alignment → Left]`

$$x \rightarrow -1.1673$$
$$x \rightarrow -0.181232 - 1.08395\ i$$
Out[35]= $\quad x \rightarrow -0.181232 + 1.08395\ i$
$$x \rightarrow 0.764884 - 0.352472\ i$$
$$x \rightarrow 0.764884 + 0.352472\ i$$

After all this you may wonder why the Solve command is ever used, since NSolve seems to be more versatile and robust. The answer is that it depends on your purposes. For numerical solutions to specific problems, NSolve is probably all you need. But for exact algebraic solutions or the derivation of general formulas, Solve is indispensable. Here are two more examples to illustrate the power of this command. The first provides the general formula for the roots of a cubic equation of the form $x^3 + b\,x + c$, where b and c may be any numbers:

In[36]:= `Clear[b, c, x];`
`Grid[Solve[x`^{3}` + b x + c == 0, x], Alignment → Left]`

$$x \rightarrow -\frac{\left(\frac{2}{3}\right)^{1/3} b}{\left(-9\,c+\sqrt{3}\ \sqrt{4\,b^3+27\,c^2}\right)^{1/3}} + \frac{\left(-9\,c+\sqrt{3}\ \sqrt{4\,b^3+27\,c^2}\right)^{1/3}}{2^{1/3}\,3^{2/3}}$$

Out[37]= $\quad x \rightarrow \dfrac{\left(1+i\,\sqrt{3}\right) b}{2^{2/3}\,3^{1/3}\left(-9\,c+\sqrt{3}\ \sqrt{4\,b^3+27\,c^2}\right)^{1/3}} - \dfrac{\left(1-i\,\sqrt{3}\right)\left(-9\,c+\sqrt{3}\ \sqrt{4\,b^3+27\,c^2}\right)^{1/3}}{2\cdot2^{1/3}\,3^{2/3}}$

$$x \rightarrow \frac{\left(1-i\,\sqrt{3}\right) b}{2^{2/3}\,3^{1/3}\left(-9\,c+\sqrt{3}\ \sqrt{4\,b^3+27\,c^2}\right)^{1/3}} - \frac{\left(1+i\,\sqrt{3}\right)\left(-9\,c+\sqrt{3}\ \sqrt{4\,b^3+27\,c^2}\right)^{1/3}}{2\cdot2^{1/3}\,3^{2/3}}$$

The next example illustrates how Solve may be used to put a given formula into a different form. It is a rather trite computation, but it illustrates the versatility of the Solve command:

In[38]:= `Clear[e, m, c];`
`Solve[e == m c`^{2}`, m]`

Out[39]= $\left\{\left\{m \rightarrow \dfrac{e}{c^2}\right\}\right\}$

One last comment about the Solve command is in order. As you may expect, it will distinguish between decimals and fractions in the input, and adjust its output to match:

In[40]:= `Solve[x`^{2}` - 0.25 == 0, x]`

Out[40]= $\{\{x \rightarrow -0.5\}, \{x \rightarrow 0.5\}\}$

In[41]:= $\text{Solve}\left[x^2 - \dfrac{1}{4} == 0, x\right]$

Out[41]= $\left\{\left\{x \to -\dfrac{1}{2}\right\}, \left\{x \to \dfrac{1}{2}\right\}\right\}$

Exercises 4.2

1. In Exercise 1 of Section 4.1 we used `Factor` to find the real roots of $f(x) = 1 + 5x + 2x^3 + 10x^4$.

   a. Use `Solve` to find the real roots of $f(x)$ and compare your solutions with the values you found in Exercise 1 of Section 4.1.

   b. Use `NSolve` to approximate the real roots of $f(x)$ and compare your solutions with the values you found in Exercise 1 of Section 4.1.

2. Use `Solve` followed by `N` to approximate the roots of the polynomial $x^3 - 15x + 2$. Then find the roots using `NSolve`. Which gives the better approximation?

3. Fix two real numbers p and q, and consider the following quadratic equation in the variable z:
   $z^2 - qz - \dfrac{1}{27}p^3 = 0$.

   a. `Solve` this equation in terms of p and q (use *Mathematica*, or work by hand using the quadratic formula).

   b. Consider the expression $\dfrac{z^2 - qz - \frac{1}{27}p^3}{z}$, which has the same roots as the quadratic above. Use replacement rules to replace z by w^3, then w by $\dfrac{1}{6}\left(3y + \sqrt{3}\ \sqrt{4p + 3y^2}\ \right)$, and then p by $\left(b - \dfrac{a^2}{3}\right)$ and q by $\left(\dfrac{-2a^3 + 9ab - 27c}{27}\right)$, and finally, y by $\left(x + \dfrac{a}{3}\right)$. `Simplify` the result and `Collect` the terms as ascending powers of x. What do you get?

   c. Use the information in parts **a** and **b** to develop a means of using the quadratic formula to solve the general cubic equation $x^3 + ax^2 + bx + c = 0$. That is, take the solution to the quadratic in part **a** and transform it into a root of the cubic $x^3 + ax^2 + bx + c$ using the transformations in part **b**. The idea to use these successive replacements for the purpose of solving a cubic was perfected in the 1500s by Italian mathematicians such as Cardano and Tartaglia.

   d. Compare the output to that of $\text{Solve}\left[x^3 + ax^2 + bx + c == 0, x\right][\![1]\!]$.

4.3 Solving Equations and Inequalities with Reduce

The `Reduce` command provides another means for solving equations. The input syntax is like that used for `Solve` and `NSolve`, but the output is expressed in a very different way.

In[1]:= $\text{Reduce}\left[x^2 == 100, x\right]$

Out[1]= $x == -10\ ||\ x == 10$

The values of *x* are given as *equations* rather than as replacement rules. The double vertical bar || stands for the word "or." So the output here reads, "Either *x* is equal to −10, or *x* is equal to 10."

The reason for the different output format is that `Reduce` is designed to consider special conditions on all parameters appearing in an equation, whereas `Solve` will ignore conditions on any parameter whose solution is not explicitly being sought. For example, the solution below only makes sense when the parameter $a \neq 0$:

In[2]:= `Solve[a x == b, x]`

Out[2]= $\left\{\left\{x \to \dfrac{b}{a}\right\}\right\}$

`Reduce` takes into account the possibility that *a* could be zero:

In[3]:= `Reduce[a x == b, x]`

Out[3]= $(b == 0 \,\&\&\, a == 0) \,||\, \left(a \neq 0 \,\&\&\, x == \dfrac{b}{a}\right)$

Note that the double ampersand && stands for the word "and," so this reads, "Either *a* and *b* are both equal to 0, or *a* is nonzero and $x = \dfrac{b}{a}$." The output syntax is designed to handle subtle expressions like this. While this syntax has many advantages, one disadvantage is that the output is not replacement rules. Luckily, we can use `ToRules` to change the output of `Reduce` (or any other such logical combination of equations) to a list of replacement rules that can then be used as input to other commands.

In[4]:= `Reduce`$\left[12 + 4\,x - 15\,x^2 - 5\,x^3 + 3\,x^4 + x^5 == 0,\ x\right]$

Out[4]= $x == -3 \,||\, x == -2 \,||\, x == -1 \,||\, x == 1 \,||\, x == 2$

In[5]:= `{ToRules[%]}`

Out[5]= $\{\{x \to -3\},\ \{x \to -2\},\ \{x \to -1\},\ \{x \to 1\},\ \{x \to 2\}\}$

Now we can check all solutions in this list are correct with great efficiency:

In[6]:= `f[x_] :=` $12 + 4\,x - 15\,x^2 - 5\,x^3 + 3\,x^4 + x^5$

In[7]:= `f[x] /.` $\{\{x \to -3\},\ \{x \to -2\},\ \{x \to -1\},\ \{x \to 1\},\ \{x \to 2\}\}$

Out[7]= $\{0, 0, 0, 0, 0\}$

As with `Solve`, we can add the optional argument `Reals` to `Reduce` to suppress complex output:

In[8]:= `Reduce`$\left[12 + 4\,x + 3\,x^2 + x^3 == 0,\ x\right]$

Out[8]= $x == -3 \,||\, x == -2\,i \,||\, x == 2\,i$

In[9]:= **Reduce** $\left[12 + 4 \text{ x} + 3 \text{ x}^2 + \text{x}^3 == 0, \text{ x, Reals}\right]$

Out[9]= $\text{X} == -3$

If there are no real solutions, Reduce will return False.

In[10]:= **Reduce** $\left[\text{x}^2 == -4, \text{ x, Reals}\right]$

Out[10]= False

Reduce is useful for simplifying inequalities:

In[11]:= **Reduce** $\left[\text{x}^2 - 1 > 0, \text{ x}\right]$

Out[11]= $\text{X} < -1 \mid\mid \text{x} > 1$

If you were asked to describe the natural domain (among all real numbers) for the function $f(x) = \frac{x^2-7x+3}{\sqrt{x^3-4x^2+2x-1}}$, you would want to know for which values of x the polynomial $x^3 - 4x^2 + 2x - 1 > 0$. Reduce can handle this:

In[12]:= **Reduce** $\left[\text{x}^3 - 4 \text{ x}^2 + 2 \text{ x} - 1 > 0, \text{ x}\right]$

Out[12]= $\text{X} > \text{Root}\left[-1 + 2 \text{ \#1} - 4 \text{ \#1}^2 + \text{\#1}^3 \, \&, \, 1\right]$

The solution is given in terms of a Root object, which at first glance may seem both intimidating and unhelpful. A careful inspection shows that Root simply writes the polynomial in the form of a pure function (see Section 8.4 for a discussion of these) for its first argument. The second argument gives an index number for the root in question. Essentially, Root objects are a means of cataloging roots of polynomials. What is important for us here is the fact that using N, we can numerically approximate any Root object with ease:

In[13]:= **Reduce** $\left[\text{x}^3 - 4 \text{ x}^2 + 2 \text{ x} - 1 > 0, \text{ x}\right] \, // \, \text{N}$

Out[13]= $\text{X} > 3.51155$

If an exact answer is preferred, one can specify for cubic or quartic polynomials that an explicit expression in radicals be given (instead of Root objects); just set the option Cubics (or Quartics in the case of a polynomial of degree 4) to True:

In[14]:= **Reduce** $\left[\text{x}^3 - 4 \text{ x}^2 + 2 \text{ x} - 1 > 0, \text{ x, Cubics} \rightarrow \text{True}\right]$

Out[14]= $\text{X} > \frac{1}{3} \left(4 + \left(\frac{83}{2} - \frac{3\sqrt{321}}{2}\right)^{1/3} + \left(\frac{1}{2}\left(83 + 3\sqrt{321}\right)\right)^{1/3}\right)$

A plot is consistent with the result that $x > 3.51$:

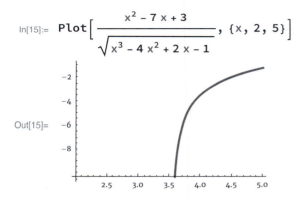

In[15]:= $\text{Plot}\left[\dfrac{x^2 - 7\,x + 3}{\sqrt{x^3 - 4\,x^2 + 2\,x - 1}},\ \{x,\ 2,\ 5\}\right]$

Let's try solving an equation with an infinite number of discrete solutions: $\cos(x) = 0$. We all know that the cosine function is equal to zero when its argument is of the form $2\,k\,\pi \pm \frac{\pi}{2}$, where k is any integer.

In[16]:= $\text{Reduce}[\text{Cos}[x] == 0,\ x]$

Out[16]= $C[1] \in \mathbb{Z} \ \&\& \ \left(x == -\dfrac{\pi}{2} + 2\,\pi\,C[1] \ || \ x == \dfrac{\pi}{2} + 2\,\pi\,C[1]\right)$

We said earlier that the solution set is composed of all numbers $2\,k\,\pi \pm \frac{\pi}{2}$, where k is an integer. *Mathematica* uses the generic name $C[1]$ (rather than k) when it has to introduce a constant. It's a rather unsightly name, but something like this is necessary. For instance, in an output where 50 such constants are needed, they will be called $C[1]$, $C[2]$, and so on; the numerical piece guarantees that the notation is capable of handling arbitrarily many such constants. The symbols $\in$ and $\mathbb{Z}$ are standard mathematical notation; $\in$ means "is an element of" and $\mathbb{Z}$ denotes the set of integers. Hence the output above says: "$C[1]$ is an element of the set of integers, and $x = 2\,\pi\,C[1] \pm \frac{\pi}{2}$." The output concisely describes *all* of the roots of the cosine function.

Mathematica can also express the output generated by Reduce using standard notation from the field of mathematical logic. In this notation, the symbol $\wedge$ means "and" and the symbol $\vee$ means "or." If you have experience with this notation, you may find it easier to read. A constant is also represented as c_1 rather than $C[1]$. To get your output in this form, simply apply TraditionalForm to the output of Reduce.

In[17]:= $\text{Reduce}[\text{Cos}[x] == 0,\ x] \ // \ \text{TraditionalForm}$
Out[17]//TraditionalForm=

$$c_1 \in \mathbb{Z} \wedge \left(x = 2\,\pi\,c_1 - \dfrac{\pi}{2} \vee x = 2\,\pi\,c_1 + \dfrac{\pi}{2}\right)$$

The output we get with Solve says the same thing in a slightly different way:

In[18]:= **Solve[Cos[x] == 0, x]**

Out[18]= $\left\{\left\{x \to \text{ConditionalExpression}\left[-\frac{\pi}{2} + 2\pi C[1], C[1] \in \mathbb{Z}\right]\right\},\right.$

$\left.\left\{x \to \text{ConditionalExpression}\left[\frac{\pi}{2} + 2\pi C[1], C[1] \in \mathbb{Z}\right]\right\}\right\}$

The command ConditionalExpression is *Mathematica*'s way of warning us that this solution is not valid for all numbers C[1]. The solution is subject to a condition, in this case C[1] must be an integer.

Here is a more complicated example in which there are two constants.

In[19]:= **Clear[ans]**

In[20]:= **ans = Solve[Sin[1 + Cos[x]] == 1, x]**

Out[20]= $\left\{\left\{x \to \text{ConditionalExpression}\left[\right.\right.\right.$

$-\text{ArcCos}\left[-1 + \frac{\pi}{2} + 2\pi C[2]\right] + 2\pi C[1], C[2] \in \mathbb{Z} \,\&\&\, C[1] \in \mathbb{Z}\right]\right\},$

$\left\{x \to \text{ConditionalExpression}\left[\text{ArcCos}\left[-1 + \frac{\pi}{2} + 2\pi C[2]\right] + 2\pi C[1],\right.\right.$

$\left.\left.\left.C[2] \in \mathbb{Z} \,\&\&\, C[1] \in \mathbb{Z}\right]\right\}\right\}$

One can replace the constants by numerical values. Here we let C[1] take on the values −1, 0, and 1 and C[2] = 0. Flatten is applied to this list to remove extra curly brackets.

In[21]:= **Clear[rules]**

In[22]:= **rules = Flatten[Table[ans /. {C[1] → k, C[2] → 0}, {k, {-1, 0, 1}}], 1]**

Out[22]= $\left\{\left\{x \to -2\pi - \text{ArcCos}\left[-1 + \frac{\pi}{2}\right]\right\}, \left\{x \to -2\pi + \text{ArcCos}\left[-1 + \frac{\pi}{2}\right]\right\},\right.$

$\left\{x \to -\text{ArcCos}\left[-1 + \frac{\pi}{2}\right]\right\}, \left\{x \to \text{ArcCos}\left[-1 + \frac{\pi}{2}\right]\right\},$

$\left.\left\{x \to 2\pi - \text{ArcCos}\left[-1 + \frac{\pi}{2}\right]\right\}, \left\{x \to 2\pi + \text{ArcCos}\left[-1 + \frac{\pi}{2}\right]\right\}\right\}$

Here, for example, is a plot of the function $f(x) = \sin(1 + \cos(x))$ with the solutions to the equation $f(x) = 1$ shown as large points via the Epilog:

In[23]:= `Plot[Sin[1 + Cos[x]], {x, -10, 10},`
    `Epilog → {PointSize[.02], Point[{x, 1}] /. rules}]`

Out[23]=

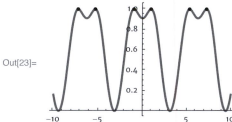

Exercises 4.3

1. Find the largest possible domain in the real numbers for the function $f(x) = \dfrac{x^3 + 5x^2 + 4x + 5}{\sqrt{x^2 + 2x - 3}}$. Make a plot of f over

 a valid domain in the *positive* real numbers, along with the function $\sqrt{x^4 + 8x^3 + 20x^2 + 34x + 58}$. What do you notice?

2. Reduce can be used to solve *systems of equations*. A system of equations is a collection of several equations, each in several variables. A *solution* to such a system is a set of values for the variables for which all the equations are satisfied.

 a. A system of equations can be entered in several ways. One can either type a list of equations, or an equation of lists like the input below. Type and enter this input.

     `Reduce[{Cos[y] Cos[x Cos[y]], -x Cos[x Cos[y]] Sin[y]} == {0, 0}, {x, y}, Reals]`

 b. The output is a bit intimidating at first. This is unavoidable for the simple reason that the solution set happens to be rather complex. If we regard a particular solution (x_0, y_0) as a point in the xy plane, then this output is composed of both discrete points and entire curves in the plane. Read the output carefully and identify the discrete points. ListPlot them in the plane.

 c. Use ContourPlot to sketch the solutions of both equations.

3. We can also use Reduce to solve a single equation with more than one variable. Use Reduce to find the set of points in the plane that are the solution of $\dfrac{8xy^2}{(1-y^2)^2} = \dfrac{4x}{1-y^2}$ and then use ContourPlot to graph the set of solutions.

4.4 Understanding Complex Output

You've noticed by now that complex numbers sometimes appear in *Mathematica*'s output. They can pop up in a variety of places, even when you don't expect them. In Section 3.2, for instance, we saw that *Mathematica* regards the cube root of a negative number as a complex number.

In[1]:= `(-8)`$^{1/3}$ `// N`
Out[1]= `1. + 1.73205 i`

In high school and early college courses it is more common to work with the *real-valued* cube root function, which would return the value -2 (instead of the complex number above) as the cube root of -8. We'll discuss the cube root function at length later in this section. Here are a few other instances where complex numbers can pop up in the context of a real computation:

In[2]:= `Log[-2]`

Out[2]= $i \pi + \text{Log}[2]$

In[3]:= `ArcSin[2.]`

Out[3]= $1.5708 - 1.31696 \, i$

Now this sort of output ought to make you hungry to learn about the complex numbers. If you are even a bit curious, ask your instructor about them. And even if you are not particularly interested in such matters, be mindful that you are now using a grown-up software package, so you are going to have to deal with them from time to time. The inputs above simply extend the domains of the logarithm and inverse sine functions beyond what we ordinarily allow. Doing so results in complex output.

A subtle issue that can arise from time to time is illustrated below:

In[4]:= $\text{Reduce}\left[x^3 - 15\,x + 2 == 0,\, x,\, \text{Cubics} \rightarrow \text{True}\right]$

Out[4]= $x == \dfrac{5}{\left(-1 + 2\,i\,\sqrt{31}\,\right)^{1/3}} + \left(-1 + 2\,i\,\sqrt{31}\,\right)^{1/3} \;||$

$\quad x == -\dfrac{5\left(1 + i\,\sqrt{3}\,\right)}{2\left(-1 + 2\,i\,\sqrt{31}\,\right)^{1/3}} - \dfrac{1}{2}\left(1 - i\,\sqrt{3}\,\right)\left(-1 + 2\,i\,\sqrt{31}\,\right)^{1/3} \;||$

$\quad x == -\dfrac{5\left(1 - i\,\sqrt{3}\,\right)}{2\left(-1 + 2\,i\,\sqrt{31}\,\right)^{1/3}} - \dfrac{1}{2}\left(1 + i\,\sqrt{3}\,\right)\left(-1 + 2\,i\,\sqrt{31}\,\right)^{1/3}$

Here Reduce has returned three expressions involving i. Yet each of these numbers is in fact a real number (one could verify this by plotting the cubic—its graph crosses the *x* axis three times). Just as one can write the real number -1 as i^2, it is possible to express other real numbers in a manner that makes use of the complex number i. That's what has happened here. In some cases it is possible to algebraically manipulate such numbers so that all the i's go away. The command that can accomplish this is called `ComplexExpand`. It will attempt to break a knotty complex number into its real and imaginary components. In this case, the imaginary part of each of the numbers above should be exactly zero. One could simply append `//ComplexExpand` to the previous input, but we will apply it just to the first root reported above to make the output easier to read:

$$\text{In[5]:=} \quad \text{ComplexExpand}\left[\frac{5}{\left(-1+2\,i\,\sqrt{31}\,\right)^{1/3}} + \left(-1+2\,i\,\sqrt{31}\,\right)^{1/3}\right]$$

$$\text{Out[5]=} \quad \sqrt{5}\,\text{Cos}\left[\frac{1}{3}\left(\pi - \text{ArcTan}\left[2\,\sqrt{31}\,\right]\right)\right] + \sqrt{5}\,\text{Cos}\left[\frac{1}{3}\left(-\pi + \text{ArcTan}\left[2\,\sqrt{31}\,\right]\right)\right] +$$
$$i\,\left(\sqrt{5}\,\text{Sin}\left[\frac{1}{3}\left(\pi - \text{ArcTan}\left[2\,\sqrt{31}\,\right]\right)\right] + \sqrt{5}\,\text{Sin}\left[\frac{1}{3}\left(-\pi + \text{ArcTan}\left[2\,\sqrt{31}\,\right]\right)\right]\right)$$

Notice the structure of the output; it is of the form $a + ib$. If this is indeed a real number, it had better be the case that $b = 0$. Now your first impression upon seeing intricate output like this may be to both marvel at what *Mathematica* can do, and simultaneously to glaze over and fail to examine the output critically. Pause for a moment to take a good look at it, and focus your attention on the imaginary component b. You will find that b is indeed zero. It is of the form $\sqrt{5}\,\sin(c) + \sqrt{5}\,\sin(-c)$, and since $\sin(-c) = -\sin(c)$, the entire quantity is zero. In the next section the `Simplify` command will be discussed. It can be invoked to carry out this simplification as well:

$$\text{In[6]:=} \quad \text{Simplify}\left[\right.$$
$$\left.\sqrt{5}\,\text{Sin}\left[\frac{1}{3}\left(\pi - \text{ArcTan}\left[2\,\sqrt{31}\,\right]\right)\right] + \sqrt{5}\,\text{Sin}\left[\frac{1}{3}\left(-\pi + \text{ArcTan}\left[2\,\sqrt{31}\,\right]\right)\right]\right]$$

$$\text{Out[6]=} \quad 0$$

Note also that the opposite issue can arise—certain non-real complex numbers may be expressed using only real numbers. At first glance they don't betray their complexity:

$$\text{In[7]:=} \quad \text{Solve}\left[x^3 == 1,\ x\right]$$

$$\text{Out[7]=} \quad \left\{\{x \to 1\},\ \left\{x \to -(-1)^{1/3}\right\},\ \left\{x \to (-1)^{2/3}\right\}\right\}$$

Again, `ComplexExpand` is the ticket for putting a complex number into standard form:

$$\text{In[8]:=} \quad \% \ // \ \text{ComplexExpand}$$

$$\text{Out[8]=} \quad \left\{\{x \to 1\},\ \left\{x \to -\frac{1}{2} - \frac{i\,\sqrt{3}}{2}\right\},\ \left\{x \to -\frac{1}{2} + \frac{i\,\sqrt{3}}{2}\right\}\right\}$$

⚠ Real-Valued versus Complex-Valued Rational Powers

We have already noted that there are different definitions of the cube root function. In precalculus and calculus courses, where the complex number system is not utilized, one defines the cube root of any real number to be its real cube root. So, for instance, $(-8)^{1/3} = -2$. *Mathematica* uses a different definition, which we will discuss in this section. Under this definition $(-8)^{1/3} = 1 + i\,\sqrt{3}$.

$$\text{In[9]:=} \quad \text{ComplexExpand}\left[(-8)^{1/3}\right]$$

$$\text{Out[9]=} \quad 1 + i\,\sqrt{3}$$

The reality is that when complex numbers are taken into account, there are *three* numbers whose cube is −8:

In[10]:= **Reduce**$\left[x^3 \mathbin{==} -8, x\right]$

Out[10]= $x \mathbin{==} -2 \mid\mid x \mathbin{==} 1 - i \sqrt{3} \mid\mid x \mathbin{==} 1 + i \sqrt{3}$

So in defining *the* cube root, one of these three must be chosen. *Mathematica* chooses the last of these, and we will soon see why. Note that the underlying command used to raise a number to a power is called `Power`:

In[11]:= x^p **// FullForm**

Out[11]//FullForm=
  `Power[x, p]`

It is the definition of this basic arithmetic operation that is at issue. When a negative number is raised to a rational power, and the denominator of that rational power is an odd number (e.g., 3 for the rational power 1/3), you might like to have a power expression evaluate to a real number, as would be expected in a precalculus or calculus course. In Section 3.2 an alternate power command called `Surd` was introduced that can be used to emulate the real-valued power functions commonly encountered in such a course.

We now discuss a topic that falls outside of the standard precalculus and calculus curricula: Why on Earth does *Mathematica* report that $(-8)^{1/3} = 1 + \sqrt{3}\,i$ when it would be so much simpler to say that the cube root of −8 is just −2? What possible reason could there be for such insanity? This will take a bit of careful thought, and a page or two of explanation, so make yourself comfortable before reading on. We'll see that there is indeed a compelling reason.

Let's suppose, for the sake of argument, that the cube root of −8 is −2. What consequences follow? Well, raising any negative real number to the power 1/3 would, in a similar manner, produce a negative real number. In fact, raising any negative real number to the power $1/n$, where n is an odd positive integer, would produce a negative real number. Now suppose we raise this result to the mth power, where m is a positive integer; that is, our original negative number is raised to the rational power m/n. If m is *odd*, the result is another negative number, while if m is *even* the result is a positive number (since squaring a negative number results in a positive number). To summarize: Raising a negative number to a positive rational power with odd denominator produces a real number. This number is negative or positive according to the parity (odd or even) of the numerator. So far so good, but there's a problem.

Just as the exponential function $g(x) = 2^x$ is continuous, in a just world we would also expect the function $f(x) = (-2)^x$ to be continuous. What happens when x is a rational number with odd denominator? Are we to accept a state of affairs in which $(-2)^{311/99}$ is a negative real number, but $(-2)^{312/99}$ is a positive real number? The two exponents are very close to each other, yet they are producing values that are not close to each other (you can check this). Furthermore, noting that $\frac{311}{99} < \pi < \frac{312}{99}$, how would we define $(-2)^\pi$? It simply cannot be done when we operate under this convention that a negative number raised to a rational power with odd denominator is real.

And of course, under such a convention it does not even make sense to raise a negative number to a rational power with *even* denominator. For instance, using the power $1/2$, the square root of a negative number is ... what? It is certainly not a real number. That's a strong indication that one may need to consult the complex number system.

The complex numbers are in fact rather simple. They include the imaginary number i, which has the property that $i^2 = -1$. There are many other complex numbers whose squares are real. For instance, $(2\,i)^2 = 2^2\,i^2 = -4$. Using multiples of i like this, one can find square roots of any negative real number. In general, a complex number has the form $a + bi$, where a and b are real. a is referred to as the *real* part of this complex number, and bi is its *imaginary* part. At this point, let's note that every complex number $a + bi$ can be represented as an ordered pair (a, b), and so can be geometrically identified with a point in the plane. The *complex plane* refers to this model of the complex numbers. The real number 1 has coordinates $(1, 0)$, and the complex number i has coordinates $(0, 1)$.

The *better* way to define powers of a negative real number necessarily entails the complex number system. Just as every positive real number has two square roots (one positive and one negative), every negative number also has two square roots. But neither of them are real numbers, both are complex. And just as we choose, for any positive real number a, *one* of its two square roots to be $a^{1/2}$ (we define $a^{1/2}$ to be the *positive* square root of a), we must also choose one of the two complex square roots of $-a$ to be $(-a)^{1/2}$. Which is *the* square root of $-a$? We choose the complex root whose argument is least, the so-called *principal* square root. That is, if one were to draw rays from the origin, one to each of the square roots of $-a$ in the complex plane, and for each measure the angle counterclockwise from the positive real axis to each ray (this angle is the *argument* of the complex number), the ray with the *smallest* angle corresponds to the principal root. Under this convention, for instance, $(-1)^{1/2} = \sqrt{-1} = i$.

Higher roots are even more subtle. In the complex number system, every nonzero number has three cube roots. One is real, and the other two are complex. The correct definition of *the* cube root of any real number a (that is, the definition of $a^{1/3}$) is the principal cube root, the one whose argument is smallest. When $a > 0$, this is the real cube root that we know and love, for its argument is zero. But when $a < 0$, the real cube root is negative, and so its argument is π radians. It so happens that one of the complex roots has argument $\pi/3$. *This* is the principal cube root of a. *This* is the one that we designate to be $a^{1/3}$. So, in particular, working in the complex numbers as *Mathematica* does, $(-8)^{1/3}$ is *not* -2. Here is a graphic showing all three roots of -8 in the complex plane. Each is shown at the end of a ray projecting from the origin. The root in the first quadrant has the smallest argument. It is the principal cube root of -8, so it is $(-8)^{1/3}$.

```
In[12]:=  roots = {Re[x], Im[x]} /. NSolve[x³ == -8, x]

Out[12]=  {{-2., 0}, {1., -1.73205}, {1., 1.73205}}
```

```
In[13]:=  Graphics[{{Thick, Gray, Table[Line[{{0, 0}, r}], {r, roots}]},
             {Black, PointSize[.03], Point[roots]}},
           Axes → True, AxesLabel → {"real", "imaginary"}]
```

Out[13]=

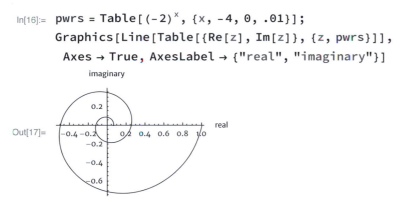

This notion of using the principal nth root as the proper definition of $a^{1/n}$ has long been accepted by the mathematical community. The most immediate benefit is the continuity of exponential functions, such as $f(x) = (-2)^x$. Note that for values of x that are close to each other, the values of this function, while complex, are also close to each other.

```
In[14]:=  N[{(-2)^311/99, (-2)^312/99}] // Column
```

Out[14]=
$$-7.96732 - 3.79246\ i$$
$$-7.89809 - 4.07175\ i$$

This means that it is possible to define powers with irrational exponents to be limits of powers with rational exponents. That is, for each irrational power (such as π), there is one and only one value of $(-2)^\pi$ that is consistent with nearby rational powers. For instance:

```
In[15]:=  N[{(-2)^311/99, (-2)^π, (-2)^312/99}] // Column
```

Out[15]=
$$-7.96732 - 3.79246\ i$$
$$-7.96618 - 3.7974\ i$$
$$-7.89809 - 4.07175\ i$$

It is easy, in fact, to witness the continuity (and the beauty) of the complex-valued function $f(x) = (-2)^x$ on the domain $-4 \leq x \leq 0$, by making a table of values for this function, and then producing a graphic of these numbers in the complex plane, joining adjacent values with line segments:

```
In[16]:=  pwrs = Table[(-2)^x, {x, -4, 0, .01}];
           Graphics[Line[Table[{Re[z], Im[z]}, {z, pwrs}]],
            Axes → True, AxesLabel → {"real", "imaginary"}]
```

Out[17]=

Note that the function assumes real values at precisely those points where this graph crosses the x axis. You would be correct to speculate that it does so on this domain when the input variable assumes the *integer* values -4 through 0. Can you calculate the values of this function at those points?

One last word regarding the complex numbers is in order. If you've made it this far, you deserve to know one final fact. This fact is so important that it is commonly known as the *fundamental theorem of algebra*. We won't prove it, but we will tell you what it says. It states simply that *every* polynomial of degree n (with real or complex coefficients) can be factored completely over the complex numbers into n linear factors. It follows that for any positive integer n, and any real number r, the polynomial $x^n - r$ has n linear factors. It so happens that the factors will all be distinct in this case. In other words, every real number r has precisely n nth roots. This is why all real numbers have three cube roots. Letting $r = -8$, we reconstruct the polynomial $x^3 - r = x^3 + 8$ from the three cube roots of -8:

In[18]:= $(x - (-2)) \left(x - \left(1 + \sqrt{3}\ \text{i}\right)\right) \left(x - \left(1 - \sqrt{3}\ \text{i}\right)\right)$ // Expand

Out[18]= $8 + x^3$

The fundamental theorem also explains why `Solve` and `NSolve` will always report n roots for a polynomial of degree n. Here is an example in which we display the eight roots of an eighth-degree polynomial as eight points in the complex plane (of which two happen to be real):

In[19]:= Graphics$\left[\{\text{Directive}[\text{Red}, \text{PointSize}[.04]],\right.$

$\qquad$ Point[{Re[x], Im[x]}] /. NSolve$\left[x^8 + 9\ x^5 - x - 1 == 0, x\right]\}$,

$\qquad$ Axes $\rightarrow$ True, PlotRange $\rightarrow$ 2$\Big]$

Out[19]=

Exercises 4.4

1. Use the following `Manipulate` to guess the value of c for which the polynomial $c - 6\ x + 8\ x^3$ has precisely *two* real roots. Test your guess. Note that by default, `TraditionalForm` is applied to the `PlotLabel` in any `Plot`.

In[1]:= `Manipulate[Plot[c - 6 x + 8 x³, {x, -1.1, 1.1},`
        `PlotLabel → Reduce[c - 6 x + 8 x³ == 0, x, Reals], PlotRange → {-4, 8}], {c, 0., 4}]`

Out[1]=

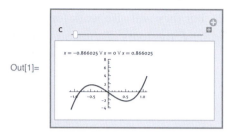

2. Use the command `Surd` introduced in Section 3.2 to produce the graph of the *real-valued* function $f(x) = x^{2/5}$ on the domain $-32 \le x \le 32$ shown below. What is $f(32)$?

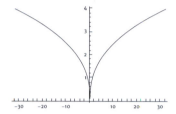

3. Use `Reduce` to find the roots of $f(x) = x^4 - x$,

   a. with the option setting `Quartics → True`.

   b. with the optional third argument `Reals`.

   c. Explain how it can be that there are no *i*s in the expressions representing the non-real roots.

   d. Redo this problem with the polynomial $f(x) = x^4 - x - 1$.

4. Consider the following input and output, and use the fundamental theorem of algebra to formulate a plausible explanation for the apparent redundancy:

   In[2]:= `Solve[(x - 2)³ == 0, x]`

   Out[2]= `{{x → 2}, {x → 2}, {x → 2}}`

5. Make a `Manipulate` that displays the roots of a fifth-degree polynomial $x^5 + ax^4 + bx^3 + cx^2 + dx + e$ in the complex plane. Make sliders for each of a, b, c, d, and e, which assume values from -2 to 2. Set the `PlotRange` to 4.

6. Make a `Manipulate` that displays the roots of the nth degree polynomial $x^n + 1$ in the complex plane, where there is a `SetterBar` displaying values of n from 1 to 10. These will be graphical depictions of all the nth roots of -1.

7. Make a `Manipulate` that displays a `Line` joining a `Table` of values for the function $(-k)^x$ on the domain $-4 \le x \le 0$ in the complex plane. Make a slider for k that assumes values from .1 to 4. Set the `PlotRange` to 2.

4.5   Working with Rational Functions

Solving Equations

The `Solve` and `NSolve` commands are built for polynomials, but they will also work for equations involving *rational functions* (quotients of polynomials). Essentially, the roots of the numerator that are not also roots of the denominator will be reported:

$$\text{In[1]:= } \text{Solve}\left[\frac{(x+3)\ (x-1)}{(x-1)} == 0,\ x\right]$$

$$\text{Out[1]= } \{\{x \to -3\}\}$$

Thus all the remarks in Section 4.2 apply to equations involving rational functions as well to those involving only polynomials.

Simplifying Rational Expressions

When you are working with a rational function, you may want to use the `Simplify` command to, well … simplify things:

$$\text{In[2]:= } \text{Simplify}\left[\frac{1-x^5}{1-x}\right]$$

$$\text{Out[2]= } 1 + x + x^2 + x^3 + x^4$$

The `Simplify` command, like `Expand` and `Factor`, takes an expression as input and returns an equivalent expression as output. `Simplify` attempts a number of transformations and returns what it believes is the most simple form. In the case of rational functions, `Simplify` will cancel the common factors appearing in the numerator and denominator. In the example above, the linear expression $1 - x$ can be factored out of the numerator. You can easily check the result:

$$\text{In[3]:= } \text{Expand}\left[(1-x)\ \left(1 + x + x^2 + x^3 + x^4\right)\right]$$

$$\text{Out[3]= } 1 - x^5$$

You can also guide *Mathematica* through such a simplification step by step. You can highlight a certain portion of an algebraic expression, and then feed that portion of the expression to one of the algebraic manipulation commands. This allows you to drive *Mathematica* step by step through an algebraic manipulation.

There is an essential difference between asking *Mathematica* to evaluate a portion of a larger input and evaluating the entire input. To work on only part of an expression, highlight that part, then rather than hitting SHIFT-ENTER to complete the computation, go to the Evaluation menu and click Evaluate in Place. If you hit SHIFT-ENTER *Mathematica* will evaluate the entire input, not just the part you highlighted.

Here, for instance, is a rational function. Rather than simplify it in one go with the `Simplify` command, let's drive through it step by step.

$$\frac{x^4 + 5\,x^3 + 8\,x^2 + 7\,x + 3}{3\,x^4 + 14\,x^3 + 18\,x^2 + 10\,x + 3}$$

First, highlight the numerator, then push the Factor button on the palette. The cell will then look like this:

$$\frac{\text{Factor}\left[x^4 + 5\,x^3 + 8\,x^2 + 7\,x + 3\right]}{3\,x^4 + 14\,x^3 + 18\,x^2 + 10\,x + 3}$$

Now highlight only the numerator by triple-clicking on the word Factor, and use Evaluate in Place from the Evaluation menu to perform the factorization. The cell will then look like this:

$$\frac{\left((1 + x)\ (3 + x)\ \left(1 + x + x^2\right)\right)}{3\,x^4 + 14\,x^3 + 18\,x^2 + 10\,x + 3}$$

Now repeat the process to factor the denominator:

$$\frac{\left((1 + x)\ (3 + x)\ \left(1 + x + x^2\right)\right)}{\left((1 + x)\ (3 + x)\ \left(1 + 2\,x + 3\,x^2\right)\right)}$$

There is clearly some cancellation that can be done. Highlight the entire expression and push Cancel[*expr*], which can be found under the More ▼ button:

In[4]:= $\text{Cancel}\left[\dfrac{\left((1 + x)\ (3 + x)\ \left(1 + x + x^2\right)\right)}{\left((1 + x)\ (3 + x)\ \left(1 + 2\,x + 3\,x^2\right)\right)}\right]$

Out[4]= $\dfrac{1 + x + x^2}{1 + 2\,x + 3\,x^2}$

The results are the same as if you had simplified the original expression using the Simplify command. The difference is that you know exactly how the simplification took place:

In[5]:= $\text{Simplify}\left[\dfrac{x^4 + 5\,x^3 + 8\,x^2 + 7\,x + 3}{3\,x^4 + 14\,x^3 + 18\,x^2 + 10\,x + 3}\right]$

Out[5]= $\dfrac{1 + x + x^2}{1 + 2\,x + 3\,x^2}$

This sort of interactive manipulation puts you in the driver's seat. You will sharpen your algebraic skills without falling into the abyss of tedium and silly mistakes (such as dropped minus signs) that can occur when performing algebraic manipulations by hand.

A rational function and the function that results from its simplification are identical, except that the original rational function will not be defined at those values of x that are roots of both the numerator and denominator. In the example above, the original function is not defined at $x = -1$ and $x = -3$, while the simplified function is defined at those points. For all other values of x the two functions are identical.

Formatting Output Using TraditionalForm

By default, *Mathematica* will always write a polynomial with ascending powers of x as you read it from left to right. It can be an annoyance reading $(-3 + x)$ rather than $(x - 3)$, but the former adheres to the ascending powers of x convention, and so that's what you will get.

```
In[6]:=  x - 3
Out[6]=  - 3 + x
```

However, any expression produced by *Mathematica* can be displayed in several ways. Append `//TraditionalForm` to any input, and it will be displayed using traditional notation (which, for a polynomial, means descending powers of x):

```
In[7]:=  x - 3 // TraditionalForm
Out[7]//TraditionalForm=
```
$$x - 3$$

You can also convert an output into `TraditionalForm` by selecting its cell bracket with your mouse, and then choosing Cell ▷ Convert To ▷ TraditionalForm in the menus.

Vertical Asymptotes

Roots of the denominator that are not also roots of the numerator will yield vertical asymptotes in the graph of a rational function. Here, for example, is a function with vertical asymptotes at $x = 3$ and $x = -3$:

```
In[8]:=  k[x_] :=
```
$$\frac{x^4 + 3\,x^3 - x^2 + 5\,x - 4}{x^2 - 9}$$

```
In[9]:=  Plot[k[x], {x, -10, 10}, Exclusions → {x² - 9 == 0},
            ExclusionsStyle → Directive[Gray, Dashed]]
```

Out[9]=

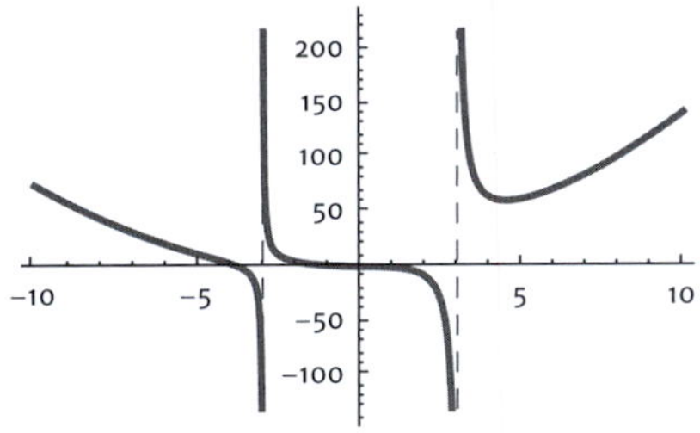

Long Division of Polynomials

Another manipulation that is useful when working with rational functions is long division. It can be done by hand, and you may have discovered that it is a tedious process. Every rational function $\frac{f(x)}{h(x)}$ can be expressed in the form $q(x) + \frac{r(x)}{h(x)}$, where $q(x)$ and $r(x)$ are polynomials, and $r(x)$ has degree less than $h(x)$. The term $q(x)$ is called the *quotient*, and the numerator $r(x)$ is called the *remainder*. When x gets sufficiently large, $\frac{r(x)}{h(x)}$ assumes values close to zero (since $r(x)$ has lesser degree than $h(x)$), so the rational function $\frac{f(x)}{h(x)}$ and the polynomial $q(x)$ are asymptotic to each other as x gets large. Here's how to get *Mathematica* to calculate the quotient and remainder:

In[10]:= $\mathsf{k\,[\,x\_\,]\ :=\ }\dfrac{x^4 + 3\,x^3 - x^2 + 5\,x - 4}{x^2 - 9}$

The commands Numerator and Denominator can be used to isolate the numerator and denominator of any fraction. You can then use these to find the quotient $q(x)$ and the remainder $r(x)$ with the commands PolynomialQuotient and PolynomialRemainder:

In[11]:= `num = Numerator[k[x]]`

Out[11]= $-4 + 5\,x - x^2 + 3\,x^3 + x^4$

In[12]:= `den = Denominator[k[x]]`

Out[12]= $-9 + x^2$

In[13]:= `q[x_] = PolynomialQuotient[num, den, x]`

Out[13]= $8 + 3\,x + x^2$

In[14]:= `r[x_] = PolynomialRemainder[num, den, x]`

Out[14]= $68 + 32\,x$

Or you can find both at once with PolynomialQuotientRemainder. The output gives the quotient followed by the remainder.

In[15]:= `PolynomialQuotientRemainder[num, den, x]`

Out[15]= $\left\{8 + 3\,x + x^2,\ 68 + 32\,x\right\}$

These commands each take three arguments. The first and second are polynomials representing the numerator and denominator of a rational function, respectively. The third is the name of the independent variable. In this example we have computed that:

$$\frac{x^4 + 3\,x^3 - x^2 + 5\,x - 4}{x^2 - 9} = \left(8 + 3\,x + x^2\right) + \frac{68 + 32\,x}{x^2 - 9}$$

You can check that *Mathematica* has done things correctly. The following computation accomplishes this. Can you see why?

In[16]:= $\texttt{Expand}\left[\left(8+3\,x+x^2\right)\,\left(x^2-9\right)+(68+32\,x)\right]$

Out[16]= $-4+5\,x-x^2+3\,x^3+x^4$

Here is a plot of k together with the quotient polynomial, which in this case is a parabola. We see that the graph of k is asymptotic to the parabola as x approaches $\pm\infty$:

In[17]:= $\texttt{Plot}\left[\{k[x], q[x]\}, \{x, -15, 15\}, \texttt{Exclusions} \rightarrow \left\{x^2-9 == 0\right\},\right.$
$\left.\texttt{ExclusionsStyle} \rightarrow \texttt{Directive}[\texttt{Gray}, \texttt{Dashed}]\right]$

Out[17]=

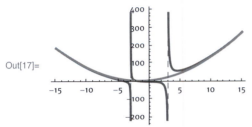

Partial Fractions

One final manipulation that is sometimes useful when working with rational functions is known as *partial fraction* decomposition. It is a fact that every rational function can be expressed as a sum of simpler rational functions, each of which has a denominator whose degree is minimal. The *Mathematica* command that can accomplish this decomposition is called $\texttt{Apart}$:

In[18]:= $\texttt{Apart}\left[\dfrac{x^4+3\,x^3-x^2+5\,x-4}{x^2-9}\right]$

Out[18]= $8+\dfrac{82}{3\,(-3+x)}+3\,x+x^2+\dfrac{14}{3\,(3+x)}$

The command that puts sums of rational expressions over a common denominator (i.e., the command that does what $\texttt{Apart}$ undoes) is $\texttt{Together}$.

In[19]:= $\texttt{Together}\left[8+\dfrac{82}{3\,(-3+x)}+3\,x+x^2+\dfrac{14}{3\,(3+x)}\right]$

Out[19]= $\dfrac{-4+5\,x-x^2+3\,x^3+x^4}{(-3+x)\,(3+x)}$

Exercises 4.5

1. The rational function $\dfrac{-6-7\,x-x^2+x^3+x^4}{-2-x+x^2}$ has no vertical asymptotes in its graph. Explain why.

2. The rational function $\frac{-6-7x-x^2+x^3+x^4}{-4-x+x^2}$ has two vertical asymptotes in its graph. Identify them, and explain why. Plot this function along with the quadratic function to which it is asymptotic for large values of x. Use $-10 \leq x \leq 10$ as your domain, and used Dashed lines for the vertical asymptotes.

4.6 Working with Other Expressions

Algebra Commands like Factor and Simplify can be applied to all sorts of expressions, not just polynomials and rational functions. In this section we give examples how some of these commands can be used.

Simplifying Things

The Simplify command can handle all types of expressions as input. Any time you have a messy expression, it won't hurt to attempt a simplification. The worst that can happen is nothing; in such cases the output will simply match the input:

```
In[1]:= Simplify[1 - (Tan[x])^4]
```

Out[1]= $\text{Cos}[2\,x]\,\text{Sec}[x]^4$

```
In[2]:= Simplify[1 + (Tan[x])^4]
```

Out[2]= $1 + \text{Tan}[x]^4$

The Simplify command can also accept a second argument specifying the domain of any variable in the expression to be simplified. For instance, consider the following example:

```
In[3]:= Simplify[Log[e^x]]
```

Out[3]= $\text{Log}[e^x]$

This seems odd; you may recall having been taught that the natural logarithm function and the exponential function are *inverses* of one another—their composition should simply yield x. The problem is that this is not necessarily true if x is a complex number, and *Mathematica* does not preclude this possibility. To restrict the domain of x to the set of real numbers, do this:

```
In[4]:= Simplify[Log[e^x], x ∈ Reals]
```

Out[4]= x

The $\in$ character can be read "is an element of." It can be found in the Typesetting section of the Basic Math Assistant palette by clicking the ⊠ tab, or you may obtain it directly by typing [ESC]elem[ESC]. This paradigm in which Simplify is called with a second argument restricting the domain of one or more parameters is extremely useful. The second argument may also be an inequality, such as $x > 0$. In this case it is implied that x is a positive *real* number. That is, including a variable in an inequality means it is not necessary to state that the variable is real.

In[5]:= `Simplify`$\left[\sqrt{x^2}\right]$

Out[5]= $\sqrt{x^2}$

In[6]:= `Simplify`$\left[\sqrt{x^2}, x > 0\right]$

Out[6]= x

In[7]:= `Simplify`$\left[\sqrt{x^2}, x < 0\right]$

Out[7]= $-x$

It is also possible to restrict variables to the set of integers. To learn about other choices for this second argument, look up `Assumptions` in the Documentation Center.

Here is another example of how the `Simplify` command might be used. Note carefully the distinct uses of := (for defining functions), == (for writing equations), and = (for assigning names):

In[8]:= `Clear[f, x];`
`f[x_] := `$x^3 - 2x + 9$

In[10]:= `Solve[f[x] == 0, x]`

Out[10]= $\left\{\left\{x \rightarrow -2\left(\dfrac{2}{3\left(81-\sqrt{6465}\right)}\right)^{1/3} - \dfrac{\left(\frac{1}{2}\left(81-\sqrt{6465}\right)\right)^{1/3}}{3^{2/3}}\right\},\right.$

$\left\{x \rightarrow \left(1+i\sqrt{3}\right)\left(\dfrac{2}{3\left(81-\sqrt{6465}\right)}\right)^{1/3} + \right.$

$\left.\dfrac{1}{2\times 3^{2/3}}\left(1-i\sqrt{3}\right)\left(\dfrac{1}{2}\left(81-\sqrt{6465}\right)\right)^{1/3}\right\},$

$\left\{x \rightarrow \left(1-i\sqrt{3}\right)\left(\dfrac{2}{3\left(81-\sqrt{6465}\right)}\right)^{1/3} + \right.$

$\left.\left.\dfrac{1}{2\times 3^{2/3}}\left(1+i\sqrt{3}\right)\left(\dfrac{1}{2}\left(81-\sqrt{6465}\right)\right)^{1/3}\right\}\right\}$

In[11]:= `realroot = x /. %[[1]]`

Out[11]= $-2\left(\dfrac{2}{3\left(81-\sqrt{6465}\right)}\right)^{1/3} - \dfrac{\left(\frac{1}{2}\left(81-\sqrt{6465}\right)\right)^{1/3}}{3^{2/3}}$

When you plug a root of a function into the function, you had better get zero:

In[12]:= **f[realroot]**

$$
\text{Out[12]= } 9 - 2\left(-2\left(\frac{2}{3\left(81 - \sqrt{6465}\right)}\right)^{1/3} - \frac{\left(\frac{1}{2}\left(81 - \sqrt{6465}\right)\right)^{1/3}}{3^{2/3}}\right) +
$$

$$
\left(-2\left(\frac{2}{3\left(81 - \sqrt{6465}\right)}\right)^{1/3} - \frac{\left(\frac{1}{2}\left(81 - \sqrt{6465}\right)\right)^{1/3}}{3^{2/3}}\right)^{3}
$$

Really?

In[13]:= **Simplify[%]**

Out[13]= 0

That's better.

The command **FullSimplify** works like **Simplify**, but it applies more transformations to the expression (and consequently it may take longer to execute). In certain instances, it will be able to reduce an expression that **Simplify** cannot.

Manipulating Trigonometric Expressions

Click on the ⎡Algebraic Trig ▾⎤ button under the Algebra Commands tab and you'll find a suite of commands specifically designed to deal with trigonometric expressions. They are **TrigExpand**, **TrigFactor**, **TrigReduce**, **ExpToTrig**, and **TrigToExp**. These commands really shine when you're working with trigonometric functions, and they're great for helping you remember your trigonometric identities:

In[14]:= **Clear[α, β, γ, x];**
TrigExpand[Cos[α + β]]

Out[15]= **Cos[α] Cos[β] - Sin[α] Sin[β]**

Of course we all know that identity. But what about this one?

In[16]:= **TrigExpand[Cos[α + β + γ]]**

Out[16]= **Cos[α] Cos[β] Cos[γ] - Cos[γ] Sin[α] Sin[β] -**
Cos[β] Sin[α] Sin[γ] - Cos[α] Sin[β] Sin[γ]

Here are examples of some other commands:

In[17]:= **TrigFactor[Cos[α] + Cos[β]]**

$$
\text{Out[17]= } 2\,\text{Cos}\left[\frac{\alpha}{2} - \frac{\beta}{2}\right]\text{Cos}\left[\frac{\alpha}{2} + \frac{\beta}{2}\right]
$$

In[18]:= `TrigReduce[1 + (Tan[x])^4]`

Out[18]= $\dfrac{1}{4} \left(3 \, \text{Sec}[x]^4 + \text{Cos}[4\,x] \, \text{Sec}[x]^4\right)$

`TrigExpand` and `TrigFactor` are analogous to `Expand` and `Factor`, but they are designed to deal with trigonometric expressions. `TrigReduce` will rewrite products and powers of trigonometric functions in terms of trigonometric functions with more complicated arguments.

Here is an example where we will demonstrate why $\cos(\pi/9)$ is a root of the polynomial $f(x) = 8\,x^3 - 6\,x - 1$. First we state the (rarely seen) triple angle formula for the cosine function:

In[19]:= `Clear[a];`
`Cos[3 a] // TrigExpand`

Out[20]= $\text{Cos}[a]^3 - 3 \, \text{Cos}[a] \, \text{Sin}[a]^2$

Next, use a replacement rule to manually replace $\sin^2(a)$ with $1 - \cos^2(a)$:

In[21]:= `(Cos[3 a] // TrigExpand) /. Sin[a]^2 → 1 - Cos[a]^2`

Out[21]= $\text{Cos}[a]^3 - 3 \, \text{Cos}[a] \left(1 - \text{Cos}[a]^2\right)$

Finally, expand this out and combine like terms:

In[22]:= `(Cos[3 a] // TrigExpand) /. Sin[a]^2 → 1 - Cos[a]^2 // Expand`

Out[22]= $-3 \, \text{Cos}[a] + 4 \, \text{Cos}[a]^3$

If $a = \frac{\pi}{9}$, then $\cos(3\,a) = \cos\left(\frac{\pi}{3}\right) = \frac{1}{2}$. Hence we have $4\cos(a)^3 - 3\cos(a) = \frac{1}{2}$. Multiply each side by 2, and we see that indeed, $\cos\left(\frac{\pi}{9}\right)$ is a root of the cubic $8\,x^3 - 6\,x - 1$. Reduce confirms this:

In[23]:= `Reduce[8 x^3 - 6 x - 1 == 0, x, Cubics → True]〚2〛 // ComplexExpand`

Out[23]= $x == \text{Cos}\left[\dfrac{\pi}{9}\right]$

As useful as these commands are, it is important to realize that they are not a panacea. Most algebraic identities are at best difficult to uncover through blind application of Algebra Commands. Rather, as in the previous example, they are best used when guided by a clear purpose. Here is another example. It is true that

$$\tfrac{\pi}{4} = \arctan\left(\tfrac{1}{2}\right) + \arctan\left(\tfrac{1}{3}\right)$$

yet no amount of manipulation of the right-hand side using Algebra Commands will produce the value $\frac{\pi}{4}$. How can these tools be used to explore, or to uncover, such an identity? The answer is subtle.

First, recognize that they are only tools. They must be used carefully, with due deliberation and forethought. Owning a hammer doesn't make one a carpenter. That's the bad news. The process is much like traditional pencil-and-paper mathematics in that you pursue an idea and see if it bears fruit. The good news is that the pursuit is made less tedious with *Mathematica* working for you.

Let's explore the identity above. First, for sanity's sake, let's see if it can possibly be true:

In[24]:= `ArcTan`$\left[\dfrac{1}{2}\right]$ `+ ArcTan`$\left[\dfrac{1}{3}\right]$ `// N`

Out[24]= `0.785398`

In[25]:= $\dfrac{\pi}{4}$ `// N`

Out[25]= `0.785398`

Okay, it's believable. Now can we derive a general formula, for which the above identity is but a special case? As a first attempt, we might try commands such as `TrigExpand`, `TrigFactor`, and `TrigReduce` on the expression `ArcTan[a] + ArcTan[b]`. We find that none has any effect. For instance:

In[26]:= `Clear[a, b];`
`ArcTan[a] + ArcTan[b] // TrigExpand`

Out[27]= `ArcTan[a] + ArcTan[b]`

Now we are at a critical juncture in our investigation. We have made no progress, except to learn that *Mathematica* does not appear to have the magic command that will provide us with the type of formula we seek. It is at this point that we need to stop and *think*. What else might we try? Well, what if we took the tangent of the expression `ArcTan[a] + ArcTan[b]`, then tried to expand that? Believe it or not, this gets us somewhere:

In[28]:= `Clear[a, b];`
`Tan[ArcTan[a] + ArcTan[b]] // TrigExpand`

Out[29]= $a \Bigg/ \left(\sqrt{1+a^2}\ \sqrt{1+b^2} \left(\dfrac{1}{\sqrt{1+a^2}\ \sqrt{1+b^2}} - \dfrac{a\,b}{\sqrt{1+a^2}\ \sqrt{1+b^2}} \right) \right) +$

$b \Bigg/ \left(\sqrt{1+a^2}\ \sqrt{1+b^2} \left(\dfrac{1}{\sqrt{1+a^2}\ \sqrt{1+b^2}} - \dfrac{a\,b}{\sqrt{1+a^2}\ \sqrt{1+b^2}} \right) \right)$

In[30]:= `% // Simplify`

Out[30]= $\dfrac{a+b}{1-a\,b}$

This tells us that

$$\frac{a+b}{1-a\,b} = \tan(\arctan(a) + \arctan(b))$$

or, taking the inverse tangent of each side, that

$$\arctan\left(\frac{a+b}{1-a\,b}\right) = \arctan(a) + \arctan(b)$$

It is a simple matter to see that when $a = \frac{1}{2}$ and $b = \frac{1}{3}$, the left-hand side is equal to $\arctan(1)$, which is $\frac{\pi}{4}$, and so this reduces to the identity mentioned previously. This formula is a generalization of that identity. The final task is determining for which values of a and b the formula is valid. We leave this task to the reader.

Exercises 4.6

1. Use `TrigExpand` to examine patterns in the nth angle formulas for the sine function, i.e., identities for $\sin(n\,x)$.

2. Use Algebraic Trig commands to derive the trigonometric identity $\frac{\sin(a\,t)+\sin((2-a)\,t)}{2\sin(t)} = \cos((1-a)\,t)$.

3. Derive a quadruple angle formula for the cosine function, and use it to show that $\cos(\pi/12)$ is a root of $16\,x^4 - 16\,x^2 + 1$.

4.7 Solving General Equations with FindRoot

The `Solve` and `NSolve` commands are built for polynomials. They will also work for equations involving rational functions, and they will sometimes work with equations involving other types of functions. `Reduce` is even more inclusive, and can sometimes be used to describe solutions to equations when `Solve` fails. These are the commands to start with when you need to solve an equation. However, there are still a few things you can do if you don't get the answer you desire.

Often `Solve` and `NSolve` can be effectively used to solve equations involving powers that are rational numbers. For instance, since raising a quantity to the power $\frac{1}{2}$ is the same as taking its square root, equations involving square roots fall into this category:

In[1]:= `Solve`$\left[\sqrt{1 + x + x^2} \,==\, 2,\ x\right]$ `// Grid`

Out[1]=
$$x \to \frac{1}{2}\left(-1 - \sqrt{13}\right)$$
$$x \to \frac{1}{2}\left(-1 + \sqrt{13}\right)$$

In[2]:= $\text{Solve}\left[x^{\frac{1}{3}} == 4 \, x, \, x\right] \, // \, \text{Grid}$

Out[2]= $\begin{array}{l} x \to 0 \\ x \to \dfrac{1}{8} \end{array}$

Solve and NSolve may be able to find solutions to simple equations with the variable appearing inside a logarithm or as an exponent:

In[3]:= $x \, /. \, \text{Solve}[400 \, \text{Log}[10, \, x] == 2, \, x]$

Out[3]= $\left\{10^{1/200}\right\}$

In[4]:= $x \, /. \, \text{Solve}[200 \, (1 + r)^x == 300, \, x]$

⋯ Solve: Inverse functions are being used by Solve, so some solutions may not be found; use Reduce for complete solution information.

Out[4]= $\left\{\dfrac{\text{Log}\left[\frac{3}{2}\right]}{\text{Log}[1 + r]}\right\}$

Here we are warned that although one solution was found, there may be more. In fact, for this example no other real solutions exist, but we have no way of knowing that on the basis of this output. Fortunately, Reduce is effective here, working either over the complex numbers (which it does by default), or over the reals where we see that the solution above is indeed unique:

In[5]:= $\text{Reduce}[200 \, (1 + r)^x == 300, \, x]$

Out[5]= $C[1] \in \mathbb{Z} \, \&\& \, 1 + r \neq 0 \, \&\& \, \text{Log}[1 + r] \neq 0 \, \&\& \, x == \dfrac{2 \, i \, \pi \, C[1] - \text{Log}[2] + \text{Log}[3]}{\text{Log}[1 + r]}$

In[6]:= $\text{Reduce}[200 \, (1 + r)^x == 300, \, x, \, \text{Reals}]$

Out[6]= $\left(-1 < r < 0 \, \&\& \, x == \dfrac{-\text{Log}[2] + \text{Log}[3]}{\text{Log}[1 + r]}\right) \, || \, \left(r > 0 \, \&\& \, x == \dfrac{-\text{Log}[2] + \text{Log}[3]}{\text{Log}[1 + r]}\right)$

On occasion these solving commands may come up empty, even when a unique solution exists:

In[7]:= $\text{Solve}\left[\text{Sin}[x] == 2 - x^2, \, x\right]$

⋯ Solve: This system cannot be solved with the methods available to Solve.

Out[7]= $\text{Solve}\left[\text{Sin}[x] == 2 - x^2, \, x\right]$

In[8]:= $\text{NSolve}\left[\text{Sin}[x] == 2 - x^2, \, x\right]$

⋯ NSolve: This system cannot be solved with the methods available to NSolve.

Out[8]= $\text{NSolve}\left[\text{Sin}[x] == 2 - x^2, \, x\right]$

In[9]:= `Reduce[Sin[x] == 2 - x², x]`

··· Reduce: This system cannot be solved with the methods available to Reduce.

Out[9]= `Reduce[Sin[x] == 2 - x², x]`

There are powerful numerical techniques for approximating solutions to equations such as these. FindRoot is the final equation-solving command that we introduce. It is your last line of defense. It is *very* robust, and adapts its methodology according to the problem it is fed. It's tenacious, but it's also old-school. To use it you must give it one or more numerical values as a starting point. Like a hound dog it will hunt down a solution for each starting value, iteratively using its current position to zero-in on each solution. It is likely to home in on the solution nearest each starting point, so choosing good starting points is key. A plot is helpful in this endeavor. A simple approach is to Plot two functions, the left side and right side of the equation you wish to solve. The solutions are the x coordinates of the points where the curves intersect. For instance, here's a view of the functions in the equation above:

In[10]:= `Plot[{Sin[x], 2 - x²}, {x, -2, 2}]`

Out[10]=

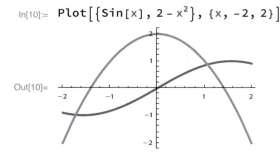

We expect solutions near $x = -1.6$ and $x = 1$. The first argument of the FindRoot command is an equation, the second is a list whose first member is the variable to be solved for, and whose second member is a single guess or list of guesses for the roots. To zero-in on a single solution once you know roughly where it is, use the FindRoot command like this:

In[11]:= `FindRoot[Sin[x] == 2 - x², {x, -1.6}]`

Out[11]= `{x → -1.72847}`

To find solutions beginning with several guesses, list them between curly brackets:

In[12]:= `FindRoot[Sin[x] == 2 - x², {x, {-1.6, 1}}]`

Out[12]= `{x → {-1.72847, 1.06155}}`

FindRoot can accept many initial guesses and will return one solution for each guess, but they may not all be unique.

In[13]:= `FindRoot[Sin[x] == 2 - x², {x, {-5, -1.6, 0, 1, 10}}]`

Out[13]= `{x → {-1.72847, -1.72847, 1.06155, 1.06155, 1.06155}}`

To have all internal calculations performed with n-digit precision you can use the optional argument `WorkingPrecision`:

In[14]:= `x /. FindRoot[Sin[x] == 2 - x², {x, 1}, WorkingPrecision → 400]`

Out[14]= `1.06154977463138382560203340351989934205887417838924148608498893580`
`932536580780136816051477221697952002055235175844381824899157523867`
`951851051980189849714178969462478131788736859073994332839024476865`
`288997963513182054066331171612084604692146632416602626438286949734`
`162187208102212531109550460260550693607930130987052525334585125583`
`233974120623830354271453579828462448472938661853701985416588367671`
`1994`

This technique of first estimating a solution with a plot and then using `FindRoot` to zero-in on it is very robust in that it will work on almost any equation you wish to solve (provided that a solution exists). It does have several drawbacks, however. First, it is a strictly numerical command; it cannot be used when there are more variables than there are equations. For instance, it won't be able to solve $x + y = 1$ for x; the solution must a number (or a list of numbers if there are several equations). Second, it may be tedious to find an appropriate domain for a plot, one in which a point of intersection resides. Third, it is often difficult to discern whether or not other intersection points might be present to the left or right of those you have already found. And finally, for some equations the algorithm will fail altogether. For instance, `FindRoot` relies at times on a well-known algorithm, the Newton–Raphson method, to produce its solutions. It is also well known that this method doesn't work for all combinations of equations and initial guesses, even when a unique solution exists:

In[15]:= `FindRoot[200 (1.05)ˣ == 300, {x, 2700}]`

••• FindRoot: Failed to converge to the requested accuracy or precision within 100 iterations.

Out[15]= `{x → 650.407}`

The output here is not correct (so the warning message is welcome). You can usually avoid this sort of thing if you make a reasonable initial guess. This sort of problem is unlikely if you follow our advice and make a few plots first, using the plots to generate reasonable initial guesses for `FindRoot`.

In[16]:= `Plot[{200 (1.05)ˣ, 300}, {x, 0, 15}]`

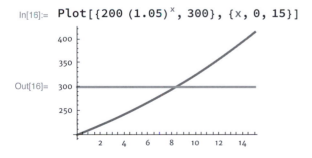

In[17]:= **FindRoot[200 (1.05)^X == 300, {x, 8}]**

Out[17]= {x → 8.31039}

Let's look at another example: solve the equation $\log(x) = x^3 - x$:

In[18]:= **Solve[Log[x] == x^3 - x, x]**

    ... Solve: This system cannot be solved with the methods available to Solve.

Out[18]= **Solve[Log[x] == -x + x^3, x]**

In[19]:= **NSolve[Log[x] == x^3 - x, x]**

    ... NSolve: This system cannot be solved with the methods available to NSolve.

Out[19]= **NSolve[Log[x] == -x + x^3, x]**

In[20]:= **Reduce[Log[x] == x^3 - x, x]**

    ... Reduce: This system cannot be solved with the methods available to Reduce.

Out[20]= **Reduce[Log[x] == -x + x^3, x]**

You shouldn't allow these outputs to cause you to give up your hunt for a solution. Solve, NSolve, and Reduce may be unable to find a solution, but that doesn't mean one does not exist. In your dealings with computers, you should live by the maxim made famous by Ronald Reagan: "Trust, but verify." In that spirit, we endeavor to make a plot and see what is going on:

In[21]:= **Plot[{Log[x], x^3 - x}, {x, 0, 10}]**

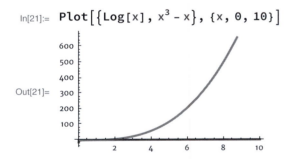

One of the functions is barely visible. It is not uncommon for one function to dwarf another when viewed over certain domains. To make things clearer, we render the Log function thick, dashed, and blue, and the cubic red.

In[22]:= `Plot[{Log[x], x³ - x}, {x, 0, 10},`
`PlotStyle → {Directive[Thick, Dashed, Blue], Red}]`

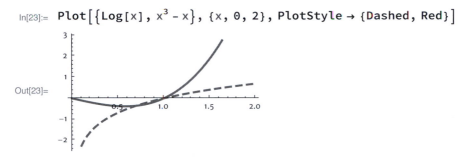

Suspicion confirmed: the `Log` function is quite flat compared to the cubic on this domain. Perhaps they intersect over on the left, somewhere between 0 and 2. Try again: Edit the iterator above, specifying the new plot domain, and reenter the cell:

In[23]:= `Plot[{Log[x], x³ - x}, {x, 0, 2}, PlotStyle → {Dashed, Red}]`

Bingo! Let's see if `FindRoot` can find these solutions:

In[24]:= `FindRoot[Log[x] == x³ - x, {x, {.7, 1}}]`

Out[24]= `{x → {0.699661, 1.}}`

Is $x = 1$ an *exact* solution? Yes: Plug it in by hand to the original equation, or do this:

In[25]:= `Log[x] == x³ - x /. x → 1`

Out[25]= `True`

It is worth noting that you can manipulate any equation into the form *expression* == 0 simply by subtracting the original quantity on the right from each side of the equation. Solving the resulting equation is then a matter of finding the roots of *expression*. The obvious advantage to this approach is that the roots are easy to read off of a plot, since they fall directly on the labeled x axis. Here is the graph for the last example when presented this way. Note that adding `PlotRange→.5` guarantees that the x axis will be included in the output graphic, even if you are unlucky enough to choose a domain on which there are no solutions.

In[26]:= `Plot[{Log[x] - x³ + x}, {x, 0, 2}, PlotRange → .5]`

Out[26]=

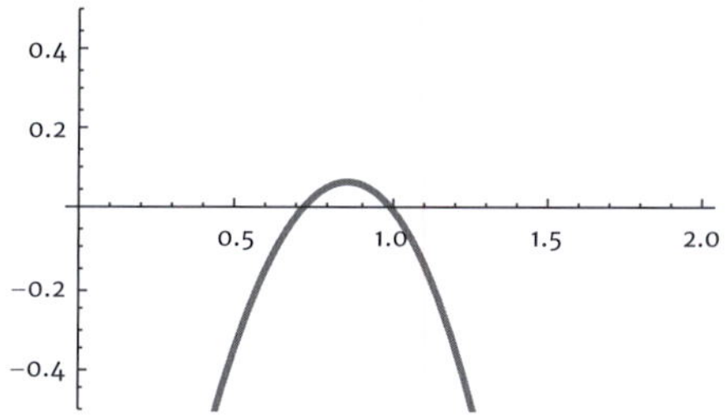

The roots, of course, are the same as the solutions we found earlier. `FindRoot` will report the same output regardless of whether you input the equation `Log[x] == -x + x³` or the equation `Log[x] - x³ + x == 0`. In fact, you can simply use `Log[x] - x³ + x` (and forgo the `== 0`) when using `FindRoot`. The name "FindRoot" makes good sense in this light. You can use whichever approach seems easier to you.

In[27]:= `FindRoot[Log[x] - x³ + x, {x, {0.7, 1}}]`

Out[27]= `{x → {0.699661, 1.}}`

Exercises 4.7

1. Approximate the solutions to the equation $1 - x^2 = \sin x$.

2. Approximate three of the solutions to the equation $e^{-x^2} = \sin x$.

3. Is it true that $e^{-\pi^2} = \sin \pi$?

4.8   Solving Difference Equations with RSolve

Difference equations (also called recurrence relations) were discussed in Section 3.13. Suppose we are given a difference equation for a sequence $a[n]$. Let's say that the nth term of the sequence is always twice the previous term, so the difference equation is $a[n] = 2\,a[n-1]$. How can we find an *explicit formula* for $a[n]$, not in terms of $a[n-1]$, but as a function of n? It is not difficult in this example to find a solution by hand, but how can *Mathematica* be employed for the purpose of solving this or any other difference equation? The command that you need is called `RSolve`.

In[1]:= `Clear[a, n];`
        `RSolve[a[n] == 2 a[n - 1], a[n], n]`

Out[2]= $\{\{a[n] \to 2^{-1+n}\,C[1]\}\}$

If no initial conditions are given (so the first argument is a difference equation and nothing else), one or more constant terms may be generated, as seen above. `C[1]` represents the constant in the output above. Any specific real or complex numerical value for this constant value will give, according to the previous output, a solution to the difference equation. The first argument may also be a list of equations. For instance, here we solve the same difference equation, but also specify the initial value $a[0] = 1/3$.

In[3]:= `RSolve[{a[n] == 2 a[n - 1], a[0] == 1 / 3}, a[n], n]`

Out[3]= $\left\{\left\{a[n] \rightarrow \dfrac{2^n}{3}\right\}\right\}$

RSolve is most useful when dealing with somewhat more complicated difference equations. Here we ask it solve the difference equation that defines the Fibonacci numbers:

In[4]:= `RSolve[{a[n] == a[n - 1] + a[n - 2], a[1] == 1, a[2] == 1}, a[n], n]`

Out[4]= `{{a[n] → Fibonacci[n]}}`

Yes, these are indeed the Fibonacci numbers:

In[5]:= `Table[a[n] /. %[[1]], {n, 10}]`

Out[5]= `{1, 1, 2, 3, 5, 8, 13, 21, 34, 55}`

Here is a logistic growth difference equation that RSolve cannot handle:

In[6]:= `RSolve[a[n + 1] == 3 a[n] - .05 a[n]`^{2}`, a[n], n]`

Out[6]= `RSolve[a[1 + n] == 3 a[n] - 0.05 a[n]`^{2}`, a[n], n]`

And here's an example of a logistic growth equation that RSolve can handle:

In[7]:= `RSolve[a[n + 1] == 2 a[n] - `$\dfrac{1}{3}$` a[n]`^{2}`, a[n], n]`

Out[7]= $\left\{\left\{a[n] \rightarrow 3 - 3\, e^{2^n\, C[1]}\right\}\right\}$

Adding an initial condition forces it to use Solve internally, and in this case it is not able to determine if it has found a unique solution. We look at the first few values as a check:

In[8]:= `RSolve[{a[n + 1] == 2 a[n] - `$\dfrac{1}{3}$` a[n]`^{2}`, a[0] == 1}, a[n], n]`

> ••• Solve: Inverse functions are being used by Solve, so some solutions may not be found; use Reduce for complete solution information.

Out[8]= $\left\{\left\{a[n] \rightarrow -3^{1-2^n}\left(2^{2^n} - 3^{2^n}\right)\right\}\right\}$

In[9]:= `Table[a[n] /. %[[1]], {n, 0, 3}]`

Out[9]= $\left\{1, \dfrac{5}{3}, \dfrac{65}{27}, \dfrac{6305}{2187}\right\}$

We can also look at the solution to the difference equation *without* the initial condition (three outputs ago), and do the solving ourselves:

In[10]:= **Reduce$\left[3 - 3\,e^{c} == 1,\, c,\, \text{Reals}\right]$**

Out[10]= $c == \text{Log}[2] - \text{Log}[3]$

So $c = \ln\frac{2}{3}$, and the solution is $a(n) = 3 - 3\,e^{2^{n}\ln\left(\frac{2}{3}\right)} = 3 - 3\,(2/3)^{2^{n}}$. It is now clear from an algebraic viewpoint that this function will quickly approach the value 3. A plot confirms this:

In[11]:= **Plot$\left[3 - 3\,(2\,/\,3)^{2^{n}},\, \{n,\, 0,\, 5\}\right]$**

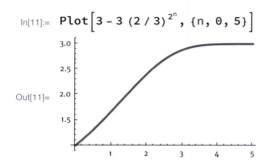

Out[11]=

Moreover, using NestList to generate the first few terms of the sequence generated by the original difference equation, we see that it agrees with our solution. The use of NestList to generate terms of a sequence defined by a difference equation is discussed at the end of Section 3.13.

In[12]:= **NestList$\left[2\,\# - \frac{1}{3}\,\#^{2}\,\&,\, 1,\, 3\right]$**

Out[12]= $\left\{1,\, \dfrac{5}{3},\, \dfrac{65}{27},\, \dfrac{6305}{2187}\right\}$

In[13]:= **Table$\left[3 - 3\,(2\,/\,3)^{2^{n}},\, \{n,\, 0,\, 3\}\right]$**

Out[13]= $\left\{1,\, \dfrac{5}{3},\, \dfrac{65}{27},\, \dfrac{6305}{2187}\right\}$

⚠ At times it may be helpful to note that the second argument to RSolve can be simply the symbol a (rather than a[n]), and the output will be a pure function expression for a. Pure functions are discussed in Section 8.4.

In[14]:= **RSolve[{a[n] == 2 a[n - 1], a[0] == 1}, a, n]**

Out[14]= $\left\{\left\{a \rightarrow \text{Function}\left[\{n\},\, 2^{n}\right]\right\}\right\}$

Exercises 4.8

1. Suppose a \$30 000 car was purchased with no money down, using a five-year loan with an annual interest rate of 7 percent, compounded monthly. This means that each month interest is compounded at the monthly rate of $\frac{.07}{12}$, while the principle is reduced by the amount p of the monthly payment.

   a. Calculate the monthly payment.

   b.   Make a table breaking down each payment as principle and interest for the 60-month loan period.

2. Suppose that the value of a new automobile is $30 000, and that it loses 10 percent of its value each year. That is, at the end of each year it is worth only 90 percent of what it was worth at the beginning of that year. When will it be worth $8000?

4.9 Solving Systems of Equations and Inequalities

It is sometimes necessary to solve several equations simultaneously. For instance, what values of x and y satisfy both $2x - 39y = 79$ and $7x + 5y = 800$? To find out, use `Solve`, `NSolve`, or `Reduce` with a *list* of equations as the first argument and a list of variables to be solved for (such as {x,y}) as the second argument:

In[1]:= `Solve[{2 x - 39 y == 79, 7 x + 5 y == 800}, {x, y}]`

Out[1]= $\left\{\left\{x \to \dfrac{31\,595}{283}, y \to \dfrac{1047}{283}\right\}\right\}$

You can leave out the second argument entirely if you want to solve for *all* the variables appearing in the equations:

In[2]:= `Solve[{2 x - 39 y == 79, 7 x + 5 y == 800}]`

Out[2]= $\left\{\left\{x \to \dfrac{31\,595}{283}, y \to \dfrac{1047}{283}\right\}\right\}$

You can easily use generic coefficients to generate a general formula for solving similar systems:

In[3]:= `Clear[a, b, c, d, e, f, x, y];`
`Solve[{a * x + b * y == c, d * x + e * y == f}, {x, y}]`

Out[4]= $\left\{\left\{x \to -\dfrac{c\,e - b\,f}{b\,d - a\,e}, y \to -\dfrac{-c\,d + a\,f}{b\,d - a\,e}\right\}\right\}$

The `Solve` command works very well for linear equations (like those above). It also does a good job with systems of polynomials. Here is an example showing the points of intersection of a circle and a parabola:

In[5]:= `ContourPlot[{x² + y² == 4, y + 1 == (x - 1)²}, {x, -2, 2}, {y, -2, 2}]`

Out[5]=

It turns out that there are two real solutions (you can see them on the plot) and two complex ones. One of the real ones is the point (2, 0). The other is:

In[6]:= **Solve[{x² + y² == 4, y + 1 == (x − 1)²}]〚2〛 // Column**

Out[6]=

$$x \to \frac{1}{3}\left(2 - \frac{1}{\left(28-3\sqrt{87}\right)^{1/3}} - \left(28 - 3\sqrt{87}\right)^{1/3}\right)$$

$$y \to \frac{1}{9}\left(-6 + \frac{1}{\left(28-3\sqrt{87}\right)^{2/3}} + \frac{2}{\left(28-3\sqrt{87}\right)^{1/3}} + 2\left(28 - 3\sqrt{87}\right)^{1/3} + \left(28 - 3\sqrt{87}\right)^{2/3}\right)$$

We won't list the complex solutions, as they're even nastier. Here's another example:

In[7]:= **ContourPlot[{y == x², y⁷ + 2 x² == 1}, {x, −2, 2}, {y, −1.5, 4}]**

Out[7]=

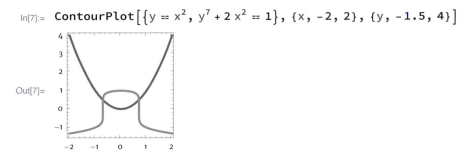

We can approximate the two real solutions seen in the plot:

In[8]:= **NSolve[{y == x², y⁷ + 2 x² == 1}, {x, y}, Reals]**

Out[8]= {{x → 0.70448, y → 0.496292}, {x → −0.70448, y → 0.496292}}

If we include complex solutions (by deleting the third argument Reals in the input above) this system has 14 solutions, which makes sense since we can substitute x^2 for y in the second equation to produce a polynomial in x of degree 14.

In[9]:= **Style[Grid[NSolve[{y == x², y⁷ + 2 x² == 1}, {x, y}],**
       Alignment → Left, Dividers → Gray], FontSize → 8]

Out[9]=

x → 0.978813 − 0.298975 i	y → 0.868688 − 0.585282 i
x → 0.978813 + 0.298975 i	y → 0.868688 + 0.585282 i
x → 0.73046 − 0.780978 i	y → −0.0763556 − 1.14095 i
x → 0.73046 + 0.780978 i	y → −0.0763556 + 1.14095 i
x → 0.268914 − 1.05489 i	y → −1.04048 − 0.56735 i
x → 0.268914 + 1.05489 i	y → −1.04048 + 0.56735 i
x → −0.268914 − 1.05489 i	y → −1.04048 + 0.56735 i
x → −0.268914 + 1.05489 i	y → −1.04048 − 0.56735 i
x → 0.70448	y → 0.496292
x → −0.73046 − 0.780978 i	y → −0.0763556 + 1.14095 i
x → −0.73046 + 0.780978 i	y → −0.0763556 − 1.14095 i
x → −0.978813 + 0.298975 i	y → 0.868688 − 0.585282 i
x → −0.978813 − 0.298975 i	y → 0.868688 + 0.585282 i
x → −0.70448	y → 0.496292

Reduce is useful for solving systems of inequalities. Consider the region bounded by the lines $y = -2x - 1$ and $y = x - 1$, and the parabola $y = x^2 + 1$.

In[10]:= `Show[RegionPlot[{y > -2 x - 1 && y > x - 2 && y < -x² + 1}, {x, -2, 2},`
`{y, -2, 2}], Plot[{-2 x - 1, x - 2, -x² + 1}, {x, -2, 2}]]`

Out[10]=

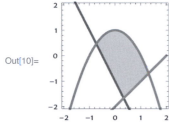

Reduce can describe the region enclosed by the curves.

In[11]:= `Reduce[{y > -2 x - 1, y > x - 2, y < x² + 1}, {x, y}]`

Out[11]= $\left(x \le \dfrac{1}{3} \ \&\& \ -1 - 2x < y < 1 + x^2 \right) \ || \ \left(x > \dfrac{1}{3} \ \&\& \ -2 + x < y < 1 + x^2 \right)$

Just as there are single equations that can foil the Reduce, Solve, and NSolve commands, there are systems of equations that can as well.

In[12]:= `Reduce[{y == eˣ, y == -x² + 2}]`

⋯ Reduce: This system cannot be solved with the methods available to Reduce.

Out[12]= `Reduce[{y == eˣ, y == 2 - x²}]`

In such situations one can use FindRoot to approximate a solution. Give as the first argument the list of equations. Follow that with an additional argument for each variable. Each of these arguments is of the form {*variable*, *guess*}, where the guess is your best estimate of the actual value for that variable. Use a plot to help you make your guess:

In[13]:= `ContourPlot[{y == eˣ, y == -x² + 2}, {x, -2, 1}, {y, 0, 3}]`

Out[13]=

In[14]:= `FindRoot[{y == eˣ, y == -x² + 2}, {x, -1.5}, {y, .2}]`

Out[14]= $\{x \to -1.31597, \ y \to 0.268213\}$

In[15]:= **FindRoot**$\left[\left\{y == e^x, y == -x^2 + 2\right\}, \{x, .5\}, \{y, 1.5\}\right]$

Out[15]= $\{x \to 0.537274, y \to 1.71134\}$

Exercises 4.9

1. Use a graph to estimate the solutions to the system of equations $y = x^2$ and $y = 4\sin(3x)$. Then find a command that will find or approximate the real-valued solutions.

5

Calculus

5.1 Computing Limits

An understanding of limits is fundamental to an understanding of calculus. Let's start by defining a couple of functions:

```
In[1]:= Clear[f, g, x];
        f[x_] := Sin[x] / x;
        g[x_] := 1 / x
```

Note that $x = 0$ is not in the domain of either of these functions. How do they behave as x approaches 0, that is, as x assumes values very close to 0? A plot is a sensible way to approach this question:

```
In[4]:= Plot[f[x], {x, -10, 10}, Exclusions → 0,
        ExclusionsStyle → {Dotted, White}, PlotTheme → "Web"]
```

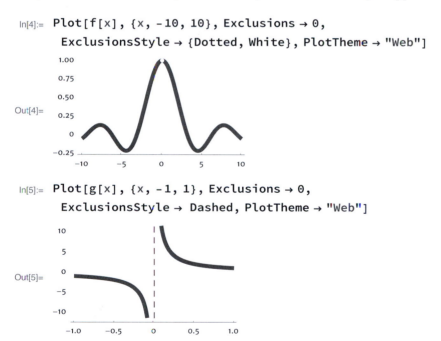

```
In[5]:= Plot[g[x], {x, -1, 1}, Exclusions → 0,
        ExclusionsStyle → Dashed, PlotTheme → "Web"]
```

The two outcomes are strikingly different, and they illustrate the likely possibilities for similar investigations. The function $f(x)$ assumes values that approach 1 as x approaches 0. The function g has a vertical asymptote at $x = 0$; as x approaches 0 from the right, g assumes values that approach $+\infty$, while as x approaches 0 from the left, g assumes values that approach $-\infty$.

We can check this numerically by making a table of values. Here is a table of values for f as x approaches 0 from the right:

In[6]:= `data = Table[{N[10^{-n}], N[f[10^{-n}], 15]}, {n, 1, 5}];`
`Text@TableForm[data, TableHeadings → {None, {"x", "f(x)"}}]`

x	$f(x)$
0.1	0.998334166468282
0.01	0.999983333416666
0.001	0.999999833333342
0.0001	0.999999998333333
0.00001	0.999999999983333

Out[6]=

A button for the Limit command can be found under the Calculus Commands tab $d\int\Sigma$ in the Basic Commands section of the Basic Math Assistant palette. The `Limit` command provides an easy way to investigate the behavior of functions as the independent variable approaches some particular value (such as 0). The first argument to the `Limit` command is the expression for which you wish to find a limiting value. The second argument ($x \to 0$ in these examples) specifies the independent variable and the value which it will approach.

In[7]:= `Limit[f[x], x → 0]`
Out[7]= `1`

This is a two-sided limit, which exists if and only if the limits from the left and right agree. The two-sided limit of the function g as x approaches 0 *does not exist* since the limit from the right is $+\infty$ while the limit from the left is $-\infty$.

In[8]:= `Limit[g[x], x → 0]`
Out[8]= `Indeterminate`

The output `Indeterminate` means *Mathematica* is unable to determine the value of the limit. But the one-sided limits do exist for $g(x)$ as x approaches 0. We can specify limits *from the right* by adding the optional argument `Direction → "FromAbove"`. To get limits *from the left* add `Direction → "FromBelow"`. Note that in practice you will only need to type the first few characters of Direction before a command completion popup will offer to complete the input.

In[9]:= `Limit[g[x], x → 0, Direction → "FromAbove"]`
Out[9]= ∞

In[10]:= `Limit[g[x], x → 0, Direction → "FromBelow"]`
Out[10]= $-\infty$

It is even possible to input limits in a way that looks like traditional mathematical notation. To get the lim symbol shown below, type ⎡ESC⎤ lim ⎡ESC⎤ in an input cell. Next highlight lim and click the ▪ button in the Typesetting section of the palette to create a box into which you can type $x \to 0^+$.

In[11]:= $\displaystyle\lim_{x \to 0^+} g[x]$

Out[11]= ∞

In[12]:= $\displaystyle\lim_{x \to 0^-} g[x]$

Out[12]= $-\infty$

Mathematica can also compute limits at infinity. Limits at $\pm\infty$ are always one-sided limits. You may use the ∞ symbol from the Basic Math Assistant palette, or type `Infinity`.

In[13]:= `Limit[g[x], x → Infinity]`

Out[13]= 0

In[14]:= `Limit[g[x], x → -∞]`

Out[14]= 0

Taking another glance at the graph of g, you can see that as the value of x gets large, the value of $g(x)$ approaches 0. A table of values is also useful in this regard:

In[15]:= `data = Table[N@{10ⁿ, g[10ⁿ]}, {n, 1, 5}];`
`Text@TableForm[data,`
`    TableHeadings → {None, {"x", "g(x)"}}, TableAlignments → "."]`

Out[15]=

x	g(x)
10.	0.1
100.	0.01
1000.	0.001
10 000.	0.0001
100 000.	0.00001

Note also that some functions will not have one-sided limits:

In[16]:= `Limit[Sin[x], x → ∞]`

Out[16]= `Indeterminate`

But the optional argument below provides some useful information about $\sin x$ as x approaches infinity.

In[17]:= `Limit[Sin[x], x → ∞, Method → {"AllowIndeterminateOutput" → False}]`

Out[17]= `Interval[{-1, 1}]`

The output here indicates that the sine function assumes values in the interval from −1 to 1 without approaching a single limiting value as *x* approaches infinity. This is consistent with our knowledge of the sine function; a plot provides additional confirmation:

In[18]:= `Plot[Sin[x], {x, 0, 30}]`

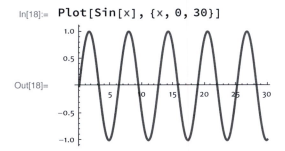

Out[18]=

Piecewise functions provide the standard examples of functions for which the left and right directional limits differ.

In[19]:= $h[x\_] := \begin{cases} x^2 + x + 1 & x \le 0 \\ \text{Sin}[x] & x > 0 \end{cases}$

In[20]:= `Plot[h[x], {x, -1, 1}]`

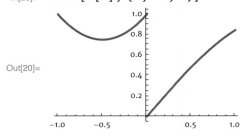

Out[20]=

In[21]:= `Limit[h[x], x → 0, Direction → "FromBelow"]`

Out[21]= 1

In[22]:= `Limit[h[x], x → 0, Direction → "FromAbove"]`

Out[22]= 0

In some cases there may be one or more parameters appearing in an expression other than the one whose limiting value we wish to determine. For instance, what happens to an expression of the form $\frac{1-x^n}{n}$ as $x \to 0$ from the right?

In[23]:= `Clear[x, n];`

$\text{Limit}\left[\dfrac{1 - x^n}{n}, x \to 0, \text{Direction} \to \text{"FromAbove"}\right]$

Out[24]= $\text{ConditionalExpression}\left[\dfrac{1}{n}, n > 0\right]$

The solution tells us that as long as $n > 0$ the limit is $\frac{1}{n}$. But what if we want the limit for a different condition? Assumptions can be specified using an optional argument of that name:

In[25]:= `Limit`$\left[\dfrac{1 - x^n}{n}, \; x \to 0, \; \text{Direction} \to \text{"FromAbove"}, \; \text{Assumptions} \to n < 0\right]$

Out[25]= ∞

Exercises 5.1

1. Use the `Limit` command to find $\lim_{x \to 2} \frac{6x-12}{x^2-4}$ and $\lim_{x \to -2} \frac{6x-12}{x^2-4}$. Then use a graph to explain these answers.

2. Use a graph to examine the behavior of functions of the form $y = x \sin\left(\frac{b}{x}\right)$ for large values of b and use your graph to predict $\lim_{x \to +\infty} x \sin\left(\frac{b}{x}\right)$. Use the `Limit` command to confirm your answer.

3. The function $f(x) = \sqrt{x^2 + 2x + 3} - x$ has very different behavior as x approaches $+\infty$ and x approaches $-\infty$. Use the `Table` command to examine this function for large positive and negative values of x.

5.2   Working with Difference Quotients

Producing and Simplifying Difference Quotients

It is easy to produce simplified difference quotients using the command `DifferenceQuotient`. Get the $\triangle$ character from the Typesetting section of the Basic Math Assistant palette, and do not put a space between it and x, for you are creating a new symbol whose name is $\triangle$x, rather than multiplying $\triangle$ by x.

In[1]:= `Clear[g, x, Δx]`
`g[x_] := x³;`
`DifferenceQuotient[g[x], {x, Δx}]`

Out[3]= $3 x^2 + 3 x \, \Delta x + \Delta x^2$

But it is much more informative to define a new command that gives an unsimplified version of the difference quotient and then simplify it step by step.

In[4]:= `Clear[diffquot, x, Δx];`
`diffquot[f_] :=` $\dfrac{f[x + \Delta x] - f[x]}{\Delta x}$

Now we can produce an unsimplified difference quotient for any function:

In[6]:= `diffquot[g]`

Out[6]= $\dfrac{-x^3 + (x + \triangle x)^3}{\triangle x}$

We can "drive" *Mathematica* through the simplification step by step using Evaluate in Place from the Evaluation dropdown menu to evaluate highlighted parts of a cell. First highlight $(x + \triangle x)^3$ in the last output, and then hit the Expand button on the palette so that the input cell looks like this:

$$\dfrac{-x^3 + \textbf{Expand}\left[(x + \triangle x)^3\right]}{\triangle x}$$

Now highlight only Expand$\left[(x + \triangle x)^3\right]$ by triple-clicking on the word Expand, and use Evaluate in Place to perform the expansion. The cell will then look like this:

$$\dfrac{-x^3 + x^3 + 3\,x^2\,\triangle x + 3\,x\,\triangle x^2 + \triangle x^3}{\triangle x}$$

If you hit SHIFT⊣ENTER *Mathematica* will evaluate the entire input, not just the part you highlighted, and your result will be different.

Now highlight the entire numerator, and hit the Simplify button. Next highlight the numerator by triple-clicking on Simplify and again use Evaluate in Place. The x^3 cancels with the $-x^3$, and $\triangle x$ is factored out of the remaining three summands. You will then have this:

$$\dfrac{\left(\triangle x\,\left(3\,x^2 + 3\,x\,\triangle x + \triangle x^2\right)\right)}{\triangle x}$$

Highlight the entire expression and push Cancel[*expr*], which can be found under the More ▼ button. The $\triangle x$ on top cancels with the one on the bottom, and your output is the simplified difference quotient.

In[7]:= $\textbf{Cancel}\left[\dfrac{\left(\triangle x\,\left(3\,x^2 + 3\,x\,\triangle x + \triangle x^2\right)\right)}{\triangle x}\right]$

Out[7]= $3\,x^2 + 3\,x\,\triangle x + \triangle x^2$

That's it! You've just simplified a difference quotient painlessly, with no dropped minus signs, and without skipping a step. We encourage you to do this for five or six functions of your choosing; you might even find it fun.

Average Rate of Change

Once you have entered the cell defining the `diffquot` command, you can work with specific values of x and Δx to find the *average* rate of change of a function as the independent variable ranges from x to $x + \Delta x$:

In[8]:= `Clear[f, x, Δx];`

$$f[x\_] := \frac{\text{Sin}[\pi\, x]}{x}$$

In[10]:= `diffquot[f]`

Out[10]= $$\frac{-\dfrac{\text{Sin}[\pi\, x]}{x} + \dfrac{\text{Sin}[\pi\,(x+\Delta x)]}{x+\Delta x}}{\Delta x}$$

You can find the average rate of change of f from $x = 2$ to $x = 2.5$ as follows:

In[11]:= `diffquot[f] /. {x → 2, Δx → 0.5}`

Out[11]= `0.8`

Recall from the last chapter (Section 4.2) that the replacement rule `/. {x → 2, Δx → 0.5}` instructs *Mathematica* to replace x by 2 and Δx by 0.5. The average rate of change of f from $x = 2$ to $x = 2.1$ is:

In[12]:= `diffquot[f] /. {x → 2, Δx → 0.1}`

Out[12]= `1.47151`

Here is a table of values for the difference quotient of f at $x = 2$ for various small values of Δx. For this example we present our table using `Grid`, but we could just as easily use `TableForm`.

In[13]:= `data = Table[{Δx, diffquot[f]} /. {x → 2, Δx → N[10⁻ⁿ]}, {n, 1, 5}];`

$$\texttt{dataWithHeadings = Prepend}\Big[\texttt{data, }\Big\{\texttt{"Δx", "}\frac{f\,(2+\Delta x) - f\,(2)}{\Delta x}\texttt{"}\Big\}\Big];$$

`Text@Grid[dataWithHeadings,`
`    Alignment → Left, Dividers → {Center, 2 → True}]`

Out[14]=

Δx	$\dfrac{f\,(2+\Delta x)-f\,(2)}{\Delta x}$
0.1	1.47151
0.01	1.56272
0.001	1.57001
0.0001	1.57072
0.00001	1.57079

Instantaneous Rate of Change

The *instantaneous* rate of change at $x = 2$ is found by taking the limit as Δx approaches 0 of the difference quotient at $x = 2$:

In[15]:= `diffquot[f] /. x → 2`

Out[15]= $\dfrac{\text{Sin}[\pi\ (2 + \Delta x)]}{\Delta x\ (2 + \Delta x)}$

In[16]:= `Limit[%, Δx → 0]`

Out[16]= $\dfrac{\pi}{2}$

In[17]:= `N[%, 10]`

Out[17]= `1.570796327`

Note that this result is consistent with the table that we computed above.

Exercises 5.2

1. Find the difference quotient of $f(x) = \dfrac{1}{x^2}$ and use Evaluate in Place to simplify the expression step by step.

2. Find the limit of the difference quotient for $f(x) = \dfrac{1}{x^2}$ as $\Delta x \to 0$.

3. Find the difference quotient of $f(x) = \sqrt{x}$ and use Evaluate in Place to simplify the expression step by step.

4. Find the limit of the difference quotient for $f(x) = \sqrt{x}$ as $\Delta x \to 0$.

5.3   The Derivative

Of course there is a simpler way to take derivatives than to compute the instantaneous rate of change as above. This is an instance where the *Mathematica* syntax matches that of traditional mathematical notation. For the function f defined above, the derivative can be found as follows:

In[1]:= `f'[x]`

Out[1]= $\dfrac{\pi\ \text{Cos}[\pi\ x]}{x} - \dfrac{\text{Sin}[\pi\ x]}{x^2}$

If you check this using the quotient rule, your answer may look slightly different. You can simplify the output above by highlighting it and pushing the `Simplify` button on the palette, or by entering:

In[2]:= `Simplify[%]`

Out[2]= $\dfrac{\pi \, x \, \text{Cos}[\pi \, x] \, - \, \text{Sin}[\pi \, x]}{x^2}$

This is exactly what you would obtain if you worked by hand using the quotient rule. We can evaluate the derivative at any value of x:

In[3]:= `f'[2]`

Out[3]= $\dfrac{\pi}{2}$

A plot of a function and the tangent line to the function at a point (at $x = 2$, for example) can be produced as follows. The expression representing the line is obtained from the *point-slope* formula for a line, where the point on the line is $(2, f(2))$, and the slope of the line is $f'(2)$. You can zoom in (or out) by changing the bounds on the iterator. Try $\{x, 1.9, 2.1\}$ to zoom in on the two graphs near $x = 2$.

In[4]:= `Plot[{f[x], f[2] + f'[2] * (x - 2)}, {x, 1.5, 2.5}]`

Out[4]=

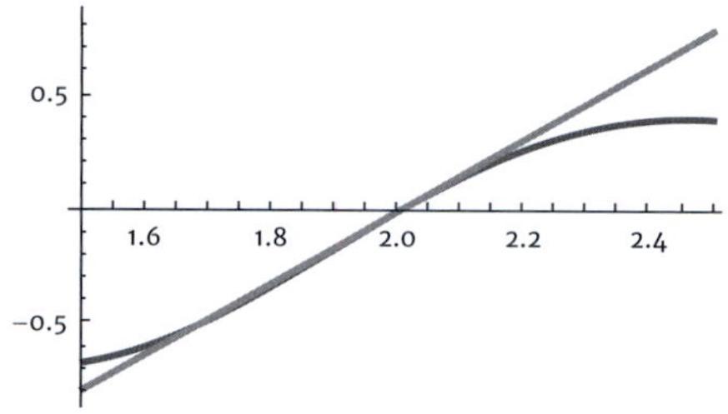

You may also find it instructive to study the graphs of a function and its derivative on the same set of axes. Here the graph of f is black, while its derivative is gray. Note that the zeros of f' correspond to the extreme values of f.

In[5]:= `Plot[{f[x], f'[x]}, {x, 0, 3},`
`PlotStyle → {Black, LightGray}]`

Out[5]=

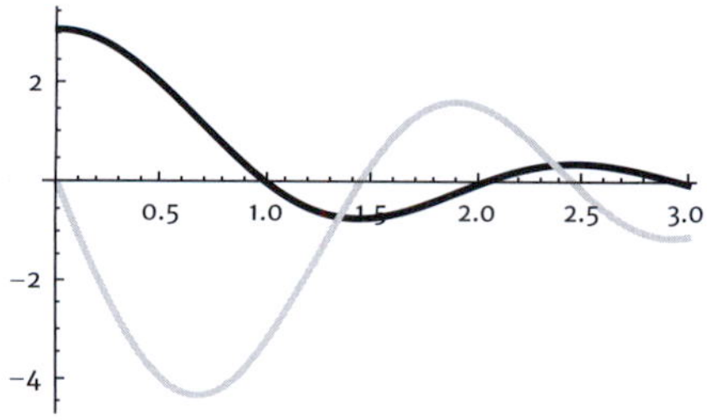

There is another way to take derivatives of expressions with *Mathematica* that is useful in many situations. The command is called D. The D button is the first item under the Calculus Commands tab $d\!\int\!\Sigma$ in the Basic Commands section of the Basic Math Assistant palette. D takes two arguments;

the first is an expression to be differentiated, and the second is the name of the variable with respect to which the differentiation is to be performed:

In[6]:= $D\left[\dfrac{Sin[\pi\,x]}{x},\ x\right]$

Out[6]= $\dfrac{\pi\,Cos[\pi\,x]}{x} - \dfrac{Sin[\pi\,x]}{x^2}$

The $\partial_\Box\,\blacksquare$ button gives a different formatting of the D command that is similar to traditional mathematics notation. Type and highlight the expression you wish to differentiate, *then* push this button. Now type x (as the subscript) to indicate that you wish to differentiate with respect to x:

In[7]:= $\partial_x\,Sin[x]$

Out[7]= $Cos[x]$

A word of warning is in order regarding this palette button. If you *first* hit the palette button and *then* enter an expression to be differentiated in the position of the placeholder, you should put grouping parentheses around the expression. Here's an example of what can happen if you don't:

In[8]:= $\partial_x\,x^2 + x^3$

Out[8]= $2\,x + x^3$

You certainly don't want to report that the derivative of $x^2 + x^3$ is $2x + x^3$! With parentheses, things are fine:

In[9]:= $\partial_x\,\left(x^2 + x^3\right)$

Out[9]= $2\,x + 3\,x^2$

When you first highlight the expression to be differentiated, and then push the palette button, *Mathematica* will add the grouping parentheses automatically.

D can be used to write out just about any differentiation rule. You just need to ask it to derive an expression involving "dummy" functions (functions which have been given no specific definition). Here is the product rule, for instance:

In[10]:= $Clear[f, g, x];$
         $D[f[x] * g[x], x]$

Out[11]= $g[x]\,f'[x] + f[x]\,g'[x]$

There are two points to remember about the D command. First, it is imperative that the variable (x in the example above) be cleared of any value before it is used in the D command. Second, if you plan to plot a derivative generated by the D command, you need to wrap it in the Evaluate command before plotting:

In[12]:= `Plot[Evaluate[{x², D[x², x]}], {x, -1, 1}]`

Out[12]=

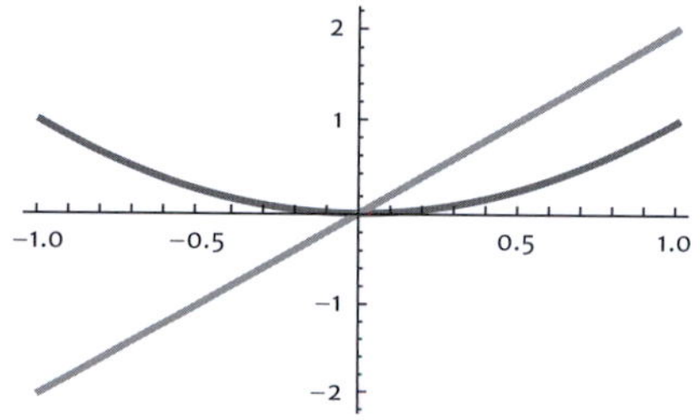

As a general rule of thumb, D is useful for differentiating unnamed expressions and for deriving general formulas. For functions to which you have already given names (such as f), the "prime" command `f'[x]` is generally easier to use than D.

Exercises 5.3

1. Make a `Manipulate` that shows the tangent line to $f(x) = \cos(x)$ at the point $x = a$ as a assumes values from -4π to 4π.

2. Graph the derivatives of $f(x) = \sin(x^n)$ for $n = 2, 3, 4$ and look for patterns in the graphs that are reflected in the expressions for their derivatives.

5.4 Visualizing Derivatives

It can be instructive to create a dynamic visualization environment, using `Manipulate`, showing the derivative function as the limit of a difference quotient. Moving the slider in the `Manipulate` below demonstrates graphically that the derivative of sin (x) is cos (x). Note the iterator for Δx is backwards; it moves from a value of 2 when the slider is positioned on the left *down* to .01 when the slider is moved all the way to the right.

In[1]:= `Manipulate[`

`Plot[{`$\dfrac{\text{Sin}[x + \Delta x] - \text{Sin}[x]}{\Delta x}$`, Cos[x]}, {x, -2 π, 2 π}], {Δx, 2, .01}]`

Out[1]=

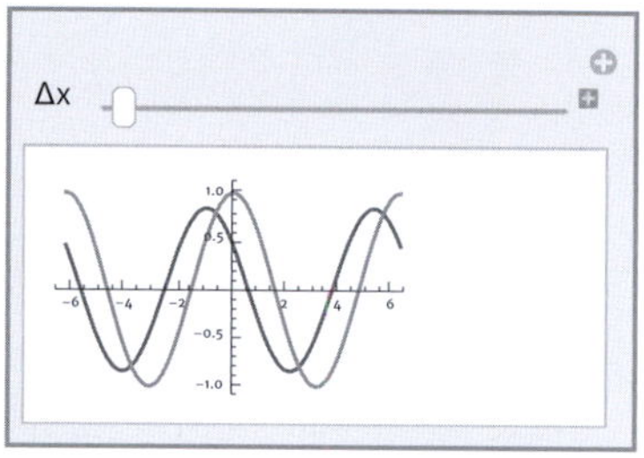

The equivalence of the instantaneous rate of change and the slope of the tangent line can be visualized by the following `Manipulate`. Here we see the graph of $f(x) = e^x$ and its tangent line at $x = 1$. As we move the slider we zoom down to the microscopic level where the curve and the tangent line become indistinguishable.

In[2]:= `Manipulate[Plot[{Exp[x], Exp'[1] (x - 1) + Exp[1]}, {x, 1 - δ, 1 + δ},`
`Frame → True, Axes → False, Epilog → {Red, Point[{1, Exp[1]}]},`
`GridLines → {Range[0, 2, .05], Range[-1, 8, .2]},`
`GridLinesStyle → Gray, FrameTicks → None,`
`Filling → {1 → {2}}], {{δ, 1, "zoom"}, 1, .01}]`

Out[2]=
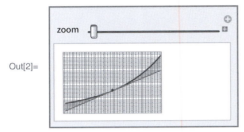

Exercises 5.4

1. Make a `Manipulate` like the first one in this section, showing the difference quotient for the natural logarithm function ln(x) converging to $\frac{1}{x}$ as $\Delta x \to 0$.

2. Modify the zooming `Manipulate` at the end of this section so that it includes a `Checkbox` control. The tangent line should display if the checkbox is checked, but not otherwise.

5.5   Higher-Order Derivatives

In[1]:= `Clear[f, x];`
$$f[x\_] := \frac{Sin[\pi x]}{x}$$

The easiest way to take a second derivative is to do this:

In[3]:= `f''[x]`

Out[3]= $-\dfrac{2\,\pi\,\text{Cos}[\pi\,x]}{x^2} + \dfrac{2\,\text{Sin}[\pi\,x]}{x^3} - \dfrac{\pi^2\,\text{Sin}[\pi\,x]}{x}$

You must use two *single* quotation marks.

Third derivatives?

In[4]:= `f'''[x]`

Out[4]= $\dfrac{6 \pi \, \text{Cos}[\pi\, x]}{x^3} - \dfrac{\pi^3 \, \text{Cos}[\pi\, x]}{x} - \dfrac{6\, \text{Sin}[\pi\, x]}{x^4} + \dfrac{3 \pi^2 \, \text{Sin}[\pi\, x]}{x^2}$

Another way to take a third derivative is to use the D command as follows:

In[5]:= `D[f[x], {x, 3}]`

Out[5]= $\dfrac{6 \pi \, \text{Cos}[\pi\, x]}{x^3} - \dfrac{\pi^3 \, \text{Cos}[\pi\, x]}{x} - \dfrac{6\, \text{Sin}[\pi\, x]}{x^4} + \dfrac{3 \pi^2 \, \text{Sin}[\pi\, x]}{x^2}$

The D command is useful for producing general formulas as in the last section. For example, here is the (seldom seen) second-derivative product rule:

In[6]:= `Clear[f, g, x]`

In[7]:= `D[f[x] * g[x], {x, 2}]`

Out[7]= `2 f'[x] g'[x] + g[x] f''[x] + f[x] g''[x]`

And here is a product rule for third derivatives. Note that the StandardForm notation for the third derivative of f[x] is f$^{(3)}$[x]. A similar notation is employed for all derivatives beyond the second.

In[8]:= `D[f[x] * g[x], {x, 3}]`

Out[8]= `3 g'[x] f''[x] + 3 f'[x] g''[x] + g[x] f`$^{(3)}$`[x] + f[x] g`$^{(3)}$`[x]`

Exercises 5.5

1. Use the D command to find a general rule for the second derivative of $y = \dfrac{f(x)}{g(x)}$.

2. Use a Table to look for patterns in the higher-order derivatives of sec(x).

5.6 Maxima and Minima

A function can only attain its relative maximum and minimum values at *critical points*, points where its graph has horizontal tangents, or where no tangent line exists (due to a sharp corner in the graph, for instance). For a differentiable function there is a unique tangent line at each point in the domain, so the critical points are all of the first type. To find a value of x for which f has a horizontal tangent, one must set the derivative equal to 0 and solve for x. Having experience with taking derivatives and solving equations with *Mathematica*, this shouldn't be too difficult. In many cases it's not. Here's an example:

In[1]:= `Clear[f, x];`
`f[x_] := x`^{3}` - 9 x + 5`

In[3]:= `Reduce[f'[x] == 0, x]`

Out[3]= $x == -\sqrt{3} \;||\; x == \sqrt{3}$

In[4]:= `Solve[f'[x] == 0, x]`

Out[4]= $\left\{\left\{x \to -\sqrt{3}\right\}, \left\{x \to \sqrt{3}\right\}\right\}$

Recall from Section 4.2 that the `Solve` command returns a list of *replacement rules*. Here is how to use that output to get a list of the two critical points, each of the form `{x, f[x]}`. These are the points in the plane where the graph of *f* assumes its extreme values:

In[5]:= `extrema = {x, f[x]} /. %`

Out[5]= $\left\{\left\{-\sqrt{3}, 5 + 6\sqrt{3}\right\}, \left\{\sqrt{3}, 5 - 6\sqrt{3}\right\}\right\}$

We can confirm that an extreme point is a maximum or a minimum by using the second derivative:

In[6]:= $f''\left[-\sqrt{3}\right] < 0$

Out[6]= `True`

The function is concave down at $x = -\sqrt{3}$ and so has a maximum at $x = -\sqrt{3}$. Similarly, the second derivative confirms that *f* has a minimum at $x = \sqrt{3}$:

In[7]:= $f''\left[\sqrt{3}\right] > 0$

Out[7]= `True`

Here is a plot of *f*, with the extreme points superimposed as large dots. They will appear as large red dots on a color display:

In[8]:= `Plot[f[x], {x, -4, 4},`
`        Epilog → {PointSize[Medium], Red, Point[extrema]}]`

Out[8]=

The `Epilog` option can be used with any command that produces graphics, such as `Plot`. It allows you to overlay *graphics primitives*, such as points, on the plot after it has been rendered. In this case, the directive `PointSize[Medium]` makes the points clearly visible, the directive `Red` makes them red, and the `Point[extrema]` transforms the list of coordinates into a `Point` object. In any event, that little bit of technical typing produces a satisfying plot, and allows you to verify visually that the points you found using the `Solve` command are really the extrema you sought.

Be mindful that a plot of some sort is important. For although relative extrema for a function f must occur at values of x that satisfy $f'(x) = 0$, satisfying this equation is no guarantee that the point in question is in fact a relative maximum or minimum. This will often happen when the equation $f'(x) = 0$ has repeated roots:

```
In[9]:=  f[x_] := 8 + 12 x - 6 x² + x³
```

```
In[10]:=  Solve[f'[x] == 0, x]
Out[10]=  {{x → 2}, {x → 2}}
```

```
In[11]:=  Plot[f[x], {x, 1, 3},
            Epilog → {PointSize[Medium], Red, Point[{2, f[2]}]}]
```

The plot suggests that even though f has a horizontal tangent when $x = 2$, f takes points immediately to the left of 2 to values smaller than $f(2)$, and f takes points immediately to the right of 2 to values greater than $f(2)$. In other words, f has no relative maximum or minimum at $x = 2$. Without a plot (or some careful mathematical reasoning) it is unclear whether a function f has extrema at those values of x satisfying $f'(x) = 0$. Note that the second derivative confirms that the function is neither concave up nor concave down at $x = 2$:

```
In[12]:=  f''[2]
Out[12]=  0
```

We next give an example of a function f for which we need to specify that we want solutions that are real numbers in order to get the critical points. We can use either `Solve` or `Reduce` with the optional argument `Reals`, but the output from `Reduce` is a little more compact. An exact solution can also be found by hand.

```
In[13]:=  f[x_] := Cos[π eˣ]
```

```
In[14]:=  f'[x]
Out[14]=  - eˣ π Sin[eˣ π]
```

In[15]:= `Solve[f'[x] == 0, x]`

··· Solve: Inverse functions are being used by Solve, so some solutions may not be found; use Reduce for complete solution information.

Out[15]= `{{x → -∞}}`

In[16]:= `Reduce[f'[x] == 0, x, Reals] // Simplify`

Out[16]= `C[1] ∈ ℤ &&`
`((C[1] ≥ 1 && x == Log[2 C[1]]) || (C[1] ≥ 0 && x == Log[1 + 2 C[1]]))`

We know from the expression for f that it will oscillate, and hence will have infinitely many local extrema. In fact, a moment's thought reveals that since the cosine function attains its extreme values when its argument is an integer multiple of π, this function will attain its extreme values when x is the natural logarithm of an integer. This is precisely what `Reduce` tells us above. Recall from Chapter 4 that C[1] ∈ ℤ means that C[1] is an element of the set of integers, the symbol && means "and," and the symbol || means "or." The solution distinguishes between the cases when the integer is even and odd. This is a remnant of the more general case when x is permitted to assume complex values, where this distinction is necessary; it also neatly divides the solutions between maxima and minima. However, when we only allow real-valued solutions, a more concise description is possible: Every solution to the equation $f'(x) = 0$ is of the form $x = \ln(c)$, where c is a positive integer. A plot confirms this:

In[17]:= `Plot[f[x], {x, -3, 3}, Epilog →`
`{PointSize[0.02], Red, Point[Table[{Log[c], f[Log[c]]}, {c, 20}]]}]`

Out[17]=

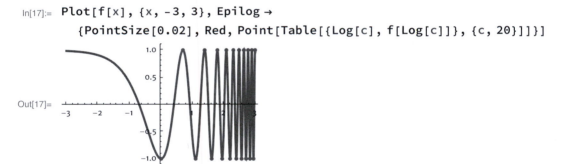

The strategy that we followed above will fail precisely when the `Solve`, `NSolve`, and `Reduce` commands are unable to solve the equation $f'(x) = 0$, typically when f is something other than a polynomial of low degree:

In[18]:= $f[x\_] := \dfrac{Sin[\pi\, x]}{x}$

In[19]:= `Reduce[f'[x] == 0, x, Reals]`

··· Reduce: This system cannot be solved with the methods available to Reduce.

Out[19]= $Reduce\left[\dfrac{\pi\, Cos[\pi\, x]}{x} - \dfrac{Sin[\pi\, x]}{x^2} == 0, x, \mathbb{R}\right]$

In[20]:= **NSolve[f'[x] == 0, x, Reals]**

   ••• NSolve: This system cannot be solved with the methods available to NSolve.

Out[20]= $\text{NSolve}\left[\dfrac{\pi\,\text{Cos}\,[\pi\,x]}{x} - \dfrac{\text{Sin}\,[\pi\,x]}{x^2} == 0,\, x,\, \mathbb{R}\right]$

This is a clue that you need to pursue an alternate strategy. One approach is to stare hard at the equation $f'(x) = 0$ and see if you can find a solution by hand. There are rare occasions in which there is an obvious solution that *Mathematica* will miss (there's an example at the end of this section). If the Solve (or NSolve) command does produce a solution, but warns you that inverse functions were used, work by hand to see if you can find other solutions. Bear in mind that this process of finding extrema cannot be reduced to a single, simple, automated procedure; you have to remain fully engaged at every step. If your efforts in solving $f'(x) = 0$ bear no fruit (as will probably be the case with the example above), don't despair. In such cases we can find *approximations* for the extrema using Plot, FindRoot, FindMinimum and FindMaximum.

The first step in this strategy is to produce a graph of f. In this example, we'll look at the graph of f between $x = -10$ and $x = 10$. If you are working on an applied problem, there is probably some specified domain. That would be a good choice for your plot.

In[21]:= **Plot[f[x], {x, -10, 10}, PlotRange → {-1, π}]**

Out[21]=

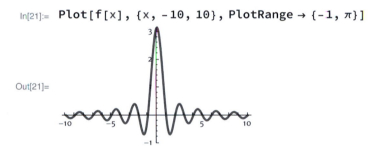

This beautiful curve has an infinite number of critical points. But be careful to note that $x = 0$ is not one of them. Since the function is not defined at $x = 0$, there is not a relative maximum at that point despite the peak that appears in the plot. The plot has a tiny hole in it precisely when $x = 0$.

The first relative minimum for a positive value of x appears near $x = 1.5$. Use that as an initial guess, and let FindRoot do the rest:

In[22]:= **FindRoot[f'[x] == 0, {x, 1.5}]**

Out[22]= $\{x \to 1.4303\}$

FindRoot can accept many initial guesses and will return one solution for each guess, but they may not all be unique.

In[23]:= **FindRoot[f'[x] == 0, {x, {1.5, 2.5, 3.5, 4.5, 4.6}}]**

Out[23]= $\{x \to \{1.4303, 2.45902, 3.47089, 4.47741, 4.47741\}\}$

Notice that the last two solutions above are the same. That happened because the initial guesses of 4.5 and 4.6 were both closest to the same solution. Careful initial guesses and a good understanding of the plot of the function are crucial when using FindRoot. Poor initial guesses can result in solutions that are not near the initial guess:

In[24]:= `FindRoot[f'[x] == 0, {x, {2, 4, 6}}]`

Out[24]= {x → {4.47741, 13.4925, 13.4925}}

While these values are critical points of f, they are not the ones closest to our initial guesses.

Mathematica has several built-in commands that go a long way toward automating the process of finding extrema, but as we will see below we must be very cautious using these tools. The commands include FindMaximum, FindMinimum, Maximize, and Minimize. Templates for these commands can be found under the More ▾ button in the Calculus Commands section of the palette by clicking the $d\int\Sigma$ tab. FindMinimum and FindMaximum search for relative extrema while Maximize and Minimize search for global extrema.

The format for FindMinimum and FindMaximum is similar to FindRoot, but with FindMinimum and FindMaximum you have the option of letting *Mathematica* select the starting point for the search. The output is a list of two items. The first gives the local minimum value of the function, while the second gives a replacement rule that indicates the point in the domain where the local minimum occurs.

In[25]:= `FindMinimum[f[x], x]`

Out[25]= {-0.68246, {x → 1.4303}}

FindMinimum and FindMaximum use different algorithms than FindRoot and are more dependable in finding a solution near your initial guess if you provide one.

In[26]:= `FindMinimum[f[x], {x, 4}]`

Out[26]= {-0.286907, {x → 3.47089}}

A disadvantage of FindMinimum and FindMaximum is that they can only search for one solution at a time. To find multiple solutions FindRoot may be faster but less dependable in finding solutions near the initial guesses.

Using the various forms of input for FindMinimum and FindMaximum you can impose constraints on your search for relative extrema. The input below will search for a relative maximum with x less than -1. But notice that since we did not specify a starting value for the search, the solution returned is not the relative maximum closest to $x = -1$.

In[27]:= `FindMaximum[{f[x], x < -1}, x]`

Out[27]= {0.222781, {x → -4.47741}}

The input below returns a value near 0 that is not a critical value. It is simply the largest value for $f(x)$ that *Mathematica* found by trying values less than 0. Examine the plot again to understand this output.

```
In[28]:= FindMaximum[{f[x], x < 0}, x]

Out[28]= {3.14159, {x → -0.000180244}}
```

The moral of this example is that the process of finding extrema is not one that can be completely automated. Rather, you must have a clear grasp of the underlying mathematical ideas, and the flexibility to combine abstract mathematical thinking with the tools that *Mathematica* provides.

A related but distinct enterprise is finding global extrema, the absolute maximum and minimum values obtained by a function on a specified domain. The commands `Maximize` and `Minimize` can find exact values for global extrema. For example, recall the first function discussed in this section.

```
In[29]:= Clear[f, x];
         f[x_] := x^3 - 9 x + 5;
         Maximize[f[x], x]
```

> ⋯ Maximize: The maximum is not attained at any point satisfying the given constraints.

```
Out[31]= {∞, {x → ∞}}
```

We saw in the graph that this function does not attain a global maximum on its full domain. But we can add constraints on the values to be considered by `Maximize` as follows:

```
In[32]:= Maximize[{f[x], -4 ≤ x ≤ 0}, x]

Out[32]= {5 + 6 √3, {x → -√3}}
```

The output is a list of two items. The first gives the maximum value of the function, while the second gives a replacement rule that indicates the point in the domain where the maximum occurs. On the same interval the minimum occurs at the left endpoint.

```
In[33]:= Minimize[{f[x], -4 ≤ x ≤ 0}, x]

Out[33]= {-23, {x → -4}}
```

Constraints can be inequalities or equations. When entering equations be sure you use double equals (==). These commands can be very useful when you want to find global extrema. Be warned that in the case of finding extreme values for transcendental functions, they may not find all solutions (this is the case for the previous example where $f(x) = \cos(\pi e^x)$; see Exercise 1). But for polynomial equations, they are bulletproof. For instance, here is an optimization word problem of the type frequently encountered in a calculus course:

> *A rectangular field is to be enclosed by a fence on three sides and by a straight stream on the fourth side. Find the dimensions of the field with maximum area that can be enclosed with 1000 feet of fence.*

Letting x and y denote the lengths of adjacent sides of the field, we want to maximize the area, $A = xy$, subject to the constraint $2x + y = 1000$.

In[34]:= `Maximize[{x * y, 2 x + y == 1000}, {x, y}]`

Out[34]= `{125 000, {x → 250, y → 500}}`

It is always a good idea to check any solution found with `Maximize` or `Minimize` by looking at a graph. As always, don't trust—verify! Here is a somewhat intricate `Manipulate` that provides a graphical confirmation by showing the rectangular field on the left and its area on the right:

In[35]:= `Manipulate[`
    `GraphicsRow[{`
      `Plot[1000 - 2 x, {x, 0, 500},`
        `AspectRatio → .5, Epilog → {Gray, EdgeForm[Black],`
          `Polygon[{{0, 0}, {x0, 0}, {x0, 1000 - 2 x0}, {0, 1000 - 2 x0}}]},`
        `AxesLabel → {"x", "y"}, Ticks → {{0, 250, 500}, Automatic}],`
      `Plot[x (1000 - 2 x), {x, 0, 500}, AspectRatio → .5,`
        `Epilog → {PointSize[Medium], Red, Point[{x0, x0 (1000 - 2 x0)}]},`
        `AxesLabel → {"x", "Area of Rectangle"}]}],`
    `{{x0, 250}, 0, 500}]`

Out[35]=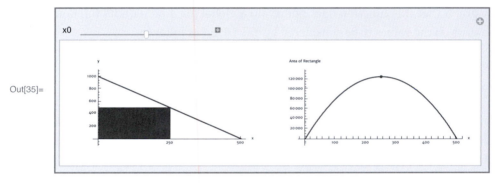

Exercises 5.6

1. Read the example concerning the function $f(x) = \cos(\pi e^x)$ in this section. Use `Maximize` to find extreme values of f on the domain $-3 \le x \le 3$. Compare the output to the graph in the text, and comment on what you find.

2. Use `Minimize` to find the x coordinate of the third occurrence of the y value -1 for the function $\sin(5 x)$ to the right of the y axis.

3. Find the dimensions of the right circular cylinder of largest volume that can be inscribed in a right circular cone with radius r and height h.

4. Find the minimum value of the function $f(x) = x^{2/3}$.

5.7 Inflection Points

```
In[1]:=  Clear[f, x];
         f[x_] := Sin[π x] / x
```

The procedure for finding points of inflection mirrors that for finding relative extrema outlined in the last section, except that second derivatives are used. A glance at the graph of f in the preceding section suggests that f has an inflection point near $x = 2$. Let's zero in on it with FindRoot:

```
In[3]:=  FindRoot[f''[x] == 0, {x, 2}]
Out[3]=  {x → 1.89088}
```

```
In[4]:=  infpt = {x, f[x]} /. %
Out[4]=  {1.89088, -0.177769}
```

```
In[5]:=  Plot[f[x], {x, 1, 3},
            Epilog → {PointSize[.02], Red, Point[infpt]}]
```

Out[5]=

The plot confirms that f has an inflection point at approximately $x = 1.89088$.

You may find it instructive to study the graph of a function and its derivatives on the same set of axes. Here is the graph of f, and the graph of its derivative with filling added. Note that f is decreasing on those intervals where f' is negative, and increasing when f' is positive. The zeros of f' correspond to the relative extrema of f.

```
In[6]:=  Plot[{f[x], f'[x]}, {x, 0, 3}, Filling → {2 → Axis}]
```

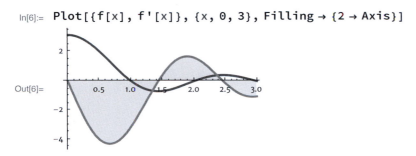

Out[6]=

And below we see f and f'' plotted together, where f'' has filling added. Note that f is concave down on those intervals where f'' is negative, and concave up where f'' is positive. The zeros of f'' correspond to the inflection points of f.

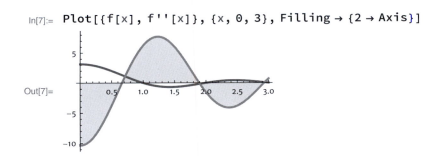

In[7]:= `Plot[{f[x], f''[x]}, {x, 0, 3}, Filling → {2 → Axis}]`

Out[7]=

Exercises 5.7

1. `Plot` the function $f(x) = \frac{\sin(\pi x)}{x}$ on the domain $-3 \le x \le 3$, then make a `ContourPlot` of the curve $f'(x) == 0$, and superimpose the two graphics using `Show`. Describe what you see.

2. `Plot` the function $f(x) = \frac{\sin(\pi x)}{x}$ on the domain $-3 \le x \le 3$, then make a `ContourPlot` of the curve $f''(x) == 0$, and superimpose the two graphics using `Show`. Describe what you see.

3. Repeat the first two exercises, but modify the `ContourPlot` input so that the first argument is not an equation but instead simply `f'[x]` or `f''[x]`. Add the option settings `Contours → {0}` and `ColorFunction → "LightTerrain"`. This will have the effect of adding color to the vertical bands. Within the `Show` command, list the `ContourPlot` first (otherwise the colored bands will be on top of, and hence obscure, the `Plot` of f).

5.8   Implicit Differentiation

Given an equation involving two variables, it is not always possible to find an expression for one variable in terms of the other. For example, we cannot solve for y as a function of x in $\cos(x^2) = y\sin(y^2)$. These types of equations are called *implicitly* defined since the dependence of y on x is implied but there is no explicit formula for this relationship. Even so, these expressions can be very interesting to study and it is still possible to find derivatives for them using a method called implicit differentiation. To produce plots of implicitly defined functions, we use `ContourPlot` (see Section 3.7.)

In[1]:= `ContourPlot[Cos[x²] == y Sin[(y)²], {x, -5, 5}, {y, -5, 5}]`

Out[1]=

The command Dt[*f*, *x*] gives the total derivative in which all variables in *f* are assumed to be functions of *x*. When doing implicit differentiation by hand we first find the derivative, keeping in mind that *y* is assumed to be a function of *x*, and hence multiplying by $\frac{dy}{dx}$ every time we take a derivative of *y*. We then solve for $\frac{dy}{dx}$. Implicit differentiation with *Mathematica* uses similar steps with the command Dt. The symbol for $\frac{dy}{dx}$ is Dt[y, x]. So to find $\frac{dy}{dx}$ for the equation $\cos(x^2) = y\sin(y^2)$ we use Dt to request the total derivative and then Solve for Dt[y, x]:

In[2]:= **Clear[x, y];**
Dt[Cos[x²] == y Sin[y²], x]

Out[3]= -2 x Sin$\left[x^2\right]$ == 2 y² Cos$\left[y^2\right]$ Dt[y, x] + Dt[y, x] Sin$\left[y^2\right]$

In[4]:= **Solve[%, Dt[y, x]]**

Out[4]= $\left\{\left\{\text{Dt}[y, x] \rightarrow -\dfrac{2 \text{ x Sin}\left[x^2\right]}{2 \text{ y}^2 \text{ Cos}\left[y^2\right] + \text{Sin}\left[y^2\right]}\right\}\right\}$

Since ($\sqrt{\dfrac{\pi}{2}}$, $\sqrt{\pi}$) is a solution of $\cos(x^2) = y\sin(y^2)$ we can use the derivative to find the equation of the tangent line at that point and then use a plot to check our answer. We compute the slope of the tangent line by plugging the coordinates of the point into the derivative we found above.

In[5]:= $-\dfrac{2 \text{ x Sin}\left[x^2\right]}{2 \text{ y}^2 \text{ Cos}\left[y^2\right] + \text{Sin}\left[y^2\right]}$ /. $\left\{x \rightarrow \sqrt{\dfrac{\pi}{2}}, y \rightarrow \sqrt{\pi}\right\}$

Out[5]= $\dfrac{1}{\sqrt{2\pi}}$

We can then use the point-slope formula to find the equation of the tangent line and produce a plot.

In[6]:= **ContourPlot$\left[\left\{\text{Cos}\left[x^2\right] == y \text{ Sin}\left[(y)^2\right], y - \sqrt{\pi} == \dfrac{1}{\sqrt{2\pi}}\left(x - \sqrt{\dfrac{\pi}{2}}\right)\right\},\right.$**

  {x, -5, 5}, {y, -5, 5},

  Epilog $\rightarrow \left\{\text{PointSize[0.04], Red, Point}\left[\left\{\sqrt{\dfrac{\pi}{2}}, \sqrt{\pi}\right\}\right]\right\}$

Out[6]=

We could also assume that x is a function of y and find $\frac{dx}{dy}$:

In[7]:= `Clear[x, y];`
`Dt[Cos[x²] == y Sin[(y)²], y]`

Out[8]= $-2 \times Dt[x, y] \, Sin[x^2] == 2 \, y^2 \, Cos[y^2] + Sin[y^2]$

In[9]:= `Solve[%, Dt[x, y]]`

Out[9]= $\left\{ \left\{ Dt[x, y] \rightarrow -\frac{1}{2 \, x} Csc[x^2] \, (2 \, y^2 \, Cos[y^2] + Sin[y^2]) \right\} \right\}$

In some instances, you may be asked to differentiate an equation such as $\cos(x^2) = y \sin(y^2)$ with respect to a third variable, such as t. In this case we assume that each of x and y are functions of t so the differentiation is carried out with respect to t:

In[10]:= `Clear[x, y, t];`
`Dt[Cos[x²] == y Sin[(y)²], t]`

Out[11]= $-2 \times Dt[x, t] \, Sin[x^2] == 2 \, y^2 \, Cos[y^2] \, Dt[y, t] + Dt[y, t] \, Sin[y^2]$

We can `Solve` for `Dt[y,t]` (i.e., $\frac{dy}{dt}$) or `Dt[x,t]` (i.e., $\frac{dx}{dt}$):

In[12]:= `Solve[%, Dt[y, t]]`

Out[12]= $\left\{ \left\{ Dt[y, t] \rightarrow -\frac{2 \, x \, Dt[x, t] \, Sin[x^2]}{2 \, y^2 \, Cos[y^2] + Sin[y^2]} \right\} \right\}$

Exercises 5.8

1. Find $\frac{dx}{dy}$ for the implicitly defined function $y \, x^3 + y = e^{xy}$.

2. Find $\frac{dy}{dx}$ for the implicitly defined function $y \, x^3 + y = e^{xy}$.

3. Find $\frac{d^2 y}{dx^2}$ for the implicitly defined function $y \, x^3 + y = e^{xy}$ and express it as a function of x and y.

4. A ten–foot ladder is leaning against a wall. The base of the ladder is sliding away from the wall at three feet per second when it is one foot from the wall. How fast is the top of the ladder sliding down the wall?

5. Use `Manipulate` to make a movie of a tangent line rolling around a unit circle.

5.9   Differential Equations

There are many applied settings in which you can observe a relationship between a function and one or more of its derivatives, even when an explicit algebraic expression for the function is unknown. In such situations, it is often possible to find the algebraic expression for the function in question by solving the *differential equation* that relates the function to its derivative(s). For instance, suppose there is a function $y(t)$ whose derivative is equal to $\frac{1}{3}$ times $y(t)$ for each value of t. This sort of situation can exist, for instance, in modeling population growth: The population at time t is denoted by $y(t)$, and the rate of growth $y'(t)$ is proportional to the population at time t. As the population gets larger, it grows faster, since there are more people available to reproduce. What kind of function is $y(t)$? What is its algebraic formula? You can solve a differential equation such as this with the DSolve command:

```
In[1]:= Clear[y, t];
```

$$\texttt{DSolve}\left[\texttt{y'[t]} \;==\; \frac{1}{3}\,\texttt{y[t]}, \texttt{y[t]}, \texttt{t}\right]$$

Out[2]= $\left\{\left\{\texttt{y[t]} \to e^{t/3}\,\texttt{C[1]}\right\}\right\}$

The DSolve command takes three arguments. The first is a differential equation, an equation that includes a derivative. The second is the function whose algebraic expression you wish to find, and the third is the name of the independent variable. The second and third arguments appear redundant in an example like this one, but in more complex situations they are needed to avoid ambiguity. In any event, you need to use them, always.

The output to DSolve is a list of replacement rules, exactly like those produced by the Solve command (see Section 4.2 in the previous chapter for a detailed description of the Solve command and replacement rules). The C[1] in the output represents a constant. It can be replaced by any number to produce an explicit solution. In applied settings, some other information is usually given that will enable you to find the value of such a constant. For instance, if we use our population growth model, we might have been told that initially, at time $t = 0$, the population was 400. Then we see that $400 = y(0) = e^0\,C[1] = C[1]$. Thus we conclude that the algebraic expression for $y(t)$ is $y(t) = 400\,e^{t/3}$.

```
In[3]:= y[t] /. %[[1]] /. C[1] → 400
```

Out[3]= $400\,e^{t/3}$

You can also use DSolve by giving a list of equations as the first argument. You can, for instance, put the differential equation *and* an initial condition in the list. This makes life very easy indeed:

```
In[4]:= Clear[y, t];
```

$$\texttt{DSolve}\left[\left\{\texttt{y'[t]} \;==\; \frac{1}{3}\,\texttt{y[t]}, \texttt{y[0]} \;==\; 400\right\}, \texttt{y[t]}, \texttt{t}\right]$$

Out[5]= $\left\{\left\{\texttt{y[t]} \to 400\,e^{t/3}\right\}\right\}$

In[6]:= `Plot[y[t] /. %, {t, 0, 10}]`

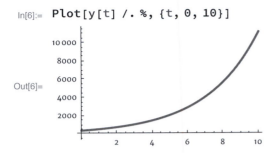

Out[6]=

Here's another example:

In[7]:= `Clear[y, t];`

$$\text{DSolve}\left[y'[t] == -\frac{1}{5} y[t] + 100, y[t], t\right]$$

Out[8]= $\left\{\left\{y[t] \to 500 + e^{-t/5} C[1]\right\}\right\}$

Here we have a family of solutions, with individual solutions determined by the values of the constant `C[1]`. For instance, here are several solutions for values of `C[1]` ranging from −500 to 500 in increments of 50:

In[9]:= `sols = Table[y[t] /. %[[1]] /. C[1] → n, {n, -500, 500, 50}]`

Out[9]= $\{500 - 500\ e^{-t/5},\ 500 - 450\ e^{-t/5},\ 500 - 400\ e^{-t/5},\ 500 - 350\ e^{-t/5},$
$500 - 300\ e^{-t/5},\ 500 - 250\ e^{-t/5},\ 500 - 200\ e^{-t/5},\ 500 - 150\ e^{-t/5},$
$500 - 100\ e^{-t/5},\ 500 - 50\ e^{-t/5},\ 500,\ 500 + 50\ e^{-t/5},\ 500 + 100\ e^{-t/5},$
$500 + 150\ e^{-t/5},\ 500 + 200\ e^{-t/5},\ 500 + 250\ e^{-t/5},\ 500 + 300\ e^{-t/5},$
$500 + 350\ e^{-t/5},\ 500 + 400\ e^{-t/5},\ 500 + 450\ e^{-t/5},\ 500 + 500\ e^{-t/5}\}$

We now have a list consisting of 21 functions, each a solution of our differential equation, and each corresponding to a different numerical value of `C[1]`. Let's plot these functions on the same set of axes.

In[10]:= `Plot[sols, {t, 0, 15}]`

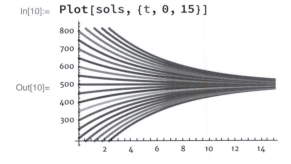

Out[10]=

Just as there is the `NSolve` command to complement the `Solve` command, there is the `NDSolve` command to complement the `DSolve` command. Use `NDSolve` in situations where the `DSolve` command is unable to provide an exact algebraic solution (or if `DSolve` seems to be taking all day). Choose Abort Evaluation in the Evaluation menu to get *Mathematica* to stop a computation.

To use NDSolve, you need to specify both a differential equation *and* an initial condition in a list for the first argument. The second argument is the function to be solved for, as with DSolve. The third argument is an iterator, specifying the name of the independent variable and the range of values it is to assume. As for the output, you will not get an explicit algebraic formula—only DSolve can provide that. Rather, you get a nebulous object known as an *interpolating function.* It is a numerical approximation to the true solution of the differential equation on the specified domain. It behaves like an ordinary function in that it can be plotted, and can be used in calculations:

In[11]:= `sol =`
`NDSolve[{y'[t] == 0.05 y[t] - 0.0001 y[t]², y[0] == 10}, y[t], {t, 0, 200}]`

Out[11]=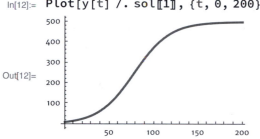

In[12]:= `Plot[y[t] /. sol⟦1⟧, {t, 0, 200}]`

Out[12]=

You can also produce a table of values for such a function:

In[13]:= `data = Table[{t, y[t] /. sol⟦1⟧}, {t, 0, 200, 20}];`
`Text@`
`Grid[Prepend[data, {"t", "y(t)"}], Alignment → ".", Dividers → Gray]`

Out[14]=

t	$y(t)$
0	10.
20	26.2797
40	65.5185
60	145.367
80	263.509
100	375.895
120	445.848
140	478.614
160	491.914
180	496.995
200	498.89

Exercises 5.9

1. Find the general solution to the differential equation $\frac{dy}{dx} = -4\,xy^2$ and then plot several solutions by choosing specific values of the constant.

2. Find the general solution for the second-order differential equation $\frac{d^2 y}{dx^2} + \frac{dy}{dx} = \cos(x)$ and then plot solutions for several values of the constants.

3. Use `NDSolve` to find the solution of $\frac{d^2 y}{dx^2} + \frac{dy}{dx} = \cos(x)$ subject to the initial conditions $y(0) = -1$ and $y'(0) = .4$ and then plot this solution.

5.10 Integration

If you haven't been impressed thus far, this is where *Mathematica* really pays for itself. Unlike differentiation, which with perseverance can always be completed by hand, integration can be exceedingly difficult. In most cases, however, if a function has a known antiderivative, *Mathematica* can find it:

In[1]:= $\displaystyle\int \frac{1}{1-x^3}\,d\,x$

Out[1]= $\displaystyle\frac{\text{ArcTan}\left[\frac{1+2\,x}{\sqrt{3}}\right]}{\sqrt{3}} - \frac{1}{3}\,\text{Log}[1-x] + \frac{1}{6}\,\text{Log}\left[1+x+x^2\right]$

The $\left|\int_{\blacksquare}d\square\right|$ button can be found under the Calculus Commands tab $\boxed{d\int\Sigma}$ in the Basic Commands section of the Basic Math Assistant palette. First type a function ($\frac{1}{1-x^3}$ in the example above), then highlight it with your mouse. Now press the $\left|\int_{\blacksquare}d\square\right|$ button on the palette. Your function will be pasted inside the integral at the position of the black square, and the cursor will be at the second placeholder. Here you type the variable with respect to which the integration will be performed (x in the example above). Now enter the cell.

If the function you wish to integrate is already on your screen (in an output cell for instance), highlight it using the mouse, then push the integration button. It will be pasted inside the integral in a new input cell. You then enter the variable with respect to which the integration is to be performed and enter the cell.

Some people find it natural to use the palette in a slightly different way, *first* pushing the integral button, and *then* typing the function in the position delimited by the first placeholder. This is okay, but be careful. If the expression you want to integrate is a sum, you need to put grouping parentheses around the whole thing. Here's what happens if you don't:

In[2]:= $\int 1 - x^2 \, dx$

• • • Integrate: $\int 1$ cannot be interpreted. Integrals are entered in the form $\int f \, dx$, $\int_a^b f \, dx$, or

$\int\limits_{\text{var} \in \text{region}} f$, where d is entered as ⎡ESC⎤dd⎡ESC⎤.

You can probably make sense of this message: *Mathematica* sees the incomplete expression $\int 1$ from which it is supposed to subtract $x^2 \, dx$. That's nonsense. With the parentheses things work fine:

In[2]:= $\int \left(1 - x^2\right) \, dx$

Out[2]= $x - \dfrac{x^3}{3}$

Note also that you must be sure to Clear any previous assignment made to the integration variable. Here's what to expect if you do not:

In[3]:= $x = 3$

Out[3]= 3

In[4]:= $\int 2 \, x \, dx$

• • • Integrate: Invalid integration variable or limit(s) in 3.

Out[4]= $\int 6 \, d3$

Clearing x is the remedy here:

In[5]:= **Clear[x]**

In[6]:= $\int 2 \, x \, dx$

Out[6]= x^2

You can produce the $\int$ symbol without the palette by typing ⎡ESC⎤ int ⎡ESC⎤, and you can produce the d symbol by typing ⎡ESC⎤ dd ⎡ESC⎤. This will allow you to type an integral entirely from the keyboard. Alternatively, you can use the Integrate command. It does the same thing as the palette button described above; in fact the palette button provides a means of utilizing the standard syntax for integrals, but when evaluated it simply calls the Integrate command. The standard *Mathematica* syntax leaves no ambiguity as to the necessity of grouping parentheses; the integrand is simply the first argument. The integration variable is the second.

In[7]:= `Integrate[ArcTan[x], x]`

Out[7]= $x \, \text{ArcTan}[x] - \dfrac{1}{2} \text{Log}\left[1 + x^2\right]$

It is important to remember that if a function has one antiderivative, it has infinitely many others. But given one, any other can be obtained by adding a constant to it. *Mathematica* always gives the most simple antiderivative, the one whose constant term is zero.

One may also use `Integrate` to produce a general formula by using an integrand that includes one or more symbolic parameters. Here, for instance, is the first integration formula one typically learns in a calculus course:

In[8]:= `Clear[n, x];`

$$\int x^n \, dx$$

Out[9]= $\dfrac{x^{1+n}}{1+n}$

Note that this formula holds for *almost* all n (it fails if $n = -1$). It is an intentional design feature to not specify special cases like this one where there is a single exception to the general formula provided. This means it is left to you, the user, to critically contemplate the output, cognizant that there may be exceptions. However, it is also possible to get a *piecewise* function as the value of an integral. This will occur when there are two or more measurable regions on which the integral assumes different values. A typical example of this behavior is when the integrand is itself a piecewise function.

In[10]:= $\displaystyle\int \left\{ \begin{array}{ll} \sqrt{n\,x} + 1 & x \geq 0 \\ e^{-n\,x} & x < 0 \end{array} \right. dx$

Out[10]= $\left\{ \begin{array}{ll} -\dfrac{e^{-n\,x}}{n} & x \leq 0 \\ -\dfrac{1}{n} + x + \dfrac{2}{3}\,x\,\sqrt{n\,x} & \text{True} \end{array} \right.$

All of the familiar integration formulas are at your fingertips. Here we see the chain rule, which is the basis for the technique of substitution:

In[11]:= `Clear[F, u, x];`

$$\int F'[u[x]] \, u'[x] \, dx$$

Out[12]= $F[u[x]]$

A more subtle feature of the `Integrate` command is the manner in which real variables are handled. By default, it is assumed that the integrand is a function that may assume complex values, and that may accept complex input. In most cases this creates no issue whatever. But there are exceptions, so it is important to know how to restrict the values of parameters to the field of real numbers. To do so, follow the syntax of this example:

In[13]:= `Assuming[t ∈ Reals, ∫√(t⁴ + 2 t² + 1) dt]`

Out[13]= $t + \dfrac{t^3}{3}$

This input reads pretty much as one would say it out loud: Assuming that t is an element of the reals, integrate the function that follows with respect to t. Equivalently, you may add an `Assumptions` option to the `Integrate` command:

In[14]:= `Integrate[√(t⁴ + 2 t² + 1), t, Assumptions → t ∈ Reals]`

Out[14]= $t + \dfrac{t^3}{3}$

The outputs above are simpler than that produced by a straight integration:

In[15]:= `∫√(t⁴ + 2 t² + 1) dt`

Out[15]= $\dfrac{t\sqrt{\left(1 + t^2\right)^2 \left(3 + t^2\right)}}{3\left(1 + t^2\right)}$

This output is different since $\sqrt{\left(1 + t^2\right)^2}$ does not necessarily simplify to $1 + t^2$ when t is a complex number. Every nonzero complex number has two square roots, and the radical indicates the *principal* square root (see Exercise 2). More examples that make use of `Assumptions` are provided in the next section.

It is also worth noting that there are numerous "special functions" that cannot be defined in terms of such elementary functions as polynomials, trigonometric functions, inverse trigonometric functions, logarithms, or exponential functions, but that can be described in terms of antiderivatives of such functions. If you use *Mathematica* to integrate a function and see in the output something you've never heard of, chances are that *Mathematica* is expressing the integral in terms of one of these special functions. Here's an example:

In[16]:= `∫Cos[x²] dx`

Out[16]= $\sqrt{\dfrac{\pi}{2}} \; \text{FresnelC}\left[\sqrt{\dfrac{2}{\pi}}\, x\right]$

Let's inquire about `FresnelC`:

In[17]:= **? FresnelC**

FresnelC[z] gives the Fresnel integral C(z). ≫

Don't be intimidated by such output. It simply says the integral you asked for cannot be expressed in terms of elementary functions. It expresses the answer in terms of another such integral, one so famous that it has its own name (like FresnelC). Augustin Fresnel (1788–1827) was a French mathematical physicist who studied this and similar integrals extensively. There is a FresnelS integral as well; it uses sine in place of cosine.

There is also the possibility that *Mathematica* will evaluate an integral producing an expression that involves complex numbers. Such numbers can be recognized by the presence of the character i in the output, which denotes $\sqrt{-1}$. In cases such as this, the Assumptions option that we mentioned earlier will not eliminate the appearance of complex numbers. Rather, they are necessary (even in the real case) to express the antiderivative.

In[18]:= **Integrate$\left[\sqrt{x + x^3}, x, \text{Assumptions} \rightarrow x \in \text{Reals}\right]$**

Out[18]= $\dfrac{1}{5\sqrt{x}} 2\sqrt{x + x^3}$

$\left(x^{3/2} + \dfrac{1}{\sqrt{1+x^2}} 2(-1)^{3/4}\left(-\text{EllipticE}\left[i\,\text{ArcSinh}\left[(-1)^{1/4}\sqrt{x}\right], -1\right] + \text{EllipticF}\left[i\,\text{ArcSinh}\left[(-1)^{1/4}\sqrt{x}\right], -1\right]\right)\right)$

In this example we also have an appearance by the special function EllipticE. What's that?

In[19]:= **? EllipticE**

EllipticE[m] gives the complete elliptic integral E(m).
EllipticE[ϕ, m] gives the elliptic integral of the second kind E(ϕ | m). ≫

If that's not helpful, don't worry about it. Suffice it to say that there is a whole universe of special functions out there, and you've just caught a glimpse of a small piece of it. The bottom line is that integration is difficult by nature. *Mathematica* doesn't know whether or not you hold a Ph.D. in mathematics. It does the best it can. You shouldn't be surprised or discouraged if you occasionally get a bit more back than you expected.

Another possibility when integrating is that *Mathematica* simply won't be able to arrive at an answer. Alas, some integrals are just that way. In such situations, the output will match the input exactly:

$$\text{In[20]:=} \quad \int \sqrt{\text{ArcTan[t]}}\ dt$$

$$\text{Out[20]=} \quad \int \sqrt{\text{ArcTan[t]}}\ dt$$

Exercises 5.10

1. Evaluate the following integrals. Note that in many cases a constant a appears in the integrand, and that in all cases the integration is with respect to the variable u. The results mimic many standard integral tables (such as those found on the inside jackets of calculus textbooks).

a. $\int \sqrt{a^2 + u^2}\ du$

b. $\int \sqrt{a^2 - u^2}\ du$

c. $\int (a^2 + u^2)^{3/2}\ du$

d. $\int u \sqrt{2au - u^2}\ du$

e. $\int \sec(u)\ du$

2. Show that for $t = 2i$, it is not the case that $\sqrt{(1 + t^2)^2} = 1 + t^2$, then find another complex number t for which the equation does not hold. Note that if t is real, then $1 + t^2 > 0$, so the equation will hold.

3. Consider the family of functions $\ln x$, $(\ln x)^2$, $(\ln x)^3$, $(\ln x)^4$, etc.

a. Integrate $(\ln x)^n$ for integers $n = 1$ through 5, identify the pattern, and propose a general formula for $\int (\ln x)^n\ dx$ for any positive integer n.

b. Using pencil and paper, *prove* that the derivative (with respect to x) of the expression in your formula reduces to $(\ln x)^n$. You will then have proved that your formula is correct. Congratulations—you have just discovered and proved a mathematical theorem!

4. Integrate the following functions, and display the results in a table. Can you find a pattern (among the latter outputs) that will enable you to predict the value of the next integral?

$$x,\ \sqrt{x+1},\ \sqrt{\sqrt{x+1}+1},\ \sqrt{\sqrt{\sqrt{x+1}+1}+1},$$

$$\sqrt{\sqrt{\sqrt{\sqrt{x+1}+1}+1}+1},\ \sqrt{\sqrt{\sqrt{\sqrt{\sqrt{x+1}+1}+1}+1}+1}$$

5.11 Definite and Improper Integrals

Computing Definite Integrals

You've probably already found the $\int_\square^\square \blacksquare\, d\square$ button on the palette. Use the [TAB] key to move from one placeholder to the next:

In[1]:= $\displaystyle\int_{-2}^{2} \left(1 - x^2\right)\, dx$

Out[1]= $-\dfrac{4}{3}$

The same comments made in the last section with regard to grouping parentheses apply here as well; in particular, if you click the palette button *before* typing the expression you wish to integrate, it may be necessary to put grouping parentheses around that expression when you type it. If you prefer typing to palettes, the command you need is `Integrate`. It works as it did in the last section, but the second argument is now an iterator giving the name of the variable and the bounds of integration.

In[2]:= `Integrate`$\left[1 - x^2,\ \{x,\ -2,\ 2\}\right]$

Out[2]= $-\dfrac{4}{3}$

Here is a plot where the value of the definite integral corresponds to the *signed area* of the shaded region—the area of the portion above the x axis minus the area of the portion below it:

In[3]:= `Plot`$\left[1 - x^2,\ \{x,\ -2,\ 2\},\ \text{Filling} \to \text{Axis}\right]$

Out[3]=

Be Careful with Odd Roots

There is a special class of function that needs discussion. We saw in Section 3.2 that using the palette button $\sqrt[\square]{\blacksquare}$ to find nth roots of negative numbers will produce complex numbers. For example, most calculus texts use the real cube root function, for which $\sqrt[3]{-8} = (-8)^{1/3} = -2$. In *Mathematica*, the principal cube root function is used instead, so that $(-8)^{1/3} = 1 + \sqrt{3}\, i$, a complex number. If we want *Mathematica* to stick to real numbers for odd roots of negative numbers, we need to use the command

Surd[x,n], which will return the real-valued *n*th root of *x*, instead of $x^{\frac{1}{n}}$ or $\sqrt[n]{x}$. Alternatively, we can use the equivalent symbol $\sqrt[n]{x}$. Notice the extra little overhang on this root symbol that differentiates it from $\sqrt[n]{x}$. To get this symbol type ESC surd ESC. Unfortunately, this real root symbol does not currently appear in the palettes.

If you are finding a definite integral of a function involving odd roots over an interval that includes negative numbers, be sure to use some form of Surd to enter the integrand. For example, the following definite integral involves complex fifth roots:

In[4]:= $N\left[\int_{-1}^{0} x^{\frac{-2}{5}}\, dx\right]$

Out[4]= $0.515028 - 1.58509\, i$

That is probably not the answer you got doing this integral by hand. Using Surd for the fifth root returns the real-valued answer:

In[5]:= $N\left[\int_{-1}^{0} Surd[x, 5]^{-2}\, dx\right]$

Out[5]= 1.66667

In[6]:= $\int_{-1}^{0} \left(\sqrt[5]{x}\right)^{-2}\, dx$

Out[6]= $\dfrac{5}{3}$

Also, notice that if we ask for an exact value of these integrals it may appear that everything is fine. But remember that *Mathematica* interprets $(-1)^{3/5}$ as a complex number. If you use this output in a further *Mathematica* computation you may encounter more unexpected complex numbers. But if you simply want the value of the integral and you interpret $(-1)^{3/5}$ as a real number that is equal to -1, then you'll be fine.

In[7]:= $\int_{-1}^{0} x^{\frac{-2}{5}}\, dx$

Out[7]= $-\dfrac{5}{3}\, (-1)^{3/5}$

In[8]:= $(-1)^{3/5}$ // ComplexExpand

Out[8]= $\dfrac{1}{4} - \dfrac{\sqrt{5}}{4} + i\sqrt{\dfrac{5}{8} + \dfrac{\sqrt{5}}{8}}$

Of course, with Surd there are no complex numbers hiding in the output:

$$\text{In[9]:=} \quad \int_{-1}^{0} \left(\sqrt[5]{x} \right)^{-2} dx$$

$$\text{Out[9]=} \quad \frac{5}{3}$$

Riemann Sums

Mathematica makes the computation of Riemann sums easy with the Sum command. Sum works very much like Table, but rather than producing a list of the specified items, it adds them:

$$\text{In[10]:=} \quad \text{Sum}\left[i^2, \{i, 1, 4\}\right]$$

$$\text{Out[10]=} \quad 30$$

This is the same as adding $1 + 4 + 9 + 16$. The advantage of using the Sum command for such additions can be seen when you want to add lots of numbers:

$$\text{In[11]:=} \quad \text{Sum}\left[i^2, \{i, 1, 100\}\right]$$

$$\text{Out[11]=} \quad 338\,350$$

There is a palette version of the Sum command under the Calculus Commands section of the palette that allows you to employ the traditional summation notation. Use the $\sum_{\square=\square}^{\square} \blacksquare$ button, and then use the

TAB key to move from one placeholder to the next:

$$\text{In[12]:=} \quad \sum_{i=1}^{100} i^2$$

$$\text{Out[12]=} \quad 338\,350$$

The cells below provide an example of a Riemann sum computation for a function f over the interval from a to b, with n rectangles and f evaluated at the left endpoint of each subinterval. The first cell sets the values of f, a, and b. It needs to be edited every time you move from one example to the next:

```
In[13]:=  Clear[f, a, b, n, x, Δx, i];
          f[x_] := Cos[x];
          a = 0;
          b = 2;
```

The following cell makes use of the values above and defines the appropriate Riemann sum as a function of *n*. It does not need to be edited as you move from one example to the next:

In[17]:=
$$\Delta x[n\_] := \frac{b - a}{n};$$

$$x[i\_, n\_] := a + i * \Delta x[n];$$

$$\texttt{leftRsum}[n\_] := \sum_{i=0}^{n-1} f[x[i, n]] * \Delta x[n] // N$$

The function $\triangle x$ returns the width of an individual rectangle—it is a function of *n* because its value depends on the number of subintervals between *a* and *b*. The function x returns the right endpoint of the *i*th subinterval. It is a function of both *i* and *n*. Lastly, leftRsum returns the Riemann sum for your function between *a* and *b*, with the function evaluated at the left endpoint of each subinterval. It is a function of *n*, for its value depends on the number of rectangles used. Here is the Riemann sum for cos(*x*) on the interval [0, 2] with 50 rectangles:

In[20]:= leftRsum[50]

Out[20]= 0.937499

Note that the values of *i* in the summation (from 0 to $n - 1$) dictate that *f* be evaluated at the *left* endpoint of each subinterval. To compute a Riemann sum with *f* evaluated at the *right* endpoint of each subinterval you can change the bounds of the summation to 1 and *n*:

In[21]:=
$$\texttt{rightRsum}[n\_] := \sum_{i=1}^{n} f[x[i, n]] * \Delta x[n] // N$$

In[22]:= rightRsum[50]

Out[22]= 0.880853

Either sum can be viewed as an approximation to the definite integral of *f* over the interval from *a* to *b*. It is not hard to modify the process to generate other approximations, such as those employing the trapezoidal rule or Simpson's rule. The approximations tend to get better as the value of *n* increases, as the following table shows:

In[23]:= `data = Table[{n, rightRsum[n]}, {n, 50, 400, 50}];`
`dataWithHeadings = Prepend[data, {"n", "Riemann Sum"}];`
`Text@Grid[dataWithHeadings,`
`    Alignment → Left, Dividers → {Center, 2 → True}]`

n	Riemann Sum
50	0.880853
100	0.895106
150	0.899843
200	0.902209
250	0.903628
300	0.904574
350	0.905249
400	0.905755

Out[24]=

Curious about the actual value of the integral?

In[25]:= $\int_0^2 f[x] \, dx \; // \; N$

Out[25]= `0.909297`

Here is a plot where the value of the definite integral corresponds to the signed area of the shaded region:

In[26]:= `Plot[f[x], {x, 0, 2}, Filling → Axis]`

Out[26]=

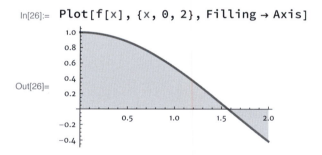

Computing Improper Integrals

If the bounds are positive or negative infinity, you may use the ∞ button in the Calculator section of the palette, type ESC `inf` ESC, or type the word `Infinity`:

In[27]:= $\int_{-\infty}^{\infty} e^{-x^2} \, dx$

Out[27]= $\sqrt{\pi}$

In[28]:= $\texttt{Integrate}\left[\dfrac{1}{x^3},\ \{x,\ 1,\ \infty\}\right]$

Out[28]= $\dfrac{1}{2}$

Of course there is the possibility that an improper integral will fail to converge. *Mathematica* will warn you in such circumstances:

In[29]:= $\displaystyle\int_1^\infty \dfrac{1}{x}\,dx$

••• Integrate: Integral of $\dfrac{1}{x}$ does not converge on $\{1, \infty\}$.

Out[29]= $\displaystyle\int_1^\infty \dfrac{1}{x}\,dx$

Other improper integrals occur when a function has a vertical asymptote between the upper and lower bounds. It is dangerous to evaluate these integrals by hand using the Fundamental Theorem of Calculus without carefully considering the behavior of the function at the asymptotes. Luckily, *Mathematica* is very careful and will tell you when these integrals do and do not converge.

In[30]:= $\displaystyle\int_{-2}^{2} \dfrac{1}{x^2}\,dx$

••• Integrate: Integral of $\dfrac{1}{x^2}$ does not converge on $\{-2, 2\}$.

Out[30]= $\displaystyle\int_{-2}^{2} \dfrac{1}{x^2}\,dx$

In[31]:= $\texttt{Plot}\left[\dfrac{1}{x^2},\ \{x,\ -2,\ 2\},\ \texttt{PlotRange} \rightarrow \{0,\ 500\},\ \texttt{Filling} \rightarrow \texttt{Axis}\right]$

Out[31]=

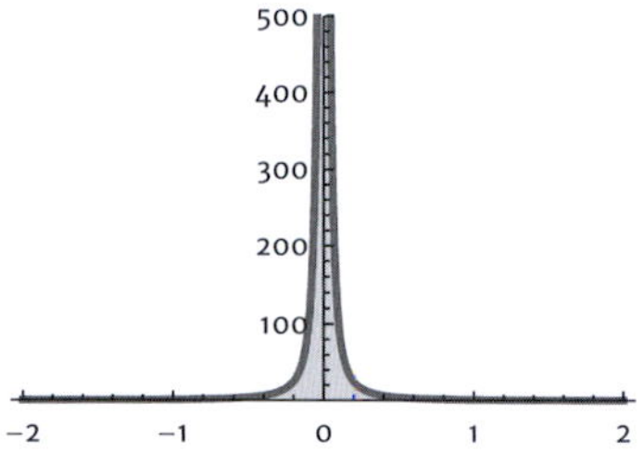

Mathematica is rightly reporting that the shaded area (were it not cut off at $y = 500$) is infinite. Here is another example:

In[32]:= $\displaystyle\int_{-\frac{\pi}{2}}^{\frac{\pi}{2}} \mathtt{Csc[x]}\ \mathtt{d}x$

⋯ Integrate: Integral of Csc[x] does not converge on $\left\{-\dfrac{\pi}{2}, \dfrac{\pi}{2}\right\}$.

Out[32]= $\displaystyle\int_{-\frac{\pi}{2}}^{\frac{\pi}{2}} \mathtt{Csc[x]}\ \mathtt{d}x$

In[33]:= $\mathtt{Plot}\left[\mathtt{Csc[x]},\ \left\{\mathtt{x},\ -\dfrac{\pi}{2},\ \dfrac{\pi}{2}\right\},\ \mathtt{PlotRange} \to \mathtt{100},\ \mathtt{Filling} \to \mathtt{Axis}\right]$

Out[33]=

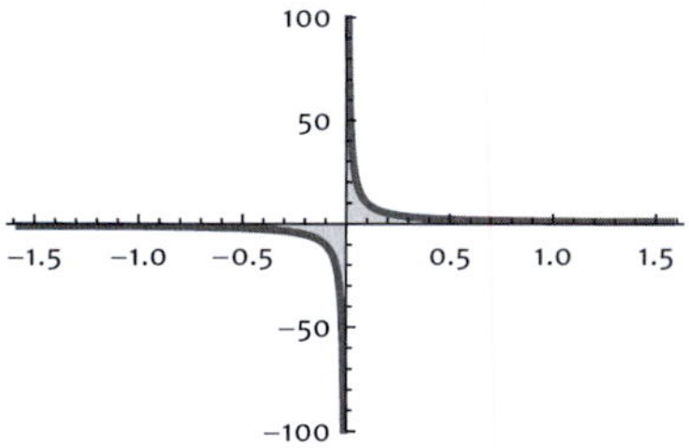

Students frequently argue that this integral should be zero due to the symmetry apparent in the graph. But *Mathematica* is returning the correct answer. Since the area to the right of $x = 0$ is not convergent, the entire integral is divergent.

In[34]:= $\mathtt{Clear[a]};$

$\mathtt{Limit}\left[\displaystyle\int_{a}^{\frac{\pi}{2}} \mathtt{Csc[x]}\ \mathtt{d}x,\ \mathtt{a} \to \mathtt{0},\ \mathtt{Direction} \to \mathtt{"FromAbove"}\right]$

⋯ Integrate: Integral of −Sec[x] does not converge on $\{0, 2\pi\}$.

⋯ Integrate: Integral of Csc[x] does not converge on $\left\{a, \dfrac{\pi}{2}\right\}$.

Out[35]= ∞

In the previous examples the functions had vertical asymptotes at $x = 0$. In the next example the interval also contains a vertical asymptote but the integral converges. Notice our use of the real cube root symbol in the integrand.

In[36]:= $\displaystyle\int_{0}^{3} \dfrac{1}{\sqrt[3]{x-2}}\ \mathtt{d}x$

Out[36]= $-\dfrac{3}{2}\left(-1 + 2^{2/3}\right)$

In[37]:= $\text{Plot}\left[\dfrac{1}{\sqrt[3]{x-2}}, \{x, 0, 3\}, \text{PlotRange} \to \{-10, 10\}, \text{Filling} \to \text{Axis}\right]$

Out[37]=

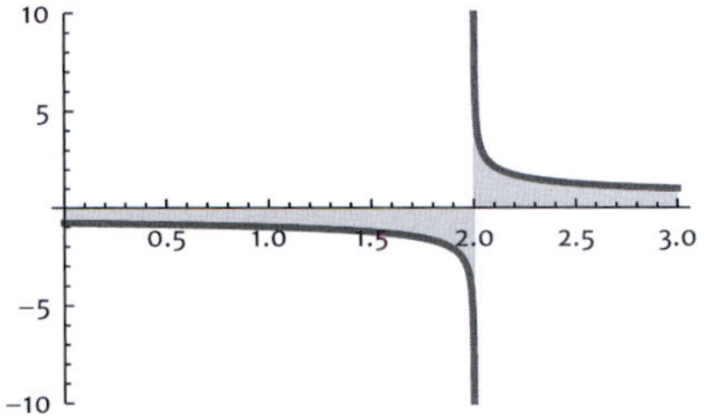

Defining Functions with Integrals

It is possible to define functions by integrating dummy variables:

In[38]:= $\text{Clear}[a, t, v, s]$
$a[t\_] := -32$

In[40]:= $v[t\_] := \displaystyle\int_0^t a[u]\, du + 20$

In[41]:= $s[t\_] := \displaystyle\int_0^t v[u]\, du + 4$

In[42]:= $s[t]$

Out[42]= $4 + 20\, t - 16\, t^2$

You simply need to remember that `Integrate` always returns the antiderivative whose constant term is equal to zero, so constants need to be included in such definitions. The function $v(t)$ above satisfies the condition that $v(0) = 20$, while the function $s(t)$ satisfies $s(0) = 4$. In the example above, $s(t)$ represents the height in feet above ground level of an object after t seconds if it is thrown vertically upward at an initial velocity of 20 feet per second and from an initial height of 4 feet; $v(t)$ is the velocity of the object at time t, and $a(t)$ is the object's acceleration. Air resistance is ignored.

Some Integrals Are Bad

And as is the case with indefinite integrals, there are functions for which there is no way to express an antiderivative in closed form, and consequently no way to evaluate the definite integral exactly:

In[43]:= $\displaystyle\int_0^1 \left(\sqrt{\text{ArcTan}[t]}\right)\, dt$

Out[43]= $\displaystyle\int_0^1 \sqrt{\text{ArcTan}[t]}\, dt$

Even in cases like this, you will often be able to get numerical approximations:

    In[44]:= **N[%]**

    Out[44]= 0.629823

The next section explores a better way to get numerical approximations of definite integrals.

Exercises 5.11

1. Make the following sketch of the graph of $f(x) = \frac{1}{x^2}$, and evaluate the definite integral of f from $x = 1$ to $x = 3$.

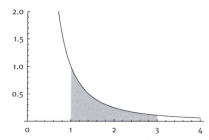

2. Evaluate the following definite integrals.

    a. $\displaystyle\int_0^1 \sqrt{t^4 + 2t^2 + 1}\; dt$

    b. $\displaystyle\int_0^1 \sqrt{t^4 + 2t^2 + 2}\; dt$

    c. $\displaystyle\int_0^\pi \cos(t)^{10}\; dt$

3. Use a Riemann sum to approximate the second of the three integrals in the previous exercise.

    a. Use $n = 100$ subintervals and left endpoints.

    b. Use $n = 100$ subintervals and right endpoints.

    c. Use $n = 100$ subintervals and midpoints.

    d. Make a Plot of $f(x) = \sqrt{x^4 + 2x^2 + 2}$ and use it to decide which of the three approximations is best.

4. Evaluate the following improper integrals using Surd for odd roots.

    a. $\int_{-5}^{5}(x^{-3/7})\,dx$

    b. $\int_{-5}^{\infty}(x^{-3/7})\,dx$

    c. $\int_{-\infty}^{-5}(x^{-7/3})\,dx$

5. Your opponent chooses a number p strictly between 0 and 1. Your opponent then chooses a second number q strictly between $\sqrt{2}$ and 2. To defeat your opponent, find a strictly increasing function on the domain $[0, 1]$ passing through $(0, 0)$ and $(1, 1)$ whose arc length exceeds q, and whose integral over $[0, 1]$ is

a. smaller than p.

b. greater than p.

Hint: Enter the following input:

```
Manipulate[
  Plot[{
      1-a
      ─── x            0 ≤ x ≤ a
       a
                                    , {x, 0, 1}, PlotRange → {{0, 1}, {0, 1}},
       a      1-2 a
      ─── x + ─────   a < x ≤ 1
      1-a      1-a

  AspectRatio → Automatic, Filling → Axis], {{a, .75}, 0, 1}]
```

6. Under what conditions on a real number n does the integral $\int_0^1 x^n \, dx$ converge?

7. Assuming that a and b are real numbers, under what specific conditions on a and b can the integral $\int_a^b \sqrt{-t} \, dt$ be evaluated? What does it evaluate to in this case?

8. Use `Integrate` to illustrate the second fundamental theorem of calculus.

9. Use `D` and `Integrate` to calculate a formula for $\frac{d}{dx} \int_a^{g(x)} f(t) \, dt$.

10. There are two absolute value functions `Abs` and `RealAbs`. `RealAbs` is clearly meant for real numbers while `Abs` works for both real and complex numbers. These built-in functions have different definitions which may cause them to produce different but equivalent forms of solutions. `Abs[x]` is the modulus function which is $\sqrt{x^2}$ if x is a real number and $\sqrt{a^2 + b^2}$ for a complex number $x = a + b\,i$. Whereas
$$\texttt{RealAbs[x]} = \begin{cases} x & x \geq 0 \\ -x & x < 0 \end{cases}.$$

a. Compute `Abs` and `RealAbs` of -2 and `Abs` of $2 + i$ and compare the outputs to the definitions given above.

In[1]:= `Abs[-2]`

Out[1]= 2

In[2]:= `Abs[-2 + i]`

Out[2]= $\sqrt{5}$

b. Enter the following inputs and discuss the different forms of the outputs.

In[3]:= `Clear[x, n];`
$$\int_{-n}^{n} \texttt{Abs[x] dx}$$

Out[4]= `ConditionalExpression`$\left[n^2, \texttt{Re[n]} > 0 \,\&\&\, \texttt{Im[n]} == 0\right]$

In[5]:= `Assuming`$\left[\texttt{x} \in \texttt{Reals}, \int_{-n}^{n} \texttt{Abs[x] dx}\right]$

Out[5]= `n Abs[n]`

In[6]:= $\text{Assuming}\left[x \in \text{Reals} \&\& n > 0, \int_{-n}^{n} \text{Abs}[x] \, dx\right]$

Out[6]= n^2

In[7]:= $\int_{-n}^{n} \text{RealAbs}[x] \, dx$

Out[7]= $-\left(\left(\begin{cases} -\dfrac{n^2}{2} & n > 0 \\ \dfrac{n^2}{2} & \text{True} \end{cases}\right) + \left(\begin{cases} -\dfrac{n^2}{2} & n \le 0 \\ \dfrac{n^2}{2} & \text{True} \end{cases}\right)\right)$

5.12 Numerical Integration

Mathematica has a numerical integration command, NIntegrate, which is extremely effective at providing numerical approximations to the values of definite integrals, even those (indeed, especially those) that the Integrate command can't handle:

In[1]:= $\text{Integrate}\left[\sqrt{\text{ArcTan}[t]}, \{t, 0, 1\}\right]$

Out[1]= $\int_{0}^{1} \sqrt{\text{ArcTan}[t]} \, dt$

In[2]:= $\text{NIntegrate}\left[\sqrt{\text{ArcTan}[t]}, \{t, 0, 1\}\right]$

Out[2]= 0.629823

NIntegrate accepts arguments exactly as Integrate does for handling definite integrals. A template for NIntegrate can be found under the   Numeric ▾   button on the Calculus Commands palette. It is important to understand that NIntegrate works in an entirely different way from Integrate. Rather than attempt symbolic manipulation, NIntegrate produces a sequence of numerical values for the integrand over the specified interval, and uses these values to produce a numerical estimate for the integral. Although the algorithm used is quite sophisticated, you can think of NIntegrate as producing something analogous to a Riemann sum. The good news is that you now have at your disposal a means for estimating some very messy integrals. The bad news is that NIntegrate can occasionally produce poor estimates. Just as the Plot command can miss features of the graph of a function that are "narrow" relative to the domain over which it is plotted, NIntegrate can miss such features also. Problems arise if points near the narrow feature are not sampled (for a discussion of the Plot command in this context, see Section 3.2). Here is an example:

In[3]:= $\texttt{Plot}\left[\texttt{e}^{-(x-2)^{2}}, \{x, -5, 5\}, \texttt{PlotRange} \to \{0, 1\}, \texttt{Filling} \to \texttt{Axis}\right]$

Out[3]=

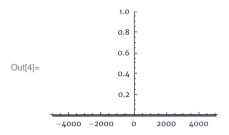

Here is the same function plotted over a much larger domain—so much larger that the bump disappears from view:

In[4]:= $\texttt{Plot}\left[\texttt{e}^{-(x-2)^{2}}, \{x, -5000, 5000\}, \texttt{PlotRange} \to \{0, 1\}, \texttt{Filling} \to \texttt{Axis}\right]$

••• General: $\text{Exp}\left[-2.5018 \times 10^{7}\right]$ is too small to represent as a normalized machine number; precision may be lost.

Out[4]=

In[5]:= $\texttt{NIntegrate}\left[\texttt{e}^{-(x-2)^{2}}, \{x, -5, 5\}\right]$

Out[5]= 1.77243

When $\texttt{NIntegrate}$ is applied to this function over the larger domain, it also misses the bump:

In[6]:= $\texttt{NIntegrate}\left[\texttt{e}^{-(x-2)^{2}}, \{x, -5000, 5000\}\right]$

••• NIntegrate: Integral and error estimates are 0 on all integration subregions. Try increasing the value of the MinRecursion option. If value of integral may be 0, specify a finite value for the AccuracyGoal option.

Out[6]= 0.

The warning messages provide a hint that something might not be right, yet an incorrect output is generated, the value of this integral is very small relative to the interval but greater than zero. This phenomenon can be even worse if the integrand has discontinuities, for in such situations the actual definite integral may not have a real value, yet $\texttt{NIntegrate}$ may report one. For example, the following integral does not converge. *Mathematica* produces warnings and then an output of 3.67657:

In[7]:= `NIntegrate[` $\frac{1}{(x - 1)}$ `, {x, 0,` $\frac{3}{2}$ `}]`

> ••• NIntegrate: Numerical integration converging too slowly; suspect one of the following: singularity, value of the integration is 0, highly oscillatory integrand, or WorkingPrecision too small.

> ••• NIntegrate: NIntegrate failed to converge to prescribed accuracy after 9 recursive bisections in x near {x} = {1.00193}. NIntegrate obtained 3.6765658596940707` and 5.363161650915528` for the integral and error estimates.

Out[7]= `3.67657`

Taking the left and right limits of the exact integral as the upper and lower bounds, respectively, approach 1 demonstrates non-convergence:

In[8]:= `Limit[` $\int_0^b \frac{1}{(x - 1)}$ `dx, b → 1, Direction → "FromBelow"]`

Out[8]= $-\infty$

In[9]:= `Limit[` $\int_a^{3/2} \frac{1}{(x - 1)}$ `dx, a → 1, Direction → "FromAbove"]`

Out[9]= ∞

If you know that the integrand has discontinuities in the interval over which you are integrating (vertical asymptotes in the graph are a giveaway), you can instruct `NIntegrate` to look out for them by replacing the iterator $\{x, xmin, xmax\}$ with $\{x, xmin, x_1, x_2, x_3, \ldots, xmax\}$, where $x_1, x_2, x_3, \ldots$ are the points of discontinuity. Sometimes this won't help, certainly not in those cases where the integral does not converge. Here we again get warnings for the divergent integral as above and a different incorrect answer.

In[10]:= `NIntegrate[` $\frac{1}{(x - 1)}$ `, {x, 0, 1,` $\frac{3}{2}$ `}]`

> ••• NIntegrate: Numerical integration converging too slowly; suspect one of the following: singularity, value of the integration is 0, highly oscillatory integrand, or WorkingPrecision too small.

> ••• NIntegrate: NIntegrate failed to converge to prescribed accuracy after 9 recursive bisections in x near {x} = {0.99999999999999999999999999999983692735662508754221254924558311692180}. NIntegrate obtained −140.395 and 25.08668778837013` for the integral and error estimates.

Out[10]= -140.395

If the integrand has discontinuities but the integral is convergent NIntegrate may still produce an incorrect solution and warnings.

In[11]:= $\mathtt{NIntegrate}\left[\dfrac{1}{\sqrt[4]{(x-1)^2}},\ \{x,\ 0,\ 3\}\right]$

> ••• NIntegrate: Numerical integration converging too slowly; suspect one of the following: singularity, value of the integration is 0, highly oscillatory integrand, or WorkingPrecision too small.

> ••• NIntegrate: NIntegrate failed to converge to prescribed accuracy after 9 recursive bisections in x near {x} = {1.00191}. NIntegrate obtained 4.810929503417521` and 0.029169629456657124` for the integral and error estimates.

Out[11]= 4.81093

Adding the points of discontinuity to the iterator allows NIntegrate to find the correct value of the integral.

In[12]:= $\mathtt{NIntegrate}\left[\dfrac{1}{\sqrt[4]{(x-1)^2}},\ \{x,\ 0,\ 1,\ 3\}\right]$

Out[12]= 4.82843

In[13]:= $\mathtt{Plot}\left[\dfrac{1}{\sqrt[4]{(x-1)^2}},\ \{x,\ 0,\ 3\},\ \mathtt{PlotRange}\rightarrow\{0,\ 14\},\ \mathtt{Filling}\rightarrow\mathtt{Axis}\right]$

Out[13]=

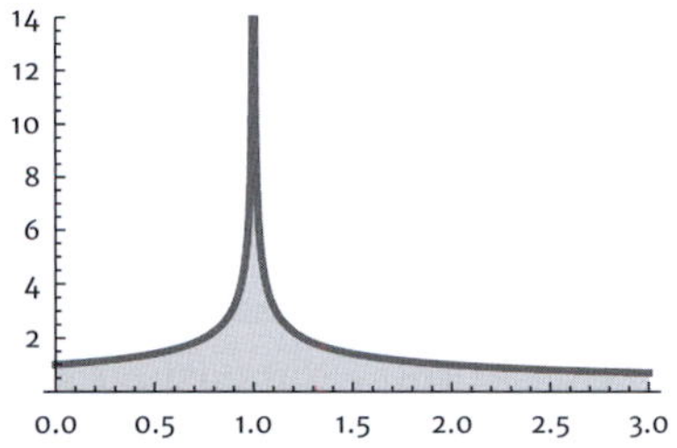

One strategy to help you determine if NIntegrate is providing an accurate answer is to examine carefully the plot of the integrand. If the numerical value provided by NIntegrate appears consistent with the area in the plot, but you still have your doubts, you might try breaking up your integral as a sum of integrals with the discontinuities as the bounds rather than between the bounds of integration.

In[14]:= $\mathtt{NIntegrate}\left[\dfrac{1}{\sqrt[4]{(x-1)^2}},\ \{x,\ 0,\ 1\}\right]$

Out[14]= 2.

In[15]:= **NIntegrate**$\left[\dfrac{1}{\sqrt[4]{(x-1)^2}}, \{x, 1, 3\}\right]$

Out[15]= 2.82843

Good. This is consistent with the previous output. As usual, it is up to you to test and decide on the efficacy of results produced with the computer.

Exercises 5.12

1. Use NIntegrate to produce a numerical approximation to $\int_{-4}^{4}\dfrac{1}{\sqrt[4]{(x-2)^2\,(x+3)^2}}\,dt.$

5.13 Surfaces of Revolution

Surfaces of revolution are often a challenge for calculus students to visualize. The command Revolu- tionPlot3D makes it easier to study these surfaces. The plot below shows x^2, for the x values 0 through 2, rotated about the vertical axis a full 360 degrees.

In[1]:= **RevolutionPlot3D**$\left[x^2, \{x, 0, 2\}\right]$

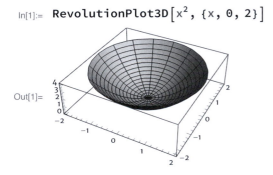

Out[1]=

RevolutionPlot3D produces a plot in three dimensions where the three axes are the x axis, y axis, and z axis. The z axis is the vertical axis. Since we are working in three dimensions the dependant variable is z and the function in the plot above is technically $z = x^2$. The curve is actually rotated about the z axis, not the y axis. But the result is visually identical to rotating a function $y = x^2$ plotted in the xy plane about the y axis.

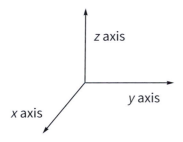

Because of the orientation of the axes, adding the optional argument RevolutionAxis → "Z" results in the same surface as above. The surface looks different below because the aspect ratio *Mathematica* selected is different for this plot.

In[2]:= `RevolutionPlot3D[x², {x, 0, 2}, RevolutionAxis → "Z"]`

Out[2]=

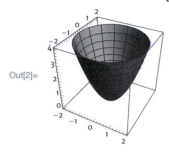

To revolve the same curve about the horizontal *x* axis, we add the optional argument RevolutionAxis → "X". Once you have generated a plot you can grab it with your mouse and rotate it to view it from any angle. Below we've rotated the image above to make the *x* axis appear horizontal.

In[3]:= `RevolutionPlot3D[x², {x, 0, 2}, RevolutionAxis → "X", Ticks → None]`

Out[3]=

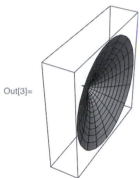

Since the function $z = f(x)$ is plotted in the xz plane, adding the optional argument RevolutionAxis → "Y" results in a flat disk in the xz plane. The spider web on the disk below is the result of rotated copies of the graph of $z = x^2$.

In[4]:= `RevolutionPlot3D[x², {x, 0, 2}, RevolutionAxis → "Y"]`

Out[4]=

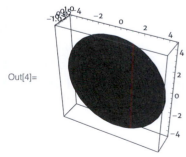

To summarize, to revolve a curve $z = f(x)$ about the vertical or "z axis," use `RevolutionPlot3D` with no options. To revolve a curve about the horizontal or "x axis" add the option setting `RevolutionAxis → "X"`. Don't use the option setting `RevolutionAxis → "Y"` unless you want a flat disk.

We can also revolve a region defined by two or more curves. Consider the region bounded by $\sin(x) + 2$ and $\cos(x) + 2$ on the interval $\frac{\pi}{4}$ to $\frac{5\pi}{4}$.

In[5]:= `Plot[{Sin[x] + 2, Cos[x] + 2}, {x, `$\frac{\pi}{4}$`, `$\frac{5\pi}{4}$`},`

`AxesOrigin → {0, 0}, Filling → {1 → {2}}]`

Out[5]=

Here is the plot of this region revolved about the vertical axis:

In[6]:= `RevolutionPlot3D[{{Sin[x] + 2}, {Cos[x] + 2}}, {x, `$\frac{\pi}{4}$`, `$\frac{5\pi}{4}$`}]`

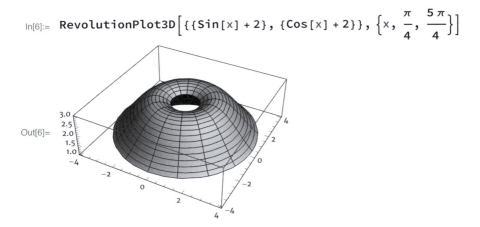

Out[6]=

It is not easy to tell from this plot that we have revolved a region rather than a single curve. It can often be easier to visualize a surface by cutting it open and peering inside. You can do this by plotting it on less than a full revolution. The plot below shows the revolution of the same region through only 270 degrees. Note that we need to use radians to indicate our angle of revolution. Also note that the two functions are each enclosed in curly brackets and then the pair is in another set of curly brackets. This is necessary since a simple list of two functions is interpreted by `RevolutionPlot3D` to be the coordinates of a parametric curve, which is not what want for this application.

In[7]:= `RevolutionPlot3D[{{Sin[x] + 2}, {Cos[x] + 2}}, {x, `$\frac{\pi}{4}$`, `$\frac{5\pi}{4}$`}, {θ, 0, `$\frac{3\pi}{2}$`}]`

Out[7]=

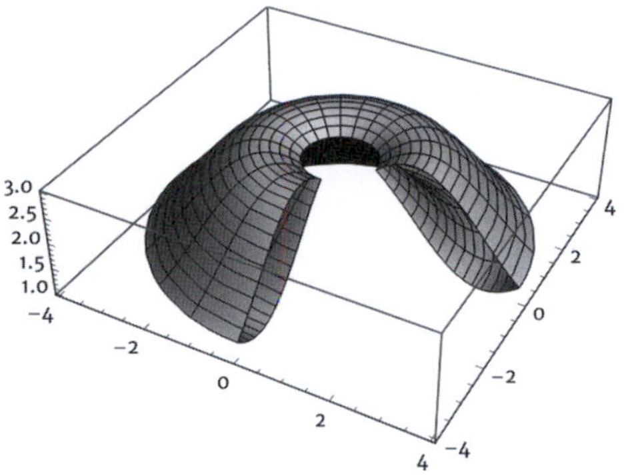

Here is the same region revolved about the x axis. We choose a different interval of 270 degrees so the missing quarter of the solid faces the viewer.

In[8]:= `RevolutionPlot3D[{{Sin[x] + 2}, {Cos[x] + 2}},`

`{x, `$\frac{\pi}{4}$`, `$\frac{5\pi}{4}$`}, {θ, `$\frac{\pi}{2}$`, 2π}, RevolutionAxis → "X"]`

Out[8]=

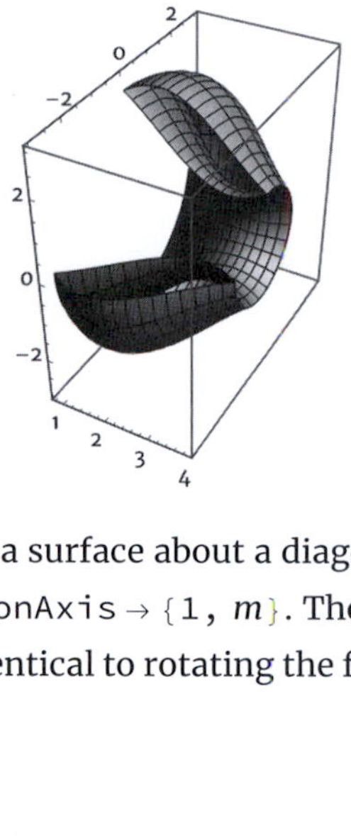

To revolve a surface about a diagonal line through the origin with slope m, use the optional argument `RevolutionAxis → {1, m}`. The plot below shows $z = x^2$ revolved about the line $z = 2x$. The result is visually identical to rotating the function $y = x^2$ plotted in the xy-plane about the line $y = 2x$.

In[9]:= `RevolutionPlot3D[x`^{2}`, {x, 0, 2}, RevolutionAxis → {1, 2}, Ticks → None]`

Out[9]=

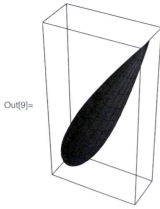

Exercises 5.13

1. Use `RevolutionPlot3D` to plot $y = \sin(x)$ on the interval 0 to 4π and revolve the surface through 330 degrees about

   a.   the vertical axis

   b.   the horizontal axis

   c.   a line through the origin at 45° to the x-axis

2. Use `RevolutionPlot3D` to plot a sphere of radius 6.

5.14 Sequences and Series

Limits of sequences can be investigated with the `DiscreteLimit` and `DiscretePlot` commands. `DiscreteLimit` calculates the limit as $n \to \infty$ over the integers.

In[1]:= `DiscreteLimit[`$\frac{n^n}{n!}$`, n → ∞]`

Out[1]= ∞

In[2]:= `DiscreteLimit[n Sin[`$\frac{\pi}{n}$`], n → ∞]`

Out[2]= π

In[3]:= `DiscreteLimit[Sin[`$\frac{n\pi}{2}$`], n → ∞]`

Out[3]= `Indeterminate`

DiscretePlot is useful for visualizing plots of sequences and their limits. For example, a plot helps explain why the sequence $\{\sin(\frac{n\pi}{2})\}$ is not convergent:

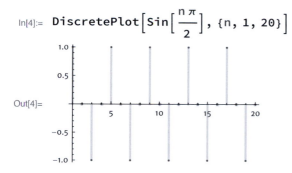

It also helps explain how the sequence $\{n\sin(\frac{\pi}{n})\}$ approaches π:

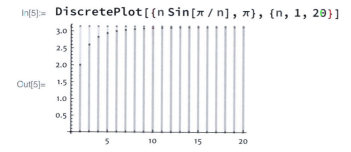

The difference between Limit and DiscreteLimit is similar to the difference between Plot and DiscretePlot. The former commands use the real numbers for the domain while the latter restrict the domain to the integers. The behavior of a function over the real numbers versus the integers can be very different, so it is important to use DiscreteLimit when finding limits of sequences. For example, $\lim_{x \to \infty} \sin(x\pi)$ does not exist while the sequence $\{\sin(n\pi)\} = \{0, 0, 0, \ldots\}$ for $n = 1, 2, 3, \ldots$, is a sequence converging to 0.

In[6]:= **DiscreteLimit[Sin[n π], n → ∞]**

Out[6]= 0

In[7]:= **Limit[Sin[n π], n → ∞]**

Out[7]= Indeterminate

A plot of the continuous function $f(x) = \sin(x\pi)$ and the sequence $\{\sin(n\pi)\}$ side by side make the distinction clear:

In[8]:= `GraphicsRow[`
　　　　　`{Plot[Sin[x π], {x, 1, 10}], DiscretePlot[Sin[n π], {n, 1, 10}]}]`

Out[8]=

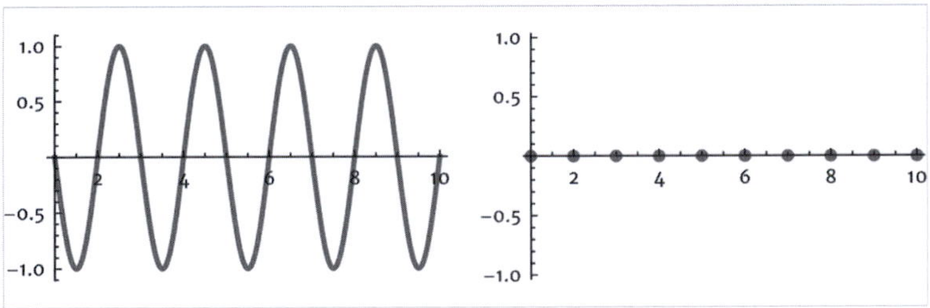

As with `Limit`, it is possible to input a `DiscreteLimit` that looks like traditional mathematical notation. To get the template shown below type ESC `dlim` ESC in an input cell.

$$\lim_{\substack{\square \to \infty \\ \mathbb{Z}}} \square$$

The $\mathbb{Z}$ below the arrow represents the integers and makes it clear this is the `DiscreteLimit` template as opposed to the `Limit` template. Notice the differences in the inputs and outputs below:

In[9]:= $\lim_{\substack{n \to \infty \\ \mathbb{Z}}} \text{Sin}[n \pi]$

Out[9]= `0`

In[10]:= $\lim_{n \to \infty} \text{Sin}[n \pi]$

Out[10]= `Indeterminate`

There are several powerful commands for dealing with series. The first and most simple is the `Sum` command, discussed earlier in this chapter—see the subsection "Riemann Sums" in Section 5.11. If you haven't yet used this command (to compute a Riemann sum, for instance), it's not hard. It works like the `Table` command, but rather than creating a list of the specified items, it adds them.

The really amazing thing about this command is that it can accept ∞ as a bound, meaning that it can find the value of an infinite series.

In[11]:= $\displaystyle\sum_{n=1}^{\infty} \frac{1}{n^2}$

Out[11]= $\dfrac{\pi^2}{6}$

Of course some series fail to converge, and others have solutions that *Mathematica* will not be able to find. Solutions to the latter type can be approximated by summing a large number of terms. Here is a series that doesn't converge:

In[12]:= $\displaystyle\sum_{n=1}^{\infty} \text{Cos}[n]$

       ••• Sum: Sum does not converge.

Out[12]= $\displaystyle\sum_{n=1}^{\infty} \text{Cos}[n]$

Here is an example of a series involving an independent variable x. Note that the keyboard version of the Sum command is more flexible than its palette counterpart in that the iterator can be adjusted to skip certain terms. Here is the sum $1 + x^2 + x^4 + \cdots$:

In[13]:= `Clear[x];`
`Sum[`x^n`, {n, 0, `∞`, 2}]`

Out[14]= $\dfrac{1}{1 - x^2}$

In this example, *Mathematica* reported a solution but did not specify which values of the independent variable x are acceptable. In particular, note that if $x = \pm 1$ the denominator will be zero, and the solution makes no sense. *Mathematica* reports the solution you most probably need in such situations, but it is up to you to determine the *region of convergence*, those values of the independent variable for which the solution is valid. In the example above, x must fall strictly between -1 and 1 for the solution to be valid.

The *Mathematica* command that more or less undoes what the Sum command does is the Series command. Here are the first few terms (those with degree not exceeding five) of the Taylor series expansion of $1/(1 - x^2)$:

In[15]:= `Series[`$\dfrac{1}{1 - x^2}$`, {x, 0, 5}]`

Out[15]= $1 + x^2 + x^4 + O[x]^6$

The Series command requires two arguments. The first is the function for which you wish to find a power series expansion. The second is a special iterator, one whose form is {*var*, *number*, *order*}, where *var* is the independent variable, *number* is the number x_0 about which the series is produced, and *order* specifies the highest power of the variable to be included in the output. The output includes a "big O" term, indicating that there are more terms in the series than those being shown. To get rid of the big O term, use the Normal command:

In[16]:= `Normal[%]`

Out[16]= $1 + x^2 + x^4$

You can produce a plot of this polynomial and the function. Note that the polynomial provides a good approximation to the function when x is near the number x_0 about which the series is produced ($x_0 = 0$ in this example):

In[17]:= $\texttt{Plot}\left[\left\{\texttt{%},\ \dfrac{1}{1-x^2}\right\},\ \{x,\ -1,\ 1\}\right]$

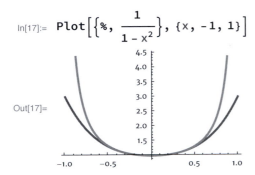

Out[17]=

Note that you can get the formula for a Taylor series expansion for an arbitrary function (such as f) about an arbitrary point (such as a). Here are the first four terms of such a series:

In[18]:= $\texttt{Clear[a, f]};$
$\texttt{Normal[Series[f[x], \{x, a, 3\}]]}$

Out[19]= $f[a] + (-a+x)\ f'[a] + \dfrac{1}{2}\ (-a+x)^2\ f''[a] + \dfrac{1}{6}\ (-a+x)^3\ f^{(3)}[a]$

In fact it is a simple matter to design a custom command for generating Taylor polynomials of degree n for the function f about the point x_0:

In[20]:= $\texttt{taylor[f\_, \{x\_, x0\_\}, n\_] := Normal[Series[f[x], \{x, x0, n\}]]}$

For example, we can now easily compute the eleventh-degree Taylor polynomial for the sine function, expanded around the point $x = 0$:

In[21]:= $\texttt{taylor[Sin, \{x, 0\}, 11]}$

Out[21]= $x - \dfrac{x^3}{6} + \dfrac{x^5}{120} - \dfrac{x^7}{5040} + \dfrac{x^9}{362\,880} - \dfrac{x^{11}}{39\,916\,800}$

Here is another example. The fourth-degree Taylor polynomial for $\cos(x)$, expanded about the point $x = \dfrac{\pi}{4}$, is given below:

In[22]:= $\texttt{taylor}\left[\texttt{Cos},\ \left\{x,\ \dfrac{\pi}{4}\right\},\ 4\right]$

Out[22]= $\dfrac{1}{\sqrt{2}} - \dfrac{-\dfrac{\pi}{4}+x}{\sqrt{2}} - \dfrac{\left(-\dfrac{\pi}{4}+x\right)^2}{2\sqrt{2}} + \dfrac{\left(-\dfrac{\pi}{4}+x\right)^3}{6\sqrt{2}} + \dfrac{\left(-\dfrac{\pi}{4}+x\right)^4}{24\sqrt{2}}$

And here is a list of the first five Taylor polynomials for $\cos(x)$, again expanded about the point $x = \frac{\pi}{4}$:

In[23]:= `Table[taylor[Cos, {x, `$\frac{\pi}{4}$`}, n], {n, 5}] // Column`

Out[23]=

$$\frac{1}{\sqrt{2}} - \frac{-\frac{\pi}{4}+x}{\sqrt{2}}$$

$$\frac{1}{\sqrt{2}} - \frac{-\frac{\pi}{4}+x}{\sqrt{2}} - \frac{\left(-\frac{\pi}{4}+x\right)^2}{2\sqrt{2}}$$

$$\frac{1}{\sqrt{2}} - \frac{-\frac{\pi}{4}+x}{\sqrt{2}} - \frac{\left(-\frac{\pi}{4}+x\right)^2}{2\sqrt{2}} + \frac{\left(-\frac{\pi}{4}+x\right)^3}{6\sqrt{2}}$$

$$\frac{1}{\sqrt{2}} - \frac{-\frac{\pi}{4}+x}{\sqrt{2}} - \frac{\left(-\frac{\pi}{4}+x\right)^2}{2\sqrt{2}} + \frac{\left(-\frac{\pi}{4}+x\right)^3}{6\sqrt{2}} + \frac{\left(-\frac{\pi}{4}+x\right)^4}{24\sqrt{2}}$$

$$\frac{1}{\sqrt{2}} - \frac{-\frac{\pi}{4}+x}{\sqrt{2}} - \frac{\left(-\frac{\pi}{4}+x\right)^2}{2\sqrt{2}} + \frac{\left(-\frac{\pi}{4}+x\right)^3}{6\sqrt{2}} + \frac{\left(-\frac{\pi}{4}+x\right)^4}{24\sqrt{2}} - \frac{\left(-\frac{\pi}{4}+x\right)^5}{120\sqrt{2}}$$

Finally, let's produce a sequence of graphics, one for each of the first 12 Taylor polynomials for the cosine function, expanded about the point $\frac{\pi}{4}$. Each plot will show the cosine function in gray, the Taylor polynomial in black, and the point $\left(\frac{\pi}{4}, \cos\left(\frac{\pi}{4}\right)\right) = \left(\frac{\pi}{4}, \frac{1}{\sqrt{2}}\right)$. The individual frames are displayed in a `Grid` below, and should be read sequentially from left to right across the rows to increase the degree of the Taylor polynomial.

In[24]:= `tlist = Table[taylor[Cos, {x, `$\frac{\pi}{4}$`}, n], {n, 12}];`

In[25]:= `plots = Table[Plot[{Cos[x], f}, {x, -2 `π`, 2 `π`},`
      `PlotRange → 3, Ticks → None, PlotStyle → {Gray, Black},`
      `Epilog → {PointSize[.04], Point[{{`$\frac{\pi}{4}$`, `$\frac{1}{\sqrt{2}}$`}]}], {f, tlist}];`

In[26]:= `GraphicsGrid[Partition[plots, 3]]`

Out[26]=

In a live session the following command is fun. Simply click on a tab to see the Taylor polynomial of that degree.

In[27]:= `TabView[Table[k → plots〚k〛, {k, 12}], ImageSize → Automatic]`

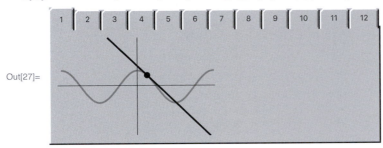

Out[27]=

Exercise 5 shows how to use the `Thread` command to construct this `TabView`.

Exercises 5.14

1. Find the limit as $n \to \infty$ of the sequence $\{n \cos(2\pi n)\}$. Use `DiscretePlot` and `Plot` to explore why the limit of this sequence is different from the limit of the continuous function $f(x) = x \cos(2\pi x)$ as $x \to \infty$.

2. Find the limit of the sequence: $\frac{2}{1}, \left(\frac{3}{2}\right)^2, \left(\frac{4}{3}\right)^3, \left(\frac{5}{4}\right)^4, \ldots$

3. Find the limit of the sequence: $\frac{1}{1}\left(\frac{1}{2}\right), \frac{1}{2}\left(\frac{2}{3}+\frac{2}{4}\right), \frac{1}{3}\left(\frac{3}{4}+\frac{3}{5}+\frac{3}{6}\right), \frac{1}{4}\left(\frac{4}{5}+\frac{4}{6}+\frac{4}{7}+\frac{4}{8}\right), \ldots$

4. Evaluate the following series.

   a. $\sum_{n=1}^{\infty} n\left(\frac{2}{3}\right)^{n-1}\left(\frac{1}{3}\right)$

   b. $\sum_{n=1}^{\infty} n\left(\frac{d}{d+1}\right)^{n-1}\left(\frac{1}{d+1}\right)$, where d is a positive integer.

5. The `Thread` command can be used to take two lists such as $\{1, 2, 3\}$ and $\{a, b, c\}$, and *thread* some command f through them to produce the list $\{f[1, a], f[2, b], f[3, c]\}$. It is particularly handy when constructing a `TabView` object, where the syntax requires a list of the form $\{label1 \to item1, label2 \to item2, label3 \to item3, \ldots\}$. In this case, f is the command `Rule` (the `FullForm` of $1 \to a$ is `Rule[1,a]`). `Thread` is discussed in greater detail in Section 8.4.

   a. Enter the following inputs to see `Thread` in action.

      `Thread[exampleFunction[{1, 2, 3}, {a, b, c}]]`

      `Thread[Rule[{1, 2, 3}, {a, b, c}]]`

      `Thread[{1, 2, 3} → {a, b, c}]`

   b. Use `Thread` rather than `Table` to create the `TabView` shown at the end of this section.

6. Create a `TabView` that displays the first ten distinct Taylor polynomials for $\sin(x)$ expanded about $x_0 = 0$.

6

Multivariable Calculus

6.1 Vectors

A standard notation for a vector in the plane is a coordinate pair, such as $\langle 2, 5 \rangle$. This represents the vector that has its tail at the origin and its head at the point with x coordinate 2 and y coordinate 5. Another standard notation for this vector is $2\vec{i} + 5\vec{j}$. Here $\vec{i}$ and $\vec{j}$ denote the unit vectors in the x and y directions, respectively.

In *Mathematica*, a vector in the plane is expressed as a *list* of length two, such as {2, 5}. Vector addition and scalar multiplication work exactly as you would expect:

```
In[1]:=  {2, 5} + {17, -4}
Out[1]=  {19, 1}
```

```
In[2]:=  -4 {2, 5}
Out[2]=  {-8, -20}
```

```
In[3]:=  i = {1, 0};
         j = {0, 1};
         2 i + 5 j
Out[5]=  {2, 5}
```

Higher-dimensional vectors are simply given as longer lists. Here is the sum of two vectors in three-space:

```
In[6]:=  {3, -57, 8} + {57, -3, π/4}
Out[6]=  {60, -60, 8 + π/4}
```

Vectors in the plane are sometimes given by their length and by the angle they make with the positive x axis. For instance, there is precisely one vector of length 3 whose direction is obtained by rotating the positive x axis 45° counterclockwise. What are the x and y coordinates of this vector? Simple trigonometry provides one means of answering this question:

In[7]:= `3 {Cos[45 Degree], Sin[45 Degree]}`

Out[7]= $\left\{ \dfrac{3}{\sqrt{2}}, \dfrac{3}{\sqrt{2}} \right\}$

The `AngleVector` command will provide such coordinates directly. Specify the polar angle (measured counterclockwise from the positive *x* direction), and it gives the unit vector pointing in that direction. This unit vector may then be scaled to any desired length.

In[8]:= `3 AngleVector[45 Degree]`

Out[8]= $\left\{ \dfrac{3}{\sqrt{2}}, \dfrac{3}{\sqrt{2}} \right\}$

The Dot Product and the Norm

The *dot product* of the vectors $\langle u_1, u_2, \ldots, u_n \rangle$ and $\langle v_1, v_2, \ldots, v_n \rangle$ is the scalar $u_1 v_1 + u_2 v_2 + \cdots + u_n v_n$. You can compute the dot product of vectors with *Mathematica* by placing a dot (a period) between them:

In[9]:= `{u₁, u₂}.{v₁, v₂}`

Out[9]= $u_1 v_1 + u_2 v_2$

In[10]:= `{3, 4}.{4, 5}`

Out[10]= 32

You can calculate the *norm* (i.e., the length or magnitude) of a vector using the `Norm` command.

In[11]:= `Norm[{3, 4}]`

Out[11]= 5

Note that you can `Normalize` a nonzero vector, that is, scale it by the reciprocal of its length and thereby obtain a unit vector. This is the same as dividing the vector by its `Norm`.

In[12]:= `Normalize[{3, 4}]`

Out[12]= $\left\{ \dfrac{3}{5}, \dfrac{4}{5} \right\}$

In[13]:= $\dfrac{\{3, 4\}}{\text{Norm}[\{3, 4\}]}$

Out[13]= $\left\{ \dfrac{3}{5}, \dfrac{4}{5} \right\}$

For any real vector $\vec{u}$, its norm is equivalent to the square root of the dot product $\vec{u}\cdot\vec{u}$:

```
In[14]:= Simplify[Norm[{u₁, u₂}], {u₁, u₂} ∈ Reals]
```

$$Out[14]= \sqrt{u_1^2 + u_2^2}$$

```
In[15]:= √({u₁, u₂}.{u₁, u₂})
```

$$Out[15]= \sqrt{u_1^2 + u_2^2}$$

> ⚠ We have made use of subscripts to represent a general vector with components u_1 and u_2. This looks very nice. However, it can get you into trouble if you try to give such a vector a name. You should never enter input such as u = {u₁, u₂}. This will throw *Mathematica* into an infinite loop. See Exercise 4. After Section 6.1 we will avoid subscripts when computing with vectors.

The dot product can also be employed to find the angle between a pair of vectors. You may recall that the cosine of the angle θ between vectors $\vec{u}$ and $\vec{v}$ is given by the formula:

$$\cos\theta = \frac{\vec{u}\cdot\vec{v}}{\|\vec{u}\|\,\|\vec{v}\|}$$

where $\|\vec{u}\|$ denotes the norm of $\vec{u}$. You can find the angle (in radians) between vectors like this:

```
In[16]:= u = {2, 4}; v = {9, -13};
         ArcCos[ u.v / (Norm[u] Norm[v]) ] // N
```

```
Out[17]= 2.0724
```

The command VectorAngle will produce the same result.

```
In[18]:= VectorAngle[u, v] // N
Out[18]= 2.0724
```

Conversion to degrees requires multiplying by the conversion factor $\frac{180}{\pi}$, or dividing by the built-in constant Degree:

```
In[19]:= % / Degree
Out[19]= 118.74
```

Rendering Vectors in the Plane

One can display vectors using the graphics primitive `Arrow`.

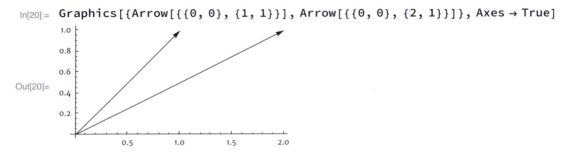

`In[20]:=` `Graphics[{Arrow[{{0, 0}, {1, 1}}], Arrow[{{0, 0}, {2, 1}}]}, Axes → True]`

`Out[20]=`

`Arrow` accepts as its argument a list of two ordered pairs. These represent the coordinates of the tail and head of the arrow, respectively. Note, however, that you can double-click on any arrow in a graphic, then drag either end of the arrow to a new location. Or you can drag the middle portion and move the entire arrow to a new location, preserving its length and direction.

But working programmatically (rather than grabbing and dragging) is advantageous for attaining precise positioning. Here we illustrate a vector sum:

```
In[21]:=  u = {1, 2}; v = {2, 1}; o = {0, 0};
          Graphics[{Arrow[{o, u}], Arrow[{o, v}],
            {Gray, Arrow[{u, u + v}], Arrow[{v, u + v}]},
            {Red, Arrow[{o, u + v}]}
          }, PlotRange → {{0, 3}, {0, 3}}, Axes → True]
```

`Out[22]=`

And after all that effort, why not drop it into a `Manipulate`? The following example has a `Locator` at the head of each of the two component vectors, so that you can drag either of those vectors by the head to move them.

```
In[23]:= Manipulate[Graphics[{
        Arrow[{{0, 0}, u}], Arrow[{{0, 0}, v}],
           {Gray, Arrow[{u, u + v}], Arrow[{v, u + v}]},
           {Red, Arrow[{{0, 0}, u + v}]}
          }, PlotRange → 3, Axes → True, Ticks → None],
         {{u, {1, 2}}, Locator, Appearance → None},
         {{v, {2, 1}}, Locator, Appearance → None}]
```

Out[23]=
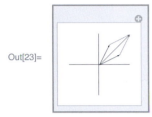

Rendering Vectors in Space

Three-dimensional vectors may be similarly produced: Each coordinate is now a 3-tuple. Just remember to use Graphics3D instead of Graphics to render the vectors.

```
In[24]:= Graphics3D[{Arrow[{{0, 0, 0}, {1, 0, 0}}], Arrow[{{0, 0, 0}, {0, 1, 0}}],
           Arrow[{{0, 0, 0}, {0, 0, 1}}], {Red, Arrow[{{0, 0, 0}, {1, 1, 1}}]}
          }]
```

Out[24]=
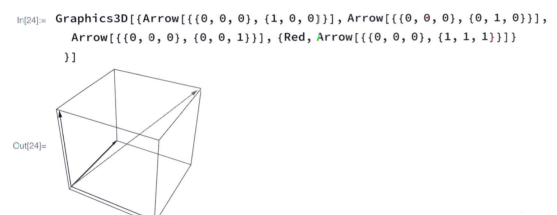

The Cross Product

Imagine a pair of vectors $\vec{u}$ and $\vec{v}$ in three-space drawn with their tails at the same point. As long as $\vec{u}$ and $\vec{v}$ are not colinear, there is a unique plane containing them. The *cross product* of $\vec{u}$ and $\vec{v}$ is a normal vector to this plane, one whose magnitude is equal to the area of the parallelogram with adjacent sides $\vec{u}$ and $\vec{v}$. If $\vec{u}$ and $\vec{v}$ are colinear, their cross product is the zero vector.

You can harness *Mathematica* to take the cross product of a pair of vectors with the command `Cross`. Here that command is used to reveal the algebraic formula for the cross product:

In[25]:= `Cross[{`u_1`, `u_2`, `u_3`}, {`v_1`, `v_2`, `v_3`}]`

Out[25]= `{-`$u_3 v_2$` + `$u_2 v_3$`, `$u_3 v_1$` - `$u_1 v_3$`, -`$u_2 v_1$` + `$u_1 v_2$`}`

And here it is used to find the cross product of a specific pair of vectors:

In[26]:= `Cross[{1, 3, 5}, {7, 9, 11}]`

Out[26]= `{-12, 24, -12}`

You can also invoke the `Cross` command in infix form by typing the first vector, then typing [ESC]cross [ESC] followed by the second vector. The input then looks like the standard notation:

In[27]:= `{1, 3, 5} × {7, 9, 11}`

Out[27]= `{-12, 24, -12}`

Don't confuse the smaller × produced above with the larger × found on the Calculator section of the Basic Math Assistant palette—that one is used for ordinary (component-wise) multiplication.

In[28]:= `{1, 3, 5} × {7, 9, 11}`

Out[28]= `{7, 27, 55}`

Exercises 6.1

1. Find an exact expression for the sine of the angle between the vectors $\langle 2, -1, 1 \rangle$ and $\langle 3, 2, 1 \rangle$.

2. Look up the `Sign` command in the Documentation Center. Explain how to use it with the dot product to determine whether the angle between a pair of vectors is acute, right, or obtuse.

3. The dot product, we learned in this section, is implemented in *Mathematica* in infix form by placing a period between a pair of vectors. As always, there is a "square bracket" version of this command. It is called `Dot`.

    a. Use `Dot` to take the dot product of `{u1,u2,u3}` with `{v1,v2,v3}`.

    b. The dot product is the most common example of an *inner product*. *Mathematica* has another command called `Inner` that can be used to create alternate inner products. Verify that the input `Inner[Times, {u1,u2,u3}, {v1,v2,v3}, Plus]` gives the same output as that produced in part a.

4. Near the beginning of this section, we did several computations using general vectors of the form $\{u_1, u_2\}$. The subscripts are obtained from the keyboard by typing, for instance, u [CTRL]-[_] 1. The `FullForm` of the resulting expression is `Subscript[u,1]`. Many textbooks will (in the course of a proof, for instance) write, "Let $\vec{u} = \langle u_1, u_2 \rangle$." While this is a convenient notation, the equal sign should not be used as part of your *Mathematica* input in this context, as you may fall into an infinite loop. If you were to enter the input $u = \{u_1, u_2\}$, what would happen? The same bad thing will happen if you enter the more simple input $u = u_1$, or even u = {u}. Try it, then explain what's going on. As the blues singer Kelly Joe Phelps put it, "It's not so far to go to find trouble."

5. Use *Mathematica* to verify the parallelogram law in $\mathbb{R}^3$: For any pair of vectors $\vec{u}$ and $\vec{v}$, the following equation is satisfied: $\left\|\vec{u} + \vec{v}\right\|^2 + \left\|\vec{u} - \vec{v}\right\|^2 = 2\left\|\vec{u}\right\|^2 + 2\left\|\vec{v}\right\|^2$.

6.2 Real-Valued Functions of Two or More Variables

One may define a real-valued function with two (or more) variables exactly as we did in Section 3.1, but with an additional variable, like this:

In[1]:= `f[x_, y_] := Sin[x² - y²]`

However, in a multivariate context we will generally find it more convenient (for reasons that will come to light shortly) to make a simple assignment like this instead:

In[2]:= `Clear[f, x, y];`
        `f = Sin[x² - y²];`

A function of three variables is dealt with similarly. Note that it is important to `Clear` any variables that have previously been assigned values.

In[4]:= `Clear[g, x, y, z];`
        `g = x² y³ - 3 x z;`

> ♡ **Multi-letter variable names**
>
> When defining a function, remember to leave a space (or to use a ⋆) between variables that you intend to multiply, otherwise *Mathematica* will interpret the multi-letter combination as a single variable. For example, note the space between the x and the z in the definition of the function g above. Said another way, one may use multi-letter variable names when defining a function; for example, names such as x1, x2, and so on are perfectly acceptable as variables.

To evaluate a function defined in this fashion, one uses replacement rules. For instance, here is $f\left(0, \sqrt{\pi/4}\,\right)$:

In[6]:= `f /. {x → 0, y → √π / 4}`

Out[6]= $-\dfrac{1}{\sqrt{2}}$

It may be useful to `Simplify` the output on some occasions. Here is $f(1 - \pi, 1 + \pi)$:

In[7]:= `f /. {x → 1 - π, y → 1 + π}`

Out[7]= `Sin[ (1 - π)² - (1 + π)² ]`

In[8]:= `Simplify[%]`

Out[8]= `0`

Plotting Functions of Two Variables with Plot3D

We plot functions of two variables with the command `Plot3D`. It works pretty much like `Plot`, but you will need an iterator specifying the span of values assumed by each of the *two* variables. The plot will be shown over the rectangular domain in the plane determined by the two iterators. When first evaluated, the positive *x* direction is to the right along the front of the plot, the positive *y* direction is to the back along the side of the plot, and the positive *z* direction is up:

In[9]:= `Plot3D[f, {x, -2, 2}, {y, -1, 1}]`

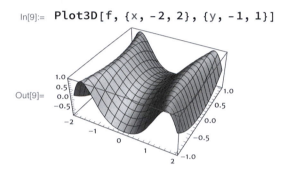

Out[9]=

Grab such a plot with your mouse and drag. This will rotate the image so that you can see it from any vantage point you like. Hold down the OPTION key while you drag and you can zoom in and out. It's a beautiful thing.

Note that it is a simple matter to produce a sketch of any vertical *cross-section* (sometimes called a trace) for such a plot in either the *x* or *y* direction. Simply set one of the two variables to a numerical value and make a `Plot` using the other as the independent variable.

In[10]:= `GraphicsRow@{Plot[f /. y → 0, {x, -2, 2}, AxesLabel → {x, z}],`
                          `Plot[f /. x → 0, {y, -1, 1}, AxesLabel → {y, z}]}`

Out[10]=

This technique may be used to find the cross-section of a plot along *any* line in the *xy* plane. For example, here is the cross-section of the plot by the line $y = \frac{1}{2}x + 1$:

In[11]:= $\text{Plot}\left[f\ /.\ y \to \dfrac{1}{2}\,x + 1,\ \{x,\ -2,\ 2\}\right]$

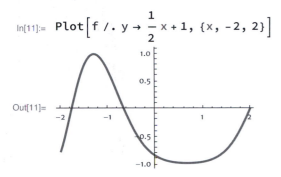

Out[11]=

We'll discuss how one can use the Mesh option to superimpose these traces onto the original Plot3D of *f* in the subsection "Controlling the Mesh Lines" later in this section of the chapter. See Exercise 6 for more on cross-sections.

Options and Themes for 3D Plotting Commands

The information in this section applies to any plotting command that generates a three-dimensional graphic. Such commands include Plot3D, ContourPlot3D, ParametricPlot3D, Spherical-Plot3D, and RevolutionPlot3D.

As with their single-variable counterparts, these commands come with pre-made themes. Each theme is a neatly packaged collection of option settings. Begin typing PlotTheme after the requisite arguments and a popup will show a thumbnail preview of the available themes. So if, for instance, you want a Plot3D that shows level curves (sometimes called contour lines) instead of the default mesh, you may simply choose the "ZMesh" theme. Or if you want a 3D-printable solid, choose the "FilledSurface" or "ThickSurface" theme.

In[12]:= $\text{GraphicsRow@Table[Plot3D}[f,\ \{x,\ -2,\ 2\},\ \{y,\ -1,\ 1\},\ \text{PlotTheme} \to \text{theme]},$
$\qquad\qquad \{\text{theme},\ \{\text{"ZMesh"},\ \text{"FilledSurface"}\}\}]$

Out[12]=

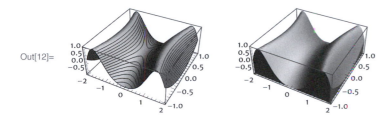

For greater control of your output, there are abundant options available. Among the options that are essentially the same as the familiar options for Plot (discussed in Section 3.3) are such common settings as AxesLabel, PlotLabel, PlotPoints, MaxRecursion and PlotRange. Other options, such as Mesh and MeshFunctions, work in a similar manner as they do in Plot, but now everything is one dimension higher. In short, they will take some getting used to.

PlotPoints, MaxRecursion, and Toggling Mesh to None or All

Note first that the simple setting `Mesh → None` will make the mesh lines disappear, while the setting `Mesh → All` will display all of the polygons produced by `Plot3D` to render the image. While the former is a popular setting that produces a beautiful image (especially when `PlotPoints` is bumped up from its default value), the latter provides a window into the means by which `Plot3D` does its stuff:

In[13]:= $\{$`Plot3D`$\left[e^{Sin[x\,y]}, \{x, -\pi, \pi\}, \{y, -\pi, \pi\}, Mesh \to None, MaxRecursion \to 4\right],$

`Plot3D`$\left[e^{Sin[x\,y]}, \{x, -\pi, \pi\}, \{y, -\pi, \pi\}, Mesh \to All, MaxRecursion \to 4\right]\}$

Out[13]=

Note that like `Plot`, `Plot3D` uses an adaptive algorithm that recursively subdivides the surface into smaller polygons in areas where the surface bends more sharply. `PlotPoints` settings control how many equally spaced points are initially sampled in each direction (so a setting of 50 will force *Mathematica* to sample $50 \times 50 = 2500$ points in the domain). `MaxRecursion` controls the number of recursive subdivisions permitted to fine-tune the image. Large settings for these options produce beautiful images, but may result in perceptibly slower rendering times, and will definitely produce larger file sizes when the notebook is saved. See Exercise 2.

Adjusting the PlotRange and BoxRatios

As is the case with the `Plot` command, `Plot3D` will sometimes clip the highest peaks and lowest valleys in a plot in order to render the middle portions with greater detail. The option setting `Clip ⁚ pingStyle → None` will remove the default horizontal planes placed into the clipped areas. `Clip ⁚ pingStyle` may also be set to a `Graphics` directive such as `Opacity[.5]`.

In[14]:= `Table`$\left[\right.$`Plot3D`$\left[\dfrac{x^2\,y^5 - x^5\,y^2}{100} + e^{-(x^2+y^2)}, \{x, -3, 3\},\right.$

$\{y, -3, 3\},$ `ClippingStyle` $\to$ k$\left.\right]$, $\{k, \{Automatic, None\}\}\left.\right]$

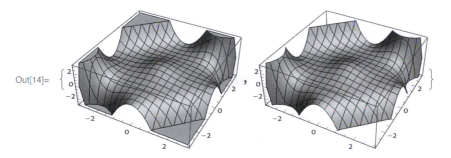

Out[14]=

The setting `PlotRange → All` will force *Mathematica* to show the entire graph with no clipping. Notice, however, that the bump in the middle of the plot vanishes from view due to the compression of the vertical axis:

In[15]:= $\text{Plot3D}\left[\dfrac{x^2\, y^5 - x^5\, y^2}{100} + e^{-(x^2+y^2)},\ \{x,\, -3,\, 3\},\ \{y,\, -3,\, 3\},\ \text{PlotRange} \to \text{All}\right]$

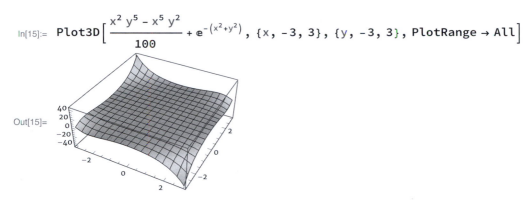

Out[15]=

The option `BoxRatios` determines the relative dimensions of the bounding box. The simple setting `BoxRatios → 1` will produce a cubical bounding box; the setting `BoxRatios → Automatic` will scale the bounding box so that all axes have the same scale. It is analogous to the option `AspectRatio` used in two-dimensional plots. Be careful to not use this setting in cases such as the one above where one axis would be dramatically longer than the others. A setting such as `BoxRatios → {1, 1, 2}` will produce a bounding box whose horizontal sides are the same length, but whose vertical dimension is twice as long.

In[16]:= `Plot3D[Sin[x Cos[y]], {x, -6, 6}, {y, -3, 3}, BoxRatios → Automatic]`

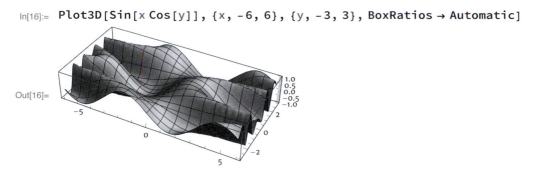

Out[16]=

The Bounding Box, Axes, and ViewPoint

The options `Boxed` and `Axes` can be used to modify the appearance of the bounding box and the tick marks that appear on three of its sides. By default, both options are set to `True`. To remove the bounding box entirely, set both to `False`. `Axes` can also be set to a list, as in the input below, to display only selected axes. The option `AxesEdge` controls in each of the three coordinate directions which of the four parallel sides of the bounding box in that direction are to be used as an axis. Each coordinate direction is specified by an ordered pair. For example, if the vertical or z axis is given the specification `{-1, -1}`, that means that the z axis will be placed on the left (negative x side) and front (negative y side).

```
In[17]:=  Plot3D[Sin[x Cos[y]], {x, -6, 6}, {y, -3, 3},
            BoxRatios → Automatic, Boxed → False, Axes → {False, False, True},
            AxesEdge → {Automatic, Automatic, {-1, -1}}]
```

`ViewPoint` specifies the position in space (relative to the center of the graphic) from which it is seen. For a plot centered at the origin, the setting `{0, 0, 4}` will give a view from above, while the setting `{3, 0, 1}` will yield a vantage point that is three units from the origin along the positive x axis, and one unit above the xy plane.

```
In[18]:=  Plot3D[Sin[x Cos[y]], {x, -6, 6}, {y, -3, 3},
            BoxRatios → Automatic, ViewPoint → {3, 0, 1}]
```

The ColorFunction

The option `ColorFunction` controls the coloring of the graph. Any of the color gradients available in the `ColorData` archive may be used to color a plot. Open the Color Schemes palette for a listing of available gradients. For instance, here we color a plot using a color gradient reminiscent of that used in topographical maps, where low regions are colored dark blue, middle regions are shaded with greens and browns, and peaks are white.

In[19]:= Plot3D$\left[\mathrm{e}^{-(x^2+y^2)}\right.$, {x, -3, 3}, {y, -3, 3}, BoxRatios → Automatic,

ColorFunction → "DarkTerrain", PlotRange → All, Mesh → None$\Big]$

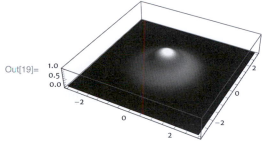

Out[19]=

ColorFunction allows you to assume complete control over the manner in which color is applied to a surface. With a bit of work, the graph of a function may be colored (using any color gradient you like) according to the values of any other function. See Exercise 1.

PlotStyle and Lighting

The PlotStyle and Lighting options provide another means of adjusting the appearance of the plot. In *Mathematica*, three-dimensional graphics are colored according to a physical lighting model that includes intrinsic surface color, the diffusive and reflective properties of the surface, and lighting (you may control the position, direction, and color of as many light sources as you like). By default, the polygons used to construct a Plot3D are all white; the lighting is responsible for all the color you see. You have total control over the output, and the possibilities are truly staggering.

PlotStyle is used to set the intrinsic surface color, and to specify the surface's diffusive and reflective properties. Several settings may be simultaneously given by wrapping them within the Direc⁚ tive command. There are three potential specifications. A straight color or opacity setting like Blue and/or Opacity[.5] can be given to set the intrinsic surface color or transparency. This color will interact with the lighting. A Glow setting, such as Glow[Red], will emanate from the surface irrespective of the color of the lighting. Finally, a Specularity setting determines the diffusive and reflective properties of the surface. Specularity can accept two arguments. The first determines the color and amount of diffusion added to reflected light. A numerical value of 1 is equivalent to a color setting of White; in this case 100% of the light is reflected back, with no alteration to its color other than that determined by the surface's color. The second argument controls the shininess of the surface. Typical values range from 1 (dull) to 50 (shiny). The setting Specularity[White, 20] is good for creating the appearance of an anodized metallic surface:

In[20]:= **Plot3D[x Cos[x y], {x, -3, 3}, {y, -2, 2}, Mesh → None, MaxRecursion → 4,
            PlotStyle → Directive[Lighter[Red], Specularity[White, 20]]]**

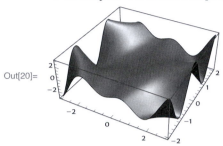

Out[20]=

Lighting can be adjusted in numerous ways. The default setting includes both ambient light and four colored light sources (although if an explicit **ColorFunction** is specified, white light from these same sources will be used instead). The simple setting **Lighting → "Neutral"** will force the use of white rather than colored lights.

In[21]:= **Plot3D[x Cos[x y], {x, -3, 3}, {y, -2, 2}, Mesh → None, MaxRecursion → 4,
            PlotStyle → Directive[Lighter[Red], Specularity[White, 20]],
            Lighting → "Neutral"]**

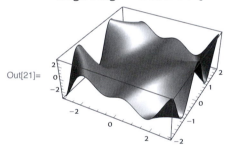

Out[21]=

The Documentation Center page for **Lighting** gives information on setting ambient, spot, and directional light sources. We note here that the setting **Lighting → {{"Ambient", White}}** is similar to the setting **Lighting → "Neutral"**, but the latter includes point light sources and the shadows they create, and so is better at giving the illusion of depth. The former may be appropriate when a **ColorFunction** is used and shadows would interfere with the information that the color provides.

Plotting over Nonrectangular Regions

A function may be plotted over any subregion of its natural domain. To illustrate how this is done, we first describe the region over which our function will be plotted. If the region is, say, the disk of unit radius centered at the origin, we may use **Disk[]**, which is the same as **Disk[{0, 0}, 1]**. Type [ESC] elem[ESC] to produce the ∈ character, which reads "is an element of."

In[22]:= **Plot3D$\left[-\sqrt{x^2+y^2}\ ,\ \{x,\ y\}\ \in\ \text{Disk}[\,]\right]$**

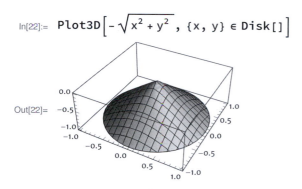

Out[22]=

Regions may be defined in a myriad of ways. The input below, for example, illustrates three equivalent ways to describe the same triangular region—you may use whichever you like. The && reads as "and," useful when listing conditions which must all be satisfied by points in the region. Type ⎡ESC⎤scT ⎡ESC⎤ to produce the $\mathcal{T}$ character, and note that $\mathcal{I}$ and $\mathcal{P}$ are obtained similarly.

In[23]:= **$\mathcal{T}$ = Triangle[{{0, 0}, {1, 0}, {0, 1}}];**
$\mathcal{I}$ = ImplicitRegion[x > 0 && y > 0 && y < 1 - x, {x, y}];
$\mathcal{P}$ = ParametricRegion[{{x, y}, 0 < x < 1 && 0 < y < 1 - x}, {x, y}];
GraphicsRow[{Region[$\mathcal{T}$], Region[$\mathcal{I}$], Region[$\mathcal{P}$]}]

Out[26]=

We may then plot our function over this region.

In[27]:= **Plot3D$\left[-\sqrt{x^2+y^2}\ ,\ \{x,\ y\}\ \in\ \mathcal{T}\right]$**

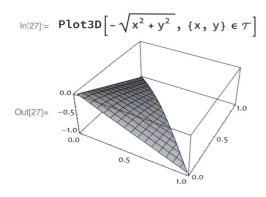

Out[27]=

If a region has holes, the function will not be plotted there.

In[28]:= $\texttt{Plot3D}\left[-\sqrt{x^2 + y^2}\ ,\right.$

$\left.\{x,\,y\} \in \texttt{MengerMesh[3, DataRange} \rightarrow \{\{-1,\,1\},\,\{-1,\,1\}\}]\right]$

Out[28]=

For a function with a discontinuity at a single point, it is often helpful to plot it over a region with a hole around that point. A classic example is the function $f(x, y) = \frac{x^2 y}{x^4 + y^2}$, which is not defined at the origin, and which has an essential discontinuity there. We remove a small disk around the origin (of radius 0.1), and get a beautiful image:

In[29]:= $\texttt{Plot3D}\left[\dfrac{x^2\,y}{x^4 + y^2},\ \{x,\,y\} \in \texttt{Annulus[\{0, 0\}, \{.1, 1\}]},\right.$

$\left.\texttt{Mesh} \rightarrow \texttt{None, MaxRecursion} \rightarrow 4\right]$

Out[29]=

Controlling the Mesh Lines

We've already discussed the two most common settings for the Mesh option, namely None and All. But much more is possible. Set Mesh to a positive integer, say 20, and there will be 20 mesh lines displayed (rather than the default 15) in each direction. Set Mesh to a list of two numbers, say {5, 30}, and there will be five mesh lines corresponding to five evenly spaced x values, and 30 mesh lines corresponding to 30 evenly spaced y values.

In[30]:= `Plot3D[`$\dfrac{x^2\,y}{x^2+y^2}$`, {x, -3, 3}, {y, -3, 3}, Mesh → {5, 30}]`

Out[30]=

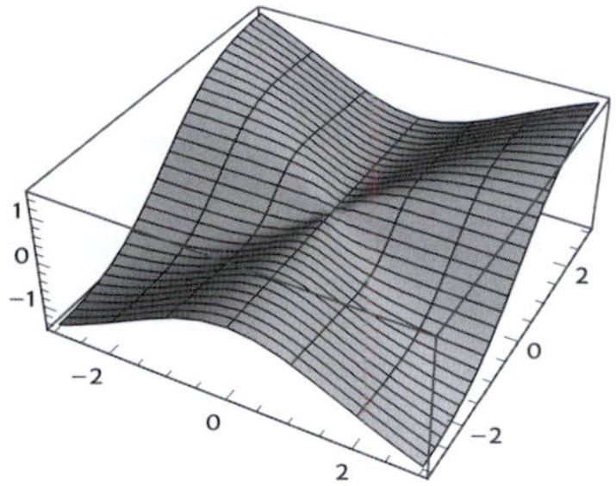

You may also specify *lists* of the specific x and y values where mesh lines should be drawn. A `Mesh` setting of `{{-2, 0, 2}, {1}}` will place mesh lines at $x = -2$, $x = 0$, and $x = 2$, and at $y = 1$. This technique can be useful for visually approximating the partial derivatives of a function at a particular point in the domain. In this case, $\dfrac{\partial f}{\partial x}$ appears to be negative at the point $(-2, 1)$ and positive at $(2, 1)$. See Exercise 6.

In[31]:= `Plot3D[`$\dfrac{x^2\,y}{x^2+y^2}$`, {x, -3, 3}, {y, -3, 3},`

           `Mesh → {{-2, 0, 2}, {1}}, Boxed → False]`

Out[31]=

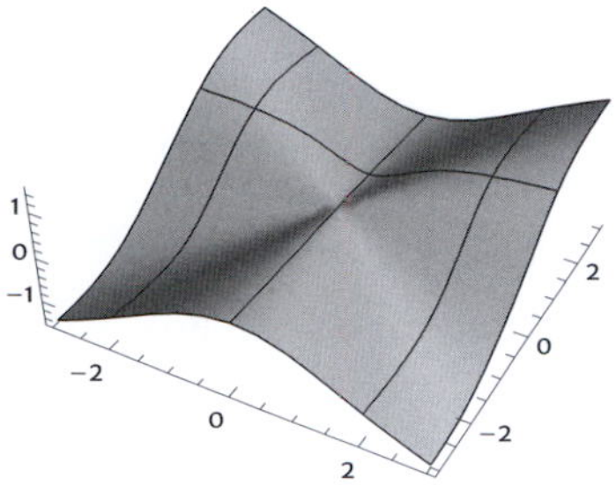

The `MeshFunctions` option gives you even more control over the rendering of the mesh lines on a plot. The price of this versatility is that it will take a bit of practice to master. Your efforts here will be well rewarded, so read on.

By default there are two mesh functions, one to produce those mesh lines corresponding to fixed x values, and one to produce the perpendicular collection of mesh lines corresponding to fixed y values. Together they form the familiar grid pattern that graces your `Plot3D` outputs. This default specification, if you were to manually type it, would read:

`MeshFuntions → {Function[{x,y,z},x], Function[{x,y,z},y]}`

It is a list of two pure functions, where each takes three arguments (one for each coordinate position in three-space). Equivalently, this default setting could be entered using the common shorthand notation: `MeshFunctions → {#1 &, #2 &}`. Pure functions are discussed in detail in Section 8.4. In any event, mesh lines will be drawn on the surface along curves where the mesh function is constant. By default, curves corresponding to 15 evenly spaced constant values will be displayed.

Perhaps the most common non-default setting is the following, which places *level curves* on your plot. That is, the third variable (we usually call it *z*) is set to 15 evenly spaced values within the plot range, and a mesh curve is added to the surface at each of these values.

In[32]:= `Plot3D[x² y³ + (x - 1)² y, {x, -2, 2}, {y, -2, 2}, MeshFunctions → {#3 &}]`

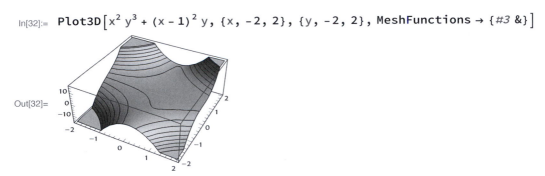

Out[32]=

As mentioned earlier, this could also be done with the option setting `PlotTheme → "ZMesh"`.

But the point of this discussion is that with `MeshFunctions`, you may define *any* mesh function you like, not only those appearing in a menu. Here we place mesh lines according to distance from the origin. In other words, each mesh line lies on the surface of an invisible sphere centered at the origin.

In[33]:= `Plot3D[x² y³ + (x - 1)² y, {x, -2, 2}, {y, -2, 2},`
          `MeshFunctions → {Norm[{#1, #2, #3}] &}, PlotRange → 2, BoxRatios → 1]`

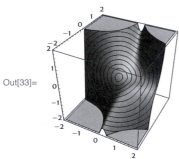

Out[33]=

MeshShading

The `MeshShading` option allows the regions between mesh lines to receive specific color directives. The setting for this option has the same list structure as `MeshFunctions`; if there is a list of two mesh functions, you should have a list of two `MeshShading` settings. Each such setting is itself a list of directives that will be used cyclically (if this list is shorter than the number of mesh regions). Setting the Lighting to "Neutral" will replace the default colored lighting with white lights, so that the colors specified in the MeshShading are accurately rendered. For instance:

In[34]:= `Plot3D[x² y³ + (x - 1)² y, {x, -3, 3}, {y, -3, 3},`
`    BoxRatios → 1, MeshFunctions → {#3 &}, Mesh → 20,`
`    MeshShading → {Red, Green}, Lighting → "Neutral"]`

Out[34]=

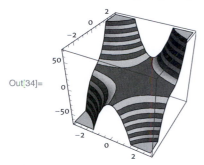

Set it to a list whose length matches the Mesh setting, and you will cycle precisely once through the list of directives. To utilize an entire color gradient, keep in mind that each color gradient function (such as ColorData["StarryNightColors"]) is defined on the domain $0 \le t \le 1$.

In[35]:= `Plot3D[x² y³ + (x - 1)² y, {x, -3, 3}, {y, -3, 3},`
`    BoxRatios → 1, MeshFunctions → {#3 &}, Mesh → 20,`
`    MeshShading → Table[ColorData["StarryNightColors"][t],`
`    {t, 0, 1, 1 / 20}], Lighting → "Neutral"]`

Out[35]=

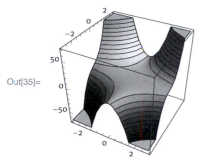

The output above is similar to that produced with ColorFunction → "StarryNightColors" (and no MeshShading or Lighting specifications). When MeshShading is used, each band between mesh lines is uniformly shaded. When ColorFunction is used, the shading varies continuously. When there are multiple MeshFunctions, the colors will criss-cross like a woven basket. Below we use the default MeshFunctions setting {#1 &, #2 &}:

In[36]:= `Plot3D[`$x^2 y^3 + (x - 1)^2 y$`, {x, -3, 3}, {y, -3, 3}, BoxRatios → 1, Mesh → 20,`
  `MeshShading → {{Yellow, Green}, {Black, White}}, Lighting → "Neutral"]`

Out[36]=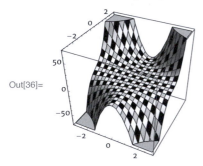

Plotting Functions of Two Variables with ContourPlot

Another commonly used command for visualizing a real-valued function of two variables is `Contour` `Plot`. A contour plot is a two-dimensional rendering of a three-dimensional surface. Imagine looking at the surface from above and placing contour lines (also called level curves) on the surface, each one a curve that is level in the sense that its height above (or below) the xy plane is constant. The contour plot is much like a topographical map—it comprises the projections of the contour lines onto the xy plane. The regions between adjacent contour lines will be shaded according to their relative height above (or below) the xy plane; darker regions are lower and lighter regions are higher.

We've previously used `ContourPlot` to plot curves representing the solutions of an *equation* (such as $\sin(x \cos y) = 0$). This solution curve can be regarded as a single level curve for the function $f(x, y) = \sin(x \cos y)$. To produce a full contour plot, use `ContourPlot` in a manner identical to that of `Plot3D`. Here we see a `ContourPlot` and a `Plot3D` of the same function, showing the same level curves and using similar shading:

In[37]:= `{ContourPlot[Sin[x Cos[y]], {x, -3, 3},`
  `{y, -3, 3}, Contours → 9, ColorFunction → "CoffeeTones"],`
  `Plot3D[Sin[x Cos[y]], {x, -3, 3}, {y, -3, 3}, MeshFunctions → {#3 &},`
  `Mesh → 9, ColorFunction → "CoffeeTones", ViewPoint → {0, -1, 2},`
  `Boxed → False, Axes → {True, True, False}]}`

Out[37]= (plots)

Perhaps the most commonly used option setting is `Contours`. Set it to a positive integer, say 20, and you will see 20 contour lines in the resulting plot. Set it to a specific *list* of values and you will see the contour lines through precisely those z values. If this list has a single value (as in the middle plot below), you will essentially be viewing the set of solutions to an equation in two variables (as in the rightmost plot below):

In[38]:= `GraphicsRow@`
`{ContourPlot[(1 + x²) (1 + y²), {x, -2, 2}, {y, -2, 2}, Contours → 20],`
`ContourPlot[(1 + x²) (1 + y²), {x, -2, 2}, {y, -2, 2}, Contours → {4}],`
`ContourPlot[(1 + x²) (1 + y²) ⩵ 4, {x, -2, 2}, {y, -2, 2}]}`

Out[38]=

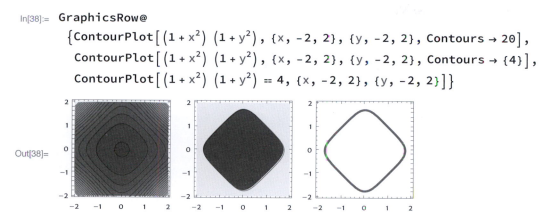

The `ContourShading` option works much like the `MeshShading` option for `Plot3D`. Note that you may set this option to `None`. As was the case with `Plot3D`, the `ColorFunction` may be set to any named color gradient.

In[39]:= `GraphicsRow@{ContourPlot[(1 + x²) (1 + y²),`
`{x, -2, 2}, {y, -2, 2}, ContourShading → {Red, Blue}],`
`ContourPlot[(1 + x²) (1 + y²), {x, -2, 2}, {y, -2, 2},`
`ContourShading → None], ContourPlot[(1 + x²) (1 + y²),`
`{x, -2, 2}, {y, -2, 2}, ColorFunction → "IslandColors"]}`

Out[39]=

Also important are `PlotPoints` and `MaxRecursion`, which, as you might expect, can be employed to improve image quality. The function $\frac{x^2}{1-x+y}$ is not defined along the line $y = x - 1$, and `ContourPlot` with its default settings has difficulty in the vicinity of this line. Increasing `PlotPoints` helps. The `Exclusions` option provides another means of dealing with such discontinuities. In the next example, we apply the `Quiet` command in postfix form to suppress warning messages that the function evaluates to $1/0$ at some points in this domain—those are points on the line $y = x - 1$.

In[40]:= $\left\{\texttt{ContourPlot}\left[\dfrac{x^2}{1-x+y}, \{x, -2, 2\}, \{y, -2, 2\}, \texttt{PlotPoints} \to 60\right],\right.$

$\texttt{ContourPlot}\left[\dfrac{x^2}{1-x+y}, \{x, -2, 2\},\right.$

$\left.\left.\{y, -2, 2\}, \texttt{Exclusions} \to \texttt{"Discontinuities"}\right]\right\} \texttt{ // Quiet}$

Out[40]= $\left\{\right.$ $\left., \right.$ $\left.\right\}$

Sometimes a Plot3D can aid in the visualization of such a function. It clearly shows the function trending toward positive infinity when (x, y) approaches the line $y = x - 1$ from one side, and negative infinity when it approaches from the other.

In[41]:= $\texttt{Plot3D}\left[\dfrac{x^2}{1-x+y}, \{x, -2, 2\}, \{y, -2, 2\}, \texttt{PlotTheme} \to \texttt{"ZMesh"}\right]$

Out[41]=

ContourPlot accepts many of the same options as Plot3D. Exceptions are those options that are specific to two-dimensional graphics. For instance, we use AspectRatio rather than BoxRatios to adjust the relative dimensions of a graphic produced by ContourPlot. Note that by default, a ContourPlot will be square.

In[42]:= `GraphicsRow@`
`{ContourPlot[Sin[x Cos[y]], {x, -6, 6}, {y, -3, 3}],`
`ContourPlot[Sin[x Cos[y]],`
`{x, -6, 6}, {y, -3, 3}, AspectRatio → Automatic]}`

Out[42]=

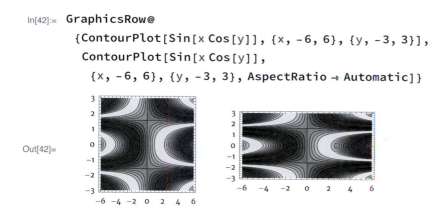

By default, `ContourPlot` will embed tooltips into its output. Position the tip of the cursor along a level curve to see the value of the z coordinate for all points on that curve. The option setting `Con` `tourLabels → All` will retain the tooltips, and will also place these values directly onto the graphic.

In[43]:= `ContourPlot[Sin[x Cos[y]], {x, -1, 1}, {y, -1, 1}, ContourLabels → All]`

Out[43]=

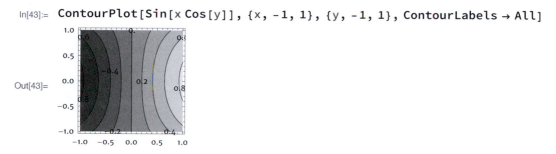

While the placement of these labels on the graphic is handled automatically, the appearance and indeed the function used to calculate the value for each label can be adjusted. Below we use the default function value (displaying the z coordinate at the point (x, y)), but we make the text red in a 6 pt font.

In[44]:= `ContourPlot[Sin[x Cos[y]], {x, -1, 1}, {y, -1, 1},`
`ContourLabels → (Style[Text[#3, {#1, #2}], Red, 6] &)]`

Out[44]=

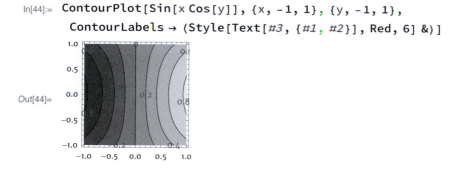

Another means to communicate the heights of the level curves in a contour plot is with the option setting PlotLegends → Automatic. This will place a legend next to your plot, like this:

In[45]:= `ContourPlot[Sin[x Cos[y]], {x, -1, 1},`
`        {y, -1, 1}, PlotLegends → Automatic]`

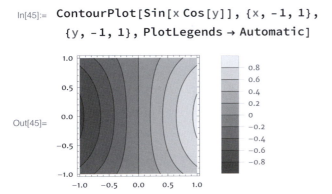

Out[45]=

In Section 3.7 we saw how to plot the curve defined by an equation in two variables using Contour-Plot. The key here is that the first argument is an *equation*, so only a single contour is rendered. For instance, here is the ellipse given by the equation $x^2 + 2y^2 = 1$.

In[46]:= `ellipse = ContourPlot[x² + 2 y² == 1, {x, -2, 2},`
`         {y, -2, 2}, ContourStyle → Directive[Thick, Green]]`

Out[46]=

We sometimes wish to superimpose such a curve with the ContourPlot of another function. It is a simple matter to use Show to display two such plots together, provided the second plot does not have any shading (if it did, it would entirely obscure the first plot beneath it). Since the ContourPlot of an equation will have no ContourShading, be sure to list it as the second plot inside Show.

$In[47]:=$ **fplot = ContourPlot$\left[x^2 - \dfrac{4 \times y}{y^2 + 1}, \{x, -2, 2\}, \{y, -2, 2\}\right]$;**

Show[fplot, ellipse]

$Out[48]=$

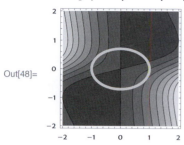

Another means for superimposing a curve on a ContourPlot is to add a custom MeshFunction to the plot. By default, ContourPlot will not display any mesh lines, so we are free to add any type of mesh we like. Below we display the ellipse $x^2 + 2y^2 = 1$ by using the mesh function Function$\left[\{x, y\}, x^2 + 2 y^2\right]$ and the single mesh value 1:

$In[49]:=$ **ContourPlot$\left[x^2 - \dfrac{4 \times y}{y^2 + 1}, \{x, -2, 2\}, \{y, -2, 2\},\right.$**

  MeshFunctions $\rightarrow \left\{\text{Function}\left[\{x, y\}, x^2 + 2 y^2\right]\right\},$

  Mesh $\rightarrow \{\{1\}\}$, MeshStyle $\rightarrow \{$Thick, Green$\}\Big]$

$Out[49]=$

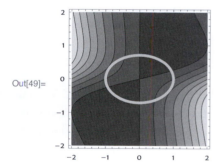

Plotting Level Surfaces with ContourPlot3D

Just as ContourPlot may be used to plot a curve defined by an equation in two variables (such as the circle $x^2 + y^2 = 1$, as outlined in Section 3.7) by using an equation as its first argument, the Contour Plot3D command may be used to plot a surface defined by an equation in three variables. Behold:

In[50]:= **ContourPlot3D$\left[x^2 + y^2 + z^2 == 1, \{x, -1, 1\}, \{y, -1, 1\}, \{z, -1, 1\}\right]$**

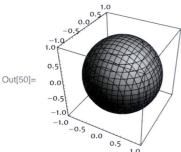

Out[50]=

And just as ContourPlot may be used to render a collection of level curves for a function of two variables (as discussed in the previous subsection of this chapter), ContourPlot3D may be used to render a collection of level surfaces for a function of three variables:

In[51]:= **ContourPlot3D$\left[x^2 + y^2 + z^2, \{x, -1, 1\}, \{y, -1, 1\},\right.$**
$\left.\{z, -1, 0\}, \text{BoxRatios} \rightarrow \{2, 2, 1\}, \text{Contours} \rightarrow 5, \text{Mesh} \rightarrow \text{None}\right]$

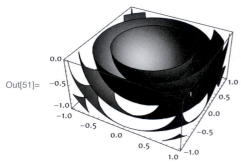

Out[51]=

Note that three iterators are needed, one for each of the three coordinate variables. Virtually all options are either identical to those of Plot3D, or can be surmised from those of ContourPlot. For instance, the Contours option works just as it does in ContourPlot. The ContourStyle option can be used to assign style directives to each level surface. The ColorFunction option can also be used for this purpose; the plot on the right uses a ColorData gradient specified by ColorFunction.

In[52]:= `GraphicsRow@{ContourPlot3D[`$x^2 + y^2 + z^2$`, {x, -1, 1},`
`{y, -1, 1}, {z, -1, 0}, BoxRatios → {2, 2, 1}, Contours → 5,`
`Mesh → None, Axes → False, ContourStyle → {White, Red}],`
`ContourPlot3D[`$x^2 + y^2 + z^2$`, {x, -1, 1}, {y, -1, 1},`
`{z, -1, 0}, BoxRatios → {2, 2, 1}, Contours → 5,`
`Mesh → None, Axes → False, ColorFunction → "Pastel"]}`

Out[52]=
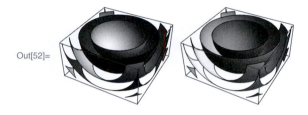

Here is a plot of the surface defined by the equation $\cos^2 x + \sin^2 y = 1 + \sin z$:

In[53]:= `ContourPlot3D[`$\cos[x]^2 + \sin[y]^2 == 1 + \cos[z]$`,`

$\left\{x, 0, 2\pi\right\}, \left\{y, \dfrac{\pi}{2}, \dfrac{5\pi}{2}\right\},$ `{z, 0, 2`π`}, Mesh → None,`

`ContourStyle → Directive[Brown, Specularity[White, 10]]]`

Out[53]=
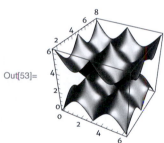

Constructing 3D plots of *solids* (rather than surfaces) can be accomplished with `RegionPlot3D`, which works much like `ContourPlot3D`. For instance, below we make a plot of the function $f(x, y, z) = y - z^2$ over the solid ball of radius 2 centered at the origin. In order to do this, we construct multiple cut-away views of this solid ball, with `MeshFunction` and `MeshShading` settings applied to color the ball according to the value of f. Note that the setting `BoxRatios → Automatic` is needed to give all axes the same scale (by default `RegionPlot3D` will scale the axes so as to create a cubical bounding box).

```
In[54]:=  GraphicsRow[Table[RegionPlot3D[Norm[{x, y, z}] ≤ 2,
              {x, -2, rightSide}, {y, -2, 2}, {z, -2, 2}, BoxRatios → Automatic,
              MeshFunctions → {Function[{x, y, z}, y - z²]}, Mesh → 10,
              MeshShading → Table[ColorData["TemperatureMap"][k], {k, 0, 1, .1}],
              Lighting → "Neutral", Axes → False],
            {rightSide, {2, 1, 0}}], ImageSize → 360]
```

Out[54]=

If $f(x, y, z)$ gives the density of the ball at the point (x, y, z), for instance, then the integral of f over the entire solid ball will give us the mass of the ball. Such integrals are discussed later in the chapter.

Graphics3D Primitives

Just as one can use the Graphics command to "manually" construct a two-dimensional graphic from primitive Point, Line, Polygon, Disk, Arrow, and Text objects, one can use the Graphics3D command to build three-dimensional graphics. The Graphics command was discussed in Section 3.0. In most cases you will use higher-level commands such as Plot3D and ContourPlot3D to generate 3D images. But there may come a time when you want to create a graphic from scratch, or to add a simple sphere or cylinder to the output of a command such as Plot3D. This section provides a basic introduction to such endeavors.

There are many primitive 3D objects that can be rendered using Graphics3D. They include familiar objects such as Point, Line, Polygon, Arrow, and Text, and 3D-specific objects such as Cone, Cuboid, Cylinder, and Sphere. In the following examples we use the Sphere and Cylinder primitives. Sphere takes two arguments: the coordinates of its center, and its radius. Cylinder also takes two arguments. The first is a list of two points: the endpoints of its central axis. The second is its radius. Most primitive objects include a default setting where no arguments are needed:

In[55]:= **GraphicsRow@**
{Graphics3D[Sphere[]], Graphics3D[Cylinder[]], Graphics3D[Cone[]]}

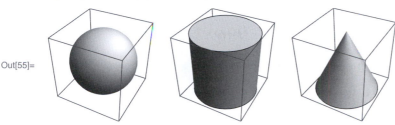

Out[55]=

In most practical applications you will want to specify the placement and size of the objects.

In[56]:= **Graphics3D[{**
Sphere[{0, 0, 6.5}, 1],
Cylinder[{{0, 0, 7.5}, {0, .5, 9}}, .8],
Cylinder[{{0, 0, 7.5}, {0, .03, 7.6}}, 1.5]
}]

Out[56]=

The overall paradigm for assembling a Graphics3D is completely analogous to that for building Graphics. The single argument given to Graphics3D is (most simply) a primitive or a list of primitives. As is the case with Graphics, you can also apply one or more *directives* to each primitive. Directives are used to customize the appearance of the individual primitive elements, and may include color, opacity, and/or specularity settings. To apply a directive to any primitive object, replace the primitive with the list {*directive*, *primitive*}. If more than one directive is to be applied, wrap them in the Directive command, as in Directive[Red, Opacity[.3]].

In[57]:= `GraphicsRow@`
    `{Graphics3D[Sphere[]], Graphics3D[{Opacity[.6], Sphere[]}],`
    `Graphics3D[{Directive[Red, Opacity[.3]], Sphere[]}]}`

Out[57]=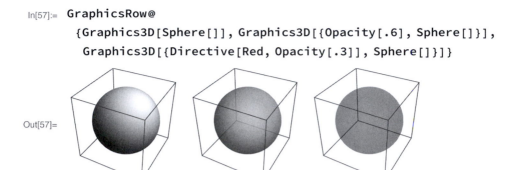

One may also add option settings to `Graphics3D`, such as `Boxed→False`. Many of these have been discussed in this section in the context of `Plot3D`. In particular, the setting `Lighting→"Neutral"` can be used to turn off the colored lights that are used by default when rendering a `Graphics3D`. This will provide a more honest rendering of any colors you introduce. Here, for instance, we make a white snowman with black hat and arms:

In[58]:= `Graphics3D[{`
        `{Lighter[Gray, .8],`
         `Sphere[{0, 0, 0}, 3],`
         `Sphere[{0, 0, 4}, 2],`
         `Sphere[{0, 0, 6.5}, 1]},`
        `{Lighter[Black],`
         `Cylinder[{{0, 0, 7.5}, {0, .5, 9}}, .8],`
         `Cylinder[{{0, 0, 7.5}, {0, .03, 7.6}}, 1.5],`
         `Cylinder[{{2, 0, 4}, {4, 0, 5}}, .2],`
         `Cylinder[{{-2, 0, 4}, {-4, 0, 5}}, .2]}`
      `}, Boxed → False, Lighting → "Neutral"]`

Out[58]=

It is straightforward to combine a `Graphics3D` with the output from one of the plotting commands. Here we use `Plot3D` to render the function $f(x, y) = \sin(xy)$ with `MeshFunctions` set to measure distance on the surface to the point $(0, 0, 2)$. The plot is colored according to this distance using `MeshShading`. We use `Graphics3D` to place a small green sphere at the point $(0, 0, 2)$. We put the two images together with `Show`:

In[59]:= Show$\Big[$

Plot3D$\Big[$Sin[x y], {x, -2, 2}, {y, -2, 2},

PlotRange → {-2.2, 2.2}, Lighting → "Neutral",

BoxRatios → Automatic, PlotPoints → 40, Mesh → 12, MeshFunctions →

$\Big\{$Function$\Big[$ {x, y, z}, $\sqrt{x^2 + y^2 + (z - 2)^2}$ $\Big]\Big\}$, MeshShading →

Table[ColorData["TemperatureMap"] [1 - k], {k, 0, 1, 1 / 12}]$\Big]$,

Graphics3D[{Darker[Green], Sphere[{0, 0, 2}, .15]}]$\Big]$

Out[59]=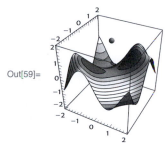

⚠ When using commands such as Plot that produce Graphics (as opposed to Graphics3D) output, it is common to add an Epilog option to place Graphics primitives directly on the image. This does not work in a 3D setting. While Epilog may also be used with commands such as Plot3D, its purpose is to add 2D elements to the notebook viewing rectangle. But Epilog cannot be used to place 3D primitives on the plot (such as the Sphere above). So in a 3D setting, Show is the best way to add primitive Graphics3D objects to another 3D image.

Limits and Derivatives of Functions of Two or More Variables

Calculating Limits

The Limit command, first discussed in Section 5.1, can be used to take limits in a multivariate setting. For a function f in the variables x and y, we can find the limiting value as (x, y) approaches $(0, 0)$ like this:

In[60]:= Clear[f, x, y];

$f = \dfrac{y - 2x + 3}{x - 1}$;

Limit[f, {x, y} → {0, 0}]

Out[62]= -3

A limit may be infinite, or it may fail to exist. In the latter case the output will be Indeterminate.

In[63]:= $\mathtt{Limit}\left[\dfrac{1}{x^2 + y^2}, \{x, y\} \to \{0, 0\}\right]$

Out[63]= ∞

In[64]:= $\mathtt{Limit[f, \{x, y\} \to \{1, -1\}]}$

Out[64]= Indeterminate

Beware that a *nested* limit is something entirely different. We can harness the Limit command to first let y approach its target, and then let x approach its target. For instance, we may first let y approach −1, and then let x approach 1.

In[65]:= $\mathtt{Limit[f, \{x \to 1, y \to -1\}]}$

Out[65]= -2

When we independently let x and y approach some targeting values like this, the rightmost target in the second argument to Limit is implemented first. So in the previous input, we are first constraining the domain to the line $y = -1$, and then approaching the point (1, −1) along this line. When we approach the point (1, −1) along a different line, we obtain a limiting value of −1.

In[66]:= $\mathtt{Limit[f, \{x \to 1, y \to x - 2\}]}$

Out[66]= -1

The two distinct limiting values of f along these two lines confirm that the limit of f as (x, y) approaches (1, −1) does not exist.

A plot can often help to illuminate the situation. The level curves for this function are lines passing through (1, −1).

In[67]:= $\mathtt{Plot3D[f, \{x, -1, 3\}, \{y, -3, 1\},}$
 $\qquad\mathtt{PlotTheme \to "ZMesh", Mesh \to 30, AxesLabel \to Automatic]}$

Out[67]=
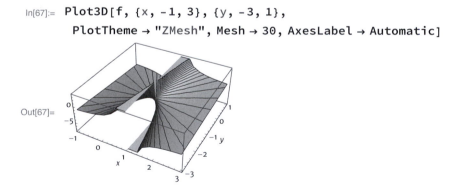

Calculating Partial Derivatives

You can calculate the partial derivatives of a function of two or more variables with the D command. This works just as in Chapter 5:

In[68]:= `Clear[f, x, y];`
`f = Sin[x² - y²];`

In[70]:= `D[f, x]`

Out[70]= $2 \times \text{Cos}\left[x^2 - y^2\right]$

In[71]:= `D[f, y]`

Out[71]= $-2 \text{ y Cos}\left[x^2 - y^2\right]$

We use replacement rules to evaluate a derivative at a particular point:

In[72]:= `% /.` $\left\{x \to 0, y \to \sqrt{\pi}\right\}$

Out[72]= $2\sqrt{\pi}$

Alternatively, you can calculate partial derivatives with the palette version of the D command by using the $\partial_{\square}$ ■ button on the Basic Math Assistant palette. Find it in the Basic Commands section of the palette under the $d \int \Sigma$ tab. The subscript indicates the variable with respect to which the derivative should be taken. Move from one placeholder to the next with the TAB key.

In[73]:= ∂_x `f`

Out[73]= $2 \times \text{Cos}\left[x^2 - y^2\right]$

If you use the palette version of D directly on a function such as $x^2 + 2xy$, it is best to first type the function expression, then highlight it, and *then* click the palette button. If you deviate from this convention by clicking the palette button *first*, be sure to put grouping parentheses around the function expression so that you don't end up only differentiating the first summand:

In[74]:= ∂_x $x^2 + 2 \times y$

Out[74]= $2 \times + 2 \times y$

In[75]:= ∂_x $\left(x^2 + 2 \times y\right)$

Out[75]= $2 \times + 2 y$

To find the second partial derivative $\frac{\partial^2 f}{\partial x^2}$, you can use the D command exactly as in Chapter 5:

In[76]:= `D[f, {x, 2}]`

Out[76]= $2 \text{ Cos}\left[x^2 - y^2\right] - 4 x^2 \text{ Sin}\left[x^2 - y^2\right]$

To find the mixed second partial derivative $\frac{\partial^2 f}{\partial x \partial y}$, simply do this:

In[77]:= **D[f, x, y]**

Out[77]= $4 \times y \sin\left[x^2 - y^2\right]$

Alternatively, you may use the $\partial_{\square,\square}\blacksquare$ key on the palette:

In[78]:= **$\partial_{x,x}$ f**

Out[78]= $2 \cos\left[x^2 - y^2\right] - 4 x^2 \sin\left[x^2 - y^2\right]$

In[79]:= **$\partial_{x,y}$ f**

Out[79]= $4 \times y \sin\left[x^2 - y^2\right]$

Derivatives beyond the second require the D command:

In[80]:= **D[f, {x, 3}, {y, 4}]**

Out[80]= $-8 x^3 \left(-12 \cos\left[x^2 - y^2\right] + 16 y^4 \cos\left[x^2 - y^2\right] - 48 y^2 \sin\left[x^2 - y^2\right]\right) -$
$12 x \left(48 y^2 \cos\left[x^2 - y^2\right] - 12 \sin\left[x^2 - y^2\right] + 16 y^4 \sin\left[x^2 - y^2\right]\right)$

The Gradient

The *gradient* of a function of two or more variables is a vector whose components are the partial derivatives of the function. For instance, for a function *f* of two variables, the gradient is the vector $\langle \partial_x f, \partial_y f \rangle$. In *Mathematica* one can simply do this:

In[81]:= **Grad[f, {x, y}]**

Out[81]= $\left\{2 x \cos\left[x^2 - y^2\right], -2 y \cos\left[x^2 - y^2\right]\right\}$

Grad takes two arguments. The first is the function whose gradient you wish to compute. The second is the list of variables used in defining the function. For example:

In[82]:= **Grad$\left[x^2 y^3, \{x, y\}\right]$**

Out[82]= $\left\{2 x y^3, 3 x^2 y^2\right\}$

In[83]:= **Grad$\left[\dfrac{x_1{}^2 x_2{}^3 x_4{}^4}{x_3{}^5}, \{x_1, x_2, x_3, x_4\}\right]$**

Out[83]= $\left\{\dfrac{2 x_1 x_2^3 x_4^4}{x_3^5}, \dfrac{3 x_1^2 x_2^2 x_4^4}{x_3^5}, -\dfrac{5 x_1^2 x_2^3 x_4^4}{x_3^6}, \dfrac{4 x_1^2 x_2^3 x_4^3}{x_3^5}\right\}$

You can evaluate the gradient at a specific point in the domain using replacement rules.

In[84]:= **Grad[f, {x, y}] /. $\left\{x \rightarrow 0, y \rightarrow \sqrt{\pi}\right\}$**

Out[84]= $\left\{0, 2\sqrt{\pi}\right\}$

The following `Manipulate` will sketch a gradient vector directly on the `ContourPlot` for a function. You click on the graphic to specify the point in the domain where the gradient should be calculated, and the gradient vector is drawn with its tail at that point. Initially it shows the gradient evaluated at the point (0.5, 0.5). The tail of the displayed gradient vector is a `Locator`; you can simply click on the graphic to move it to a new position, or you can drag it around. The geometric properties of the gradient quickly become apparent: it is perpendicular to the level curve through its tail, and it points uphill, in the direction of steepest ascent.

```
In[85]:=  Clear[f, x, y, gradf];
          f = e^(-(x²+y²)) + x y;
          gradf = Grad[f, {x, y}];
          Manipulate[
           ContourPlot[f, {x, -1, 1}, {y, -1, 1}, Contours → 20,
             Epilog → Dynamic[{Arrow[{pt, pt + gradf /. {x → pt[[1]], y → pt[[2]]}}]}]],
           {{pt, {0, .5}}, Locator,
            Appearance → Graphics[{Red, Disk[]}, ImageSize → 5]}]
```

Out[88]=

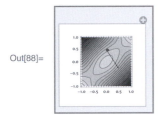

⚠ There are several interesting features in this `Manipulate`. Notice that the `Epilog` to the `ContourPlot` is wrapped in `Dynamic`. While not strictly neces-sary, this has the beneficial effect of forcing only the arrow to update as the `Locator` is moved, rather than having the `ContourPlot` itself (which does not change) be re-rendered every time the `Locator` is moved. This makes the action more "zippy." For more information, search for "Advanced Manipulate Functionality" in the Documentation Center and follow the link to the tutorial of that name. Finally, note that we use the `Appearance` option to change the appearance of the `Locator` from its default crosshair icon to a simple red disk that is 5 printer's points in diameter. This option allows you to make a `Locator` appear exactly the way you like.

Given a function of two or three variables, there is a simple means for simultaneously plotting an array of its gradient vectors over a given domain. See Section 6.5 for a discussion of the `VectorPlot` and `VectorPlot3D` commands.

You can take a *directional derivative* by taking the dot product of the gradient with a unit vector in the indicated direction. Here, for example, is an expression representing the directional derivative of the function $f(x, y) = x^2 y^3$ in the direction of the vector $3\,\vec{i} - \vec{j}$:

In[89]:= `Grad[x² y³, {x, y}].Normalize[{3, -1}]`

Out[89]= $-\dfrac{3\,x^2\,y^2}{\sqrt{10}} + 3\sqrt{\dfrac{2}{5}}\,x\,y^3$

To evaluate the directional derivative at a specific point in the domain, use replacement rules:

In[90]:= `% /. {x → 2, y → 3}`

Out[90]= $108\sqrt{\dfrac{2}{5}}$

Differentials

For a function $f(x, y)$, the *differential* is $df = (\partial_x f)\,dx + (\partial_y f)\,dy$. The differential approximates the change in the value of f, where dx represents a small change in x and dy represents a small change in y. The command `Dt` provides a simple way to compute differentials.

In[91]:= `Clear[x, y, f];`
`f = x² y³;`
`Dt[f]`

Out[93]= $2\,x\,y^3\,Dt[x] + 3\,x^2\,y^2\,Dt[y]$

The `Dt[x]` in the output represents dx, and the `Dt[y]` represents dy. So, for instance, at the point $(x, y) = (2, 3)$, if x were to increase by .03 and y were to decrease by .01, the change in f would be approximated by the differential.

In[94]:= `% /. {Dt[x] → .03, Dt[y] → -.01, x → 2, y → 3}`

Out[94]= `2.16`

In this case, it is a simple matter to find the *exact* change in f:

In[95]:= `(f /. {x → 2.03, y → 2.99}) - (f /. {x → 2, y → 3})`

Out[95]= `2.15536`

The quotient $\dfrac{df}{f}$ approximates the *proportional* change in f, typically expressed as a percentage. Similarly, the quotients $\dfrac{dx}{x}$ and $\dfrac{dy}{y}$ represent small proportional changes in x and y.

In[96]:= $\dfrac{Dt[f]}{f}$ `// Simplify`

Out[96]= $\dfrac{2\,Dt[x]}{x} + \dfrac{3\,Dt[y]}{y}$

This tells us that a small percentage change in y is $3/2$ more consequential to the value of f than an equivalent percentage change in x.

Optimization

There are numerous methods for finding extreme values of multivariate functions. It is certainly possible to mimic the basic techniques presented in a standard calculus course, with *Mathematica* doing the heavy lifting when the algebra gets tough. We outline such an approach in this section. There are also the high-level commands Maximize and Minimize, which can completely automate the process but which also have inherent limitations. We'll begin with these built-in commands, and then discuss the traditional approach using critical points and second derivatives.

The commands Maximize, Minimize, and their numerical counterparts NMaximize and NMinimize (first introduced in Section 5.6), all use the same syntax—understand how to use one and you understand them all. In the most simple setting, where your function is not overly complicated and happens to have a single extremum in its largest natural domain, these commands make light work of optimization:

In[97]:= `Maximize[-85 + 16 x - 4 x`^{2}` - 4 y - 4 y`^{2}` + 40 z - 4 z`^{2}`, {x, y, z}]`

Out[97]= $\left\{32, \left\{x \to 2, y \to -\dfrac{1}{2}, z \to 5\right\}\right\}$

But be aware that for some functions an extreme value may not exist. The function in the previous example has no minimum value, for instance, as all three of the dominant terms x^2, y^2, and z^2 have negative coefficients; this function assumes arbitrarily large negative values as the point (x, y, z) moves away from the origin. Here is what happens if you ask *Mathematica* for an extremum like this that does not exist:

In[98]:= `Minimize[-85 + 16 x - 4 x`^{2}` - 4 y - 4 y`^{2}` + 40 z - 4 z`^{2}`, {x, y, z}]`

⋯ Minimize: The minimum is not attained at any point satisfying the given constraints.

Out[98]= $\left\{-\infty, \left\{x \to -\infty, y \to -\dfrac{12}{5}, z \to -\dfrac{1}{2}\right\}\right\}$

The first item listed here is the important one: If the function can assume values that are both negative and of arbitrarily large magnitude, Minimize will return $-\infty$ here. You are being told this function does not have a minimum value.

These optimization commands attempt to find *global* extrema. They can be adapted to hunt for *local* extrema by adding constraints. To do this, simply use a list of the form {*function*, *constraint*} as the first argument, where the second member of the list is an equation or inequality (or any logical combination of these):

In[99]:= `f = 12 y`^{3}` + 4 x`^{2}` - 10 x y;`

In[100]:= `Minimize[{f, -1 ≤ x ≤ 1 && -1 ≤ y ≤ 1}, {x, y}]`

Out[100]= {- 18, {x → -1, y → -1}}

In[101]:= `ContourPlot[f, {x, -1, 1}, {y, -1, 1},`
`    Epilog → {Red, PointSize[Medium], Point[{x, y} /. Last[%]]}]`

Out[101]=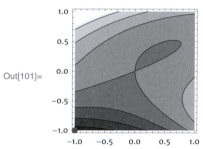

Here the minimum occurs on the boundary, at a corner of the square region. But the plot suggests there should be a *local* minimum inside the closed "loop," near (0.5, 0.25). To find it using `Minimize`, we must search within a smaller region, a region where that local minimum is also the absolute minimum. Let's restrict our search to the upper-right quarter of the previous square:

In[102]:= `f = 12 y³ + 4 x² - 10 x y;`
`    Minimize[{f, 0 ≤ x ≤ 1 && 0 ≤ y ≤ 1}, {x, y}]`

Out[103]= $\left\{-\dfrac{15\,625}{62\,208}, \left\{x \to \dfrac{125}{288}, y \to \dfrac{25}{72}\right\}\right\}$

In[104]:= `ContourPlot[f, {x, 0, 1}, {y, 0, 1},`
`    Epilog → {Red, PointSize[Medium], Point[{x, y} /. Last[%]]}]`

Out[104]=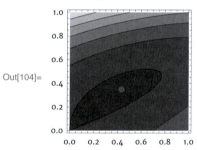

Bingo! This technique, where we inspect a plot and gradually zoom in to a small region containing a local extremum, may require multiple iterations to home in on a single extremum, but it can be very effective. Here we conclude that f has a local minimum at the point $\left(\frac{125}{288}, \frac{25}{72}\right)$, where it assumes the value $-\frac{15\,625}{62\,208}$. Who knew?

As an alternate approach to the procedure above, traditionally analytical methods can be used to find this local minimum. That analytical approach, when it can be effectively implemented, has the big advantage that it will find all extrema at once, rather than pursuing them one at a time. So if your goal is to find *all* extrema for a differentiable function (as it often is in a calculus course), your first line of attack comes right out of your calculus textbook: The *critical points* for a function are those points where the first partials are both zero (i.e., the gradient of the function is the zero vector), or where one or both partials do not exist. If a function assumes a relative minimum or maximum value in the interior of its domain, it does so at a critical point. So all we have to do is find all the critical points for a given function, and we know the extrema lie in that collection.

Mathematica provides a compellingly simple way to visualize where critical points occur for a function of two variables. Below we consider the function $f(x, y) = x^2 - \frac{4xy}{y^2+1}$, and display in dashed red the curve where the partial derivative with respect to x is zero, and in yellow the curves (lines in this case) where the partial derivative with respect to y is equal to zero. The critical points, and hence maxima and minima for $f(x, y)$ on this domain, occur at the three intersection points of the solid and dashed curves, as these are the points where *both* partials are equal to zero.

```
In[105]:= Clear[f, x, y, fplot, xcrit, ycrit];
          f = x² - (4 x y)/(y² + 1);
          fplot = ContourPlot[f, {x, -2, 2}, {y, -2, 2}];
          xcrit = ContourPlot[Evaluate[D[f, x] == 0], {x, -2, 2},
                  {y, -2, 2}, ContourStyle → Directive[Thick, Dashed, Red]];
          ycrit = ContourPlot[Evaluate[D[f, y] == 0], {x, -2, 2},
                  {y, -2, 2}, ContourStyle → Directive[Thick, Yellow]];
          Show[fplot, xcrit, ycrit]
```

Out[110]=

It is often possible to find critical points with `Solve`, `NSolve`, or `Reduce`. The setting here is just as it was in Section 4.9, where we used these commands to solve systems of equations. Recall that these commands are designed primarily to solve polynomial equations, but can sometimes solve more general classes of equations. Here we return to our earlier example, using `Solve` to find the critical points of this polynomial:

In[111]:= f = 12 y³ + 4 x² − 10 x y;

crPts = Solve[Grad[f, {x, y}] == {0, 0}, {x, y}]

Out[112]= $\left\{ \{x \to 0, y \to 0\}, \left\{x \to \dfrac{125}{288}, y \to \dfrac{25}{72}\right\}\right\}$

You will often be able to determine whether f has a relative minimum or maximum or saddle at a particular critical point in a purely algebraic fashion by examining the *discriminant*, using the second partials evaluated at this critical point. Recall that the discriminant of f is the expression

$$\Delta_f = \left(\partial_{x,x} f\right)\left(\partial_{y,y} f\right) - \left(\partial_{x,y} f\right)^2.$$

The standard test to determine the status of the critical point (x, y) is as follows:

- If $\Delta_f > 0$ and $\partial_{x,x} f > 0$, then (x, y) is a relative minimum.

- If $\Delta_f > 0$ and $\partial_{x,x} f < 0$, then (x, y) is a relative maximum.

- If $\Delta_f < 0$, then (x, y) is a saddle point.

- If $\Delta_f = 0$, then the test is inconclusive.

Let's carry out this test for the two critical points found in our previous example.

In[113]:= $\left(\partial_{x,x} f\right) \left(\partial_{y,y} f\right) - \left(\partial_{x,y} f\right)^2$ /. crPts // N

Out[113]= {−100., 100.}

The first critical point, $(0, 0)$, is therefore a saddle point, while the second is either a maximum or minimum. Which is it?

In[114]:= $\partial_{x,x} f$ /. crPts[[2]] // N

Out[114]= 8.

The positive value indicates that there is upward concavity in the x direction at this point. Since this point is an extreme value, it must be a minimum. A ContourPlot shows both critical points clearly, confirming this analysis: f has a saddle at the origin, and a local minimum at $\left(\frac{125}{288}, \frac{25}{72}\right)$.

In[115]:= `ContourPlot[f, {x, -1, 1}, {y, -1, 1},`
`Epilog → {Red, PointSize[Medium], Point[{x, y} /. crPts]}]`

Out[115]=

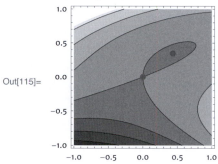

Finally, we can evaluate f at the critical points as follows:

In[116]:= `f /. crPts`

Out[116]= $\left\{0, -\dfrac{15\,625}{62\,208}\right\}$

In this example we used `Solve` to find the critical points, but `Reduce` could have been used instead:

In[117]:= `Reduce[Grad[f, {x, y}] == {0, 0}, {x, y}]`

Out[117]= $\left(x == 0 \mid\mid x == \dfrac{125}{288}\right) \&\& y == \dfrac{4\,x}{5}$

Here is a second example, where we point out something that is rarely emphasized in calculus texts: The set of critical points for a multivariate function may be *far* more complex than a few isolated points (like the two critical points we found in the previous example). For instance:

In[118]:= `f = Sin[x Cos[y]];`
`Short[Solve[Grad[f, {x, y}] == {0, 0}, {x, y}, Reals], 9]`

••• Solve: Equations may not give solutions for all "solve" variables.

Out[119]//Short= $\left\{\left\{y \rightarrow \text{ConditionalExpression}\left[-\text{ArcCos}\left[\dfrac{-\pi + 4\,\pi\,\text{C}[1]}{2\,x}\right] + 2\,\pi\,\text{C}[2],\right.\right.\right.$

$((\text{C}[1] \mid \text{C}[2]) \in \mathbb{Z} \&\& -\pi + 2\,x + 4\,\pi\,\text{C}[1] \geq 0 \&\& \text{C}[1] \leq 0) \mid\mid$
$((\text{C}[1] \mid \text{C}[2]) \in \mathbb{Z} \&\& -\pi + 2\,x + 4\,\pi\,\text{C}[1] \leq 0 \&\& \text{C}[1] \geq 1) \mid\mid$
$((\text{C}[1] \mid \text{C}[2]) \in \mathbb{Z} \&\& \text{C}[1] \geq 1 \&\& \pi + 2\,x - 4\,\pi\,\text{C}[1] \geq 0) \mid\mid$
$\left.((\text{C}[1] \mid \text{C}[2]) \in \mathbb{Z} \&\& \text{C}[1] \leq 0 \&\& \pi + 2\,x - 4\,\pi\,\text{C}[1] \leq 0)\right]\right\},$

$\ll 4 \gg, \left\{x \rightarrow \text{ConditionalExpression}[0, \text{C}[1] \in \mathbb{Z}],\right.$

$\left.\left.y \rightarrow \text{ConditionalExpression}\left[\dfrac{\pi}{2} + 2\,\pi\,\text{C}[1], \text{C}[1] \in \mathbb{Z}\right]\right\}\right\}$

Note that we invoked the optional third argument Reals, so that nonreal solutions are not reported. There are six solutions reported, but only the first and last are shown (since we wrapped the input above in Short to save space, the four missing solutions are indicated by «4»). Even the abbreviated output is a bit intimidating. Note that there are two constants, C[1] and C[2], both integers. Solve has found an infinite family of points and curves, parameterized by these two constants. If you are only concerned with critical points within a *bounded* domain the output can be greatly simplified, often with such constants removed. Below we include in the list of equations some *bounds* on both *x* and *y*. The constants are then no longer needed.

In[120]:= `f = Sin[x Cos[y]];`
`Solve[{Grad[f, {x, y}] == {0, 0}, -3 ≤ x ≤ 3, -3 ≤ y ≤ 3}, {x, y}, Reals]`

••• Solve: Equations may not give solutions for all "solve" variables.

Out[121]= $\left\{\left\{y \to \text{ConditionalExpression}\left[-\text{ArcCos}\left[-\frac{\pi}{2x}\right], -3 \le x \le -\frac{\pi}{2} \,||\, -\frac{1}{2}\pi\,\text{Sec}[3] \le x \le 3\right]\right\},\right.$

$\left\{y \to \text{ConditionalExpression}\left[\text{ArcCos}\left[-\frac{\pi}{2x}\right], -3 \le x \le -\frac{\pi}{2} \,||\, -\frac{1}{2}\pi\,\text{Sec}[3] \le x \le 3\right]\right\},$

$\left\{y \to \text{ConditionalExpression}\left[-\text{ArcCos}\left[\frac{\pi}{2x}\right], -3 \le x \le \frac{1}{2}\pi\,\text{Sec}[3] \,||\, \frac{\pi}{2} \le x \le 3\right]\right\}, \left\{y \to\right.$

$\left.\text{ConditionalExpression}\left[\text{ArcCos}\left[\frac{\pi}{2x}\right], -3 \le x \le \frac{1}{2}\pi\,\text{Sec}[3] \,||\, \frac{\pi}{2} \le x \le 3\right]\right\},$

$\left.\left\{x \to 0, y \to -\frac{\pi}{2}\right\}, \left\{x \to 0, y \to \frac{\pi}{2}\right\}\right\}$

Okay, this is still rather intimidating. But now we have the full output (not a shortened version) and it rewards careful reading. The very last line shows two discrete critical points, at $\left(0, -\frac{\pi}{2}\right)$ and $\left(0, \frac{\pi}{2}\right)$. Each of the other solutions presents *y* as a function of *x*, where *x* is constrained to a pair of intervals (recall that || denotes the word "or"). In other words, the other critical points are composed of *curves*.

Let's embark on a brief visual investigation to clarify all this. In the following graphic, the solid mesh lines are curves where the partial derivative with respect to *x* is zero, and dotted mesh lines are curves where the partial derivative with respect to *y* is zero. The critical points are those points where both partials are simultaneously zero. These can be discrete *points* (where the solid and dotted lines cross), or *curves* (where they coincide). This function has both types.

In[122]:= $\{fx, fy\} = \{\partial_x\, f, \partial_y\, f\};$

```
In[123]:=  Plot3D[f, {x, -3, 3}, {y, -3, 3}, BoxRatios → Automatic,
              MeshFunctions → {Function[{x, y}, fx], Function[{x, y}, fy]},
              MeshStyle → {Directive[Thickness[.01], Red],
                 Directive[Thick, Dotted]}, Mesh → {{0}, {0}}, Boxed → False,
              Axes → {True, True, False}, ViewPoint → {.1, -1, 3}]
```

Out[123]=
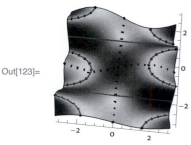

Do you see the two discrete critical points that we identified earlier? They lie on the intersection of the solid and dotted lines. They appear to be saddles. We confirm this below:

```
In[124]:=  (∂x,x f) (∂y,y f) - (∂x,y f)² /. {{x → 0, y → -π / 2}, {x → 0, y → π / 2}}
```

Out[124]= {-1, -1}

So to summarize: If you know that a function has a single extreme value, then Maximize and Minimize are hard to beat. But when you are tasked with finding *all* extrema for a function and you don't know how many there are, then identifying and classifying its critical points is the better approach. Remember that Maximize and Minimize always return a single extremum, even when there are infinitely many, as shown in the next input. Clearly, finding and classifying all the critical points is a more comprehensive approach.

```
In[125]:=  Maximize[{f, -3 ≤ x ≤ 3 && -3 ≤ y ≤ 3}, {x, y}]
```

Out[125]= $\left\{1, \left\{x \to -\frac{21}{8}, y \to -\text{ArcCos}\left[-\frac{4\pi}{21}\right]\right\}\right\}$

The remainder of this section deals with what to do if the approaches outlined above fail. For instance, Minimize has trouble with the likes of $f(x, y) = e^{\sin(x y)} + \cos\left(\frac{5x}{y^2+1}\right)\sin\left(\frac{3y}{x^2+1}\right)$. And so do Solve and Reduce when trying to find its critical points. To put it plainly, this is a nasty function. Take a look and see for yourself:

In[126]:= `Clear[f, x, y];`

$$f = e^{Sin[x\,y]} + Cos\left[\frac{5\,x}{y^2 + 1}\right] Sin\left[\frac{3\,y}{x^2 + 1}\right];$$

`ContourPlot[f, {x, -2, 2}, {y, -2, 2}]`

Out[128]=

In cases where `Minimize`, `Solve`, and `Reduce` cannot find exact values, we may draw instead from a strong line-up of numerical commands. For instance, we may use `NSolve` to find numerical approximations to the critical points. The rest of the procedure for classifying critical points should then work without a hitch. But for the truly nasty functions, such as our function *f* above, even `NSolve` can fail to return solutions. When that happens, we are forced to hunt for individual extrema one by one, much like we did earlier in Chapter 5: Use a `ContourPlot` to roughly locate a candidate extremum, and then use a numerical command to zero in on it.

The commands at your disposal are `NMaximize`, `NMinimize`, `FindMaximum`, and `FindMinimum`. Like the command `FindRoot` (introduced in Section 4.7), these are your weapons of last resort. All are strictly numerical tools—the solution they provide is approximate. Their true merit lies in their robust nature. They are fast and highly effective for all but the most pathological of functions. Our example function *f* above will pose no difficulty whatever.

Look at the contour plot for *f*. There appears to be a tiny island near (1, −1), suggesting that *f* assumes a relative maximum value there. Now that we have it in our sights, let's zero in on it. `NMaximize` works just like `Maximize`; we must constrain our search to a sufficiently small neighborhood of the desired extremum, so small that no other extremum lives in that neighborhood:

In[129]:= `NMaximize[{f, .5 < x < 1 && -1 < y < 0}, {x, y}]`

Out[129]= `{1.51106, {x → 0.740375, y → -0.529412}}`

`FindMaximum` is a little simpler to use. Rather than put boundaries around the search area, you give it a starting value for each variable. Again, use your `ContourPlot` to choose a starting value as close as possible to the target extremum. It will likely converge rapidly to that target:

In[130]:= `FindMaximum[f, {x, 1}, {y, -1}]`

Out[130]= `{1.51106, {x → 0.740375, y → -0.529412}}`

Similarly, there appears to be a relative minimum near (−1, 1); let's zero in on it. Both `NMinimum` and `FindMinimum` succeed in finding it.

```
In[131]:= NMinimize[{f, -2 ≤ x ≤ -1 && .5 ≤ y ≤ 1.5}, {x, y}]

Out[131]= {-0.551724, {x → -1.30697, y → 1.09308}}
```

```
In[132]:= FindMinimum[f, {x, -1}, {y, 1}]

Out[132]= {-0.551724, {x → -1.30697, y → 1.09308}}
```

Constrained Optimization

The technique of Lagrange multipliers is easily implemented in *Mathematica*. Suppose the function you wish to optimize is called f, while the constraint is of the form $g = 0$. We wish to solve the system $\nabla f = \lambda \nabla g$, for some real constant λ, together with the constraint equation $g = 0$. Here's a simple example: Maximize the quantity $4xy$ under the constraint that $4x^2 + y^2 = 8$.

```
In[133]:= Clear[f, g, x, y, λ];
          f = 4 x * y;
          g = 4 x² + y² - 8;
```

```
In[136]:= sols = Solve[Grad[f - λ * g, {x, y, λ}] == {0, 0, 0}, {x, y, λ}, Reals]

Out[136]= {{x → -1, y → -2, λ → 1}, {x → -1, y → 2, λ → -1},
           {x → 1, y → -2, λ → -1}, {x → 1, y → 2, λ → 1}}
```

This single `Solve` input solves the system, as the three partial derivatives of the function $L(x, y, \lambda) = f(x, y) - \lambda g(x, y)$ are zero precisely when $\nabla f = \lambda \nabla g$ and $g = 0$. We then evaluate the function at the solution points:

```
In[137]:= {x, y} /. sols

Out[137]= {{-1, -2}, {-1, 2}, {1, -2}, {1, 2}}
```

```
In[138]:= f /. sols

Out[138]= {8, -8, -8, 8}
```

A `ContourPlot` provides visual verification. The solutions are shown as red dots:

```
In[139]:= Show[ContourPlot[f, {x, -2, 2}, {y, -3, 3}],
             ContourPlot[g == 0, {x, -2, 2}, {y, -3, 3},
               ContourStyle → Directive[Thick, Yellow]],
               Epilog → {Red, PointSize[Medium], Point[{x, y} /. sols]}]
```

Note that the `Maximize`, `Minimize`, `NMaximize`, and `NMinimize` commands will do this all in one go, but they will only find a single solution. If that's all you need, there is no easier way to get there:

In[140]:= `Maximize[{f, g == 0}, {x, y}]`

Out[140]= $\{8, \{x \to -1, y \to -2\}\}$

In[141]:= `Minimize[{f, g == 0}, {x, y}]`

Out[141]= $\{-8, \{x \to -1, y \to 2\}\}$

Integration of Functions of Two or More Variables

In a standard calculus course, double and triple, in fact all multiple integrals are evaluated as *iterated* integrals. Evaluating iterated integrals over rectangular regions is easy when such regions have sides parallel to the coordinate axes; you use the same `Integrate` command (from Section 5.10), adding another iterator (for definite integrals) or another variable (for indefinite integrals):

In[142]:= $\texttt{Integrate}\left[5 - x^2\, y^2,\ \{y, 1, 3\}, \{x, 0, 2\}\right]$

Out[142]= $-\dfrac{28}{9}$

In[143]:= $\texttt{Integrate}\left[5 - x^2\, y^2,\ y,\ x\right]$

Out[143]= $5\, x\, y - \dfrac{x^3\, y^3}{9}$

In the examples above we integrated first with respect to x, then with respect to y. That is, the variables are listed within `Integrate` in the same order that the *integral signs* are written in standard mathematical notation. Or said another way, the first variable listed corresponds to the *outermost* integral. The palette version of the `Integrate` command makes the order of integration more transparent. First type and highlight the function you wish to integrate, then click the appropriate integration button on the Basic Math Assistant palette and fill in the placeholders for the *innermost* integral, using the ⌨TAB key to move from one placeholder to the next. Now highlight the entire expression representing the inner integral and click the integration button a second time, fill in the placeholders, and enter:

In[144]:= $\displaystyle\int_1^3 \left(\int_0^2 \left(5 - x^2\, y^2\right)\, dx\right)\, dy$

Out[144]= $-\dfrac{28}{9}$

In[145]:= $\displaystyle\int \left(\int \left(5 - x^2\, y^2\right)\, dx\right)\, dy$

Out[145]= $5\, x\, y - \dfrac{x^3\, y^3}{9}$

To evaluate a definite integral over a nonrectangular region in the plane, the simplest approach is to forgo the decomposition into an iterated integral and calculate directly. For example, suppose we wish to integrate this same function $f(x, y) = 5 - x^2 y^2$ over the triangular region in the xy plane with corners $(0, 0)$, $(3, 0)$, and $(0, 2)$. We may use Integrate as above, but replace the iterators for x and y with an appropriate region specification. The syntax is exactly like it is for Plot3D.

In[146]:= `Integrate[5 - x² y², {x, y} ∈ Triangle[{{0, 0}, {3, 0}, {0, 2}}]]`

Out[146]= $\dfrac{69}{5}$

In[147]:= `Plot3D[5 - x² y², {x, y} ∈ Triangle[{{0, 0}, {3, 0}, {0, 2}}],`
        `Filling → Axis, PlotRange → {0, 5}, BoxRatios → {1, 1, 1}]`

Out[147]=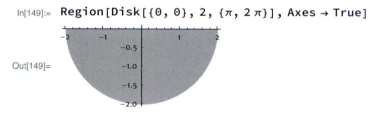

Or we may wish to integrate over the sector of the disk $x^2 + y^2 \le 4$ that lies in the lower half-plane:

In[148]:= `Integrate[5 - x² y², {x, y} ∈ Disk[{0, 0}, 2, {π, 2 π}]]`

Out[148]= $\dfrac{26\,\pi}{3}$

If you wish to view your region (for instance, to be sure it looks like it's supposed to), use Region:

In[149]:= `Region[Disk[{0, 0}, 2, {π, 2 π}], Axes → True]`

Out[149]=

And here is a view of the volume that this double integral represents. We use Plot3D with a Filling setting (to show a translucent solid region under the graph of the integrand). We could have instead used PlotTheme → "FilledSurface" for this purpose. Note also that PlotRange is needed to extend the image all the way down to the xy plane.

In[150]:= $\texttt{Plot3D}\left[\texttt{5 - x}^2\,\texttt{y}^2,\ \{\texttt{x, y}\}\in\texttt{Disk}[\{\texttt{0, 0}\},\ \texttt{2},\ \{\pi,\ \texttt{2}\,\pi\}],\ \texttt{Mesh}\to\texttt{None},$

$\qquad\texttt{Filling}\to\texttt{Axis, PlotRange}\to\{\texttt{0, 5}\},\ \texttt{BoxRatios}\to\{\texttt{2, 1, 1}\}\big]$

Out[150]=

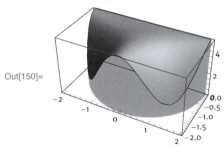

In a traditional multivariate calculus course, multiple integrals are usually evaluated by setting up the appropriate *iterated* integral. This entails breaking down the region of integration into appropriate bounds for each variable. *Mathematica* can take care of this decomposition for you; the command `CylindricalDecomposition` is designed expressly for this purpose. But in most cases, `Reduce` will accomplish this task just as well. These two commands use the same syntax:

In[151]:= $\texttt{CylindricalDecomposition}[\{\texttt{x, y}\}\in\texttt{Disk}[\{\texttt{0, 0}\},\ \texttt{2},\ \{\pi,\ \texttt{2}\,\pi\}],\ \{\texttt{x, y}\}]$

Out[151]= $(\texttt{x} == -2\ \&\&\ \texttt{y} == 0)\ ||\ \left(-2 < \texttt{x} < 2\ \&\&\ -\sqrt{4 - \texttt{x}^2} \le \texttt{y} \le 0\right)\ ||\ (\texttt{x} == 2\ \&\&\ \texttt{y} == 0)$

In[152]:= $\texttt{Reduce}[\{\texttt{x, y}\}\in\texttt{Disk}[\{\texttt{0, 0}\},\ \texttt{2},\ \{\pi,\ \texttt{2}\,\pi\}],\ \{\texttt{x, y}\}]$

Out[152]= $(\texttt{x} == -2\ \&\&\ \texttt{y} == 0)\ ||\ \left(-2 < \texttt{x} < 2\ \&\&\ -\sqrt{4 - \texttt{x}^2} \le \texttt{y} \le 0\right)\ ||\ (\texttt{x} == 2\ \&\&\ \texttt{y} == 0)$

The individual points in the outputs contribute nothing to the integral, so we ignore them and use the inequalities in the middle portion of the output to set up our bounds of integration. The resulting iterated integral gives the same value we obtained earlier:

In[153]:= $\displaystyle\int_{-2}^{2}\left(\int_{-\sqrt{4-x^2}}^{0}\left(5 - x^2\,y^2\right)\,dy\right)dx$

Out[153]= $\displaystyle\frac{26\,\pi}{3}$

To reverse the order of integration, simply use $\{\texttt{y},\texttt{x}\}$ for the second argument instead of $\{\texttt{x},\texttt{y}\}$ when obtaining the decomposition:

In[154]:= $\texttt{Reduce}[\{\texttt{x, y}\}\in\texttt{Disk}[\{\texttt{0, 0}\},\ \texttt{2},\ \{\pi,\ \texttt{2}\,\pi\}],\ \{\texttt{y, x}\}]$

Out[154]= $(\texttt{y} == -2\ \&\&\ \texttt{x} == 0)\ ||\ \left(-2 < \texttt{y} \le 0\ \&\&\ -\sqrt{4 - \texttt{y}^2} \le \texttt{x} \le \sqrt{4 - \texttt{y}^2}\right)$

In[155]:= $\int_{-2}^{0} \left(\int_{-\sqrt{4-y^2}}^{\sqrt{4-y^2}} (5 - x^2 \, y^2) \, dx \right) dy$

Out[155]= $\dfrac{26\,\pi}{3}$

An analogous process works in higher dimensions. Here we integrate the function $f(x, y, z) = xy - z^2$ over the region inside a ball of radius 2 centered at the origin:

In[156]:= **Integrate** $\left[x\,y - z^2, \{x, y, z\} \in \text{Ball}[\{0, 0, 0\}, 2]\right]$

Out[156]= $-\dfrac{128\,\pi}{15}$

And here we obtain the same result using an iterated integral:

In[157]:= **Reduce** $[\{x, y, z\} \in \text{Ball}[\{0, 0, 0\}, 2], \{z, y, x\}]$

Out[157]= $-2 \le z \le 2 \, \&\& \left(\left(y == -\sqrt{4 - z^2} \, \&\& x == 0\right) \, || \right.$

$\left(-\sqrt{4 - z^2} < y < \sqrt{4 - z^2} \, \&\& -\sqrt{4 - y^2 - z^2} \le x \le \sqrt{4 - y^2 - z^2}\right) \, ||$

$\left. \left(y == \sqrt{4 - z^2} \, \&\& x == 0\right) \right)$

In[158]:= $\int_{-2}^{2} \left(\int_{-\sqrt{4-z^2}}^{\sqrt{4-z^2}} \left(\int_{-\sqrt{4-y^2-z^2}}^{\sqrt{4-y^2-z^2}} (x\,y - z^2) \, dx \right) dy \right) dz$

Out[158]= $-\dfrac{128\,\pi}{15}$

This last integral may take a few moments to evaluate. A more sensible approach, even with a tool as powerful as *Mathematica*, is to use a spherical coordinate system to evaluate this iterated integral. See the subsection "Integration in Other Coordinate Systems" in Section 6.4, where we will return to this example.

As a final example, we embark on a problem where our efforts are focused on translating the problem as stated to a collection of concrete inputs that yield a solution:

> *Find the volume of the solid region bounded by the plane $z = 6 - x - 2y$ and the three coordinate planes $x = 0$, $y = 0$, and $z = 0$.*

The main difficulty with such a problem lies in turning that verbal description of the solid into a region we can enter into *Mathematica*. There are many ways to tackle this. Here is one way to whittle it down piece by piece: The solid is bounded by the four given planes. Each collection of three of these planes intersects in a point, and these points are easy to find. For instance, if a point lies on the three planes $x = 0$ and $y = 0$ and $z = 0$, then that point must be $(0, 0, 0)$. Similarly, if a point lies on the planes $x = 0$, $y = 0$, and $z = 6 - x - 2y$, then $z = 6 - 0 - 0 = 6$, and so the point must be $(0, 0, 6)$. The remaining two "corner" points of the solid are derived in a similar manner: (0, 3, 0) and (6, 0, 0). The solid is a tetrahedron (a four-sided polyhedron) so we can enter it into *Mathematica* like this:

In[159]:= `solid = Tetrahedron[{{0, 0, 0}, {0, 0, 6}, {0, 3, 0}, {6, 0, 0}}];`
`Graphics3D[{Opacity[.5], solid},`
`    Axes → True, AxesLabel → {"x", "y", "z"}]`

Out[160]=

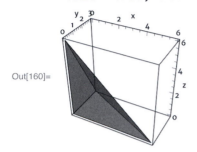

We can ask for its volume directly:

In[161]:= `Volume[solid]`

Out[161]= 18

Or we may integrate the function $f(x, y, z) = 1$ over the solid tetrahedron.

In[162]:= `Integrate[1, {x, y, z} ∈ solid]`

Out[162]= 18

Yet another approach is to describe the two-dimensional region in the xy plane over which the solid resides. By steps similar to our initial work above, we see this region of the xy plane is the triangle with vertices (0, 0), (6, 0), and (0, 3). So we integrate $f(x, y) = 6 - x - 2y$ over this triangle to obtain the desired volume.

In[163]:= `Integrate[6 - x - 2 y, {x, y} ∈ Triangle[{{0, 3}, {6, 0}, {0, 0}}]]`

Out[163]= 18

The point of showing these different approaches is to make clear that for all but the most basic of problems there is "front end" conceptual work that must be done to distill the central question into a form amenable to computation. This is a skill that requires practice, practice, and more practice.

Exercises 6.2

1. In this exercise you will explore the `ColorFunction` option for `Plot3D`. `ColorFunction` may be set to any pure function with three variables (one for each coordinate position). Pure functions are discussed in Section 8.4. By default, each of the input values for this function are scaled from the actual coordinate values to span the range from 0 to 1. In order to use the actual coordinate values, the additional option setting `ColorFunctionScaling → False` must be added. Moreover the output of the `ColorFunction` must be a `Hue`, `RGBColor`, or other color directive (such as a named gradient like `ColorData["StarryNightCol`
`ors"]`). The inputs to functions such as `Hue` should span the values from 0 to 1. In practice, this means that most "interesting" color functions will have to be `Rescaled` before being suitable for input to `Hue` or whichever color rendering function you plan to use.

   a. Make a `Plot3D` of the function $e^{\sin(x\,y)}$ on the domain $-2 \le x \le 2, -2 \le y \le 2$ with the option setting `ColorFunction → (#1&)`. Repeat for `(#2&)` and `(#3&)`. Note that by setting an explicit color function, the default `Lighting` setting switches to using white light only, so as not to interfere with your choice of color.

   b. Make a `Plot3D` of the function $e^{\sin(x\,y)}\sqrt{(x\cos(x\,y))^2 + (y\cos(x\,y))^2}$ on the domain $-2 \le x \le 2$, $-2 \le y \le 2$ with the option setting `PlotRange → All`. Estimate the minimum and maximum values obtained by the function on this domain.

   c. Repeat the previous part, but this time plot the function
   `Rescale[`$e^{\text{Sin}[x\,y]}\sqrt{(x\,\text{Cos}[x\,y])^2 + (y\,\text{Cos}[x\,y])^2}$`,{0,4}]`. What do you notice about its minimum and maximum values?

   d. The function above is suitable for input into a color rendering command such as `Hue` or `ColorData["S`
   `tarryNightColors"]`. Let's do it; enter the following input, and comment on the coloring. What this shows is that (with a little work) the graph of one function can be colored according to the values of any other function.

   In[1]:= `Plot3D[`$e^{\text{Sin}[x\,y]}$`, {x, -2, 2}, {y, -2, 2}, ColorFunctionScaling → False,`

         `ColorFunction → Function[{x, y, z}, ColorData["StarryNightColors"][`

              `Rescale[`$e^{\text{Sin}[x\,y]}\sqrt{(x\,\text{Cos}[x\,y])^2 + (y\,\text{Cos}[x\,y])^2}$`, {0, 4}]]], Mesh → None]`

   Out[1]=

   e. The following output wraps the color rendering function in `Glow`, which means that it will not react with any `Lighting`. Can you see any difference from the last input?

In[2]:= $\texttt{Plot3D}\Big[e^{\texttt{Sin}[x\,y]}, \{x, -2, 2\}, \{y, -2, 2\}, \texttt{ColorFunctionScaling} \to \texttt{False},$

$\quad\texttt{ColorFunction} \to \texttt{Function}\Big[\{x, y, z\}, \texttt{Glow@ColorData}[\texttt{"StarryNightColors"}]\Big[$

$\quad\quad\texttt{Rescale}\Big[e^{\texttt{Sin}[x\,y]}\sqrt{(x\,\texttt{Cos}[x\,y])^2 + (y\,\texttt{Cos}[x\,y])^2}, \{0, 4\}\Big]\Big]\Big], \texttt{Mesh} \to \texttt{None}\Big]$

Out[2]=

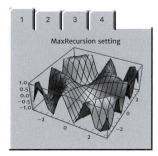

2. Use `TabView` to construct a dynamic display of a `Plot3D` object like the one shown below where `MaxRecursion` may be set to any of the values 0 to 3.

3. Make a plot of the function $f(x, y) = \dfrac{x\,y}{x^2+y^2}$ over the annular domain $.1 \le \sqrt{x^2 + y^2} \le 1$. Add `Filling` to the bottom of the bounding box. Repeat for $f(x, y) = \dfrac{x\,y^2}{x^2+y^2}$. Comment on the behavior of these functions near the origin.

4. Make two images side by side, one showing a `ContourPlot` of your favorite function, and the other a `Plot3D` of that same function on the same domain. Use `MeshFunctions` to display level curves in the `Plot3D`. Use a specific `Range` of values for the `Contours` settings on the `ContourPlot`, and use that same collection of values for `Mesh` settings on the `Plot3D`. This way you will synchronize the level curves being shown in each plot. Use a `ColorFunction` or `MeshShading` to apply `"LakeColors"` to your `Plot3D`.

5. Plot the function $f(x, y) = x^2 - y^2$ over the square region bounded by the lines $y = x - 2$, $y = x + 2$, $y = -x - 2$, and $y = -x + 2$. Then integrate f over this square region.

6. Consider the function $f(x, y) = \sin(x^2 - y^2)$ on the domain $-2 \le x \le 2$, $-1 \le y \le 1$. In this exercise you will explore several methods of illustrating *cross-sections* for this function. That is, you will set one of the coordinate variables equal to a constant. For instance, if $x = 1$ this means geometrically that you slice the graph of f with the vertical plane $x = 1$.

   a. Make a `Manipulate` that will display a `Plot` of the cross-section $y = c$ for f, as c ranges from -1 to 1. For those familiar with medical imaging, this is a bit like an MRI scan of the 3D plot of f.

   b. Make a `Manipulate` that will display a `Plot` of the cross-section $x = c$ for f, as c ranges from -2 to 2.

c. Make the `Manipulate` shown below that shows both of the cross-sections together with a `Plot3D` of f with appropriate `Mesh` lines.

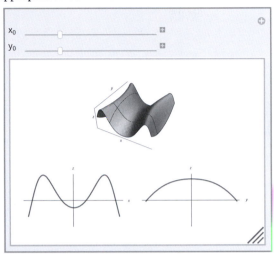

7. Describe the set of critical points for the function $f(x, y) = \sin(x^2 - y^2)$ on the domain $-2 \le x \le 2$ and $-1 \le y \le 1$. Use `Reduce` with the second argument set to $\{y, x\}$ and again with the second argument set to $\{x, y\}$. Is one output easier to interpret?

8. Consider the function $f(x, y) = x \cos(xy)$.

a. Show that f has no critical points. Make a `ContourPlot` with `MeshFunctions` and `Mesh` settings to display the curves where the partial derivative with respect to x is zero, and those where the partial derivative with respect to y is zero. Confirm visually that these two sets of curves never cross.

b. Show that for any direction measured by the polar angle θ, and any real number $r > 0$, the function f has a point (x_0, y_0) in its domain where the directional derivative in the direction of θ exceeds r, and another point (x_1, y_1) where the directional derivative in the direction of θ is less than $-r$. Essentially, the steepness of this function is unbounded in *every* direction, despite being defined on the entire plane, and having no relative minima, maxima, or saddle points.

9. Explain how to use `ContourPlot3D` to view the graph of any real-valued function of two variables, such as $f(x, y) = 2xy$ on the domain $-1 \le x \le 1$, $-1 \le y \le 1$. How does this differ from using the `Plot3D` command to produce such a graph?

10. Maximize the quantity $x^{1/3} y^{2/3}$ under the constraint that $40x + 50y = 10\,000$.

11. Find *all* point(s) on the surface $z = xy$ closest to the point $(0, 0, 3)$. Make a `ContourPlot3D` of this surface, colored (via `MeshShading`) according to how close points are to $(0, 0, 3)$.

12. Consider the function $f(x, y) = 2\sqrt{1 - x^2}$ defined over the unit disk in the xy plane centered at the origin.

a. Make a `Plot3D` of f over this circular region, and use `Filling` to display the solid under the graph of f and above the xy plane.

b. Find the volume of this solid.

c. Make the following `Manipulate`, showing the graph from part **a** together with a movable square cross-section. If one first integrates with respect to y, the inner integral is equal to the area of this square cross-section.

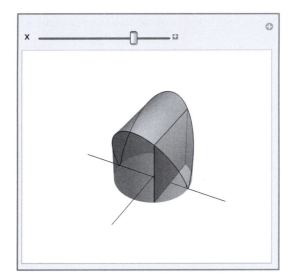

13. Find the *approximate* value of the double integral of the function $f(x, y) = 2x - y$ over the region $\mathcal{R}$ in the xy plane bounded by $y = \sin x$ and $y = 1 - x^2$. Make a three-dimensional sketch of the signed volume that this integral represents.

14. Use `RegionPlot3D` to view the solid torus $z^2 + \left(\sqrt{x^2 + y^2} - 3\right)^2 \le 1$. Use `MeshShading` to color the torus according to distance from the origin, with points closest to the origin appearing red, and the most distant points appearing blue (The `ColorData["TemperatureMap"]` gradient is perfect for this). Finally, display that portion of the surface with $-2 \le x \le 4$ and $0 \le y \le 4$.

6.3 Parametric Curves and Surfaces

Parametric Curves in the Plane

A parametric representation of a curve is a continuous vector-valued function of one variable; for each value of a variable t, the function returns a vector $\langle x(t), y(t) \rangle$ in the plane. As t varies continuously through an interval, the vectors trace out a curve. Since a vector in *Mathematica* is represented as a `List`, a parametric curve can be defined as a `List` of two or more real-valued functions. The first function represents the x coordinate, the second the y coordinate. Since there is only one variable, we revert to the paradigm for defining functions used in Chapters 3 through 5, with an underscore after the independent variable on the left side, and using `SetDelayed (:=)`.

```
In[1]:= s[t_] := {Cos[t] + t, Sin[t]}
```

You can now find your position in the plane for any value of t:

```
In[2]:= s[π/4]
```

$$\text{Out[2]}= \left\{ \frac{1}{\sqrt{2}} + \frac{\pi}{4}, \frac{1}{\sqrt{2}} \right\}$$

To plot a parametric function, use the command `ParametricPlot`:

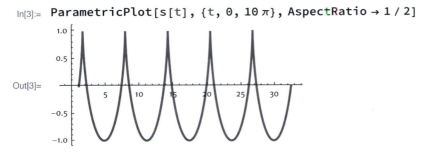

`In[3]:= ParametricPlot[s[t], {t, 0, 10 π}, AspectRatio → 1 / 2]`

`ParametricPlot` takes two arguments. The first is the function you wish to plot, and the second is an iterator for the independent variable (`t` in this example). `ParametricPlot` will tend to give both axes the same scale unless you explicitly tell it not to. Many curves, circles for instance, look better that way, so that's what happens by default. Be aware that in plots like the one above where one axis is far longer than the other, an `AspectRatio` setting will be in order.

You need not restrict yourself to simple functions. `ParametricPlot` works well on `Piecewise` functions, and even on interesting curves like this:

$$In[4]:= \quad c[t\_] = \left\{ \int_0^t \mathrm{Sin}[u^2]\, du, \int_0^t \mathrm{Cos}[u^2]\, du \right\};$$

`In[5]:= ParametricPlot[c[t], {t, -10, 10}]`

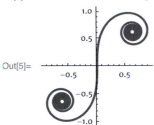

⚠ Note that the definition of c(t) above uses `Set` (`=`) rather than `SetDelayed` (`:=`). This causes the two integrals on the right side of the definition to be evaluated once, when the `c[t_]=` cell is entered. It is the expressions that are the values of these integrals (they happen to be Fresnel functions) that are assigned to c(t), and that are then plotted. If `SetDelayed` had been used in defining c(t), then the integrals would have to be re-evaluated for each input value t used to create the plot (and there are several hundred such values). It would slow the process of plotting by several orders of magnitude.

While a `ParametricPlot` shows the set of points of the form $(x(t), y(t))$ as t runs through all values in an interval, it does not give any indication of which point goes with which input. `Manipulate` can be harnessed to trace out a parametric curve, with a slider to control the independent variable. Here, for instance, is a standard parameterization of the unit circle. Note the `PlotRange` setting (which keeps the plot range fixed as t varies), and the small but positive starting value 0.01 for the endpoint t (one needs *distinct* starting and ending values for the independent variable in any `ParametricPlot`).

In[6]:= `Manipulate[Show[`
          `ParametricPlot[{Cos[θ], Sin[θ]}, {θ, 0, t}, PlotRange → 1],`
          `Graphics[Arrow[{{0, 0}, {Cos[t], Sin[t]}}]]`
         `],`
         `{{t, 5.}, 0.01, 2 π}]`

Out[6]=

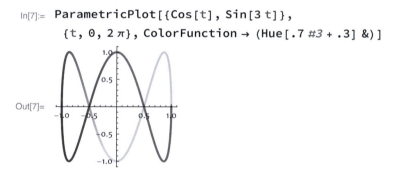

It is not hard to define a custom parametric plotting command that will apply a color gradient to the curve, so that it will, for instance, start in green and gradually progress through the color gradient to end in red. Thinking green for go, red for stop, the resulting plot shows both the curve and its orientation relative to the parameterization. Here's a simple implementation, but you'll need to try it in order to see the colors on your display.

In[7]:= `ParametricPlot[{Cos[t], Sin[3 t]},`
          `{t, 0, 2 π}, ColorFunction → (Hue[.7 #3 + .3] &)]`

Out[7]=

> ⚠ The `ColorFunction` accepts any or all of three arguments. The first two are the x and y coordinates of the parametric curve. The third (#3 used above) is the independent variable t. By default, the values of t will be scaled to run from 0 to 1 before being input to the `ColorFunction`, regardless of the domain you choose. Hence the option setting above produces a color gradient that starts at `Hue[.3]` (green) and ends at `Hue[1.]` (red). So the same setting used here may be used to color any `ParametricPlot` to start green and end red. Exercise 4 shows how to color a parametric curve according to its curvature.

We note that `ParametricPlot` accepts most of the options accepted by other two-dimensional plotting commands such as `Plot`. The `PlotPoints` option, for example, can be set to a numerical value (such as 100) if you see jagged segments where you suspect they should not be. However, the adaptive algorithm employed by `ParametricPlot` is both speedy and robust; it is rare to find cases where it does anything less than an excellent job. The following `Manipulate` may help to convince you of this:

```
In[8]:= Manipulate[ParametricPlot[
          {Cos[t] + 1/2 Cos[7 t] + 1/2 Sin[a t], Sin[t] + 1/2 Sin[7 t] + 1/2 Cos[b t]},
          {t, 0, 2 π}, Axes → False, PlotRange → 2],
          {{a, 17}, 5, 25}, {{b, 12}, 5, 25}]
```

Out[8]=

The derivative of the parametric function $\langle x(t), y(t) \rangle$ is $\langle x'(t), y'(t) \rangle$. You can differentiate a parametric function just as you did a single-variable function in Chapter 5, or like we did for multivariable functions in the previous section of this chapter, using ∂:

```
In[9]:= D[s[t], t]
Out[9]= {1 - Sin[t], Cos[t]}
```

```
In[10]:= s'[t]
Out[10]= {1 - Sin[t], Cos[t]}
```

```
In[11]:= ∂_t s[t]
Out[11]= {1 - Sin[t], Cos[t]}
```

Note that while the `ParametricPlot` of $\vec{s}(t)$ has sharp corners (it is the first plot shown at the beginning of this section), its derivative is defined everywhere. This can happen. The `Manipulate` below shows the derivative vector $\vec{s}'(t)$ with its tail at the point $s(t)$, as t varies. When t is $\pi/2$ or $5\pi/2$, $\sin t = 1$ and $\cos t = 0$, and so the derivative is the zero vector. This happens at the top of each sharp corner in the plot.

```
In[12]:= Manipulate[Module[{s},
           s[t_] = {t + Cos[t], Sin[t]};
           Show[
             ParametricPlot[s[t], {t, 0, 10}, PlotRange → {{0, 10}, {-2, 2}}],
             Graphics[{Arrow[{s[t0], s[t0] + s'[t0]}],
               {Red, PointSize[.015], Point[s[t0]]}}]
           ]],
           {{t0, 4, "t₀"}, 0, 10}]
```

Out[12]=

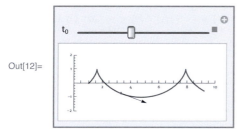

⚠ In this `Manipulate`, the entire first argument is wrapped in a `Module`. This has
the effect of localizing the variable s, so that it is immune to any updates. For
more information, search for "Advanced Manipulate Functionality" in the
Documentation Center and follow the link to the tutorial of that name. The
`Module` command is discussed in Section 8.6.

If $\vec{s}(t)$ represents the position of a particle at time t, then its *velocity* vector is $\vec{s}'(t)$, and its *speed* is the
magnitude of this vector. To compute speed, say at time $t = 3$, you can do this:

```
In[13]:= Norm[s'[3]] // N
```
```
Out[13]= 1.31063
```

You can even get a formula for speed as a function of t. Here we produce and `Simplify` the formula,
using the optional second argument for `Simplify` in order to specify that t is permitted to assume
only real values (as opposed to complex values). We could have given the second argument as
`Element[t, Reals]`. The infix form of the `Element` command is invoked with the $\in$ symbol, which
can be found in the Typesetting section of the Basic Math Assistant palette under the $\times$ tab.

```
In[14]:= Simplify[Norm[s'[t]], t ∈ Reals]
```
$$Out[14]= \sqrt{2 - 2\,Sin[t]}$$

Note that this is consistent with the `Manipulate` above; speed is zero precisely when t is $\pi/2$, $5\pi/2$,
etc.

Unit tangent vectors are constructed exactly as you would expect. The use of `Simplify` as above will generally serve you well.

```
In[15]:=  unitTangent[s_, t_] := Simplify[Normalize[D[s, t]], t ∈ Reals]
```

```
In[16]:=  s[t_] = {t + Cos[t], Sin[t]};
          unitTangent[s[t], t]
```

$$Out[17]= \left\{ \frac{\sqrt{1-\mathrm{Sin}[t]}}{\sqrt{2}}, \frac{\mathrm{Cos}[t]}{\sqrt{2-2\,\mathrm{Sin}[t]}} \right\}$$

The unit tangent vector at a specific value of *t* can then be obtained via a simple replacement:

```
In[18]:=  unitTangent[s[t], t] /. t → 1.2
```

```
Out[18]=  {0.184338, 0.982863}
```

Unit normal vectors can be formed in a similar way (although `FullSimplify` tends to do a better job than `Simplify` in this case):

```
In[19]:=  unitNormal[s_, t_] :=
              FullSimplify[Normalize[D[unitTangent[s, t], t]], t ∈ Reals]
```

```
In[20]:=  unitNormal[s[t], t]
```

$$Out[20]= \left\{ -\frac{\mathrm{Cos}[t]}{\sqrt{2-2\,\mathrm{Sin}[t]}}, \frac{\sqrt{1-\mathrm{Sin}[t]}}{\sqrt{2}} \right\}$$

Even though neither the unit tangent nor the unit normal is defined when $t = \pi/2$ or $t = 5\pi/2$ (since the derivative is the zero vector and hence cannot be normalized), the following `Manipulate` works fine, as it is unlikely to sample these precise values. We define auxiliary commands `ut` and `un` so that `unitTangent` and `unitNormal` only need to be evaluated once (they are slow, after all, since they use `Simplify` and `FullSimplify`, respectively, each time they are called). The auxiliary commands `ut` and `un` are defined using `Set` (=). So they use the *formulas* generated by `unitTangent` and `unitNormal`. They are speedy!

In[21]:= `Manipulate[Module[{s, ut, un},`
`    s[t_] = {t + Cos[t], Sin[t]};`
`    ut[t_] = unitTangent[s[t], t];`
`    un[t_] = unitNormal[s[t], t];`
`    Show[ParametricPlot[s[t], {t, 0, 10}, PlotRange → {{0, 10}, {-2, 2}}],`
`      Graphics[{Blue, Arrow[{s[t0], s[t0] + ut[t0]}]}],`
`      Graphics[{Red, Arrow[{s[t0], s[t0] + un[t0]}]}]]], {{t0, 4}, 0, 10}]`

Out[21]=

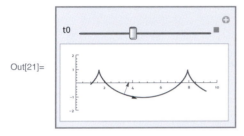

Curvature is also a simple calculation. We use the Greek letter κ (kappa) to denote this quantity. Find κ on the Basic Math Assistant palette, or type ⎋ k ⎋.

In[22]:= `κ[s_, t_] :=`
`    FullSimplify[Norm[D[unitTangent[s, t], t]] / Norm[D[s, t]], t ∈ Reals]`

In[23]:= `κ[s[t], t]`

Out[23]=
$$\frac{1}{2\sqrt{2 - 2\,\text{Sin}[t]}}$$

And so the *radius of curvature* is the reciprocal of this quantity, $2\sqrt{2 - 2\sin t}$. At the sharp corners (when t is $\pi/2$, $5\pi/2$, etc.) the curvature is undefined, and the radius of curvature approaches zero. The `Manipulate` below shows the *osculating circle* for any value of t. This illustrates that the radius of curvature approaches zero very rapidly as t approaches $5\pi/2$.

In[24]:= `Manipulate[Module[{s, un, curv},`

`    s[t_] = {t + Cos[t], Sin[t]};`
`    un[t_] = unitNormal[s[t], t];`
`    curv[t_] = κ[s[t], t];`
`    Show[`
`      ParametricPlot[s[t], {t, 0, 10}, PlotRange → {{-4, 12}, {-2, 6}}],`

$$\texttt{Graphics}\left[\left\{\texttt{Gray, Circle}\left[\texttt{s[t0]} + \frac{1}{\texttt{curv[t0]}} \texttt{un[t0]}, \frac{1}{\texttt{curv[t0]}}\right]\right\}\right],$$

$$\texttt{Graphics}\left[\left\{\texttt{Red, Arrow}\left[\left\{\texttt{s[t0]} + \frac{1}{\texttt{curv[t0]}} \texttt{un[t0]}, \texttt{s[t0]}\right\}\right]\right\}\right]$$

`    ]], {{t0, 7.}, 0, 10}]`

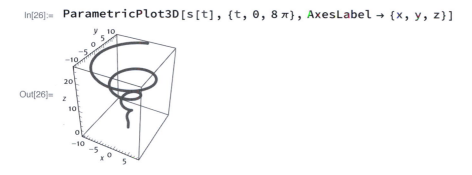

Out[24]=

Parametric Curves in Space

Parametric curves in three-space are just like parametric curves in the plane, except that they are constructed as a list of *three* real-valued functions. The first function represents the x coordinate, the second represents the y coordinate, and the third represents the z coordinate.

In[25]:= $\texttt{s[t\_] := }\left\{\frac{t^2}{50}\texttt{ Sin[t], }\frac{t^2}{50}\texttt{ Cos[t], }t\right\}$

To plot a parametric function in space, use the command `ParametricPlot3D`:

In[26]:= `ParametricPlot3D[s[t], {t, 0, 8 π}, AxesLabel → {x, y, z}]`

Out[26]=

ParametricPlot3D takes two arguments. The first is the function you wish to plot (a List of three coordinate functions), and the second is an iterator for the independent variable. Adding an AxesLabel option makes it easy to identify which direction is which after you rotate the figure with your mouse. Many of the same options for the other 3D plotting commands are applicable here; see the subsection of Section 6.2 called "Options for 3D Plotting Commands." Also, one can use MeshShading or ColorFunction settings in exactly the same manner as for 2D parametric plots. For example, here we color a curve according to the value of the independent variable:

In[27]:= **ParametricPlot3D[s[t], {t, 0, 8 π},**
          AxesLabel → {x, y, z}, ColorFunction → (Hue[.3 + .7 #3] &)]

Out[27]=

Differentiation, integration, unit tangents, unit normals, and curvature work exactly as for 2D parametric functions (see the previous subsection). In the case of three-space, however, there is a well-known alternate formula for curvature based on the cross-product. It is a simple matter to program a command based on this formula:

In[28]:= **curvature[r_, t_] :=**
$$\textbf{FullSimplify}\left[\frac{\textbf{Norm[Cross[}r\textbf{'[t]}, r\textbf{''[t]]]}}{\textbf{Norm[}r\textbf{'[t]]}^3}, t \in \textbf{Reals}\right]$$

We may now calculate curvature for any function, at any point *t* in its domain:

In[29]:= **curvature[s, π]**

Out[29]= $\left(50 \sqrt{\left(10\,000 + 30\,000\,\pi^2 + 2536\,\pi^4 + 12\,\pi^6 + \pi^8\right)}\right) \Big/ \left(2500 + 4\,\pi^2 + \pi^4\right)^{3/2}$

In[30]:= **curvature[s, t]**

Out[30]= $50 \sqrt{\left(\left(10\,000 + 30\,000\,t^2 + 2536\,t^4 + 12\,t^6 + t^8\right) \Big/ \left(2500 + 4\,t^2 + t^4\right)^3\right)}$

Parametric Surfaces in Space

A surface in space can be parameterized much like a curve in space, but rather than using a single independent variable *t*, we use a pair of independent variables *u* and *v*. Whereas a parameterization of a curve in space is a continuous function from an *interval* of the real line to three-space, a parameterization of a surface is a continuous function from a *rectangle* in the plane to three-space. The image of each coordinate pair (*u*, *v*) is a point in space, a 3-tuple (*x*(*u*, *v*), *y*(*u*, *v*), *z*(*u*, *v*)), where *x*, *y*, and *z* are real-valued coordinate functions.

Mathematica is instrumental in visualizing the amazing spectrum of surfaces that can be constructed in this manner. Here is an example. It illustrates that just as a parametrically defined curve can intersect itself (if the coordinate functions assume the same values at two or more distinct values of *t*), so too can a parametrically defined surface intersect itself. This surface is known as the *Whitney umbrella*, named after the American mathematician Hassler Whitney (1907−1989).

```
In[31]:= Clear[Φ, u, v];
        Φ = {u v, u, v²}
```
```
Out[32]= {u v, u, v²}
```
```
In[33]:= ParametricPlot3D[Φ, {u, -3, 3}, {v, -2, 2}]
```

Out[33]=

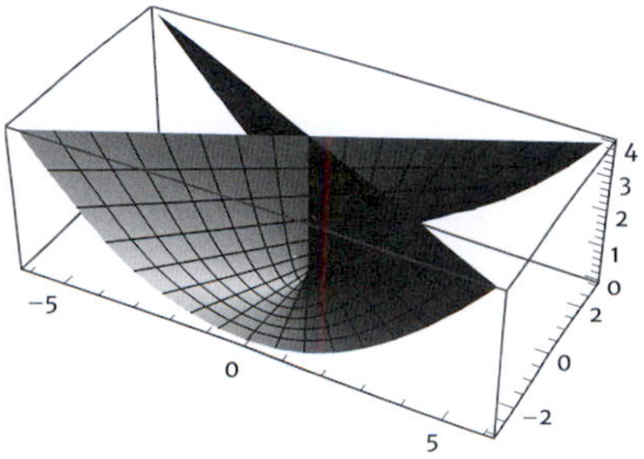

The rectangular region in the *uv* plane with $-3 \le u \le 3$ and $-2 \le v \le 2$ is mapped continuously via Φ to the surface in $\mathbb{R}^3$ shown above. As with parametric curves, the plot does not show the domain, but only the image of the domain after the parametric function is applied.

Here's another example. We map a rectangle in the *uv* plane to a torus:

```
In[34]:= Φ = {Cos[u] (2 + Cos[v]), Sin[u] (2 + Cos[v]), Sin[v]};
```
```
In[35]:= ParametricPlot3D[Φ, {u, 0, 2 π}, {v, 0, 2 π}]
```

Out[35]=

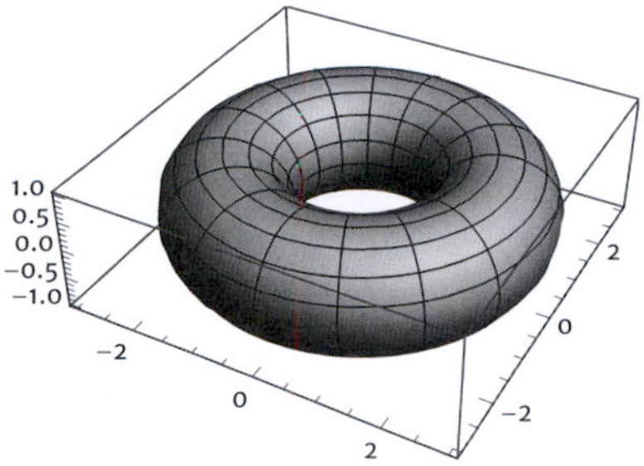

For parametric surfaces, a mesh function can accept up to five arguments. In order, the arguments are *x*, *y*, *z*, *u*, and *v*. The first three are the coordinates in space of the surface, while the last two are the independent variables. The default setting for the MeshFunctions option is {#4 &, #5 &}, meaning that the image under Φ of uniformly spaced rectangular grid lines on the domain rectangle are shown. More information can be gained by using Mesh, MeshFunctions, and MeshShading to apply a color gradient according to increasing values of one of the independent variables. This is accomplished in exactly the same way as described in the subsection of Section 6.2 called "Options for

3D Plotting Commands." Below we do this for the first independent variable, u, used in the torus. The "seam" is easily visible (on a color screen) as the sharp boundary between red and blue.

```
In[36]:= ParametricPlot3D[Φ, {u, 0, 2 π},
           {v, 0, 2 π}, Mesh → 10, MeshFunctions → {#4 &},
           MeshShading → Table[ColorData["TemperatureMap"][k], {k, 0, 1, .1}],
           Lighting → "Neutral"]
```

Out[36]=

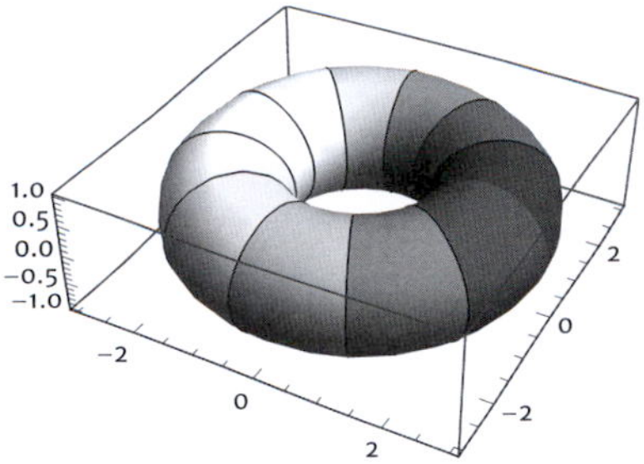

Differentiation works just as with parameterized curves. Here is the partial derivative with respect to v:

```
In[37]:= ∂_v Φ
```

Out[37]= $\{-Cos[u] Sin[v], -Sin[u] Sin[v], Cos[v]\}$

It is easy to use the concept of a parametric surface to generate a *surface of revolution*. You may recall surfaces of revolution from single-variable calculus; indeed, in Section 5.13 we discussed the built-in command RevolutionPlot3D, which will plot the surface of revolution obtained from revolving the function $z = f(x)$ about the z axis by default, but other axes may be specified. For example, here we rotate a parabola about the x axis:

```
In[38]:= f[x_] := 1 - x²;
           GraphicsRow[{Plot[f[x], {x, -1, 1}],
              RevolutionPlot3D[f[x], {x, -1, 1}, RevolutionAxis → "X"]}]
```

Out[39]=

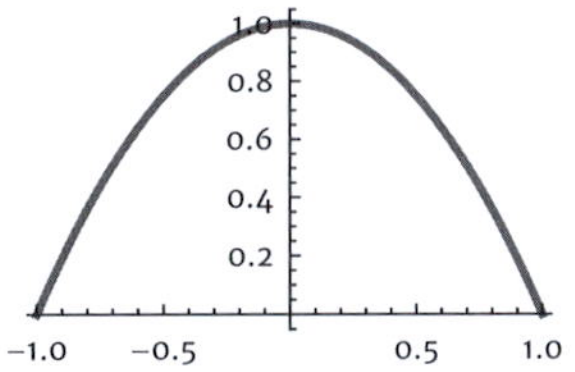

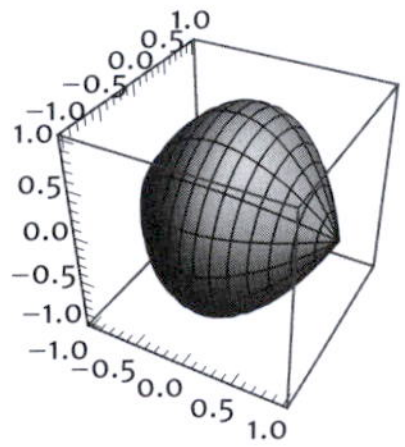

Using ParametricPlot3D, it is straightforward to write a custom command for rotating the graph of a function $f(x)$ around the x axis:

```
In[40]:= xRevolutionPlot3D[f_, {x_, xmin_, xmax_}] :=
           ParametricPlot3D[{x, f Cos[θ], f Sin[θ]}, {x, xmin, xmax}, {θ, 0, 2 π}]
```

In[41]:= **xRevolutionPlot3D[f[x], {x, -1, 1}]**

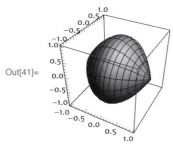

Out[41]=

Exercises 6.3

1. Explain how to use `ParametricPlot` to view the graph of any real-valued function of a single variable, such as $f(x) = x^2 - 1$. How does this differ from using the `Plot` command to produce such a graph?

2. There are many different parameterizations of the same curve. A standard parameterization of the unit circle is $\langle \cos t, \sin t \rangle$, where $0 \le t \le 2\pi$. Verify that the parametric function $\left\langle \dfrac{\sin(4\,t)+\sin(6\,t)}{2\sin(5\,t)}, \dfrac{\cos(4\,t)-\cos(6\,t)}{2\sin(5\,t)} \right\rangle$, where $0 < t < 2\pi$, also parameterizes the unit circle for those values of t where it is defined (e.g., it is not defined at integer multiples of $t = \pi/5$).

3. Consider the vector-valued function $\vec{r}(t) = \langle 2\sin(t), \cos(t), \sin(2\,t) \rangle$.

   a. Superimpose a `ParametricPlot3D` of $\vec{r}(t)$ with a `ContourPlot3D` of the surface $z = x\,y$. Use the option `Mesh → None` in your plot of the surface. What do you find?

   b. Explain why the curve lies on the surface. Hint: You will need the double-angle formula for the sine function. If you have forgotten it, type `TrigExpand[Sin[2t]]`.

4. Use `ColorFunction` to color a `ParametricPlot` of the function $\left\langle t,\ e^{-t^2} \right\rangle$ on the domain $-2 \le t \le 2$ according to its *curvature* with the `"TemperatureMap"` color gradient. While this method produces continuous color transitions (as opposed to the discrete color values produced when using `MeshFunctions` for this purpose), it requires your knowing the maximum and minimum curvature values for your specific function on your specific domain.

5. Use `MeshShading` to shade a `ParametricPlot3D` of the torus,

$$\Phi(u, v) = \langle \cos(u)\,(\cos(v) + 2),\ \sin(u)\,(\cos(v) + 2),\ \sin(v) \rangle$$

   where each independent variable ranges from 0 to 2π, according to values of the independent variable v. Use the color gradient `ColorData["TemperatureMap"]` with ten gradations. Use the resulting graphic to identify the "seam" in the torus created by this variable.

6.4 Other Coordinate Systems

Polar Coordinates

Conversion to and from Polar Coordinates

A point in polar coordinates is represented as an ordered pair (r, θ), where r is the distance from the point to the origin, and the angle θ is measured in radians, counterclockwise, from the positive x axis to the segment connecting the origin to the point.

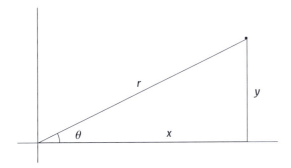

To convert between polar and Cartesian coordinates, one makes use of the above triangle and some basic trigonometry. So in converting from polar to Cartesian coordinates, one uses the formulas $x = r \cos \theta$ and $y = r \sin \theta$. *Mathematica*'s FromPolarCoordinates command does precisely this.

```
In[1]:=  Clear[x, y, z, r, θ];
         FromPolarCoordinates[{r, θ}]

Out[2]=  {r Cos[θ], r Sin[θ]}
```

So, for example, it is a simple matter to convert a point in polar coordinates to Cartesian coordinates.

```
In[3]:=  FromPolarCoordinates[{10, π/12}]
```

$$\text{Out[3]}= \left\{ \frac{5\left(1+\sqrt{3}\right)}{\sqrt{2}}, \frac{5\left(-1+\sqrt{3}\right)}{\sqrt{2}} \right\}$$

In converting from Cartesian to polar coordinates, one uses the formula $r = \sqrt{x^2 + y^2}$, and so long as $x \neq 0$, $\tan \theta = y/x$. This last equation, when solved for θ, can be expressed as follows:

$$\theta = \begin{cases} \arctan(y/x) & x > 0 \\ \arctan(y/x) + \pi & x < 0 \text{ and } y \geq 0 \\ \arctan(y/x) - \pi & x < 0 \text{ and } y < 0 \\ \pi/2 & x = 0 \text{ and } y > 0 \\ -\pi/2 & x = 0 \text{ and } y < 0 \end{cases}$$

This expression for θ is clearly a bit messy. The formula above will produce a value of θ with $-\pi < \theta \leq \pi$. *Mathematica* makes the calculation of θ much easier with its ArcTan command. The ArcTan command usually takes a single number as its argument, and returns a value between $-\pi/2$ and $\pi/2$, the arc tangent of that number. But you can also feed it an xy pair. ArcTan[x, y] will return the polar angle θ for the point with Cartesian coordinates (x, y), with $-\pi < \theta \leq \pi$. That is, it will essentially invoke the complicated piecewise formula above. So life is easy after all: In converting from Cartesian to polar coordinates, $\theta = \text{ArcTan[x, y]}$. For instance:

In[4]:= `{ArcTan[1, 1], ArcTan[0, 1], ArcTan[-1, 1], ArcTan[-1, -1]}`

Out[4]= $\left\{ \dfrac{\pi}{4}, \dfrac{\pi}{2}, \dfrac{3\pi}{4}, -\dfrac{3\pi}{4} \right\}$

Mathematica's ToPolarCoordinates command utilizes the two-argument form of ArcTan.

In[5]:= `ToPolarCoordinates[{x, y}]`

Out[5]= $\left\{ \sqrt{x^2 + y^2}, \text{ArcTan}[x, y] \right\}$

So, for example:

In[6]:= `ToPolarCoordinates[{-1, √3}]`

Out[6]= $\left\{ 2, \dfrac{2\pi}{3} \right\}$

We note that there is a more general coordinate transformation command that can do the work of ToPolarCoordinates and FromPolarCoordinates, and much more. The command is called CoordinateTransform. Here are two quick examples to demonstrate its syntax:

In[7]:= `CoordinateTransform["Polar" → "Cartesian", {r, θ}]`

Out[7]= `{r Cos[θ], r Sin[θ]}`

In[8]:= `CoordinateTransform["Cartesian" → "Polar", {-1, √3}]`

Out[8]= $\left\{ 2, \dfrac{2\pi}{3} \right\}$

Plotting in Polar Coordinates

The built-in command `PolarPlot` can be used to view the graph of the polar function $r = f(\theta)$. For example:

In[9]:= `PolarPlot`$\left[\dfrac{1}{1 - \text{Sin}[\theta]}, \left\{\theta, \dfrac{-5\pi}{4}, \dfrac{\pi}{4}\right\}\right]$

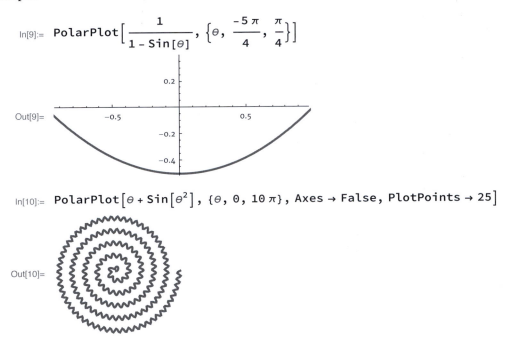

In[10]:= `PolarPlot`$\left[\theta + \text{Sin}\left[\theta^2\right], \{\theta, 0, 10\pi\}, \text{Axes} \to \text{False}, \text{PlotPoints} \to 25\right]$

Like `Plot`, `PolarPlot` will accept a *list* of functions as its first argument (so that multiple functions can be simultaneously plotted). It accepts most of the same options accepted by `Plot`, so you will be pleased to find that you're already an expert in its usage. For example:

In[11]:= `PolarPlot`$\left[\left\{\sqrt{\theta}, -\sqrt{\theta}\right\}, \{\theta, 0, 4\pi\}, \right.$

$\left. \text{Axes} \to \text{False}, \text{PlotStyle} \to \{\text{Gray}, \text{Dashed}\}\right]$

Parametric Plotting in Polar Coordinates

There is no built-in command for this, but it is easy to write the command yourself. If r and θ are each functions of the parameter t, then $x = r\cos\theta$ and $y = r\sin\theta$ are also functions of t, and so can be plotted using `ParametricPlot`. Here's how we can formalize this notion:

```
In[12]:=  polarParametricPlot[{r_, θ_}, args__] :=
            ParametricPlot[{r*Cos[θ], r*Sin[θ]}, args]
```

Put *two* underscores after `args` on the left side of the definition (two underscores means that `args` represents one *or more* arguments, separated by commas). In this case args stands for the required iterator for the independent variable *and* for any options that might be added. Here's an example:

```
In[13]:=  Clear[r, θ, t];
            r[t_] := t Sin[t];
            θ[t_] := e^t
```

```
In[16]:=  polarParametricPlot[{r[t], θ[t]}, {t, 0, π}, Axes → False]
```

Out[16]=

Cylindrical and Spherical Coordinates

Conversion to and from Cartesian Coordinates

When translating from one coordinate system to another it is imperative that you understand the geometry and trigonometry underlying the translation. Otherwise, you will be placing your faith entirely in the computer, which is never a good idea. However, it would be nice to be able to automate the process, or to be able to ask *Mathematica* for a conversion formula that you might have forgotten.

Translation between different coordinate systems is best handled by `CoordinateTransform`:

```
In[17]:=  CoordinateTransform[ "Cartesian" → "Cylindrical", {x, y, z}]
```

$$Out[17]= \left\{ \sqrt{x^2 + y^2}, \text{ArcTan}[x, y], z \right\}$$

```
In[18]:=  CoordinateTransform[ "Cartesian" → "Cylindrical", {-√2, √2, 3}]
```

$$Out[18]= \left\{ 2, \frac{3\pi}{4}, 3 \right\}$$

```
In[19]:=  CoordinateTransform[ "Cylindrical" → "Cartesian", {r, θ, z}]
```

$$Out[19]= \{r \text{ Cos}[θ], r \text{ Sin}[θ], z\}$$

Working with spherical coordinates demands that you pay careful attention to *Mathematica*'s conventions for this coordinate system. By default, nonzero points expressed in spherical coordinates are of the form $\{\rho, \phi, \theta\}$, where ρ is the distance from the point to the origin, ϕ is the angle from the positive z axis to the vector from the origin to the point, and θ is the angle used in polar and cylindrical coordinates. Note that at the north pole of the unit sphere $\phi = 0$, and at the south pole $\phi = \pi$. The second and third coordinate positions are transposed in many standard calculus texts, so beware!

```
In[20]:= CoordinateTransform[ "Spherical" → "Cartesian", {10, π / 3, π / 4}]
```

$$\text{Out[20]}= \left\{ 5 \sqrt{\frac{3}{2}} \, , \, 5 \sqrt{\frac{3}{2}} \, , \, 5 \right\}$$

```
In[21]:= CoordinateTransform[ "Spherical" → "Cartesian", {10, 2 π / 3, π / 4}]
```

$$\text{Out[21]}= \left\{ 5 \sqrt{\frac{3}{2}} \, , \, 5 \sqrt{\frac{3}{2}} \, , \, -5 \right\}$$

```
In[22]:= CoordinateTransform[ "Cartesian" → "Spherical" , {1, 1, 1}]
```

$$\text{Out[22]}= \left\{ \sqrt{3} \, , \, \text{ArcTan}\left[\sqrt{2} \right], \, \frac{\pi}{4} \right\}$$

Best of all, you can use these conversion commands to help you remember the conversion formulas:

```
In[23]:= Clear[ρ, φ, θ];
        CoordinateTransform[ "Spherical" → "Cartesian", {ρ, φ, θ}]
```

$$\text{Out[24]}= \{ \rho \, \text{Cos}[\theta] \, \text{Sin}[\phi], \, \rho \, \text{Sin}[\theta] \, \text{Sin}[\phi], \, \rho \, \text{Cos}[\phi] \}$$

```
In[25]:= Clear[x, y, z];
        CoordinateTransform[ "Cartesian" → "Spherical" , {x, y, z}]
```

$$\text{Out[26]}= \left\{ \sqrt{x^2 + y^2 + z^2} \, , \, \text{ArcTan}\left[z, \, \sqrt{x^2 + y^2} \right], \, \text{ArcTan}[x, y] \right\}$$

If you are not familiar with the `ArcTan[x,y]` convention, see the subsection "Polar Coordinates" at the beginning of this section.

Plotting in Cylindrical Coordinates

Suppose you have a function given in cylindrical coordinates, that is, where $z = f(r, \theta)$ is expressed as a function of the radius r and polar angle θ. The command `RevolutionPlot3D` (first introduced in Section 5.13 for the purpose of plotting a surface of revolution) can be used to produce the graph of such a function. It works much like `Plot3D`: The first argument is the expression for z in the variables r and θ, and the second and third arguments are iterators for r and θ, respectively.

In[27]:= `RevolutionPlot3D[θ, {r, 0, 3}, {θ, 0, 2 π}, BoxRatios → 1]`

Out[27]=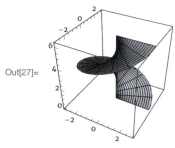

Here we plot the paraboloid $f(x, y) = x^2 + y^2$, shown over a circular domain of radius 2, with polar angle θ between 0 and $3\pi/2$:

In[28]:= `RevolutionPlot3D[r², {r, 0, 2}, {θ, 0, 3 π / 2},`
`BoxRatios → {1, 1, 1}, Boxed → False, Axes → False]`

Out[28]=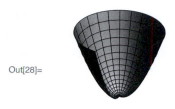

Parametric Plotting in Cylindrical Coordinates

If r, θ, and z are each parameterized by a variable such as t, you may wish to plot the curve that results from the parameterization. While there is no built-in command for this, you can create the command `parametricCylindricalPlot3D` as follows:

In[29]:= `parametricCylindricalPlot3D[{r_, θ_, z_}, args__] :=`
`ParametricPlot3D[{r * Cos[θ], r * Sin[θ], z}, args]`

This command simply invokes `ParametricPlot3D` after converting the arguments from cylindrical to Cartesian coordinates. Be sure to put two underscores after `args` on the left side of the defining equation; two underscores mean that `args` stands for a sequence of one *or more* arguments. In this case, `args` represents the required iterator for the independent variable *t and* any options you might add—this will allow you to use any of the options allowed by `ParametricPlot3D`.

Here is an example of a curve that resides along the cylinder whose equation in cylindrical coordinates is $r = 1$:

In[30]:= `parametricCylindricalPlot3D[{1, t, Cos[20 t]},`
         `{t, 0, 2 π}, Boxed → False, Axes → False]`

Out[30]=

Plotting in Spherical Coordinates

If, in spherical coordinates, ρ is a function of ϕ and θ, you can produce a plot of this function with the command `SphericalPlot3D`. Using this command is much like using `Plot3D`—the first argument is the expression for the radius ρ given in terms of ϕ and θ. The second and third arguments are iterators for ϕ and θ, respectively (note that ϕ, the angle from the positive z axis, comes *first*). Here are two hemispheres, each with the equation $\rho = 2$:

In[31]:= `SphericalPlot3D[2, {ϕ, 0, π / 2}, {θ, 0, 2 π}]`

Out[31]=

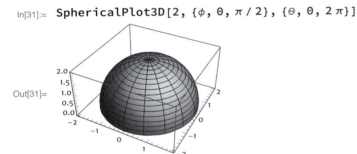

In[32]:= `SphericalPlot3D[2, {ϕ, 0, π}, {θ, 0, π}]`

Out[32]=

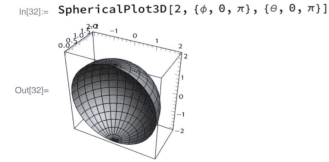

And here is a plot of the surface with the simple equation $\rho = \theta$:

```
SphericalPlot3D[θ, {φ, 0, π}, {θ, 0, 7π/2}, Boxed → False, Axes → False]
```

Out[33]=

Most of the options that can be used with the command `Plot3D` will also work for `Spherical Plot3D`. A discussion of these options can be found in the subsection "Options for 3D Plotting Commands" of Section 6.2.

Parametric Plotting in Spherical Coordinates

If ρ and ϕ and θ are each parameterized by a variable such as t, you may wish to plot the curve that results from this parameterization. While there is no built-in command for this, you can create the command `parametricSphericalPlot3D` as follows:

In[34]:=
```
parametricSphericalPlot3D[{ρ_, φ_, θ_}, args__] := ParametricPlot3D[
    {ρ*Sin[φ]*Cos[θ], ρ*Sin[φ]*Sin[θ], ρ*Cos[φ]}, args]
```

This command simply invokes `ParametricPlot3D` after converting the arguments from spherical to Cartesian coordinates. Be sure to put two underscores after `args` on the left side of the defining equation; two underscores mean that `args` stands for a sequence of one *or more* arguments. In this case, `args` represents the required iterator for the independent variable *t and* any options you might add—this will allow you to use any of the options allowed by `ParametricPlot3D`.

Here is an example of a curve that resides on the sphere whose equation in spherical coordinates is $\rho = 1$:

In[35]:=
```
parametricSphericalPlot3D[{1, t, 20 t},
    {t, 0, π}, Boxed → False, Axes → False]
```

Out[35]=

Integration in Other Coordinate Systems

No new *Mathematica* commands are needed to evaluate integrals in other coordinate systems. You simply need to know the underlying conversion formulas in order to set up such an integral.

For example, back in the subsection "Integration of Functions of Two or More Variables" of Section 6.2 we evaluated the double integral of the function $f(x, y) = 5 - x^2 y^2$ over the portion of the disk of radius 2 centered at the origin that lies in the lower half-plane. This is more easily handled in polar coordinates. We convert the integrand into polar coordinates as follows:

```
In[36]:= Clear[x, y, r, θ];
         5 - x² y² /. {x → r * Cos[θ], y → r * Sin[θ]}
```
$$Out[37]= 5 - r^4 \cos[\theta]^2 \sin[\theta]^2$$

We can now integrate, replacing $dx\,dy$ with $r\,dr\,d\theta$. Since the region of integration is a half-disk of radius 2 residing below the x axis, the bounds of integration are easily described in polar coordinates: $0 \le r \le 2$ and $\pi \le \theta \le 2\pi$.

```
In[38]:=    ∫π²π ( ∫0² % r dr ) dθ
```
$$Out[38]= \frac{26\,\pi}{3}$$

And how about the triple integral of the function $f(x, y, z) = y - z^2$ over the region bounded by a sphere of radius 2 centered at the origin? We did this one in Cartesian coordinates earlier as well. We accomplish the same result in spherical coordinates as follows. We first convert the integrand into spherical coordinates. Now what were those conversion formulas?

```
In[39]:= Clear[x, y, z, ρ, ϕ, θ];
         CoordinateTransform["Spherical" → "Cartesian", {ρ, ϕ, θ}]
```
$$Out[40]= \{\rho \cos[\theta] \sin[\phi],\ \rho \sin[\theta] \sin[\phi],\ \rho \cos[\phi]\}$$

We can make replacement rules from these conversions like so:

```
In[41]:= Thread[{x, y, z} → %]
```
$$Out[41]= \{x \to \rho \cos[\theta] \sin[\phi],\ y \to \rho \sin[\theta] \sin[\phi],\ z \to \rho \cos[\phi]\}$$

> ⚠ The Thread command is used here to "thread" Rule (→) over the lists of
> variables and conversion expressions. The FullForm of the input above is
> Thread[Rule[List[x, y, z], List[⋯]]]. Thread has the effect of distribut-
> ing Rule over the lists, producing a list of rules rather than a rule of lists. So the
> output has the form List[Rule[x, ⋯], Rule[y, ⋯], Rule[z, ⋯]]. Thread
> is discussed in Section 8.4.

Here is the converted integrand:

In[42]:= `y - z^2 /. %`

Out[42]= $-\rho^2 \, \text{Cos}[\phi]^2 + \rho \, \text{Sin}[\theta] \, \text{Sin}[\phi]$

And now we integrate, replacing $dx\,dy\,dz$ with $\rho^2 \sin(\phi)\,d\rho\,d\phi\,d\theta$. Since we wish to integrate over a sphere of radius 2 centered at the origin, we choose as our bounds of integration $0 \le \rho \le 2$, $0 \le \phi \le \pi$, and $0 \le \theta \le 2\pi$. The result agrees with our earlier output, but it evaluates far more quickly due to the simpler bounds of integration.

In[43]:= $\int_0^{2\pi} \left(\int_0^{\pi} \left(\int_0^{2} \% * \rho^2 \, \text{Sin}[\phi] \, d\rho \right) d\phi \right) d\theta$

Out[43]= $-\dfrac{128\,\pi}{15}$

Change of Variables

When integrating a real-valued function in polar coordinates, we essentially replace $dx\,dy$ with $r\,dr\,d\theta$. The extra factor r is the Jacobian for this change of variables. In general, if $x = g(u, v)$ and $y = h(u, v)$ represent a change of variables, then when integrating in the uv coordinate system, the required "extra factor" is the absolute value of the *Jacobian*, defined as

$$\text{Det}\begin{pmatrix} g_u & g_v \\ h_u & h_v \end{pmatrix}.$$

Here's an example. Suppose you are tasked with integrating $f(x, y) = x - \frac{1}{2}y$ over the region $\mathcal{R}$ shown below—the parallelogram with vertices $(0, 0)$, $(3, 1)$, $(5, 5)$, $(2, 4)$. You can type `ESC scR ESC` to produce the script $\mathcal{R}$ character.

In[44]:= `R = Polygon[{{0, 0}, {3, 1}, {5, 5}, {2, 4}}];`
`Graphics[{LightBlue, EdgeForm[Black], R}, Axes → True]`

Out[45]=

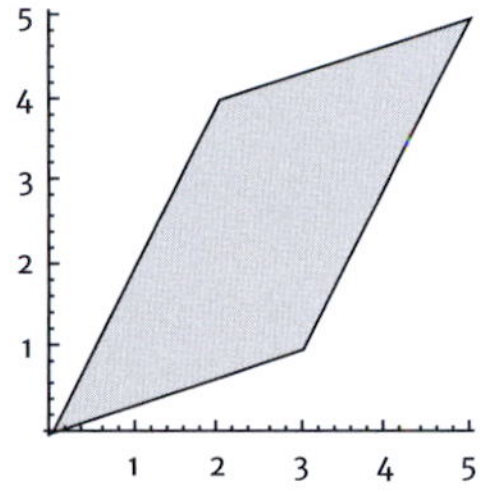

In *Mathematica*, the integration is as simple as can be: We use the "square bracket" version of the `Integrate` command, and use the region $\mathcal{R}$ as the region of integration. No change of variables is required!

In[46]:= `Clear[x, y];`

$$\text{Integrate}\left[x - \frac{1}{2}y, \{x, y\} \in \mathcal{R}\right]$$

Out[47]= $\dfrac{25}{2}$

But in a traditional calculus course, where you typically evaluate integrals by hand, you may be asked to carry out a change of variables in order to simplify the calculation (which would otherwise require the region to be broken into several pieces, with a separate integration required for each). Let us walk through the change of variable procedure, using *Mathematica* to help with the grunt work.

The lines demarcating the left and right sides of $\mathcal{R}$ have equations $y = 2x$ and $y = 2x - 5$ (found using the corner points of $\mathcal{R}$). Note that we may write these as $2x - y = 0$ and $2x - y = 5$. Set $u = 2x - y$. For this region we have $0 \le u \le 5$.

The lines demarcating the top and bottom sides of $\mathcal{R}$ have equations $y = \frac{1}{3}x$ and $y = \frac{1}{3}x + \frac{10}{3}$. Note that we may write these as $y - \frac{1}{3}x = 0$ and $y - \frac{1}{3}x = \frac{10}{3}$. Set $v = y - \frac{1}{3}x$. For this region we have $0 \le v \le \frac{10}{3}$.

We are now ready to find the transformations $x = g(u, v)$ and $y = h(u, v)$. We may solve the system of equations by hand, or ask *Mathematica* to do it:

In[48]:= $\text{Solve}\left[\left\{u == 2x - y, v == y - \frac{1}{3}x\right\}, \{x, y\}\right]$

Out[48]= $\left\{\left\{x \to \dfrac{3(u + v)}{5}, y \to \dfrac{1}{5}(u + 6v)\right\}\right\}$

In[49]:= $g = \dfrac{3(u + v)}{5};$

In[50]:= $h = \dfrac{1}{5}(u + 6v);$

This is an easy way to visually confirm that we have the right transformation functions: We see that the transformed rectangle in the *uv* plane is precisely the region $\mathcal{R}$.

In[51]:= $\text{ParametricPlot}\left[\{g, h\}, \{u, 0, 5\}, \left\{v, 0, \dfrac{10}{3}\right\}\right]$

Out[51]=

We may now calculate the Jacobian.

In[52]:= `jacobian = Det[(` $\begin{pmatrix} \text{D[g, u]} & \text{D[g, v]} \\ \text{D[h, u]} & \text{D[h, v]} \end{pmatrix}$ `)]`

Out[52]= $\dfrac{3}{5}$

And lastly, we write $f(x, y) = x - \dfrac{1}{2} y$ in terms of u and v, and integrate:

In[53]:= `x - ` $\dfrac{1}{2}$ `y /. {x → g, y → h} // Simplify`

Out[53]= $\dfrac{u}{2}$

In[54]:= $\int_0^{10/3} \left(\int_0^5 \dfrac{u}{2} \text{ Abs[jacobian] d}u \right) \text{d}v$

Out[54]= $\dfrac{25}{2}$

This agrees with our earlier answer! We note that regions bounded by curves (as opposed to straight line segments) will need to be specified with `ImplicitRegion` or `ParametricRegion`, rather than with `Polygon`.

Exercises 6.4

1. Make a `Manipulate` with two controllers that displays a graph of the polar function $r = f(\theta) = \sin(n\,\theta)$, where n is allowed to vary from .01 to 3, and the variable θ assumes values from 0 to *length*, where *length* is permitted to vary from 2π to 100π. The resulting curves are known as *roses*.

2. Explain how to use `ParametricPlot` to produce the same output as that produced by `PolarPlot` to view the graph of the polar function $r = f(\theta)$. Test your solution on the function $f(\theta) = \theta$.

3. Explain how to use `ParametricPlot` to produce the graph of the inverse polar function $\theta = f(r)$. Carry this out on the function $f(r) = r^2 - 2r + 1$ as r goes from 0 to 2.

4. Integrate the function $f(x, y) = x^2 - y^2 + 2x + 1$ over the region bounded by the parabolas $y = x^2$ and $y = x^2 + 2$, and the lines $x = 0$ and $x = 1$. Make a plot of this region.

5. Make a `Manipulate` to view various `PolarPlots` of the *superformula* with polar equation $r(\theta) = \left(\left| \cos\left(\dfrac{m\theta}{4} \right) \right|^{n_2} + \left| \sin\left(\dfrac{m\theta}{4} \right) \right|^{n_3} \right)^{\frac{-1}{n_1}}$. Use sliders that allow m, n_1, n_2, and n_3 to range from 1 to 20. Restrict m to assume only integer values in this range.

6. A *homotopy* between two surfaces is a smooth deformation from one surface to the other governed by a single real parameter t ranging from 0 to 1. Make a `Manipulate` that illustrates the homotopy from the Roman surface ($t = 0$) to the Boy surface ($t = 1$) given by:

$$x = \frac{\sqrt{2}\,\cos(2\,u)\cos^2 v + \cos u \sin(2\,v)}{2-t\,\sqrt{2}\,\sin(3\,u)\sin(2\,v)},$$

$$y = \frac{\sqrt{2}\,\sin(2\,u)\cos^2 v - \sin u \sin(2\,v)}{2-t\,\sqrt{2}\,\sin(3\,u)\sin(2\,v)},$$

$$z = \frac{3\cos^2 v}{2-t\,\sqrt{2}\,\sin(3\,u)\sin(2\,v)},$$

where $-\frac{\pi}{2} \le u \le \frac{\pi}{2}$ and $0 \le v \le \pi$.

6.5 Vector Fields

Defining a Vector Field

Recall that a parameterized curve is a vector-valued function of one variable. That is, it's a function taking $\mathbb{R} \to \mathbb{R}^2$ or $\mathbb{R} \to \mathbb{R}^3$. A *vector field* is a vector-valued function of two or more variables. It is a function taking $\mathbb{R}^2 \to \mathbb{R}^2$ or $\mathbb{R}^3 \to \mathbb{R}^3$ (or in general: $\mathbb{R}^n \to \mathbb{R}^n$). You define a vector field $\mathcal{F}$ exactly as you might expect (type ESC scF ESC to get the script $\mathcal{F}$ character).

```
In[1]:=  Clear[F, x, y];
         F = {x⁴ + y⁴ - 6 x² y² - 1, 4 x³ y - 4 x y³}
Out[2]=  {-1 + x⁴ - 6 x² y² + y⁴, 4 x³ y - 4 x y³}
```

A three-dimensional vector field has three coordinate functions:

```
In[3]:=  Clear[G, x, y, z];
         G = {y - z, z - x, x - y}
Out[4]=  {y - z, -x + z, x - y}
```

Plotting a Vector Field

Use the command `VectorPlot` to view a two-dimensional vector field. You may use iterators for x and y to view it over a rectangular region, or use the $\{x,\ y\} \in \mathcal{R}$ paradigm to view it over a region $\mathcal{R}$.

```
In[5]:= GraphicsRow[{
         VectorPlot[{y, x}, {x, -1, 1}, {y, -1, 1}],
         VectorPlot[{y, x}, {x, y} ∈ Disk[]]
       }]
```

Out[5]=

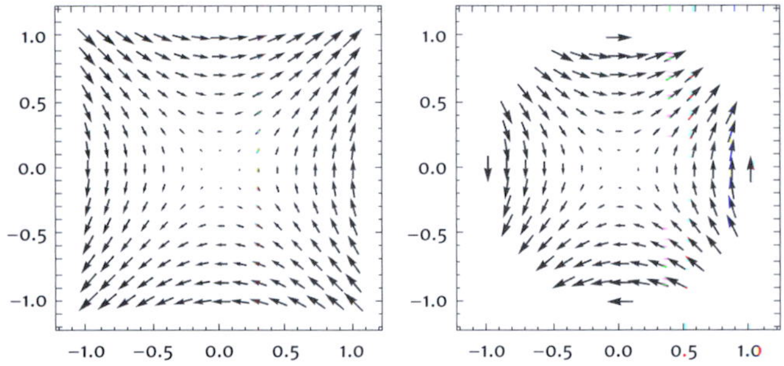

When the region is rectangular, each side is subdivided into 15 equal pieces. At each of the $15 \times 15 = 225$ points of the resulting grid, the tail of a vector is placed, the vector being the value of the vector field at that point. The lengths of the vectors are scaled uniformly so that the vectors will not overlap one another. You can change the number of vectors displayed with the VectorPoints option. Set it to a positive integer such as 10 to view a 10×10 array of vectors. Set it to a list of two such integers such as {10, 5} to view ten columns and five rows of vectors. Lower PlotPoints settings will speed up the evaluation time, and in some cases this can produce a more readable image. Note that by default the same scale is given to each axis.

```
In[6]:= GraphicsRow[{
         VectorPlot[{y, x}, {x, -1, 1}, {y, -1, 1}, VectorPoints → 10],
         VectorPlot[{y, x}, {x, -1, 1}, {y, -1, 1}, VectorPoints → {10, 5}]
       }]
```

Out[6]=

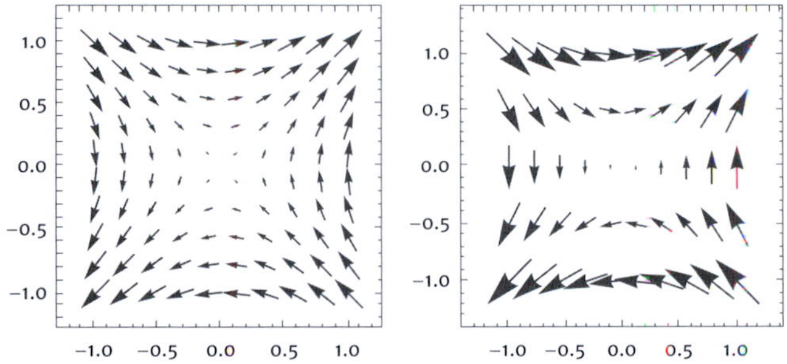

A related and sometimes useful command is `StreamPlot`, which will place the vectors to better suggest the *flow lines* in the plot. The syntax for this command is identical to that of `VectorPlot`.

In[3]:= **StreamPlot[{y, x}, {x, -1, 1}, {y, -1, 1}]**

Out[3]=
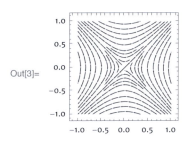

A vector field is *conservative* precisely if it is the gradient of a real-valued function. The example above is the gradient of $f(x, y) = xy$, for instance, and hence is conservative. The flow lines for a conservative field are orthogonal to the level curves of f, since the gradient evaluated at any point will be orthogonal to the level curve passing through that point. It is a simple matter to visualize this phenomenon:

In[4]:= **Show[**
  ContourPlot[x y, {x, -1, 1}, {y, -1, 1}, Contours → 20],
  StreamPlot[{y, x}, {x, -1, 1}, {y, -1, 1}, StreamStyle → Yellow]
]

Out[4]=

Note that it is important to list the `ContourPlot` first to create this graphic. Had it been listed second, the contour plot would be overlaid on *top* of the vector field plot and would obscure the `StreamPlot` beneath it.

The command `VectorPlot3D` is used to plot three-dimensional vector fields. The option setting `VectorStyle → Arrowheads[size]` can be used to resize arrowheads, which sometimes improves the readability of the plot. Use size 0 to remove arrowheads completely.

```
In[7]:= GraphicsRow[{
          VectorPlot3D[{x, y, z}, {x, -1, 1}, {y, -1, 1}, {z, -1, 1}],
          VectorPlot3D[{x, y, z}, {x, -1, 1},
            {y, -1, 1}, {z, -1, 1}, VectorStyle → Arrowheads[0]]
        }]
```

Out[7]=

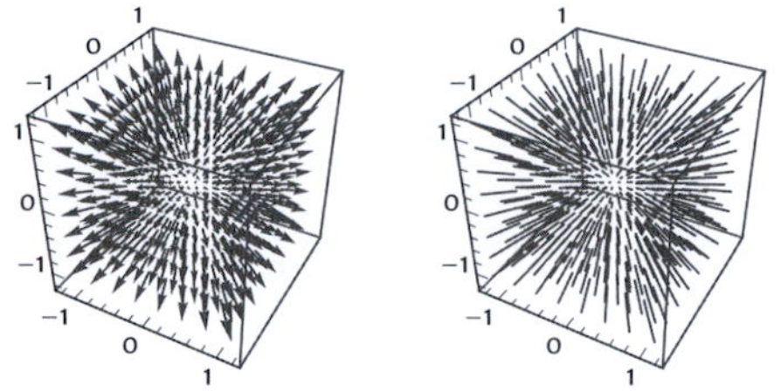

By default, there are eight vectors drawn in each coordinate direction, for a total of $8^3 = 512$ vectors in the plot. As before, this behavior can be modified via the VectorPoints option.

Below we show the gradient field for the function $f(x, y, z) = x^2 y - z$, and then we add five level surfaces for this function and display them together. Again, the gradient vectors are orthogonal to the level surfaces, and they point in the direction of maximal increase of f.

```
In[8]:= Grad[x² y - z, {x, y, z}]
```

$$Out[8]= \{2 x y, x^2, -1\}$$

```
In[9]:= VectorPlot3D[{2 x y, x², -1}, {x, 0, 1}, {y, 0, 1},
          {z, 0, 1}, VectorPoints → 4, VectorStyle → Arrowheads[.02]]
```

Out[9]=

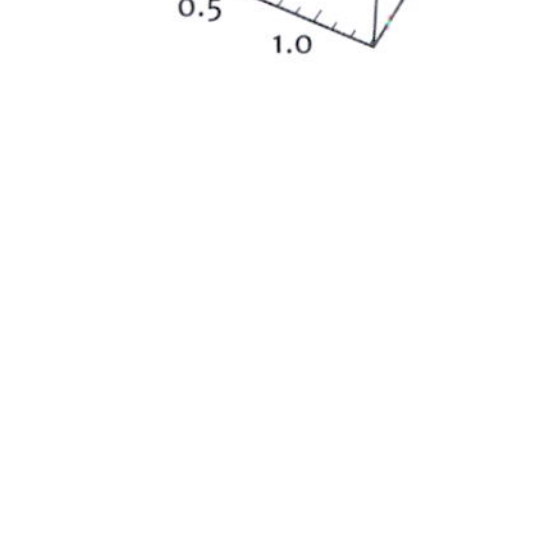

In[10]:= `GraphicsRow[{`
     `vp = VectorPlot3D[{2 x y, x², -1}, {x, 0, 1}, {y, 0, 1},`
         `{z, 0, 1}, VectorPoints → 4, VectorStyle → Arrowheads[.02]],`
     `cp = ContourPlot3D[x² y - z, {x, 0, 1}, {y, 0, 1}, {z, 0, 1},`
         `Contours → 5, Mesh → None, ContourStyle → Opacity[.8]],`
     `Show[vp, cp]}, ImageSize → 300]`

Out[10]=

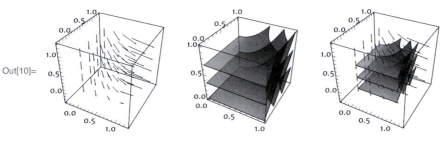

Divergence and Curl of a Three-Dimensional Vector Field

Given a three-dimensional vector field $f(x, y, z) = f_1(x, y, z)\,\vec{i} + f_2(x, y, z)\,\vec{j} + f_3(x, y, z)\,\vec{k}$, its *divergence* is the real-valued function

$$\operatorname{div} f(x, y, z) = \partial_x f_1 + \partial_y f_2 + \partial_z f_3$$

The *curl* of f is the three-dimensional vector field

$$\operatorname{curl} f(x, y, z) = \left(\partial_y f_3 - \partial_z f_2\right)\vec{i} + \left(\partial_z f_1 - \partial_x f_3\right)\vec{j} + \left(\partial_x f_2 - \partial_y f_1\right)\vec{k}$$

The easiest way to compute divergence and curl with *Mathematica* is with the `Div` and `Curl` commands.

In[11]:= `Div[{x² y, z, x y z}, {x, y, z}]`

Out[11]= `3 x y`

In[12]:= `Curl[{x² y, z, x y z}, {x, y, z}]`

Out[12]= $\{-1 + x\,z, -y\,z, -x^2\}$

If you are doing calculations in other coordinate systems, you simply set the coordinate system and the coordinate variable names you want to use. Typical choices are `"Polar"` in two dimensions (for the two-dimensional version of `Div`), and `"Cylindrical"` and `"Spherical"` in three dimensions.

In[13]:= `Div[{r², -r θ}, {r, θ}, "Polar"]`

Out[13]= $2\,r + \dfrac{-r + r^2}{r}$

In[14]:= `Div[{r² z, -θ, z}, {r, θ, z}, "Cylindrical"]`

Out[14]= $1 + 2\ r\ z + \dfrac{-1 + r^2\ z}{r}$

In[13]:= `Curl[{r² z, -θ, z}, {r, θ, z}, "Cylindrical"]`

Out[13]= $\left\{0,\ r^2,\ -\dfrac{\theta}{r}\right\}$

In[14]:= `Curl[{ρ, π - φ, ρ θ / 10}, {ρ, φ, θ}, "Spherical"]`

Out[14]= $\left\{\dfrac{1}{10}\ \theta\ \text{Cot}[\phi],\ -\dfrac{\theta}{5},\ -\dfrac{-\pi + \phi}{\rho}\right\}$

Note that `Div` has an alternate syntax: You may type $\nabla_{\{x,y,z\}} \cdot f$ instead of `Div[f, {x, y, z}]`, where `f` is a vector field. Use ESC del ESC to produce the ∇ character, and use CTRL _ to get to the sub-script position.

In[15]:= `Div[{x² y, z, x y z}, {x, y, z}]`

Out[15]= `3 x y`

In[16]:= $\nabla_{\{x,y,z\}} \cdot \{x^2\ y,\ z,\ x\ y\ z\}$

Out[16]= `3 x y`

Exercises 6.5

1. The option setting `VectorScale → None` may be added to `VectorPlot` input to turn off the automatic scaling of vectors. While the vector fields are then drawn with perfect accuracy, the vectors may overlap one another. This exercise will illustrate that overlapping vectors can be confusing to view. This is why the default settings include vector scaling that prevents overlapping vectors.

   a. Sketch the vector field $F(x,\ y) = \langle y,\ x \rangle$, without vector scaling.

   b. Show that for this field, the head of *every* vector lies on the line $y = x$.

2. Use *Mathematica* to verify that the divergence of the curl of *any* vector field is zero.

6.6 Line Integrals and Surface Integrals

Line Integrals
Here is a parameterization of a curve $\vec{r}(t)$ that joins the point $(-1, -1)$ to the point $(2, 2)$ as t runs from -1 to 2:

```
In[1]:= Clear[r, x, y, t];
        x[t_] := t;
        y[t_] := t³ - t² - t;
        r[t_] := {x[t], y[t]}
```

```
In[5]:= curve = ParametricPlot[r[t], {t, -1, 2}]
```

Out[5]=

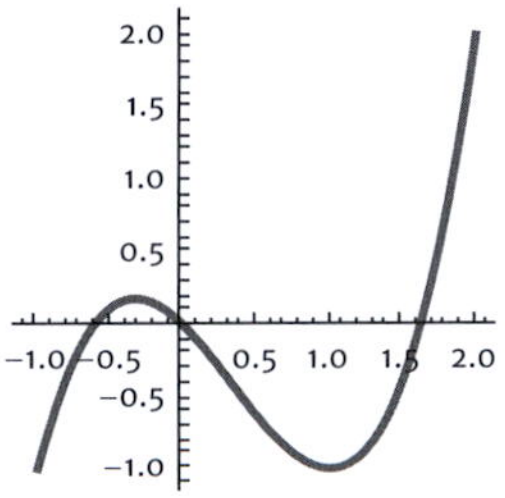

Here is a vector field in the plane:

```
In[6]:= Clear[𝓕];
        𝓕 = {x - y, y²}
```

Out[7]= $\{x - y, y^2\}$

And here we superimpose a plot of the vector field with a plot of the curve:

```
In[8]:= Show[curve, VectorPlot[𝓕, {x, -1, 2}, {y, -1, 2},
            VectorPoints → 10, VectorStyle → Arrowheads[.02]]]
```

Out[8]=

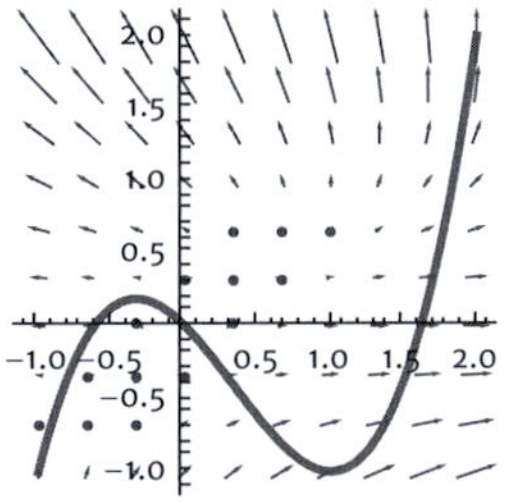

The calculation of the line integral $\int \vec{\mathcal{F}} \cdot d\vec{r}$ is straightforward. Here is the integrand:

```
In[9]:= (𝓕 /. {x → x[t], y → y[t]}).r'[t] // Simplify
```

Out[9]= $t \left(2 - 5 t^2 + 10 t^4 - 8 t^6 + 3 t^7\right)$

And here is the integral:

```
In[10]:= ∫₋₁² t (2 - 5 t² + 10 t⁴ - 8 t⁶ + 3 t⁷) ⅆt
```

Out[10]= $\dfrac{21}{4}$

Line integrals in three or more dimensions are just as easy to evaluate. Plots for three dimensions will require the commands `ParametricPlot3D` and `VectorPlot3D`.

Surface Integrals

Here is a surface:

```
In[11]:=  Clear[Φ, u, v, x, y, z];
          x[u_, v_] := (1 - v²) Sin[u];
          y[u_, v_] := (1 - v²) Sin[2 u];
          z[u_, v_] := v;
          Φ[u_, v_] := {x[u, v], y[u, v], z[u, v]}
```

```
In[16]:=  surface = ParametricPlot3D[Φ[u, v], {u, 0, 2 π},
             {v, -1, 1}, Mesh → None, PlotStyle → Opacity[.8]]
```

Out[16]=

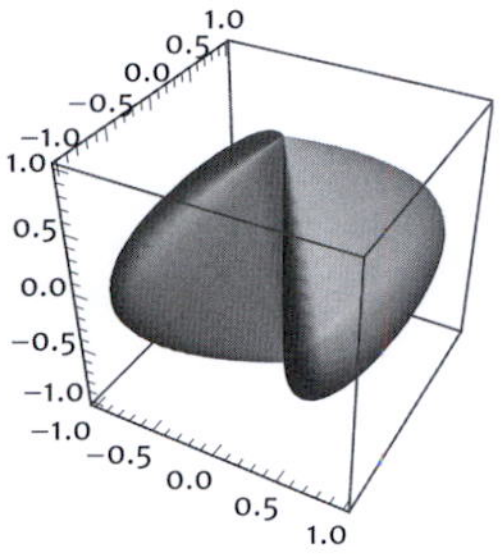

And here is a three-dimensional vector field:

```
In[17]:=  Clear[ℱ];
          ℱ = {2 x, 2 x y, 1/z}
```

Out[18]= $\left\{2\,x,\ 2\,x\,y,\ \dfrac{1}{z}\right\}$

```
In[19]:=  Show[VectorPlot3D[ℱ, {x, -1, 1}, {y, -1, 1},
             {z, -1, 1}, VectorStyle → Arrowheads[.01]], surface]
```

Out[19]=

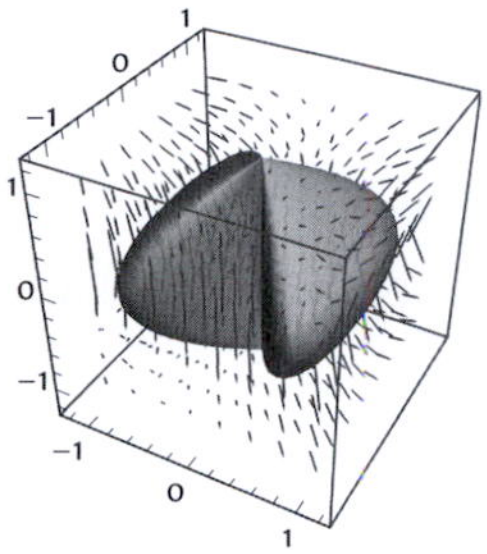

The surface integral can be evaluated with ease. Here is the integrand. Be sure to use the cross product (×) and not the (larger) multiplication operator (×) when pulling that symbol from the Basic Math Assistant palette.

In[20]:= $(\mathcal{F}\ /.\ \{x \to x[u, v], y \to y[u, v], z \to z[u, v]\}).(\partial_u \Phi[u, v] \times \partial_v \Phi[u, v])$

Out[20]= $2 (1 - v^2) (2 \cos[2u] - 2 v^2 \cos[2u]) \sin[u] +$
$2 (1 - v^2)^2 (-\cos[u] + v^2 \cos[u]) \sin[u] \sin[2u] +$
$\frac{1}{v} (4 v \cos[2u] \sin[u] - 4 v^3 \cos[2u] \sin[u] -$
$2 v \cos[u] \sin[2u] + 2 v^3 \cos[u] \sin[2u])$

In[21]:= Simplify[%]

Out[21]= $(-1 + v^2) \sin[u] (2 + (-6 + 4 v^2) \cos[2u] +$
$(-1 + v^2)^2 \sin[u] + \sin[3u] - 2 v^2 \sin[3u] + v^4 \sin[3u])$

And here we evaluate the integral:

In[22]:= $\int_{-1}^{1} \left(\int_0^{2\pi} \% \, du \right) dv$

Out[22]= $-\frac{32\pi}{35}$

Exercises 6.6

1. Consider the vector field $\vec{\mathcal{F}}(x, y) = \frac{\langle -y, x \rangle}{\sqrt{x^2 + y^2}}$.

   a. Plot this vector field on the domain $-2 \le x \le 2, -2 \le y \le 2$.
   b. Let $r(t) = \langle t, t \rangle$. Sketch this curve for $0 \le t \le 2$, and superimpose it with the plot above.
   c. Evaluate the line integral $\int \vec{\mathcal{F}} \cdot d\vec{r}$ for $0 \le t \le 2$.
   d. Let $r(t) = \langle t, t^3 - t^2 - t \rangle$. Sketch this curve for $0 \le t \le 2$, and superimpose it with the plot from part **a**.
   e. Evaluate the line integral $\int \vec{\mathcal{F}} \cdot d\vec{r}$ for $0 \le t \le 2$.

2. Consider the vector field $\vec{\mathcal{F}}(x, y) = \langle \cos(y) \cos(x \cos(y)), -x \cos(x \cos(y)) \sin(y) \rangle$.

   a. Show that this is a gradient field, and superimpose its plot with a contour plot of its potential function on the domain $-2 \le x \le 2, -2 \le y \le 2$.
   b. Evaluate the line integral $\int \vec{\mathcal{F}} \cdot d\vec{r}$ for any curve $\vec{r}(t)$ from $(-\pi/2, 0)$ to $(\pi/2, 0)$.

7

Linear Algebra

7.1 Matrices

Entering Matrices

Traditionally, matrices are denoted by capital letters, but in *Mathematica* you should be careful to avoid using single-letter symbols such as C, D, E, I, K, and N when naming a matrix, as these letters already have a designated purpose. For instance, E is the base of the natural logarithm, and N is the numerical approximation command. Of course, lowercase letters are fine for naming matrices. But if you really can't live in a world where matrices are denoted by lowercase letters, there is a simple solution: Use script or Greek uppercase letters. For example, a script $\mathcal{M}$ or a Greek A is perfectly acceptable. Type the former with the key combination [ESC] scM [ESC]. This approach works for any script letter; just change the uppercase M to whichever script letter you like. Type [ESC] A [ESC] for a capital alpha. This works for other Greek letters as well.

To enter a matrix in *Mathematica* first type a name for your matrix followed by an equal sign. Then select Table/Matrix ▷ New... in the Insert menu. A dialog box will appear. Select Matrix and enter the correct number of rows and columns, then click OK. A matrix of the appropriate dimensions will appear in your input cell with a placeholder for each entry. Click on the first placeholder and type a value, and then use the [TAB] key to move to the next entry. Enter the cell when you have finished:

$$\text{In[1]:= } \mathcal{M} = \begin{pmatrix} 2 & 3 & 4 & 5 & 6 & 7 \\ 1 & 1 & 1 & 1 & 1 & 1 \\ 4 & 5 & 4 & 5 & 4 & 5 \\ 11 & 2 & 2 & 2 & 2 & 2 \\ 0 & 0 & 0 & 0 & 0 & 1 \end{pmatrix}$$

Out[1]= {{2, 3, 4, 5, 6, 7}, {1, 1, 1, 1, 1, 1},
{4, 5, 4, 5, 4, 5}, {11, 2, 2, 2, 2, 2}, {0, 0, 0, 0, 0, 1}}

Look carefully at the output above. *Mathematica* thinks of a matrix as a list of lists. Each row is enclosed in curly brackets with entries separated by commas, the rows are separated by commas, and the entire matrix is enclosed in curly brackets. You can enter a matrix in this form but it can be a little messy:

In[2]:= N = {{1, 2, 3}, {3, 4, 5}, {5, 6, 7}}

Out[2]= {{1, 2, 3}, {3, 4, 5}, {5, 6, 7}}

You can also enter matrices using the palette button , which is found in the Linear Algebra and

Matrices section which opens when you click the tab in the Basic Commands section of the

Basic Math Assistant palette. When you click this button a 2×2 matrix template will appear. You can add more rows or columns by clicking the buttons `Add Row` or `Add Column`. Or use `CTRL`-`⏎` to add rows and `CTRL`-`,` to add columns. You can also use these buttons to add more rows or columns to existing matrices. Just click above where you want the new row to appear or where you want the new column and use the buttons or key strokes. If the original matrix appeared in a output cell, the modified matrix will appear in a new input cell.

The command `MatrixForm` will display any matrix as a formatted rectangular array with brackets on the sides, the way humans are used to seeing them. It is best not to use the `MatrixForm` command when defining a matrix, as it would then be impossible to perform some operations. It is better to simply request that the output be in `MatrixForm` whenever you want a nice look at your matrix:

> In[3]:= `N // MatrixForm`
>
> Out[3]//MatrixForm=
> $$\begin{pmatrix} 1 & 2 & 3 \\ 3 & 4 & 5 \\ 5 & 6 & 7 \end{pmatrix}$$

You can request that *Mathematica* output every matrix in `MatrixForm` by typing the following command at the beginning of a session:

> In[4]:= `$Post := If[MatrixQ[#], MatrixForm[#], #] &`
>
> In[5]:= `M`
>
> Out[5]//MatrixForm=
> $$\begin{pmatrix} 2 & 3 & 4 & 5 & 6 & 7 \\ 1 & 1 & 1 & 1 & 1 & 1 \\ 4 & 5 & 4 & 5 & 4 & 5 \\ 11 & 2 & 2 & 2 & 2 & 2 \\ 0 & 0 & 0 & 0 & 0 & 1 \end{pmatrix}$$

In order to avoid confusion we will continue to affix `//MatrixForm` to all our inputs in this chapter.

⚠ `$Post` is a global variable whose value, if set, is a function that will be applied to every output generated in the current session. The simplest setting would be something like `$Post := MatrixForm`, which would put every output cell into `MatrixForm`. This would work if every output were a matrix, but it could produce unwanted behavior if nonmatrix output were generated. Hence the rather intimidating setting above.

The command `If[MatrixQ[#], MatrixForm[#], #] &` is an example of something called a pure function. It looks rather fancy and cryptic, but the idea of a pure function is quite simple, and from the perspective of programming, is also quite elegant. In order to understand the working of a pure function, you need to understand the two symbols # and &. The symbol # represents the argument of the function, and the symbol & is used to separate the definition of the function from the argument. So, for instance, the input (# + 1) &[3] would produce the output 4. In essence, we have created a function whose name (# + 1) & reveals precisely what it does. See Section 8.4 for a meatier discussion of pure functions.

In the If[MatrixQ[#], MatrixForm[#], #] & example above, things are only a little more complicated. Understand first that the argument # will represent an output generated in the current session. The effect of the function will be to put matrix output into MatrixForm, but to leave non-matrix output alone. This is accomplished with the If command, which takes three arguments. The first is a condition. The second is what is returned if the condition is true. The third is what is returned if the condition is false. The condition is checked with the MatrixQ command. MatrixQ[x] returns True if x is a matrix and False otherwise.

Enter $Post =. to turn off all post-processing.

Mathematica is happy to report the dimensions of your matrix. When fed a matrix as input, the Dimensions command returns a list containing the number of rows and columns in the matrix, respectively:

In[6]:= **Dimensions[M]**

Out[6]= {5, 6}

There are several commands that produce matrices quickly. To get a 3×5 matrix with random integer entries between 0 and 50, type:

In[7]:= **RandomInteger[50, {3, 5}] // MatrixForm**

Out[7]//MatrixForm=

$$\begin{pmatrix} 0 & 28 & 44 & 15 & 50 \\ 16 & 6 & 19 & 40 & 16 \\ 48 & 1 & 8 & 12 & 21 \end{pmatrix}$$

The Table command can be used to enter matrices. The next command gives a 5×5 matrix whose i, jth entry (the entry in row i and column j) is $i + 2j$:

In[8]:= **Table[i + 2 j, {i, 5}, {j, 5}] // MatrixForm**

Out[8]//MatrixForm=

$$\begin{pmatrix} 3 & 5 & 7 & 9 & 11 \\ 4 & 6 & 8 & 10 & 12 \\ 5 & 7 & 9 & 11 & 13 \\ 6 & 8 & 10 & 12 & 14 \\ 7 & 9 & 11 & 13 & 15 \end{pmatrix}$$

The iterators can be set to start at values other than 1:

```
In[9]:= Table[i + 2 j, {i, -2, 3}, {j, 0, 2}] // MatrixForm
```
Out[9]//MatrixForm=

$$\begin{pmatrix} -2 & 0 & 2 \\ -1 & 1 & 3 \\ 0 & 2 & 4 \\ 1 & 3 & 5 \\ 2 & 4 & 6 \\ 3 & 5 & 7 \end{pmatrix}$$

To get a 3×4 zero matrix you can type this:

```
In[10]:= Table[0, {3}, {4}] // MatrixForm
```
Out[10]//MatrixForm=

$$\begin{pmatrix} 0 & 0 & 0 & 0 \\ 0 & 0 & 0 & 0 \\ 0 & 0 & 0 & 0 \end{pmatrix}$$

You can also produce a zero matrix by using Table/Matrix ▷ New... in the Insert menu. Just check the Fill with 0 box. Yet another way is to use the command `ConstantArray`, like this:

```
In[11]:= ConstantArray[π, {3, 5}] // MatrixForm
```
Out[11]//MatrixForm=

$$\begin{pmatrix} \pi & \pi & \pi & \pi & \pi \\ \pi & \pi & \pi & \pi & \pi \\ \pi & \pi & \pi & \pi & \pi \end{pmatrix}$$

We can produce a 4×4 lower triangular matrix with entries on and below the diagonal equal to $i + 2j$, and above the diagonal equal to 0, by typing:

```
In[12]:= Table[If[i ≥ j, i + 2 j, 0], {i, 4}, {j, 4}] // MatrixForm
```
Out[12]//MatrixForm=

$$\begin{pmatrix} 3 & 0 & 0 & 0 \\ 4 & 6 & 0 & 0 \\ 5 & 7 & 9 & 0 \\ 6 & 8 & 10 & 12 \end{pmatrix}$$

The `If` command takes three arguments. The first is a condition or predicate, i.e., an expression that evaluates to either `True` or `False`. The second is the expression to evaluate if the condition is true. The third is the expression to evaluate if the condition is false. `If` is discussed in Section 8.5.

The `Array` command works much like the `Table` command but uses a function (either built-in or user-defined) rather than an expression to compute the entries. For a function f that takes two arguments, the command `Array[f, {m, n}]` gives the $m \times n$ matrix whose i, jth entry is $f(i, j)$. For example, using the built-in function `Min` for f produces a matrix where each entry is the minimum of the row number and column number of that entry's position:

```
In[13]:=  Array[Min, {4, 5}] // MatrixForm
```
Out[13]//MatrixForm=

$$\begin{pmatrix} 1 & 1 & 1 & 1 & 1 \\ 1 & 2 & 2 & 2 & 2 \\ 1 & 2 & 3 & 3 & 3 \\ 1 & 2 & 3 & 4 & 4 \end{pmatrix}$$

Here is a second example, this time with a user-defined function:

```
In[14]:=  Clear[f];
          f[i_, j_] := i³ + j²;
          Array[f, {2, 3}] // MatrixForm
```
Out[16]//MatrixForm=

$$\begin{pmatrix} 2 & 5 & 10 \\ 9 & 12 & 17 \end{pmatrix}$$

We can use the Array command to produce a general 3×4 matrix whose i, jth entry is a_{ij}.

```
In[17]:=  Clear[a, mat];
          mat = Array[a## &, {3, 4}]; mat // MatrixForm
```
Out[18]//MatrixForm=

$$\begin{pmatrix} a_{1,1} & a_{1,2} & a_{1,3} & a_{1,4} \\ a_{2,1} & a_{2,2} & a_{2,3} & a_{2,4} \\ a_{3,1} & a_{3,2} & a_{3,3} & a_{3,4} \end{pmatrix}$$

The command below returns an identity matrix of the specified size.

```
In[19]:=  IdentityMatrix[4] // MatrixForm
```
Out[19]//MatrixForm=

$$\begin{pmatrix} 1 & 0 & 0 & 0 \\ 0 & 1 & 0 & 0 \\ 0 & 0 & 1 & 0 \\ 0 & 0 & 0 & 1 \end{pmatrix}$$

This can also be accomplished using Table/Matrix ▷ New... in the Insert menu by checking the Fill with 0 and Fill Diagonal with 1 boxes.

The following command gives a diagonal matrix with the enclosed list on the diagonal:

```
In[20]:=  DiagonalMatrix[{a, b, c, d}] // MatrixForm
```
Out[20]//MatrixForm=

$$\begin{pmatrix} a & 0 & 0 & 0 \\ 0 & b & 0 & 0 \\ 0 & 0 & c & 0 \\ 0 & 0 & 0 & d \end{pmatrix}$$

We can also use `DiagonalMatrix` to create a superdiagonal matrix.

In[21]:= **DiagonalMatrix[{a, b, c}, 1] // MatrixForm**

Out[21]//MatrixForm=

$$\begin{pmatrix} 0 & a & 0 & 0 \\ 0 & 0 & b & 0 \\ 0 & 0 & 0 & c \\ 0 & 0 & 0 & 0 \end{pmatrix}$$

Or a subdiagonal matrix:

In[22]:= **DiagonalMatrix[{a, b, c}, -1] // MatrixForm**

Out[22]//MatrixForm=

$$\begin{pmatrix} 0 & 0 & 0 & 0 \\ a & 0 & 0 & 0 \\ 0 & b & 0 & 0 \\ 0 & 0 & c & 0 \end{pmatrix}$$

Combining Matrices

A handy way to build a new matrix from existing matrices is with the command `ArrayFlatten`. This command allows us to treat entire matrices as if they are individual entries in a matrix. For instance, the following command will stack the matrices `mat1` and `mat2` on top of each other. We use curly brackets, {}, to indicate that each matrix should be treated as a row in the new matrix and then "flattened" into a single matrix. This command will only return a matrix if the input matrices have the same number of columns.

In[23]:= **mat1 = RandomInteger[9, {3, 4}];**

mat1 // MatrixForm

Out[24]//MatrixForm=

$$\begin{pmatrix} 5 & 1 & 7 & 1 \\ 7 & 0 & 6 & 2 \\ 8 & 4 & 3 & 7 \end{pmatrix}$$

In[25]:= **mat2 = RandomInteger[9, {3, 4}];**

mat2 // MatrixForm

Out[26]//MatrixForm=

$$\begin{pmatrix} 5 & 3 & 0 & 5 \\ 1 & 9 & 9 & 7 \\ 8 & 6 & 8 & 9 \end{pmatrix}$$

```
In[27]:= ArrayFlatten[{{mat1}, {mat2}}] // MatrixForm
```
Out[27]//MatrixForm=

$$\begin{pmatrix} 5 & 1 & 7 & 1 \\ 7 & 0 & 6 & 2 \\ 8 & 4 & 3 & 7 \\ 5 & 3 & 0 & 5 \\ 1 & 9 & 9 & 7 \\ 8 & 6 & 8 & 9 \end{pmatrix}$$

To form the matrix consisting of mat1 and mat2 side by side we use curly brackets to indicate that the individual matrices should form a single row.

```
In[28]:= ArrayFlatten[{{mat1, mat2}}] // MatrixForm
```
Out[28]//MatrixForm=

$$\begin{pmatrix} 5 & 1 & 7 & 1 & 5 & 3 & 0 & 5 \\ 7 & 0 & 6 & 2 & 1 & 9 & 9 & 7 \\ 8 & 4 & 3 & 7 & 8 & 6 & 8 & 9 \end{pmatrix}$$

One can also form a *block matrix*. Below we have a matrix composed of four blocks, where mat1 appears in the upper left position, and mat2 appears in the lower right position. The remaining positions are composed entirely of zeros.

```
In[29]:= bm = ArrayFlatten[{{mat1, 0}, {0, mat2}}];
         bm // MatrixForm
```
Out[30]//MatrixForm=

$$\begin{pmatrix} 5 & 1 & 7 & 1 & 0 & 0 & 0 & 0 \\ 7 & 0 & 6 & 2 & 0 & 0 & 0 & 0 \\ 8 & 4 & 3 & 7 & 0 & 0 & 0 & 0 \\ 0 & 0 & 0 & 0 & 5 & 3 & 0 & 5 \\ 0 & 0 & 0 & 0 & 1 & 9 & 9 & 7 \\ 0 & 0 & 0 & 0 & 8 & 6 & 8 & 9 \end{pmatrix}$$

Using Grid instead of MatrixForm to display the matrix, we can make the blocks easily visible:

```
In[31]:= Grid[bm, Dividers → {{5 → True}, {4 → True}}, Frame → True]
```

Out[31]=

5	1	7	1	0	0	0	0
7	0	6	2	0	0	0	0
8	4	3	7	0	0	0	0
0	0	0	0	5	3	0	5
0	0	0	0	1	9	9	7
0	0	0	0	8	6	8	9

Extracting Parts of Matrices

Always remember that internally *Mathematica* thinks of a matrix as a list of lists. So to refer to a part of a matrix we use the same notation discussed in Section 3.11. The basic rule is that you use double square brackets to refer to individual items in a list:

```
In[32]:= mat1 // MatrixForm
Out[32]//MatrixForm=
```

$$\begin{pmatrix} 5 & 1 & 7 & 1 \\ 7 & 0 & 6 & 2 \\ 8 & 4 & 3 & 7 \end{pmatrix}$$

To get the second row, we simply take the second `Part`, whose infix form is double square brackets:

```
In[33]:= mat1[[2]]
Out[33]= {7, 0, 6, 2}
```

There are palette buttons for tidier versions of the left and right double brackets in the Typesetting section of the Basic Math Assistant palette. Click on the ⌫ tab to reveal the section containing the buttons 〚 and 〛. You may also type ESC [[ESC to get a left double bracket and ESC]] ESC to produce the right double bracket. We'll do this for the remainder of the chapter, since it looks a bit nicer than plain double brackets:

```
In[34]:= mat1〚2〛
Out[34]= {7, 0, 6, 2}
```

To retrieve the entry in row 3, column 4, type:

```
In[35]:= mat1〚3, 4〛
Out[35]= 7
```

To extract a single column, indicate that you want `All` rows. For example, to get the third column type:

```
In[36]:= mat1〚All, 3〛
Out[36]= {7, 6, 3}
```

Use `Span`, whose infix form is `;;`, to specify a span of rows and/or columns. Here we take the second through fourth columns:

```
In[37]:= mat1〚All, 2 ;; 4〛 // MatrixForm
Out[37]//MatrixForm=
```

$$\begin{pmatrix} 1 & 7 & 1 \\ 0 & 6 & 2 \\ 4 & 3 & 7 \end{pmatrix}$$

The Take command can also be used to extract submatrices of a given matrix. We'll use a general 5×5 matrix to get a good look at what is happening:

```
In[38]:= Clear[a, mat];
         mat = Array[a## &, {5, 5}]; mat // MatrixForm
```

Out[39]//MatrixForm=

$$\begin{pmatrix} a_{1,1} & a_{1,2} & a_{1,3} & a_{1,4} & a_{1,5} \\ a_{2,1} & a_{2,2} & a_{2,3} & a_{2,4} & a_{2,5} \\ a_{3,1} & a_{3,2} & a_{3,3} & a_{3,4} & a_{3,5} \\ a_{4,1} & a_{4,2} & a_{4,3} & a_{4,4} & a_{4,5} \\ a_{5,1} & a_{5,2} & a_{5,3} & a_{5,4} & a_{5,5} \end{pmatrix}$$

Take can be used with two or three arguments. The first argument is a matrix, the second indicates which rows are desired, the optional third argument indicates the columns. The following command will return the first three rows of the matrix mat:

```
In[40]:= Take[mat, 3] // MatrixForm
```

Out[40]//MatrixForm=

$$\begin{pmatrix} a_{1,1} & a_{1,2} & a_{1,3} & a_{1,4} & a_{1,5} \\ a_{2,1} & a_{2,2} & a_{2,3} & a_{2,4} & a_{2,5} \\ a_{3,1} & a_{3,2} & a_{3,3} & a_{3,4} & a_{3,5} \end{pmatrix}$$

This command will return the last two rows:

```
In[41]:= Take[mat, -2] // MatrixForm
```

Out[41]//MatrixForm=

$$\begin{pmatrix} a_{4,1} & a_{4,2} & a_{4,3} & a_{4,4} & a_{4,5} \\ a_{5,1} & a_{5,2} & a_{5,3} & a_{5,4} & a_{5,5} \end{pmatrix}$$

To get rows 2 through 4 we use a list:

```
In[42]:= Take[mat, {2, 4}] // MatrixForm
```

Out[42]//MatrixForm=

$$\begin{pmatrix} a_{2,1} & a_{2,2} & a_{2,3} & a_{2,4} & a_{2,5} \\ a_{3,1} & a_{3,2} & a_{3,3} & a_{3,4} & a_{3,5} \\ a_{4,1} & a_{4,2} & a_{4,3} & a_{4,4} & a_{4,5} \end{pmatrix}$$

If we want every other row we can enter:

```
In[43]:= Take[mat, {1, -1, 2}] // MatrixForm
```

Out[43]//MatrixForm=

$$\begin{pmatrix} a_{1,1} & a_{1,2} & a_{1,3} & a_{1,4} & a_{1,5} \\ a_{3,1} & a_{3,2} & a_{3,3} & a_{3,4} & a_{3,5} \\ a_{5,1} & a_{5,2} & a_{5,3} & a_{5,4} & a_{5,5} \end{pmatrix}$$

The list $\{1, -1, 2\}$ above indicates that we want to start at the first row, end at the last row, and increment the index of the selected rows by two. In a matrix with five rows you could equivalently use the list $\{1, 5, 2\}$.

If we use three arguments we can select rows and columns.

In[44]:= `Take[mat, 2, -4] // MatrixForm`
Out[44]//MatrixForm=

$$
\begin{pmatrix}
a_{1,2} & a_{1,3} & a_{1,4} & a_{1,5} \\
a_{2,2} & a_{2,3} & a_{2,4} & a_{2,5}
\end{pmatrix}
$$

In order to extract complete columns, use `All` for the second entry. So to get the last three columns enter:

In[45]:= `Take[mat, All, -3] // MatrixForm`
Out[45]//MatrixForm=

$$
\begin{pmatrix}
a_{1,3} & a_{1,4} & a_{1,5} \\
a_{2,3} & a_{2,4} & a_{2,5} \\
a_{3,3} & a_{3,4} & a_{3,5} \\
a_{4,3} & a_{4,4} & a_{4,5} \\
a_{5,3} & a_{5,4} & a_{5,5}
\end{pmatrix}
$$

We can extract a submatrix by indicating a range of values for the rows and columns in lists,

In[46]:= `Take[mat, {2, 4}, {3, 5}] // MatrixForm`
Out[46]//MatrixForm=

$$
\begin{pmatrix}
a_{2,3} & a_{2,4} & a_{2,5} \\
a_{3,3} & a_{3,4} & a_{3,5} \\
a_{4,3} & a_{4,4} & a_{4,5}
\end{pmatrix}
$$

Or we could ask for the submatrix consisting of only the first and fourth rows and the second and fourth columns.

In[47]:= `Take[mat, {1, 4, 3}, {2, 4, 2}] // MatrixForm`
Out[47]//MatrixForm=

$$
\begin{pmatrix}
a_{1,2} & a_{1,4} \\
a_{4,2} & a_{4,4}
\end{pmatrix}
$$

The `Part` and `Span` commands may be used together as an alternative to `Take`. The previous `Take` command is equivalent to the following:

In[48]:= `mat[[1 ;; 4 ;; 3, 2 ;; 4 ;; 2]] // MatrixForm`
Out[48]//MatrixForm=

$$
\begin{pmatrix}
a_{1,2} & a_{1,4} \\
a_{4,2} & a_{4,4}
\end{pmatrix}
$$

Exercises 7.1

1. Use the `Table` command to enter a matrix with the integers 1 through 10 on the diagonal, 0 below the diagonal, and 1 above the diagonal.

2. Consider the matrix shown below. Write a custom command called `wellMatrix` that will generate matrices of this form in any size. For instance, the output below should result from `wellMatrix[5]//MatrixForm`. (The name `wellMatrix` stems from an ancient Chinese problem about rope lengths needed to reach the bottom of a well. See Section 7.6, Exercise 3.)

$$\begin{pmatrix} 2 & 1 & 0 & 0 & 0 \\ 0 & 3 & 1 & 0 & 0 \\ 0 & 0 & 4 & 1 & 0 \\ 0 & 0 & 0 & 5 & 1 \\ 1 & 0 & 0 & 0 & 6 \end{pmatrix}$$

3. Consider the block matrix shown below. Write a custom command called `blockMatrix` that will generate matrices of this form of any size. For instance, the output below should result from `blockMatrix[5]//MatrixForm`.

$$\begin{pmatrix} 1 & 0 & 0 & 0 & 0 & 0 & 0 & 0 & 0 & 0 & 0 & 0 & 0 & 0 & 0 \\ 0 & 2 & 2 & 0 & 0 & 0 & 0 & 0 & 0 & 0 & 0 & 0 & 0 & 0 & 0 \\ 0 & 2 & 2 & 0 & 0 & 0 & 0 & 0 & 0 & 0 & 0 & 0 & 0 & 0 & 0 \\ 0 & 0 & 0 & 3 & 3 & 3 & 0 & 0 & 0 & 0 & 0 & 0 & 0 & 0 & 0 \\ 0 & 0 & 0 & 3 & 3 & 3 & 0 & 0 & 0 & 0 & 0 & 0 & 0 & 0 & 0 \\ 0 & 0 & 0 & 3 & 3 & 3 & 0 & 0 & 0 & 0 & 0 & 0 & 0 & 0 & 0 \\ 0 & 0 & 0 & 0 & 0 & 0 & 4 & 4 & 4 & 4 & 0 & 0 & 0 & 0 & 0 \\ 0 & 0 & 0 & 0 & 0 & 0 & 4 & 4 & 4 & 4 & 0 & 0 & 0 & 0 & 0 \\ 0 & 0 & 0 & 0 & 0 & 0 & 4 & 4 & 4 & 4 & 0 & 0 & 0 & 0 & 0 \\ 0 & 0 & 0 & 0 & 0 & 0 & 4 & 4 & 4 & 4 & 0 & 0 & 0 & 0 & 0 \\ 0 & 0 & 0 & 0 & 0 & 0 & 0 & 0 & 0 & 0 & 5 & 5 & 5 & 5 & 5 \\ 0 & 0 & 0 & 0 & 0 & 0 & 0 & 0 & 0 & 0 & 5 & 5 & 5 & 5 & 5 \\ 0 & 0 & 0 & 0 & 0 & 0 & 0 & 0 & 0 & 0 & 5 & 5 & 5 & 5 & 5 \\ 0 & 0 & 0 & 0 & 0 & 0 & 0 & 0 & 0 & 0 & 5 & 5 & 5 & 5 & 5 \\ 0 & 0 & 0 & 0 & 0 & 0 & 0 & 0 & 0 & 0 & 5 & 5 & 5 & 5 & 5 \end{pmatrix}$$

7.2 Performing Gaussian Elimination

A matrix is in *reduced row echelon form* if the first nonzero entry in each row is a 1 with only 0s above and beneath it. Furthermore, the rows must be arranged so that if one row begins with more 0s than another, then that row appears beneath the other. Any matrix can be put into reduced row echelon form by performing successive elementary row operations: multiplying a row by a nonzero constant, replacing a row by its sum with a multiple of another row, or interchanging two rows.

You can ask *Mathematica* to find the reduced row echelon form of a matrix by using the command RowReduce:

In[1]:= `Clear[𝒟];`

$$\mathcal{D} = \begin{pmatrix} 1 & 1 & 4 & 25 \\ 2 & 1 & 0 & 7 \\ -3 & 0 & 1 & -1 \end{pmatrix};$$

`RowReduce[𝒟] // MatrixForm`

Out[3]//MatrixForm=

$$\begin{pmatrix} 1 & 0 & 0 & 2 \\ 0 & 1 & 0 & 3 \\ 0 & 0 & 1 & 5 \end{pmatrix}$$

You can also perform "manual" row reduction. Use `mat⟦i⟧` to refer to the *i*th row of the matrix `mat`, as explained in the last section. To replace the second row with the sum of the second row and -2 times the first row, type:

In[4]:= `𝒟⟦2⟧ = 𝒟⟦2⟧ - 2 𝒟⟦1⟧;`
`𝒟 // MatrixForm`

Out[5]//MatrixForm=

$$\begin{pmatrix} 1 & 1 & 4 & 25 \\ 0 & -1 & -8 & -43 \\ -3 & 0 & 1 & -1 \end{pmatrix}$$

The first line performed the operation, and the semicolon suppressed the output; the second line asked *Mathematica* to display the revised matrix in `MatrixForm`. Next we can replace the third row with the sum of three times the first row and the third row; and we can replace the first row with the sum of the second and the first row:

In[6]:= `𝒟⟦3⟧ = 𝒟⟦3⟧ + 3 𝒟⟦1⟧;`
`𝒟⟦1⟧ = 𝒟⟦1⟧ + 𝒟⟦2⟧;`
`𝒟 // MatrixForm`

Out[8]//MatrixForm=

$$\begin{pmatrix} 1 & 0 & -4 & -18 \\ 0 & -1 & -8 & -43 \\ 0 & 3 & 13 & 74 \end{pmatrix}$$

Now add three times the second row to the third row:

In[9]:= `𝒟⟦3⟧ = 𝒟⟦3⟧ + 3 𝒟⟦2⟧;`
`𝒟 // MatrixForm`

Out[10]//MatrixForm=

$$\begin{pmatrix} 1 & 0 & -4 & -18 \\ 0 & -1 & -8 & -43 \\ 0 & 0 & -11 & -55 \end{pmatrix}$$

Finally, we can multiply the third row by $-\frac{1}{11}$, multiply the second row by -1, add -8 times the third row to the second row, and add four times the third row to the first row:

```
In[11]:=  𝒟[[3]] = (- 1/11) 𝒟[[3]];
          𝒟[[2]] = -1 𝒟[[2]];
          𝒟[[2]] = 𝒟[[2]] - 8 𝒟[[3]];
          𝒟[[1]] = 𝒟[[1]] + 4 𝒟[[3]];
          𝒟 // MatrixForm
```

Out[15]//MatrixForm=

$$\begin{pmatrix} 1 & 0 & 0 & 2 \\ 0 & 1 & 0 & 3 \\ 0 & 0 & 1 & 5 \end{pmatrix}$$

Exercises 7.2

1. Use row operations to write the matrix $\begin{pmatrix} 1 & 2 \\ 3 & 4 \end{pmatrix}$ as the product of an upper triangular matrix and an *elementary matrix*. An elementary matrix is a matrix that differs from the identity matrix by a single row operation.

2. Use row operations to row reduce the matrix shown below.

$$\begin{pmatrix} 2 & 1 & 0 & 0 & 0 & 721 \\ 0 & 3 & 1 & 0 & 0 & 721 \\ 0 & 0 & 4 & 1 & 0 & 721 \\ 0 & 0 & 0 & 5 & 1 & 721 \\ 1 & 0 & 0 & 0 & 6 & 721 \end{pmatrix}$$

7.3 Matrix Operations

If two matrices have the same dimensions, we can compute their sum by adding the corresponding entries of the two matrices. In *Mathematica*, as in ordinary mathematical notation, we use the + operator for matrix sums:

```
In[1]:=  C = ( 1   0   0 )       ( 2  2  3 )
             ( 2   3   4 ); 𝒟 = ( 0  0  1 );
             (-1   5  -1 )       ( 5  5  5 )

In[2]:=  C + 𝒟 // MatrixForm
```

Out[2]//MatrixForm=

$$\begin{pmatrix} 3 & 2 & 3 \\ 2 & 3 & 5 \\ 4 & 10 & 4 \end{pmatrix}$$

We can also find their difference:

```
In[3]:=  C - D // MatrixForm
```
Out[3]//MatrixForm=
$$\begin{pmatrix} -1 & -2 & -3 \\ 2 & 3 & 3 \\ -6 & 0 & -6 \end{pmatrix}$$

We can perform scalar multiplication:

```
In[4]:=  7 * C // MatrixForm
```
Out[4]//MatrixForm=
$$\begin{pmatrix} 7 & 0 & 0 \\ 14 & 21 & 28 \\ -7 & 35 & -7 \end{pmatrix}$$

And we can multiply matrices. The i,jth entry of the *product* of the matrix C with the matrix D is the dot product of the ith row of C with the jth column of D. Multiplication is only possible if the number of columns of C is equal to the number of rows of D.

In *Mathematica*, use the dot (i.e., the period) to take the product of matrices:

```
In[5]:=  C.D // MatrixForm
```
Out[5]//MatrixForm=
$$\begin{pmatrix} 2 & 2 & 3 \\ 24 & 24 & 29 \\ -7 & -7 & -3 \end{pmatrix}$$

Be careful to use the dot to perform matrix multiplication. The symbol $*$ will simply multiply corresponding entries in the two matrices (which is *not* the same as the matrix product):

```
In[6]:=  C * D // MatrixForm
```
Out[6]//MatrixForm=
$$\begin{pmatrix} 2 & 0 & 0 \\ 0 & 0 & 4 \\ -5 & 25 & -5 \end{pmatrix}$$

The `Transpose` command will produce the transpose of a matrix—the matrix obtained by switching the rows and columns of that matrix:

```
In[7]:=  Transpose[C] // MatrixForm
```
Out[7]//MatrixForm=
$$\begin{pmatrix} 1 & 2 & -1 \\ 0 & 3 & 5 \\ 0 & 4 & -1 \end{pmatrix}$$

To find a power of a matrix, use the command `MatrixPower`. The first argument is the matrix, and the second argument is the desired power:

In[8]:= `MatrixPower[C, 10] // MatrixForm`

Out[8]//MatrixForm=

$$\begin{pmatrix} 1 & 0 & 0 \\ 10\,249\,364 & 36\,166\,989 & 20\,498\,728 \\ 7\,834\,130 & 25\,623\,410 & 15\,668\,261 \end{pmatrix}$$

The *inverse* of a square matrix, if it exists, is the matrix whose product with the original matrix is the identity matrix. A matrix that has an inverse is said to be *nonsingular*. You can find the inverse of a nonsingular matrix with the `Inverse` command:

In[9]:= `Inverse[C] // MatrixForm`

Out[9]//MatrixForm=

$$\begin{pmatrix} 1 & 0 & 0 \\ \dfrac{2}{23} & \dfrac{1}{23} & \dfrac{4}{23} \\ -\dfrac{13}{23} & \dfrac{5}{23} & -\dfrac{3}{23} \end{pmatrix}$$

It is a simple matter to check that the product of a matrix with its inverse is the identity:

In[10]:= `%.C // MatrixForm`

Out[10]//MatrixForm=

$$\begin{pmatrix} 1 & 0 & 0 \\ 0 & 1 & 0 \\ 0 & 0 & 1 \end{pmatrix}$$

⚠ Note that the % in the last input represents the inverse of *C* rather than the `MatrixForm` of that inverse. This is the reason for the cell tag Out[10]//MatrixForm=. If you refer to any such output cell (with % or %%, for instance), *Mathematica* will use the output generated before `MatrixForm` was applied. In other words, although it is displayed in `MatrixForm`, the actual output is the raw underlying matrix. This makes it easy to incorporate `MatrixForm` output into new input.

The *determinant* of a square matrix is a number that is nonzero if and only if the matrix is nonsingular. Determinants are notoriously tedious to compute by hand, but are a snap with *Mathematica*'s `Det` command:

In[11]:= `Det[C]`

Out[11]= -23

Matrix operations can be performed on matrices whose entries are numeric, and also on matrices whose entries are purely symbolic. For example, you can find the formula for the determinant of a general 3×3 matrix by asking for it:

In[12]:= `Clear[a]; 𝒜 = Array[a## &, {3, 3}]; 𝒜 // MatrixForm`

Out[12]//MatrixForm=

$$\begin{pmatrix} a_{1,1} & a_{1,2} & a_{1,3} \\ a_{2,1} & a_{2,2} & a_{2,3} \\ a_{3,1} & a_{3,2} & a_{3,3} \end{pmatrix}$$

In[13]:= `Det[𝒜]`

Out[13]= $-a_{1,3}\,a_{2,2}\,a_{3,1} + a_{1,2}\,a_{2,3}\,a_{3,1} + a_{1,3}\,a_{2,1}\,a_{3,2} - a_{1,1}\,a_{2,3}\,a_{3,2} - a_{1,2}\,a_{2,1}\,a_{3,3} + a_{1,1}\,a_{2,2}\,a_{3,3}$

Notice how the determinant arises naturally in the inverse of a matrix. Here is the entry in the first row and first column of the inverse of `mat5`:

In[14]:= `Inverse[𝒜][[1, 1]]`

Out[14]= $\left(-a_{2,3}\,a_{3,2} + a_{2,2}\,a_{3,3}\right) \Big/ \big(-a_{1,3}\,a_{2,2}\,a_{3,1} + a_{1,2}\,a_{2,3}\,a_{3,1} + a_{1,3}\,a_{2,1}\,a_{3,2} - a_{1,1}\,a_{2,3}\,a_{3,2} - a_{1,2}\,a_{2,1}\,a_{3,3} + a_{1,1}\,a_{2,2}\,a_{3,3}\big)$

Here is the same entry with the determinant replaced by the symbol `det`:

In[15]:= `Inverse[𝒜][[1, 1]] /. Det[𝒜] → det`

Out[15]= $\dfrac{-a_{2,3}\,a_{3,2} + a_{2,2}\,a_{3,3}}{det}$

The *trace* of a matrix is the sum of the entries along the main diagonal. The trace of a matrix may be calculated with the command `Tr`:

In[16]:= `Tr[𝒜]`

Out[16]= $a_{1,1} + a_{2,2} + a_{3,3}$

Be careful, there is a command whose name is `Trace`, but it has nothing to do with linear algebra; don't use it to compute the trace of a matrix.

Exercises 7.3

1. Using the `Dividers` option to the `Grid` command, find a way to format a matrix with vertical bars on the sides instead of parentheses. It is handy to be able to do this when typesetting, as vertical bars are traditionally used to denote the determinant of the matrix they enclose. Use your result to typeset the following equation:

$$\begin{vmatrix} 1 & 2 \\ 3 & 4 \end{vmatrix} = -2.$$

2. Find the inverse of the matrix $\begin{pmatrix} 1 & 7 & 5 & 0 \\ 5 & 8 & 6 & 9 \\ 2 & 1 & 6 & 4 \\ 8 & 1 & 2 & 4 \end{pmatrix}$ by appending the identity matrix to the right side of this matrix

and then using Gaussian elimination to find the inverse.

7.4 Minors and Cofactors

Another command to be wary of is `Minors`. This command computes determinants of submatrices, but not according to the traditional definition of minors. Traditionally, if A is a square matrix then the *minor* M_{ij} of entry a_{ij} is the determinant of the submatrix that remains after the ith row and jth column are deleted from A. If we create $M = (M_{ij})$ we have the matrix of minors. But the command `Minors` will return a matrix whose i,jth entry is the determinant of the submatrix that remains after the $(n - i + 1)$st row and $(n - j + 1)$st column are deleted from A. Yes, this is really confusing, but see if you can spot the difference in the examples below.

```
In[1]:=  Clear[a]; mat5 = Array[a## &, {3, 3}]; mat5 // MatrixForm
```
Out[1]//MatrixForm=
$$\begin{pmatrix} a_{1,1} & a_{1,2} & a_{1,3} \\ a_{2,1} & a_{2,2} & a_{2,3} \\ a_{3,1} & a_{3,2} & a_{3,3} \end{pmatrix}$$

This is the matrix returned by the built-in `Minors` command:

```
In[2]:=  Minors[mat5] // MatrixForm
```
Out[2]//MatrixForm=
$$\begin{pmatrix} -a_{1,2}\,a_{2,1} + a_{1,1}\,a_{2,2} & -a_{1,3}\,a_{2,1} + a_{1,1}\,a_{2,3} & -a_{1,3}\,a_{2,2} + a_{1,2}\,a_{2,3} \\ -a_{1,2}\,a_{3,1} + a_{1,1}\,a_{3,2} & -a_{1,3}\,a_{3,1} + a_{1,1}\,a_{3,3} & -a_{1,3}\,a_{3,2} + a_{1,2}\,a_{3,3} \\ -a_{2,2}\,a_{3,1} + a_{2,1}\,a_{3,2} & -a_{2,3}\,a_{3,1} + a_{2,1}\,a_{3,3} & -a_{2,3}\,a_{3,2} + a_{2,2}\,a_{3,3} \end{pmatrix}$$

The custom command below will give us the traditional matrix of minors. Notice that the entries are the "reverse" of the entries above. The `Map` command is discussed in Section 8.4.

```
In[3]:=  minorsMatrix[m_List?MatrixQ]  := Map[Reverse, Minors[m], {0, 1}]
```

```
In[4]:=  minorsMatrix[mat5] // MatrixForm
```
Out[4]//MatrixForm=
$$\begin{pmatrix} -a_{2,3}\,a_{3,2} + a_{2,2}\,a_{3,3} & -a_{2,3}\,a_{3,1} + a_{2,1}\,a_{3,3} & -a_{2,2}\,a_{3,1} + a_{2,1}\,a_{3,2} \\ -a_{1,3}\,a_{3,2} + a_{1,2}\,a_{3,3} & -a_{1,3}\,a_{3,1} + a_{1,1}\,a_{3,3} & -a_{1,2}\,a_{3,1} + a_{1,1}\,a_{3,2} \\ -a_{1,3}\,a_{2,2} + a_{1,2}\,a_{2,3} & -a_{1,3}\,a_{2,1} + a_{1,1}\,a_{2,3} & -a_{1,2}\,a_{2,1} + a_{1,1}\,a_{2,2} \end{pmatrix}$$

To get a single minor, say M_{23}, we can simply ask for that entry from the output of the `minorsMa`trix command.

In[5]:= `minorsMatrix[mat5][[2, 3]]`

Out[5]= $-a_{1,2}\, a_{3,1} + a_{1,1}\, a_{3,2}$

The *matrix of cofactors* is the matrix whose ijth entry is $(-1)^{i+j}\, M_{ij}$. We can use our `minorsMatrix` command to compute a matrix of cofactors.

In[6]:= `cofactorsMatrix[m_List?MatrixQ] :=`
   `Table[(-1)`$^{i+j}$`, {i, Length[m]}, {j, Length[m]}] * minorsMatrix[m]`

Notice that the `*` above will multiply the corresponding entries of the two matrices.

In[7]:= `cofactorsMatrix[mat5] // MatrixForm`

Out[7]//MatrixForm=

$$\begin{pmatrix} -a_{2,3}\,a_{3,2} + a_{2,2}\,a_{3,3} & a_{2,3}\,a_{3,1} - a_{2,1}\,a_{3,3} & -a_{2,2}\,a_{3,1} + a_{2,1}\,a_{3,2} \\ a_{1,3}\,a_{3,2} - a_{1,2}\,a_{3,3} & -a_{1,3}\,a_{3,1} + a_{1,1}\,a_{3,3} & a_{1,2}\,a_{3,1} - a_{1,1}\,a_{3,2} \\ -a_{1,3}\,a_{2,2} + a_{1,2}\,a_{2,3} & a_{1,3}\,a_{2,1} - a_{1,1}\,a_{2,3} & -a_{1,2}\,a_{2,1} + a_{1,1}\,a_{2,2} \end{pmatrix}$$

Finally, recall that the *adjoint* of a matrix is the transpose of its matrix of cofactors. There is a lovely relationship between the inverse of a matrix and its adjoint: $A^{-1} = \frac{1}{\det(A)}\,\mathrm{adj}(A)$. Let's use an example to illustrate this fact.

In[8]:= `Clear[mat];`
   `mat = RandomInteger[9, {4, 4}];`
   `mat // MatrixForm`

Out[10]//MatrixForm=

$$\begin{pmatrix} 1 & 2 & 4 & 8 \\ 9 & 7 & 4 & 3 \\ 9 & 8 & 0 & 2 \\ 8 & 8 & 6 & 3 \end{pmatrix}$$

In[11]:= $\left(\dfrac{1}{\texttt{Det[mat]}}\right)$ `Transpose[cofactorsMatrix[mat]] // MatrixForm`

Out[11]//MatrixForm=

$$\begin{pmatrix} -\dfrac{7}{151} & \dfrac{82}{151} & -\dfrac{20}{151} & \dfrac{50}{151} \\ \dfrac{5}{302} & -\dfrac{94}{151} & \dfrac{79}{302} & \dfrac{61}{151} \\ -\dfrac{19}{604} & \dfrac{25}{302} & \dfrac{119}{604} & \dfrac{20}{151} \\ \dfrac{43}{302} & \dfrac{7}{151} & \dfrac{15}{302} & -\dfrac{19}{151} \end{pmatrix}$$

Did we get the correct inverse?

In[12]:= %.mat // MatrixForm

Out[12]//MatrixForm=

$$\begin{pmatrix} 1 & 0 & 0 & 0 \\ 0 & 1 & 0 & 0 \\ 0 & 0 & 1 & 0 \\ 0 & 0 & 0 & 1 \end{pmatrix}$$

We did indeed!

Exercises 7.4

1. Find the adjoint of $A = \begin{pmatrix} 8 & 0 & 3 & 7 \\ 9 & 4 & 2 & 9 \\ 2 & 8 & 0 & 7 \\ 8 & 9 & 7 & 0 \end{pmatrix}$ using the determinant and the inverse of A, then check your answer

   using the cofactorsMatrix command.

2. Write a command to find the determinant of a matrix by cofactor expansion along the first row.

7.5 Working with Large Matrices

If you have a large matrix with only a few nonzero entries you can use the SparseArray command to enter, store, and work with the matrix efficiently. To create a SparseArray simply give the position and value for each nonzero entry of the matrix as follows:

```
In[1]:= Clear[a, b, c, d];
        s1 = SparseArray[{{1, 1} → a, {2, 3} → b, {5, 2} → c, {6, 7} → d}]
```

Out[2]= SparseArray[⊞ ▦ Specified elements: 4
                              Dimensions: {6, 7}]

The output from the SparseArray command gives us the number of nonzero entries and then the dimensions of the matrix we've created. We can use MatrixForm to get a look at this matrix.

In[3]:= s1 // MatrixForm

Out[3]//MatrixForm=

$$\begin{pmatrix} a & 0 & 0 & 0 & 0 & 0 & 0 \\ 0 & 0 & b & 0 & 0 & 0 & 0 \\ 0 & 0 & 0 & 0 & 0 & 0 & 0 \\ 0 & 0 & 0 & 0 & 0 & 0 & 0 \\ 0 & c & 0 & 0 & 0 & 0 & 0 \\ 0 & 0 & 0 & 0 & 0 & 0 & d \end{pmatrix}$$

Equivalently, we can enter a list of positions and a list of corresponding values.

In[4]:= `s2 = SparseArray[{{1, 1}, {2, 3}, {5, 2}, {6, 7}} → {a, b, c, d}]`

Out[4]= SparseArray[⊞ ▪ Specified elements: 4
                            Dimensions: {6, 7}]

In[5]:= `s2 // MatrixForm`
Out[5]//MatrixForm=

$$\begin{pmatrix} a & 0 & 0 & 0 & 0 & 0 & 0 \\ 0 & 0 & b & 0 & 0 & 0 & 0 \\ 0 & 0 & 0 & 0 & 0 & 0 & 0 \\ 0 & 0 & 0 & 0 & 0 & 0 & 0 \\ 0 & c & 0 & 0 & 0 & 0 & 0 \\ 0 & 0 & 0 & 0 & 0 & 0 & d \end{pmatrix}$$

SparseArray will create a matrix that fits all the nonzero entries we specify. We can also specify a matrix of a larger size.

In[6]:= `s3 = SparseArray[{{1, 1}, {2, 3}, {5, 2}, {6, 7}} → {a, b, c, d}, {8, 10}]`

Out[6]= SparseArray[⊞ ▪ Specified elements: 4
                            Dimensions: {8, 10}]

In[7]:= `s3 // MatrixForm`
Out[7]//MatrixForm=

$$\begin{pmatrix} a & 0 & 0 & 0 & 0 & 0 & 0 & 0 & 0 & 0 \\ 0 & 0 & b & 0 & 0 & 0 & 0 & 0 & 0 & 0 \\ 0 & 0 & 0 & 0 & 0 & 0 & 0 & 0 & 0 & 0 \\ 0 & 0 & 0 & 0 & 0 & 0 & 0 & 0 & 0 & 0 \\ 0 & c & 0 & 0 & 0 & 0 & 0 & 0 & 0 & 0 \\ 0 & 0 & 0 & 0 & 0 & 0 & d & 0 & 0 & 0 \\ 0 & 0 & 0 & 0 & 0 & 0 & 0 & 0 & 0 & 0 \\ 0 & 0 & 0 & 0 & 0 & 0 & 0 & 0 & 0 & 0 \end{pmatrix}$$

We can create a SparseArray in which the unspecified entries have a value other than zero.

In[8]:= `s4 = SparseArray[{{1, 1} → a, {2, 3} → b, {5, 2} → c}, {5, 5}, 2]`

Out[8]= SparseArray[⊞ ▪ Specified elements: 3
                            Dimensions: {5, 5}
                            Default: 2]

In[9]:= **s4 // MatrixForm**

Out[9]//MatrixForm=

$$\begin{pmatrix} a & 2 & 2 & 2 & 2 \\ 2 & 2 & b & 2 & 2 \\ 2 & 2 & 2 & 2 & 2 \\ 2 & 2 & 2 & 2 & 2 \\ 2 & c & 2 & 2 & 2 \end{pmatrix}$$

The Normal command will convert the output of SparseArray to the list form of a matrix.

In[10]:= **Normal[s4]**

Out[10]= {{a, 2, 2, 2, 2}, {2, 2, b, 2, 2},

{2, 2, 2, 2, 2}, {2, 2, 2, 2, 2}, {2, c, 2, 2, 2}}

We can use Table to help us list the nonzero entries of a large matrix. For example the command below creates a 16×12 matrix with 1 in positions (2, 3), (4, 6), (8, 9), and (16, 12).

In[11]:= **s5 = SparseArray[Table[{2^i, 3 i} → 1, {i, 4}]]**

Out[11]= SparseArray[⊞ ▪ Specified elements: 4
Dimensions: {16, 12}]

Since a large matrix in MatrixForm can be difficult to read, a picture can be more informative. MatrixPlot is designed for this purpose.

In[12]:= **s5 // MatrixPlot**

Out[12]=

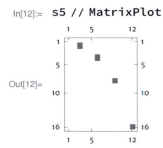

Values of larger magnitude will be displayed in a darker color, while zeros are pure white. Positive numbers are orange by default, and negative numbers are blue.

Sparse arrays can have more than two dimensions.

In[13]:= **s6 = SparseArray[Table[{2^i, 3 i, i + 1} → i, {i, 4}]]**

Out[13]= SparseArray[⊞ ▪ Specified elements: 4
Dimensions: {16, 12, 5}]

ArrayRules will return the positions and values we gave for a sparse array.

```
In[14]:=  ArrayRules[s6]

Out[14]=  {{2, 3, 2} → 1, {4, 6, 3} → 2, {8, 9, 4} → 3, {16, 12, 5} → 4, {_, _, _} → 0}
```

Band can be used with SparseArray to give a matrix in which a single value is present in each position on a diagonal beginning at the given starting position.

```
In[15]:=  Clear[b];
          SparseArray[{Band[{3, 2}] → 3, Band[{1, 4}] → b}, {6, 6}]
```

Out[16]= SparseArray[⊞ ▨ Specified elements: 7
                              Dimensions: {6, 6}]

```
In[17]:=  % // MatrixForm
```

Out[17]//MatrixForm=

$$
\begin{pmatrix}
0 & 0 & 0 & b & 0 & 0 \\
0 & 0 & 0 & 0 & b & 0 \\
0 & 3 & 0 & 0 & 0 & b \\
0 & 0 & 3 & 0 & 0 & 0 \\
0 & 0 & 0 & 3 & 0 & 0 \\
0 & 0 & 0 & 0 & 3 & 0
\end{pmatrix}
$$

Or a band can be a list of values.

```
In[18]:=  SparseArray[Band[{3, 2}] → {2, 4, 6, 8}, {6, 6}]
```

Out[18]= SparseArray[⊞ ▨ Specified elements: 4
                              Dimensions: {6, 6}]

```
In[19]:=  % // MatrixForm
```

Out[19]//MatrixForm=

$$
\begin{pmatrix}
0 & 0 & 0 & 0 & 0 & 0 \\
0 & 0 & 0 & 0 & 0 & 0 \\
0 & 2 & 0 & 0 & 0 & 0 \\
0 & 0 & 4 & 0 & 0 & 0 \\
0 & 0 & 0 & 6 & 0 & 0 \\
0 & 0 & 0 & 0 & 8 & 0
\end{pmatrix}
$$

Exercises 7.5

1. Use SparseArray to create the following picture:

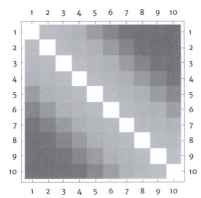

2. Use SparseArray to create the following matrix:

$$\begin{pmatrix} 1 & 2 & 0 & 0 & 0 & 0 & 0 & 0 & 0 & 0 & 0 & 0 \\ 3 & 4 & 0 & 0 & 0 & 0 & 0 & 0 & 0 & 0 & 0 & 0 \\ 0 & 0 & 1 & 2 & 0 & 0 & 0 & 0 & 0 & 0 & 0 & 0 \\ 0 & 0 & 3 & 4 & 0 & 0 & 0 & 0 & 0 & 0 & 0 & 0 \\ 0 & 0 & 0 & 0 & 1 & 2 & 0 & 0 & 0 & 0 & 0 & 0 \\ 0 & 0 & 0 & 0 & 3 & 4 & 0 & 0 & 0 & 0 & 0 & 0 \\ 0 & 0 & 0 & 0 & 0 & 0 & 1 & 2 & 0 & 0 & 0 & 0 \\ 0 & 0 & 0 & 0 & 0 & 0 & 3 & 4 & 0 & 0 & 0 & 0 \\ 0 & 0 & 0 & 0 & 0 & 0 & 0 & 0 & 1 & 2 & 0 & 0 \\ 0 & 0 & 0 & 0 & 0 & 0 & 0 & 0 & 3 & 4 & 0 & 0 \\ 0 & 0 & 0 & 0 & 0 & 0 & 0 & 0 & 0 & 0 & 1 & 2 \\ 0 & 0 & 0 & 0 & 0 & 0 & 0 & 0 & 0 & 0 & 3 & 4 \end{pmatrix}$$

7.6 Solving Systems of Linear Equations

Nonhomogeneous Systems of Linear Equations

Suppose we want to solve a system of linear equations in the form $m\,x = b$, where m is the coefficient matrix, x is a column vector of variables, and b is a column vector. Such a system is called *nonhomogeneous* when b is a vector with at least one nonzero entry. *Mathematica* offers several options for solving such a system, and we will explore each in turn. In this first example m is a nonsingular matrix and the system has a unique solution. Enter the equation $m\,x = b$ by typing m.x == b. Note how *Mathematica* interprets this equation:

In[1]:= `Clear[m, x, x1, x2, x3, x4, b];`

$$m = \begin{pmatrix} 1 & 5 & -4 & 1 \\ 3 & 4 & -1 & 2 \\ 3 & 2 & 1 & 5 \\ 0 & -6 & 7 & 1 \end{pmatrix}; \; x = \begin{pmatrix} x1 \\ x2 \\ x3 \\ x4 \end{pmatrix}; \; b = \begin{pmatrix} 1 \\ 2 \\ 3 \\ 4 \end{pmatrix};$$

`m.x == b`

Out[3]= `{{x1 + 5 x2 - 4 x3 + x4}, {3 x1 + 4 x2 - x3 + 2 x4},`
`{3 x1 + 2 x2 + x3 + 5 x4}, {-6 x2 + 7 x3 + x4}} == {{1}, {2}, {3}, {4}}`

We can interpret this as a list of four linear equations, each in four variables. Just to be sure there is a unique solution, let's check that m is nonsingular (i.e., its determinant is nonzero):

In[4]:= `Det[m]`

Out[4]= `35`

We now use the command `ArrayFlatten` to form the augmented matrix, and the command `RowRe` duce to find the reduced row echelon form of the matrix.

In[5]:= `ArrayFlatten[{{m, b}}] // MatrixForm`

Out[5]//MatrixForm=

$$\begin{pmatrix} 1 & 5 & -4 & 1 & 1 \\ 3 & 4 & -1 & 2 & 2 \\ 3 & 2 & 1 & 5 & 3 \\ 0 & -6 & 7 & 1 & 4 \end{pmatrix}$$

In[6]:= `RowReduce[%] // MatrixForm`

Out[6]//MatrixForm=

$$\begin{pmatrix} 1 & 0 & 0 & 0 & -\frac{127}{35} \\ 0 & 1 & 0 & 0 & \frac{141}{35} \\ 0 & 0 & 1 & 0 & \frac{139}{35} \\ 0 & 0 & 0 & 1 & \frac{13}{35} \end{pmatrix}$$

We conclude that $x_1 = -\frac{127}{35}, x_2 = \frac{141}{35}, x_3 = \frac{139}{35}, x_4 = \frac{13}{35}$.

The command `LinearSolve` provides a quick means for solving systems that have a single solution:

In[7]:= `LinearSolve[m, b]`

Out[7]= $\left\{\left\{-\frac{127}{35}\right\}, \left\{\frac{141}{35}\right\}, \left\{\frac{139}{35}\right\}, \left\{\frac{13}{35}\right\}\right\}$

We can also use the `LinearSolve` command to form a function for matrix *m* that can be applied to any vector *b*. This is handy if the same matrix is used multiple times with different vectors *b*.

In[8]:= `Clear[f]; f = LinearSolve[m]`

Out[8]= `LinearSolveFunction[` ▦ ▦$^{-1}$ `Matrix dimensions: {4, 4}` `]`

In[9]:= `f[b]`

Out[9]= $\left\{\left\{-\dfrac{127}{35}\right\}, \left\{\dfrac{141}{35}\right\}, \left\{\dfrac{139}{35}\right\}, \left\{\dfrac{13}{35}\right\}\right\}$

Or we can solve the system $m\,x = b$ for x by multiplying both sides on the left by m^{-1}, to get $x = m^{-1}\,b$.

In[10]:= `Inverse[m].b`

Out[10]= $\left\{\left\{-\dfrac{127}{35}\right\}, \left\{\dfrac{141}{35}\right\}, \left\{\dfrac{139}{35}\right\}, \left\{\dfrac{13}{35}\right\}\right\}$

Finally, we can use the command `Solve` to solve this system, just as in Section 4.9. But we have to be careful using `Solve`. When we use the Table/Matrix ▷ New… dialog box to create m, x, and b, both $m\,x$ and b are lists of lists. The `Solve` command takes a list of equations as its first argument and a list of variables as its second argument—it unfortunately cannot accept lists of lists. There is a simple solution: We will have to reenter x and b without using the Table/Matrix ▷ New… dialog box, expressing each as a single list. If we do this, the equation `m.x == b` is acceptable as input to the `Solve` command. Note how *Mathematica* interprets the equation `m.x == b` as a single list of equations when x and b are entered this way:

In[11]:= `Clear[x, b]; x = {x1, x2, x3, x4}; b = {1, 2, 3, 4}; m.x == b`

Out[11]= `{x1 + 5 x2 - 4 x3 + x4, 3 x1 + 4 x2 - x3 + 2 x4,`
  `3 x1 + 2 x2 + x3 + 5 x4, -6 x2 + 7 x3 + x4} == {1, 2, 3, 4}`

In[12]:= `Solve[m.x == b, x]`

Out[12]= $\left\{\left\{x1 \to -\dfrac{127}{35}, \; x2 \to \dfrac{141}{35}, \; x3 \to \dfrac{139}{35}, \; x4 \to \dfrac{13}{35}\right\}\right\}$

An *inconsistent* system of equations has no solutions. If we use the `Solve` command on such a system, the output will be an empty set of curly brackets:

In[13]:= `Clear[m, x, b];`

$m = \begin{pmatrix} 1 & 1 & 1 \\ 1 & 1 & 1 \\ 1 & -1 & -1 \end{pmatrix}$ `; x = {x1, x2, x3}; b = {1, 2, -1};`

`Solve[m.x == b, x]`

Out[15]= `{}`

However, if we row-reduce, we can see the inconsistency in the system:

```
In[16]:= ArrayFlatten[{{m, Transpose[{b}]}}]

Out[16]= {{1, 1, 1, 1}, {1, 1, 1, 2}, {1, -1, -1, -1}}
```

```
In[17]:= RowReduce[%] // MatrixForm
```
Out[17]//MatrixForm=
$$\begin{pmatrix} 1 & 0 & 0 & 0 \\ 0 & 1 & 1 & 0 \\ 0 & 0 & 0 & 1 \end{pmatrix}$$

The last row represents the impossible equation $0 = 1$.

If you use the LinearSolve command with an inconsistent system, you will be told off:

```
In[18]:= LinearSolve[m, b]
```

••• LinearSolve: Linear equation encountered that has no solution.

```
Out[18]= LinearSolve[{{1, 1, 1}, {1, 1, 1}, {1, -1, -1}}, {1, 2, -1}]
```

And if you try to find the inverse of m you will be told off again:

```
In[19]:= Inverse[m].b
```

••• Inverse: Matrix {{1, 1, 1}, {1, 1, 1}, {1, –1, –1}} is singular.

```
Out[19]= Inverse[{{1, 1, 1}, {1, 1, 1}, {1, -1, -1}}].{1, 2, -1}
```

The remaining possibility for a system of equations is that there are an infinite number of solutions. The Solve command nicely displays the solution set in this situation. The warning message can be safely ignored here:

```
In[20]:= Clear[m, x, b];
```

$$m = \begin{pmatrix} 2 & 3 & -4 \\ 4 & 6 & -8 \\ 1 & -1 & -1 \end{pmatrix}; \ x = \{x1, x2, x3\}; \ b = \{8, 16, 1\};$$

```
Solve[m.x == b, x]
```

••• Solve: Equations may not give solutions for all "solve" variables.

Out[22]= $\left\{\left\{x2 \to \dfrac{4}{7} + \dfrac{2\,x1}{7}, \ x3 \to -\dfrac{11}{7} + \dfrac{5\,x1}{7}\right\}\right\}$

Be very careful when using the LinearSolve command. In a system having an infinite number of solutions it will return only one of them, giving no indication that there are others. In this example it returns only the solution where $x_3 = 0$:

In[23]:= **LinearSolve[m, b]**

Out[23]= $\left\{\dfrac{11}{5}, \dfrac{6}{5}, 0\right\}$

Row reduction gives the solution with little possibility for confusion:

In[24]:= **ArrayFlatten[{{m, Transpose[{b}]}}]**

Out[24]= $\{\{2, 3, -4, 8\}, \{4, 6, -8, 16\}, \{1, -1, -1, 1\}\}$

In[25]:= **RowReduce[%] // MatrixForm**

Out[25]//MatrixForm=

$$\begin{pmatrix} 1 & 0 & -\dfrac{7}{5} & \dfrac{11}{5} \\ 0 & 1 & -\dfrac{2}{5} & \dfrac{6}{5} \\ 0 & 0 & 0 & 0 \end{pmatrix}$$

Thus, for each real value assumed by x_3, there is a solution with $x_1 = \dfrac{11}{5} + \dfrac{7}{5} x_3$, and $x_2 = \dfrac{6}{5} + \dfrac{2}{5} x_3$.

The moral is that you should be very careful using the command LinearSolve unless you know you have a nonsingular matrix and hence a single solution. To check this condition, you can use the Det command, keeping in mind that a singular matrix has determinant zero. When in doubt it is best to use row reduction and your knowledge of linear algebra to find the solution vectors.

Homogeneous Systems of Equations

A *homogeneous* system of equations has the form $m\,x = \mathbf{0}$, where m is a coefficient matrix, x is a column vector of variables, and $\mathbf{0}$ is the zero vector. Note that $x = \mathbf{0}$ is a solution to any homogeneous system. Now suppose m is a square matrix. Recall that such a system of linear equations has a unique solution if and only if m is nonsingular. Hence, we see that if m is nonsingular, a homogeneous system will have only the *trivial* solution $x = \mathbf{0}$, while if m is singular the system will have an infinite number of solutions. The set of all solutions to a homogeneous system is called the *null space* of m:

In[26]:= **Clear[m, x, b];**

$$m = \begin{pmatrix} 0 & 2 & 2 & 4 \\ 1 & 0 & -1 & -3 \\ 2 & 3 & 1 & 1 \\ -2 & 1 & 3 & -2 \end{pmatrix}; \; x = \begin{pmatrix} x1 \\ x2 \\ x3 \\ x4 \end{pmatrix}; \; b = \begin{pmatrix} 0 \\ 0 \\ 0 \\ 0 \end{pmatrix}; \; \textbf{Det[m]}$$

Out[27]= 0

```
In[28]:= RowReduce[ArrayFlatten[{{m, b}}]] // MatrixForm
```
Out[28]//MatrixForm=
$$\begin{pmatrix} 1 & 0 & -1 & 0 & 0 \\ 0 & 1 & 1 & 0 & 0 \\ 0 & 0 & 0 & 1 & 0 \\ 0 & 0 & 0 & 0 & 0 \end{pmatrix}$$

This reduced form of the augmented matrix tells us that $x_1 = x_3$, $x_2 = -x_3$, and $x_4 = 0$. That is, any vector of the form $(t, -t, t, 0)$, where t is a real number, is a solution, and the vector $(1, -1, 1, 0)$ forms a *basis* for the solution space. Bases are discussed in the next section of this chapter.

The command NullSpace gives a set of basis vectors for the solution space of the homogeneous equation $m\,x = 0$:

```
In[29]:= NullSpace[m]
```
Out[29]= $\{\{1, -1, 1, 0\}\}$

Using LinearSolve and NullSpace to Solve Nonhomogeneous Systems

We have seen that the LinearSolve command will only return one solution when a matrix equation $m\,x = b$ has an infinite number of solutions. This can be confusing at first, but you should understand that there is a reason for its behavior. If you were to take the sum of the solution vector provided by LinearSolve with any vector in the null space of m, you would get another solution vector. Moreover, every solution vector is of this form. Here's an example:

```
In[30]:= Clear[m, b];
```
$$m = \begin{pmatrix} 0 & 2 & 2 & 4 \\ 1 & 0 & -1 & -3 \\ 2 & 3 & 1 & 1 \end{pmatrix}; b = \begin{pmatrix} 2 \\ 0 \\ 0 \end{pmatrix};$$

```
In[32]:= LinearSolve[m, b]
```
Out[32]= $\{\{-9\}, \{7\}, \{0\}, \{-3\}\}$

```
In[33]:= NullSpace[m]
```
Out[33]= $\{\{1, -1, 1, 0\}\}$

This tells us that there are an infinite number of solutions. For each real number t, there is a solution $(-9, 7, 0, -3) + t(1, -1, 1, 0)$. In other words, $x_1 = -9 + t$, $x_2 = 7 - t$, $x_3 = t$, and $x_4 = -3$. This is exactly what row reduction tells us, in slightly different language:

```
In[34]:= RowReduce[ArrayFlatten[{{m, b}}]] // MatrixForm
```
Out[34]//MatrixForm=
$$\begin{pmatrix} 1 & 0 & -1 & 0 & -9 \\ 0 & 1 & 1 & 0 & 7 \\ 0 & 0 & 0 & 1 & -3 \end{pmatrix}$$

Exercises 7.6

1. For which values of a will the following system of linear equations have no solutions, one solution, or an infinite number of solutions?

$$
\begin{aligned}
x + 2y - 3z &= 4 \\
2x - y + 5z &= 2 \\
4x + 3y + a^2 z &= a + 3
\end{aligned}
$$

2. Find the equation of the circle that contains the points $(4, -3), (-4, 5)$, and $(-2, 7)$.

3. The following is a 2000-year-old problem from China: Five families, A, B, C, D, E, share a well. Family A has two well ropes, B has three, C has four, D has five, and E has six; for each family, their ropes have the same positive integer length. The deficit of A's ropes is the length of one of B's (meaning that A's two ropes and one of B's equals the depth of the well). The deficit of B's ropes is the length of one of C's. The deficit of C's ropes is the length of one of D's. The deficit of D's ropes is the length of one of E's. The deficit of E's ropes is the length of one of A's. Find the depth w of the well, and the lengths a, b, c, d, and e of the ropes belonging to each of the five families. Hint: See Exercise 2 in Section 7.1. Source: R. Hart, *The Chinese Roots of Linear Algebra*. Johns Hopkins University Press, 2011.

7.7 Vector Spaces

Span and Linear Independence

Suppose we are given a set $\{v_1, v_2, v_3, \ldots, v_n\}$ of vectors. Any vector that can be expressed in the form $a_1 v_1 + a_2 v_2 + a_3 v_3 + \cdots + a_n v_n$ is said to be in the *span* of the vectors $v_1, v_2, v_3, \ldots, v_n$, where the coefficients a_i are scalars.

We can determine whether a given vector b is in the span of the vectors $v_1, v_2, v_3, \ldots, v_n$ by letting m be the matrix whose columns are $v_1, v_2, v_3, \ldots, v_n$, and then determining whether the equation $m x = b$ has a solution. A solution x, if it exists, provides values for the scalars a_i.

For example, in real three-space, is the vector $b = (1, 2, 3)$ in the span of the vectors $v_1 = (10, 4, 5)$, $v_2 = (4, 4, 7)$, and $v_3 = (8, 1, 0)$?

```
In[1]:= Clear[v1, v2, v, b, m, c];
        v1 = {10, 4, 5};
        v2 = {4, 4, 7};
        v3 = {8, 1, 0};
        b = {1, 2, 3};
        m = Transpose[{v1, v2, v3}];
        c = LinearSolve[m, b]
```

$$
\text{Out[7]}= \left\{ \frac{3}{2}, -\frac{9}{14}, -\frac{10}{7} \right\}
$$

We can check that $\frac{3}{2} v_1 - \frac{9}{14} v_2 - \frac{10}{7} v_3 = b$, so yes, b is in the span of the three vectors.

```
In[8]:=  c[[1]] v1 + c[[2]] v2 + c[[3]] v3
Out[8]=  {1, 2, 3}
```

A set of vectors $\{v_1, v_2, v_3, \ldots, v_n\}$ is said to be *linearly independent* if every vector in their span can be expressed in a unique way as a linear combination $a_1 v_1 + a_2 v_2 + a_3 v_3 + \cdots + a_n v_n$. Put another way, this means that the only way to express the zero vector as such a linear combination is to have each coefficient $a_i = 0$. If it is possible to write $a_1 v_1 + a_2 v_2 + a_3 v_3 + \cdots + a_n v_n = 0$ with at least one of the $a_i \neq 0$, then the set of vectors $\{v_1, v_2, v_3, \ldots, v_n\}$ is linearly *dependent*.

To check whether a set of vectors $\{v_1, v_2, v_3, \ldots, v_n\}$ is linearly independent, let m be the matrix whose columns are $v_1, v_2, v_3, \ldots, v_n$, and check that the equation $m x = 0$ has only the trivial solution:

```
In[9]:=  NullSpace[m]
Out[9]=  {}
```

Yes, these are independent vectors. Alternatively, we could check that the matrix whose rows (or columns) are $v_1, v_2, v_3, \ldots, v_n$, is nonsingular:

```
In[10]:=  Det[{v1, v2, v3}]
Out[10]=  14
```

Bases

A *basis* for a vector space is a set of linearly independent vectors whose span includes every vector in the vector space. Given a spanning set of vectors $\{v_1, v_2, v_3, \ldots, v_n\}$ for a vector space we can easily obtain a basis for that space. Form a matrix whose rows are the vectors $v_1, v_2, v_3, \ldots, v_n$, and row-reduce:

```
In[11]:=  Clear[v1, v2, v3, v4, m, a, b, c];
          v1 = {2, 1, 15, 10, 6};
          v2 = {2, -5, -3, -2, 6};
          v3 = {0, 5, 15, 10, 0};
          v4 = {2, 6, 18, 8, 6};
          m = {v1, v2, v3, v4};
          RowReduce[m] // MatrixForm
Out[17]//MatrixForm=
          ( 1  0  0  -2   3 )
          ( 0  1  0  -1   0 )
          ( 0  0  1   1   0 )
          ( 0  0  0   0   0 )
```

The nonzero rows of this matrix form a basis for the space spanned by the set $\{v_1, v_2, v_3, v_4\}$. This space is also called the *row space* of the matrix m.

We can also find a basis consisting of a subset of the original vectors. If we row-reduce the matrix whose columns are the vectors v_1, v_2, v_3, ..., v_n, then the columns containing the *leading 1s* will form a basis for the column space, and the corresponding columns from the original matrix will also form a basis for the column space. (An entry in a row-reduced matrix is called a leading 1 if the entry is a 1 and it has only zeros to its left.)

```
In[18]:=  Clear[v1, v2, v3, v4, m];
          v1 = {2, 1, 15, 10, 6};
          v2 = {2, -5, -3, -2, 6};
          v3 = {0, 5, 15, 10, 0};
          v4 = {2, 6, 18, 8, 6};
In[23]:=  m = Transpose[{v1, v2, v3, v4}];
          RowReduce[m] // MatrixForm
Out[24]//MatrixForm=
```

$$\begin{pmatrix} 1 & 0 & \frac{5}{6} & 0 \\ 0 & 1 & -\frac{5}{6} & 0 \\ 0 & 0 & 0 & 1 \\ 0 & 0 & 0 & 0 \\ 0 & 0 & 0 & 0 \end{pmatrix}$$

The vectors $(1, 0, 0, 0, 0)$, $(0, 1, 0, 0, 0)$, and $(0, 0, 1, 0, 0)$ form a basis for the column space of *m*. The vectors from the same columns in *m* will also form a basis for the column space. Hence v_1, v_2, and v_4 will form a basis for the space spanned by the set $\{v_1, v_2, v_3, v_4\}$. We can confirm that $\{v_1, v_2, v_4\}$ independent set:

```
In[25]:=  NullSpace[Transpose[{v1, v2, v4}]]
Out[25]=  {}
```

We see here an example of a general truth: A vector space may have many distinct bases. The number of vectors in any basis for that vector space, however, will always be the same. This number is called the *dimension* of the vector space.

Rank and Nullity

The dimension of the null space of a matrix is called the *nullity* of the matrix. We can find the nullity by using the Length command to count the vectors in a basis for the null space:

```
In[26]:=  Length[NullSpace[m]]
Out[26]=  1
```

The *rank* of a matrix is the common dimension of the row space and the column space. The rank plus the nullity must equal the number of columns in a matrix.

In[27]:= `MatrixRank[m]`

Out[27]= 3

Orthonormal Bases and the Gram–Schmidt Process

Given a set of vectors it is frequently desirable to find a collection of vectors with the same span that have some special properties.

In[28]:= `Clear[v1, v2, v3, u1, w1, w2, w3];`
`v1 = {2, 3, -4, 1, 0};`
`v2 = {1, 5, -6, 10, -3};`
`v3 = {7, -2, 1, 1, 1};`

It is easy to find a *unit vector*, a vector whose length or norm is 1, in the same direction as a given vector. We simply need to divide each component by the norm of the vector. The command `Normal`ize does this automatically.

In[32]:= `Norm[v1]`

Out[32]= $\sqrt{30}$

In[33]:= `u1 = Normalize[v1]`

Out[33]= $\left\{ \sqrt{\dfrac{2}{15}}, \sqrt{\dfrac{3}{10}}, -2\sqrt{\dfrac{2}{15}}, \dfrac{1}{\sqrt{30}}, 0 \right\}$

In[34]:= `Norm[u1]`

Out[34]= 1

A collection of vectors is *orthogonal* if the vectors are mutually perpendicular, i.e., if the dot product of every pair is 0. The set is *orthonormal* if in addition each vector has norm 1. Given a basis for a vector space, we can use the `Orthogonalize` command to find an orthonormal basis. `Orthogonalize` uses the Gram–Schmidt process unless another method is specified using the `Method` option. The argument for the command `Orthogonalize` is a list of linearly independent vectors. The output is a list of mutually orthogonal unit vectors with the same span:

Before we apply `Orthogonalize`, let's check that our vectors are linearly independent:

In[35]:= `NullSpace[Transpose[{v1, v2, v3}]]`

Out[35]= { }

Good, we are free to proceed.

In[36]:= `{w1, w2, w3} = Orthogonalize[{v1, v2, v3}];`

`{w1, w2, w3} // MatrixForm`

Out[37]//MatrixForm=

$$\begin{pmatrix} \sqrt{\frac{2}{15}} & \sqrt{\frac{3}{10}} & -2\sqrt{\frac{2}{15}} & \frac{1}{\sqrt{30}} & 0 \\ -4\sqrt{\frac{6}{1405}} & -\frac{1}{\sqrt{8430}} & 4\sqrt{\frac{2}{4215}} & \frac{83}{\sqrt{8430}} & -\sqrt{\frac{30}{281}} \\ \frac{5368}{\sqrt{38\,274\,729}} & -706\sqrt{\frac{3}{12\,758\,243}} & \frac{1489}{\sqrt{38\,274\,729}} & \frac{1574}{\sqrt{38\,274\,729}} & 176\sqrt{\frac{3}{12\,758\,243}} \end{pmatrix}$$

It is easy to check that any pair of these vectors is orthogonal. Just enter a list whose items are dot products of every possible pair of distinct vectors. The output will be a list of zeros if the vectors in each pair are orthogonal:

In[38]:= `{w1.w2, w2.w3, w3.w1}`

Out[38]= `{0, 0, 0}`

And here we check that they are all unit vectors:

In[39]:= `{Norm[w1], Norm[w2], Norm[w3]}`

Out[39]= `{1, 1, 1}`

The familiar concepts of vector length and the angle between pairs of vectors in Euclidean vector spaces can be generalized to other vector spaces that admit an *inner product*—a generalization of the dot product. As with the dot product, two vectors whose inner product is zero are said to be orthogonal. And a vector whose inner product with itself is 1 is said to be a unit vector.

For example, consider the vector space P_3 of polynomials in the variable x of degree at most three with real coefficients. Given two polynomials p and q in P_3 we can form their inner product using the function f defined below:

In[40]:= `Clear[f, p, q]`

In[41]:= $f[p\_, q\_] := \int_{-1}^{1} p * q \, dx$

Applying f to the vector w_1 below we see that $w_1 = \frac{1}{\sqrt{2}}$ is a unit vector in the inner product space P_3.

In[42]:= `Clear[x, w1, w2, w3, w4];`

$w1 = \frac{1}{\sqrt{2}};\ w2 = x;\ w3 = x^2;\ w4 = x^3;$

In[44]:= `f[w1, w1]`

Out[44]= `1`

And we can see that the vectors w_1 and w_2 are orthogonal.

In[45]:= **f[w1, w2]**

Out[45]= 0

The `Orthogonalize` command can be applied in any inner product space. The default inner product for `Orthogonalize` is the dot product, but a different inner product function can be specified as an optional second argument.

In[46]:= **{v1, v2, v3, v4} = Orthogonalize[{w1, w2, w3, w4}, f]**

Out[46]= $\left\{ \dfrac{1}{\sqrt{2}}, \sqrt{\dfrac{3}{2}}\, x, \dfrac{3}{2}\sqrt{\dfrac{5}{2}}\left(-\dfrac{1}{3} + x^2\right), \dfrac{5}{2}\sqrt{\dfrac{7}{2}}\left(-\dfrac{3\,x}{5} + x^3\right) \right\}$

We can apply the inner product to these vectors to check that they are pairwise orthogonal unit vectors.

In[47]:= **f[v3, v3]**

Out[47]= 1

In[48]:= **f[v2, v3]**

Out[48]= 0

QR−Decomposition

The QR-decomposition of a matrix is a factorization of a matrix with linearly independent column vectors, into a product of a matrix Q that has orthonormal column vectors and a matrix R that is invertible and upper triangular. The matrix Q is obtained by applying the Gram−Schmidt process to the column vectors of the matrix. The matrix R is then uniquely determined.

Consider the matrix m.

In[49]:= **m =** $\begin{pmatrix} 1 & 0 & 0 \\ -1 & 2 & 0 \\ 0 & 1 & 3 \end{pmatrix}$ **;**

In[50]:= **Det[m]**

Out[50]= 6

In[51]:= `q = Transpose[Orthogonalize[Transpose[m]]];`
`MatrixForm[q]`

Out[52]//MatrixForm=

$$\begin{pmatrix} \dfrac{1}{\sqrt{2}} & \dfrac{1}{\sqrt{3}} & -\dfrac{1}{\sqrt{6}} \\[2ex] -\dfrac{1}{\sqrt{2}} & \dfrac{1}{\sqrt{3}} & -\dfrac{1}{\sqrt{6}} \\[2ex] 0 & \dfrac{1}{\sqrt{3}} & \sqrt{\dfrac{2}{3}} \end{pmatrix}$$

In[53]:= `r = Inverse[q].m // Simplify;`
`MatrixForm[r]`

Out[54]//MatrixForm=

$$\begin{pmatrix} \sqrt{2} & -\sqrt{2} & 0 \\ 0 & \sqrt{3} & \sqrt{3} \\ 0 & 0 & \sqrt{6} \end{pmatrix}$$

In[55]:= `q.r // MatrixForm`

Out[55]//MatrixForm=

$$\begin{pmatrix} 1 & 0 & 0 \\ -1 & 2 & 0 \\ 0 & 1 & 3 \end{pmatrix}$$

The command QRDecomposition automates the process.

In[56]:= `qr = QRDecomposition[m]`

Out[56]= $\left\{\left\{\left\{\dfrac{1}{\sqrt{2}}, -\dfrac{1}{\sqrt{2}}, 0\right\}, \left\{\dfrac{1}{\sqrt{3}}, \dfrac{1}{\sqrt{3}}, \dfrac{1}{\sqrt{3}}\right\}, \left\{-\dfrac{1}{\sqrt{6}}, -\dfrac{1}{\sqrt{6}}, \sqrt{\dfrac{2}{3}}\right\}\right\},\right.$

$\left.\left\{\left\{\sqrt{2}, -\sqrt{2}, 0\right\}, \left\{0, \sqrt{3}, \sqrt{3}\right\}, \left\{0, 0, \sqrt{6}\right\}\right\}\right\}$

In[57]:= `Map[MatrixForm, qr]`

Out[57]= $\left\{\begin{pmatrix} \dfrac{1}{\sqrt{2}} & -\dfrac{1}{\sqrt{2}} & 0 \\[2ex] \dfrac{1}{\sqrt{3}} & \dfrac{1}{\sqrt{3}} & \dfrac{1}{\sqrt{3}} \\[2ex] -\dfrac{1}{\sqrt{6}} & -\dfrac{1}{\sqrt{6}} & \sqrt{\dfrac{2}{3}} \end{pmatrix}, \begin{pmatrix} \sqrt{2} & -\sqrt{2} & 0 \\ 0 & \sqrt{3} & \sqrt{3} \\ 0 & 0 & \sqrt{6} \end{pmatrix}\right\}$

The command `QRDecomposition` returns two matrices, q and r, where $q^t r$ is equal to the original matrix. Notice that the first matrix in this list is the transpose of our matrix q above.

```
In[58]:= Transpose[qr[[1]]].qr[[2]]
```

```
Out[58]= {{1, 0, 0}, {-1, 2, 0}, {0, 1, 3}}
```

Exercises 7.7

1. Consider the vector space V spanned by the vectors $v_1 = (1, 2, 3)$, $v_2 = (4, 5, 6)$, and $v_3 = (7, 7, 8)$ in $\mathbb{R}^3$.

   a. Find an orthonormal basis for V and let O be the matrix whose rows are the three basis vectors. Show that the product of O with its transpose is the identity matrix.

   b. Show that the product of any orthonormal matrix with its transpose is the identity matrix.

7.8 Eigenvalues and Eigenvectors

Given an $n \times n$ matrix m, the nonzero vectors v_i such that $m\, v_i = \lambda_i\, v_i$ are the *eigenvectors* of m, and the scalars λ_i are the *eigenvalues* of m. There are at most n eigenvalues. First we will use the commands `Eigenvalues`, `Eigenvectors`, and `Eigensystem` to find eigenvalues and eigenvectors. Then we will walk through the process "manually."

Finding Eigenvalues and Eigenvectors Automatically
Here is a simple matrix:

```
In[1]:= Clear[m];
        m = Array[Min, {2, 2}]; m // MatrixForm
```

Out[2]//MatrixForm=
$$\begin{pmatrix} 1 & 1 \\ 1 & 2 \end{pmatrix}$$

To get the eigenvalues, type the following command (look for λ in the Typesetting section of the Basic Math Assistant palette):

```
In[3]:= {λ1, λ2} = Eigenvalues[m]
```

Out[3]= $\left\{ \dfrac{1}{2}\left(3 + \sqrt{5}\right), \ \dfrac{1}{2}\left(3 - \sqrt{5}\right) \right\}$

For the eigenvectors, type:

```
In[4]:= {v1, v2} = Eigenvectors[m]
```

Out[4]= $\left\{ \left\{ \dfrac{1}{2}\left(-1 + \sqrt{5}\right), 1 \right\}, \ \left\{ \dfrac{1}{2}\left(-1 - \sqrt{5}\right), 1 \right\} \right\}$

We find two eigenvalues and two eigenvectors. Let's check that $m\,v_1 = \lambda_1\,v_1$:

In[5]:= **m.v1 // Simplify**

Out[5]= $\left\{ \dfrac{1}{2}\left(1 + \sqrt{5}\,\right),\ \dfrac{1}{2}\left(3 + \sqrt{5}\,\right)\right\}$

In[6]:= **λ1 * v1 // Simplify**

Out[6]= $\left\{ \dfrac{1}{2}\left(1 + \sqrt{5}\,\right),\ \dfrac{1}{2}\left(3 + \sqrt{5}\,\right)\right\}$

In[7]:= **m.v1 == λ1 * v1**

Out[7]= True

You can easily check that $m\,v_2 = \lambda_2\,v_2$ as well.

The command `Eigensystem` gives both the eigenvalues and the eigenvectors. The output is a list whose first item is a list of eigenvalues and whose second item is a list of corresponding eigenvectors:

In[8]:= **Eigensystem[m]**

Out[8]= $\left\{\left\{ \dfrac{1}{2}\left(3 + \sqrt{5}\,\right),\ \dfrac{1}{2}\left(3 - \sqrt{5}\,\right)\right\},\ \left\{\left\{\dfrac{1}{2}\left(-1 + \sqrt{5}\,\right),\ 1\right\},\ \left\{\dfrac{1}{2}\left(-1 - \sqrt{5}\,\right),\ 1\right\}\right\}\right\}$

We can ask that the output of any of these commands be numerical approximations by replacing m with N[m]:

In[9]:= **Eigensystem[N[m]]**

Out[9]= {{2.61803, 0.381966}, {{0.525731, 0.850651}, {-0.850651, 0.525731}}}

Even for a simple matrix with integer entries, the eigenvalues can be quite complicated and involve complex numbers:

In[10]:= **Clear[m];**
m = Array[Min, {3, 3}]; m // MatrixForm

Out[11]//MatrixForm=

$\begin{pmatrix} 1 & 1 & 1 \\ 1 & 2 & 2 \\ 1 & 2 & 3 \end{pmatrix}$

In[12]:= **Eigenvalues[m]**

Out[12]= $\left\{ \text{Root}\left[-1 + 5\,\#1 - 6\,\#1^2 + \#1^3\ \&,\ 3\right],\right.$
$\left.\text{Root}\left[-1 + 5\,\#1 - 6\,\#1^2 + \#1^3\ \&,\ 2\right],\ \text{Root}\left[-1 + 5\,\#1 - 6\,\#1^2 + \#1^3\ \&,\ 1\right]\right\}$

The eigenvalues here are returned as `Root` objects, in this case the three roots of the characteristic polynomial $-1 + 5\,x - 6\,x^2 + x^3$. The option setting `Cubics → True` will permit the display of such roots in terms of radicals.

In[13]:= `Eigenvalues[m, Cubics → True]`

Out[13]= $\left\{ 2 + \dfrac{7^{2/3}}{\left(\frac{3}{2}\left(9 + i\,\sqrt{3}\right)\right)^{1/3}} + \dfrac{\left(\frac{7}{2}\left(9 + i\,\sqrt{3}\right)\right)^{1/3}}{3^{2/3}}, \right.$

$2 - \dfrac{7^{2/3}\left(1 - i\,\sqrt{3}\right)}{2^{2/3}\left(3\left(9 + i\,\sqrt{3}\right)\right)^{1/3}} - \dfrac{\left(1 + i\,\sqrt{3}\right)\left(\frac{7}{2}\left(9 + i\,\sqrt{3}\right)\right)^{1/3}}{2 \times 3^{2/3}},$

$\left. 2 - \dfrac{7^{2/3}\left(1 + i\,\sqrt{3}\right)}{2^{2/3}\left(3\left(9 + i\,\sqrt{3}\right)\right)^{1/3}} - \dfrac{\left(1 - i\,\sqrt{3}\right)\left(\frac{7}{2}\left(9 + i\,\sqrt{3}\right)\right)^{1/3}}{2 \times 3^{2/3}} \right\}$

There is a similar option setting for quartics. One may also get a numerical approximation of the eigenvalues as follows:

In[14]:= `Eigenvalues[m] // N`

Out[14]= `{5.04892, 0.643104, 0.307979}`

For an $n \times n$ matrix *Mathematica* will always return n eigenvalues even if they are not all distinct. The eigenvalues will occur in the same frequency as the roots of the characteristic polynomial (as explained in the next subsection). *Mathematica* will also output n eigenvectors. If there are fewer than n linearly independent eigenvectors, the output may contain one or more zero vectors. These zero vectors are there for bookkeeping only; actual eigenvectors are nonzero by definition:

In[15]:= `Clear[m];`

$$m = \begin{pmatrix} 2 & 1 & 0 \\ 0 & 2 & 0 \\ 0 & 0 & 0 \end{pmatrix};$$

`Eigensystem[m]`

Out[17]= `{{2, 2, 0}, {{1, 0, 0}, {0, 0, 0}, {0, 0, 1}}}`

Finding Eigenvalues and Eigenvectors Manually

Even though *Mathematica* can produce eigenvalues and eigenvectors very quickly, it is still sometimes enlightening to go through the process "manually." To find the eigenvalues we first form the *characteristic polynomial*, which is the determinant of the matrix $\lambda I - m$, where m is a square matrix, λ is an indeterminate, and I is the identity matrix of the same dimensions as m:

In[18]:= `Clear[m];`

$$m = \begin{pmatrix} 2 & -1 & 0 \\ -1 & 2 & 0 \\ 0 & 0 & 3 \end{pmatrix};$$

`c = Det[λ IdentityMatrix[3] - m]`

Out[20]= $(-3 + \lambda) \left(3 - 4\lambda + \lambda^2\right)$

Then we find the roots of the characteristic polynomial:

In[21]:= `Solve[c == 0, λ]`

Out[21]= $\{\{\lambda \to 1\}, \{\lambda \to 3\}, \{\lambda \to 3\}\}$

There are two eigenvalues $\lambda = 1$ and $\lambda = 3$. The eigenvalue 3 is reported twice because it occurs twice as a root of the characteristic polynomial c. We can see this clearly by factoring c:

In[22]:= `Factor[c]`

Out[22]= $(-3 + \lambda)^2 (-1 + \lambda)$

Of course, most characteristic polynomials will not factor so nicely. To find the eigenspace of each eigenvalue λ_i we will find the null space of the matrix $\lambda_i I - m$:

In[23]:= `NullSpace[1 * IdentityMatrix[3] - m]`

Out[23]= $\{\{1, 1, 0\}\}$

In[24]:= `NullSpace[3 * IdentityMatrix[3] - m]`

Out[24]= $\{\{0, 0, 1\}, \{-1, 1, 0\}\}$

The eigenspace for the eigenvalue $\lambda = 1$ has one basis vector: (1, 1, 0). The eigenspace for the eigenvalue $\lambda = 3$ has two basis vectors: (0, 0, 1) and (−1, 1, 0).

Let's have *Mathematica* check our work:

In[25]:= `Eigensystem[m]`

Out[25]= $\{\{3, 3, 1\}, \{\{0, 0, 1\}, \{-1, 1, 0\}, \{1, 1, 0\}\}\}$

Diagonalization

A square matrix m is *diagonalizable* if there exists a diagonal matrix d and an invertible matrix p such that $m = p\,d\,p^{-1}$. In this case, the expression on the right-hand side is called a *Jordan decomposition* or *diagonalization* of m. An $n \times n$ matrix is diagonalizable if and only if it has n linearly independent eigenvectors. In this case the matrix p will be the matrix whose columns are the eigenvectors of m and the matrix d will have the eigenvalues of m along the diagonal (and zeros everywhere else):

We can use `Eigensystem` to find the eigenvalues and eigenvectors and then form the matrices *p* and *d* ourselves or use `JordanDecomposition` and have *Mathematica* compute the matrices *p* and *d*. Notice that the matrices we get by each method are slightly different. The order in which the eigenvalues and eigenvectors are listed causes this difference.

In[26]:= `Clear[m, p, c, d];`

$$m = \begin{pmatrix} 2 & -1 & 0 \\ -1 & 2 & 0 \\ 0 & 0 & 3 \end{pmatrix};$$

In[28]:= `{evals, evecs} = Eigensystem[m]`

Out[28]= `{{3, 3, 1}, {{0, 0, 1}, {-1, 1, 0}, {1, 1, 0}}}`

In[29]:= `d = DiagonalMatrix[evals];`
`d // MatrixForm`

Out[30]//MatrixForm=
$$\begin{pmatrix} 3 & 0 & 0 \\ 0 & 3 & 0 \\ 0 & 0 & 1 \end{pmatrix}$$

In[31]:= `p = Transpose[evecs];`
`p // MatrixForm`

Out[32]//MatrixForm=
$$\begin{pmatrix} 0 & -1 & 1 \\ 0 & 1 & 1 \\ 1 & 0 & 0 \end{pmatrix}$$

In[33]:= `p.d.Inverse[p] // MatrixForm`

Out[33]//MatrixForm=
$$\begin{pmatrix} 2 & -1 & 0 \\ -1 & 2 & 0 \\ 0 & 0 & 3 \end{pmatrix}$$

In[34]:= `Clear[p, d];`
`{p, d} = JordanDecomposition[m]`

Out[35]= `{{{1, 0, -1}, {1, 0, 1}, {0, 1, 0}}, {{1, 0, 0}, {0, 3, 0}, {0, 0, 3}}}`

In[36]:= `Map[MatrixForm, %]`

Out[36]= $\left\{ \begin{pmatrix} 1 & 0 & -1 \\ 1 & 0 & 1 \\ 0 & 1 & 0 \end{pmatrix}, \begin{pmatrix} 1 & 0 & 0 \\ 0 & 3 & 0 \\ 0 & 0 & 3 \end{pmatrix} \right\}$

In[37]:= **p.d.Inverse[p] // MatrixForm**

Out[37]//MatrixForm=

$$\begin{pmatrix} 2 & -1 & 0 \\ -1 & 2 & 0 \\ 0 & 0 & 3 \end{pmatrix}$$

Exercises 7.8

1. Form the LU-decomposition of the matrix $m = \begin{pmatrix} 2 & -1 & 0 \\ -1 & 2 & 0 \\ 0 & 0 & 3 \end{pmatrix}$.

7.9 Visualizing Linear Transformations

A *linear transformation F* is a function from one vector space to another such that for all vectors *u* and *v* in the domain, $F(u + v) = F(u) + F(v)$, and for all scalars *k*, $F(k\,v) = k\,F(v)$. Once bases have been specified for each vector space, a linear transformation *F* can be represented as multiplication by a matrix *m*, so that $F(v) = m.v$ for all vectors *v* in the domain of *F*.

We can better understand a linear transformation by studying the effect it has on geometric figures in its domain. *Mathematica* can be used to visualize the effect of a linear transformation from $\mathbb{R}^2$ to $\mathbb{R}^2$ on a geometric object in the plane. We first produce a polygonal shape by specifying the coordinates of its vertices. We can then apply a linear transformation to each of these points and see where they land. Examining the geometric changes tells us how the linear transformation behaves.

To produce a figure on which to demonstrate transformations, go to the Graphics menu and select New Graphic. Next, bring up the drawing tools via Graphics ▷ Drawing Tools, and select the line segments tool (push the appropriate button, or type the letter s). Now click on the graphic repeatedly to draw a picture, being careful not to click on any previous points (to close the loop) until you are done. Don't get too fancy; just a single closed loop is all that is needed. For instance, here is a stunning portrait of our dog, Zoe:

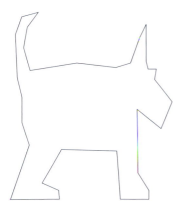

Now click on the graphic so that the orange border is showing, copy it to the clipboard (Edit ▷ Copy) and paste it into the following command:

In[1]:= `dog = First@Cases`  `, Line[pts_] → pts, Infinity]`

Out[1]= {{0, 0}, {0.237841, 0.700376}, {0.145025, 0.981963},
        {0.145025, 1.30109}, {0.087015, 1.54514}, {0.063811, 2.08954},
        {0.145025, 2.31481}, {0.353861, 2.37112}, {0.214637, 2.1834},
        {0.168229, 1.92058}, {0.249443, 1.639}, {0.841145, 1.73286},
        {1.32843, 1.67654}, {1.51406, 1.73286}, {1.63008, 2.05199},
        {1.7113, 2.22094}, {1.7113, 1.75163}, {1.7345, 1.65777},
        {1.83892, 1.65777}, {1.81571, 1.52636}, {2.03615, 1.24478},
        {1.89693, 0.906873}, {1.59528, 1.15091}, {1.60688, 0.3437},
        {1.7461, 0.118431}, {1.7461, 0.00579624}, {1.38644, 0.00579624},
        {1.34003, 0.625287}, {0.643911, 0.644059}, {0.400269, 0.212293},
        {0.609105, 0.118431}, {0.620707, 0.00579624}, {0, 0}}

The details of how the `Cases` command works are discussed in Section 8.8. But what it produces is simply the list of Zoe's coordinates. Her picture is easily recovered from this coordinate list, either as a `Line` or `Polygon` object:

In[2]:= `{Graphics[Line[dog]], Graphics[{Brown, Polygon[dog]}]}`

Out[2]=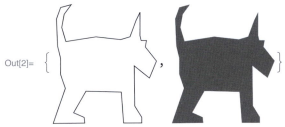

⚠ If, when constructing a graphic, you invoke the line segments tool more than once, you will produce a graphic with more than one `Line` object in it. Things are a bit more complicated here. In such cases do not apply `First` to the `Cases` input above. `Cases` will produce a list containing multiple lists of points. Give this master list a name (such as `dog`). To display this list, instead of `Graphics[Line[dog]]`, use `Graphics[Map[Line,dog]]` (or equivalently: `Graphics[Table[Line[s],{s,dog}]]`). To multiply the matrix `m` by each vertex in

the dog lists, we use `Map[m.#&,dog,{2}]`. This "maps" the `Func:-`
`tion[v,m.v]` over the dog list at the second level. `Map` and `Function` are
described in detail in Section 8.4. Finally, to display the transformed image, put
this all together to get:

```
Graphics[{Brown, Map[Line, Map[m.#&, dog, {2}]]}]
```

You will probably not want to use `Polygon` to render an image made from multiple
`Line` objects.

We can reflect Zoe about the y axis using the matrix $\begin{pmatrix} -1 & 0 \\ 0 & 1 \end{pmatrix}$. We simply multiply each of Zoe's coordinates by this matrix, then make a `Polygon` from the transformed coordinates. Both the original and transformed figures are shown below:

In[3]:= `Graphics[{{Brown, Polygon[Table[`$\begin{pmatrix} -1 & 0 \\ 0 & 1 \end{pmatrix}$`.v, {v, dog}]]}, Line[dog]},`

`Axes → True]`

Out[3]=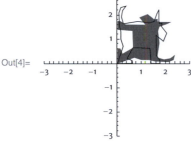

Here Zoe is reflected about the line $y = x$, using the matrix $\begin{pmatrix} 0 & 1 \\ 1 & 0 \end{pmatrix}$:

In[4]:= `Graphics[{{Brown, Polygon[Table[`$\begin{pmatrix} 0 & 1 \\ 1 & 0 \end{pmatrix}$`.v, {v, dog}]]}, Line[dog]},`

`Axes → True, PlotRange → 3]`

Out[4]=

The most simple type of linear transformation is a dilation or contraction. The standard matrix for this type of transformation is $\begin{pmatrix} c & 0 \\ 0 & c \end{pmatrix}$. If $0 < c < 1$ we have a contraction, while if $c > 1$, we have a dilation. Using `Manipulate` we allow c to vary dynamically. Below we display the dilation matrix together with the graphical output. Toward this end, we introduce a `displayMatrix` command that will round all matrix entries to two decimal places, leave room in front of each entry for a minus sign, and generally make the matrix entries easy to read as the parameter c is manipulated.

```
In[5]:= displayMatrix[m_] :=
          MatrixForm@Map[NumberForm[Chop[N[#], 10^-3], {3, 2},
             NumberSigns → {"-", " "}] &, m, {2}]
```

> ⚠ The `displayMatrix` command utilizes both `Map` and `Function`, which are discussed in Section 8.4, in order to operate individually on each matrix entry. It also makes use of `NumberForm`, which is used to regulate the display of numbers, and `Chop`, which is used to round sufficiently small numbers to zero. `NumberForm` is discussed in Section 8.3.

```
In[6]:= Manipulate[Labeled[
          Graphics[{{Brown, Polygon[Table[( c 0
                                            0 c ).v, {v, dog}]]}}, Line[dog]},
             Axes → True, PlotRange → 10], (* the label *)
          ( c 0
            0 c ) // displayMatrix, {{Right, Top}}],
          {{c, 2.75}, .2, 5}]
```

Out[6]=

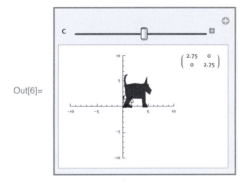

We can rotate a figure in two dimensions through an angle θ using the standard rotation matrix.

```
In[7]:= RotationMatrix[θ] // MatrixForm
```
Out[7]//MatrixForm=
$$\begin{pmatrix} \cos[\theta] & -\sin[\theta] \\ \sin[\theta] & \cos[\theta] \end{pmatrix}$$

```
In[8]:= Manipulate[Labeled[
          Graphics[{{Brown, Polygon[Table[RotationMatrix[θ].v, {v, dog}]]},
            Line[dog]}, Axes → True, PlotRange → 4, PlotLabel → "Bad Dog"],
          (* the label *)RotationMatrix[θ] // displayMatrix, {{Right, Top}}],
          {{θ, .8}, 0, 2 π}]
```

Out[8]=

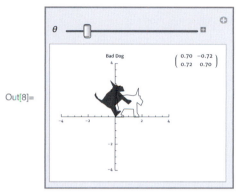

We can compose linear transformations by multiplying the individual matrices for the transformations. Below we've combined a reflection about the *x* axis with a dilation and a rotation.

```
In[9]:= Manipulate[With[{m = (1  0 ) . (c  0) . RotationMatrix[θ]},
                        (0 -1)   (0  c)
          Labeled[Graphics[{{Brown, Polygon[Table[m.v, {v, dog}]]},
            Line[dog]}, Axes → True, PlotRange → 10],
          (* the label *)
          Row[{MatrixForm[(1  0 )], ".", displayMatrix[(c  0)], ".",
                          (0 -1)                        (0  c)
            displayMatrix[RotationMatrix[θ]], "=", displayMatrix[m]}],
          Top]], {{θ, 2}, 0, 2 π}, {{c, 2.5}, 1, 4}]
```

Out[9]=

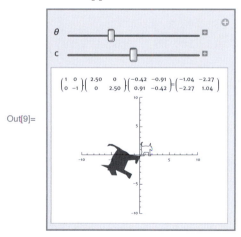

In three dimensions, we can easily access any of the dozens of polyhedra available in the Polyhedron Data collection, or any of the Geometry3D objects in the ExampleData collection. Here, for instance, is the *space shuttle*:

In[11]:= **ExampleData[{"Geometry3D", "SpaceShuttle"}]**

Out[11]=

We can easily extract its vertex coordinates as follows (to save space we display only the first few):

In[12]:= **vertices =**
    N@ExampleData[{"Geometry3D", "SpaceShuttle"}, "VertexData"];
    Take[vertices, 10]

Out[13]= {{-4.99949, -0.68171, 0.569242}, {-4.99976, -0.491153, 0.805206},
    {-5.34948, -0.470935, 0.566062}, {-4.99976, 0.491153, 0.805206},
    {-4.90671, 0.620194, 0.686502}, {-4.99949, 0.68171, 0.569242},
    {-5.29975, -0.147914, 0.811038}, {-5.56803, -0.1192, 0.568687},
    {-4.90671, -0.620194, 0.686502}, {-5.56803, 0.1192, 0.568687}}

Collections of these vertices are assembled to make the polygonal faces. The first face, for instance, is a triangle composed of the first, second, and third vertices in the above list. The third face utilizes vertices three, seven, and eight.

In[14]:= **faces = ExampleData[{"Geometry3D", "SpaceShuttle"}, "PolygonData"];**
    Take[faces, 10]

Out[15]= {{1, 2, 3}, {4, 5, 6}, {3, 7, 8}, {1, 9, 2}, {7, 3, 2},
    {10, 11, 12}, {12, 4, 6}, {12, 11, 4}, {13, 14, 15}, {16, 17, 18}}

In total there are 310 vertices and 393 faces:

In[16]:= **{Length[vertices], Length[faces]}**

Out[16]= {310, 393}

We can reassemble this information into a three-dimensional graphic using GraphicsComplex, like this:

In[17]:= `Graphics3D[{EdgeForm[], GraphicsComplex[vertices, Polygon[faces]]}]`

Out[17]=

So, proceeding as in the two-dimensional case, we dynamically display the figure resulting from the application of a linear transformation to each of the vertices of the figure above. For instance, below we show the effect of composing rotations about each of the three coordinate axes, respectively:

In[18]:=
```
Manipulate[
    With[{m = RotationMatrix[θ, {1, 0, 0}].RotationMatrix[ϕ, {0, 1, 0}].
        RotationMatrix[φ, {0, 0, 1}], vertices =
      N@ExampleData[{"Geometry3D", "SpaceShuttle"}, "VertexData"],
      faces = ExampleData[{"Geometry3D", "SpaceShuttle"},
        "PolygonData"]},
     Labeled[
      Graphics3D[{EdgeForm[],
        GraphicsComplex[Table[m.v, {v, vertices}], Polygon[faces]]},
        PlotRange → 8], displayMatrix[m], {{Right, Top}}]],
    {{θ, .5}, 0, 2 π}, {ϕ, 0, 2 π}, {φ, 0, 2 π}]
```

Out[18]=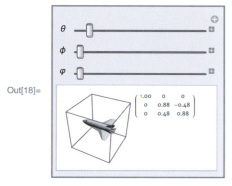

Exercises 7.9

1. Make a simple line drawing and construct its reflection about the x axis using an appropriate linear transformation.

2. One can apply matrix transformations to each vertex in any of the objects in the `PolyhedronData` collection.

    a. Enter the input below to render a *square gyrobicupola*:

        `PolyhedronData["SquareGyrobicupola"]`

    b. Extract the vertices and face indices for this polyhedron. Hint: A similar extraction was carried out in the text for the *space shuttle*. The syntax is slightly different here, however. The relevant properties are now called `"VertexCoordinates"` and `"FaceIndices"`. Type `PolyhedronData["SquareGyro` `bicupola","Properties"]` for a listing of *all* available properties.

    c. How many vertices and faces are there in this example?

    d. Construct a `Manipulate` that will enable you to rotate the polyhedron about any of the three coordinate axes.

8

Programming

8.1 Introduction

When you put several commands together to accomplish some purpose beyond the capacity of any individual command, you are *programming*. The Wolfram Language is intentionally designed for this purpose. Like anything else, getting good at programming takes practice. But it is also exceedingly handy to have familiarity with commands that lend themselves to such greater enterprises. We've seen plenty of *Mathematica* in the first seven chapters; in this chapter we'll discuss commands that are especially useful for programming. Keep in mind that we only have room here for a brief introduction to these concepts. Entire books, much longer than this one, have been written on this subject. Think of this chapter as a gentle introduction.

We begin in Section 8.2 with some important background material, a consideration of the *internal* form of any and every Wolfram Language expression. Every expression, input, output (or a cell, or an entire notebook) is highly structured. Before it is possible to operate on any such expression, you simply have to know what you are dealing with. You have to understand its *structure*.

Some of the most fundamental structures in the Wolfram Language are the various types of numbers. These are addressed in Section 8.3. The internal forms of the various types of numbers are discussed, along with notions such as precision and accuracy. *Mathematica* has the capacity to carry out calculations to arbitrarily high precision. In this section we also discuss a myriad of possibilities for the display of numbers.

Section 8.4 introduces the workhorses of *functional programming*, commands like Map and Function and MapThread. Section 8.5 introduces the staples of procedural programming, with predicate commands (that return True or False), and control structures and looping commands such as If, Do, While, and For. These commands instruct *Mathematica* to carry out a sequence of instructions, and similar commands are often among the first encountered when one learns an elementary programming language.

Section 8.6 discusses commands that limit the scope of auxiliary functions and symbols that are sometimes needed in programming. These *scoping commands* are essential to insulate local definitions from any global assignments that a user might make. Section 8.7 introduces the essential commands that facilitate iteration, such as NestList, NestWhileList, FoldList, and Fixed‑PointList. Finally, Section 8.8 discusses patterns and pattern matching in the context of defining commands, making replacements, and for use in specific commands like Cases.

8.2 FullForm: What the Kernel Sees

Every Wolfram Language expression is either an *atom* or a *nested expression*. An atom is the most simple type of expression: a number, a symbol, a string. It is an expression that cannot be decomposed into simpler component pieces. The AtomQ command will tell you if an expression is atomic. Here are a few examples:

In[1]:= `Clear[a, x];`
`Grid[Table[{exp, AtomQ[exp]}, {exp, {2, 2.0, 2 / 3, 2 + 3 i, π,`
`    a, Plot3D, Sin, "a string", 2 + a, a[x]}}], Dividers → Gray]`

Out[2]=

2	True
2.	True
$\frac{2}{3}$	True
2 + 3 i	True
π	True
a	True
Plot3D	True
Sin	True
a string	True
2 + a	False
a[x]	False

A nested expression has the form head[*arg1*, *arg2*, ...]. The head is typically atomic (it is usually a command name, although it may itself be a nested expression), and the arguments are either nested expressions or atoms. The arguments are enclosed in square brackets (typically there are one or more arguments, but zero arguments are permitted). The command Head will display the head of any nested expression. Here are a few examples (for each expression in the left column, its head appears in the right column):

In[3]:= `Clear[a, b, c, g, x, y, myCommand];`
`Grid[Table[{exp, Head[exp]}, {exp,`
`    {myCommand[x], g[x, y], a[b[x, y], c], a[b][c]}}], Dividers → Gray]`

Out[3]=

myCommand[x]	myCommand
g[x, y]	g
a[b[x, y], c]	a
a[b][c]	a[b]

Even the expression a[b][c] qualifies as a legitimate nested expression. The head is the nested expression a[b].

Every non-atomic Wolfram Language expression has this form, a head followed by square brackets enclosing zero or more arguments.

That last statement should give you pause. Consider the expression 2 + a. It is not atomic (we saw this in the second to last output above), so what is the head? Where are the square brackets? What are the arguments? It does not appear to have the form head[*arg1*, *arg2*, ...]. What gives?

> In[4]:= **Head[2 + a]**
>
> Out[4]= Plus

What's going on is that the internal or FullForm of this expression is not revealed when we type 2 + a. These paltry three characters are parsed into the following before being sent to the kernel for evaluation:

> In[5]:= **2 + a // FullForm**
>
> Out[5]//FullForm=
>
> Plus[2, a]

Ah, so this expression *does* have the form of a nested expression after all, and the head is indeed Plus. *Mathematica* allows you to type 2 + a because you're a human, and that's what you're used to (this is called the *infix form* of the Plus command). In this and in dozens of other cases you are permitted to create expressions that do not look like proper nested expressions. This flexibility is granted simply to make your interactions with *Mathematica* more natural, and to make the typing as simple as possible. But in each of these cases your input is parsed into a properly structured nested expression before being sent to the kernel. It is crucial to understand this fact if you are to program effectively in *Mathematica*. FullForm is a great tool for peeking under the hood to view the internal form of any *Mathematica* expression. Here are some other examples (for each expression in the left column we show its FullForm in the right column):

> In[6]:= **Grid[Table[{exp, FullForm[exp]}, {exp,**
>
> **{2 + a, 2 * a, -a, 2^a, $\sqrt{a}$, 2 / a, π, e, {2, a}, _, a_, a__, a[[1]],**
>
> **a && b, a || b, ! a, a → 2, a /. b, a //. b, a == b, a ≠ b, a < b, a ≤ b,**
>
> **a ∈ Reals, a ~~ b, a'[x], $\int$a[x] dx}}], Dividers → Gray] // Quiet**

2 + a	Plus[2, a]
2 a	Times[2, a]
- a	Times[-1, a]
2^a	Power[2, a]
$\sqrt{a}$	Power[a, Rational[1, 2]]
$\frac{2}{a}$	Times[2, Power[a, -1]]
π	Pi
e	E
{2, a}	List[2, a]
_	Blank[]
a_	Pattern[a, Blank[]]
a__	Pattern[a, BlankSequence[]]
a⟦1⟧	Part[a, 1]
a && b	And[a, b]
a || b	Or[a, b]
! a	Not[a]
a → 2	Rule[a, 2]
a /.b	ReplaceAll[a, b]
a //.b	ReplaceRepeated[a, b]
a == b	Equal[a, b]
a ≠ b	Unequal[a, b]
a < b	Less[a, b]
a ≤ b	LessEqual[a, b]
a ∈ Reals	Element[a, Reals]
a ~~ b	StringExpression[a, b]
a′[x]	Derivative[1][a][x]
∫a[x] dx	Integrate[a[x], x]

Out[6]=

⚠ Note that Quiet has been applied (in postfix form) in the previous input. This suppresses all warning messages. In this case, for instance, the a /. b input generates a warning message that b is neither a replacement rule nor a list of replacement rules.

Note that FullForm can be subtle to use in some cases, as an expression may evaluate before Full: Form is applied. If one enters FullForm[a = b], for instance, the expression a = b evaluates and returns b, and then the FullForm of b (which is simply b) is displayed. In fact, the FullForm of a = b is Set[a, b]. In such cases, wrapping the expression in Defer will prevent this sort of premature evaluation.

In[7]:= **FullForm[a = b]**

Out[7]//FullForm=

    b

```
In[8]:=  Defer[FullForm[a = b]]
Out[8]=  Set[a, b]
```

```
In[9]:=  Defer[FullForm[a := b]]
Out[9]=  SetDelayed[a, b]
```

Understanding the structure of the Wolfram Language allows you to do many things. One clearly sees at this point, for instance, the internal distinctions between the symbols =, :=, and ==. They correspond respectively to the commands Set, SetDelayed, and Equal. You will soon be able to harness your knowledge of the structure of expressions to operate in interesting ways on complex expressions. This is the essence of programming in the Wolfram Language.

One last symbol deserves our attention in this context: the semicolon. We have used this symbol to suppress output on many occasions. It also allows us to evaluate several commands in a single input cell, like this:

```
In[10]:=  a = 3; 2 a
Out[10]=  6
```

The FullForm of the input above can be seen via Defer:

```
In[11]:=  Defer[FullForm[a = 3; 2 a]]
Out[11]=  CompoundExpression[Set[a, 3], Times[2, a]]
```

And here is the FullForm of an expression that *ends* in a semicolon:

```
In[12]:=  Defer[FullForm[a = 3;]]
Out[12]=  CompoundExpression[Set[a, 3], Null]
```

The command is CompoundExpression, and each argument is itself an expression. The arguments are evaluated in turn, but only the output associated with the expression in the final argument is displayed. CompoundExpression is an invaluable tool in writing *Mathematica* programs, for it allows several inputs to be evaluated in turn, one after the other, with only the output of the last input displayed.

Here's one more example that may be revealing. Copy any graphic you like into an input cell, and ask for its FullForm or InputForm to see its underlying structure. In this case we used the Drawing Tools palette to create a simple image with the Line Segments tool.

In[13]:= ⟩⟨⟩ // FullForm

Out[13]//FullForm=

```
Graphics[
  List[Line[List[List[0.21111111111111117`, 0.8333333333333334`],
      List[0.2972222222222223`, 0.5972222222222223`],
      List[0.18611111111111114`, 0.41666666666666674`],
      List[0.31666666666666665`, 0.1972222222222222`]]],
    Line[List[List[0.5611111111111111`, 0.8361111111111111`],
      List[0.4722222222222222`, 0.6027777777777779`],
      List[0.5722222222222222`, 0.40000000000000013`],
      List[0.4833333333333334`, 0.19999999999999996`]]],
    Line[List[List[0.7527777777777778`, 0.8305555555555556`],
      List[0.8611111111111112`, 0.6222222222222222`],
      List[0.7361111111111112`, 0.3944444444444444`],
      List[0.8166666666666667`, 0.18055555555555558`]]]],
  Rule[PlotRange, List[List[0, 1], List[0, 1]]]]]
```

⚠ In fact, Mathematica notebooks are themselves valid nested expressions. If you
were to open a Mathematica notebook in a text editor, you would see a plain
text file with the structure Notebook[arg1, arg2, ...]. The individual arguments in a notebook are cells, and every cell is a nested expression in its own
right, of the form Cell[arg1, arg2, ...], and so on. This state of affairs is most
definitely intentional, and is even a little bit devious. It is devious in that the
FrontEnd does not reveal the highly structured nature of the underlying document, just as it does not reveal the FullForm of expressions such as $\sqrt{a}$,
unless you for ask it. But underneath, the structure is there. The benefit (and a
distinguishing feature of Mathematica) is that you have access to this underlying
form. Because cells and even entire notebooks have the structure of a valid
expression, it is possible to program Mathematica to operate on an entire
notebook. This was done, for example, in the writing of this book. Each chapter
in this book is a Mathematica notebook. The entire notebook expressions for all
of the chapter files were sent to the kernel to programmatically generate the
table of contents. They were sent again to make the index, and so on. While the
details of these specific techniques lie beyond the scope of this book, it is
important to understand the potential for operating programmatically on an
entire notebook.

Exercises 8.2

1. Find the Head of each of the following expressions:

   a.   x → 2

   b. $\sqrt{2}$

   c.   {1, 2, 3}

   d.   # + 1 &

2. Find the FullForm of each of the following expressions:

   a.   x → 2

   b.   1/2

   c. $\sqrt{2}$

   d.   {1, 2, 3}

3. What is the head of the expression a'[x]? Find its FullForm, and base your answer on what you see. Check your answer with Head.

4. What is the FullForm of the expression 2x + 1 /. x → 3? Use Defer and FullForm to find out.

5. What is the FullForm of the expression x = 3; 2x? Use Defer and FullForm to find out.

6. The command TreeForm produces a visual representation of the FullForm of any expression. Find the TreeForm of the expression 2x + 1 /. x → 3.

7. The Part command was introduced in Chapter 3 to extract a part of a list. It is typically invoked via typing double square brackets. For instance the input {a, b, c}[[2]] will produce the output b. But Part can also be used to extract parts of compound Wolfram Language expressions.

   a.   Apply TreeForm to the input a ∗ b + c ∗ d².

   b.   Extract the zeroth, first, and second parts of this same input.

   c.   Find parts [[2,1]] and [[2,2]].

   d.   Find parts [[2,2,1]] and [[2,2,2]].

8. Go to the Graphics menu, create a new graphic, bring up the Drawing Tools palette, and draw an arrow. Copy the arrow graphic into a new input cell, and apply TreeForm to the result.

9. A String in the Wolfram Language is any collection of characters or symbols enclosed in double quotations. Strings are atomic expressions. There are many commands available to operate on strings, but one of the most basic is StringExpression. StringExpression[*string1*, *string2*] will concatenate the two strings *string1* and *string2* into a single string. The infix form of StringExpression is ~~. That is, one may invoke StringExpression by typing *string1*~~*string2*.

   a.   Type and enter a string. What do you see? What do you see if you apply FullForm to the input?

   b.   Apply FullForm to the input "I am"~~" putting strings together."

   c.   Apply Defer to the input FullForm["a"~~"b"].

d.   The command `ToString` will take any expression and convert it to a string. It is often used in conjunction with `StringExpression` to create a string that depends on some external input. Use `ToString` and `StringExpression` to create a command that will take a numerical input *n* and return the string `"n is my favorite number."`

10. A notebook is composed of cells. Each cell expression in a notebook has the head `Cell`. To see the underlying form of a `Cell` expression requires a special technique, as the FrontEnd will display `Cell` expressions nicely, that is, in a manner which hides the underlying structure of the expression.

a.   Click anywhere in any cell in any notebook, and in the menus go to Cell ▷ ShowExpression. The underlying cell structure will be revealed. In this state, you can edit it directly if you like. Then toggle it back to normal with the same technique. Try this on several different cells in one of your notebooks.

b.   A `Cell` is a versatile structure, capable of many forms, from input to output to text to graphics. So it may not be surprising to learn that `Cell` accepts a myriad of options. How many options would you guess `Cell` can accept? Test your answer using the `Options` command.

8.3   Numbers

Types of Numbers: Integer, Rational, Real, and Complex

When working with a calculator or spreadsheet, one is typically not concerned with whether one enters a whole number (such as 12) or a decimal number (such as 12.0). These are, after all, the same number. In *Mathematica*, however, they are treated very differently, and for a good reason. Decimal numbers are cursed with an inherent ambiguity stemming from the fact that while there are an infinite number of decimal places, we cannot possibly write them all. There are two distinct ways to interpret a decimal number presented with finitely many decimal places. In one, we interpret the number as an approximation, such as when writing $\pi \approx 3.14159$. We understand that we are seeing only a few digits in the expansion, and that we are not seeing the remaining digits. In the other interpretation, we agree that all digits beyond those that are displayed are zero, such as when writing $1/4 = .25$. Unfortunately, when one gives a computer a decimal number such as 3.14159 or .25, there is no way for the computer to know which situation you are in. When you type .25, should the computer interpret that to mean $1/4$, or should it instead read it as the first two digits of some potentially longer number, whose other decimal places are not known? *Mathematica* chooses the latter: It treats all decimal numbers as *approximations*, where only the given decimal digits are known, and where all additional decimal digits are treated as unknown. *Mathematica* refers to such numbers as `Real` numbers.

By contrast, an `Integer`, or whole number, is exact. There is no ambiguity. Likewise, fractions with integer numerator and denominator are also exact. Such fractions are called `Rational` numbers. While all numbers are atomic expressions in the Wolfram Language, the `Head` command (introduced in the last section) can be used to distinguish them.

```
In[1]:=  Head[12.0]
Out[1]=  Real
```

In[2]:= **Head[12]**

Out[2]= Integer

In[3]:= **Head[12 / 7]**

Out[3]= Rational

It is often a shock for new *Mathematica* users to encounter output such as the following:

In[4]:= $\dfrac{22}{7}$

Out[4]= $\dfrac{22}{7}$

Mathematica simply will not convert an Integer or Rational number to a Real, unless instructed to do so. In cases where you seek a decimal output, either enter at least one Real number in the input, or use the N command to convert it for you. Note that typing 22. is the same as writing 22.0.

In[5]:= $\dfrac{22.}{7}$

Out[5]= 3.14286

In[6]:= $\dfrac{22}{7}$ **// N**

Out[6]= 3.14286

In addition to Integer, Rational, and Real numbers, there are also complex numbers, such as 2+3i, where i represents the square root of −1. Regardless of which type of numbers comprise the individual real and imaginary components of such a number, *Mathematica* treats the entire expression as a Complex number.

In[7]:= **Head[2 + 3 i]**

Out[7]= Complex

In[8]:= **Head[2.0 + 3.0 i]**

Out[8]= Complex

Displaying Numbers

It is important to understand that while real (decimal) numbers are by default *displayed* with six significant digits, internally they are stored to at least machine precision (usually 16 significant digits). Perhaps you have already discovered this; if you copy a real number from an output cell and then paste it into a new input cell you will see the "full" machine representation of the number. Alternately, you can use the command InputForm to display all the digits of a real number.

```
In[9]:=  N[π]
Out[9]=  3.14159
```

```
In[10]:=  N[π] // InputForm
Out[10]//InputForm=
          3.141592653589793
```

Note *Mathematica*'s InputForm for scientific notation:

```
In[11]:=  N[π * 10²⁰] // InputForm
Out[11]//InputForm=
          3.1415926535897933*^20
```

It is possible to display all the digits of a real number in any format you can imagine. While *Mathematica*'s InputForm is handy for peeking under the hood, a more practical command for displaying numbers is NumberForm. Here, for example, we see the first 12 digits of π (including the digit to the left of the decimal point).

```
In[12]:=  NumberForm[N[π], 12]
Out[12]//NumberForm=
          3.14159265359
```

This is not too exciting, as it looks like the output for N[π,12]. However, if the second argument to NumberForm is a list of *two* positive integers, the first number specifies the total number of digits to be displayed and the second specifies the number of digits to the *right of the decimal.* This can be very useful. Here we see the first ten decimal places of π (compare the output carefully with the output above; NumberForm displays the number *rounded* to the correct number of specified digits):

```
In[13]:=  NumberForm[N[π], {11, 10}]
Out[13]//NumberForm=
          3.1415926536
```

Unneeded digits on the left will not be displayed.

```
In[14]:=  NumberForm[1.0, {10, 5}]
Out[14]//NumberForm=
          1.00000
```

However the option NumberPadding allows you to specify characters to pad the areas to the left and right of the displayed digits.

```
In[15]:=  NumberForm[1.0, {10, 5}, NumberPadding → {"□", "0"}]
Out[15]//NumberForm=
          □□□□□□1.00000
```

The padding on the left in the output above appears to have one extra character; this is the space reserved for the sign character in the case of negative numbers:

In[16]:= `NumberForm[-1.0, {10, 5}, NumberPadding → {"▫", "0"}]`

Out[16]//NumberForm=

▫ ▫ ▫ ▫ -1.00000

A similar command is `PaddedForm`, which works essentially the same way as `NumberForm`, but it will also "pad" the number with white space on the left, leaving room to accommodate all the requested digits (and the sign character). Using `PaddedForm` will often free you from having to add a `Number` `Padding` option to `NumberForm`.

In[17]:= `NumberForm[1.0, {10, 5}]`
`NumberForm[1.0, {10, 5}, NumberPadding → {" ", "0"}]`
`PaddedForm[1.0, {10, 5}]`

Out[17]//NumberForm=

1.00000

Out[18]//NumberForm=

1.00000

Out[19]//PaddedForm=

1.00000

`PaddedForm` is useful for displaying numbers in a table so that numbers in a column are all displayed with the same number of places to the right of the decimal, and with decimal points aligned.

In[20]:= `Table[{n, PaddedForm[N[n * π], {5, 2}]}, {n, 0, 6}] // Grid`

0	0.00
1	3.14
2	6.28
3	9.42
4	12.57
5	15.71
6	18.85

Out[20]=

Numbers that are very small or very large, however, will disturb the neat display above. Such numbers will (sensibly enough) be displayed in scientific notation (with the requested two places shown to the right of the decimal):

In[21]:= `PaddedForm[.000001234, {12, 2}]`

Out[21]//PaddedForm=

$$1.23 \times 10^{-6}$$

In[22]:= `PaddedForm[1 001 234.5678, {12, 2}]`

Out[22]//PaddedForm=

$$1.00 \times 10^{6}$$

If you do not want such numbers represented in scientific notation (for instance, if you are displaying monetary values and want your answer in dollars and cents), both `NumberForm` and `PaddedForm` accept the option setting `ExponentFunction → (Null&)`, which prohibits the display of exponents.

In[23]:= `PaddedForm[.000001234, {12, 2}, ExponentFunction → (Null &)]`

Out[23]//PaddedForm=

                              0.00

In[24]:= `PaddedForm[1 001 234.5678, {12, 2}, ExponentFunction → (Null &)]`

Out[24]//PaddedForm=

                      1001234.57

If your goal is to avoid the exponents of scientific notation, but you don't need number padding on the left side, `DecimalForm` provides a simpler option.

In[25]:= `DecimalForm[.000001234, {12, 2}]`

Out[25]//DecimalForm=

              0.00

In[26]:= `DecimalForm[1 001 234.5678, {12, 2}]`

Out[26]//DecimalForm=

              1001234.57

This mechanism provides a sensible means of representing quantities such as money, where precisely two decimal places should be displayed. The following command could be used whenever a monetary value x is to be shown. This particular implementation allows for at most ten digits to the left of the decimal.

In[27]:= `Clear[dollar];`
         `dollar[x_] := PaddedForm[N[x], {12, 2}, ExponentFunction → (Null &)]`

In[29]:= `{dollar[0.0049], dollar[0.0050], dollar[π], dollar[10⁹ π]} // Column`

Out[29]=

                      0.00
                      0.01
                      3.14
              3141592653.59

Suppose you have one dollar, and it loses 1/3 of its value each year. Here's what happens to your dollar over time. The second column shows the numerical value to the default six significant digits, while the third column displays this same value rounded to the nearest cent:

In[30]:= `Grid[Table[{n, N[(2/3)`^{n}`], dollar[(2/3)`^{n}`]}, {n, 0, 15}],`
`Alignment → ".", Dividers → Gray]`

Out[30]=

0	1.	1.00
1	0.666667	0.67
2	0.444444	0.44
3	0.296296	0.30
4	0.197531	0.20
5	0.131687	0.13
6	0.0877915	0.09
7	0.0585277	0.06
8	0.0390184	0.04
9	0.0260123	0.03
10	0.0173415	0.02
11	0.011561	0.01
12	0.00770735	0.01
13	0.00513823	0.01
14	0.00342549	0.00
15	0.00228366	0.00

More complex structures such as loan amortization tables can be built in a similar fashion.

If the number we wish to display is an *exact* integer (no decimal point) we need not specify digits of precision, and scientific notation will not be used.

In[31]:= `NumberForm[10`^{30}`]`

Out[31]//NumberForm=

`1000000000000000000000000000000`

But very large numbers are easier for humans to read if the digits are blocked in, say, groups of three. `NumberForm` and `PaddedForm` have an option called `DigitBlock` to allow for this sort of display. In fact there are a host of options that allow you full control over the display of numbers. Look up `NumberForm` in the Documentation Center for more information.

In[32]:= `NumberForm[10`^{30}`, DigitBlock → 3]`
`NumberForm[10`^{30}`, DigitBlock → 5, NumberSeparator → " "]`

Out[32]//NumberForm=

`1,000,000,000,000,000,000,000,000,000,000`

Out[33]//NumberForm=

`1 00000 00000 00000 00000 00000 00000`

Note that in desktop versions you can go into *Mathematica*'s Preferences panel and make global adjustments to these settings. In the Preferences panel, look under Appearance ▷ Numbers ▷ Format‐ ting, and tweak to your heart's content. This will invoke your display preferences for every session.

In this example we modify the command `dollar` to use three-digit blocks:

```
In[34]:= Clear[dollar];
        dollar[x_] :=
          PaddedForm[N[x], {12, 2}, ExponentFunction → (Null &), DigitBlock → 3]
In[36]:= dollar[10⁹]
```
Out[36]//PaddedForm=

        1,000,000,000.00

`NumberForm` and its cousin `PaddedForm` have several other close relatives, including `DecimalForm`, `ScientificForm`, `EngineeringForm`, and `AccountingForm`. These work in much the same way, but have different default settings. Information can be found in the Documentation Center.

Precision and Accuracy

Here's an experiment. Find another program on your computer that is capable of doing arithmetic, for instance a calculator program or a spreadsheet. Ask that program to evaluate 2^{1023} and 2^{1024}. Now try it in *Mathematica*. As with any calculation, with *Mathematica* you can ask for a numerical approximation or an exact answer:

```
In[37]:= N[2^1023, 10]
```
Out[37]= $8.988465674 \times 10^{307}$

```
In[38]:= 2^1024
```
Out[38]= 179 769 313 486 231 590 772 930 519 078 902 473 361 797 697 894 230 657 273 430 ⸱
          081 157 732 675 805 500 963 132 708 477 322 407 536 021 120 113 879 871 393 357 ⸱
          658 789 768 814 416 622 492 847 430 639 474 124 377 767 893 424 865 485 276 302 ⸱
          219 601 246 094 119 453 082 952 085 005 768 838 150 682 342 462 881 473 913 110 ⸱
          540 827 237 163 350 510 684 586 298 239 947 245 938 479 716 304 835 356 329 624 ⸱
          224 137 216

In most cases you'll find that other programs will give an answer like the output above for 2^{1023}, but they will choke on 2^{1024}, and fail to produce an answer. This is because most programs rely on your computer's hardware, in particular on its floating point unit (FPU), to carry out arithmetic operations. And this number is simply too big for most FPUs commonly in use at the time of this writing. It's a matter that most of us rarely think about, but while the real number system is infinite, the number system utilized by most FPUs (commonly IEEE double–precision floating point arithmetic) is finite. That is, there is a finite quantity of numbers available in this system, and so there is necessarily a *largest* number. In most systems it happens to be just under 2^{1024}. The boundary occurs at a power of two since the FPU converts numbers to base 2 before operating on them. You can have *Mathematica* query your hardware and determine the largest number supported by the FPU on your machine by entering the following:

In[39]:= `$MaxMachineNumber`

Out[39]= 1.79769×10^{308}

In[40]:= `N[2^1024]`

Out[40]= $1.797693134862316 \times 10^{308}$

Mathematica handles numbers differently than most other programs. It will make use of your computer's FPU whenever possible in order to save time, since hardware is generally several orders of magnitude faster than software. But when you input a real number too large, too small, or too precise for the FPU to handle, or if the result of evaluating your input produces such a number, *Mathematica* will seamlessly switch into high−precision mode, abandoning the FPU and carrying out the calculation itself. In one sense you never need to worry about it, for it happens automatically. In another sense, it is useful to understand just how *Mathematica* interprets real numbers so that you can better understand its output, and so that you can manually switch to high−precision arithmetic should you desire to do so.

For instance, enter the following input. Then select the output with your mouse, copy it, and paste it into a new input cell. This is what you will see:

In[41]:= `N[π]`

Out[41]= `3.14159`

```
3.141592653589793`
```
This procedure causes *Mathematica* to give you a peek under the hood at how it views this number. You can also force *Mathematica* to show it to you with the command `FullForm` (the command `Input Form` will also display all the digits of the number, but it does not display the backquote character `` ` ``).

In[42]:= `N[π] // FullForm`

Out[42]//FullForm=
```
3.141592653589793`
```

We already know that the `N` command will by default display only six significant digits of a number, while internally there is a machine number lurking underneath. Machine numbers, that is, numbers accessible to your computer's FPU, never have more than a fixed number of significant digits, usually 16. We will use the term *precision* to indicate how many significant digits a real number has, and hence we say that machine numbers generally have a precision of 16. Machine numbers are identified (in `FullForm`) by the backquote `` ` `` appearing as the final character. If you ever copy and paste a number and see these extra digits and backquote character, don't worry. Numbers can be input in this form and the output is no different than it would otherwise be.

In[43]:= `100 * 3.15159`

Out[43]= `315.159`

```
In[44]:= 100 * 3.141592653589793`
```
```
Out[44]= 314.159
```

One way to input a high−precision number is to type a decimal number with a total of more than 16 digits. Another is to use N, specifying (with the second argument) more than 16 digits of precision.

```
In[45]:= N[2, 40]
```
```
Out[45]= 2.000000000000000000000000000000000000000
```

If you copy and paste the output above, or apply FullForm to it, you will see the internal structure of a high−precision number:

```
In[46]:= N[2, 40] // FullForm
```
```
Out[46]//FullForm=
        2.`40.
```

The FullForm of a high precision number is the number itself followed by the backquote character ` followed by the number's precision. High−precision numbers may also be entered directly this way:

```
In[47]:= 2`40
```
```
Out[47]= 2.000000000000000000000000000000000000000
```

In order to understand the internal form for *any* high−precision number, we just combine the notation above with the internal form for scientific notation (discussed in the previous subsection). For example:

```
In[48]:= N[2 * 10^100, 40] // FullForm
```
```
Out[48]//FullForm=
        2.`40.*^100
```

A simple way to force *Mathematica* to jump into high−precision mode when evaluating an input is to make sure *every* number appearing in the input is a high−precision number. If any single number in the input has only machine precision, the answer can be no more precise. The Precision command displays the precision of any quantity.

```
In[49]:= Precision[2`40]
```
```
Out[49]= 40.
```

```
In[50]:= Precision[N[2, 40]]
```
```
Out[50]= 40.
```

```
In[51]:= Precision[2.]
```
```
Out[51]= MachinePrecision
```

When high−precision numbers are combined arithmetically, the precision is no greater than that of the least precise number in the input.

In[52]:= `N[2, 40] * N[2, 30]`

Out[52]= `4.0000000000000000000000000000000`

In[53]:= `Precision[%]`

Out[53]= `30.`

However, with some operations the precision can decrease below that of the least precise number in the input. In the following example it is useful to think of each number as an infinite decimal number, the first few digits of which are 2 followed by 29 or 39 zeros. When subtracted, their difference begins 0.000000 … (with 29 zeros after the decimal point), but beyond that nothing is known. No *significant* digits of the difference can be surmised. The precision is 0.

In[54]:= `N[2, 30] – N[2, 40]`

Out[54]= $0. \times 10^{-30}$

In[55]:= `Precision[%]`

Out[55]= `0.`

This may seem unfair. However, we do know that the result is zero to 29 decimal places, even though we don't know any of the actual nonzero digits of the difference. The command `Accuracy` will tell you (roughly) how many digits to the right of the decimal point are known to be correct.

In[56]:= `Accuracy[%%]`

Out[56]= `29.699`

The following won't give a high–precision number, since the machine precision number 2.0 appears in the input. You cannot take a machine precision real number and increase its precision. In fact, you cannot do any operation involving a machine precision number and end up with high precision output.

In[57]:= `N[2., 40]`

Out[57]= `2.`

In[58]:= `Precision[%]`

Out[58]= `MachinePrecision`

Finally, note that exact numbers have infinite precision:

In[59]:= `Precision[2]`

Out[59]= ∞

In[60]:= `Precision[`π`]`

Out[60]= ∞

Exercises 8.3

1. You may be familiar with the parable about the peasant who is to be rewarded by the king with many sacks of rice. The peasant says, "Why don't you simply give me one grain of rice the first day, two the second day, four the third day, and so on, each day giving me twice the quantity of the previous day, and do this for one month?" The king, thinking this will cost less, agrees. Make a table showing how many grains of rice the king owes each day, from day one to day 31. Use `DigitBlocks` of length three to make the numbers easy to read.

2. In this section we advocate the use of `PaddedForm` to display numbers in a table or column, each with the same number of decimal places and with the decimal points aligned. Another technique for accomplishing such alignment without necessarily restricting the number of decimal places is with the `Alignment` option in the `Grid` and `Column` commands. Look up this option in the Documentation Center, and use it to display the `Table` below in a column. You may also wish to consult Exercise 6 in Section 3.5.

In[1]:= `Table[10`^{n}` * N[`π`], {n, 0, 5}]`

Out[1]= `{3.14159, 31.4159, 314.159, 3141.59, 31415.9, 314159.}`

8.4 Map and Function

Two fundamental programming commands, `Map` and `Function`, are introduced in this section. An understanding of these commands is something that distinguishes a Wolfram Language power user from a casual user. They will facilitate your being able to do powerful list manipulations, and expand your capability to perform certain tasks with great efficiency. We'll tackle them one at a time, then show how they can be used together.

`Map` is a command for applying a function to each member of a list. For instance, we can test a list of numbers to see which of the numbers are primes:

In[1]:= `Map[PrimeQ, {2, 3, 4, 5, 6}]`

Out[1]= `{True, True, False, True, False}`

Or we can apply an undefined function to a list of undefined quantities:

In[2]:= `Clear[f, a, b, c];`
        `Map[f, {a, b, c}]`

Out[3]= `{f[a], f[b], f[c]}`

The first argument of `Map` is a function or command. The second argument is a list. The members of the list are fed to the function, one by one, and the resulting list of values is returned.

There is a commonly used infix syntax for `Map`. Instead of typing `Map[`*f*`, `*list*`]`, one can instead type *f* `/@` *list*. Effectively, one can `Map` a function over a list with just two keystrokes:

In[4]:= `f /@ {a, b, c}`

Out[4]= `{f[a], f[b], f[c]}`

This will seem strange at first, but it is akin to typing $2 + 3$ instead of the more formal `Plus[2, 3]`. It departs from the standard "square bracket" notation employed by most *Mathematica* commands. With a bit of practice, however, it's quite natural.

We now turn our attention to a second command, `Function`, which is typically used to construct functions that are used only once (for instance, functions to be `Map`ped over a list). In order to create a function that squares its argument, for example, and apply it to every item in a list, either of these inputs will do:

In[5]:= `Map[Function[x, x²], {a, b, c}]`

Out[5]= $\{a^2, b^2, c^2\}$

In[6]:= `Function[x, x²] /@ {a, b, c}`

Out[6]= $\{a^2, b^2, c^2\}$

This may seem like overkill; we've typed more input than the output we produced. But the idea is extremely powerful, as we can now map *any* function over *any* list. We'll explore more interesting examples shortly.

In general, to create a function one types `Function[input,output]`. The input variable x above could be replaced by any symbol; it's simply a dummy variable. An alternate syntax is commonly used that both minimizes typing and standardizes the name of the dummy variable to be the `Slot` character #. To define a `Function` using this syntax, use only one argument: the output expression (using # for the variable):

In[7]:= `Map[Function[#²], {a, b, c}]`

Out[7]= $\{a^2, b^2, c^2\}$

Even more brevity in typing can be attained by disposing entirely of the `Function` command name. One may simply type the output expression (again using only # for the variable) and then type the ampersand character & to mark the end of the function. It's a bit odd at first, but you'll pick up on it quickly. Instead of `Function[#²]`, for example, one instead may type a paltry three characters: #² &. For instance:

In[8]:= `Map[#² &, {a, b, c}]`

Out[8]= $\{a^2, b^2, c^2\}$

Or even better:

```
In[9]:= #^2 & /@ {a, b, c}
Out[9]= {a^2, b^2, c^2}
```

This last form is the most cryptic, but it is also the quickest to type, and is by far the most commonly encountered syntax convention for mapping a function over a list. You will see it frequently in examples in the Documentation Center. Here are a few examples. Remember the Slot character # is simply a stand-in for each member of the list that follows.

```
In[10]:= Column[N[π, #] & /@ Range[20]]
         3.
         3.1
         3.14
         3.142
         3.1416
         3.14159
         3.141593
         3.1415927
         3.14159265
         3.141592654
Out[10]=
         3.1415926536
         3.14159265359
         3.141592653590
         3.1415926535898
         3.14159265358979
         3.141592653589793
         3.1415926535897932
         3.14159265358979324
         3.141592653589793238
         3.1415926535897932385
```

```
In[11]:= GraphicsRow[
           Plot[Sin[x^4], {x, 0, 2}, PlotStyle -> #] & /@ {Dashed, Dotted, Thick}]
```

In[12]:= `Plot[x`#` & /@ {1 / 6, 1 / 5, 1 / 4, 1 / 3, 1 / 2, 1, 2, 3, 4, 5, 6},`
`{x, 0, 1}, Ticks → None, AspectRatio → 1]`

Out[12]=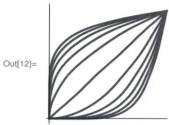

In[13]:= `GraphicsRow[Plot[x`#`, {x, 0, 1},`
`Ticks → None, AspectRatio → 1, AxesOrigin → {0, 0}] & /@`
`{1 / 6, 1 / 5, 1 / 4, 1 / 3, 1 / 2, 1, 2, 3, 4, 5, 6}]`

Out[13]=

In[14]:= `Text@Style[Grid[{#, "= ", Expand[#]} & /@ Table[(1 + x)`ⁿ`, {n, 9}],`
`Alignment → Left], "TraditionalForm"]`

$$1 + x \quad = \quad 1 + x$$
$$(1 + x)^2 \quad = \quad 1 + 2x + x^2$$
$$(1 + x)^3 \quad = \quad 1 + 3x + 3x^2 + x^3$$
$$(1 + x)^4 \quad = \quad 1 + 4x + 6x^2 + 4x^3 + x^4$$
Out[14]= $(1 + x)^5 \quad = \quad 1 + 5x + 10x^2 + 10x^3 + 5x^4 + x^5$
$$(1 + x)^6 \quad = \quad 1 + 6x + 15x^2 + 20x^3 + 15x^4 + 6x^5 + x^6$$
$$(1 + x)^7 \quad = \quad 1 + 7x + 21x^2 + 35x^3 + 35x^4 + 21x^5 + 7x^6 + x^7$$
$$(1 + x)^8 \quad = \quad 1 + 8x + 28x^2 + 56x^3 + 70x^4 + 56x^5 + 28x^6 + 8x^7 + x^8$$
$$(1 + x)^9 \quad = \quad 1 + 9x + 36x^2 + 84x^3 + 126x^4 + 126x^5 + 84x^6 + 36x^7 + 9x^8 + x^9$$

Note that it is possible to Map a Function over a list without using either command. Use the special iterator form {x, *list*} in a Table to accomplish the same thing. In fact, this idea has been used repeatedly throughout this book. For instance:

In[15]:= `Table[x`²`, {x, {a, b, c}}]`

Out[15]= $\{a^2, b^2, c^2\}$

In[16]:= `GraphicsRow[Table[Plot[Sin[x⁴], {x, 0, 2}, PlotStyle → sty],`
`{sty, {Dashed, Dotted, Thick}}]]`

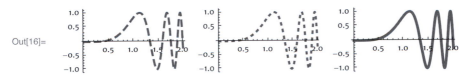

Out[16]=

Keep in mind, however, that *Mathematica* has been around since the late 1980s. Prior to version 6, when this type of iterator was first used in `Table`, the `Map-Function` combo was ubiquitous. Its use still pervades examples in the Documentation Center, and is found in much of the code you are likely to see. And it is more than a relic. With a little practice, it is very easy both to type and to read. It avoids the use of naming a dummy variable (like the `sty` variable in the example above). And in cases where the list being mapped over is generated by `Table`, the `Map-Function` combo negates the need to nest one `Table` inside another.

It should also be noted that both `Function` and `Map` are widely used independently of each other. In short, both are essential programming tools.

A `Function` can be given multiple arguments. This form is required by the `Sort` command, which is used to sort a given list. For instance:

In[17]:= `myList = RandomInteger[100, 15]`

Out[17]= `{69, 55, 9, 24, 90, 91, 9, 18, 10, 23, 15, 21, 41, 89, 53}`

In[18]:= `Sort[myList]`

Out[18]= `{9, 9, 10, 15, 18, 21, 23, 24, 41, 53, 55, 69, 89, 90, 91}`

The sorting may be accomplished via a sorting function, given in an optional second argument, which returns `True` precisely when its two arguments are given in the desired order. Each of the notations below accomplish the same thing: they put the list in reverse order:

In[19]:= `Sort[myList, Function[{x, y}, x > y]]`

Out[19]= `{91, 90, 89, 69, 55, 53, 41, 24, 23, 21, 18, 15, 10, 9, 9}`

In[20]:= `Sort[myList, Function[#1 > #2]]`

Out[20]= `{91, 90, 89, 69, 55, 53, 41, 24, 23, 21, 18, 15, 10, 9, 9}`

In[21]:= `Sort[myList, #1 > #2 &]`

Out[21]= `{91, 90, 89, 69, 55, 53, 41, 24, 23, 21, 18, 15, 10, 9, 9}`

Note that there are many other ways to accomplish this. For instance, one could `Reverse` the list after it is sorted in ascending order, or one could call the built-in `Greater` command, which accomplishes the same thing as our `Function` above:

In[22]:= `Reverse[Sort[myList]]`

Out[22]= {91, 90, 89, 69, 55, 53, 41, 24, 23, 21, 18, 15, 10, 9, 9}

In[23]:= `Sort[myList, Greater]`

Out[23]= {91, 90, 89, 69, 55, 53, 41, 24, 23, 21, 18, 15, 10, 9, 9}

But here we sort a list of vectors according to their Norm. There is no better way to accomplish this feat than with a sorting Function:

In[24]:= `myList = RandomInteger[100, {10, 3}]`

Out[24]= {{22, 15, 87}, {21, 70, 1}, {1, 68, 19}, {35, 50, 33}, {31, 57, 23},
{23, 18, 67}, {27, 52, 46}, {1, 2, 21}, {33, 78, 73}, {95, 14, 85}}

In[25]:= `Sort[myList, Norm[#1] < Norm[#2] &]`

Out[25]= {{1, 2, 21}, {31, 57, 23}, {35, 50, 33}, {1, 68, 19}, {23, 18, 67},
{21, 70, 1}, {27, 52, 46}, {22, 15, 87}, {33, 78, 73}, {95, 14, 85}}

And here we sort the same list of vectors according to the value of the third coordinate:

In[26]:= `Sort[myList, #1〚3〛 < #2〚3〛 &]`

Out[26]= {{21, 70, 1}, {1, 68, 19}, {1, 2, 21}, {31, 57, 23}, {35, 50, 33},
{27, 52, 46}, {23, 18, 67}, {33, 78, 73}, {95, 14, 85}, {22, 15, 87}}

In[27]:= `Clear[myList]`

RegionFunction and MeshFunctions specifications in 3D plotting commands are typically each given as a Function with multiple arguments. In this setting the Slot values #1, #2, and #3 stand for the coordinate values x, y, and z respectively. Below, the RegionFunction setting specifies that the domain includes only negative x values within a disk of radius 2, while the MeshFunctions setting specifies that Mesh lines will be drawn at equally spaced z values.

In[28]:= `Plot3D[e^{-(x^2+y^2)}, {x, y} ∈ Disk[{0, 0}, 2],`
`RegionFunction → (#1 < 0 &), MeshFunctions → {#3 &}, PlotPoints → 30]`

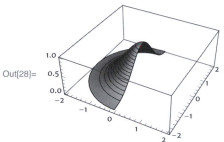

Out[28]=

Functional Programming

Mathematica is a *functional programming* language. That is, unlike languages such as BASIC and C, *Mathematica* commands can operate not only on specific types of numbers and data structures, but on arbitrary expressions. In particular, the argument to one function may be another function. This provides a powerful and elegant paradigm for programming. While we will not provide a philosophical discussion on the advantages and nature of functional programming, suffice it to say that if you've read and followed this section to this point you're already doing it. `Map` and `Function` are your point of entry. Commands such as `Apply`, `Thread`, and `MapThread` (introduced below) will expand your horizons, while `Nest`, `Fold`, replacement rules, and pattern matching (introduced later in the chapter) will take you to the next level.

A useful command that is similar to `Map` is `Apply`. Like `Map`, `Apply` takes two arguments: a function and an expression (often a list). The output is the second argument, with its head *replaced* by the function in the first argument. That's it; `Apply` will pluck the head off of any expression and replace it with something else. For example, `Apply[Times, List[a,b,c]]` will return `Times[a,b,c]`:

In[29]:= `Apply[Times, {a, b, c}]`

Out[29]= a b c

`Apply` can be given in infix form via `@@`.

In[30]:= `Times @@ {a, b, c}`

Out[30]= a b c

Here's another example. We randomly generate 40 points in the plane (ordered pairs of numbers, with each coordinate between −1 and 1), then replace `Point` by `Line` to connect the individual points with line segments, and by `Polygon` to fill the resulting regions. Finally, we display all three together.

In[31]:= `pts = Point[RandomReal[{-1, 1}, {40, 2}]];`
`Graphics[pts]`

Out[32]=

```
In[33]:=  GraphicsRow[
            {Graphics[Line @@ pts], Graphics[{Gray, Polygon @@ pts}],
             Graphics[{{Gray, Polygon @@ pts}, Line @@ pts, pts}]},
            Dividers → All]
```

Out[33]=

```
In[34]:=  Clear[pts]
```

The command Thread can be used to "thread" a function over several lists. In the example below, the (undefined) function is called f. It is called with two arguments, each of which is a list. Wrapping this expression in Thread causes f to be called on corresponding members of the two lists, with the output being a list of the results:

```
In[35]:=  Thread[f[{a, b, c}, {1, 2, 3}]]
Out[35]=  {f[a, 1], f[b, 2], f[c, 3]}
```

Here are two applications. The first shows how to use Thread to programmatically create a list of rules from a list of left-side values and a list of right-side values. In this case, the command Rule plays the role of the function f above. The second example illustrates that Thread has the same effect as Transpose on a list of lists (i.e., on a matrix). In this case List plays the role of the function f above.

```
In[36]:=  Thread[{a, b, c} → {1, 2, 3}]
Out[36]=  {a → 1, b → 2, c → 3}
```

```
In[37]:=  Thread[{{a, b, c}, {1, 2, 3}}]
Out[37]=  {{a, 1}, {b, 2}, {c, 3}}
```

The command MapThread combines the functionality of Map and Thread. The example below illustrates a typical implementation. It essentially does what Thread does, but there are two arguments, with the function (in this case f) being given alone as the first argument.

```
In[38]:=  MapThread[f, {{a, b, c}, {1, 2, 3}}]
Out[38]=  {f[a, 1], f[b, 2], f[c, 3]}
```

An example that illustrates the utility of MapThread follows. Suppose you wish to construct a 3D graphic of a right cylinder whose top and bottom are regular polygons. These polygons are easily constructed (we utilize Map to add the third coordinate to each vertex):

```
In[39]:=  n = 10;
          pts = Table[{Cos[t], Sin[t]}, {t, 0, 2 π, (2 π)/n}];
          bottom = Append[#, 0] & /@ pts;
          top = Append[#, 1] & /@ pts;
          Graphics3D[Polygon /@ {top, bottom}]
```

Out[43]=

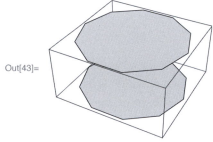

The rub is constructing the *n* rectangles that make up the sides. Suppose that $\{b_1, b_2\}$ is a list of two adjacent vertices on the bottom polygon, and that $\{t_1, t_2\}$ are the vertices on the top polygon directly above these. The side of the cylinder with these four vertices will have the form Polygon[$\{b_1, b_2, t_2, t_1\}$]. To get this, we will Partition the top and bottom vertices into sublists of length 2 with an offset (or overlap) of 1, and Reverse each ordered pair of vertices on the top. We'll then use MapThread to Join the corresponding lists. Here's an illustration of the idea:

```
In[44]:=  Partition[{b1, b2, b3}, 2, 1]
Out[44]=  {{b1, b2}, {b2, b3}}

In[45]:=  Reverse /@ Partition[{t1, t2, t3}, 2, 1]
Out[45]=  {{t2, t1}, {t3, t2}}

In[46]:=  MapThread[Join, {%%, %}]
Out[46]=  {{b1, b2, t2, t1}, {b2, b3, t3, t2}}
```

Here's the finished product:

In[47]:= `sides = MapThread[Join,`
`        {Partition[bottom, 2, 1], Reverse /@ Partition[top, 2, 1]}];`
`    Graphics3D[Polygon /@ Join[{top, bottom}, sides]]`

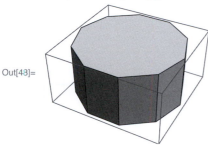

Out[48]=

In[49]:= `Clear[n, pts, top, bottom, sides]`

Exercises 8.4

1. The command `First`, when applied to a list, will return the first item in the list. More generally, `First[f[a,b,c]]` will return the first argument a for any command f. Compare the outputs of the commands `Options[NSolve]` and `First/@Options[NSolve]`. What is the command f to which `First` is being applied in this case?

2. Use `Function` to define a command which when given an integer argument n between 1 and 26 will return the nth letter of the alphabet. Use it to find the 19th letter of the alphabet.

3. What is the `FullForm` of the pure function $\#^2$ `&`?

4. What is the `FullForm` of the pure function `Norm[{#1, #2}] < 3`?

5. One could have, back at the beginning of Chapter 3, taken a different approach to defining a function such as $f(x) = x^2 + 3x - 1$ in *Mathematica*. Back then we advocated the following convention to define this function: `f[x_] := x^2 + 3 x - 1.` In this exercise we'll consider an alternate approach: `f = Function[x, x^2 + 3 x - 1].`

   a. Define f using `Function`, then make a `Plot` of f on the domain $-5 \le x \le 2$.

   b. Use *Mathematica* to differentiate and integrate f.

6. How would you use `Function` to define the multivariable real-valued function $f(x, y) = x^2 y - x + 3 y$?

7. How would you use `Function` to define the vector field $f(x, y) = \langle x^2 y - x + 3 y, \cos x \rangle$?

8. `Map`, `Function`, and `Apply` can be used to transform a simple `Table` into a sophisticated display. In this exercise you will work with the table below, where each row holds the left and right sides of a trigonometric identity.

   `Clear[a, k, t];`
   `t = Table[{Tan[k a], Together[TrigExpand[Tan[k a]]]}, {k, 2, 9}];`

a.   Use `Map`, `Function`, `Apply`, and `Equal` on `t`, and display the result with `Column` and `Traditional⁚ Form` to produce the output below:

$$\tan(2\,a) = \frac{2\cos(a)\sin(a)}{\cos^2(a) - \sin^2(a)}$$

$$\tan(3\,a) = \frac{\sec(a)\left(3\cos^2(a)\sin(a) - \sin^3(a)\right)}{\cos^2(a) - 3\sin^2(a)}$$

$$\tan(4\,a) = \frac{4\left(\cos^3(a)\sin(a) - \cos(a)\sin^3(a)\right)}{\cos^4(a) - 6\sin^2(a)\cos^2(a) + \sin^4(a)}$$

$$\tan(5\,a) = \frac{\sec(a)\left(\sin^5(a) - 10\cos^2(a)\sin^3(a) + 5\cos^4(a)\sin(a)\right)}{\cos^4(a) - 10\sin^2(a)\cos^2(a) + 5\sin^4(a)}$$

$$\tan(6\,a) = \left(2\left(3\sin(a)\cos^5(a) - 10\sin^3(a)\cos^3(a) + 3\sin^5(a)\cos(a)\right)\right) \Big/$$
$$\left(\cos^6(a) - 15\sin^2(a)\cos^4(a) + 15\sin^4(a)\cos^2(a) - \sin^6(a)\right)$$

$$\tan(7\,a) = \left(\sec(a)\left(-\sin^7(a) + 21\cos^2(a)\sin^5(a) - 35\cos^4(a)\sin^3(a) + 7\cos^6(a)\sin(a)\right)\right) \Big/$$
$$\left(\cos^6(a) - 21\sin^2(a)\cos^4(a) + 35\sin^4(a)\cos^2(a) - 7\sin^6(a)\right)$$

$$\tan(8\,a) = \left(8\left(\sin(a)\cos^7(a) - 7\sin^3(a)\cos^5(a) + 7\sin^5(a)\cos^3(a) - \sin^7(a)\cos(a)\right)\right) \Big/$$
$$\left(\cos^8(a) - 28\sin^2(a)\cos^6(a) + 70\sin^4(a)\cos^4(a) - 28\sin^6(a)\cos^2(a) + \sin^8(a)\right)$$

$$\tan(9\,a) = \left(\sec(a)\left(\sin^9(a) - 36\cos^2(a)\sin^7(a) +\right.\right.$$
$$126\cos^4(a)\sin^5(a) - 84\cos^6(a)\sin^3(a) + 9\cos^8(a)\sin(a)\left.\left.\right)\right) \Big/$$
$$\left(\cos^8(a) - 36\sin^2(a)\cos^6(a) + 126\sin^4(a)\cos^4(a) - 84\sin^6(a)\cos^2(a) + 9\sin^8(a)\right)$$

b.   Use `Map`, `Function`, `Apply`, and `Rule` on `t`, and display the result with `TabView` and `Traditional⁚ Form` to produce the output below:

$\tan(2\,a)$	$\tan(3\,a)$	$\tan(4\,a)$	$\tan(5\,a)$	$\tan(6\,a)$	$\tan(7\,a)$	$\tan(8\,a)$	$\tan(9\,a)$

$$\frac{2\sin(a)\cos(a)}{\cos^2(a) - \sin^2(a)}$$

9. Look up the term *functional programming* on Wikipedia, and contrast it with *procedural programming*.

10. A *cipher* is an encryption scheme whereby each individual character in the message is replaced by some other character or symbol. For instance, one could encode a message by replacing every *a* with *b*, every *b* with *c*, and in general replacing each letter with the next letter, except for *z* which is replaced with *a*. A cipher such as this that is based on a simple shift (replacing each letter with the letter a fixed number of characters to its right) is called a *Caesar cipher*.

a.   Use `StringReplace`, `CharacterRange`, `Thread`, and `RotateLeft` to build a command encode that will implement this cipher on any `String` composed of lowercase letters.

b.   Create a decode command to decode an encrypted message (you may wish to use `RotateRight`).

11. Modify the commands in the previous exercise so that a second argument controls the number of places that each character is shifted to the left in the encryption process.

8.5 Control Structures and Looping

In contrast to the techniques introduced in the previous section, *procedural programming* is a paradigm in which one gives step-by-step instructions to the computer. This is often the first type of programming one encounters, using a language such as BASIC or C. *Mathematica* supports this style of programming with looping commands such as Do, For, and While, and control structures such as If and Which. In this section we'll discuss the use of these commands.

The most simple looping command is Do. Its syntax is like that of Table; the first argument is an expression, and additional arguments are iterators. The expression is evaluated once for each value assumed by the iterated variable. For example:

```
In[1]:= myList = {};
        Do[PrependTo[myList, k], {k, 10}];
        myList
Out[3]= {10, 9, 8, 7, 6, 5, 4, 3, 2, 1}
```

Above we begin with an empty list myList, and then PrependTo (put at the beginning of) this list each of the first ten whole numbers in turn, beginning with 1. While effective, this procedural code is certainly not the easiest way to produce this list. Here's another way:

```
In[4]:= Reverse[Range[10]]
Out[4]= {10, 9, 8, 7, 6, 5, 4, 3, 2, 1}
```

As a second example, we use Do to write a procedural program for calculating the factorial of any integer. Yes, there is a built-in command Factorial (!) that does this already; the point is simply to illustrate how Do works. We begin by having Do calculate 4 factorial. First the dummy variable x is set to 1. Then as k assumes the integer values 1 to 4 in turn, x is set to k times its current value. So first x becomes $1 \times 1 = 1$, then $2 \times 1 = 2$, then $3 \times 2 = 6$, then $4 \times 6 = 24$.

```
In[5]:= x = 1;
        Do[x = k * x, {k, 4}];
        x
Out[7]= 24
```

We use this idea to create a command fac to calculate the factorial of any positive integer n. We use SetDelayed (:=) for we do not want to evaluate the right side until fac is called.

```
In[8]:= fac[n_] := (x = 1; Do[x = k * x, {k, n}]; x)
```

For example:

In[9]:= `TabView[Table[ToString[n] ~~ "!" → fac[n], {n, 15}], 13]`

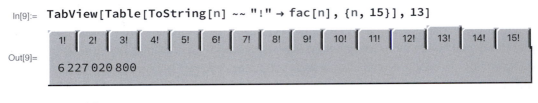

Out[9]=

6 227 020 800

In[10]:= `Clear[fac, x]`

Note that the first argument to Do can be a CompoundExpression (a sequence of commands separated by semicolons). This allows you to Do more than one thing, or to organize your code into simple steps. For instance, below we get serious and harness Do to implement the *secant method* for approximating the root of an equation $f(x) = 0$. You may recall that this method begins with two points x_0 and x_1 near the root in question. One then builds a sequence of values $x_1, x_2, x_3, \ldots$ that (one hopes) will be successively better approximations to the actual root. The sequence is constructed recursively via the second-order difference equation

$$x_{n+1} = x_n - \frac{x_n - x_{n-1}}{f(x_n) - f(x_{n-1})} f(x_n)$$

Below we harness Do to carry out nine steps of this process on the cubic $f(x) = x^3 - 2x + 2$ (you can check that f has only one real root), starting at $x_0 = -1$ and $x_1 = -3/2$. In this implementation we use x0 and x1 to represent the current values of x_{n-1} and x_n, respectively, in the equation above. We use xtemp to temporarily hold the value of x_n so that x_{n-1} may assume this value in the next iteration. Note also that the iterator for Do in this case is the ultra-simple {9}, which simply means, "do this nine times."

In[11]:= `f[x_] := x³ - 2 x + 2`

In[12]:= `x0 = -1;`
`x1 = -3 / 2;`
`Do[xtemp = x1;`

$$x1 = x1 - \frac{x1 - x0}{f[x1] - f[x0]} \, f[x1];$$

`x0 = xtemp;`
`Print[N[x1, 40]], {9}]`

-2.090909090909090909090909090909090909091

-1.709454061251664447403462050599201065246

-1.757205908865359830981764868540767091628

-1.769832257373596686295309726912982898092

-1.769287639221607075547801570536291382136

$$-1.76929235241102486011047855370896541502 8$$

$$-1.76929235423863760357466469734811639797 0$$

$$-1.76929235423863141524040134233144251410 7$$

$$-1.76929235423863141524040946433503349263 4$$

In this case we obtain 38-digit precision, for the actual real root (to 40-digit precision) looks like this:

In[15]:= `N[Reduce[f[x] == 0, x, Reals], 40]`

Out[15]= `x == -1.769292354238631415240409464335033492671`

While `Do` is effective, the secant method and the Newton–Raphson method for approximating roots can be implemented more efficiently using `NestList`. Such an implementation for Newton–Raphson can be found in Section 8.7, and Exercise 6 of that section asks you for an implementation of the secant method.

`Do` can also accept more than one iterator. Below, `k` assumes integer values from 0 to 3, while `m` assumes the values `a`, `b`, and `c`.

In[16]:= `myList = {};`
`Do[AppendTo[myList, k + m], {k, 0, 3}, {m, {a, b, c}}];`
`myList`

Out[18]= `{a, b, c, 1 + a, 1 + b, 1 + c, 2 + a, 2 + b, 2 + c, 3 + a, 3 + b, 3 + c}`

In[19]:= `Clear[myList]`

Predicates

Many control structures rely on conditions that are either true or false. If a condition is true, a certain set of instructions are given, while if the condition is false, an alternate set of instructions are given. In logic, a statement that is either true or false is called a *predicate*. In computer science, a command that returns one of the values true or false is sometimes referred to as a *query*. Mathematica has many predicate commands, which often end in the letter Q (for query). These commands return either the symbol `True` or the symbol `False`.

In[20]:= `PrimeQ[2^16 + 1]`

Out[20]= `True`

In[21]:= `Table[EvenQ[n], {n, 10}]`

Out[21]= `{False, True, False, True, False, True, False, True, False, True}`

Another useful predicate command is `FreeQ`, which will return `True` if the expression appearing in its first argument is completely free of the pattern or expression in its second argument. Note that for atomic expressions (such as numbers), one can use their `Head` (e.g., `Integer`, `Rational`, `Real`, `Complex`) for the second argument.

In[22]:= **FreeQ[{2, 3, 4}, Complex]**

Out[22]= True

In[23]:= **FreeQ[{2, 3, 4 + 2 𝕚}, Complex]**

Out[23]= False

In[24]:= **FreeQ[Solve[$x^3 + 34 x^2 - 9 x + 1 == 0$, x], Complex]**

Out[24]= False

An equation can be a useful predicate.

In[25]:= **2 == 3**

Out[25]= False

In[26]:= **N[π] == 1.0 ∗ π**

Out[26]= True

Note also that one can reverse the output of a predicate command by wrapping it in Not. The prefix form of Not[*expr*] is !*expr*.

In[27]:= **! False**

Out[27]= True

In[28]:= **! PrimeQ[8]**

Out[28]= True

In the case of equations, one may type != for Unequal, or use the ≠ button on the Basic Math Assistant palette.

In[29]:= **2 ≠ 3**

Out[29]= True

Here's an application that requires predicates: the Select command is used to select those items from a list that satisfy a condition. More precisely, a predicate command is applied to each member of the given list, and Select returns those items in the list for which the predicate is True. Here we Select all integers from 1 to 30 that are prime:

In[30]:= **Select[Range[30], PrimeQ]**

Out[30]= {2, 3, 5, 7, 11, 13, 17, 19, 23, 29}

It is common to use a Function to create a specialized predicate. Here we select those items in the given list whose value is at least 4:

```
In[31]:= Select[{1, 2, 3, 4, 5, 6}, # ≥ 4 &]
Out[31]= {4, 5, 6}
```

Here are all integers from 1 to 1000 with more than three distinct prime factors:

```
In[32]:= Select[Range[1000], Length[FactorInteger[#]] > 3 &]
Out[32]= {210, 330, 390, 420, 462, 510, 546, 570, 630, 660, 690,
          714, 770, 780, 798, 840, 858, 870, 910, 924, 930, 966, 990}
```

Select is useful for extracting numerical items from long lists. For instance, a few of the countries listed in CountryData do not currently have life expectancy figures available.

```
In[33]:= CountryData["VaticanCity", "LifeExpectancy"]
Out[33]= Missing[NotAvailable]
```

Recalling that CountryData[] returns a list of all countries in the dataset, the input and output below reveals that (at the time of this writing) there are 240 countries in the world, and there are life expectancy values given as Quantity objects for 230 of these, while these data are missing for the remaining 10.

```
In[34]:= Length /@ {CountryData[], Select[CountryData[],
            QuantityQ[CountryData[#, "LifeExpectancy"]] &],
          Select[CountryData[],
            CountryData[#, "LifeExpectancy"] == Missing["NotAvailable"] &]}
Out[34]= {240, 230, 10}
```

Control Structures: If, Which, Piecewise

The most basic control structure is the If command. Usage is straightforward: it accepts three arguments. The first is a predicate. The second is what is to be evaluated if the predicate is True, and the third is what is to be evaluated if the predicate is False. Here, for example, we test a few nearby numbers for primality, and display the results in a table:

In[35]:= `Text@Grid[`
`        Table[{k, If[PrimeQ[k], "prime", "composite"]}, {k, 101, 117, 2}],`
`        Dividers → Gray]`

Out[35]=

101	prime
103	prime
105	composite
107	prime
109	prime
111	composite
113	prime
115	composite
117	composite

Here's an example in which we combine an `If` control structure with a `Do` loop to investigate a conjecture made by Leibniz himself in the field of number theory. Leibniz observed that:

$$\left(2^2 - 1\right) \text{ is divisible by 3,}$$

$$\left(2^4 - 1\right) \text{ is divisible by 5,}$$

$$\left(2^6 - 1\right) \text{ is divisible by 7,}$$

$$\left(2^8 - 1\right) \text{ is NOT divisible by 9,}$$

$$\left(2^{10} - 1\right) \text{ is divisible by 11,}$$

$$\left(2^{12} - 1\right) \text{ is divisible by 13,}$$

$$\left(2^{14} - 1\right) \text{ is NOT divisible by 15,}$$

$$\left(2^{16} - 1\right) \text{ is divisible by 17, and so on.}$$

He conjectured that $2^n - 1$ will be evenly divisible by $n + 1$ if and only if $n + 1$ is an odd prime. The numbers on the right in these examples, after all, are primes precisely in those cases where divisibility occurs. One can restate this conjecture as follows: $\frac{2^n - 1}{n+1}$ will be an integer precisely when $n + 1$ is an odd prime. Here we check it for the values of n up to 200. It would appear that Leibniz was on to something!

In[36]:= $\text{Table}\left[\text{If}\left[\text{PrimeQ}[n + 1] == \text{IntegerQ}\left[\frac{2^n - 1}{n + 1}\right], \text{True}, \text{False}\right], \{n, 2, 200, 2\}\right]$

Out[36]= {True, True, True, True, True, True, True, True, True, True, True, True,
True, True, True, True, True, True, True, True, True, True, True,
True, True, True, True, True, True, True, True, True, True, True,
True, True, True, True, True, True, True, True, True, True, True,
True, True, True, True, True, True, True, True, True, True, True,
True, True, True, True, True, True, True, True, True, True, True,
True, True, True, True, True, True, True, True, True, True, True,
True, True, True, True, True, True, True, True, True, True, True,
True, True, True, True, True, True, True, True, True, True, True}

The predicate above (the first argument in the If command) in this case is an equation with one of True or False appearing on each side. It will be True if and only if the two symbols agree. For instance:

In[37]:= {True == True, True == False, False == True, False == False}

Out[37]= {True, False, False, True}

A quick way to make sure a long list (such as the Table above) contains only the symbol True is to Apply the And command to it. And gives True only if each of its arguments is True. We see, for instance, that Leibniz was correct up through $n = 338$:

In[38]:= **And @@**

$\quad\quad \text{Table}\left[\text{If}\left[\text{PrimeQ}[n + 1] == \text{IntegerQ}\left[\frac{2^n - 1}{n + 1}\right], \text{True}, \text{False}\right], \{n, 2, 338, 2\}\right]$

Out[38]= True

But, unfortunately, when $n = 340$ the conjecture fails. And it fails for several larger values of n as well. Here are the values of $n + 1$ for which it fails up through 10 000:

In[39]:= **counterExamples = {};**

$\quad\quad \text{Do}\left[\text{If}\left[\text{PrimeQ}[n + 1] \mathbin{!=} \text{IntegerQ}\left[\frac{2^n - 1}{n + 1}\right],\right.$

$\quad\quad\quad \left.\text{AppendTo}[\text{counterExamples}, n + 1]\right], \{n, 2, 10\,000, 2\}\right];$

$\quad\quad$ **counterExamples**

Out[41]= {341, 561, 645, 1105, 1387, 1729, 1905, 2047, 2465, 2701, 2821,
3277, 4033, 4369, 4371, 4681, 5461, 6601, 7957, 8321, 8481, 8911}

So the conjecture, despite its promising start, is most definitely false. How exactly does it fail? Either 341 is not prime while $\frac{2^{340}-1}{341}$ is an integer, *or* 341 is prime while $\frac{2^{34}-1}{341}$ is not an integer. It turns out to be the former:

```
In[42]:= PrimeQ[341]

Out[42]= False
```

```
In[43]:= IntegerQ[ (2^n - 1)/(n + 1) /. n → 340]

Out[43]= True
```

All of our counterexamples fail this way:

```
In[44]:= PrimeQ /@ counterExamples

Out[44]= {False, False, False, False, False, False, False, False, False, False, False,
          False, False, False, False, False, False, False, False, False, False}
```

Does it never fail the other way? That is, if p is an odd prime, must it be the case that $\frac{2^{p-1}-1}{p}$ is an integer? The answer is *yes*. This is a consequence of Fermat's little theorem (which you can look up online at MathWorld). So to his credit, Leibniz was half right. If he had access to *Mathematica*, he certainly would have been able to see the folly of his original conjecture. Since the first counterexample occurs at $n = 340$, and involves checking that $2^{340} - 1$ is divisible by 341, it is understandable that he believed this conjecture. And given that you have access to *Mathematica*, it is a reasonably simple matter for you to make investigations of this nature to peer deeply into the world of numbers.

`Which` is similar to `If`. The arguments come in pairs. The first argument in each pair is a predicate, and the second is an expression to evaluate if that predicate is `True`. `Which` will return the output associated with the *first* predicate that is `True`. For instance:

```
In[45]:= Text@Grid[Table[
            {n, Which[n == 1, "is a unit", PrimeQ[n], "is a prime", EvenQ[n],
              "is an even composite", OddQ[n], "is an odd composite"]},
            {n, 10}], Alignment → {{Right, Left}}]

Out[45]=    1  is a unit
            2  is a prime
            3  is a prime
            4  is an even composite
            5  is a prime
            6  is an even composite
            7  is a prime
            8  is an even composite
            9  is an odd composite
           10  is an even composite
```

The number $n = 1$ satisfies the first and last predicate; in such cases it is the expression corresponding to the first predicate that returns True that is evaluated.

Similar to Which is the Piecewise command, introduced in Section 3.6 It has the advantage of reading very nicely when its infix form is utilized. Type ⎡ESC⎤pw⎡ESC⎤ followed by one or more ⎡CTRL⎤⎡RET⎤ (Mac OS) or ⎡CTRL⎤⎡ENTER⎤ (Windows), one for each additional line.

$$
\text{In[46]:= } \mathtt{Text@Grid\Big[Table\Big[\Big\{n, \begin{bmatrix} \text{"is a unit"} & n == 1 \\ \text{"is a prime"} & \text{PrimeQ[n]} \\ \text{"is an even composite"} & \text{EvenQ[n]} \\ \text{"is an odd composite"} & \text{OddQ[n]} \end{bmatrix}\Big\}, \{n, 10\}\Big],}
$$

$$
\mathtt{Alignment \rightarrow \{\{Right, Left\}\}\Big]}
$$

Out[46]=
```
 1  is a unit
 2  is a prime
 3  is a prime
 4  is an even composite
 5  is a prime
 6  is an even composite
 7  is a prime
 8  is an even composite
 9  is an odd composite
10  is an even composite
```

Looping with While and For

The most basic looping command is Do. The commands While and For also allow you repeat a procedure, but rather than using an iterator to control the body of the loop, a predicate is utilized instead. Each of these procedural commands closely mirrors its counterpart in the C language.

The While command takes two arguments. The first is a predicate. The second is the body, which will be evaluated repeatedly until the predicate returns False. Here we use a While loop to find the first prime number greater than 1000. We Set a dummy variable k to be 1000, and then Increment k (increase its value by 1) until it is a prime. The value of this prime (the current value of k) is then returned.

```
In[47]:= k = 1000;
         While[ ! PrimeQ[k], Increment[k]];
         k
```

Out[49]= 1009

Note that the Increment command has the alternate postfix syntax ++. That is, Increment[k] can be typed as k++. Here, for instance, we use the same technique to find the first prime greater than one million:

In[50]:= `k = 1 000 000;`
`While[ ! PrimeQ[k], k++];`
`k`

Out[52]= `1 000 003`

The `For` command accepts four arguments (no pun intended), although three will suffice if the body is empty. You can, for instance, use `For` to write a procedure like those above to find the first prime number exceeding 1000: for k starting at 1000, and as long as k is not a prime, continue incrementing k by one. At this point, return the value of k. Here is how to implement this program:

In[53]:= `For[k = 1000, ! PrimeQ[k], k++]; k`

Out[53]= `1009`

The general syntax takes the form `For[`*start*, *test*, *increment*, *body*`]`. Upon entry, *start* is evaluated, and then the *increment* and *body* are evaluated repeatedly until the *test* returns `False`. In the example below, we take a starting number and repeatedly divide it by 2 until the result is no longer an integer. The body makes use of the `Print` command, which forces the value of k to be printed at each step.

In[54]:= `For[k = 1296, IntegerQ[k], k = k/2, Print[k]]`

1296

648

324

162

81

Exercises 8.5

1. Enter the input `?*Q` to get a listing of all commands that end with a capital Q. Here you will find many of the basic predicate commands that will output one of the symbols `True` or `False`.

2. The great French mathematician Pierre de Fermat (1601–1665) postulated that every number exceeding by 1 the quantity 2 raised to a power of 2 must be a prime number. That is, every number of the form $2^{(2^n)} + 1$ is prime according to Fermat. It was about a century later that he was proved wrong, by none other than Leonard Euler. Find the first counterexample to Fermat's famous conjecture.

3. The two most commonly used methods for incrementing a dummy variable are `Increment` (postfix form `++`), described in this section, and `PreIncrement` (*prefix* form `++`). Enter the commands `j = 1; j++` and `k = 1; ++k`, and describe the difference.

4. Find the smallest positive integer n with the property that $\int_0^{21/20-1/n} x^n \, dx > \frac{1}{10}$.

5. Write a `For` loop to carry out the following procedure: Beginning with the number 1, keep adding a random integer chosen between 1 and 100 to the current value until such time as the result is a prime.

   a. Write the loop so that all intermediate results are displayed.

   b. Write the loop so that a *list* of all intermediate values, including the last, is displayed.

   c. Write the loop so that only the number of iterations required is displayed.

   d. Run the procedure from part **c** 1000 times (using `Table`), and `Tally` the results.

8.6 Scoping Constructs: With and Module

When writing a program it is common to make one or more intermediate assignments. See, for instance, the example at the end of Section 8.4, where we wrote a program to display a 3D graphic of a right cylinder whose base is a regular n-gon. In that example, assignments were made to the symbols `n`, `pts`, `top`, `bottom`, and `sides`. These assignments were only used to create the image, and were not needed afterward. Another example appears below. It provides a means of drawing a regular n-gon for any integer $n > 2$. Note that we could use `CirclePoints` in place of the `Table` below, except our table duplicates the first and last point in the list so that `Line` will include the final line segment and "close the loop."

In[1]:= `n = 10;`

`Graphics[Line[Table[{Cos[t], Sin[t]}, {t, 0, 2 π, `$\frac{2\,\pi}{n}$`}]]]`

Out[2]=

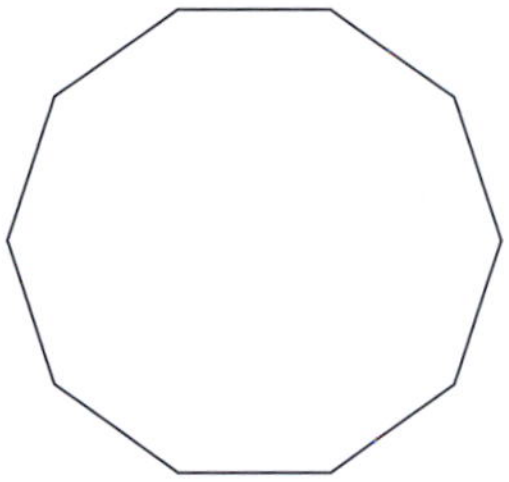

The only potentially bad consequence of this construction is that the symbol `n` has been `Set` to the value 10. This has the potential to interfere with subsequent evaluations involving this symbol that you might try to make. For instance, if after entering the input above, you try to `Solve` an equation for n you will run into trouble:

In[3]:= `Solve[3 n + 1 == 22, n]`

••• Solve: 10 is not a valid variable.

Out[3]= `Solve[False, 10]`

Essentially, you must be diligent in `Clearing` all such assignments before using such symbols in another setting. A better practice is to make assignments *locally*. This is easily accomplished by putting them inside of a *scoping* command, such as `With` or `Module`. Whatever is assigned in a scoping command *stays* in the scoping command.

In[4]:= `Clear[n];`
`With[{n = 5},`

$$\mathtt{Graphics[Line[Table[\{Cos[t], Sin[t]\}, \{t, 0, 2\,\pi, \frac{2\,\pi}{n}\}]]]]}$$

Out[5]=

In this case, n has not been assigned a value in the Global` context:

In[6]:= `n`

Out[6]= `n`

This means that the local assignment made to the symbol n will not interfere with subsequent evaluations:

In[7]:= `Solve[3 n + 1 == 22, n]`

Out[7]= `{{n → 7}}`

With accepts two arguments. Its first argument is a list of local assignments. Its second argument is an expression. The assignments given in the first argument are local to the expression appearing in the second argument. The assignments do not persist afterward, nor do they affect any previous assignments. The command name With suggests its use; you can read the input code like a sentence that begins, "With $n = 10$, do the following…" Here's another example. Note how the With statement does not affect the earlier assignment n = 3, and how this assignment does not affect the n appearing within the With statement.

In[8]:= `n = 3;`
`With[{n = 10}, n²]`

Out[9]= `100`

In[10]:= `n`

Out[10]= `3`

Another useful scoping construct, and indeed a more general one, is Module. It works much like With, insulating any symbols you have already defined from its own local variables, and vice-versa. The main difference between Module and With (from the user's perspective) is that the local variables in a Module do not need to be assigned in the first argument (although they do have to be listed there). Delayed assignments (:=) may also be used in a Module, while only immediate assignments

(=) can be used in With. Here's a simple example:

We're going to draw a star shape. We'll begin with a list of $2n$ points equally spaced around the unit circle (again, with the first point repeated at the end). We then multiply every second point (as we move clockwise around the circle) by a scalar, to move it farther from the origin along its radial axis. Finally, we connect the resulting list of points with line segments. Let's do this step by step with $n = 5$:

In[11]:= **n = 5;**

$$\text{pts = Table}\left[\{\text{Sin}[t], \text{Cos}[t]\}, \left\{t, 0, 2\pi, \frac{2\pi}{2n}\right\}\right]$$

Out[12]= $\left\{ \{0, 1\}, \left\{ \sqrt{\frac{5}{8} - \frac{\sqrt{5}}{8}}, \frac{1}{4}\left(1 + \sqrt{5}\right)\right\}, \left\{ \sqrt{\frac{5}{8} + \frac{\sqrt{5}}{8}}, \frac{1}{4}\left(-1 + \sqrt{5}\right)\right\},\right.$

$\left\{ \sqrt{\frac{5}{8} + \frac{\sqrt{5}}{8}}, \frac{1}{4}\left(1 - \sqrt{5}\right)\right\}, \left\{ \sqrt{\frac{5}{8} - \frac{\sqrt{5}}{8}}, \frac{1}{4}\left(-1 - \sqrt{5}\right)\right\}, \{0, -1\},$

$\left\{ -\sqrt{\frac{5}{8} - \frac{\sqrt{5}}{8}}, \frac{1}{4}\left(-1 - \sqrt{5}\right)\right\}, \left\{ -\sqrt{\frac{5}{8} + \frac{\sqrt{5}}{8}}, \frac{1}{4}\left(1 - \sqrt{5}\right)\right\},$

$\left. \left\{ -\sqrt{\frac{5}{8} + \frac{\sqrt{5}}{8}}, \frac{1}{4}\left(-1 + \sqrt{5}\right)\right\}, \left\{ -\sqrt{\frac{5}{8} - \frac{\sqrt{5}}{8}}, \frac{1}{4}\left(1 + \sqrt{5}\right)\right\}, \{0, 1\}\right\}$

Note how our list has $2n + 1 = 11$ points, with the first equal to the last. To get a corresponding list of scale factors for each of these points, we utilize the Riffle command to intersperse a scale-factor of 2.5 at every second position in a list of $n + 1 = 6$ ones. The resulting list has length $2n + 1$ to match our list of points.

In[13]:= **scaleList = Riffle[Table[1, {n + 1}], 2.5]**
Out[13]= {1, 2.5, 1, 2.5, 1, 2.5, 1, 2.5, 1, 2.5, 1}

The final picture is obtained by multiplying the two lists (which multiplies their corresponding members), and wrapping the resulting list of points in the Line command:

In[14]:= **Graphics[Line[scaleList * pts]]**

Out[14]=

In[15]:= `Clear[n, pts, scaleList]`

Here is how we could organize the individual commands above into a coherent piece of code, all in a single input cell, and in such a way that none of the local variables interferes with a global symbol of the same name. Note that while n and `scaleFactor` are assigned in the first argument, the other local variables `pts` and `scaleList` are listed but not assigned there. Rather, they are assigned in the body of the `Module`. This body (the second argument to `Module`) is a `CompoundExpression` (expressions separated by semicolons). The first two such expressions define the local variables `pts` and `scaleList`, and the third creates the `Graphics`. Note also that the values assigned to `pts` and `scaleList` depend on the values of n and `scaleFactor`. This would be impossible using `With`, where all local variables must be assigned in the first argument, and independently of one another.

$$\text{Module}\Big[\{n = 5,\ \text{scaleFactor} = 2.5,\ \text{pts},\ \text{scaleList}\},$$
$$\text{pts} = \text{Table}\Big[\{\text{Sin}[t],\ \text{Cos}[t]\},\ \Big\{t,\ 0,\ 2\,\pi,\ \frac{2\,\pi}{2\,n}\Big\}\Big];$$
$$\text{scaleList} = \text{Riffle}[\text{Table}[1,\ \{n+1\}],\ \text{scaleFactor}];$$
$$\text{Graphics}[\text{Line}[\text{scaleList} * \text{pts}]]\Big]$$

Finally, we can use this code to create a command for sketching stars, letting the user select values for *n* and the scale factor.

In[16]:= $$\text{star}[n\_,\ \textit{scaleFactor}\_] := \text{Module}\Big[\{\text{pts},\ \text{scaleList}\},$$
$$\text{pts} = \text{Table}\Big[\{\text{Sin}[t],\ \text{Cos}[t]\},\ \Big\{t,\ 0,\ 2\,\pi,\ \frac{2\,\pi}{2\,n}\Big\}\Big];$$
$$\text{scaleList} = \text{Riffle}[\text{Table}[1,\ \{n+1\}],\ \textit{scaleFactor}];$$
$$\text{Graphics}[\text{Line}[\text{scaleList} * \text{pts}]]\Big]$$

For instance:

In[17]:= `GraphicsGrid[Table[star[n, k], {n, 5, 7}, {k, 1, 4, .5}]]`

Out[17]=

Note that it is not *necessary* to use any local variables in the definition above, and hence not necessary to use a `Module` at all. One could just do the following:

```
In[18]:= star[n_, scale_] :=
           Graphics[Line[Riffle[Table[1, {n + 1}], scale] *
               Table[{Sin[t], Cos[t]}, {t, 0, 2 π, (2 π)/(2 n)}]]]
```

This is essentially just the last line of code in the earlier `Module`, with local variables `pts` and `scaleList` replaced by their definitions. While more elegant in one sense, some would find the code more difficult to read. A `Module` lets you break a complex set of instructions into smaller pieces, with each one easy to read and understand. In more complex settings, a `Module` can actually be a more efficient way to code. For instance, if a single large `Table` appears more than once in a program, it is generally more efficient to assign a local variable to represent it (so the `Table` is evaluated only once), and then use that local variable every time the `Table` is needed.

This happens in the example provided below, where the local variable `circlePts` is used twice.

```
In[19]:= Manipulate[
           Module[{circlePts = CirclePoints[100], bottomPts, topPts},
             bottomPts = Map[Append[#, -h/2.] &, r2 * circlePts];
             topPts = Map[Append[#, h/2.] &, r1 * circlePts];
             Graphics3D[{EdgeForm[],
               Polygon /@ MapThread[Join, {Partition[bottomPts, 2, 1, 1],
                   Reverse /@ Partition[topPts, 2, 1, 1]}]},
               PlotRange → 1, Boxed → False, ImageSize → {200},
               PlotLabel → Style["surface area =\n π (r_1+r_2) √(h² + (r_1 - r_2)²) =" ~~
                 ToString[PaddedForm[π (r1 + r2) √(h² + (r1 - r2)²), {4, 2}]]]]],
           {{r1, .6, "r_1"}, .01, 1, Appearance → "Labeled"},
           {{r2, 1., "r_2"}, .01, 1, Appearance → "Labeled"},
           {{h, 1.}, 0, 2, Appearance → "Labeled"}, Alignment → Center]
```

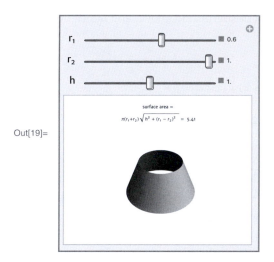

Out[19]=

This example shows code to produce illustrations of a *circular frustum* (loosely speaking, a cone with its tip cut off). The output is a Manipulate in which the user controls the top and bottom radii and the height *h* between them. The code is based on the example given at the end of Section 8.4. In this case the top and bottom circles are approximated by 100-sided polygons.

Scoping and Dynamic Elements

Most of the dynamic interfaces and controls that we have seen, such as sliders and buttons, have been generated by the Manipulate command. As you might expect, Manipulate makes calls to a host of lower-level commands that do the real magic, and you have access to these commands as well. The fundamental command at the heart of all such live interactive interfaces is Dynamic. Wrap an expression in Dynamic and the front end will automatically update it whenever its value changes. Below, for example, we make a Slider that ranges from 0 to 3, and that is used to control the values assumed by the symbol x.

```
In[20]:= {Slider[Dynamic[x], {0, 3}], Dynamic[x]}
```

Out[20]= { ⬤——————————————————————— , 0. }

Note that moving the slider (we moved the one above to 1.78) will actually make an assignment to the symbol x:

```
In[21]:= x
```

Out[21]= 1.78

The construction of dynamic interfaces with *Mathematica*, while remarkably simple compared with most other programming languages, is a vast subject that falls beyond the scope of this book. The tutorials in the Documentation Center titled "Introduction to Dynamic" and "Advanced Dynamic Functionality" are excellent resources for those who wish to explore this arena. Our purpose here is to introduce the DynamicModule command, and to understand its role in the context of the other scoping commands. Like Module, any symbols declared in a DynamicModule will be insulated from

assignments made elsewhere. Below, for instance, we duplicate the input above within a
`DynamicModule`.

```
In[22]:= DynamicModule[{x = 2.5},
           {Slider[Dynamic[x], {0, 3}], Dynamic[x]}]
```

Out[22]= { ——————————————————————◯———— , 2.5}

The dynamic content is now completely insulated from the global variable x, whose value is still 1.78:

```
In[23]:= x
```

Out[23]= 1.78

Here's a simple but more interesting example. Below we take a thick, orange `PolarPlot` whose
independent variable tops out at the dynamically controlled quantity u, and superimpose it with the
same (but thin) `PolarPlot` on the full domain $0 \le \theta \le 2\pi$. A slider allows you to adjust u, so that you
can follow the parameterization from 0 to 2π.

```
In[24]:= DynamicModule[{u = 4.5},
           Column[{Slider[Dynamic[u], {.01, 2 π}],
             Dynamic@Show[PolarPlot[Cos[θ] - 2 Cos[4 θ] + 3 Sin[5 θ], {θ, 0, 2 π}],
               PolarPlot[Cos[θ] - 2 Cos[4 θ] + 3 Sin[5 θ], {θ, 0, u},
                 PlotStyle → Directive[Thick, Orange]]]}, Frame → Gray]]
```

Out[24]=

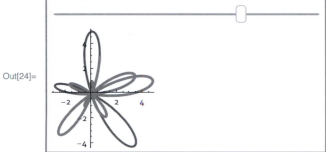

This example illustrates once again the powerful implications of working in a functional programming environment. The `Dynamic` command accepts general *Mathematica* expressions (such as the
`Show` expression above), and permits them to be dynamically updated.

The interface and input code above is nearly identical to what one could produce using `Manipulate`.
The *real* benefit of using dynamic programming constructions (instead of `Manipulate`) is the precise
control that is afforded regarding which quantities get dynamically updated and which do not. This is
controlled by careful placement of `Dynamic` elements. Above, *both* the static polar plot and the
dynamic orange plot are re-evaluated whenever the slider is moved. This is a consequence of wrapping the entire `Show` expression in `Dynamic`. An alternate and slightly more sophisticated input that

produces the same output follows. In this case, the static plot is evaluated only once. Only the thick, orange plot is dynamically updated by the controller.

```
In[25]:= DynamicModule[{u = 4.5, dynamicPlt},
           dynamicPlt = Dynamic@First@PolarPlot[Cos[θ] - 2 Cos[4 θ] + 3 Sin[5 θ],
               {θ, 0, u}, PlotStyle → Directive[Thick, Orange]];
           Column[{Slider[Dynamic[u], {.01, 2 π}],
               Show[PolarPlot[Cos[θ] - 2 Cos[4 θ] + 3 Sin[5 θ], {θ, 0, 2 π}],
                   Graphics[dynamicPlt]]}, Frame → Gray]]
```

Out[25]=

In the input above we applied First to the thick, orange PolarPlot. This returns the first argument of the Graphics generated by PolarPlot (essentially a Line object with dozens or hundreds of points). Dynamic is applied to this quantity, and it is later displayed (by wrapping it in Graphics) together with the static plot. The behavior of this output and the previous one are essentially the same, but in principle this latter one is zippier and more responsive as the slider is moved, as fewer items need to be dynamically updated. If you were to add a static but complicated ContourPlot to the Show argument in each of the last two inputs, the relative zippiness provided by this latter approach would be obvious.

DynamicModule, unlike Module, stores its information in the Front End. If you save a notebook with the output cell above included and re-open it later, it will display properly and the slider will still work, even if you do not re-evaluate the input. Moreover, you could copy the output above and paste it in several different places. Each pasted copy would work independently of the others. In essence, the DynamicModule can be thought of as providing insulation in such a way that it stakes out specific real estate in a notebook in which the localizations take place.

Exercises 8.6

1. Here is one way to generate the nth partial sum $1 + \frac{1}{2} + \frac{1}{3} + \cdots + \frac{1}{n}$ of the harmonic series. Explain how it works, and use it to calculate the 100th partial sum of the harmonic series. Compare the output with that of the built-in command HarmonicNumber. See also Section 8.7 for an alternate definition using Fold.

$$\text{harmonicNumber}[n\_] := \text{Module}\left[\{s = 0\}, \text{For}\left[i = 1, i \leq n, i++, s = s + \frac{1}{i}\right];\right.$$
$$\left.s\right]$$

2. A local variable named x within a Module creates a symbol with a name such as x$30075, where the stuff to the right of the local variable name is the current value of the system variable $ModuleNumber. This variable is incremented each time any Module is called. Create a Do loop that will evaluate the expression Module[{x}, Print[x]] ten times.

3. In addition to With and Module, there is a third scoping command called Block, whose syntax and purpose matches that of Module. Block uses a slightly different approach to insulate its local variables. To illustrate how it works, suppose that you have entered x = 3 in a session, and then create a Block with the local assignment x = 2. No new symbols will be created. Rather, when the Block is evaluated the value of x will be temporarily cleared and the local assignment will be utilized. After Block is finished the old value of x will be restored.

a. Enter the input below to see Block in action.

    x = 3; Block[{x = 2}, Print[x]]; x

b. Enter the inputs below and explain the different outputs.

    Clear[x]; expr = x + 1

    Block[{x = 2}, x + expr]

    Module[{x = 2}, x + expr]

    Clear[expr]

8.7 Iterations: Nest and Fold

Consider the following input:

In[1]:= Clear[f, x];
        NestList[f, x, 3]
Out[2]= {x, f[x], f[f[x]], f[f[f[x]]]}

The command NestList is a fundamental tool for iterating a function. When one enters the command NestList[*command*, *start*, *n*], a list of length $n + 1$ is created with *start* as the first entry. This is followed by the result of applying *command* to *start* and then the result of applying *command* to this result, and so on, up through *n* applications of *command*. The command Nest is similar, but it will output only the last item in this list.

In[3]:= Nest[f, x, 3]
Out[3]= f[f[f[x]]]

Here is a famous example of a type of problem that is especially amenable to computer exploration using iterations. It is known as the reverse-add problem, or sometimes as the *versum* problem (this being a derivative of "reverse sum"). Take a positive integer and add it to the integer obtained by writing the digits of the original number in reverse order. For instance, if the original number is 29, one adds $29 + 92 = 121$. The result in this case is a *palindrome*, a number that reads the same forward and backward. If you start with 39 and carry out this procedure you get $39 + 93 = 132$, which is not a palindrome. However, apply the procedure to 132 and you get the palindrome 363. It was conjectured long ago that no matter what the starting number, a palindrome will eventually result when this procedure is iterated.

Here is a means of using *Mathematica* to carry out the reverse-add procedure. Each step of the procedure can be accomplished by extracting the digits of the input number (IntegerDigits), reversing this list of digits (Reverse), then converting the reversed digit list back to a number (FromDigits) and finally adding it to the original.

```
In[4]:= Clear[step];
        step[n_] := n + FromDigits[Reverse[IntegerDigits[n]]]
```

For example:

```
In[6]:= {39, step[39], step[step[39]]}
Out[6]= {39, 132, 363}
```

```
In[7]:= NestList[step, 39, 2]
Out[7]= {39, 132, 363}
```

To explore the conjecture (that every input will lead eventually to a palindrome), let's make a command that will identify palindromes. The command palStyle accepts an integer as input and outputs that integer with a frame around it if it is a palindrome and in black otherwise.

```
In[8]:= palStyle[n_] :=
          If[IntegerDigits[n] == Reverse[IntegerDigits[n]], Framed[n], n]
```

For example, starting with 79 we see three palindromes in the first 20 iterations:

```
In[9]:= palStyle /@ NestList[step, 79, 20]
```

Out[9]= { 79, 176, 847, 1595, 7546, 14 003, 44 044 , 88 088 , 176 176, 847 847,

1 596 595, 7 553 546, 14 007 103, 44 177 144 , 88 354 288, 176 599 676,

853 595 347, 1 597 190 705, 6 668 108 656, 13 236 127 322, 35 608 290 553}

For this particular application it would be nice to have a mechanism whereby the iterations would stop as soon as a palindrome is produced, for it is simply not clear how many iterations may be required. The command NestWhileList (or NestWhile if only the last item is to be output) is the ticket. The syntax is like that of NestList, but instead of using a positive integer for the third argument to indicate the number of iterations, use a predicate instead. The iterations will continue as long as the predicate returns True. Here, for instance, we set up a pure function for this purpose:

```
In[10]:= NestWhileList[step, 79,
            IntegerDigits[#] ≠ Reverse[IntegerDigits[#]] &]

Out[10]= {79, 176, 847, 1595, 7546, 14 003, 44 044}
```

And here we see the number of iterations required to reach a palindrome for each of the first 195 integers. That is, above each integer *n* on the horizontal axis we see a vertical bar indicating the minimal number of iterations required to reach a palindrome. Integers *n* that are palindromes appear directly on the horizontal axis:

```
In[11]:= ListPlot[Table[{n, Length[NestWhileList[step, n,
            IntegerDigits[#] ≠ Reverse[IntegerDigits[#]] &]] - 1}, {n, 195}],
          Filling → Axis, PlotStyle → PointSize[.002], PlotRange → All,
          AspectRatio → 1 / 3, AxesOrigin → {0, 0}]
```

We stopped at 195 here for a very good reason. The number 196 will not produce a palindrome even after *millions* of iterations. For this reason it is strongly suspected that the original conjecture is false, although at the time of this writing this has not been proved. In other words, no one really knows if after enough iterations of this procedure starting at 196 a palindrome will be produced. All that is known is that a palindrome will not be produced quickly. If you were to call our NestWhileList input with 196 as the starting value, it would run (if you let it) for days, weeks, maybe years. Suffice it to say that you might get bored waiting. For this reason it is possible to add an escape mechanism to NestWhileList so that after a certain number of iterations it will stop, regardless of whether the predicate is True or not. The following input accomplishes this. The fourth argument (1 in the input below) indicates that the predicate needs to test only one item (the last result computed). The final argument (50 in the input below) specifies the maximal number of iterations to allow. Here we see that there are no palindromes in the first 50 iterations when one starts with 196:

In[12]:= `palStyle /@ NestWhileList[step, 196,`
`    IntegerDigits[#] ≠ Reverse[IntegerDigits[#]] &, 1, 50]`

Out[12]= {196, 887, 1675, 7436, 13 783, 52 514, 94 039, 187 088, 1 067 869, 10 755 470,
18 211 171, 35 322 452, 60 744 805, 111 589 511, 227 574 622, 454 050 344,
897 100 798, 1 794 102 596, 8 746 117 567, 16 403 234 045, 70 446 464 506,
130 992 928 913, 450 822 227 944, 900 544 455 998, 1 800 098 901 007,
8 801 197 801 088, 17 602 285 712 176, 84 724 043 932 847, 159 547 977 975 595,
755 127 757 721 546, 1 400 255 515 443 103, 4 413 700 670 963 144,
8 827 391 431 036 288, 17 653 692 772 973 576, 85 191 620 502 609 247,
159 482 241 005 228 405, 664 304 741 147 513 356, 1 317 620 482 294 916 822,
3 603 815 405 135 183 953, 7 197 630 720 180 367 016, 13 305 261 530 450 734 933,
47 248 966 933 966 985 264, 93 507 933 867 933 969 538,
177 104 867 844 767 940 077, 947 154 635 293 536 341 848,
1 795 298 270 686 072 793 597, 9 749 270 977 546 801 719 568,
18 408 442 064 004 592 449 047, 92 502 871 604 050 616 929 528,
175 095 833 209 091 234 750 057, 925 153 265 399 993 573 340 628}

Let's apply this procedure to each of the first thousand numbers and make a list of the results:

In[13]:= `data = Table[NestWhileList[step, n,`
`    IntegerDigits[#] ≠ Reverse[IntegerDigits[#]] &, 1, 50], {n, 1000}];`

For example:

In[14]:= `palStyle /@ data〚485〛`

Out[14]= {485, 1069, 10 670, 18 271, 35 552, 61 105, 111 221, │ 233 332 │}

Here is a `ListPlot` like that produced earlier, but with a `Tooltip` added which will display the coordinates of a data point as you mouseover it.

In[15]:= `ListPlot[Tooltip@{First[#], Length[#] - 1} & /@ data,`
`    Filling → Axis, PlotStyle → PointSize[.002],`
`    AspectRatio → 1 / 3, PlotRange → All, AxesOrigin → {0, 0}]`

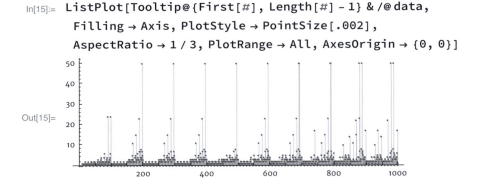

Below are all numbers between 1 and 1000 that, like 196, do not produce a palindrome after 50 iterations. In fact, even with many more iterations none of these numbers have ever produced a palindrome. See Exercise 2.

```
In[16]:= First /@ Select[data, Length[#] == 51 &]

Out[16]= {196, 295, 394, 493, 592, 689, 691, 788, 790, 879, 887, 978, 986}
```

```
In[17]:= Clear[data]
```

For a second example of programming iteratively, consider the Newton–Raphson method for approximating a root of an equation $f(x) = 0$, where f is a differentiable function. The technique, you may recall, entails making an initial guess x_0 for the root, and then calculating a sequence of (what we hope will be) successively better approximations $x_1, x_2, x_3, \ldots$ via the iterative formula

$$x_{n+1} = x_n - \frac{f(x_n)}{f'(x_n)}$$

Here is a command `newtonStep` that can be iterated with `NestList`. In order that it may be iterated, it needs to accept a *single* numerical input. But we would also like to be able to specify the function f whose root we wish to approximate. We accommodate both of these demands by using the syntax below:

```
In[18]:= Clear[newtonStep, f, x];

         newtonStep[f_] = Function[x, Simplify[x - f[x]/f'[x]]];
```

We can now specify a function f explicitly like this:

```
In[20]:= f[x_] := 2 - x^2;
         newtonStep[f][x]
```

$$Out[21]= \frac{1}{x} + \frac{x}{2}$$

Or as a pure function, like this:

```
In[22]:= newtonStep[2 - #^2 &][x]
```

$$Out[22]= \frac{1}{x} + \frac{x}{2}$$

Either way, we know that the function $f(x) = 2 - x^2$ has a positive root at $x = \sqrt{2}$. Here we use the Newton–Raphson technique to approximate this root, using the initial value of `N[1,40]`:

```
In[23]:= NestList[newtonStep[f], N[1, 40], 8] // Column
         1.0000000000000000000000000000000000000000
         1.5000000000000000000000000000000000000000
         1.4166666666666666666666666666666666666667
         1.4142156862745098039215686274509803921
Out[23]= 1.4142135623746899106262955788901349012
         1.4142135623730950488016896235025302436
         1.4142135623730950488016887242096980786
         1.4142135623730950488016887242096980786
         1.4142135623730950488016887242096980786
```

We see that seven iterations are sufficient to give 38-digit accuracy in this case (since the last two rows—the seventh and eight iterates—agree at every digit, and since two digits of precision were lost during the iteration process). This agrees with our knowledge of the root:

```
In[24]:= N[√2 , 38]
Out[24]= 1.4142135623730950488016887242096980786
```

It may be worth recalling that the built-in command FindRoot is designed to be used in cases such as this, where a good approximation to the root of a function is desired. Programming the Newton–Raphson method is intended to shed light on the behavior of this algorithm. We don't mean to imply that it is the best and only tool for this purpose.

```
In[25]:= FindRoot[2 - x² == 0, {x, 1}, WorkingPrecision → 40]
Out[25]= {x → 1.414213562373095048801688724209698078570}
```

There are several other iteration commands available beyond Nest and NestList. One of the most useful is FixedPointList. This is a special case of NestWhileList that halts when the outputs become indistinguishable from one another. That is, it provides a simpler means of doing what the NestWhileList input below does:

```
In[26]:= NestWhileList[newtonStep[f], N[1, 40], UnsameQ, 2] // Column
         1.0000000000000000000000000000000000000000
         1.5000000000000000000000000000000000000000
         1.4166666666666666666666666666666666666667
         1.4142156862745098039215686274509803921
Out[26]= 1.4142135623746899106262955788901349012
         1.4142135623730950488016896235025302436
         1.4142135623730950488016887242096980786
         1.4142135623730950488016887242096980786
```

```
In[27]:=  FixedPointList[newtonStep[f], N[1, 40]] // Column
```
```
        1.0000000000000000000000000000000000000000
        1.5000000000000000000000000000000000000000
        1.4166666666666666666666666666666666666667
Out[27]= 1.4142156862745098039215686274509803921 6
        1.4142135623746899106262955788901349101 2
        1.4142135623730950488016896235025302436 1
        1.4142135623730950488016887242096980785 7
        1.4142135623730950488016887242096980786
```

And, as you would expect, there is a FixedPoint command that simply returns the final value:

```
In[28]:=  FixedPoint[newtonStep[f], N[1, 40]]
```
```
Out[28]=  1.4142135623730950488016887242096980786
```

Here we use Newton's method to give an approximation of $\pi/4$ (i.e., as a root of $f(x) = \sin x - \cos x$).

```
In[29]:=  FixedPoint[newtonStep[Sin[#] - Cos[#] &], N[1, 40]]
```
```
Out[29]=  0.78539816339744830961566084581987572105
```

```
In[30]:=  N[π / 4, 38]
```
```
Out[30]=  0.78539816339744830961566084581987572105
```

Note that FixedPoint and FixedPointList can accept a third argument, which specifies the maximal number of iterations. This is useful when it is not clear in advance that the iteration process will terminate.

The commands Fold and FoldList are used to iterate a function of two variables over its first variable, while the second variable assumes successive values in a given list. That sounds worse than it is. The input below illustrates the idea. The first argument is the function to be iterated, the second argument is the starting value for this function's first variable, and the third argument is the list of values for the function's second variable. The length of this list controls the number of iterations to perform:

```
In[31]:=  Clear[f, a];
          FoldList[f, a, {1, 2, 3}]
```
```
Out[32]=  {a, f[a, 1], f[f[a, 1], 2], f[f[f[a, 1], 2], 3]}
```

```
In[33]:=  Fold[f, a, {1, 2, 3}]
```
```
Out[33]=  f[f[f[a, 1], 2], 3]
```

Here is how to use FoldList to create a list whose nth member is the nth partial sum $1 + \frac{1}{2} + \frac{1}{3} + \cdots + \frac{1}{n}$ of the harmonic series:

In[34]:= `FoldList[#1 + 1/#2 &, 1, Range[2, 10]]`

Out[34]= $\left\{1, \dfrac{3}{2}, \dfrac{11}{6}, \dfrac{25}{12}, \dfrac{137}{60}, \dfrac{49}{20}, \dfrac{363}{140}, \dfrac{761}{280}, \dfrac{7129}{2520}, \dfrac{7381}{2520}\right\}$

Notice that changing the initial value from 1 to 1. causes numerical approximations to be used throughout. This increases the speed of computation and produces results sufficient for plotting:

In[35]:= `FoldList[#1 + 1/#2 &, 1., Range[2, 10]]`

Out[35]= {1., 1.5, 1.83333, 2.08333, 2.28333,
          2.45, 2.59286, 2.71786, 2.82897, 2.92897}

In[36]:= `ListPlot@FoldList[#1 + 1/#2 &, 1., Range[2, 200]]`

Out[36]=

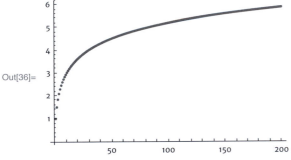

An even simpler means of calculating partial sums is via the `Accumulate` command. Given a finite list {a, b, c, ...}, `Accumulate` will return a list containing the partial sums: {a, a + b, a + b + c, ...}.

In[37]:= `Accumulate[Table[1 / n, {n, 10}]]`

Out[37]= $\left\{1, \dfrac{3}{2}, \dfrac{11}{6}, \dfrac{25}{12}, \dfrac{137}{60}, \dfrac{49}{20}, \dfrac{363}{140}, \dfrac{761}{280}, \dfrac{7129}{2520}, \dfrac{7381}{2520}\right\}$

Another useful iteration command is `Differences`, which will return the differences between successive members in a list.

In[38]:= `Differences[{1, 4, 9, 16}]`

Out[38]= {3, 5, 7}

Whereas one could use `Nest` to iterate this command, it will accept a second argument (specifying the number of iterations desired) to save you the trouble:

In[39]:= `Range[10]^2`

Out[39]= {1, 4, 9, 16, 25, 36, 49, 64, 81, 100}

In[40]:= **Differences$\left[\text{Range}[10]^2\right]$**

Out[40]= {3, 5, 7, 9, 11, 13, 15, 17, 19}

In[41]:= **Differences$\left[\text{Range}[10]^2, 2\right]$**

Out[41]= {2, 2, 2, 2, 2, 2, 2, 2}

In[42]:= **Differences$\left[\text{Range}[10]^2, 3\right]$**

Out[42]= {0, 0, 0, 0, 0, 0, 0}

The input below shows a means of displaying successive differences for the first ten terms in the harmonic sequence, where each row after the first represents the differences for the row above. The display is a Column with each row aligned at its center. Individual rows are Grids (each with only one row), where the ItemSize option is utilized to guarantee a fixed width for each item. It is this fixed width that is needed to produce an easy-to-read display. Exercise 11 in Section 8.8 will have you build a command to automate this procedure for any initial list.

In[43]:= **Column[**
 Table[Grid[{Differences[Table[1 / n, {n, 10}], k]}, ItemSize → 3.25],
 {k, 0, 9}], Alignment → Center]

Out[43]=

$$
\begin{array}{cccccccccc}
1 & \frac{1}{2} & \frac{1}{3} & \frac{1}{4} & \frac{1}{5} & \frac{1}{6} & \frac{1}{7} & \frac{1}{8} & \frac{1}{9} & \frac{1}{10} \\
 & -\frac{1}{2} & -\frac{1}{6} & -\frac{1}{12} & -\frac{1}{20} & -\frac{1}{30} & -\frac{1}{42} & -\frac{1}{56} & -\frac{1}{72} & -\frac{1}{90} \\
 & & \frac{1}{3} & \frac{1}{12} & \frac{1}{30} & \frac{1}{60} & \frac{1}{105} & \frac{1}{168} & \frac{1}{252} & \frac{1}{360} \\
 & & & -\frac{1}{4} & -\frac{1}{20} & -\frac{1}{60} & -\frac{1}{140} & -\frac{1}{280} & -\frac{1}{504} & -\frac{1}{840} \\
 & & & & \frac{1}{5} & \frac{1}{30} & \frac{1}{105} & \frac{1}{280} & \frac{1}{630} & \frac{1}{1260} \\
 & & & & & -\frac{1}{6} & -\frac{1}{42} & -\frac{1}{168} & -\frac{1}{504} & -\frac{1}{1260} \\
 & & & & & & \frac{1}{7} & \frac{1}{56} & \frac{1}{252} & \frac{1}{840} \\
 & & & & & & & -\frac{1}{8} & -\frac{1}{72} & -\frac{1}{360} \\
 & & & & & & & & \frac{1}{9} & \frac{1}{90} \\
 & & & & & & & & & -\frac{1}{10}
\end{array}
$$

Exercises 8.7

1. If one were to set f = Function[x, 2x], then the input Nest[f, x, 4] would produce the output 16x. Give the definition of a Function called f so that Nest[f, x, 4] produces the outputs below. Be sure to check your answers.

   a. 10000 x

   b. x^{16}

c. $\sqrt{1 + \sqrt{1 + \sqrt{1 + \sqrt{1 + x}}}}$

d. $\cfrac{1}{1+\cfrac{1}{1+\cfrac{1}{1+\cfrac{1}{1+x}}}}$

2. When the reverse-add procedure is applied to some numbers, a palindrome is not produced even after millions of iterations. It is suspected (although it has not yet been proved) that a palindrome will *never* result with these numbers. The numbers in this class are known as the *Lychrel numbers* (do an internet search for A023108 and follow the link to the Online Encyclopedia of Integer Sequences for more information). Carry out an investigation of the orbit of the number 196 under 10 000 iterations of the reverse-add procedure, and confirm that no palindrome is produced.

3. When an iteration scheme has a fixed point, it is often a matter of interest to understand how quickly the fixed point is approached. Does it take many iterations to get (for instance) 100 digits of precision, or just a few? A very simple means for garnering a qualitative assessment of the rate of convergence for an iterative sequence of real numbers can be had as follows: Make an `ArrayPlot` where each row represents an iterate, and where each digit is represented by a different tonal value. When a particular decimal position stabilizes to its final value, the column in the array representing that position will be monotone from that point on down. This concept is illustrated below:

   a.   Use `NestList` to iterate the function $f(x) = \dfrac{1}{x} + \dfrac{x}{2}$ ten times, with a starting value of `N[1,20]`.

   b.   Map the function `First[RealDigits[#]]&` over the output above to convert each number into a list of its digits.

   c.   Wrap the output above with `ArrayPlot` to produce a visual representation.

   d.   Repeat parts **a** through **c** in a single input, but where the initial value is `N[1,100]`.

   e.   Repeat part **d**, where the function to be iterated is $f(x) = \dfrac{1}{x} + \dfrac{x}{3}$, and where there are 200 (as opposed to 10) iterations in total. Contrast the results to those of part **d**.

4. Add the option setting `ColorFunction → "Rainbow"` to your favorite `ArrayPlot` and see what happens.

5. When a function f is iterated and converges to a fixed point x^*, it must be the case that $f(x^*) = x^*$ (why?). Geometrically, this means that the point (x^*, x^*) is the intersection of the graphs of $y = f(x)$ and $y = x$. One often illustrates the convergence of the iteration from a particular starting value x_0 by making a *cobweb* diagram. This is composed of the graphs of $y = f(x)$ and $y = x$, together with line segments joining the points (x_0, x_0), $(x_0, f(x_0))$, $(f(x_0), f(x_0))$, $(f(x_0), f(f(x_0)))$, and so on, with alternating vertical and horizontal segments heading ever deeper into the iteration scheme. An illustration is provided below for the function $f(x) = 2.9\, x(1 - x)$, starting point $x_0 = 0.5$. Program *Mathematica* to produce such a diagram.

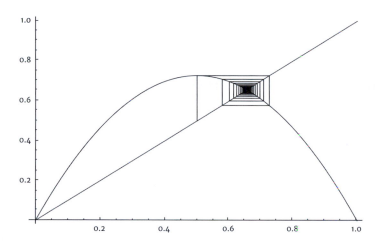

6. The secant method for finding a real root of an equation $f(x) = 0$ was discussed in Section 8.5, where it was implemented via a Do loop. If you go online and visit *MathWorld* (www.mathworld.com) and look up "secant method," you will find the Wolfram Language code shown below for implementing the secant method using NestList. Explain how the code works, and run nine iterations on the function $f(x) = x^3 - 2x + 2$ with starting values $x_0 = -1$ and $x_1 = -3/2$. Does it give the same result as the implementation using Do?

```
In[44]:=  secantMethodList[f_, {x_, x0_, x1_}, n_] :=
            NestList[Last[#] - {0, (Function[x, f][Last[#]] * Subtract @@ #) /
              Subtract @@ Function[x, f] /@ #} &, {x0, x1}, n]
```

7. Make a Manipulate showing cobweb diagrams (like that of the previous exercise) for the family of functions $f(x) = a\,x(1 - x)$, with a slider for a ranging from 2.5 to 3.7, and a second slider for the starting point x_0 ranging from .1 to .9.

8. The command ContinuedFraction will accept a real number as input and will output a list of integers that specifies the *simple continued fraction* form of the input (provided a finite or repeating continued fraction exists). The output $\{1,2,3\}$, for example, represents the continued fraction $1 + \cfrac{1}{2 + \cfrac{1}{3}}$.

   a. Enter ContinuedFraction[10/7], and check that $\dfrac{10}{7} = 1 + \cfrac{1}{2 + \cfrac{1}{3}}$.

   b. Use Fold and Defer to write a command named displayCF that will accept a (finite) digit list as input and will display the simple continued fraction corresponding to that digit list. For instance, displayCF[{1,2,3}] should return $1 + \cfrac{1}{2 + \cfrac{1}{3}}$. Moreover (by using Defer), you will be able to click on and then enter the output to evaluate it.

   c. Use displayCF to display a continued fraction that approximates π to within 10^{-20}. You can use ContinuedFraction$\left[\text{Rationalize}\left[\pi, 10^{-20}\right]\right]$, for instance, to find a continued fraction sequence for a rational number close to π.

9. Use `Accumulate` to find the first ten partial sums of the series $1 + \frac{1}{4} + \frac{1}{9} + \frac{1}{16} + \frac{1}{25} + \cdots$. Euler showed this series converges to $\frac{\pi^2}{6}$ in 1735, solving a decades-old problem (known as the *Basel problem*) and securing fame for himself in the process. Make a `ListPlot` of the first 1000 partial sums together with a horizontal line at height $\frac{\pi^2}{6}$. Comment on the rate of convergence.

8.8 Patterns

For those who wish to program with *Mathematica*, patterns are often the most inaccessible aspect of the language. They are the last frontier to be conquered. For those who "get it," on the other hand, patterns are most definitely a source of power. With an understanding of the fundamentals of patterns, there is the possibility of developing toward power-user status. Without such an understanding, there is little hope.

The first thing to recognize is that you have been using patterns for a quite a while. The most typical instance is in a function definition that includes an underscore (_) on the left-hand side, like the first input shown below. While the subject of patterns is far too vast to adequately cover here, our hope is to be able to convey enough basic knowledge and some illustrative examples so that you will be able to recognize the power of patterns and replacement rules as you go about your work.

A *pattern* is a structure that can be used to represent an entire class of expressions. *Mathematica* has extensive tools for building sophisticated patterns, for detecting when a particular expression matches a given pattern, and for making replacements according to criteria given as patterns. We have already used the most basic type of pattern when defining functions. The x_ on the left side of the definition below, for example, is a pattern.

```
In[1]:= Clear[f, g, u];
        f[x_] := x + 1
```

Here is the `FullForm` of this definition:

```
In[3]:= Defer[FullForm[f[x_] := x + 1]]
Out[3]= SetDelayed[f[Pattern[x, Blank[]]], Plus[x, 1]]
```

The pattern itself, x_, is show below:

```
In[4]:= FullForm[x_]
Out[4]//FullForm=
        Pattern[x, Blank[]]
```

We already have a pretty clear sense that this means x is the independent variable. If the function f above is called with a numerical argument, say for instance that the user enters f[2], then the expression on the right side of the definition will be evaluated with 2 replacing the x and the result is 3. In the broader context of *Mathematica* itself, the pattern x_ can represent *any* structurally valid expression (either an atom or a nested expression, as discussed in Section 8.2). For instance:

```
In[5]:=  f[g[u]]
Out[5]=  1 + g[u]
```

One important use of patterns is to restrict the class of expressions that will match the left side of a definition. If, for instance, one wanted to define a function f that would only work with numeric arguments, this structure would do the trick:

```
In[6]:=  Clear[f];
         f[x_ ?NumericQ] := x + 1

In[8]:=  f[24]
Out[8]=  25
```

Non-numeric input does not match the pattern x_?NumericQ, and so the definition given above is not applied; rather, the expression is returned unevaluated:

```
In[9]:=  f[g[u]]
Out[9]=  f[g[u]]
```

There is much to say here. First, note the structure of the pattern. The name of the pattern (we used x) can be, of course, whatever you like. It is simply the name used to refer to the pattern on the right side of the definition. The underscore is essential; we'll discuss this soon. The ? can be followed by any predicate command. An expression matches the pattern if and only if the predicate returns True for that expression. A handy way to explore this idea is with the command MatchQ. The first argument is an expression and the second is a pattern.

```
In[10]:=  MatchQ[g[u], x_ ?NumericQ]
Out[10]=  False

In[11]:=  MatchQ[24, x_ ?NumericQ]
Out[11]=  True
```

For the purpose of matching, the name x is not even necessary. The underscore (Blank[]) suffices:

```
In[12]:=  MatchQ[24, _ ?NumericQ]
Out[12]=  True
```

Next, note that the same symbol f may be given a different definition for a different form of input. Recall that the function f when given numeric input x outputs the number x + 1. We can add another definition for an input that is a string; f will then return an output corresponding to *either* type of input.

```
In[13]:=  f[x_ ?StringQ] := "YOUR INPUT WAS: " ~~ x
```

In[14]:= `f["blah blah blah"]`

Out[14]= `YOUR INPUT WAS: blah blah blah`

In[15]:= `f[3]`

Out[15]= `4`

In[16]:= `f[apple]`

Out[16]= `f[apple]`

Since apple is neither a string nor numeric (its head is Symbol), f returns unevaluated.

This notion of multiple definitions, one for each of several forms of input, can be useful. For example, consider the famous *Collatz conjecture* (for Lothar Collatz, who proposed it in 1937). Start with a positive integer n. If n is even, return $n/2$. If n is odd, return $3n + 1$. Iterate this process while the result is not 1. The conjecture states that regardless of the starting number, the process will eventually lead to the number 1. The conjecture has been tested extensively, and while it appears to be true, it has not been proven. But programming the function to be iterated is a snap:

In[17]:=
```
Clear[f];
f[n_ ?EvenQ] := n / 2;
f[n_ ?OddQ] := 3 n + 1
```

Here, for example, is the orbit of the starting number 342. It takes a while, but it eventually gets to 1. See Exercise 5 to further explore this conjecture.

In[20]:= `NestWhileList[f, 342, # ≠ 1 &]`

Out[20]= `{342, 171, 514, 257, 772, 386, 193, 580, 290, 145, 436, 218, 109, 328, 164,`
`82, 41, 124, 62, 31, 94, 47, 142, 71, 214, 107, 322, 161, 484, 242,`
`121, 364, 182, 91, 274, 137, 412, 206, 103, 310, 155, 466, 233, 700,`
`350, 175, 526, 263, 790, 395, 1186, 593, 1780, 890, 445, 1336, 668,`
`334, 167, 502, 251, 754, 377, 1132, 566, 283, 850, 425, 1276, 638,`
`319, 958, 479, 1438, 719, 2158, 1079, 3238, 1619, 4858, 2429, 7288,`
`3644, 1822, 911, 2734, 1367, 4102, 2051, 6154, 3077, 9232, 4616, 2308,`
`1154, 577, 1732, 866, 433, 1300, 650, 325, 976, 488, 244, 122, 61,`
`184, 92, 46, 23, 70, 35, 106, 53, 160, 80, 40, 20, 10, 5, 16, 8, 4, 2, 1}`

Now the function f above could also effectively be defined as a Piecewise function. Patterns in this case provide an alternate approach. There are other cases where patterns provide a uniquely elegant means of identifying a pertinent class of expression. In order to see such examples it is necessary to broaden our knowledge of pattern structures. The next fundamental pattern structure we introduce is a _ (Blank[]) followed immediately by a symbol, typically a command name. Any expression having that symbol as its Head will match this pattern. It is the internal FullForm of the expression (discussed in Section 8.2) that determines a match.

```
In[21]:= MatchQ[{1, 2, 3}, _List]
Out[21]= True
```

```
In[22]:= MatchQ[{1, 2, 3}, _Times]
Out[22]= False
```

If a particular expression (such as {1,2,3} below) matches two patterns, the more specific will generally be used first:

```
In[23]:= Clear[f];
         f[x_List] := Apply[Times, x];
         f[x_] := x
```

```
In[26]:= f[{1, 2, 3}]
Out[26]= 6
```

```
In[27]:= f[g[u]]
Out[27]= g[u]
```

Note that the evaluation sequence is important. Structurally, the input 23^2 is represented as Power[23, 2] before evaluation. Its head is Power. After evaluation it becomes 529, and its head is Integer. Expressions will be evaluated *before* being matched to a pattern.

```
In[28]:= Defer[FullForm[23^2]]
Out[28]= Power[23, 2]
```

```
In[29]:= MatchQ[#, _Integer] & /@ {23, 23^2, ∫_0^1 2 t ⅆt, ∫_0^1 t ⅆt}
Out[29]= {True, True, True, False}
```

One may combine the two pattern structures discussed above. Suppose, for instance, you wish to create a function which will only accept a positive integer as its argument. This can be accomplished with the pattern _Integer?Positive. It will only match an expression that evaluates to an Integer, and which returns True when the predicate command Positive is applied.

```
In[30]:= MatchQ[#, _Integer?Positive] & /@ {23, -23, 23.}
Out[30]= {True, False, False}
```

```
In[31]:= Clear[f];
         f[x_Integer?Positive] := 3 x + 1
```

```
In[33]:= f /@ {23, -23, 23.}
Out[33]= {70, f[-23], f[23.]}
```

In case you were wondering, yes, this could also be accomplished via the slightly more cumbersome pattern `_?(Positive[#]&&IntegerQ[#]&)`.

```
In[34]:= MatchQ[#, _?(Positive[#] && IntegerQ[#] &)] & /@ {23, -23, 23.}
Out[34]= {True, False, False}
```

Beginning in *Mathematica* version 12, the number domain `PositiveIntegers` has been added to the language, so the pattern `_?(Element[#,PositiveIntegers]&)` may also be used.

We next consider the various kinds of underscores. While a single underscore `_` (`Blank[]`) will match any expression, a double underscore `__` (two underscores back-to-back, full name `BlankSe`quence`[]`) is an object that will match any *sequence* of one or more expressions (i.e., expressions separated by commas). Just as with the single underscore, it can be preceded by a name (e.g., `x__`) and it can be followed by either a question mark and predicate, or by a command name. For instance, consider the following definition. The pattern `x__Integer` will be matched by a sequence of one or more integers. Every argument in the sequence must be an integer in order for there to be a match. The name `x` refers to the entire sequence.

```
In[35]:= Clear[f, a];
         f[x__Integer] := Times[x]

In[37]:= f[1, 2, 3]
Out[37]= 6

In[38]:= f[3]
Out[38]= 3

In[39]:= f[1, 2, a]
Out[39]= f[1, 2, a]
```

Using the double underscore, you can easily create a command that is based on a built-in command. For instance, below we create a command f that simply invokes `ParametricPlot3D` with the same arguments. It produces two versions of the same image. The pattern `args__` represents the *entire* sequence of arguments.

```
In[40]:= Clear[f, t];
         f[args__] := GraphicsRow[{ParametricPlot3D[args],
             ParametricPlot3D[args, PlotStyle → Dotted]}, ImageSize → 280]
```

In[42]:= **f[{Sin[t] Cos[50 t], Sin[t] Sin[50 t], t},**
    {t, 0, π}, BoxRatios → 1, Boxed → False, Axes → False]

Out[42]=

Finally, there is the *triple* underscore ___ (BlankNullSequence[]), which will match any sequence of *zero* or more expressions. This is especially useful for adding optional arguments to a user-defined command. For example, the command myPlot will call the Plot command with some specific option settings, including a PlotLabel and AxesLabel that are based on the values of the requisite arguments. In the definition below, f and iter represent the requisite arguments for the Plot command, while opts represents any additional option settings the user wishes to add. Since such settings have the head Rule, we demand this via the pattern opts___Rule. The triple underscore is appropriate here since myPlot might be called without any options.

In[43]:= **Clear[myPlot];**
    myPlot[f_, iter_List, opts___Rule] :=
      Plot[f, iter, opts, PlotStyle → Thick, PlotLabel →
        "y = " ~~ ToString[TraditionalForm[f]], AxesLabel → {iter[[1]], "y"}]

In[45]:= **myPlot[1 - x², {x, -1, 1}]**

Out[45]=

$$y = 1 - x^2$$

Note that the PlotLabel and AxesLabels are based on the values provided to the myPlot command's requisite arguments (in the example below, for instance, the variable *t* is used instead of *x*). Note also that because opts appears on the right side of the myPlot definition *before* the specific option settings (e.g., PlotStyle → Thick), any user-supplied option settings will override these defaults. For instance, here a different PlotStyle is specified:

In[46]:= `myPlot[`e^t`, {t, 0, 3}, PlotStyle → Dashed]`

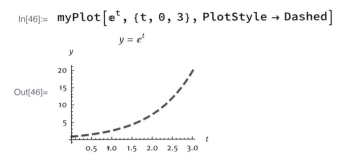

Out[46]=

In Exercise 7 we show another way to add optional arguments to a user-defined command using `OptionsPattern`.

The three types of underscores can also be used in a `StringExpression` (`~~`). The inputs below demonstrate their use in this setting. Given several strings, `StringExpression` will concatenate them into a single string, as in the `PlotLabel` setting for `myPlot` above. Below, the command `DictionaryLookup` is used to scour the dictionary for words that begin with "angle." In the first case it finds all such words that have a single additional character (there are three). In the second case it finds all such words with one or more additional letters (there are seven, including the three from the first output). In the last it finds all such words with zero or more additional letters. The output is the same as the second case with one exception: the word "angle" itself is also present.

In[47]:= `DictionaryLookup["angle" ~~ _]`

Out[47]= `{angled, angler, angles}`

In[48]:= `DictionaryLookup["angle" ~~ __]`

Out[48]= `{angled, anglepoise, angler, anglers, angles, angleworm, angleworms}`

In[49]:= `DictionaryLookup["angle" ~~ ___]`

Out[49]= `{angle, angled, anglepoise, angler,`
`             anglers, angles, angleworm, angleworms}`

So far we have discussed the three types of underscores, that it is permissible to name a pattern by preceding any type of underscore with a symbol (e.g., `x_`), and that it is possible to restrict the type of expression that will match a pattern in one of two ways: by following the underscore with either a command name (such as `x_Integer`), or with a question mark followed by a predicate command (such as `x_?NonNegative`). When defining your own commands this knowledge will get you a long way, as patterns like these are very common on the left side of definitions. But patterns have *many* other uses, and there are countless cases where more sophisticated pattern objects are needed. The next order of business will be to explain how such objects are constructed.

We will do this by introducing the `Cases` command. Like `Select`, this command is used to extract items from a list. Unlike `Select` (which applies a predicate command to the list items and returns those for which the predicate is `True`), `Cases` returns those items from the list that match a pattern. For instance:

In[50]:= `Cases[{0, 2, -2, 4, -4, 6, -6}, _?NonNegative]`

Out[50]= `{0, 2, 4, 6}`

In[51]:= `Select[{0, 2, -2, 4, -4, 6, -6}, NonNegative]`

Out[51]= `{0, 2, 4, 6}`

For the most basic use of Cases, the first argument is the list, and the second is a pattern object. It is the multitude of possible variations for this second argument we wish to address. Here are some illustrative examples:

In[52]:= `Clear[x, g, a, b, c];`
`Cases[x /. NSolve[3 x^4 - x^3 + 5 x^2 + 7 x + 1, x], _Real]`

Out[53]= `{-0.758966, -0.162674}`

In[54]:= `Cases[NSolve[3 x^4 - x^3 + 5 x^2 + 7 x + 1, x], {x -> _Real}]`

Out[54]= `{{x -> -0.758966}, {x -> -0.162674}}`

In[55]:= `Cases[{1, a, a^2, a^3, a^π, a^4}, Power[a, _]]`

Out[55]= `{a^2, a^3, a^π, a^4}`

In[56]:= `Cases[{1, a, a^2, a^3, a^π, a^4}, a^_?(#>3&)]`

Out[56]= `{a^π, a^4}`

In[57]:= `Cases[{1, a, a^2, a^3, a^π, a^4}, a^_Integer]`

Out[57]= `{a^2, a^3, a^4}`

In[58]:= `Cases[{g[1], g[a], g[a, b], g[a, b, c]}, g[_]]`

Out[58]= `{g[1], g[a]}`

In[59]:= `Cases[{g[1], g[a], g[a, b], g[a, b, c]}, g[_Symbol]]`

Out[59]= `{g[a]}`

In[60]:= `Cases[{g[1], g[a], g[a, b], g[a, b, c]}, g[__Symbol]]`

Out[60]= `{g[a], g[a, b], g[a, b, c]}`

In[61]:= `Cases[{g[1], g[a], g[a, b], g[a, b, c]}, g[___, b, ___]]`

Out[61]= `{g[a, b], g[a, b, c]}`

The point here is that a pattern object can be any ordinary expression, but typically it will contain one or more of the various underscores.

Pattern objects can also make use of a number of special commands. For instance, Except[*pattern*] is a pattern object that will match any expression except those that match *pattern*. It is useful in cases when it is more convenient to say what something isn't rather than what it is. The input below is a simplified example of a list where some members have the form `Missing["Not Available"]`. For instance, many of the curated data commands such as `CountryData` will use this symbol when there are missing data. `Cases` and `Except` can be used to extract those data values that are not missing.

```
In[62]:=  Cases[{1, 2, Missing["Not Available"]}, Except[Missing[_]]]
Out[62]=  {1, 2}
```

The `Repeated (..)` command is useful for matching repeating sequences of objects. In the first input below we find all cases of a list composed of the same expression *a* repeated multiple times. In the next input we find all cases of a list composed only of integers.

```
In[63]:=  Cases[{{.12, 2, 3}, {2, 2, 2}, {3, 2, 3}}, {(a_) ..}]
Out[63]=  {{2, 2, 2}}
```

```
In[64]:=  Cases[{{.12, 2, 3}, {2, 2, 2}, {3, 2, 3}}, {_Integer ..}]
Out[64]=  {{2, 2, 2}, {3, 2, 3}}
```

Other such pattern commands include `Longest`, `Shortest`, `Condition`, and `PatternSequence`.

Most of the pattern objects used in the `Cases` examples above were not named. Another setting that often makes use of pattern objects is that of making replacements, and this enterprise generally requires that patterns be named. Here are two simple examples. In the first, no patterns are used. In the second, a simple named pattern is used to make the replacements:

```
In[65]:=  1 + x + x² + x³ /. x → x²
Out[65]=  1 + x² + x⁴ + x⁶
```

```
In[66]:=  1 + x + x² + x³ /. a_Integer → a + 1
Out[66]=  2 + x + x³ + x⁴
```

In the second example every integer in the expression is increased by 1. It is important to make clear that the x in the expression does not get transformed to x^2 under this replacement (even though x is mathematically equivalent to x^1). Rather, patterns are matched to the underlying `FullForm` of the expression in question.

Now imagine that in the last example you wish to increase by 1 only the *exponents* (not the 1 at the far left). The pattern object `Power[x, n_]` will match the exponents, or equivalently x^{n_-}. Note that you need to name the pattern (in this case n) in order to refer to it on the right side of the rule.

```
In[67]:=  1 + x + x² + x³ /. xⁿ⁻ → xⁿ⁺¹
Out[67]=  1 + x + x³ + x⁴
```

⚠ If you want to increase the exponent on every term with an x, the simplest means of doing so is with the pattern object `Power[x,n_.]`. Note the dot (a simple period) after the underscore. The `n_.` represents an optional argument to a command, and it will assume the default value if the argument is omitted. For the `Power` command, the default value for the second argument is 1. In other words, `MatchQ[x,Power[x,n_.]]` will return `True`. So the rule `Power[x, n_.] → Power[x,n+1]` will do the trick.

In the example below, a simple replacement rule is used to turn an integer into a row of a table:

In[68]:= `Grid[Range[10] /. n_Integer → {Defer[n!], "=", n!},`
`      Alignment → Right] // TraditionalForm`

Out[68]//TraditionalForm=

$$
\begin{array}{rcr}
1! & = & 1 \\
2! & = & 2 \\
3! & = & 6 \\
4! & = & 24 \\
5! & = & 120 \\
6! & = & 720 \\
7! & = & 5040 \\
8! & = & 40\,320 \\
9! & = & 362\,880 \\
10! & = & 3\,628\,800
\end{array}
$$

Here is yet another example of named patterns being used in the context of making replacements. We begin with a table, where on any row you will find two mathematically equivalent trigonometric expressions.

In[69]:= `Clear[a, k, n];`
`      Grid[`
`        Table[{Cos[k a], TrigExpand[Cos[k a]]}, {k, 2, 9}],`
`        Alignment → Left, Dividers → Gray`
`      ] // TraditionalForm`

Out[70]//TraditionalForm=

$\cos(2\,a)$	$\cos^2(a) - \sin^2(a)$
$\cos(3\,a)$	$\cos^3(a) - 3\sin^2(a)\cos(a)$
$\cos(4\,a)$	$\sin^4(a) + \cos^4(a) - 6\sin^2(a)\cos^2(a)$
$\cos(5\,a)$	$\cos^5(a) - 10\sin^2(a)\cos^3(a) + 5\sin^4(a)\cos(a)$
$\cos(6\,a)$	$-\sin^6(a) + \cos^6(a) - 15\sin^2(a)\cos^4(a) + 15\sin^4(a)\cos^2(a)$
$\cos(7\,a)$	$\cos^7(a) - 21\sin^2(a)\cos^5(a) + 35\sin^4(a)\cos^3(a) - 7\sin^6(a)\cos(a)$
$\cos(8\,a)$	$\sin^8(a) + \cos^8(a) - 28\sin^2(a)\cos^6(a) + 70\sin^4(a)\cos^4(a) - 28\sin^6(a)\cos^2(a)$
$\cos(9\,a)$	$\cos^9(a) - 36\sin^2(a)\cos^7(a) +$ $126\sin^4(a)\cos^5(a) - 84\sin^6(a)\cos^3(a) + 9\sin^8(a)\cos(a)$

Looking carefully at the expanded expressions in the right column, we observe that the sine function only occurs with an even exponent. This means we can easily eliminate all sine functions from the expressions on the right: use the fact that $\sin^2(a) = 1 - \cos^2(a)$. Or raising each side of this identity to an arbitrary integer power n, we have $\sin^{2n}(a) = (1 - \cos^2(a))^n$. Here is how one could make such a replacement:

In[71]:= `TrigExpand[Cos[7 a]] /. Sin[a]`$^{n\_?EvenQ}$ `→ `$(1 - Cos[a]^2)^{n/2}$

Out[71]= $\text{Cos}[a]^7 - 21\,\text{Cos}[a]^5\,(1 - \text{Cos}[a]^2) +$
$35\,\text{Cos}[a]^3\,(1 - \text{Cos}[a]^2)^2 - 7\,\text{Cos}[a]\,(1 - \text{Cos}[a]^2)^3$

Finally, we `Expand` this to get a nice expression for $\cos(7\,a)$ as a polynomial in $\cos(a)$:

In[72]:= `Expand[%]`

Out[72]= $-7\,\text{Cos}[a] + 56\,\text{Cos}[a]^3 - 112\,\text{Cos}[a]^5 + 64\,\text{Cos}[a]^7$

Here is the table that results from this procedure:

In[73]:= `Grid[`
        `Table[{Cos[k a], TrigExpand[Cos[k a]] /.`
              `Sin[a]`$^{n\_?EvenQ}$ `→ `$(1 - Cos[a]^2)^{n/2}$ `// Expand}, {k, 2, 9}],`
        `Alignment → Left, Dividers → Gray`
        `] // TraditionalForm`

Out[73]//TraditionalForm=

$\cos(2\,a)$	$2\cos^2(a) - 1$
$\cos(3\,a)$	$4\cos^3(a) - 3\cos(a)$
$\cos(4\,a)$	$8\cos^4(a) - 8\cos^2(a) + 1$
$\cos(5\,a)$	$16\cos^5(a) - 20\cos^3(a) + 5\cos(a)$
$\cos(6\,a)$	$32\cos^6(a) - 48\cos^4(a) + 18\cos^2(a) - 1$
$\cos(7\,a)$	$64\cos^7(a) - 112\cos^5(a) + 56\cos^3(a) - 7\cos(a)$
$\cos(8\,a)$	$128\cos^8(a) - 256\cos^6(a) + 160\cos^4(a) - 32\cos^2(a) + 1$
$\cos(9\,a)$	$256\cos^9(a) - 576\cos^7(a) + 432\cos^5(a) - 120\cos^3(a) + 9\cos(a)$

Exercise 6 asks you to use this table to prove that $\cos(\pi/21)$ is a root of the polynomial $f(x) = 1 + 16\,x + 32\,x^2 - 48\,x^3 - 96\,x^4 + 32\,x^5 + 64\,x^6$.

The `Cases` command discussed earlier in this section can also make replacements. That is, one can find all cases within a list (or indeed any expression) of subexpressions that match a particular pattern, and replace each of these by something else. It sounds a bit far-fetched, but it's actually incredibly powerful and useful. There was an example in Section 7.9, for instance, where we extracted all `Line` objects from a graphic and replaced each with the underlying list of points. Let's recreate an example like that one:

In[74]:= Cases[⟨⟨⟨ , Line[*pts_*] → pts, Infinity]

Out[74]= {{{0.211111, 0.833333}, {0.297222, 0.597222},
          {0.186111, 0.416667}, {0.316667, 0.197222}},
         {{0.561111, 0.836111}, {0.472222, 0.602778}, {0.572222, 0.4},
          {0.483333, 0.2}}, {{0.752778, 0.830556}, {0.861111, 0.622222},
          {0.736111, 0.394444}, {0.816667, 0.180556}}}

The first argument to Cases here is not a list, but rather a Graphics that was produced with the Drawing Tools palette. Note the third argument to Cases is Infinity. Cases goes into the FullForm of the Graphics and searches at *every* level (since the third argument is Infinity) for subexpressions matching the pattern object Line[pts_]. Each matching expression is replaced by pts, and a list of all such matching expressions is returned. The result in this case is three lists of points (or more precisely, a *list* of three lists of points).

When making replacements, it is often desirable to assign a name to an entire pattern object. The Pattern command is used for this purpose. The infix form of this command is the colon (:). An expression of the form *name*:*pattern* is used to associate *name* with *pattern*. In the (simple but common) setting where the pattern object is a simple underscore, the colon can be eliminated altogether. That is, the expression x_ (that is so commonly seen) is equivalent to x:_. The colon is essential when naming a more intricate pattern object. Consider, for instance, the example below in which every row that begins with 1 in a matrix gets replaced with that same row multiplied by 3:

In[75]:= $\begin{pmatrix} 1 & 3 & 5 & 7 \\ 7 & 9 & 1 & 8 \\ 1 & 2 & 3 & 4 \\ 2 & 5 & 9 & 1 \end{pmatrix}$ /. a : {1, __} → 3 a // MatrixForm

Out[75]//MatrixForm=
$\begin{pmatrix} 3 & 9 & 15 & 21 \\ 7 & 9 & 1 & 8 \\ 3 & 6 & 9 & 12 \\ 2 & 5 & 9 & 1 \end{pmatrix}$

The name a is associated with the pattern object {1, __}. So 3 a represents the scalar 3 times this list, which has the effect of multiplying every member of the list by 3.

Note that when you make a replacement via ReplaceAll (/.), the very first item in the evaluation sequence will be the right side of the Rule. That is, when you enter the cell containing a replacement, the right side of the Rule is evaluated first. In the example below (which is just like the previous example, except here we Reverse each row in the matrix that begins with 1) this is problematic. The input Reverse[a] generates an error message (because a is a Symbol, not a List). The output, however, is correct.

In[76]:= $\begin{pmatrix} 1 & 3 & 5 & 7 \\ 7 & 9 & 1 & 8 \\ 1 & 2 & 3 & 4 \\ 2 & 5 & 9 & 1 \end{pmatrix}$ /. a : {1, __} → Reverse[a] // MatrixForm

    ▪▪▪ Reverse: Nonatomic expression expected at position 1 in Reverse[a].

Out[76]//MatrixForm=
$\begin{pmatrix} 7 & 5 & 3 & 1 \\ 7 & 9 & 1 & 8 \\ 4 & 3 & 2 & 1 \\ 2 & 5 & 9 & 1 \end{pmatrix}$

In a case such as this, it is better to *delay* evaluation of the right side of the Rule until *after* the replacements have been made. Then Reverse will be applied only to an actual list, and all is fine. The key to doing this is to use RuleDelayed (:> or :→) instead of Rule:

In[77]:= $\begin{pmatrix} 1 & 3 & 5 & 7 \\ 7 & 9 & 1 & 8 \\ 1 & 2 & 3 & 4 \\ 2 & 5 & 9 & 1 \end{pmatrix}$ /. a : {1, __} :→ Reverse[a] // MatrixForm

Out[77]//MatrixForm=
$\begin{pmatrix} 7 & 5 & 3 & 1 \\ 7 & 9 & 1 & 8 \\ 4 & 3 & 2 & 1 \\ 2 & 5 & 9 & 1 \end{pmatrix}$

Another example may help to clarify the distinction between Rule and RuleDelayed. In the first input below, the right side of Rule is evaluated prior to making the replacements. Hence every replacement receives the same random integer. In the second input, the right side of RuleDelayed is not evaluated until after the replacements have been made. Hence RandomInteger[100] is evaluated three times.

In[78]:= {a, a, a} /. a → RandomInteger[100]
Out[78]= {31, 31, 31}

In[79]:= {a, a, a} /. a :→ RandomInteger[100]
Out[79]= {43, 7, 89}

⚠ In order to understand the evaluation sequence upon entering a particular expression, wrap the expression with `Trace`. The result will be a list of every expression that is encountered during the evaluation process, with the final item being the output. In the case of an expression with head `ReplaceAll` whose second argument is a `Rule`, the right side of the `Rule` will be the first thing evaluated.

The final pattern command that we will introduce is called `Optional`. This allows you to build a command with an optional argument. `Optional` accepts a pattern object as its first argument, and the default value to be used if that pattern is omitted as its second argument. For instance, this command will draw a random sample from the list x. If a second argument is given, that will be the size of the sample. If no second argument is given, a random sample of size three will be generated.

In[80]:= `randomSample[x_List, Optional[y_, 3]] := RandomSample[x, y]`

In[81]:= `randomSample[Range[100], 5]`

Out[81]= `{69, 20, 39, 54, 86}`

In[82]:= `randomSample[Range[100]]`

Out[82]= `{69, 79, 83}`

⚠ The infix form of `Optional` is a colon (`:`). There are two distinct commands whose infix form is given by a colon (`:`). For an expression matching the form symbol`:`pattern, the meaning is `Pattern[symbol, pattern]`. On the other hand, for an expression matching the form pattern`:`expression, the meaning is `Optional[pattern, expression]`. So the left side of the definition above could have been entered as `randomSample[x_List, y_:3]`. This can be confusing to someone trying learn about patterns, but it never leads to syntactic ambiguity, for the first argument to `Pattern` must be symbol, while the first argument to `Optional` should be a pattern object. Mercifully, this dual use of a single symbol is exceedingly rare (another example is `!`, which is used for both `Factorial` and the logical negation command `Not`).

Exercises 8.8

1. Define a function f with a single argument. The function will return unevaluated unless

   a. the argument is an even integer greater than 10. In this case the function returns the string `"success"`.

   b. the argument is either an even integer, or is greater than 10. In this case the function returns the string `"success"`.

2. Explain the following output. Doesn't x_1 represent a pattern that will only match the number 1?

```
In[1]:=  Clear[f];
         f[x_ 1] := "success";
         f /@ {1, 2, 2., "donkey"}

Out[1]=  {success, success, success, success}
```

3. Find a word that contains the five letters "angle" (contiguous, and in that order), and which begins with the letter "q" and ends with the letter "s."

4. A DNA molecule is composed of two *complementary* strands twisted into a double helix, where each strand may be represented as an ordered sequence of the letters A, C, G, and T. The complementary strand is built from a given strand by replacing every A by T, every T by A, every G by C, and every C by G. In other words, A is swapped with T, and C is swapped with G. Define a command `complementaryDNA` that will take a list of character strings from the four-letter alphabet "A","C","G", and "T" (which is how we will represent a strand of DNA) and return the complementary strand, in which all As and Ts are switched, and in which all Gs and Cs are switched.

5. This exercise concerns the Collatz conjecture, which was discussed in this section.

   a. Write a command `collatz`, that when given a positive integer will return the orbit of that integer under the iterated Collatz process. The conjecture states that every orbit ends at 1, so use `NestWhileList` with iterations occurring as long as the iterated function does not return 1. To be safe, put a cap on it so that it will never carry out more than 1000 iterations.

   b. Run the `collatz` command on each of the first 20 integers, and make a `Table` of the results. Map the command `Length` over this table to see how many iterations were carried out for each input. Make a `ListPlot` of the results. Did any number require all 1000 possible iterations? If not, we can be confident that every orbit ends in 1.

   c. Map the `Partition` command over your data table to replace an orbit such as {5,16,8,4,2,1} with a list of pairs of successive numbers, like this: {{5,16},{16,8},{8,4},{4,2},{2,1}}.

   d. `Flatten` the result at level 1 to produce a single list of pairs, then feed that list of pairs to the `Union` command (to eliminate duplicate pairs). The list should end like this: {...{88,44},{106,53},{160,80}}.

   e. Use `Map` to `Apply` the command `Rule` to each pair from part **c** to obtain an amalgamated list of all orbits. It should end like this: {..., 88 → 44, 106 → 53, 160 → 80}. Now feed the result to the command `GraphPlot` to get a visualization of the orbit space for the Collatz process.

   f. Repeat the entire exercise for the first 100 integers (rather than just the first 20). Do it yet again for the first 1000.

6. Use the trigonometric expressions for $\cos(ka)$ from this section to prove that $\cos(\pi/21)$ is a root of the polynomial $f(x) = 1 + 16 x + 32 x^2 - 48 x^3 - 96 x^4 + 32 x^5 + 64 x^6$. You may wish to take a look at the example for $\cos(3a)$ in Section 4.6.

7. The commands `Optional` and `OptionsPattern[]` may be used in place of `___Rule` when writing a user-defined command that permits optional arguments. Rewrite the command `myPlot` defined in this section using `opts : OptionsPattern[]` in place of `opts___Rule`.

8. Make a replacement to `Range[15]` and wrap the result in `TabView` to produce the output shown below.

362 880

9. Make a command `scaleRuns` that will take a list $\mathcal{L}$ of 0s and 1s, and return a list in which every run of k consecutive 1s in $\mathcal{L}$ is replaced with k consecutive ks. For instance, the input {1,1,0,1,1,1,0,0} should produce the output {2,2,0,3,3,3,0,0}. You may want to make use of the `Split` command and the `Repeated` command.

10. Use the `scaleRuns` command of the previous exercise to build a command that will take a list of 0s and 1s and display it using an `ArrayPlot` with a single row (with one item in the array for each member of the list), and where each consecutive run of 1s is shaded according to the length of the run. Use `Partition` to modify this command so that it will break a long sequence (say with more than 50 elements) into several rows.

11. Make a command `differenceTable` that will accept two arguments. The first is a list. The second is an optional argument (with default value 3) that specifies the `ItemSize` for each item in a `Grid`. The output will be a difference table display like the one appearing at the end of Section 8.7. You can model the command on the input for the example given there.

9

3D Printing

9.1 Introduction

Mathematica is not a CAD program, nor was it designed with 3D printing in mind. But its intrinsic capabilities make it well suited to creating a wide variety of 3D-printable objects, especially those of a mathematical nature and those accessible in the Wolfram Knowledgebase. In this chapter we will provide an introduction to the commands that are most useful for this purpose, and give you a sense of how they can be used together to produce a quality print. We provide numerous examples with the goal of allowing you to pursue your own projects.

We note at the outset that it is important to design your models with a particular printing technology in mind. Most printers available in educational settings use a process called fused deposition modelling, or FDM, where thin layers of material are added, one atop the next, to build a 3D object. If you will use an FDM printer, it will typically not matter if you make your object "solid" or "hollow," as only its outer surface will be considered by the printer's slicing software. By contrast, most online print services, such as Shapeways or Sculpteo, use a process called selective laser sintering (SLS). With this process, it is often advantageous to hollow out an object *and* leave a hole somewhere in it where leftover sintering powder can be evacuated after printing. This can greatly reduce the cost of printing, but it is up to you to specify the thickness of the model's outer surface and to place the hole in the model.

9.2 3D Printing Basics

The most basic workflow for 3D printing is to render an object via a plotting command, and then call `Printout3D`. For example, here is a printable model of a paraboloid generated with `Plot3D`. We thicken the surface with the option setting `PlotTheme → "ThickSurface"`, and use the setting `BoxRatios → Automatic` to give all three axes the same scale, ensuring that the on-screen rendering accurately reflects the true dimensions of the object.

In[1]:= **paraboloid = Plot3D$\left[x^2 + y^2, \{x, y\} \in \text{Disk}[], \right.$**
           PlotTheme → "ThickSurface", BoxRatios → Automatic$\left.\right]$

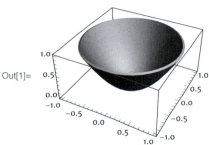

Out[1]=

The paraboloid is now ready to print. If you have not done so already, save your working notebook in its own directory so you can export your print files to that same directory.

Now call `Printout3D`. This will do several things. It first discretizes the output above, turning it into a `MeshRegion` (these will be discussed in the next section). It then runs some diagnostics and if necessary repairs the resulting mesh. Finally, it can either write the printable output to an STL, OBJ, or DAE file for local printing, or it can upload the file directly to a third-party print service such as Shapeways or Sculpteo. To create a file for printing locally, just specify a filename (with appropriate suffix, in this case .stl) as the second argument, and the appropriate file will be created.

In[2]:= **Printout3D[paraboloid, NotebookDirectory[] <> "paraboid.stl"]**

Out[2]=

Status	Successful
Image	
Size	2.1 in × 2.1 in × 1.1 in
FileName	File⌈ /Users/btorrence/Library/Mathematica/Applications/SIM3/paraboid.stl » ⌉
Report	. . .

If instead the second argument is the name of a print service, the file will be uploaded to that service and the price will be displayed. Click the URL in the output to be directed to your object on the print service's website.

In[3]:= **Printout3D[paraboloid, "Sculpteo"]**

Out[3]=

Status	Successful
Service	sculpteo
Image	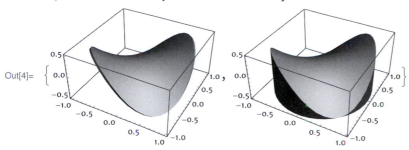
Size	2.1 in × 2.1 in × 1.1 in
Material	Multicolor
Price	—
URL	http://www.sculpteo.com/gallery/design/ext/avCXy64...
Report	...

There are two common plot themes that are useful for 3D printing. We've just seen that the "ThickSurface" theme will add thickness to a two-dimensional surface so that it can be printed. It will work for any 3D plotting command that produces a surface, such as Plot3D, ContourPlot3D, ParametricPlot3D, SphericalPlot3D, and so on.

The theme "FilledSurface" will fill in the volume below a surface generated by Plot3D or ListPlot3D:

In[4]:= **Plot3D[x y, {x, y} ∈ Disk[], PlotTheme → #, BoxRatios → Automatic] & /@**
{"ThickSurface", "FilledSurface"}

Out[4]=

When using the "FilledSurface" theme, the PlotRange setting can be used to specify how far down the fill goes.

```
In[5]:= ListPlot3D[Table[.1 x y, {x, -10, 10}, {y, -10, 10}],
        PlotRange → {#, 10}, PlotTheme → "FilledSurface",
        BoxRatios → Automatic, ClippingStyle → None] & /@ {-15, -10, -5}
```

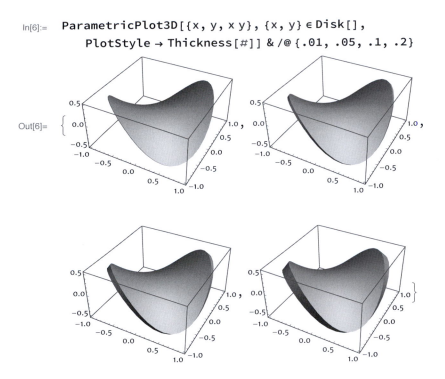

We note that when plotting a surface with ParametricPlot3D, you may set the PlotStyle option to a Thickness of the desired amount. This gives you the ability to control the thickness of the surface.

```
In[6]:= ParametricPlot3D[{x, y, x y}, {x, y} ∈ Disk[],
        PlotStyle → Thickness[#]] & /@ {.01, .05, .1, .2}
```

Another common setting involves thickening a curve in space. To thicken a curve rendered with ParametricPlot3D, set the PlotStyle option to a Tube of the desired radius. You may need to manually set PlotRange to All to prevent clipping if the Tube is sufficiently thick.

```
In[7]:=  ParametricPlot3D[{.1 t, Sin[t], Cos[t]},
           {t, 0, 20 π}, PlotStyle → Tube[.1], PlotRange → All]
```

Out[7]=

9.3 MeshRegions

When `Printout3D` is called, the first thing it does is *discretize* its argument in an effort to create a "watertight mesh," a discrete approximation to the outer surface of the object that can be processed and printed. The discretization step can be accomplished separately with such commands as `Dis⌇cretizeGraphics` or `DiscretizeRegion`. These commands afford you some control over the discretization process, allowing you to fine-tune your mesh to balance its resolution and the resulting file size. In order to do this and a host of other useful things, it is important to first understand the structure of a `MeshRegion`.

Let's step back for a moment and consider the information contained in a standard 3D print file format, STL. While this suffix was originally an acronym for "stereolithography," a more apt and commonly applied descriptor is "standard triangle language." The idea is to represent the surface of the object to be printed as a collection of triangles in 3-space. And indeed, that is what an STL file contains: a long list of triangles, each of whose vertices is a 3-tuple of real numbers. Moreover, each of these triangles has an *orientation*, a designation of a front face and a back face (determined by the direction of a normal vector to the face). The triangles in a printable STL file fit together to form a sort of chain-mail skin around the outer surface of the object to be printed. Each triangle in the mesh has its front face facing outward.

More precisely, the triangles in a mesh should be assembled edge-to-edge so that each edge is shared by precisely two triangles. Moreover, no pair of triangles should intersect unless they share a common edge or a common vertex (no triangle stabbings). Finally, the triangles incident with an individual vertex must form a neighborhood that is a topological disk. (A violation of this last condition would be, say, two cubes that share a common corner; the common corner is the bad vertex.) Such an assemblage is commonly referred to as a "watertight mesh," as it completely encloses the object like a skin. Below is an illustration of three different watertight triangular meshes that, with varying degrees of accuracy, approximate the outer surface of a ball:

In[1]:= `GraphicsRow[`
          `DiscretizeRegion[Sphere[], MaxCellMeasure → #, PrecisionGoal → 0] & /@`
          `{.1, .01, .001}]`

Out[1]=

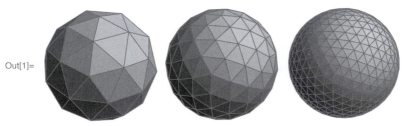

And here is a mesh that approximates the "Stanford bunny," an object often used for testing algorithms in computational geometry:

In[2]:= `ExampleData[{"Geometry3D", "StanfordBunny"}, "MeshRegion"]`

Out[2]=

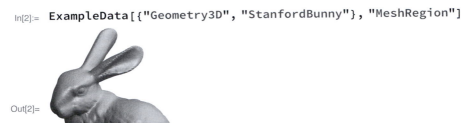

Mathematica represents these meshes as `MeshRegion` objects. Think of these as *Mathematica*'s souped-up version of an STL file. Note that you can click once on the image of a `MeshRegion` to get a handy contextual menu. The information tab provides a host of useful information, such as the number of vertices, edges, and faces in the mesh, the dimensions of its bounding box, and more. Other tabs allow you to change the display settings for the mesh, or to perform basic modifications such as rotations and reflections.

We will examine the internal representation of a `MeshRegion` shortly, but let us first describe some means for constructing one from common objects in *Mathematica*. There are two powerful methods: One is to first create a `Graphics3D` object (say, with `SphericalPlot3D`), and then apply `DiscretizeGraphics` to the result. The other is to first define a region (say, with `ImplicitRegion`), and then apply `DiscretizeRegion` to the result.

In[3]:= `SphericalPlot3D[-θ - φ, {φ, 0, π},`
          `{θ, 0, 2π}, PlotTheme → "ThickSurface",`
          `BoxRatios → Automatic] // DiscretizeGraphics`

Out[3]=

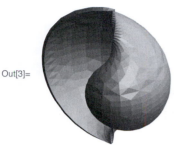

When applying `DiscretizeGraphics` to the output of a plotting command, the simplest means for adjusting the quality of the mesh is to adjust the resolution in the plotting command. For instance, increasing `PlotPoints` to 60 in the input above produces a mesh with more and smaller triangles—it is a better approximation to the true object.

In[4]:= `SphericalPlot3D[-θ - φ, {φ, 0, π}, {θ, 0, 2π},`
          `PlotTheme → "ThickSurface", BoxRatios → Automatic,`
          `PlotPoints → 60] // DiscretizeGraphics`

Out[4]=

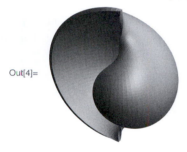

⚠ There is a balance to be struck between the quality of a mesh and the size of the resulting print file. Beyond a certain point, a finer mesh will not produce a better print, as eventually the printer's maximal resolution will be surpassed. Too fine a mesh can produce a huge print file, too large to upload to a print service, or too large to be processed by slicing software. It takes experience with a particular printer to find the right balance, but the rule of thumb is to use the coarsest mesh (and smallest file size) that gives satisfactory results.

The lesson here is that when printing an object created by a plotting command, you can effectively control the quality of the mesh directly from the plotting command. The discretization step permits a close inspection of the resulting mesh, but it is not a necessary step in the workflow. For prints like that of the previous output, it suffices to produce a nice plot and send it directly to `Printout3D`.

The other common method for producing a mesh is `DiscretizeRegion`, which will attempt to discretize any well-defined region. Regions can be built-in primitive graphics objects such as `Ball`, `Sphere`, `Cylinder`, `Cuboid`, `Cone`, etc., or those produced by `ImplicitRegion` or `ParametricRe`-gion. A region may be *solid*:

In[5]:= `ImplicitRegion`$[x^2 + y^2 \le z^4, \{\{x, -1, 1\}, \{y, -1, 1\}, \{z, 0, 1\}\}]$ `//`
        `DiscretizeRegion`

Out[5]=

Solid regions are three-dimensional. The discretization is composed of "3-cells." Think of these as small solid bricks, usually in the shape of tetrahedra.

In[6]:= `RegionDimension[%]`

Out[6]= 3

But a region can also be the *boundary surface* of a solid in three-space. The interior is empty. When discretized, the mesh is composed of triangles or polygons, sometimes called "2-cells." The command `RegionBoundary` may be used to extract the boundary from a solid region.

In[7]:= `RegionBoundary`$[$`ImplicitRegion`$[x^2 + y^2 \le z^4,$
        $\{\{x, -1, 1\}, \{y, -1, 1\}, \{z, 0, 1\}\}]]$ `// DiscretizeRegion`

Out[7]=

In[8]:= `RegionDimension[%]`

Out[8]= 2

Note that if we replace the inequality $x^2 + y^2 \le z^4$ in the previous input with the equation $x^2 + y^2 == z^4$ and dispense with `RegionBoundary`, we get almost the same result, but with the important distinction that the closed disk on the top of the object is no longer included. The resulting mesh is no longer watertight, since each triangle incident with the top boundary circle has an edge that is not incident with another triangle in the mesh. Rule of thumb: If both the front and back side of a triangle in a mesh is visible, the mesh is *not* watertight.

In[9]:= `ImplicitRegion`$[x^2 + y^2 == z^4, \{\{x, -1, 1\}, \{y, -1, 1\}, \{z, 0, 1\}\}]$ //
    `DiscretizeRegion`

Out[9]=

In order to print this object, it must first be thickened. A simple approach is to use `ContourPlot3D` to render the object using the `"ThickSurface"` theme, and then discretize the result.

In[10]:= `ContourPlot3D`$[x^2 + y^2 == z^4, \{x, -1, 1\}, \{y, -1, 1\},$
    $\{z, 0, 1\}$, `BoxRatios` → `Automatic`, `PlotTheme` → `"ThickSurface"`,
    `PlotPoints` → 40] // `DiscretizeGraphics`

Out[10]=

At the `MeshRegion` level, the "thickened" object is obtained from the pure two-dimensional surface by adding a second layer of triangular faces (essentially parallel to the first), and then joining the two layers "around the boundary rim" with a row of triangles. The resulting mesh is two-dimensional and watertight, ready for printing.

In[11]:= `RegionDimension[%]`

Out[11]= 2

Since primitive graphics objects (such as a `Cylinder`) may be treated directly as regions and discretized with `DiscretizeRegion`, keep in mind that a `Sphere` and a `Tube` are two-dimensional, while a `Ball` and a `Cylinder` are three-dimensional (solid). Other solid primitives are `Cone`, `Cuboid`, `Hexahedron`, `Prism`, `Pyramid`, and `Tetrahedron`.

It is useful to understand that most common file formats for 3D printing do not permit 3-cells. So when a solid 3D object is sent to `Printout3D`, only the triangles of its boundary surface are recorded. So in one sense, it does not matter if you produce a solid object or the boundary surface of that object in *Mathematica*; when you export either type of object to STL (or most other printing formats) the results will be the same. That said, we will for the sake of consistency strive to produce watertight meshes, comprising just the two-dimensional boundary surface of the underlying solid object.

When discretizing a region, use options such as `MaxCellMeasure` to set the maximum area of each triangle in a mesh, and/or `PrecisionGoal` to set the desired precision of the resulting mesh relative to the region that it approximates. With `PrecisionGoal` set to 0, the effect of `MaxCellMeasure` can be clearly seen:

```
In[12]:= GraphicsRow[
            DiscretizeRegion[RegionBoundary[Cylinder[]], MaxCellMeasure → #,
                PrecisionGoal → 0] & /@ {1, .1, .01, .001}]
```

Out[12]=

> ⚠ When the individual triangles in a mesh are sufficiently small, Mathematica will no longer render the face edges, as the proliferation of such edges in extreme cases can can completely obscure the faces. In the preceding output, the first three meshes display the face edges, while the one on the far right does not. If you would like to see the edges in a mesh, just use `HiglightMesh[mesh,Style[1,Gray]]`.

The Structure of a MeshRegion

A `MeshRegion` is in principle a simple construction. There are two arguments. The first is a list of all vertices (the corners of all triangles) in the mesh. The second, for the case of a 3D-printable watertight mesh, is a list of `Triangle` and/or `Polygon` objects. A simple example is provided by a tetrahedron—a solid polyhedron with four triangular faces.

```
In[13]:= MeshRegion[{{0., 0., 0.}, {1., 0., 0.}, {0., 1., 0.}, {0., 0., 1.}},
            {Polygon[{{1, 2, 3}, {1, 2, 4}, {1, 3, 4}, {2, 3, 4}}]}];
```

Use `HighlightMesh` to style or label elements in a mesh. Here we label the vertices, or 0-cells, by their position in the vertex list.

In[14]:= `HighlightMesh[%, Labeled[0, "Index"]]`

Out[14]=

Each triangular face is specified by a triple of whole numbers, such as {1, 2, 3}. These are vertex *indices*, meaning that the first, second, and third vertices in the vertex list determine a triangular face (in this case, the "bottom" face of the tetrahedron).

We can build our own `MeshRegion` easily. Consider, for example, the standard *regular tetrahedron* centered at the origin: It has unit-length sides and equilateral triangular faces. We typed CTRL = followed by "regular tetrahedron" to call up the regular tetrahedron entity from the Wolfram Knowledgebase. While we could just ask for the "MeshRegion" property of this entity, here we instead ask for its vertex list and face indices so we can build it ourselves.

In[15]:= v = (regular tetrahedron POLYHEDRON) `["VertexCoordinates"]`

$$
\text{Out[15]=} \quad \left\{ \left\{ 0, 0, \sqrt{\frac{2}{3}} - \frac{1}{2\sqrt{6}} \right\}, \left\{ -\frac{1}{2\sqrt{3}}, -\frac{1}{2}, -\frac{1}{2\sqrt{6}} \right\}, \right.
$$

$$
\left. \left\{ -\frac{1}{2\sqrt{3}}, \frac{1}{2}, -\frac{1}{2\sqrt{6}} \right\}, \left\{ \frac{1}{\sqrt{3}}, 0, -\frac{1}{2\sqrt{6}} \right\} \right\}
$$

In[16]:= f = (regular tetrahedron POLYHEDRON) `["Faces"]`

Out[16]= {{2, 3, 4}, {3, 2, 1}, {4, 1, 2}, {1, 4, 3}}

We can check that the distance between any two vertices is exactly 1:

In[17]:= `EuclideanDistance @@@ Subsets[v, {2}]`

Out[17]= {1, 1, 1, 1, 1, 1}

The `MeshRegion` with these four triangular faces can be expressed like this:

In[18]:= `tetMesh = MeshRegion[v, Polygon[f]]`

Out[18]=

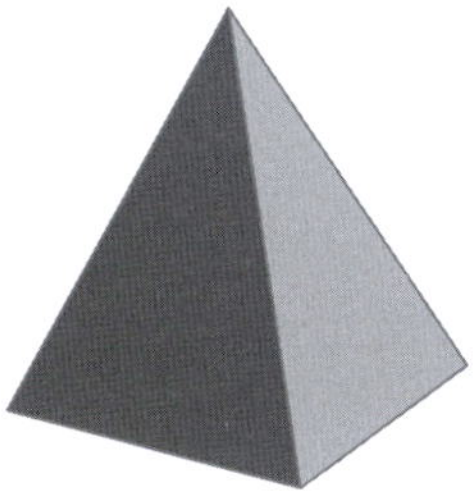

Notice that `MeshRegion` objects use numerical approximations to store vertex coordinates, as this can greatly reduce both computation time and storage space.

In[19]:= `tetMesh // InputForm`

Out[19]//InputForm=

```
MeshRegion[{{0., 0., 0.6123724356957945}, {-0.2886751345948129,
   -0.5, -0.20412414523193154}, {-0.2886751345948129, 0.5,
   -0.20412414523193154}, {0.5773502691896258, 0.,
   -0.2041241452319354}}, {Polygon[{{2, 3, 4}, {3, 2, 1}, {4, 1,
   2}, {1, 4, 3}}]}]
```

Understanding the structure of a `MeshRegion` gives you a simple and powerful platform to create a new mesh from an existing mesh. For instance, you could apply a transformation to the vertices while maintaining the same face indices. Let us illustrate this with a slightly more complex example: a cylinder of radius 1 whose central axis runs from (0, 0, 0) to (3, 0, 0). We use `RegionBoundary` to extract the boundary surface from the solid cylinder.

In[20]:= `cylMesh =`
       `DiscretizeRegion[RegionBoundary[Cylinder[{{0, 0, 0}, {3, 0, 0}}, 1]]]`

Out[20]=

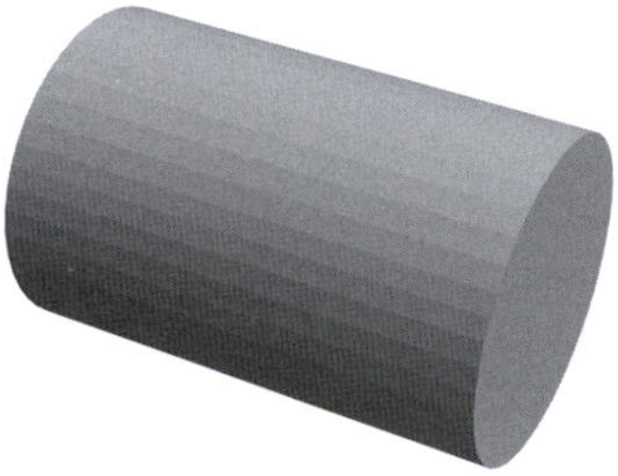

We can retrieve the individual vertex coordinates and face indices from any `MeshRegion` using the commands `MeshCoordinates` and `MeshCells`. The second argument to `MeshCells` is set to 2, so it will return all two-dimensional mesh cells, the faces.

In[21]:= `verts = MeshCoordinates[cylMesh];`
       `faces = MeshCells[cylMesh, 2];`

We may now, for instance, apply a shearing transformation to the vertices, keeping the face indices unchanged, to obtain a new mesh:

In[23]:= **MeshRegion[**
          ShearingTransform[-π/6, {1, 0, 0}, {0, 0, 1}][verts], faces]

Out[23]=

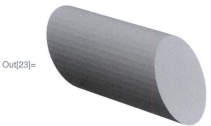

A straightforward application of this idea is to Rescale the vertex coordinates of a given mesh to produce a new mesh with the object sized differently. Rescale applied to the vertex list will scale the vertices proportionally so that the longest edge in the bounding box for the object ranges from 0 to 1. To resize, it is best to first translate the coordinates so that all are nonnegative. Use RegionBounds to get the current x, y, and z bounds for the object so you know how much to translate it (or click on the mesh in your notebook to bring up the contextual menu, and look in the information tab).

In[24]:= **RegionBounds[cylMesh]**

Out[24]= {{0., 3.}, {-0.996616, 0.996616}, {-1., 1.}}

The output tells us we should add 1 to all the y and z coordinates to make them nonnegative. Now apply Rescale and multiply this normalized vertex list by whatever scaling factor you like. For instance, if our goal is to make a cylinder that is 20 cm in length, we may resize our cylinder so that the longest x, y, or z span is 20 units:

In[25]:= **MeshRegion[**
          20 * Rescale[Plus[#, {0, 1, 1}] & /@ verts], faces, Axes → True]

Out[25]=

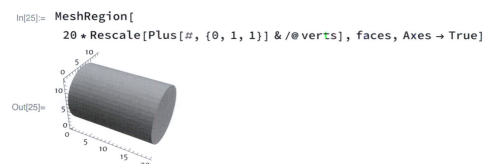

The option setting TargetUnits → "Centimeters" can then be set in Printout3D to ensure a properly sized print.

We note also that the structure of a MeshRegion is analogous to that of a GraphicsComplex. Both take two arguments: a list of vertices, and a list of polygons (or other primitive graphics objects) specified by vertex indices.

In[26]:= `Graphics3D[GraphicsComplex[verts, faces]]`

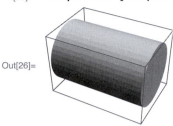

Out[26]=

Many plotting commands, like `Plot3D`, `ParametricPlot3D`, and `ContourPlot3D`, produce a `GraphicsComplex` as their output, and in such cases it is a simple matter for `DiscretizeGraphics` to turn that into a `MeshRegion`, essentially using the same vertices and face indices. This is why increasing the resolution of a plot, say by increasing the value of `PlotPoints`, leads to a finer mesh.

Face Orientation

Each face, or "2-cell," in a `MeshRegion` has two sides—a front side and a back side—and the designation of which side is which is the face's *orientation*. Recall that for a watertight mesh, we want only the front side of the faces to be visible. Recall also that a face is specified as a list of vertex indices, such as {2, 3, 4}. The order in which the vertex indices are listed determines a face's orientation. The front side of a face is determined by a right-hand rule: If you place the wrist of your right hand on vertex 2, and curl your fingers so that from wrist to fingertip you visit vertices 2, 3, and 4, then your thumb points outward from the *front* of the face. Or said another way: The perimeter path that visits the vertices in the order 2, 3, 4, 2 will traverse the front side of the face in counterclockwise fashion. How can we show the face orientations in a given mesh?

A simple method is to use `HighlightMesh` to reveal the orientations of the faces in a `MeshRegion`. This command is used to change the display settings for any individual element (face, edge, or vertex) in a mesh, or all elements of a particular type (such as all faces). We will use `HighlightMesh` to color the front and back sides of faces differently, so we can be assured that the front sides are facing outward. In the next input we color the front side of each 2-cell yellow, and the back side black. The second argument says "style every 2-cell with yellow on the front side and black on the back." We see that the faces of our tetrahedron are correctly oriented for printing, but those of the cylinder are backwards:

In[27]:= `HighlightMesh[#, Style[2, FaceForm[Yellow, Black]]] & /@`
          `{tetMesh, cylMesh}`

Out[27]= {  }

To flip the all the faces in a `MeshRegion` object, one simply needs to `Reverse` the ordering of the vertex indices in each face. Here is a simple command for doing that:

```
In[28]:=  flipFaces[mesh_] :=
            MeshRegion[MeshCoordinates[mesh],
              Polygon[Reverse @@@ MeshCells[mesh, 2]]]
```

```
In[29]:=  HighlightMesh[#, Style[2, FaceForm[Yellow, Black]]] & /@
            {cylMesh, flipFaces[cylMesh]}
```

Out[29]=

It is good practice when preparing a model for 3D printing to first discretize the model and check the orientation of its faces. Once a watertight, properly oriented `MeshRegion` is created, it may be exported directly as an STL, OBJ, or DAE file with `Export` instead of running the more thorough `Printout3D`.

```
In[30]:=  Export[NotebookDirectory[] <> "cylinder.stl", flipFaces[cylMesh]];
```

Exercises 9.3

1. This exercise will explore how the `PlotPoints` option can be used in `ParametricPlot3D` on a function of a single variable (a curve in space) to fine-tune the fidelity of the mesh obtained from the discretization of its output. In each input, include the options `PlotStyle→Tube[.2]`, `MaxRecursion→0` and `PlotRange→ All`.

   a. Make a `ParametricPlot` of the function $\{Cos[t], Sin[t], .1\,t\}$ for $0 \le t \le 6\pi$.

   b. Make a `ParametricPlot` of the function $\{Cos[t], Sin[t], .1\,t\}$ for $0 \le t \le 6\pi$, but now set `PlotPoints` to 13.

   c. Make a `ParametricPlot` of the function $\{Cos[t], Sin[t], .1\,t\}$ for $0 \le t \le 6\pi$, but now set `PlotPoints` to 130.

   d. Make a `ParametricPlot` of the function $\{Cos[t], Sin[t], .1\,t\}$ for $0 \le t \le 6\pi$, keep `PlotPoints` set to 130, but now change the `PlotStyle` setting to `Tube[.2, PlotPoints → 4]`.

   e. Make a `ParametricPlot` of the function $\{Cos[t], Sin[t], .1\,t\}$ for $0 \le t \le 6\pi$, keep `PlotPoints` set to 130, but now change the `PlotStyle` setting to `Tube[.2, PlotPoints → 24]`. Apply `DiscretizeGraphics` to the result, and explain how the two `PlotPoints` settings affect the mesh.

2. This exercise will explore how the `PlotPoints` option can be used in `ParametricPlot3D` on a function of two variables (a surface in space) to fine-tune the fidelity of the mesh obtained from the discretization of its output. In each input, include the options `PlotStyle → Thickness[.2]`, `MaxRecursion → 0` and `Mesh → All`.

    a. Make a `ParametricPlot` of the function `{Cos[t], Sin[t], u}` for $0 \le t \le 2\pi$ and $0 \le u \le 1$.

    b. Make a `ParametricPlot` of the function `{Cos[t], Sin[t], u}` for $0 \le t \le 2\pi$ and $0 \le u \le 1$, but now set `PlotPoints` to 5.

    c. Make a `ParametricPlot` of the function `{Cos[t], Sin[t], u}` for $0 \le t \le 2\pi$ and $0 \le u \le 1$, but now set `PlotPoints` to `{20, 5}`. Explain how the numbers 20 and 5 affect the output.

9.4   MeshRegions from the Wolfram Knowledgebase

The Wolfram Knowledgebase is teaming with pre-made meshes for all manner of objects. To access them simply type ⌞CTRL⌟`=` followed by a query in natural language, such as "mesh region of femur." That query produces this:

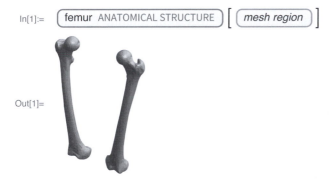

The input `AnatomyData["Femur"]["MeshRegion"]` will produce the same result. `AnatomyData` provides an extensive library with tens of thousands of anatomical structures. One may use `Anatomy⁚Plot3D` to display several anatomical entities together, and then discretize the entire assemblage for printing.

In[2]:= `model = AnatomyPlot3D[`

{ femur ANATOMICAL STRUCTURE , pelvis ANATOMICAL STRUCTURE }];

`DiscretizeGraphics[model]`

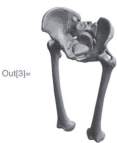

Out[3]=

`ChemicalData` holds another huge repository of pre-made meshes, watertight and ready for printing.

In[4]:= `ChemicalData["Aspirin", "MeshRegion"]`

Out[4]=

There is also a beautiful repository containing hundreds of polyhedra and complexes of polyhedra in `PolyhedronData`. The `MeshRegion` for a polyhedron will result in a solid mesh, rather than the watertight two-dimensional mesh we seek for printing.

In[5]:= snub cube POLYHEDRON `["MeshRegion"]`

Out[5]=

In[6]:= `RegionDimension[%]`

Out[6]= 3

One may simply ask for the RegionBoundary of such a mesh. Doing so produces a mesh with more triangles than are needed, but it produces a lovely print.

In[7]:= `RegionBoundary[ ( snub cube POLYHEDRON ) ["MeshRegion"] ]`

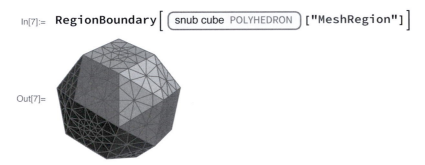

Out[7]=

Alternatively, it is a simple matter to create lists of a polyhedron's vertices and faces, and then assemble these into a mesh. The resulting mesh has precisely the same faces as the polyhedron. Here we build such a mesh for the snub cube and confirm that its faces are correctly oriented.

In[8]:= `v = ( snub cube POLYHEDRON ) ["VertexCoordinates"];`

`f = ( snub cube POLYHEDRON ) ["Faces"];`

`snubCube = MeshRegion[v, Polygon[f]];`

`HighlightMesh[snubCube, Style[2, FaceForm[Yellow, Black]]]`

Out[11]=

Since STL files are built from triangles, exporting this mesh requires splitting the square faces into triangles. Export will take care of this, as we can see by importing the STL file it produces. This STL is a tiny file with just 44 triangles, and it produces a perfect print.

In[12]:= `Import[Export["snubCube.stl", snubCube]]`

Out[12]=

The approach of building a `MeshRegion` from the vertices and faces of a polyhedron also makes it possible to print the "frame" of a polyhedron (replacing the edges with cylindrical "struts" and eliminating the faces), which uses far less material. We will explore methods for accomplishing this in the next section.

Yet another repository for pre-made meshes is `KnotData`. The `"MeshRegion"` property will again produce a solid mesh, so use `RegionBoundary` to produce a watertight, two-dimensional mesh.

In[13]:= `RegionBoundary[KnotData[#, "MeshRegion"]] & /@`
         `{"Trefoil", {"TorusKnot", {3, 2}}}`

Out[13]= {

}

In[14]:= `HighlightMesh[Last[%], Style[2, FaceForm[Yellow, Black]]]`

Out[14]=

The Wolfram Knowledgebase is always expanding, and surely more meshes from entirely new classes of objects will be added in the future.

9.5   Mesh Assembly, Modification, and Diagnostics

Modifying a Mesh

It is always possible to modify an existing mesh or region to get something entirely new. Consider, for example, the *icosidodecahedron*, an Archimedean solid with regular pentagonal and triangular faces that may be found in `PolyhedronData`:

In[1]:=   `( icosidodecahedron POLYHEDRON )["MeshRegion"]`

Out[1]=

We will extract the lower half of this object, and thicken it to make a bowl. Before we get started, note that the mesh is centered at the origin (click on it and look in the information tab, or take the mean of its vertices as we do below).

In[2]:=   `v = PolyhedronData["Icosidodecahedron", "VertexCoordinates"];`
          `Mean[v] // FullSimplify`

Out[3]=   `{0, 0, 0}`

To retrieve the faces on the lower half, we discard from the face list for the icosidodecahedron any face that includes a vertex with positive z coordinate, as these faces lie above the "equator." This leaves the 16 lower faces.

In[4]:=   `f = Select[PolyhedronData["Icosidodecahedron", "FaceIndices"],`
          `    ContainsNone[#, Flatten[Position[v, {_, _, _?Positive}], 1]] &]`

Out[4]=   `{{12, 13, 4, 17, 3}, {3, 17, 9}, {17, 4, 10}, {4, 13, 28},`
          `  {13, 12, 11}, {12, 3, 27}, {27, 1, 18}, {9, 22, 15}, {10, 16, 23},`
          `  {28, 19, 2}, {11, 20, 21}, {27, 3, 9, 15, 1}, {9, 17, 10, 23, 22},`
          `  {10, 4, 28, 2, 16}, {28, 13, 11, 21, 19}, {11, 12, 27, 18, 20}}`

Next, we form meshes for the inner and outer surfaces of the bowl. Both will have the faces f, but for the outer layer we scale up the vertices slightly, pushing them outward from the origin. We then use `RegionUnion` to combine the two individual meshes into a single new `MeshRegion`. This means combining the two vertex lists into one, and hence re-indexing all the face polygons. We use `High⁚ lightMesh` to reveal the new vertex indices.

In[5]:= `inner = MeshRegion[v, Polygon[f]];`
`outer = MeshRegion[1.2 v, Polygon[f]];`
`union = RegionUnion[inner, outer];`
`HighlightMesh[union, Labeled[0, "Index"]]`

Out[8]=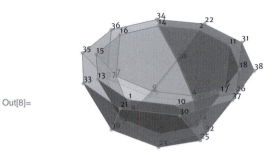

As a final step, we make this mesh watertight by adding polygons that join the inner and outer surfaces along the rim. Using the indices shown above, it is a simple matter to do this manually. We give each quadrilateral a counterclockwise orientation when viewed from above so these faces will have their front sides facing up.

In[9]:= `bowlMesh =`
`MeshRegion[MeshCoordinates[union], Join[MeshCells[union, 2],`
`Polygon /@ {{1, 21, 30, 10}, {10, 30, 37, 17}, {17, 37, 38, 18},`
`{18, 38, 31, 11}, {11, 31, 22, 2}, {2, 22, 34, 14}, {14, 34, 36, 16},`
`{16, 36, 35, 15}, {15, 35, 33, 13}, {13, 33, 21, 1}}]]`

Out[9]=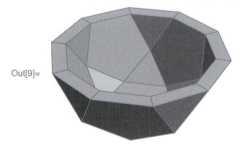

The result looks perfect, but looks can be deceiving. Fortunately, there is a powerful diagnostic tool for meshes: `FindMeshDefects`. Feed it a mesh and it will flag issues, if there are any, that prevent the mesh from being watertight.

In[10]:= `FindMeshDefects[bowlMesh]`

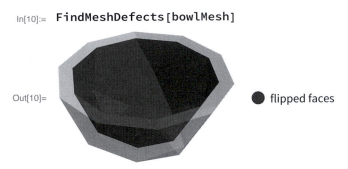

Out[10]=   ● flipped faces

Here we see that the faces of the inner surface are not oriented correctly. In hindsight, this should be obvious; since the inner and outer surfaces have the same face indices, they are similarly oriented. But the bowl needs the polygons on its outer surface facing away from the origin, and those on its inner surface facing toward it. Fortunately, `RepairMesh` is equipped to reorient polygons in situations such as this.

In[11]:= `bowlMeshFinal = RepairMesh[bowlMesh, "FlippedFaces"];`
`HighlightMesh[bowlMeshFinal, Style[2, FaceForm[Yellow, Black]]]`

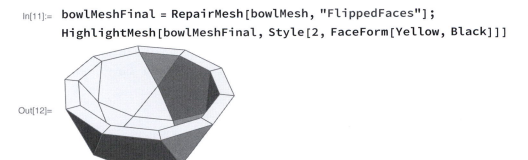

Out[12]=

We note that the mesh above has triangular, trapezoidal, and pentagonal faces. This is permissible in a `MeshRegion`, but not for an STL file where all faces must be triangular. Both `Export` and `Print`out3D will add edges to triangulate any faces with more than three sides when creating an STL file, so it's not something that needs to be addressed when building a model. The bowl above is ready for printing.

In[13]:= `SetDirectory[NotebookDirectory[]];`
`Export["icosidodecaBowl.stl", bowlMeshFinal]`

Out[14]= `icosidodecaBowl.stl`

We note also that while `RepairMesh` does not require a second argument, it is generally best to employ it with one so that it fixes precisely the problem at hand. In the input above, for instance, without a second argument `RepairMesh` will eliminate all non-triangular faces in the mesh—not what we want! See Exercise 1.

There are typically many approaches to realize a three-dimensional design objective. A very different approach for this model is to take the two-dimensional `inner` mesh, and then use `RegionDistance` to make a solid object comprising all points in space that are sufficiently close to it. The fidelity of the resulting mesh can be tuned with the `MaxCellMeasure` option in `DiscretizeRegion`.

In[15]:= `thickenedRegion =`
`    ImplicitRegion[RegionDistance[inner, {x, y, z}] ≤ .1, {x, y, z}];`
`model = DiscretizeRegion[thickenedRegion,`
`    RegionBounds[thickenedRegion], MaxCellMeasure → .001]`

Out[16]=

Among the commonly encountered mesh defects are "hole edges," sometimes called "boundary edges," where some triangles in the mesh have an edge that does not belong to any other triangle. Such a mesh is unprintable. A simple example is provided by discretizing the plot of a real-valued function of two variables over a compact domain such as a rectangle or disk. The outer rim of the resulting mesh has triangles that do not share an edge with any other triangles, so the mesh is not watertight. The image on the left in the following output shows the boundary as a thick, dashed curve.

In[17]:= `plot = Plot3D[x² + y², {x, y} ∈ Disk[], Mesh → None,`
`    BoundaryStyle → {Thick, Dashed}, Axes → False,`
`    Boxed → False, BoxRatios → Automatic, ImageSize → 250];`
`meshWithBoundary = DiscretizeGraphics[plot];`
`{plot, meshWithBoundary}`

Out[19]=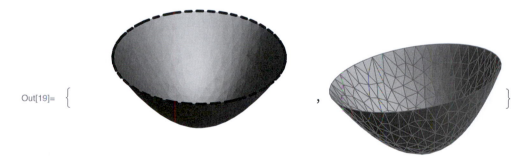

⚠ Note the option setting Mesh → None in the previous input. The placement of the mesh lines in a 3D plot will affect the triangulation used to render it, and this in turn will affect the discretization. So when using `DiscretizeGraphics` on such a plot, the output will be affected by the Mesh settings in that plot. It is often the case that eliminating mesh specifications in a plot (by setting Mesh to All or None) improves the discretization.

Running `FindMeshDefects` on this mesh reveals the offending edges—the edges along the rim of the bowl are highlighted, and the legend tells us that these are "hole edges."

In[20]:= `FindMeshDefects[meshWithBoundary]`

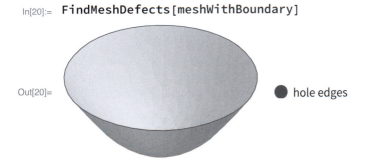

Out[20]=   ● hole edges

`RepairMesh` will in this case seal the "hole," although this may not be the result you seek.

In[21]:= `RepairMesh[meshWithBoundary, "HoleEdges"]`

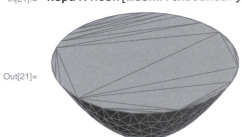

Out[21]=

Meshes obtained from 3D scanning software, or imported from third parties, are often rife with defects. There can be isolated vertices, not connected to any faces. There can be edges that belong to no faces, sticking out like strands of hair. There can be three or more triangles sharing a common edge. Running `FindMeshDefects` can in many cases reveal such issues, and running `RepairMesh` can in many cases fix them.

Overlapping Faces and Torus Knots

There are a myriad of ways in which a mesh can fail to be watertight. Some are disqualifying, some are easily repaired, and others may not even be worth fussing about. A commonly encountered issue that is often not worth fussing about is that of "overlapping faces." Let us explore this phenomenon more carefully by introducing the family of *torus knots*, closed curves that wrap around the surface of a torus.

In the previous section of this chapter we showed how to access knots in the Wolfram Knowledge-base, including torus knots. If your goal is to make a simple model of a knot, the most direct method is to ask for the "MeshRegion" property of the appropriate knot. But our goal here is to illustrate general methods for working with closed curves, and torus knots provide a rich setting for such endeavors.

Torus knots are indexed by a pair of positive integers m and n. The (m, n) torus knot wraps around the "doughnut hole" of the torus m times, and wraps around the circular cross-section n times. If the underlying torus has radius $r_1 = 2$ (from the center of the doughnut hole to the center of the circular cross-section) and if the cross-section has radius $r_2 = 1$, the standard parameterization of a torus is given as follows:

```
In[22]:=  torus = ParametricPlot3D[
            2 {Cos[u], Sin[u], 0} + {Cos[u] Cos[v], Sin[u] Cos[v], Sin[v]},
            {u, 0, 2 Pi}, {v, 0, 2 Pi}, Mesh → All,
            MaxRecursion → 0, PlotPoints → {40, 20}]
```

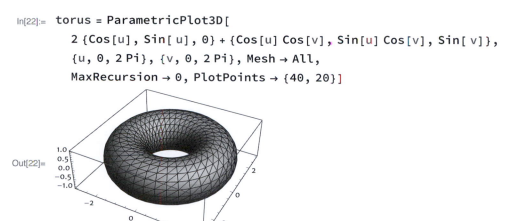

The (m, n) torus knot is obtained from the standard parameterization of a torus by replacing the "around the doughnut hole" parameter u by $m*t$ and the "around the cross-section" parameter v by $n*t$, where the parameter t ranges from 0 to 2π.

```
In[23]:=  torusKnot[r1_, r2_, m_, n_][t_] := r1 {Cos[m t], Sin[m t], 0} +
            r2 {Cos[m t] Cos[n t], Sin[m t] Cos[n t], Sin[n t]}
```

So, for example, the (2, 1) torus knot may be rendered with `ParametricPlot3D` and discretized as follows:

```
In[24]:=  knot = ParametricPlot3D[torusKnot[2, 1, 2, 1][t],
            {t, 0, 2 π}, PlotStyle → Tube[.25, PlotPoints → 25],
            PlotPoints → 100, PlotRange → All];
          {Show[torus, knot, PlotRange → All], knot, DiscretizeGraphics[knot]}
```

Out[25]=

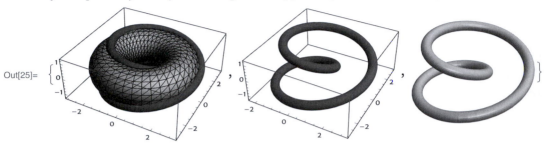

If we allow t to run from 0 to something short of 2π, the discretized mesh is watertight. But when t is permitted to reach or exceed 2π, the end of the mesh overlaps with its beginning, introducing what are called "overlapping faces."

```
In[26]:=  DiscretizeGraphics[ParametricPlot3D[torusKnot[2, 1, 2, 1][u],
            {u, 0, 2 π + #}, PlotStyle → Tube[.25, PlotPoints → 25],
            PlotPoints → 100, PlotRange → All]] & /@ {-.2, 0, .2}
```

Out[26]=

For printing on an FDM printer, any of these meshes is appropriate, even though the two rightmost meshes have overlapping faces. In fact, letting t advance slightly past 2π is likely to create a stronger print; we have seen prints of such closed curves "break at the seam" when there is no overlap, as the model is essentially watertight with the two closed ends of the tube just butting up against each other. They often can be easily pulled apart.

With a bit more work, we can produce a perfectly watertight mesh for *any* smooth, closed, parameterized curve embedded in three-space, and moreover we can control every aspect of the model. We illustrate the ideas with torus knots.

The idea is straightforward: Partition a curve $f(t)$ into a list of p points $f(t_1)$, $f(t_2)$, ..., $f(t_p)$. At each point $f(t_i)$, calculate the unit normal and binormal vectors (as discussed in Section 6.3), and use them as basis vectors to trace out q equally spaced points to form the vertices for the cross-section at $f(t_i)$. Here we use `FrenetSerretSystem` to calculate general expressions for the unit normal and binormal vectors in terms of the parameter t for the $(3, 2)$ torus knot.

```
In[27]:= Clear[f, t];
         f[t_] := torusKnot[2, 1, 3, 2][t];
         {{curvature, torsion}, {tangent, normal, binormal}} =
             Simplify[FrenetSerretSystem[f[t], t]];
```

Each of the five quantities defined on the last line above is an expression in *t*. For example, here is the unit tangent vector:

```
In[30]:= tangent
```

$$
\text{Out[30]= } \left\{ -\frac{\text{Sin}[t] + 12\,\text{Sin}[3\,t] + 5\,\text{Sin}[5\,t]}{\sqrt{2}\,\sqrt{89 + 72\,\text{Cos}[2\,t] + 9\,\text{Cos}[4\,t]}}, \right.
$$

$$
\left. \frac{\text{Cos}[t] + 12\,\text{Cos}[3\,t] + 5\,\text{Cos}[5\,t]}{\sqrt{2}\,\sqrt{89 + 72\,\text{Cos}[2\,t] + 9\,\text{Cos}[4\,t]}}, \frac{2\,\sqrt{2}\,\text{Cos}[2\,t]}{\sqrt{89 + 72\,\text{Cos}[2\,t] + 9\,\text{Cos}[4\,t]}} \right\}
$$

Here are the vertices for our model of $f(t)$ when we subdivide the curve into $p = 200$ parts, where each cross-section has $q = 15$ points:

```
In[31]:= Module[{a = 0, b = 2 π, p = 200, q = 15, radius = .25, δ},
            δ = (b - a) / p;
            vertices = Join @@ Table[
                f[t] + radius * (Cos[2. π k / q] normal + Sin[2. π k / q] binormal) /.
                    t → ti, {ti, a, b - δ, δ}, {k, 1, q}];
            Graphics3D[{PointSize[Tiny], Point[vertices]}]
         ]
```

There are several ways to build a watertight mesh around these vertices. The simplest is to use ListSurfacePlot3D, which will attempt to build a surface from a list of points in space.

```
In[32]:= lsp = ListSurfacePlot3D[vertices, Mesh → None, MaxPlotPoints → 50];
       {lsp, DiscretizeGraphics[lsp]}
```

Out[33]=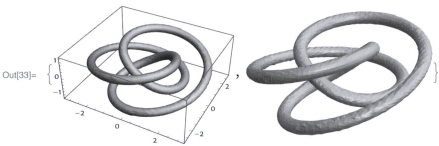

The discretization is watertight, although it is a good idea to run `FindMeshDefects` to be sure. There are more robust and systematic means to build a mesh from such a nicely structured list of vertices, but these take a bit more work. See Exercises 7 and 8.

A lovely modification to a torus knot is to imagine that for each value of the parameter t we run a line segment from the point at t to the point at $t + \pi$. If we introduce a second parameter s to do this, the result is a surface rather than a curve. This construction turns the (2, 1) torus knot into a Möbius band. The knot itself runs along the boundary edge of the Möbius band, and the line segments run between pairs of points on the knot.

```
In[34]:= mobius = ParametricPlot3D[s * torusKnot[2, 1, 2, 1][t + π] +
           (1 - s) torusKnot[2, 1, 2, 1][t], {t, 0, π}, {s, 0, 1},
          Mesh → All, MaxRecursion → 0, PlotPoints → {50, 10},
          PlotStyle → {Thickness[.15], FaceForm[Yellow, Black]},
          Boxed → False, Axes → False, ImageSize → 250];
       {Show[mobius, knot, PlotRange → All], mobius,
        DiscretizeGraphics[mobius]}
```

Out[35]=

Note that we let t range from 0 to π (rather than 2π) so that each connecting line segment is added only once. The discretization looks watertight, but like the knot itself it has a seam. The seam is easily visible in the middle image above at roughly 3 o'clock when viewed from above—note how the "diagonal" edges in the mesh meet. These overlapping faces are invisible in the final print, so there is no compelling reason to attempt a repair.

A more dramatic illustration of overlapping faces is obtained from a similar construction on the (4, 1) torus knot:

```
In[36]:=  mobius2 = ParametricPlot3D[s * torusKnot[2, 1, 4, 1][t + π] +
              (1 - s) torusKnot[2, 1, 4, 1][t], {t, 0, π}, {s, 0, 1},
            Mesh → All, MaxRecursion → 0, PlotPoints → {100, 10},
            PlotStyle → {Thickness[.15], FaceForm[Yellow, Black]},
            Boxed → False, Axes → False, ImageSize → 250];
          {mobius2, DiscretizeGraphics[mobius2]}
```

Out[37]=

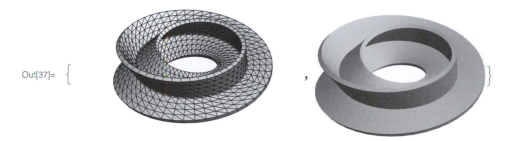

Again, the discretization looks watertight, but it is not. This has the same seam as the previous example, and in addition each line segment joining two points on the knot intersects another such line segment at a right angle. This causes faces to pass through one another along the central circle where $s = 1/2$. To be clear, the points where $s = 1/2$ do indeed form a circle:

```
In[38]:=  1
          ─ torusKnot[2, 1, 4, 1][t + π] + 1
          2                                 ─ torusKnot[2, 1, 4, 1][t] // Simplify
                                            2
Out[38]=  {2 Cos[4 t], 2 Sin[4 t], 0}
```

Again, despite the overlapping faces, there is no compelling reason to attempt a repair. A print rendered from such a mesh will be fine.

Solid Unions

It is often the case that a model is constructed from several individual components. A useful paradigm for combining disparate objects is to first make the individual components solid, then take the desired union, intersection, or other Boolean operation, and finally take the RegionBoundary of the result. We illustrate the ideas with the well-known *compound of five cubes*, which can be found in PolyhedronData. It is a special configuration of five superimposed cubes, where each "corner" is shared by precisely two cubes.

In[39]:= ⌈ cube 5-compound POLYHEDRON ⌉ ["Image"]

Out[39]=

The outer surface of the complex comprises a large number of triangular faces. But a close look at the vertices and faces of the compound reveals something very different.

In[40]:= **vertices = N**⌈ ⌈ cube 5-compound POLYHEDRON ⌉ ["VertexCoordinates"]⌉;

Length[vertices]

Out[41]= **20**

In[42]:= **faces =** ⌈ cube 5-compound POLYHEDRON ⌉ ["Faces"]

Out[42]= {{19, 11, 4, 8}, {14, 20, 9, 1}, {19, 1, 9, 11},
         {4, 20, 14, 8}, {19, 8, 14, 1}, {9, 20, 4, 11}, {7, 3, 12, 19},
         {2, 10, 20, 13}, {12, 10, 2, 19}, {7, 13, 20, 3},
         {2, 13, 7, 19}, {12, 3, 20, 10}, {5, 15, 12, 8}, {18, 6, 9, 13},
         {5, 13, 9, 15}, {12, 6, 18, 8}, {5, 8, 18, 13}, {9, 6, 12, 15},
         {7, 11, 16, 5}, {14, 10, 6, 17}, {16, 10, 14, 5}, {7, 17, 6, 11},
         {14, 17, 7, 5}, {16, 11, 6, 10}, {15, 16, 2, 1}, {17, 18, 4, 3},
         {15, 3, 4, 16}, {2, 18, 17, 1}, {15, 1, 17, 3}, {4, 18, 2, 16}}

What we have here is literally five overlapping cubes, with a total of $5 \times 6 = 30$ square faces and $(5 \times 8)/2 = 20$ vertices (since each cube has eight vertices, and each vertex is shared by two cubes). A simple MeshRegion with these vertices and faces is *not* watertight. Each square face cuts through other square faces, creating a profound tangle of overlapping faces.

While not watertight, as in previous examples nothing prevents us from creating an STL file directly from such a mesh. So despite the flawed mesh, this approach may be practical if your goal is to make a print of this object on an FDM printer. Let's take a peek at what the STL file contains by importing it back into *Mathematica*.

In[43]:= `Printout3D[MeshRegion[vertices, Polygon[faces]],`
`NotebookDirectory[] <> "fiveCubes.stl"]`

Out[43]=

Status	Successful
Image	
Size	1.7 in × 1.6 in × 1.4 in
FileName	File /Users/btorrence/Library/Mathematica/Applications/SIM3/fiveCubes.stl »
Report	...

In[44]:= `test = Import[NotebookDirectory[] <> "fiveCubes.stl"];`
`MeshCellCount[test]`

Out[45]= `{20, 90, 60}`

It's not hard to understand what has happened: The exported mesh has the 20 vertices we started with, 90 edges, and 60 faces. The number of faces is twice the number of square faces on the five cubes, which makes sense since each square face must be split into two triangles (as an STL file can only contain triangles). There were $12 \times 5 = 60$ edges in the original compound, and now there are $6 \times 5 = 30$ additional edges due to splitting the square faces, for a total of 90 edges. So the triangular faces in this mesh are not those of the outer surface of the compound; they are derived from the square faces of the five cubes by splitting each square face in half. Thus the "overlapping faces" issue is still present. Nonetheless, the STL file is easily processed by standard slicing software such as Cura or MakerBot Print, and it produces a beautiful print.

But it is always possible that some printer or print service may be unable to process a non-watertight mesh. Or you may just be curious: Can I turn this into a watertight mesh? The answer is yes, and it is not hard to accomplish: First make a solid version of each of the five cubes, then take their union, and finally take the `RegionBoundary` of the result.

This is simpler than it sounds. The faces in the original mesh happen to be laid out so that each sequential set of six faces belongs to a separate cube. To make a solid version of an individual cube, we use `BoundaryMeshRegion` on its vertices and faces instead of `MeshRegion`. When given the vertices and faces of a watertight two-dimensional mesh that bounds a solid region, `Bound aryMeshRegion` will give the *solid* region. To illustrate, we produce the first two cubes and use `RegionUnion` to take their union. To get a two-dimensional watertight mesh, apply `RegionBound ary` to the union.

```
In[46]:= cube1 = BoundaryMeshRegion[vertices, Polygon[faces[[1 ;; 6]]]];
        cube2 = BoundaryMeshRegion[vertices, Polygon[faces[[7 ;; 12]]]];
        twoCubes = RegionBoundary[RegionUnion[cube1, cube2]]
```

Out[48]=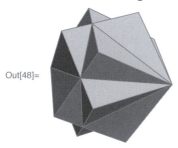

```
In[49]:= RegionDimension /@ {cube1, cube2, twoCubes}
```

Out[49]= {3, 3, 2}

Let's count vertices and faces: The two cubes have 16 vertices in total, but two of these are shared, giving a total of 14. The mesh above also includes six additional vertices where the edges of the two cubes intersect, giving a total of 20 vertices. The faces are the 36 triangles that comprise the outer surface of the assemblage. This is indeed a watertight mesh.

```
In[50]:= MeshCellCount[twoCubes]
```

Out[50]= {20, 54, 36}

Using RegionIntersection in place of RegionUnion results in a watertight mesh for the intersection of the two cubes.

```
In[51]:= RegionBoundary[RegionIntersection[cube1, cube2]]
```

•••   MeshRegion: Degenerate cells including Polygon[{6, 2, 3}] have been removed.

Out[51]=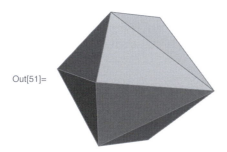

A watertight mesh for the full union (or intersection) of five cubes can easily be produced using this technique. See Exercises 2, 3, and 4.

An interesting contrast to the compound of five cubes is provided by the *small stellated dodecahedron*. This is not a compound of several polyhedra, it is just a polyhedron that looks like it is built from lots of identical triangular faces:

In[52]:= | small stellated dodecahedron POLYHEDRON | ["Image"]

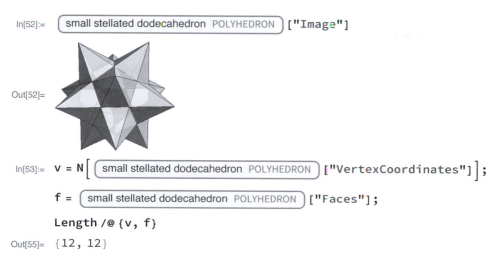

Out[52]=

In[53]:= v = N[| small stellated dodecahedron POLYHEDRON | ["VertexCoordinates"]];

f = | small stellated dodecahedron POLYHEDRON | ["Faces"];

Length /@ {v, f}

Out[55]= {12, 12}

That there are only 12 vertices and 12 faces is telling. The vertices are the 12 outermost points, while each face is a pentagram joining five vertices. Because of the way *Mathematica* interprets polygons with edges that cross, the center pentagon is missing from each face. The next input shows a single face (left), two adjacent faces (center), and the entire complex (right).

In[56]:= {HighlightMesh[MeshRegion[v, Polygon[f[[3]]]],
        Style[0, PointSize[Medium]]],
      MeshRegion[v, Polygon[f[[5 ;; 6]]]], HighlightMesh[
        MeshRegion[v, Polygon[f]], Style[2, FaceForm[Yellow, Black]]]]}

Out[56]=

Hence the mesh with vertices v and faces f is indeed watertight, and moreover the faces are correctly oriented. This mesh is ready for printing!

Another useful application of these ideas is to remove the face surfaces from a mesh, and then "thicken" its edges into struts, producing what is essentially a thickened wireframe version of the original mesh. Such a construction requires very little material to print, and can produce a stunningly intricate print on a SLS printer from an online print service.

One approach that may be applied to any mesh is to render each vertex as a Ball and each edge as a Cylinder. Recall that a GraphicsComplex works essentially like a MeshRegion, so we can build our structure with a bounding box that is ten units per side as follows:

In[57]:= e = (small stellated dodecahedron POLYHEDRON)["Edges"];

frame = Graphics3D[GraphicsComplex[10 Rescale[v], {Ball[#, .25] & /@
Range[Length[v]], Cylinder[#, .25] & /@ e}], Axes → True]

Out[57]=

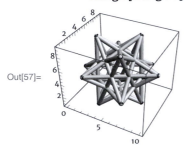

Since every Cylinder and Ball intersects several other components, the STL file that is produced from the boundary surface of this rendering has overlapping faces and so is not watertight. But as that is the only issue, this approach gives a simple means for building a workable thickened wireframe model from the vertices and edges of virtually any mesh.

In[58]:= Printout3D[frame,
NotebookDirectory[] <> "smStellatedDodecahedron.stl",
TargetUnits → "Centimeters"]

Out[58]=

Status	Successful
Image	
Size	10.9 cm × 10.0 cm × 9.7 cm
FileName	File[/Users/btorrence/Library/Mathematica/Applications/SIM3/smStellatedDodecahedror
Report	...

In order to produce a truly watertight mesh, however, more work is needed. One approach is to mimic what we did for the compound of five cubes: Make the struts solid, take their RegionUnion, and then take the RegionBoundary of the result. Here we specify each Ball and Cylinder using the *actual* vertex coordinates rather than the *indices* for the coordinates, so that we can regard them as independent regions and hence take their RegionUnion. To get the edges in this form, we use MeshPrimi‐tives[*mesh region*, 1].

In[59]:= mesh = MeshRegion[10 Rescale[v], Line[e]];
MeshPrimitives[mesh, 1] // First

Out[60]= Line[{{0., 5., 4.04508}, {7.5, 0.669873, 4.04508}}]

```
In[61]:= With[{r = .25},
          balls = Ball[#, r] & /@ (10 Rescale[v]);
          cylinders = MeshPrimitives[mesh, 1] /. Line[pts_] :> Cylinder[pts, r]
         ];
        ru = RegionUnion @@ Join[cylinders, balls];
        smStellatedDodecahedron = RegionBoundary[
          DiscretizeRegion[ru, MaxCellMeasure → {"Length" → .25}]]
```

Out[63]=

⚠ Note the setting for MaxCellMeasure used in DiscretizeRegion. When set
to a pure number, it represents the maximal area of a face in the mesh. Here we
instead limit the length of each side of a face to .2. Some experimentation may
be called for to finesse the quality of the mesh; in this case, limiting the lengths
of the sides of triangles prevents overly long and thin triangles from appearing in
the mesh.

This mesh, while a bit jaggy, is watertight and correctly oriented. It is ready to print.

Exercises 9.5

1. Enter the command RepairMesh[bowlMesh] after building the bowlMesh described at the beginning of
   this section, and describe what happens.

2. Make a watertight mesh for the *union* of the five cubes, "CubeFiveCompound" in PolyhedronData.

3. Make a watertight mesh for the *intersection* of the five cubes in the "CubeFiveCompound" in Polyhedron-
   Data. The result is a well-known polyhedron whose faces are identical rhombi. What is the name of this
   polyhedron?

4. Make a Manipulate with a single slider for *n* that will render the first *n* triangular faces of the watertight
   mesh (from Exercise 2) for the compound of five cubes. How many triangles are in the mesh?

5. Make a watertight mesh for the *union* of the two tetrahedra in the "TetrahedronTwoCompound" in
   PolyhedronData.

6. Make a watertight mesh for the *intersection* of the five tetrahedra in the "TetrahedronFiveCompound" in PolyhedronData. The result is a Platonic solid. Which solid is it?

7. In this section we showed how to take a smooth, closed, parameterized curve $f(t)$ and generate a list of vertices by subdividing the curve into p pieces, and building a cross-section with q vertices at each juncture in the subdivision, for a total of $p*q$ vertices. Recall that in the *Functional Programming* subsection of Section 8.5 we showed how to use MapThread, Join, and Partition to construct four-sided polygons to build "side walls" between a pair of parallel q-gons. Thinking of those q-gons as adjacent cross-sections, modify that technique to build a watertight triangular mesh around $f(t)$, and use it to build a mesh around the curve $f(t) = \langle \cos(t), \sin(t), \sin(2t) \rangle$ for $0 \le t \le 2\pi$ like those shown below ($p = 200$ and $q = 3$, left; $p = 200$ and $q = 20$, right).

8. Modify the technique used in the previous exercise so that the triangular faces are constructed directly using Table (rather than using MapThread and Partition).

9. Modify the technique used in the previous two exercises so that the radius of each cross-section is proportional to the radius of curvature at that point. The watertight mesh for the (2, 5) torus knot shown below uses $q = 3$ points for each cross-section, with radius 0.5*curvature.

10. Given that $\mathcal{R}$ is the MeshRegion representation of a surface, one can produce a list of its faces with MeshCells[$\mathcal{R}$,2], and a list of its edges with MeshCells[$\mathcal{R}$,1]. Write a program that will determine how many faces—one or two—is incident with each edge in $\mathcal{R}$. Note: If $\mathcal{R}$ is a watertight mesh, this routine should output a list of 2s, as every edge will lie on precisely two faces.

11. Make a watertight mesh for the thickened wireframe version of the *truncated tetrahedron*, like that shown below.

12. Make a watertight mesh for the *union* of the edges of the five tetrahedra in the "TetrahedronFiveCompound" in `PolyhedronData`, so that each edge is replaced by a `Cylinder`, and each vertex is replaced by `Ball`.

13. Use a (5, 2) torus knot and add line segments joining the point at t to the point at $t + \pi$ for each t from 0 to π. Thicken the surface to make a printable model. It should look like this:

14. Use a (9, 1) torus knot and a sphere to make a printable model of a ball trapped within a wireframe torus, as shown below.

15. Use `FindMeshDefects` to check the `"MeshRegion"` representation of a caffeine molecule in `Chemical` `Data` for defects. Is this a watertight mesh?

9.6 Extrusion

A common technique for the design of three-dimensional objects is to take a planar figure and *extrude* or thicken it into the third dimension, much like a pasta machine extrudes a disk-shape to produce a cylindrical strand of spaghetti. In essence, each point (x, y) in the planar figure is replaced by a vertical line segment of the form (x, y, z), where the z coordinate ranges between fixed lower and upper bounds. In mathematical parlance, we are taking the *product* of the planar figure with a line segment. Products are easily produced with the `RegionProduct` command.

```
In[1]:=  base =
            DiscretizeRegion[Annulus[{0, 0}, {10., 15.}], MaxCellMeasure → 1.];
         {base, RegionProduct[base, Line[{{0.}, {10.}}]]}
```

Out[2]=
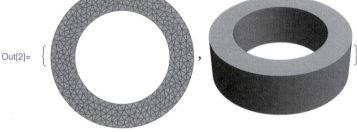

The product in this case is a solid object; each triangle in the discretization of the two-dimensional annulus is replaced by a solid triangular prism standing upright on its triangular end. In general, the `RegionDimension` of a `RegionProduct` is the sum of the corresponding dimensions of its factors. In the previous example, the annulus is two-dimensional and the line segment is one-dimensional, so the product is solid, i.e., three-dimensional. Its `RegionBoundary` is a watertight mesh, albeit with some rectangular faces. Upon export to STL (or any format that requires triangular faces), each rectangular face will be subdivided into two or more triangles.

```
In[3]:=  HighlightMesh[
            RegionBoundary@RegionProduct[base, Line[{{0.}, {10.}}]],
            Style[2, FaceForm[Yellow, Black]]]
```

Out[3]=
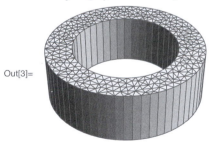

Of equal importance, the EmbeddingDimension of a RegionProduct is the sum of the corresponding embedding dimensions of its factors. For instance, a circle has RegionDimension 1 and Embedding Dimension 2 (since it lives in the plane). So its product with the line segment used above has RegionDimension 2 and EmbeddingDimension 3. Keep in mind that every object suitable for 3D printing has EmbeddingDimension 3.

In[4]:= `{RegionBoundary[base],`
`RegionProduct[RegionBoundary[base], Line[{{0.}, {10.}}]]}`

Out[4]=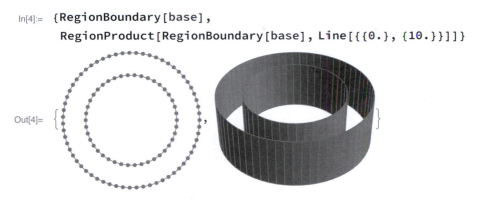

There are rich possibilities for the creation of a 3D model by extruding a planar figure. Indeed, we may do so for any planar figure that can be discretized into a mesh. One source of such planar figures is the extensive collection of LaminaData. Most of the two-dimensional lamina entities have a "MeshRegion" property that is a function with one or more parameters to determine the dimensions of the resulting mesh.

In[5]:= [pentagram LAMINA] `["MeshRegion"][50.]`

Out[5]=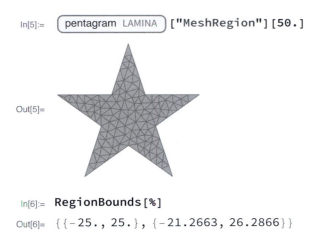

In[6]:= `RegionBounds[%]`
Out[6]= `{{-25., 25.}, {-21.2663, 26.2866}}`

Just as DiscretizeGraphics may be used to discretize a three-dimensional Graphics3D object, it may just as easily be used to create a two-dimensional mesh from a Graphics object, which may then be extruded.

```
In[7]:= rectangle = DiscretizeGraphics[Rectangle[{-20, -10}, {20, 10}]];
        disk = DiscretizeGraphics[Disk[{0, 0}, 5]];
        mesh2D = RegionDifference[rectangle, disk];
        {mesh2D, RegionProduct[mesh2D, Line[{{0.}, {10.}}]]}
```

Out[10]=

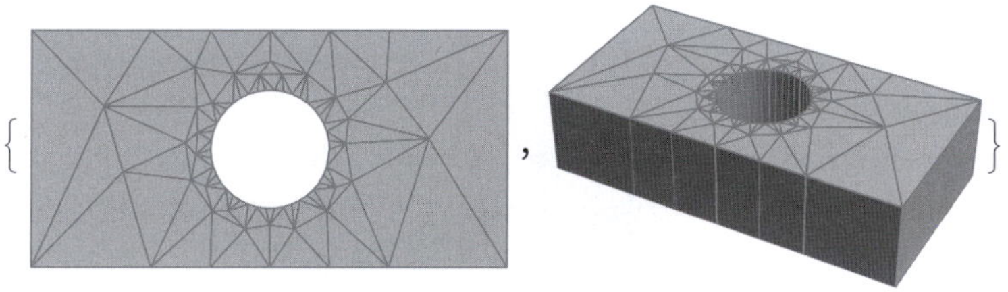

```
In[11]:= ct = DiscretizeGraphics[
             ⬭ Connecticut, United States ADMINISTRATIVE DIVISION ["Polygon"]];
         {ct, RegionProduct[ct, Line[{{0.}, {.1}}]]}
```

Out[12]=

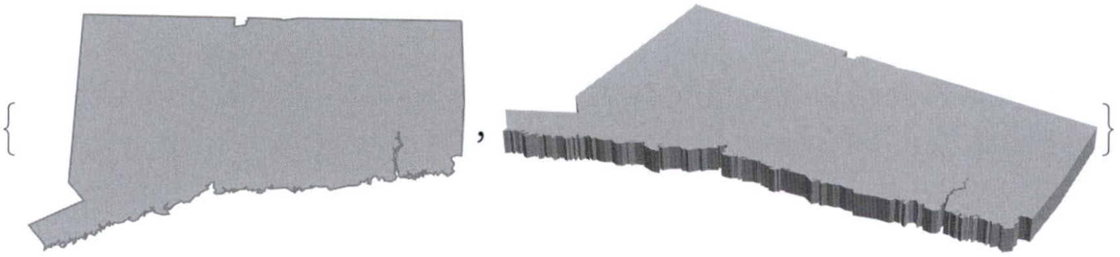

Note that BoundaryDiscretizeGraphics may be applied to a closed plane curve to create a two-dimensional planar region comprising the curve and its interior. The result is two-dimensional BoundaryMeshRegion, which may then be extruded.

```
In[13]:= outline = ⬭ first heart curve PLANE CURVE ["Graphics"];
         heart = BoundaryDiscretizeGraphics[outline];
         {outline, heart, RegionProduct[heart, Line[{{0.}, {.3}}]]}
```

Out[15]=

Note that DiscretizeGraphics and BoundaryDiscretizeGraphics permit an optional second argument. This argument is a Pattern specifying which Graphics objects should be discretized. This is particularly useful for discretizing text.

```
In[16]:= {three, d} = BoundaryDiscretizeGraphics[Text[
             Style[#, FontFamily → "Futura", Bold]], _Text] & /@ {"3", "D"};
         {three, d, RegionProduct[three, Line[{{0.}, {3.}}]],
          RegionProduct[d, Line[{{0.}, {3.}}]]]}
```

Out[17]=

In fact, it is straightforward to extrude letters in different directions and combine them. Below we extrude "3" in the *y* direction and "D" in the *x* direction, then take their intersection. We first Rescale them so they have the same height. (See Exercise 3 for a "perfect square" rescaling and the construction of a "letter cube" from three letters.)

```
In[18]:= RegionBounds /@ {three, d} // Column
```

Out[18]=
{{-2.80781, 2.80781}, {-3.74367, 3.74367}}
{{-3.08859, 3.08859}, {-3.53828, 3.53828}}

```
In[19]:= dRescaled =
           BoundaryMeshRegion[Rescale@MeshCoordinates[d], MeshCells[d, 1]];
         threeRescaled = BoundaryMeshRegion[
           Rescale@MeshCoordinates[three], MeshCells[three, 1]];
         RegionBounds /@ {threeRescaled, dRescaled} // Column
```

Out[21]=
{{0.124992, 0.875008}, {0., 1.}}
{{0.0635462, 0.936454}, {0., 1.}}

The replacement rule in the third line below switches the *y* and *z* coordinates, so the extrusion for "3" is in the *y* direction.

```
In[22]:= dMesh = RegionProduct[Line[{{-1.}, {1.}}], dRescaled];
         threeMesh = RegionProduct[threeRescaled, Line[{{-1.}, {1.}}]];
         threeMesh = MeshRegion[MeshCoordinates[threeMesh] /.
             {x_, y_, z_} → {x, z, y}, MeshCells[threeMesh, 3]];
         threeD = RegionIntersection[threeMesh, dMesh];
         {threeD, Show[threeD, ViewPoint → Front],
          Show[threeD, ViewPoint → Right]}
```

Out[26]=

Yet another class of 2D meshes are those derived from an `Image`, such as a digital photo or a scan of a handmade drawing. Use `ImageMesh` to convert an image into a mesh. Below we use `Morphologi``calBinarize` to reduce a photograph to pure black and pure white, and `ColorNegate` to switch the roles of black and white (white has value 1, and only pixels with value 1 are included in the region produced by `ImageMesh`).

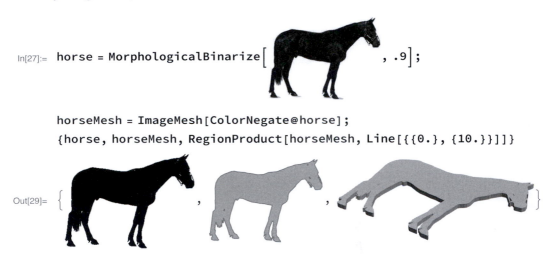

```
In[27]:=  horse = MorphologicalBinarize[           , .9];

          horseMesh = ImageMesh[ColorNegate@horse];
          {horse, horseMesh, RegionProduct[horseMesh, Line[{{0.}, {10.}}]]}
```

```
Out[29]=  {           ,           ,           }
```

It is also possible, via `RegionImage`, to transform a planar region into an `Image`. By nesting the composition `ImageMesh[RegionImage[#]]&`, one may alternately transform region to image and back several times, with a delightful degradation in quality as the number of iterations increases. This provides a simple method for introducing noise into a region.

```
In[30]:=  text = "3D Print Lab";
          meshText = BoundaryDiscretizeGraphics[
            Text[Style[text, FontFamily → "Lucida Bright", Bold]], _Text]
```

```
Out[31]=  3D Print Lab
```

```
In[32]:=  meshTextDegraded = Nest[ImageMesh[RegionImage[#]] &, meshText, 4]
```

```
Out[32]=  3D Print Lab
```

In[33]:= `RegionProduct[meshTextDegraded, Line[{{0.}, {5.}}]]`

Out[33]=

An alternate means for extruding an image employs `Image3D`. Give it a list of two-dimensional images of the same size and color space, and it will stack them, one atop the next, to create a three-dimensional image. This concept is common in medical imaging, for instance, when layers of CAT scan images are "stacked" to provide a 3D model. When given an `Image3D` object, `ImageMesh` will produce a solid three-dimensional mesh of the object. Here is an example: We first take the two-dimensional text mesh above and convert it to an image, and then change the color space of that image to RGB.

In[34]:= `textImage = ColorConvert[RegionImage[meshTextDegraded], "RGB"]`

Out[34]= **3D Print Lab**

Now make a base plate of the same size as this text image. This will be a constant (white) image in the RGB color space.

In[35]:= `baseImage =`
`    ColorConvert[ConstantImage[1., ImageDimensions[textImage]], "RGB"];`

We then stack 15 copies of the text image on top of five copies of the base image, and feed it to `Image3D`:

In[36]:= `stack = Image3D@Join[`
`        ConstantArray[textImage, 15],`
`        ConstantArray[baseImage, 5]`
`    ]`

Out[36]=

Finally, use `ImageMesh` to convert the `Image3D` to a solid mesh. The `"DualMarchingCubes"` method tends to smooth out jagged pixelation in an image. The `RegionBoundary` of the solid mesh is watertight and ready for printing.

In[37]:= `model = RegionBoundary@ImageMesh[stack, Method → "DualMarchingCubes"]`

Out[37]=

As an example of using extrusion to build a more complex watertight mesh, we next consider the Penrose kite and dart tiles. An illustration of these two tile shapes is shown below. Note that $\phi = \left(1 + \sqrt{5}\right)\big/2$ is the `GoldenRatio`, approximately 1.618. In the 1970s, Roger Penrose showed that it is possible to tile the plane with these two tile shapes under the constraint that tiles may be placed edge-to-edge only when the circular arcs match. (So, for example, the tiles as shown in the image below cannot be moved horizontally together since the arcs would not match.) Moreover, any infinite tiling produced in this fashion is *aperiodic*, meaning the tiling pattern does not have translational symmetry.

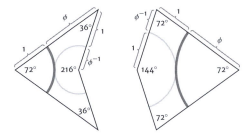

We will use extrusion to produce a model for the *kite* tile, shown on the right above. (See Exercise 1 for tips on constructing the *dart*, shown left.) We will extrude the two-dimensional kite shape, and further extrude the arcs from the upper face of the kite, with one arc thicker than the other to distinguish it.

Since the kite has mirror symmetry along a horizontal axis, we begin by establishing the vertex coordinates for its "top" triangle, above the symmetry axis. Using the "side−angle−side" information provided in the measurements from the figure, we obtain coordinates for its vertices:

In[39]:= `SASTriangle[1 + GoldenRatio,`
         `    72 Degree, 1 + 1/GoldenRatio] // FullSimplify`

Out[39]= $\text{Triangle}\left[\left\{\{0, 0\}, \left\{\frac{1}{2}\left(3 + \sqrt{5}\right), 0\right\}, \left\{\frac{1}{2}, \frac{1}{2}\sqrt{5 + 2\sqrt{5}}\right\}\right\}\right]$

Using these vertices and mirror symmetry, we construct a two-dimensional mesh for the kite shape. We simply take the BoundaryMeshRegion of a path around its perimeter.

In[40]:= kite2D = BoundaryMeshRegion$\left[\left\{\{0, 0\}, \left\{\frac{1}{2}, \frac{1}{2}\sqrt{5 + 2\sqrt{5}}\right\},\right.\right.$

$\left.\left.\left\{\frac{1}{2}\left(3 + \sqrt{5}\right), 0\right\}, \left\{\frac{1}{2}, -\frac{1}{2}\sqrt{5 + 2\sqrt{5}}\right\}\right\}, \text{Line}[\{1, 4, 3, 2, 1\}]\right]$

Out[40]=

We next extrude the boundary of the kite mesh by taking its product with a line segment. We use the RegionBounds for the 2D kite mesh to get a sense of its scale. This information is used to choose an appropriate length for the line segment used in the RegionProduct.

In[41]:= RegionBounds[kite2D]
Out[41]= {{0., 2.61803}, {-1.53884, 1.53884}}

In[42]:= kiteWalls = RegionProduct[RegionBoundary[kite2D], Line[{{0}, {.1}}]]

Out[42]=

We next use Annulus to produce a two-dimensional mesh for the two arcs, making one arc twice the width of the other, and being careful to make sure both arcs lie entirely inside the boundary of the kite (without touching the boundary).

In[43]:= `With[{δ = .1}, arc1 = DiscretizeGraphics[`
`Annulus[{0, 0}, {1 - δ / 4, 1 + δ / 4}, {-71 Degree, 71 Degree}]];`
`arc2 = DiscretizeGraphics[Annulus[{1/2 (3 + √5), 0}, {GoldenRatio - δ / 2,`
`GoldenRatio + δ / 2}, {145 Degree, (144 + 71) Degree}]];`
`kiteArcs = RegionUnion[arc1, arc2]]`

Out[43]=

We form the top face of the kite tile by removing the arcs from the kite shape.

In[44]:= `kite2Dtop = RegionDifference[kite2D, kiteArcs]`

Out[44]=

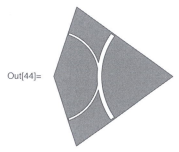

We may now extrude the `RegionBoundary` of the `kiteArcs` to build its walls.

In[45]:= `arcWalls = RegionProduct[RegionBoundary[kiteArcs], Line[{{.1}, {.2}}]]`

Out[45]=

The tile is now ready for assembly. We take the `RegionProduct` of each 2D mesh with a point (`RegionDimension` 0 and `EmbeddingDimension` 1) to embed the 2D mesh in 3D space. The value of the `Point` determines the *z* coordinate in the embedding.

```
In[46]:=  kite3D = DiscretizeGraphics[Show[
            RegionProduct[kite2D, Point[{0.}]],
            kiteWalls,
            RegionProduct[kite2Dtop, Point[{.1}]],
            arcWalls,
            RegionProduct[kiteArcs, Point[{.2}]]
          ]]
```

Out[46]=

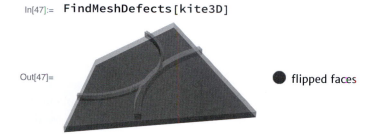

There are a host of subtleties in this construction. The most important is that by defining the `kite2D` mesh as a `BoundaryMeshRegion`, when we constructed the `kiteWalls` from its boundary, the vertex coordinates from the `kite2D` were used. So the triangles on the bottom and side meshes of the kite model line up perfectly. The same principle is applied to the top of the kite and the arcs to produce a watertight mesh. The only defect, in fact, is that the bottom of the model is facing upward rather than downward.

```
In[47]:=  FindMeshDefects[kite3D]
```

Out[47]=

● flipped faces

But this is easily repaired:

```
In[48]:=  kite3DFinal = RepairMesh[kite3D, "FlippedFaces"];
          HighlightMesh[kite3DFinal, Style[2, FaceForm[Yellow, Black]]]
```

Out[49]=

Exercises 9.6

1. Use extrusion and the techniques outlined in this section to make a model for the Penrose *dart* tile.

2. Place the text "3D Print Lab" on a base plate using the same extrusion technique outlined in this section for building the Penrose kite.

3. Extrude the letter "G" along the *x* axis, the letter "E" along the *y* axis, and the letter "B" along the *z* axis, then superimpose and take their intersection. It is helpful to first rescale each letter so that its `RegionBounds` are {{−1, 1}, {−1, 1}}. The result, shown below, should look like the illustration on the cover of the classic bestselling book, *Gödel, Escher, Bach: An Eternal Golden Brai*d, by Douglas R. Hofstadter.

4. As an alternative to taking the `RegionProduct` of a 2D curve and a line segment to extrude the 2D curve, one could use `ParametricPlot3D` (with two parameters) instead. Use parameter *t* to render the curve, and parameter *u* to extrude it, by applying `ParametricPlot3D` to `{Sin[t], Cos[3 t], u}`.

5. Make a table showing a graphical representation of every object in `LaminaData`.

9.7 Printing a Solid of Revolution

Suppose you wish to print a solid of revolution, the 3D shape obtained by revolving a planar figure about an axis in three-space. In Chapter 5 we discussed how to find the volume of such solids, and how to visualize them with `RevolutionPlot3D`. But how can we print one? For example, consider the surface obtained by revolving the graph of $f(x) = -x \sin(x)$ with $0 \le x \le 3\pi/2$ about the *y* axis.

```
In[1]:= Plot[-x Sin[x], {x, 0, 3 π / 2}, AspectRatio → Automatic]
```

Out[1]=

Using `RevolutionPlot3D` with the option setting `PlotTheme → "ThickSurface"` thickens the surface to make it printable. We bump up the `PlotPoints` setting to produce a smoother graph.

In[2]:= `RevolutionPlot3D[-x Sin[x], {x, 0, 3 π / 2}, PlotPoints → 60,`
         `PlotTheme → "ThickSurface", BoxRatios → {10, 10, 7}]`

Out[2]=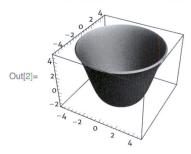

For greater control, parameterize the surface and render it with `ParametricPlot3D`, and then `PlotStyle` may be set to any desired `Thickness`. Setting `Mesh` to `All` will reveal the fidelity of the discretization, and setting `MaxRecursion` to 0 will prevent triangles from being subdivided beyond the amount specified by `PlotPoints`.

In[3]:= `rev = ParametricPlot3D[{r Cos[θ], r Sin[θ], -r Sin[r]}, {r, 0, 3 π / 2},`
         `{θ, 0, 2 π}, PlotPoints → 60, PlotStyle → Thickness[.4],`
         `Mesh → All, MaxRecursion → 0, BoxRatios → Automatic]`

Out[3]=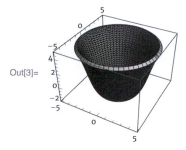

The situation is more subtle when a solid of revolution is formed by revolving a planar region that is constructed from two or more curves. For instance, consider the solid of revolution obtained by revolving around the x axis the region in the xy plane bounded by the curves $y = x^2 + 1$ and $y = -x^2 + 2x + 5$. As above, we may use `RevolutionPlot3D` to view the solid. We first find the x values where the two curves intersect, and use those as the bounds for x in the plot:

In[4]:= `Reduce[x² + 1 == -x² + 2 x + 5, x]`

Out[4]= `x == -1 || x == 2`

So the planar region to be revolved looks like this:

```
In[5]:= R = ImplicitRegion[x^2 + 1 ≤ y ≤ -x^2 + 2 x + 5, {{x, -1, 2}, y}];

Region[R, Axes → True]
```

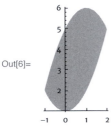

Out[6]=

Note that we could get a similar picture by simply plotting the two curves. (The input is below, but we suppress the output to save space.)

```
Plot[{x^2 + 1, -x^2 + 2 x + 5}, {x, -1, 2},
    Filling → {1 → {2}}, AspectRatio → Automatic]
```

In any event, when the region is rotated about the *x* axis, the resulting solid looks like this:

```
In[7]:= rev = RevolutionPlot3D[{{x^2 + 1}, {-x^2 + 2 x + 5}},
            {x, -1, 2}, RevolutionAxis → {1, 0, 0}]
```

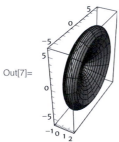

Out[7]=

While we have produced a beautiful on-screen rendering of the solid, more work is required to produce a printable model. The reason is that the Graphics3D object we produced comprises two distinct surfaces: One is obtained by revolving $y = x^2 + 1$ about the *x* axis, and the other by revolving $y = -x^2 + 2x - 5$. Internally, RevolutionPlot3D treats the surfaces individually; they remain entirely distinct entities.

```
In[8]:= ConnectedMeshComponents[DiscretizeGraphics[rev]]
```

Out[8]=

For printing purposes, each surface component has two "holes" that need sealing. That is because each surface can be continuously deformed into a cylinder, and a cylinder has a hole at each end. `RepairMesh` will identify and effectively seal all those holes.

In[9]:= `DiscretizeGraphics[rev] // RepairMesh`

Out[9]=

Since calling `Printout3D` on the `RevolutionPlot3D` output will first discretize the graphic into a mesh (with those two distinct components), and then repair that mesh (by sealing the holes), the result will be a model that looks like the image above—not what we want. A simple workaround is to use `DiscretizeGraphics` on `rev` and then use `Export` rather than `Printout3D` to generate a print file.

In[10]:= `SetDirectory[NotebookDirectory[]];`
`Export["rev.stl", DiscretizeGraphics[rev]]`

Out[11]= `rev.stl`

This will bypass any mesh repair, exporting the mesh with its two distinct connected components. While not technically watertight, the two components butt tightly against each other, and the slicing software for most FDM printers will have no problem making a great print from it.

To produce a truly watertight mesh, a solution is easily had if we forgo the use of `Revolution`‑`Plot3D`. Instead, describe the outer surface of the solid of revolution implicitly as those points (x, y, z) with $-1 \le x \le 2$ and either $(x^2 + 1)^2 = y^2 + z^2$ or $(-x^2 + 2x + 5)^2 = y^2 + z^2$. This is because for any point (x, y, z) in space, the distance to the x axis is $\sqrt{y^2 + z^2}$. In order for (x, y, z) to lie on the surface of the solid of revolution, this distance must be either $x^2 + 1$ or $-x^2 + 2x + 5$. We may thus use `Implic`‑`itRegion` to create the boundary surface of the solid of revolution. While we could view the result immediately with `Region`, we instead opt for delayed gratification and only render it after it is discretized.

In[12]:= `R = ImplicitRegion[`
`(x² + 1)² == y² + z² || (-x² + 2 x + 5)² == y² + z², {{x, -1, 2}, y, z}];`

We now discretize the boundary surface into a triangular mesh using `DiscretizeRegion`. The `MaxCellMeasure` option determines the maximum area of the triangles used in the mesh. Smaller settings yield more and smaller triangles, producing a more accurate model (and a larger file size—the discretized model below has over 28 000 triangles).

In[13]:= **dRev = DiscretizeRegion[ℛ, MaxCellMeasure → .005]**

Out[13]=

In[14]:= **MeshCellCount[dRev, 2]**

Out[14]= 28 416

The important difference with this approach, as opposed to using RevolutionPlot3D, is that the mesh has only one connected component:

In[15]:= **ConnectedMeshComponents[dRev] // Length**

Out[15]= 1

Let's check that the faces are properly oriented:

In[16]:= **HighlightMesh[#, Style[2, FaceForm[Yellow, Black]]] & /@**
          {dRev, RepairMesh[dRev, "FlippedFaces"]}

Out[16]= {  }

While the faces on one surface in dRev are backwards (left image), RepairMesh reorients them correctly (right image), so the repaired mesh is ready for printing.

Exercises 9.7

1. Make a printable model of the solid obtained by rotating the region bounded by $y = x^2 - 2x$ and $y = x$ about the line $y = 4$.

2. Make a printable model of the solid obtained by rotating the region bounded by $y = x^2 - 2x$ and $y = x$ about the y axis.

3. Make a printable model of a *torus* by rotating the unit circle $(x - 2)^2 + y^2 = 1$ about the y axis.

9.8   Printing a 3D Terrain Map

Suppose you want to make a 3D terrain map to illustrate the topography for some region of the globe: a country, state, city, mountain, island—any location for which there is elevation data. With its extensive access to geographic data, the Wolfram Language is well suited to such an endeavor. For our first example we will create a terrain map of a rectangular region in the Shenandoah mountains of Virginia. Next we will create a model of the island of Kauai, the oldest of the five major Hawaiian islands. Through these examples you should gain the ability to make a 3D model of virtually any geographic region.

The basic idea will be to use GeoElevationData to create a matrix of elevation data for your region. Technically, this matrix is a QuantityArray, a matrix where each entry carries a common unit (of elevation). We then use ListPlot3D to render the elevations as a watertight model suitable for printing.

Rectangular Regions

For our first example, we specify a rectangular patch of the globe using the {*latitude, longitude*} coordinates for a pair of opposite corners. We used a web browser and Google Maps for this task, dropping a pin at the southwest and northeast corners and reading off the coordinates. The coordinates may be entered in degrees, exactly as they are presented on the map.

```
In[1]:=  {lat1, lon1} = {37.78, -79.19} (* sw corner *);
         {lat2, lon2} = {38.0, -78.86} (* ne corner *);
```

The most direct way to construct a 3D model from this information is the following, which produces a BoundaryMeshRegion ready for printing:

```
In[3]:=  GeoElevationData[
             GeoBoundsRegion[{{lat1, lat2}, {lon1, lon2}}], Automatic, "Region"]
```

Out[3]=

Unfortunately, for this region the aspect ratio of the rectangular footprint is incorrect. This is because the distance between adjacent elevation measurements in the elevation data array in the east–west direction is not the same as the distance between successive north–south measurements. But if that doesn't matter to you, then you're done: Just call Printout3D and have at it. But if you want to correct the aspect ratio of the rectangular footprint, enhance the vertical scale, or thicken the base of the model to make it less fragile, a more refined approach is needed.

While not strictly necessary, we next instruct `GeoElevationData` to report elevations in meters. Working in the U.S., the default unit for elevation is feet, and we prefer meters for the simple reason that we will ultimately use the same units for all three directions (east–west, north–south, up–down) in order to produce a plot with the proper `BoxRatios`. Meters are slightly easier to read for the horizontal directions since they are so easily converted to kilometers.

In[4]:= `SetOptions[GeoElevationData, UnitSystem → "Metric"]`

Out[4]= `{GeoModel → Automatic, GeoZoomLevel → Automatic, UnitSystem → Metric}`

The `SetOptions` command can also be used to set the `GeoZoomLevel`, which allows you to produce a plot with finer or coarser resolution (settings range from 1 to 12). In our experience, the default setting generally works quite well.

Whether feet or meters, let's name our distance unit.

In[5]:= `distUnit = QuantityUnit[GeoElevationData[{lat1, lon1}]]`

Out[5]= `Meters`

This is a matrix of elevation data, measured in meters above sea level.

In[6]:= `elevArray = Reverse[GeoElevationData[{{lat1, lon1}, {lat2, lon2}}]]`

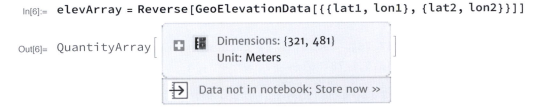

Out[6]= QuantityArray[Dimensions: {321, 481} Unit: Meters]

Data not in notebook; Store now »

Successive rows of a `GeoElevationData` array correspond to *decreasing* latitude. We applied `Reverse` to the array to reverse the order of its rows. This is because we will create a 3D rendering of the data using `ListPlot3D`, which by default takes the *x* and *y* coordinate values for each data point to be successive integers starting at 1, meaning rows correspond to *increasing* latitude. If we did not apply `Reverse`, the 3D model would be a mirror image of the real world. The dimensions of the matrix will depend on the granularity of the elevation data available for the region, the `GeoZoomLevel`, and the region's size. In this example, we get a 321×481 array of elevation data (read it directly off the icon for the array above). Each entry in the array is a `Quantity` expression such as `Quantity[909., "Meters"]`.

In[7]:= `elevArray[[1, 1]] // InputForm`

Out[7]//InputForm=
          `Quantity[909., "Meters"]`

In order to accurately scale the east–west and north–south dimensions of the 3D model, we express them in the same distance units as the elevations. Since east–west distances between two fixed longitudes vary with latitude, we will approximate the east–west distance by measuring it at the mean latitude.

```
In[8]:=  m = Mean[{lat1, lat2}];
         ewDistance =
           UnitConvert[GeoDistance[{m, lon1}, {m, lon2}], distUnit];
         nsDistance = UnitConvert[
           GeoDistance[{lat1, lon1}, {lat2, lon1}], distUnit];
         {ewDistance, nsDistance}
```

```
Out[11]=  { 29 027.9 m ,  24 418.8 m }
```

So our region is roughly 29 km from east to west, and 24 km from south to north. We are now ready to render it with ListPlot3D. Terrain maps often exaggerate the vertical scale, as this makes the terrain features easier to read, and the result is also a bit more dramatic. We'll use a vertical scaling factor of 2.5 for this model. We add some extra thickness to the base of the model by extending the PlotRange 500 meters below the minimum elevation in the data. QuantityMagnitude is used to strip the units from the Quantity expressions, turning them into pure numbers. By setting DataRange to the true distances for the east–west and north–south measurements, we obtain a model whose rectangular footprint has the proper aspect ratio. We set PlotTheme to "FilledSurface" to create a watertight model. Finally, always use the BoxRatios → Automatic option setting to ensure that the on-screen rendering accurately reflects the dimensions as they will be printed.

```
In[12]:=  s = 2.5;
          extraThickness = 500;
          model = ListPlot3D[s * elevArray,
            PlotRange → {QuantityMagnitude[Min[s * elevArray]] - extraThickness,
              QuantityMagnitude[Max[s * elevArray]]},
            DataRange → {{0, QuantityMagnitude@ewDistance},
              {0, QuantityMagnitude@nsDistance}},
            PlotTheme → "FilledSurface", BoxRatios → Automatic]
```

A call to Printout3D, as discussed previously, will discretize the model (this may take a few minutes) and save it as an STL, OBJ, or DAE file.

As an aside, we mention that it is a simple matter to add color to the model. One way to do this is to add the option ColorFunction → "GreenBrownTerrain" to the ListPlot3D. (Of course, you may use whichever color gradient you like.) This will color the map by elevation, with green at lower elevations, moving through brown and finally white at the highest elevations. Another method is to apply a texture to the map, like this:

In[15]:= `texture = GeoGraphics[GeoRange → {{lat1, lat2}, {lon1, lon2}},`
        `    GeoBackground → GeoStyling["StreetMap"], GeoZoomLevel → 12]`

Out[15]=

Now add the option PlotStyle → Texture[texture] to the ListPlot3D, and the texture graphic above will be fused to the terrain surface. It creates a stunning on-screen map, but at the time of this writing the texture will not be included in an exported OBJ or DAE file. The shaded area in this example represents the George Washington National Forest.

In[16]:= `s = 2.5;`
        `extraThickness = 500;`
        `model = ListPlot3D[s * elevArray,`
        `    PlotRange → {QuantityMagnitude[Min[s * elevArray]] - extraThickness,`
        `      QuantityMagnitude[Max[s * elevArray]]},`
        `    DataRange → {{0, QuantityMagnitude@ewDistance},`
        `      {0, QuantityMagnitude@nsDistance}}, PlotTheme → "FilledSurface",`
        `    BoxRatios → Automatic, PlotStyle → Texture[texture]]`

Out[18]=

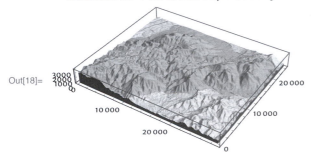

Printing an Island

An island presents an added challenge, as the elevation data include negative values for points below sea level. We need to chop off all such points, leaving only the island. We will also thicken the base, for otherwise the model may be too fragile, or too thin to remove from the build-plate of a FDM printer.

Our example will be the island of Kauai in the Pacific island chain of Hawaii. We first use ⌷CTRL⌷=⌷ to create a freeform input to describe the region of interest in ordinary language. For this example we typed "kauai." Check the checkbox when the correct entity is created.

In[19]:= [Kauai ISLAND] [{"Latitude", "Longitude"}]

Out[19]= { 22.083° , -159.5° }

The island fits in a disk of radius 35 kilometers:

In[20]:= GeoGraphics[GeoDisk[(Kauai ISLAND), 35 km],
          GeoGridLines → Quantity[.1, "AngularDegrees"],
          GeoScaleBar → { 0 km , 25 km , 50 km }]

Out[20]=

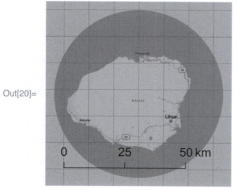

Using the latitude and longitude coordinates for Kauai's center obtained above, and noting that the grid lines on the map are spaced at 1/10 degree, we specify as before the GeoElevationData for a rectangle delimited by the {*latitude, longitude*} coordinates of its northeast and southwest corners. In this case, we just need to be sure our rectangle is sufficiently large to include the entire island.

In[21]:= {lat1, lon1} = {21.8, -159.9}(* sw corner *);
          {lat2, lon2} = {22.3, -159.2}(* ne corner *);
In[23]:= distUnit = QuantityUnit[GeoElevationData[{lat1, lon1}]]
Out[23]= Meters

In[24]:= elevArray = Reverse[GeoElevationData[{{lat1, lon1}, {lat2, lon2}}]]

Out[24]= QuantityArray[⊞ ▤ Dimensions: {364, 510}
                              Unit: Meters   ]

          ⇥ Data not in notebook; Store now »

```
In[25]:=  m = Mean[{lat1, lat2}];
          ewDistance =
             UnitConvert[GeoDistance[{m, lon1}, {m, lon2}], distUnit];
          nsDistance = UnitConvert[
             GeoDistance[{lat1, lon1}, {lat2, lon1}], distUnit];
          {ewDistance, nsDistance}
```

```
Out[28]=  { 72 258.1 m , 55 365.5 m }
```

We see that our elevation data spans a rectangle measuring 72 km from east to west, and 55 km from north to south. But the elevation data includes negative measurements for points below sea level, as is clearly shown in a `ReliefPlot`:

```
In[29]:=  ReliefPlot[elevArray]
```

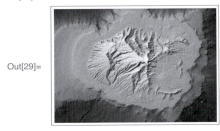

```
Out[29]=
```

We can remove the ocean floor from our `ListPlot3D` by setting the lower `PlotRange` value to 0. We also add the option `ClippingStyle → None` so that the ocean surface is not included as a flat plane spanning the full rectangular footprint. We also scale the vertical elevation data by a factor of 4 to make a more dramatic model.

```
In[30]:=  s = 4.0;
          ListPlot3D[s * elevArray,
            PlotRange → {0, QuantityMagnitude[Max[s * elevArray]]},
            DataRange → {{0, QuantityMagnitude@ewDistance},
               {0, QuantityMagnitude@nsDistance}}, PlotTheme → "FilledSurface",
            BoxRatios → Automatic, ClippingStyle → None]
```

```
Out[31]=
```

The model is paper-thin around the coastline. The task of thickening the base of the model to make it less fragile is slightly more complicated for an island than it was in the first example, for simply extending the lower bound on the PlotRange would have the effect of including land that resides below sea level. Instead, we will add 200 meters to all elevations that are above sea level using a replacement rule, after first stripping the data of its units with QuantityMagnitude. (See Section 8.8 for a primer on patterns and replacement rules.)

```
In[32]:= newArray = QuantityMagnitude[elevArray] /. x_ ?Positive → x + 200;
```

For fun, we add some color to the final model.

```
In[33]:= s = 4.0;
        model = ListPlot3D[s * newArray, PlotRange → {0, Max[s * newArray]},
           DataRange → {{0, QuantityMagnitude@ewDistance},
              {0, QuantityMagnitude@nsDistance}}, PlotTheme → "FilledSurface",
           BoxRatios → Automatic, ClippingStyle → None,
           ColorFunction → (ColorData["GreenBrownTerrain"][.1 + .9 (1 − #3)] &)]
```

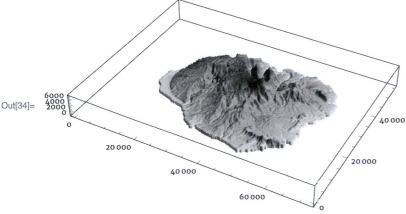

Out[34]=

The model can now be sent to Printout3D for printing.

Non-rectangular Footprints

We present a third and final example to illustrate a method for creating a 3D terrain map for a region with a non-rectangular footprint, such as a national park, a state, or a country. But unlike an island, suppose the surrounding regions are not at sea level.

We will illustrate the ideas using the mountainous country of Nepal. In the process we will introduce a different paradigm for using ListPlot3D: We do not give it an *array* of elevation data, but rather a simple list of {*longitude, latitude, elevation*} triples. We carefully choose only triples residing within the country, along its boundary, and in a narrow halo just outside the borders. The points outside the borders will be assigned negative elevations so that the boundary of the country forms a crisp vertical wall for our model.

We begin by retrieving a polygonal footprint for Nepal:

In[35]:= [Nepal COUNTRY]["Polygon"]

Out[35]= Polygon[GeoPosition[

> Number of points: 796
> Dimensions: {1, 796}
> Lat bounds: {26.3, 30.4}
> Lon bounds: {80.1, 88.2}

]]

In[36]:= Graphics[%, Axes → True]

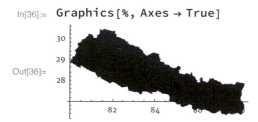

Out[36]=

We see that the *x* coordinates are longitudes and the *y* coordinates are latitudes. Later we will need to determine if a given {*longitude*, *latitude*} point is inside or outside Nepal. Let's turn the graphic into a region so that we can use RegionMember to check this.

In[37]:= nepalMR = DiscretizeGraphics[%]

Out[37]=

As in our earlier examples, we mark a pair of opposing corners for a bounding geo-rectangle. We can read the coordinates off of the first output above, where we created the polygon. We add 0.1 degree to the outermost corners to ensure we include a small halo around the entire country. And as in our earlier examples, we use the metric system for all distances.

In[38]:= {lat1, lon1} = {26.2, 80.0}(* sw corner *);
          {lat2, lon2} = {30.5, 88.3}(* ne corner *);
In[40]:= SetOptions[GeoElevationData, UnitSystem → "Metric"]
Out[40]= {GeoModel → Automatic, GeoZoomLevel → Automatic, UnitSystem → Metric}

Some countries and states have islands. It's a simple matter to check that with Nepal we have a single connected component.

In[41]:= ConnectedMeshComponents[nepalMR] // Length
Out[41]= 1

We will next work to produce two distinct sets of elevation data: one for the points that define Nepal's boundary polygon, and a second comprising an elevation array for the entire geo-rectangle. We want our model to have a crisp border, so that's the reason for the first dataset. The second will give us the elevations inside the borders, and just outside them as well.

The paradigm we use will require that each data point is of the form {*longitude, latitude, elevation*}, and moreover we will need to have a common distance unit (we will use meters) for all three coordinates. That means we need to convert the degrees of latitude and longitude into meters. We will set the southwest corner of the geo-rectangle to have coordinates {0, 0}, and measure horizontal distances in meters from there.

To convert degrees to meters, we first pick a point near the center of the country:

In[42]:= (Nepal COUNTRY) [{"Longitude", "Latitude"}]

Out[42]= { 84.° , 28.° }

In[43]:= Show[nepalMR, Graphics[{PointSize[.02], Red, Point[{84, 28}]}]]

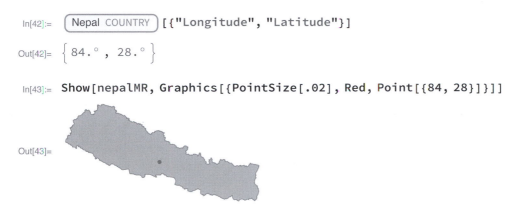

Out[43]=

At that location, one degree of latitude corresponds to roughly 111 km in the north–south direction:

In[44]:= UnitConvert[GeoDistance[{27.5, 84}, {28.5, 84}], "Meters"]

Out[44]= 110 819. m

In[45]:= ns = QuantityMagnitude[%]
        (* north-south meters per degree of latitude *)

Out[45]= 110 819.

And one degree of longitude corresponds to roughly 98 km in the east–west direction:

In[46]:= UnitConvert[GeoDistance[{28, 83.5}, {28, 84.5}], "Meters"]

Out[46]= 98 361.6 m

In[47]:= ew = QuantityMagnitude[%]
        (* east-west meters per degree of longitude *)

Out[47]= 98 361.6

Our desired horizontal distance units will be obtained by subtracting {*lon1, lat1*} from all {*longitude, latitude*} coordinates, so that the southwest corner of the enclosing geo-rectangle has coordinates {0, 0}, and then scaling the result by ns in the first coordinate and ew in the second (to convert degrees to meters). This approach makes the simplifying assumption that the degrees-to-meters scale factors are constant throughout Nepal. While this is not exactly true, it is nearly so, and will be for any geo-rectangular region that is not too tall longitudinally and not too close to the poles.

To illustrate the ideas, here are the first few points on the boundary, in their standard {*longitude, latitude*} coordinates:

```
In[48]:= MeshCoordinates[nepalMR][[1 ;; 3]]
```

```
Out[48]= {{81.0322, 30.1967}, {81.0344, 30.1972}, {81.0366, 30.1968}}
```

We will need to reverse the order of reach pair to {*latitude, longitude*} in order to compute the elevation:

```
In[49]:= GeoElevationData[{30.1, 81.0}]
```

```
Out[49]= 4606. m
```

So for each of the 796 boundary coordinates, we create a triple with all units in meters. Here are the first three points along the boundary:

```
In[50]:= Map[{ew (First[#] - lon1), ns (Last[#] - lat1),
            QuantityMagnitude@GeoElevationData[Reverse[#]]} &,
         MeshCoordinates[nepalMR][[1 ;; 3]]]
```

```
Out[50]= {{101 527., 442 910., 5551.},
          {101 748., 442 968., 5538.}, {101 960., 442 918., 5387.}}
```

And here's the whole batch. This will take a few minutes.

```
In[51]:= boundaryElevDataMeters =
            Map[{ew (First[#] - lon1), ns (Last[#] - lat1), QuantityMagnitude@
               GeoElevationData[Reverse[#]]} &, MeshCoordinates[nepalMR]];
```

Since that takes some time, after it is finished you can save the resulting data to the notebook (without having to display it all) by iconizing it. Then the data are stored in the notebook, so they can be used in a later session without having to duplicate that lengthy computation.

```
In[52]:= Iconize[boundaryElevDataMeters]
```

```
Out[52]= {...}  List  +
```

Having completed the boundary elevation data list, our next task is to make a second list of elevations for points within and slightly beyond the borders of Nepal. As in our earlier examples, we first make an array of elevation data, but here we use "GeoPosition" as a third argument to give us an array of *triples* of the form {*latitude, longitude, elevation*}.

```
In[53]:=  GeoElevationData[{{lat1, lon1}, {lat2, lon2}},
            Automatic, "GeoPosition"]
```

Out[53]= GeoPosition
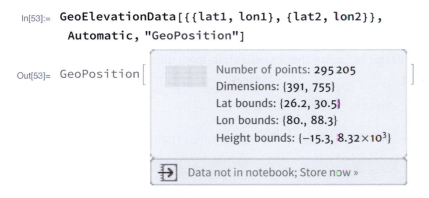

Number of points: 295 205
Dimensions: {391, 755}
Lat bounds: {26.2, 30.5}
Lon bounds: {80., 88.3}
Height bounds: {−15.3, 8.32×10^3}

Data not in notebook; Store now »

The actual 391×755 array is wrapped in GeoPosition, so let's dispense with the wrapper and just get the numerical data. We name it elevArray.

```
In[54]:=  elevArray = First[%]
```

Out[54]= {{{30.4926, 80.0079, 5653.6}, {30.4926, 80.0189, 5573.51},
          ⋯ 752 ⋯ , {30.4926, 88.2916, 5422.57}}, ⋯ 389 ⋯ , { ⋯ 1 ⋯ }}

large output | show less | show more | show all | set size limit...

We will need to do several things to get the array into the form we require. For instance, we must switch the first two coordinates of each data point to put it in {*longitude*, *latitude*, *elevation*} form:

```
In[55]:=  elevArray[[1, 1]] /. {lat_, lon_, elev_} :> {lon, lat, elev}
```

Out[55]= {80.0079, 30.4926, 5653.6}

We will use RegionMember on the first two coordinates to decide if a position lies within Nepal. Here is an example:

```
In[56]:=  RegionMember[nepalMR, {84, 28}]
```

Out[56]= True

Unlike our examples in the Shenandoah mountains and Kauai, we will flatten the array structure of the elevation data, turning it into a simple list of 3-tuples. The first three data points in the resulting list are:

```
In[57]:=  Flatten[elevArray, 1][[1 ;; 3]]
```

Out[57]= {{30.4926, 80.0079, 5653.6},
          {30.4926, 80.0189, 5573.51}, {30.4926, 80.0299, 5070.43}}

The reason for flattening the array is that the country of Nepal occupies only a small portion of a large geo-rectangle, so we will discard elevation data taken from portions of the geo-rectangle that are sufficiently far from Nepal. This is a somewhat subtle process: We will ultimately assign negative elevations (far below the elevation of any point in Nepal) to points outside Nepal but near its borders, as this will result in a crisp, near-vertical outline of the country's borders in the terrain map. But we will discard all data that are far from the borders for the sake of efficiency. There are tens of thousands of data points out there, and including them would slow down the rendering of the terrain map significantly.

We begin by taking the `ConvexHull` of the Nepal mesh.

In[58]:= `chNepal = ConvexHullMesh[MeshCoordinates[nepalMR]]`

Out[58]=

We now discard from the data array those points that are at least .3 (in degree units) from the convex hull.

In[59]:= `RegionDistance[chNepal, {81, 30}] < .3`

Out[59]= `True`

In[60]:= `RegionDistance[chNepal, {81, 27}] < .3`

Out[60]= `False`

In[61]:= `interiorElevData = Select[Flatten[elevArray, 1],`
         `RegionDistance[chNepal, {#[[2]], #[[1]]}] < .3 &];`

We have reduced the number of data points from roughly 295 000 to 187 000:

In[62]:= `{Length[Flatten[elevArray, 1]], Length[interiorElevData]}`

Out[62]= `{295 205, 187 052}`

Having parsed the data, we now convert the east–west and north–south units from degrees to (approximate) meters, just as we did for the boundary data. At the same time, we assign an elevation of −1000 meters to any data points that lie outside the true borders of the country. Again, the purpose of these negative elevations for points just outside the borders is to ensure a near-vertical edge at the border of the model.

In[63]:= `interiorElevDataMeters =`
         `(interiorElevData /. {lat_, lon_, elev_} :> If[RegionMember[nepalMR,`
            `{lon, lat}], {ew (lon - lon1), ns (lat - lat1), elev},`
             `{ew (lon - lon1), ns (lat - lat1), -1000}]);`

We now join the 796 data points from the boundary with the 187 052 data points in `interiorElevDa-taMeters`:

```
In[64]:= nepalElevDataMeters =
            Join[boundaryElevDataMeters, interiorElevDataMeters];
In[65]:= Length[nepalElevDataMeters]
Out[65]= 187 848
```

As a final step, we may wish to scale the vertical elevations in our model. How do we scale the third coordinate of each 3-tuple? We illustrate with a small sample from the data:

```
In[66]:= test = RandomSample[nepalElevDataMeters, 5]
Out[66]= {{551 903., 211 501., 4738.77},
            {797 207., 146 974., -1000}, {598 370., 201 761., 5566.27},
            {332 535., 171 324., 771.83}, {692 385., 271 159., -1000}}
```

We can multiply the coordinates of each triple by 1, 1, and 10, respectively, like this:

```
In[67]:= {1, 1, 10} # & /@ test
Out[67]= {{551 903., 211 501., 47 387.7},
            {797 207., 146 974., -10 000}, {598 370., 201 761., 55 662.7},
            {332 535., 171 324., 7718.3}, {692 385., 271 159., -10 000}}
```

We are finally ready to make the model. In order to get a quick preview so we may iteratively tweak the vertical scale factor and the extra thickness for the base, it is helpful to work with a reduced set of data. Here we randomly select 10 000 interior points and join them with the full set of 796 boundary points. The resulting `ListPlot3D` will be low-res, but it will render in just a few seconds. Try a bunch of different values for the vertical scale and extra thickness, until it looks right.

```
In[68]:= nepalTest = Join[boundaryElevDataMeters,
            RandomSample[interiorElevDataMeters, 10 000]];
In[69]:= s = 5; (* vertical scale factor *)
         extraThickness = 900;
         ListPlot3D[{1, 1, s} * # & /@ nepalTest,
            PlotRange → {All, All, s * {-extraThickness, 9000}},
            ClippingStyle → None, PlotTheme → "FilledSurface",
            BoxRatios → Automatic]
```

Out[71]=

Once the parameters are finalized, construct the full model by copying the input above and replacing elevTest with nepalElevDataMeters.

```
In[72]:=  s = 5; (* vertical scale factor *)
          extraThickness = 900;
          nepalModel = ListPlot3D[{1, 1, s} * # & /@ nepalElevDataMeters,
            PlotRange → {All, All, s * {-extraThickness, 9000}}, ClippingStyle →
            None, PlotTheme → "FilledSurface", BoxRatios → Automatic]
```

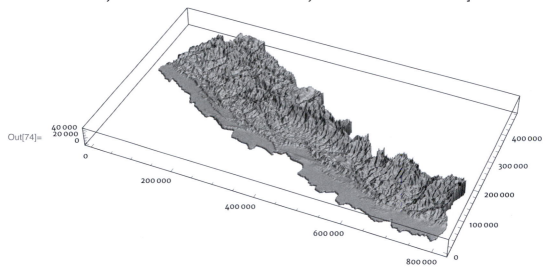

The resulting STL file is approximately 24 MB in size, so it will take a few minutes to export. It makes a beautiful model!

```
In[75]:=  SetDirectory[NotebookDirectory[]];
          Export["nepal.stl", nepalModel]
Out[76]=  nepal.stl
```

Exercises 9.8

1. Write a command that will add 10 to every *positive* value in the 5×5 matrix Table[RandomInte⋮ger[{-50,50}],{5},{5}]. Your command should leave the non-positive entries alone.